SCIENCE IN ARCHAEOLOGY

SCIENCE IN ARCHAEOLOGY

A Comprehensive Survey of Progress and Research

Edited by
DON BROTHWELL
British Museum (Natural History),
London

and ERIC HIGGS
Department of Archaeology and
Anthropology
University of Cambridge

With a Foreword by
GRAHAME CLARK
Disney Professor of Archaeology
University of Cambridge

95 photographs, 92 line drawings and 66 tables

THAMES AND HUDSON

First published 1963

Second impression 1965

© Thames and Hudson 1963

Printed in the United States of America

Contents

6   CONTENTS

List of Plates

Illustrations in the Text

PREFACE

ARCHAEOLOGICAL STUDIES are now increasingly dependent upon a variety of scientific disciplines for valuable information. This relationship between excavator and specialist is, however, usually obscured by the fact that the scientific studies appear either as papers in specialized scientific journals divorced from any archaeological test, or in the form of a note or appendix in an archaeological report. The importance of bringing together the various scientific aspects is obvious, and there is no doubt that archaeo-scientific work will eventually mature into a discipline of its own. Although we make no claim to be the first to collect together essays of this nature for the guidance of archaeologists we have attempted to produce a first really general reader. Obviously, in a book of this size, some minor topics must be excluded, or be of chapter size, even though whole books could be written about them. Similarly, subjects bordering on the scientific such as aerial photography and surveying have had to be excluded, although we fully appreciate that there are some arguments for including them in a general treatise of this kind.

It becomes clear that not to use the scientific methods now available to archaeology, is to commit the worst of archaeological crimes, to ignore available evidence or during excavation to destroy it. So far the scientist has acted in the main as a consultant, to advise on finds which happen to fit into his field. There are in fact few archaeological institutions or bodies which are equipped with the right kind of personnel to pose the questions which science can answer, and which should be posed before excavation begins. Few, too, are the archaeologists who have sufficient scientific knowledge to cast a discriminating eye over the mass of scientific evidence upon which much of the ultimate conclusions will in the future depend. This book will serve some purpose if it helps to indicate the task in hand, for the knowledge of prehistoric peoples derived by scientific methods will before long overwhelm the information which has been gained from the study of artifacts in relative isolation.

It is inevitable that, when dealing with such a variety of subjects and authors, there will be a considerable range of literary styles. Rather than attempt any rigid standardization we have considered it to be to the general well-being of the book as a whole to have individuality of this sort.

Rather than amalgamate the references into a general bibliography, we have thought it advisable to have them at the end of each contribution. Again, we have been faced with the problem of whether or not to standardize rigidly the system of references, but we have decided that minor differences in bibliographical form are not likely to reduce the value of the reading lists. Owing to the constant necessity to consider book size, the titles of papers in the majority of periodicals have been omitted.

We should like to take this opportunity of thanking all those who have contributed so willingly and promptly to our invitation, and to Dr Glyn Daniel for his enthusiasm and encouragement during the preparation of this work.

Individual acknowledgements are to be found at the end of the particular contribution in question.

DON BROTHWELL

ERIC HIGGS

FOREWORD

GRAHAME CLARK

IN HIS MODE OF WORK and in his general approach the archaeologist resembles in several significant respects the detective. Like the disciples of Sherlock Holmes he seeks to recover the activities of men in past time from clues which compensate for their incomplete and often vestigial character by abundance and diversity. Most of this evidence is necessarily circumstantial—it can only be made to speak by bringing upon it the resources of natural science; and the more effectively these can be harnessed the more complete the information likely to be won from traces, which in themselves may appear to the layman to be almost as slight as the bloodstains and finger-prints used by skilled detectives to reconstruct crimes. The correct interpretation of the data wrung by scientific means from material that may at first sight appear unpromising still depends on the genius, perspicacity and breadth of sympathy of the investigator; but the range of information on which his conclusions are based will be limited by the technical means at his disposal. What the archaeologist is able to learn about the past depends to a great extent on the completeness and discrimination with which he avails himself of the resources being made available on an ever more generous scale by his colleagues in a growing range of scientific disciplines.

It is a prime object of this book to provide a systematic conspectus of the bearing of the natural sciences on archaeological investigation. The book is addressed not merely to students of archaeology and of the various branches of natural science, but to all those who follow with growing fascination the unfolding of new and ever-widening perspectives of human history. It aims to show precisely how the different branches and techniques of natural science, many of them quite recently developed, are able to make their own peculiar contributions to our understanding of the past, allowing us to view the achievements of our forebears in altogether greater depth and detail than was possible only a few years ago.

It is logical for such a book to open with the scientific methods and techniques concerned with chronology, since without an ordered frame of reference the reconstruction of human history can hardly begin. Although both are concerned with past events, the archaeologist is as a rule concerned with a much greater depth in time. It is true that archaeology is capable of throwing important light on quite recent periods of history even in highly literate societies, particularly in spheres which for one reason or another have not been adequately recorded in writing; but the fact remains that many of the most important and exciting discoveries made by archaeologists relate to the vast and

in many respects decisive phases of human history entirely or almost entirely unillumina-
ted by the written word. Although this does not alter in any fundamental way the
essential process of detection, it does affect the emphasis placed on chronology and for
the remoter periods of prehistory in particular it implies the deployment of numerous
scientific techniques, some of them only recently brought into use or still in process of
development.

Like all other forms of life, man exists in a physical environment and we have to take
full account of this if we are to understand how he lived. This is very far from saying
that human life even at a material level can be explained in terms of external circumstances: environment certainly does not determine, but it does impose limits to the
possibilities open to people at any particular stage of culture; and by the same token the
stage of cultural development can itself be measured, at least in economic terms, by the
use made of the environment. In studying societies that flourished long ago the archaeologist—and more particularly the prehistoric archaeologist—has to consider the ecological conditions that prevailed at the relevant time and place. He can only do so by the
help of scientific colleagues technically equipped on the one hand to reconstitute the
climate and soil that together form the habitat and on the other to recover vegetation
and animals that constitute the biome and provide man in the most literal sense with the
basis of his subsistence.

Since the archaeologist, like the criminal detective with whom we have compared
him, is concerned with human activities, it follows that his interest centres more on man
and his culture than on his environment. He wants to know as much as he can about the
biological aspects of men, as individuals and as populations, and to obtain this he turns
to experts in various branches of human anatomy and physiology. The knowledge to be
won by investigating the physical remains of early man far transcends the biological
level, important though this undoubtedly is: in sometimes unexpected ways it throws
light on economic, social and even spiritual aspects of life. This only goes to show how
important it is to subject human burials—still after all among the most abundant finds
made by the archaeologist—to the scrutiny of those best equipped to extract the fullest
information from them.

When all is said, the archaeologist is primarily and specifically concerned with artifacts—the structures, tools, weapons, utensils, ornaments and gear that form his traditional stock-in-trade and provide him with his own insight into the life of earlier days.
All too commonly these have been studied from a merely morphological point of view,
as a means of distinguishing one culture from another and successive stages of development within each. Such methods of analysis, proper to art history, while sure of a place
in the archaeologist's armoury, are no longer his principal weapon even in the most
backward areas. Today the emphasis falls more on the effort to understand how the
various peoples of antiquity in fact lived and artifacts are being studied more and more
as sources of information about such broad topics as economy, technology, warfare,
settlement, social organization and religion. The effect of this shift of emphasis has once
more been to draw archaeology and the natural sciences closer together: whereas stylistic
analysis requires no more than intuitive appreciation, it requires a wide range of more or

less highly specialized scientific techniques and procedures to elicit full information about such things as the precise character and sources of raw materials, the techniques used to convert these into artifacts and the uses to which finished objects were put.

The growing involvement of archaeologists with colleagues in a wide range of sciences, whether in relation to dating, environment, man or material culture, does more than complicate their task of liaison: it is subtly changing their whole outlook. This can be illustrated in two ways, each exemplified in this book. First, there is a growing tendency to supplement qualitative by quantitative assessment and measurement. Secondly, and in some ways more fundamentally, there is a notable change of attitude towards the process of discovery on which archaeologists depend for their basic clues. Modern archaeologists have taken on something of the questing spirit of science: they no longer dig merely to accumulate data but to solve problems. For this reason they are not content to wait on accidental discoveries or even to dig into monuments merely because they happen to be visible: instead they strive to recover the precise evidence they need wherever this may exist. For this as well as for more prosaic reasons, archaeologists are eagerly availing themselves of new techniques of detection, techniques which have commonly been brought to an advanced stage of development in the course of prospecting for oil or for military purposes. As archaeologists learn to share in the great adventure of purposive research, they are coming to appreciate proton magneto-meter and resistivity surveys not merely as useful accessories but as tools of fundamental importance.

To sum up, the archaeologist, despite all his triumphs, remains almost at the beginning of his task: immense fields of knowledge remain to be opened up, not merely in remote parts of the world, but even in the lands where archaeology passed through its initial primitive stages of development; and in gaining the deeper insights which only fresh data will make possible, he depends increasingly on harnessing the resources of modern science and technology. By drawing attention to some of the scientific methods and procedures now available to archaeology, the editors and authors of this book point the way to further progress in unfolding the common past of mankind.

SECTION I DATING

1 *Archaeology and Dating*

C. B. M. McBURNEY

IN THE EXPRESSED VIEW of a number of students of human history in the widest sense—that is to say of the whole pattern of human development and the evolution of civilization—archaeology is a technique and not in the strict meaning a study in its own right. On this view, archaeology merely serves to extend, and in some circumstances amplify, the conclusions based on written documents. The technique is admittedly often uncertain and inadequate for the purpose, but it is the best available. With this view the writer finds himself wholly at variance. It is indeed sometimes evident that the use of archaeological methods supplies the historian with a few facts of the kind he is accustomed to deal with and enables him to draw somewhat tentative conclusions of a 'historical' nature. But many of the most significant conclusions reached by archaeology, and many others potentially attainable, fall quite outside the range of problems tackled by the student of written history. The heart of prehistoric studies, whence the real impetus derives, lies in the attempt to understand man and not men, the deliberate attack on the broad problems of human *Werdegang*, with the conscious objective of gaining some insight into that immense and profoundly significant pattern of culture change which lies outside the field of the historian in the strict sense. Twenty, even ten years ago, such an enterprise might have been regarded as unrealistic but today, precisely owing to co-operation with other sciences, it is no longer so.

For successful combined research mutual understanding is essential and the lack of it the cause of many inadequate, abortive or prematurely abandoned projects. Since earlier works, excellent in their way and for their time, such as Laming's *La Découverte du Passé* (1952) and others of the post-war period, there are striking signs of a steady progress in this respect. But much still remains to be done. Far too many scientists regard archaeology merely as an uncertain form of dating and are apparently unaware of the preoccupation of archaeologists with fundamental problems and patterns of culture growth of which dating is but one of many by-products. On the other hand archaeologists are to be found whose attitude, say, to radiocarbon dating might be described as hesitant belief in a sort of magic whose spells sometimes do and sometimes do not 'work', without any attempt to understand the real nature of the factors of uncertainty involved.

Pride of place in the matter of dating must of course go to radiocarbon. Here progress in supplying an absolute framework of chronology in the different periods and different areas occupied by man in the past is perhaps the most exciting single development achieved in archaeology by our generation of workers. The practical effect of such dating when adequately checked is of course far more than the mere satisfaction of curiosity on the age of this or that striking find. The far-reaching lines of inquiry suggested by differential dating of a given culture in separate areas of its distribution are particularly significant. Not only does this set the distribution maps in motion, affording a first indication of the place and time of origin, and direction of spread, but in the long run by bringing such processes gradually into sharper focus we may hope to discover something of the actual causative factors in the spread of ethnic groups and of culture complexes.

Again a wholly new field is offered by the possibility of the measurement of long-term changes within a given cultural tradition. Many different types of assumption regarding the nature of such evolutionary (or devolutionary) trends are implicit in current theories of typology and interpretations of observed changes. By supplying an absolute time scale, radiocarbon now makes it possible to study these more in a manner which may lead ultimately to a more exact understanding of their dynamics. Typical questions in this field which can be pertinently asked and may well prove answerable are, for instance, whether elaboration normally proceeds as a smooth process or by sudden jumps like 'mutations' in organic evolution. What in a word are the relative importance of 'inventions' as opposed to gradual improvements? Few archaeologists who have considered the matter would care to deny that such questions are fundamental to a wide variety of interpretative problems.

The validity of a system of dating that is based on such an apparently remote phenomenon as radioactive disintegration is likely to remain in the back of the minds of many archaeologists. Within precisely what limit, apart from the built-in statistical margin, can the archaeologist rely fully on the results of his physicist colleague? In many cases the field worker with some general understanding of the laboratory tests is probably in a better position, or at least as good a one, to spot possible causes of distortion than the physicist working remote from the actual conditions of collection. Yet the archaeological world in general is only interested in the reliability of the final result; how can this best be tested in the last resort? The reasonableness or otherwise of some crucial test is in itself a highly subjective criterion unless applied with the maximum of rigorous logic. Various other methods are available in particular cases. In the early days for instance the age of the Postglacial climatic phases in northern Europe could only be compared with varve estimates. With the multiplication of results however a sensitive alternative is offered by the mere internal consistency of readings. Thus elaborate repeated tests of the age of episodes in the Postglacial botanical history of the British Isles, whose sequence is checked at many points, reveals at once the simultaneous consistency of the two patterns and a satisfactory degree of correlation with the earlier varve results.

The same process of testing consistency with events in a known sequence will probably become steadily more important as dates, particularly those of greater antiquity, are multiplied. In this process up to about 50,000 years ago, or even slightly before, much will depend on the accuracy of identification of the episodes, and in this recent experience has shown that geological interpretation particularly for the earlier episodes is of very variable reliability. Nevertheless there is good hope that in time the mere accumulation of readings will enable a correlation between the two kinds of data to be established within useful limits, and to that extent eliminate the possibility of systematic error or alternatively reveal its presence. It should be stated however that so far none of the ingenious theories whereby a systematic error could have been introduced— a case in point is that of fluctuations in the earth's magnetic field or the rate of bombardment of the outer atmosphere—has so far achieved any positive support.

Neither obsidian dating nor the argon method, nor thermoluminescence, nor dating by any other isotope has yet produced results in sufficient quantities to enable them to be tested exhaustively one against the other on a sequential basis. Probably, one of these methods will produce an absolute and reliable chronology for the Lower and Middle Pleistocene. As for the alternative method based on the extrapolated solar radiation curve devised by M. Milankovitch, in its final stages estimates for the age of various cultural events, such as the Aurignacian in Europe, are widely divergent from those of radiocarbon. This fact alone hardly serves to inspire reliance on estimates of much earlier climatic events, although a certain degree of correspondence with some calculations on purely geological bases has been noted by some writers. Probably the most hopeful approach at present to Lower and Middle Palaeolithic chronology is towards a purely relative chronology based on the refinement of such studies as Quaternary geology and palaeontology.

Finally tribute should be paid to fluorine and nitrogen, dendrochronology and archaeomagnetism, which although restricted in their application have added each in their different way to refinements of prehistoric chronology and are a valuable check upon other methods of dating.

Other lines of investigation, those which amplify our knowledge of the climatic or biological context of human activity, give us a fuller, more vivid impression of the human situation at the time, or act as a chronological check at one remove. As these inquiries develop, more fundamental objectives come into view concerning both the aetiology of particular cultural events and even, we may hope, of classes of event and long-sustained trends of change involving devolution as well as evolution. Further, in these more advanced levels of investigation, the proper application of statistical methods will play a part.

In a word then co-operation with specialized scientific fields appears to widen and not narrow the field of inquiry of the archaeologist and that to a degree promising greater co-ordination within the subject and a realization of problems of an ever more fundamental and significant kind. If prehistory is to come of age as a subject of basic philosophical import it is along these lines that the most hopeful signs of advance lie. But such advance clearly cannot be through one-sided efforts. If the prehistorian is to make fullest use of the help offered by his scientific colleagues, he will need not merely to lean upon them, or even to acquire an understanding of their methods, but above all to define significant problems in the field of human past and also to take an informed part in initiating combined inquiries.

2 Analytical Methods of Dating Bones

KENNETH P. OAKLEY

A CONSIDERABLE AMOUNT OF PROGRESS has been made during the last decade in the dating of bones, and a number of new techniques for this purpose have been developed. In briefly surveying them in this chapter it is important at the outset to distinguish two main types of dating, for a technique applicable in one type of dating may be quite inappropriate in another. The first type of dating is *relative dating*. This places a specimen, event or deposit in relation to an established sequence. Of course one may know the relative age of a specimen and yet have very little or no idea of its age in years (e.g. the Swanscombe skull). Where it is possible to measure actual age of a specimen, or of the contemporaneous matrix, the procedure is now usually referred to as *chronometric dating*.*

There is an ageing process inherent in organic materials which was discovered about 1947 by Professor W. F. Libby, then at the Institute of Nuclear Studies, Chicago, and within certain limits this makes it possible to determine the exact antiquity of some specimens in years. All living matter contains a small but practically constant proportion of the radioactive isotope of carbon, C^{14}, which is produced by cosmic-ray bombardment of nitrogen atoms in the outer atmosphere. When an animal or plant dies, the radioactive carbon in its tissues is no longer replenished from the atmosphere, and it disintegrates at a constant rate—the quantity is halved in 5,600 years. Thus by measuring the radioactivity of the carbon extracted from an ancient specimen of organic material, its age can be calculated. After a certain lapse of time the radioactivity is too weak to be measured.

With existing techniques the backward limit of the radiocarbon method is between 60,000 and 70,000 years, but the range is gradually being increased with the development of the device known as isotopic enrichment in a diffusion column, having converted the carbon first into carbon dioxide.

Another very practical limitation of radiocarbon dating is the fact that a certain minimum quantity of organic carbon must be available in the specimen or sample. Thus calcined bone is undatable whereas charred bone is potentially datable. The amount required depends partly on the level of age—the older the material the more the carbon required for an accurate dating—but the techniques are being improved in this as in

* Some authors have used 'absolute dating' as synonymous with 'dating in years', but this usage is gradually dropping out of currency because it makes no distinction between placing a specimen in a time bracket (e.g. determining its age as $40,000\pm2,000$ years) and placing it on a time-line. Where it is possible to establish that two deposits in widely separated areas were formed contemporaneously (e.g. if they both contain the same fall of cosmic tektites), they could be said to be of the same 'absolute' age even if their antiquity in *years* is quite unknown.

other respects. Thus in 1953 when the antiquity of the Piltdown jawbone was doubted on the score of its fluorine and nitrogen content (*infra*), it would have been impossible to date it by C[14] because at that time about 6 grams of carbon were demanded by the laboratories using the method, and as this is approximately its total carbon content, the exercise would have involved the total destruction of this 'historic' specimen, suspected by then to have been probably fabricated out of a modern orang-utan jawbone. By 1959, however, the late Professor H. de Vries in the Groningen Laboratory undertook at the author's request to date it by C[14], and he was able to do so closely enough to confirm that it was geologically recent.[1] This was on the basis of testing one gram of the bone, cut out of the corpus mandibulae, which yielded, after grinding and treatment in the Government Laboratory for the purpose of removing all possible traces of preservative, and after decalcification in Groningen, 0·1 gram of organic carbon. Measurement of its radioactivity showed that the jaw was a few centuries old, perhaps not so surprising when one recalls that the modern Dyaks preserve trophy orang-utan skulls for centuries in their longhouses and in ritual deposits in caves.

The absolute age of a skull or mandible is usually obtained indirectly, as when it comes from a deposit containing other material more suitable for radiocarbon dating, or other bones more easily expended. Thus the Palaeolithic skull found in spring-deposits at Florisbad, in the Orange Free State, has been dated as about 37,000 years old on the basis of radiocarbon dating of a seam of peat within the same deposit.[2]

Dating a specimen by the age of the containing deposit of course makes the assumption that they are contemporaneous and obviously this is not always justifiable, particularly where human remains are concerned, because of man's long-established practice of burying the dead.

The fluorine test (and other tests working on the same principle described below) was mainly devised for the purpose of checking the age-relation between bones and the deposit in which they have been found or to which they are attributed. Frequently it has been misunderstood. Thus, when it was stated a few years ago in a newspaper report that 'the fluorine test indicated that the Swanscombe skull was more than 100,000 years old', this was merely a way of saying that the test had confirmed its contemporaneity with the gravel in which it was found, and that geologists' current assessment of the antiquity of the gravel was 'more than 100,000 years old'.

The relative age of a fossil bone can be determined by comparing its chemical composition with that of other fossil bones of known ages from the same site or from the same area if they have been preserved under comparable conditions. As soon as bones are buried their composition is subject to chemical changes, some rapid, others much slower. The organic matter in bone consists mainly of fats and protein (collagen). The fatty matter of bone is lost quite rapidly after burial, but the protein disappears much more slowly, and under some conditions, where the soil is permanently frozen or where bacteria and air are excluded, it may persist for tens of thousands of years. Collagen fibres have been demonstrated in fossil ivory (Plate Ia) from Siberia, and in the humerus of a woolly rhinoceros excavated from Pleistocene clay on the site of the Lloyd's Building in Leadenhall Street in the City of London (Plate Ib).

The appearance or texture of a bone is not a reliable guide to how much organic matter it contains. During excavations at Gibraltar in the last century, the skeleton of a horse was encountered a few feet below the surface. It was taken at first to be the remains of a fossil horse, for the bones appeared to have lost the greater part of their organic matter; but, when the foot bones were exhumed, the shoes with which the animal had been shod were found still in position. It was in fact the remains of an Arab charger buried only 25 years earlier.

With such cases in mind the organic content of fossil bones had become widely regarded as an unreliable criterion of their antiquity, but extensive analytical studies carried out since the Second World War[3] have shown that some bones which appear to be well fossilized have in fact retained considerable amounts of protein. As bones lose their protein at a slow and, under the same conditions, fairly uniform rate, the relative ages of bones at some sites can be determined by comparing their organic contents—nitrogen, carbon, and chemically-bound water—or the quantity of mineral ash after burning, which becomes greater with age.

It is usually found most convenient to assess the residual organic matter in fossil bone or dentine by determining its nitrogen content by the method of chemical analysis known as micro-kjeldahl. As bone protein or collagen decays in course of fossilization, it is broken down into the various component amino-acids which are leached out or retained for varying lengths of time depending on the local conditions.[4,5] Some amino-acids were found surviving even in the bones of fossil fishes embedded in hard shales of a Devonian formation nearly 300 million years old in Ohio. In order to assess the degree of degradation of collagen in fossil bone, a sample is first dissolved in a suitable acid, and the amino-acids present in the resulting hydrolysate are then determined by means of paper-chromatography. A chromatogram (Plate Ib) prepared from a sample of the ulna of woolly rhinoceros in clay from the Lloyd's site showed all the amino-acids composing collagen; whereas the Galley Hill skeleton, although only Bronze Age, preserved in gravelly matrix showed these amino-acids in reduced strength.

Changes in the mineral matter of buried bones and teeth depend on the composition of the percolating ground-water. They are of two kinds: (1) alteration of the phosphatic material of which bones are mainly composed (hydroxy-apatite), and (2) addition of new mineral matter (e.g. lime or iron oxide) in the pores of the bone. Changes of the latter kind involving an increase in weight are what people usually mean by 'fossilization', but they are often misleading as a means of relative dating. For this purpose, the more valuable change is the slow, invisible, weightless alteration which occurs through the irreversible substitution of one element for another in the hydroxy-apatite. The two elements which accumulate in this way are fluorine and uranium.

Of these elements fluorine is widely distributed in the form of soluble fluorides which occur in trace quantities in almost all ground-waters. When fluorine ions come into contact with bones and teeth, they are absorbed and become locked in through replacing the hydroxyl ions in the ultramicroscopic crystals of hydroxy-apatite. Fluor-apatite is less soluble than hydroxy-apatite, so that when fluorine atoms have once been fixed in bone, they are not readily dissolved out. With the passage of time, bones and teeth in permeable deposits accumulate fluorine progressively. The rate at which the fluorine content increases varies from place to place, but bones which have lain for the same period of time in a particular deposit will have approximately the same fluorine content. As the fluorine fixed in bone is not readily removed, a specimen which has been washed out of a more ancient deposit and redeposited in another at a later date will show a much higher fluorine content than bones contemporary with the bed. Bones artificially interred in the same deposit at a later date may have come to resemble the fossils of the bed in appearance, but will have accumulated substantially less fluorine. This is the basis of the fluorine-dating method,[6,7] the usefulness of which was demonstrated in 1948 when it was applied to the Galley Hill skeleton[8] and the Swanscombe skull.

The Galley Hill skeleton is that of a man of modern type but with certain allegedly primitive traits. It was discovered in 1888 at a depth (it was said) of 8 ft in the river terrace gravels near Swanscombe, which contain Lower Palaeolithic hand-axes together with remains of extinct elephant and which certainly date from before the time of Neanderthal man. In these same gravels the bones of the Swanscombe skull were found in 1935–36 at a depth of 24 ft. The fluorine content of the Galley Hill skeleton, of the Swanscombe skull, and of fossil animal bones from the same gravels was determined by chemical analysis in the Government Chemist's Department. The results confirmed the antiquity of the Swanscombe skull and indicated that the Galley Hill skeleton was an intrusive burial considerably later than the Middle Pleistocene gravels in which it lay.

These fluorine results were later cross-checked by measurements of the nitrogen content of the same bones. The two sets of results are shown together in Table A.

TABLE A

Fluorine and nitrogen contents of the Galley Hill skeleton and the Swanscombe skull.

	Fluorine	Nitrogen
	%	%
Neolithic skull, Coldrum, Kent	0·3	1·9
Galley Hill skeleton	0·5	1·6
Swanscombe skull	1·7	trace
Bones of fossil mammals from Swanscombe gravel	1·5	trace

It will be seen that bones which have accumulated little fluorine have retained much nitrogen, and vice versa. Although the Galley Hill skeleton was clearly much later than the gravel in which it lay, the question of how much later, even in general terms, could not be solved by the fluorine or nitrogen methods of relative dating, because no bones in a similar matrix known to be Late Palaeolithic, Mesolithic, Neolithic, Bronze Age or of precise later date were available in the locality for comparison. However, the nitrogen tests showed that sufficient degraded collagen occurred in the skeleton to enable its age to be determined directly by the radiocarbon method if a portion of this famous specimen were sacrificed to this end. As the ratio C/N in collagen is approximately 2·5 : 1, it was estimated that 100 grams of the skeleton would yield about 4 grams of carbon. Accordingly in 1959 it was decided to make an accurate cast of one of the limb-bones, and then to drill out of it about 100 grams of tissue.

The bone powder was repeatedly washed in warm water and acetone (by Mr E. J. Johnson of the Government Chemist's Department) to remove any possible traces of celluloid or glue which might have been applied to the skeleton after excavation, and then it was submitted to the Research Laboratory of the British Museum, where Mr H. Barker[9] determined its age as 3,310±150 years old, indicating that it was most probably an Early Bronze Age burial. This is probably the first instance in which an allegedly 'fossil' human skeleton has been dated directly by the radiocarbon method.

The solving of another outstanding problem, that of 'Piltdown Man', was also begun by means of relative dating techniques,[10] and was completed by the chronometric method of radiocarbon (p. 24). The unravelling of this complicated problem[11] (described by one distinguished scholar in 1948 as one that would probably never be solved) began in 1949 with the application of the fluorine-dating method to all the vertebrate specimens from the Piltdown gravel. In addition to the jawbone, canine or eye tooth, and fragments of human braincase, 17 fossil mammalian specimens had been recorded from the pit. These appeared to be of two ages: an older group originally called Pliocene, including pieces of the grinding teeth of a rare type of elephant which died out early in the Pleistocene—that is, more than 600,000 years ago according to conventional geological estimates; and a much later group including remains of beaver, red deer, and perhaps hippopotamus, dating from just before the last glaciation of about 60,000 years ago. It appeared that fossils of two formations had been washed together, through some strange chance. Those authorities who could not believe that the jawbone belonged to the skull held the view that the jaw belonged to the 'Pliocene' group, and the skull to the later.

Samples of all these specimens were submitted to the Government Chemist's Department, where they were analysed by Dr C. R. Hoskins. The fossils of the older group proved to contain a great deal of fluorine, 2 to 3% (3·8% is the theoretical maximum). In striking contrast the amount of fluorine in small samples of the famous skull, jawbone, and canine tooth proved to be only between 0·1 and 0·4%. It was not immediately obvious that these remains were bogus, because there did not appear to be any significant difference in fluorine content between the jawbone and skull, or between the skull and an associated molar tooth of hippopotamus (extinct in Britain since before the last glaciation).

In 1953, in order to test Dr J. S. Weiner's hypothesis that the jawbone and canine tooth were modern specimens faked to match fossilized human skull bones, larger samples were removed and submitted to the Government Chemist's Department, where they were analysed by Mr C. F. M. Fryd, who devised a way of measuring smaller amounts of fluorine than could be measured in 1949.[12] The jawbone and canine tooth proved to contain no more fluorine than fresh bones and teeth, whereas the human skull bones contained just enough to indicate that they were ancient. The nitrogen content of the jawbone and teeth was also determined, and proved to be the same as in fresh specimens.

The nitrogen content would not have proved the modernity of the jawbone conclusively without the cross-check provided by fluorine. The woolly rhinoceros bone from clay below the Lloyd's site (in which collagen fibres have been detected—p. 25) has the same nitrogen content as the Piltdown jawbone, yet it is undoubtedly fossil. The reason for its remarkable preservation is that it was embedded in clay which has provided an anaerobic and sterile environment since the Late Pleistocene. A fragment of mammoth bone from the same site, but from a layer of sand, contains almost no nitrogen. Fortunately the fluorine content of buried bones increases at about the same rate in sand (or gravel) and in clay. Thus these rhinoceros and mammoth bones both contain about 1% fluorine, as expected in alluvial deposits of Upper Pleistocene age in southern England. Thus if for the sake of argument it were supposed that the Piltdown jawbone had been encased in clay since Pleistocene times, and that this had prevented its organic content from being degraded, its fluorine content should nevertheless be higher than in modern bone. In fact, the matrix was gravel.

The fluorine content of the Piltdown skull bones is lower than that of fossils from any other Pleistocene gravels in Britain. But so long as the hippopotamus tooth with the same low fluorine content was accepted as a local fossil it could be argued that the ground-water at Piltdown had been exceptionally deficient in fluorine since the Ice Age; the exposed dentine of a tooth and compact bone absorb fluorine at about the same rate. When evidence came to light that the hippopotamus tooth had been artificially stained, and therefore was a fraudulent introduction, the provisional dating of the Piltdown cranium as Late Pleistocene lost its foundation.

Further chemical studies of the Piltdown hippopotamus molar showed that its organic content is almost negligible, indicating that it is a fossil of considerable antiquity— whereas its low fluorine content suggested that it was not very ancient. It has now been found that in limestone cave deposits passage of fluorine ions is inhibited but that decay of organic matter proceeds at normal rates. Hippopotamus remains are rare in cave deposits, except in Mediterranean islands, for example Malta—which may be where the 'Piltdown' specimen came from originally.

A new method of relative dating of bones and teeth has been tried with considerable success on the Piltdown specimens: the method of radiometric assay developed by Professor C. F. Davidson and Mr S. H. U. Bowie while working together in the Atomic Energy Division of the Geological Survey. It was established by Lord Rayleigh in 1908 that mineral phosphates, including fossil bones, contain uranium. Recent medical researches have shown that uranium circulating in the blood stream is fixed in the mineral matter of bones, probably through replacement of the calcium ions in the hydroxy-apatite. The same process of replacement occurs in bones buried in deposits through which ground-water percolates with traces of uranium. The longer a bone has lain in that deposit the more uranium it will have absorbed. Uranium is radio-active, and consequently it is possible to estimate the uranium content of a fossil by making a count, under suitable conditions, of the amount of radioactive breakdown that is proceeding. Radiometric assays of fossil bones carried out at the Geological Survey have shown that, although there is a wide variation in the radioactivity of fossils of the same age from different sites, there is a progressive build-up in the average radioactivity of fossils with increasing geological age. Moreover, contemporaneous bones and teeth from a single site show only a small range of radioactivity (although the radioactivity of the enamel of a tooth is generally less than that of dentine or cementum, which are more absorptive). Fossil bones and teeth from limestone formations and clays contain less uranium than specimens of the same age from gravels and sands. The radiometric assay can sometimes serve in the same way as fluorine analysis to distinguish between specimens which, for whatever reasons, are older or younger than the bed they are found in and those which are contemporaneous. It has an advantage over the fluorine method of dating in that it does not involve destruction of material.

When Bowie and Davidson carried out a radiometric assay of the Piltdown speci-mens[13] the results agreed with those obtained by fluorine analysis, indicating that the cranium is post-Pleistocene, and that the animal remains have been derived from very

TABLE B

Fluorine, nitrogen and uranium contents of human and mammal remains from Europe and North Africa.

	Fluorine	Nitrogen	'Uranium' $(e.U_3O_3)$
	%	%	p.p.m.*
Fresh bone	0·03	4·0	0
Piltdown jawbone	<0·03	3·9	0
Neolithic skull, Kent	0·3	1·9	–
Piltdown skull	0·1	1·4	1
Piltdown hippopotamus molar†	<0·1	<0·1	3
Malta hippopotamus molar†	0·1	<0·1	7
Swanscombe skull	1·7	trace	27
Suffolk Red Crag *Mastodon* molar†	1·9	trace	46
Piltdown '*Elephas* cf. *planifrons*' molar†	2·7	nil	610
Ichkeul '*Elephas* cf. *planifrons*' molar†	2·7	trace	580

* Equivalent uranium oxide content, estimated in parts per million on basis of beta-radiations per minute. That all this radiation is due to uranium is an assump-tion; in fact some is undoubtedly due to uranium 'daughter elements'. However, chemical analysis of the dentine of the Piltdown molar of *E.* cf. *planifrons* showed that it contained *c.* 1,000 p.p.m. of uranium oxide according to A. D. Baynes–Cope (*Bull. B.M. (N.H.), Geol.* vol. 2, no. 6, 1955, pp. 283–4).
† Samples of dentine or cementum.

varied geological sources. The most striking additional information concerned the fragments of molar teeth of an extinct elephant—similar to *Elephas planifrons*, which lived
early in the Pleistocene, and has been rarely if ever recorded elsewhere in Britain. These
fragments proved to have a radioactivity far higher than that of any Tertiary or Pleistocene fossils from Britain that have been tested, and higher than that of fossil elephant
teeth of the same age from foreign localities, with the exception only of a specimen
of '*Elephas* cf. *planifrons*' from Ichkeul, in Tunisia, now referred to as *Archidiskodon
africanavus*, an African member of the *Elephas planifrons* group.

Some summarized results obtained by the fluorine, nitrogen, and uranium methods
are shown in Table B.

There are so many variables affecting the composition of fossil bones and teeth that
it is usually impossible to use either fluorine content or radioactivity as more than a
rough guide to the geological age of an isolated specimen. However, these methods,
combined where necessary with nitrogen analysis, are useful in (a) establishing the
relative ages of a variety of vertebrate remains occurring in comparable circumstances
at the same or neighbouring sites, and (b) tracing the most likely origin of specimens
derived from several possible sources. The usefulness of the combined techniques is
well illustrated by the results obtained through applying them to the problem of the
relative age and origin of remains of 'sabre-tooth tiger'—strictly speaking, they should
be termed sabre-tooth *cats*—reported from British cave deposits.

In 1876 a canine tooth of '*Machaerodus*' (*Epimachaerodus*) was found in an Upper
Palaeolithic layer at Robin Hood's Cave, Creswell Crags, Derbyshire. Some authorities
have doubted whether this was a genuine find, suspecting that it had been fraudulently
planted at the site, and that it had really originated in alluvial deposits of earliest
Pleistocene (Villafranchian) age in France or Italy, where specimens of this genus
are not uncommon. Comparison of the fluorine content of the Creswell tooth
with that of Villafranchian specimens from the main Continental localities appears

TABLE C

Fluorine, nitrogen and uranium contents of Epimachaerodus *teeth from
Creswell Crags and other European sites.*

Source of Epimachaerodus dentine tested	Nitrogen	Fluorine	$\%F/\%P_2O_5$ ($\times 100$)	'Uranium' $(e.U_3O_8)^*$
	%	%		p.p.m.
Val d'Arno, Italy	0·2	1·6	5·3	35
Mt Perrier, France	nil	1·9	6·3	30
Doveholes, Derbyshire	nil	2·5	8·6	68
Creswell, Derbyshire	2·1	0·2	0·8	< 1
Kent's Cavern, Devon	1·2	<0·01	<0·1	5

* Equivalent uranium oxide content (estimated on basis of net β-radiations per
minute).

to dispel this suggestion (Table C). Other possibilities had to be considered. Was the Creswell canine derived from a Lower Pleistocene deposit in Derbyshire and brought into the Robin Hood's Cave by prehistoric man? There are many instances of fossils having been treasured during the Stone Age and transported many miles from their natural source—the most famous example is the Silurian trilobite found in a Magdalenian layer in Grotte du Trilobite at Arcy-sur-Cure (Yonne). Moreover, *Epimachaerodus* canines (but specifically different from the Creswell specimen) have been found in association with Villafranchian fossils in a fissure deposit at Doveholes, which is also in Derbyshire. Yet their lack of organic matter, high fluorine content and high radioactivity contrast sharply with the Creswell specimen, whose composition agrees with that of local Upper Pleistocene cave mammals.

If it were still to be maintained that the Creswell canine had been fraudulently planted in the cave, its composition could only be accounted for by supposing that it had been obtained from some other similar *cave* deposit elsewhere; for in our experience it is only in limestone cave deposits that Pleistocene vertebrate specimens are so deficient in fluorine as this one is. Teeth of *Epimachaerodus* (a genus confined to the Old World) have in fact been reported from Upper Pleistocene ('Mousterian') cave-earth in Kent's Cavern, Torquay. It has generally been assumed by vertebrate palaeontologists in recent years that these specimens were residues from some much older deposit in the Torquay Cave system. The composition of one of the Kent's Cavern canines was therefore tested. The fluorine content of the dentine proved to be negligible, and the uranium content very low. The failure of these elements to circulate in calcareous cave deposits is of course recognized, but if these specimens were considerably older than the undoubtedly Upper Pleistocene mammoth teeth found in the same cave-earth they should contain substantially less organic matter. In fact they prove to contain just as much (*see* Table D).

TABLE D

Fluorine and nitrogen content of mammalian teeth from Kent's Cavern.

Specimens of dentine from Kent's Cavern	Nitrogen	$\%F/\%P_2O_5$ ($\times$ 100)
Epimachaerodus canine (BMNH. Pal. 14954); cave-earth	% 1·2[*]	< 0·1
Mammoth molar; cave-earth	0·8	< 0.1
Bear molar; basal breccia	0·2	< 0·1

Washing the sample in warm water and then in acetone to remove any possible traces of nitrogenous preservative effected no reduction in the nitrogen content.

Thus it may be inferred provisionally that sabre-tooth cats survived as rarities in some areas in Britain until Upper Pleistocene times, and that the last of them were contemporary with Middle Palaeolithic and possibly even with the earliest Upper Palaeolithic

(a) Collagen fibres in fossil ivory from Siberia.

SOLVENT FRONT

↑

SOLVENT "B"

← LEUCINE →

← VALINE →

PROLINE

ALANINE

OH-PROLINE

← GLYCINE →

← ARGENINE →

LYSINE
GLUTAMIC ACID }?

MIXTURE OF MARKERS

LLOYD'S RHINO BONE

(b) Chromatogram of amino-acids in hydrolysate from the ulna of a woolly rhinoceros found on the site of the Lloyd's Building, City of London.

(see page 24) PLATE I

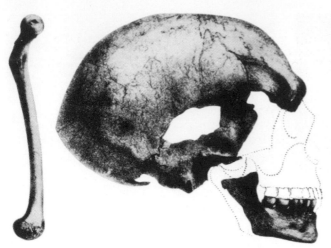

(a) Femur and skull of Galley Hill Man found in the Swanscombe Gravels in 1888. Fluorine and nitrogen tests indicated that this skeleton was an intrusive (post–Pleistocene) burial, that is, less than 10,000 years old. Radiocarbon dating of the residual collagen confirmed this, showing that the skeleton had an antiquity of between 3,000 and 4,000 years.

(b) The Swanscombe skull: the three known bones (found in 1935, 1936 and 1955) articulated and shown from behind. Fluorine, nitrogen and uranium analyses confirmed the contemporaneity of the skull with the Second Interglacial fauna in these gravels, indicating an antiquity of about a quarter of a million years. Photo courtesy Trustees of the British Museum (Natural History).

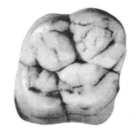

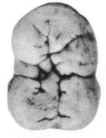

(c) Upper and lower molars of (left to right) man, orang-utan and *Gigantopithecus* ($\times \frac{3}{2}$), the last bought with a prescription for 'Dragon's Teeth' at Chinese drugstores. The Middle Pleistocene date of *Gigantopithecus* has been confirmed by radiometric assays. Photo courtesy Professor G. H. R. von Koenigswald.

PLATE II (see page 24)

men. Surprising as this may seem, it should be recalled that the survival of *Epimachaero-dus* into late Middle Pleistocene times on the Continent is already well established.[14]

Some years ago I suggested[15] that it might be possible to solve the question of the relative antiquity of the enormous hominoid teeth (*Gigantopithecus*) bought by Professor G. H. R. von Koenigswald from Chinese drugstores along with other so-called dragons' teeth which are in fact recognizably the teeth of various fossil mammalia in three main age-groups, Lower Pliocene and Lower and Middle Pleistocene, and obtainable only from certain limited areas in China. The type-specimens (Plate IIc) of *Gigantopithecus* have been regarded as too precious to drill for the purpose of applying the full range of the F-U-N relative dating techniques (fluorine, uranium and nitrogen analyses); but their uranium content at least could be assessed by the method of radiometric assay since it involves no destruction of material. This has now been done through Professor von Koenigswald's courtesy in bringing two of the type specimens to the British Museum (Nat. Hist.) for the purpose. In each case the base of the tooth (largely dentine/cementum) was assayed. The results considered in conjunction with assays on drugstore specimens of known geological ages left no reasonable doubt that the type-specimens of *Gigantopithecus* belong to the Middle Pleistocene group of drugstore fossils.

TABLE E

Uranium content of Gigantopithecus *teeth and other Drugstore and Chinese Fossils of known ages.*

	$e. U_3O_8$ p.p.m.
Drugstore Fossils	
Lower Pliocene group	
Hipparion dentine	130
Hipparion dentine (second specimen)	80
Lower Pleistocene group	
Equus sanamensis dentine*	30
Middle Pleistocene group	
Ailuropoda dentine	<1
Gigantopithecus	
Type specimens (from Drugstores)	
Lower molar	1
Upper molar	10
Liucheng Cave molar	<1
Liucheng Cave-earth fauna (including	
Mastodon) early Middle Pleistocene	$<1-10$

* Made available through the courtesy of Mr Tom Harrisson, Curator of the Sarawak Museum. Further analyses are required in this and in other groups before the ranges of fluctuation will be known.

This conclusion agrees well with the recent discovery by Pei-Wen-Chung of examples of *Gigantopithecus* in a cave deposit with Middle Pleistocene fauna at Liucheng in the Kwangsi Province of southern China.[16] The Chinese scientists generously sent one of the original Liucheng molars of *Gigantopithecus* together with eight associated fossil mammalian specimens for testing in our laboratories in London, and a summary of the results is included in Table E.

Thus the new relative dating techniques both by supplementing the methods of 'absolute' (chronometric) dating, and by helping to establish the stratigraphical origins of specimens of doubtful provenance, are bringing a new element of certainty where previously much has been so uncertain.

REFERENCES AND NOTES

1 DE VRIES, H. and OAKLEY, K. P. 1959. *Nature 184*, 224–6
2 ZINDEREN-BAKKER, E. M. VAN 1957. *Proc. 3rd Pan-Afr. Congr. Prehist. 1955*, London, 237
3 For example, COOK, S. F. and HEIZER, R. F. 1947. *Am. J. Phys. Anth.* 5, 201–20
4 ABELSON, P. H. 1955. *Yearbook Carnegie Inst., Washington 54*, 107–9
5 —— 1956. *Scientific American 195* (1), 83
6 MIDDLETON, J. 1844. *Proc. Geol. Soc. Lond.* 4, 431–3
7 CARNOT, A. 1893. *Ann. de Mines. Mémoires* 9ème sér., *3*, 155–95
8 OAKLEY, K. P. and MONTAGU, M.F.A. 1949. *Bull. Brit. Mus. (Nat. Hist.) Geol.* 1 (2), 25–48
9 BARKER, H. and MACKEY, J. 1961. *Radiocarbon 3*, 41
10 The application of fluorine dating to 'Piltdown Man' was proposed in OAKLEY, K. P. 1948. *Advancement of Science 16*, 336–7. The first results were described in OAKLEY, K. P. and HOSKINS, C. R. 1950. *Nature 165*, 379–82, and further results leading to exposure of the forgery in WEINER, J. S., OAKLEY, K. P. and LE GROS CLARK, W. E. 1953. *Bull. Brit. Mus. (Nat. Hist.) Geol.* 2 (3), 139–46; and the final relative dating by these and nine other authors in 1955. *Ibid.* 2 (6), 225–87
11 For a convenient summary in 1955 see *American Scientist 43* (4), 573–83
12 FRYD, C. F. M. 1955. *Bull. Brit. Mus. (Nat. Hist.) Geol.* 2 (6), 266–7
13 DAVIDSON, C. F. and BOWIE, S. H. U. 1955. *Ibid.* 2 (6), 276–82
14 ADAM, K. D. 1961. *Stuttgarter Beiträge z. Naturkunde 78*, 29
15 OAKLEY, K. P. 1954. *The Times Sci. Rev. 13*, 16
16 PEI, W. C. 1957. *Vertebrata Palasiatica 1* (2), 65–70

3 Radiocarbon Dating

E. H. WILLIS

FEW AIDS TO ARCHAEOLOGICAL INVESTIGATIONS can have contributed as much to our knowledge of the time scale of past events as the radiocarbon dating method. Its global and universal application coupled with the relatively high degree of accuracy on samples of known age makes it the paramount dating method in the age range over which it is practical to use it. Scientific imagination was stirred by the first tentative measurements of Willard Libby, then of the Institute of Nuclear Studies, Chicago, who predicted the existence of radiocarbon in the atmosphere on purely theoretical grounds.[1] The early experiments were quick to be exploited, and the value of the method and the theoretical perception behind it were recognized in 1960 by the award to Professor Libby of the Nobel Prize for Chemistry.

The method relies on certain fundamental assumptions and these, as described below, may be criticized on the grounds that their validity might either be incorrect or might need serious modification. From time to time, notably when the radiocarbon chronology has been at variance with previously conceived chronologies, such criticism has aroused a certain amount of support. The physicists for their part have been most sensitive to the possibility of variations in the fundamental parameters of the method, and have devoted a considerable amount of their research effort to establish the validity of the prime assumptions. As frequently occurs in research of this nature, the by-products have themselves had considerable significance, particularly in the fields of isotopic fractionation of plant material, the turnover times of the stratosphere, troposphere and the oceans; and the past behaviour of the cosmic ray flux. It is therefore pertinent at the outset of this account to examine the validity of the assumptions that Libby first made, and to see under what circumstances it might be necessary to modify them to avoid serious errors in the estimation of the age of an unknown sample. It is perhaps a testimonial to Libby's original notion that the modifications, although important, detract little from the positive value of the method as a dating device.

THE FUNDAMENTAL ASSUMPTIONS

Libby,[2] in postulating the idea that the cosmic ray-produced radiocarbon might provide a valuable means of age determination, supposed that the C^{14} atoms would be readily oxidized to carbon dioxide and would mix freely with the atmospheric carbon dioxide. As a consequence of the rapid turnover of the earth's atmosphere, radiocarbon-labelled carbon dioxide would achieve a uniform global distribution, and might be expected to be taken up in the same proportion by all plant life during the process of photosynthesis. All animal life, derived directly or indirectly from plant material, would also be expected to contain the same universal specific activity. Sea life would be similarly affected, since the carbon dioxide of the atmosphere is in exchange equilibrium with the oceans which in turn reach equilibrium with the atmospheric carbon dioxide. He argued that these equilibria are reached quickly compared with the half-life of C^{14}. Upon the death of an organism, further uptake or exchange of radiocarbon would cease, leaving the trapped radiocarbon to decay exponentially with time.

If the specific activity of organic material has been constant over many thousands of years, then ancient organic material would have exhibited the same specific activity at the time of its death as organic material at the present time. If, then, it were possible to measure the activity of such an ancient sample and compare it with the activity of a modern sample, it would be possible, knowing the half-life of radiocarbon, to calculate the time that has elapsed since the ancient sample was in isotopic exchange equilibrium with the carbon reservoir.

The time t since the death of the organism would be given by

$$t = \frac{1}{\lambda} \log_e \frac{I_o}{I} \quad \dots\dots\dots\dots\dots\dots\dots\dots\dots (1)$$

where λ is the decay constant of radiocarbon; I is the measured activity of the ancient sample; and I_o is the measured activity of modern organic material.

As we have said, criticisms of the method have been made on the ground that one or another of the fundamental assumptions is either not valid, or required serious modification. The more controversial assumptions are:

(1) That the specific activity of living organic material has been constant over a very long period, and further that the contemporary assay is universal.

(2) That the biological materials which are to be assayed have retained their true original composition and ceased exchanging with reservoir carbon at the time of death.

(3) That the half-life of radiocarbon has been accurately determined.

1. *The constancy of the contemporary specific activity.* The specific activity of contemporary plant carbon will depend upon the concentration of radiocarbon in the atmosphere and also the extent of any isotopic fractionation which occurs during photosynthesis, and subsequent metabolism. The constancy of the atmospheric activity will depend in turn on the constancy of radiocarbon production and the rates of isotopic equilibrium within the components of the carbon reservoir.

To the first approximation the dates obtained using the method have been shown to be empirically correct. Nevertheless, with the refinement of the technique, de Vries [3] has shown that variations of the order of $\pm 1\%$ have occurred since AD 1500. This conclusion was reached by measuring the initial activity of carefully dated tree rings taking into account the radioactive decay. Following a similar technique, Willis, Münnich and Tauber,[4] conducting parallel measurement on the same sequoia tree in three separate laboratories, have extended the pattern of variations back to AD 600 with good agreement, and have observed the order of variations described by de Vries. Such variations would lead to errors, independent of the error due to counting statistics, of ± 100 years. Thus it could be that materials of one, three, or even five, finite ages could exhibit the same radiocarbon activity and then be ascribed to one common radiocarbon date. The implications are particularly troublesome for the archaeologist, who often requires a more precise age for his samples.

The variation in the specific activity might imply that the production rate of atmospheric radiocarbon has varied with time and thus the cosmic ray flux likewise, or, that in some way the equilibrium of the carbon reservoir has been disturbed. Stuiver[5] has correlated the variations described above with sunspot activity and has shown a distinct correlation between the two. Whether this is in fact a case of cause and effect still remains to be established.

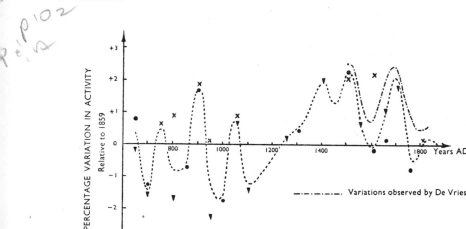

Fig. 1 The result of a combined experiment by the Copenhagen, Heidelberg and Cambridge dating laboratories on the fluctuation of the atmospheric radiocarbon content in the past 1,300 years using the tree rings of a Giant Sequoia as an index

(a) *Equilibrium between the parts of the reservoir.* Craig,[6] Broecker[7] and others have postulated a dynamic model to describe the equilibrium of the radiocarbon reservoir. This model represents a considerable simplification of the natural processes, but nevertheless affords an assessment to be made of the turnover times of the various phases of the reservoir.

The reservoir is continually being replenished by the radiocarbon production from cosmic radiation, and depleted by radioactive decay and sedimentation in the oceans. If the system has reached isotopic equilibrium, the rate of loss will equal the replenishment. The phases are represented by the atmosphere, the biosphere, the upper ocean above the thermocline, and the deep sea. A certain amount of radiocarbon will leak out of the exchange reservoir by becoming entombed in the ocean sediment. This description is known as the chain model. A refinement of this interpretation, known as the cyclic model, has been made to include the direct exchange between deep ocean water and the atmosphere when the former rises to the surface in polar regions. De Vries [8] has described an electrical analogy of Craig's model by considering the phases to constitute an interconnected network of condensers with parallel resistance leak paths.

The specific activity of the contemporary carbon in the different phases will depend largely on the mean residence time of a radiocarbon atom in each phase. As the exchange between growing plant life and the atmosphere is rapid, the contemporary activity of the biosphere will reflect the activity of the atmosphere almost exactly. The two activities will not, however, be identical since an isotopic enrichment in C^{12} is observed during the process of photosynthesis. The mean age of a radiocarbon atom in the surface ocean layers will be much larger than in the atmosphere, since it may have exchanged once or twice with the deep sea. This will mean that the specific activity of the upper ocean would be lower than the atmosphere if there were no isotopic fractionation. Because the latter effect enriches the ocean in radiocarbon, the activity is in fact nearly the same as that found in modern wood.

Similarly, the deep sea will exhibit a specific activity of an even lower value, since its large bulk means that the mean time spent by a radiocarbon atom in this phase is relatively large. Broecker [9] and colleagues at the Lamont Geological Observatory have utilized the apparent age of ocean water to extend our knowledge of the simple turnover model referred to earlier, and in particular to throw some light upon the turnover processes of the oceans themselves.

Isotopic fractionation. The accuracy of the solid carbon method for the contemporary assay was $\pm 2\%$. Kulp [10] found that in practice even this accuracy was difficult to obtain. The effects of isotopic fractionation, which had been demonstrated for several natural processes by Craig [11] for C^{13}, and predicted by extrapolation for C^{14}, were masked by this large error in the assay. The increased efficiency of gas proportional counting has led to the quantitative detection of these effects, especially by Suess,[12] Rafter [13] and Brannon *et al.*[14]

Craig had already shown by mass spectrometric measurements that the atmospheric carbon dioxide showed an enrichment of C^{13} with respect to modern wood of $1 \cdot 84\%$. On this basis Craig predicted that the C^{14} enrichment would be twice the value, namely $3 \cdot 6\%$. Rafter has measured the specific activity of air from Makaia, New Zealand, and obtained results in good agreement with the predicted figure of Craig. Brannon *et al.* have confirmed this figure, which seems well established.

Besides the natural isotopic fractionation that occurs during the growth of the organism, fractionation may also be introduced during the combustion and subsequent processing of the sample for counting. This fractionation is nearly always present if the overall yield of carbon from the original sample is less than 100%. As a consequence, corrections for this effect must be always taken into account during the calculation of the age of a sample. The fractionation of C^{14} with respect to C^{12} is almost exactly twice that of C^{13}, and since this stable isotope of carbon occurs naturally with an abundance of about 1% of C^{12}, the ratio between the two may be determined directly with a suitable mass spectrometer using double beam collection.

(b) *The fossil fuel effect.* These natural processes are further complicated by the large amounts of fossil fuel, containing no residual radiocarbon, which have been burned during the past century. This addition to the carbon reservoir has diluted the atmosphere with C^{12}. A corresponding lowering of the specific activity of modern wood has been observed,[12] but much of the effect has been buffered by exchange with the sea; there, however, the effect has been quite small.

The effect of the fossil fuel dilution influences dating considerably, since samples older than 100 years would exhibit a greater contemporary specific activity than 1960 wood. Moreover, the effect could conceivably be greater in some industrial areas, and dates published by different laboratories may be based on significantly different values for the specific contemporary activity. Before the recognition of this effect, such variations did in fact exist and the need for amending date lists was recognized by de Vries.[15]

Brannon[16] *et al.* have estimated a total combustion of $3 \cdot 3 \times 10^{17}$ gm of fossil fuel since 1860, from Putnam's [17] figures for world coal production, cumulative petroleum production, and natural gas (from the ratio of gas to oil production). This sum is equivalent to 14% of the total amount of carbon dioxide in the atmosphere, which would have exhibited a similar percentage increase in C^{12} in the absence of exchange with the other phases. In fact, as has been shown, this exchange does exist, and the observed dilution was only of the order of 3%.

(c) *Weapon testing effects.* The high neutron flux which occurs during the detonation of a thermonuclear bomb has a similar effect to the naturally occurring neutrons produced by cosmic radiation. Radiocarbon has been added to the atmosphere to such an extent that the dilution effect of the fossil fuel has been far more than compensated.

The cessation of weapon testing after the conclusion of a very intense series by all three interested nations has allowed the fate of a relatively large stratospheric injection of radiocarbon to be observed by samples taken over wide areas. The immediate response was a sharp rise in the spring of 1959 corresponding to the annual flushing of stratospheric air through the tropopause gap. This effect had been demonstrated in previous years by Münnich and Vogel [18] for radiocarbon and by other workers for other fall-out products. The rise of 1959 came to a peak at midsummer with a level in NW. Europe of about 32% of 1953 values,[19, 20] the Northern Hemisphere average being slightly less at around 26%.[21] In 1960, a continuous sampling programme at Cambridge showed no pronounced seasonal variation, and the midsummer level had dropped to 22% above 1953 values, and in 1961 a further drop of 2% was observed. The violation of the moratorium in the autumn of 1961, however, must inevitably lead to a reversal of this trend.

The effects of recent additions of both active and inactive carbon to the reservoir can largely be overcome for dating purposes by using a piece of wood over 100 years old as a standard for the contemporary activity, and this procedure is now common practice.

Standards. To offset any possible variation in the activity of contemporary samples used by different dating laboratories, the National Bureau of Standards, Washington,

D.C., now holds a batch of oxalic acid which is available as a universal reference against which laboratory standards may be checked. Similarly a standard is required for carbon 13/12 determinations, and the sample established by custom for this purpose is the belemnite sample used by Craig. There is an NBS C^{13}/C^{12} standard, however, and Craig [22] has shown a variation of $1 \cdot 1$ per mil between this and the belemnite standard.

The difference between the C^{13}/C^{12} ratio of a counting sample and that of the standard may be expressed by δC^{13}, thus:[23]

$$\delta C^{13} = \left(\frac{C^{13}/C^{12} \text{ sample} - C^{13}/C^{12} \text{ standard}}{C^{13}/C^{12} \text{ standard}} \right) \times 1{,}000 \quad \ldots \ldots \ldots (2)$$

The oxalic acid C^{14}/C^{12} standard is itself affected by the rise in activity due to nuclear weapon testing and is therefore higher than an 'ideal' contemporary sample might be. It transpires however from experience that wood of AD 1890, that is just prior to the industrial revolution, exhibits an activity equal to approximately 95% of the activity of the oxalic acid. This activity, designated in literature as $0 \cdot 95 \, A_{ox}$, is the accepted standard.

The oxalic acid standard must always be used with due reference to the C^{13}/C^{12} standard mentioned above. Craig [24] has measured about 20 samples of carbon dioxide gas made from the oxalic acid by a number of laboratories and the average C^{13}/C^{12} deviation from the standard is close to $-19 \cdot 0 \, \%_{oo}$, and by agreement, this value is the established ratio for the oxalic acid. Since the oxidation, either wet or dry, is very prone to introduce further fractionation in the laboratory, it is essential that each batch of gas prepared from the NBS standard be assayed for C^{13}/C^{12} and due allowance made before using it as a reference for dating.

The corrected value for the oxalic acid standard activity, $0 \cdot 95 \, A_{ox}$, will be given by

$$0 \cdot 95 \, A_{ox} = 0 \cdot 95 \, A^{1}_{ox} \left(1 - \frac{2 \left(19 \cdot 0 + \delta C^{13}_{ox} \right)}{1{,}000} \right) \quad \ldots \ldots \ldots \ldots (3)$$

where A^{1}_{ox} is the observed radiocarbon activity.[23]

19.0 is the average per millage C^{13}/C^{12} deviation of oxalic acid from the Chicago standard.

δC^{13}_{ox} is the measured C^{13}/C^{12} deviation of the sample of gas prepared from the oxalic acid.

It thus follows that if the measured value of the laboratory sample is -19%, then $0 \cdot 95 \, A_{ox} = 0.95 \, A^{1}_{ox}$, and there is no correction.

Calculation of the activity of an unknown sample with respect to the standard. If δC^{14} is the measured deviation between the radiocarbon activity of the unknown sample and that of the standard as computed above, and expressed by

$$\delta C^{14} = \left(\frac{A \text{ sample} - 0 \cdot 95 \, A_{ox}}{0 \cdot 95 \, A_{ox}} \right) \times 1{,}000 \ldots \ldots \ldots \ldots (4)$$

then the true deviation of the activity of the unknown sample when isotopic fractionation is taken into account may be expressed as Δ, given by

$$\Delta = \delta C^{14} - \left(2\delta C^{13} + 50\right)\left(1 + \frac{\delta C^{14}}{1,000}\right) \quad \dots\dots\dots\dots (5)$$

This value is then equivalent to $\left(\frac{I - I_o}{I_o}\right) \times 1,000$ using the symbols of equation (1),

and the age of the sample may be computed directly, since

$$\frac{I}{I_o} = \frac{\Delta + 1,000}{1,000}$$

$$\text{and } t = \frac{1}{\lambda}\log_e \frac{(\Delta + 1,000)}{1,000} \quad \dots\dots\dots\dots (6)$$

2. *Absence of exchange: the retention by biological materials of their original compositions.* Barghorn [25] has shown that under anaerobic conditions there are no known bacteria which will attack lignin. The cellulose fraction of plant material, however, can be the subject of degradative processes. Unfortunately, the more resistant lignin fraction is appreciably soluble and material of similar chemical composition may migrate and be redeposited in another place. Since the more chemically stable cellulose fraction is depleted by degradation processes, the situation can easily arise where redeposited material forms a major source of contamination. Where such a contamination is suspected, the intrusive colloidal material may be extracted with alkali, and this material when assayed invariably yields a much younger age than the residue.

The intrusion of secondary material into a sample can be seen readily in many stratigraphic sections where growing roots have penetrated many feet below the contemporary horizon.[26] Where such intrusion is recognized by fresh rootlets, these can be largely mechanically removed, but perhaps the case is more serious where the secondary intrusion has itself been humified and is indistinguishable from the primary material. Errors of this nature have the greater significance the greater the age of the deposit, and may prove to be one of the limiting factors of the method.

Intrusions do not necessarily have to be of younger origin. In areas such as Britain where there are large outcrops of Palaeozoic or Mesozoic coal, the boulder clays can be shown to contain much comminuted material derived from them,[27] and lake deposits, such as are often employed in dating the Late Glacial period, may contain enough inactive carbon from this source to increase the true dates appreciably.

It has been clearly shown by Deevey *et al.*[28] and Münnich[29] that when the prime source of organic lake mud is by the photosynthesis of submerged plants in hard water, the ancient carbon brought into lakes from limestone formations as soluble bicarbonate may be incorporated into the carbohydrates made by green plants. If this were the only source of carbon for the photosynthetic fixation of submerged aquatic plants in hard water lakes, the dating of their remains might be expected to yield a spurious activity of one half-life of radiocarbon, namely, about 5,000 years. In practice, however, this figure is rarely realized since there is a constant exchange of carbon dioxide in the lake with the atmosphere, especially if it is shallow; this exchange will tend to restore a fraction of the C^{14} deficit.

3. *The half-life of radiocarbon*. The half-life of radiocarbon has been variously determined at values ranging from 7,200 to 4,700 yr. The evaluation of this quantity is essential to the method if radiocarbon ages are to be truly identified with solar years. The present internationally accepted half-life is 5,568 ± 30 yr, and is derived from the weighted average of three determinations. They are 5,580 ± 45 yr (Engelkeimer, Hammil, Inghram, and Libby[30]), 5,589 ± 75 yr (Jones[31]), and 5,513 ± 165 yr (Miller, Ballentine, Bernstein, Friedman, Nier, and Evans[32]). Each of these three values was derived from absolute gas counting methods and considerable trouble was taken to evaluate the efficiency of the counters used. In all three cases, mass spectrometric methods were used for the isotopic composition of the sample.

Later values (Caswell et al.,[33] Manor and Curtiss[34]) gave 5,900 ± 250 and 5,370 ± 210 yr, respectively, although the higher probable error signifies the lower accuracy of the measurements.

Since the three estimations from which the weighted average was taken were made on three different sets of apparatus, it seems probable that the accepted value for the half-life has a real error greater than the ± 30 yr quoted, which is based on statistics. Ralph[35] drew attention to the fact that measurements made on samples of known age back to 2000 BC indicated that the half-life of 5,568 years was not the best fit for the distribution of the points obtained when known age was plotted against measured age. Crowe[36] had earlier observed that samples of known age plotted on Libby's exponential decay curve in his book *Radiocarbon Dating*[37] tended to fall to one side of the curve. Indeed, a recent announcement by the U.S. National Bureau of Standards indicates that this value of 5,568, accepted universally for the past 10 years, is probably incorrect. Since several physical laboratories are known to be working on the same redetermination, it has been agreed to suspend a recalculation of existing published dates until international agreement has been reached. The redetermination is not likely to entail more than a few per cent alteration, and recalculation of previously published dates would be quite simple.

COUNTING METHODS

The process of establishing the activity of an ancient sample, comparing it with that of a contemporary sample, and thus computing the age in accordance with the formula quoted, should in theory be extremely simple. It is, however, far from simple, for radiocarbon is a weak β particle emitter and even the most energetic of its particles are easily stopped by a metal foil. Furthermore, the amount of radiation involved is extremely small, even for a modern sample. These two factors make it impossible to measure by the simplest form of radioactive measurement, namely by placing the sample on a tray under an end window Geiger counter, but in some circumstances it is possible to place a liquid, synthesized from the sample, in front of a scintillation counter. This technique has achieved comparatively little success until recently because of the difficult chemistry, but at the time of writing a substantial advance seems to have been made, and the technique holds much for the future. In general, however, the sample has to be introduced inside the counting chamber itself, and in one form or another the majority of dates produced so far have been obtained in this way.

Libby's original solution to the counting problems was the most direct way possible. He introduced the sample as elementary carbon into a specially constructed screen wall Geiger counter.[39] The carbon was spread evenly over the inner surface of a brass cylinder, and inserted into the counter. The ends were sealed in place, the counter evacuated, and then filled with a normal filling mixture of argon and ethylene. The filling mixture provides a Geiger counter with good counting characteristics, but although reliable from this point of view, the counting efficiency proved extremely low and counting errors correspondingly large. Twenty thousand years was consequently a generous upper limit to this technique. Furthermore, a source of error which soon became sufficiently large to cause the abandonment of solid carbon counting was the liability to contamination by both naturally occurring atmospheric radioactivities and to the ever-increasing fission products from nuclear tests. The need for higher accuracy with smaller sample requirement and freedom from outside contamination led to the examination of other methods of counting.

The most obvious course to take was the conversion of the sample carbon into the gas phase, and introducing it into a counting chamber as the filling gas. Since it is desirable to get as much sample into the counter as possible to achieve the maximum count rate, higher filling pressures than are normally used in Geiger counting are necessary and counting is generally carried out in the proportional region. The difference between the two is simply that in the Geiger counter the discharge resulting from the ionization of the gas spreads throughout the chamber and results in a large pulse no matter what energy the initial ionizing radiation possessed, whilst in a proportional counter, as its name implies, the final pulse obtained is proportional to the initial energy expended by the ionizing radiation. Weak ionizations produce weak pulses and strong ionizations produce strong pulses.

The choice of gas which is to be used as the counting medium will be influenced by the factors of ease of synthesis of the gas from the raw sample, the manner in which it behaves as a counting gas and how many atoms of carbon each molecule of the gas contains.

The Michigan laboratory [40] uses a mixture of carbon disulphide and carbon dioxide at relatively low gas pressures and is able to use this arrangement as a Geiger counter. It has proved very reliable and simple to operate but the efficiency of this method is, however, somewhat low since the operating pressure is limited.

Carbon dioxide is by far the easiest gas to synthesize, since it is obtained by direct combustion of the sample in a stream of oxygen. It would have few challengers but for the stringent purity requirements for reliable counting characteristics. It had long been held that carbon dioxide was useless as a counting medium, but by rigorous purification of all electronegative impurities it has been demonstrated to be completely reliable.[41] Fergusson [42] has estimated that one part of chlorine in ten million parts of carbon dioxide is sufficient to affect the counting characteristics appreciably. The greater number of laboratories at present producing dates rely on this method.

Methane is more tolerant to impurities and therefore satisfies the second requirement admirably. Its synthesis from carbon dioxide requires additional chemical processes which to some extent detract from its obvious counting qualities. It has one particular advantage over other gases, however, since it requires a much lower working voltage and can be operated at high pressures. At similar pressure with carbon dioxide, high voltage corona discharges become increasingly apparent.

Both acetylene and ethylene are diatomic in carbon and thus have an immediate advantage over both carbon dioxide and methane.[43-45] Syntheses are again more complex, but acetylene in particular has proved popular with a number of laboratories, and is more tolerant to impurities than carbon dioxide.

In practice, the size of counters and hence the amount of gas to fill them is limited largely by the availability of carbon from the sample. Archaeologists are naturally reluctant to part with quantities of precious samples, and the carbon content of geological samples, such as lake muds, is often in small supply. A small counter filled to a high pressure with a relatively low background will best meet the need for small sample size and accuracy of counting. The overall sensitivity of the counter is dependent upon the square of its contemporary count rate divided by its background.

Scintillation counting offers the attractive possibility of introducing much larger quantities of carbon into the counting system than with either of the two previous methods; again supposing sufficient sample to be available.

Routine measurements of natural radiocarbon have been successfully carried out by McAulay and associates[46] at Trinity College, Dublin, using methanol as a solvent. The decision to use scintillation counting in this case was influenced by the non-availability of liquid nitrogen supplies, which makes the use of gaseous systems involving vacuum line technique quite impossible. One of the limiting factors in the scintillation technique has hitherto been the synthesis of a suitable solvent. In most solvents prepared for radiocarbon dating, only one atom in the final molecule originates from the sample, but recently the synthesis of benzene has been reported[47] which derives all its carbon atoms from the raw sample. The syntheses in most forms of scintillation counting are more complex than gas proportional counting, but with the pressing need for age determinations greater than the 70,000 years obtained by the late Hessel de Vries by isotopic enrichment,[48] this method might promise a significant advance.

PUBLICATION OF DATES

The growing number of dates produced by the thirty or more laboratories now in operation presents a formidable amount of data to assimilate. There has thus been a great need for a medium through which dates may be published quickly and in a uniform manner. Two organizations have been created for this specific purpose, the one being complementary to the other.

The first is an offshoot from the *American Journal of Science*, formerly issued as a Supplement to that journal, but now published under the title of 'Radiocarbon'.

Published annually, this journal is supported by nearly every working laboratory, and serves as a source book for all radiocarbon dates. Each sample and its date is accompanied by a brief description of its provenance and significance, and is designated by the sample number and laboratory prefix letter.

The other medium is 'Radiocarbon Dates Inc.', a non-profit-making organization concerned with the distribution of dates on a punched card system. Each card, an example of which is shown in Plate III, contains all the relevant information, and may be sorted under a wide range of headings. Inquiries should be addressed to Radiocarbon Dates Inc., R. S. Peabody Museum for Archaeology, Andover, Mass., U.S.A., and for the journal, Sterling Tower, Yale University, New Haven, Conn., U.S.A.

Both organizations provide an excellent service, and by their very existence demonstrate the contribution that the method has made to the advancement of our knowledge of man's past history.

REFERENCES

1 LIBBY, W. F. 1946. *Phys. Rev. 69*, 671
2 —— 1955. *Radiocarbon Dating*, Chicago
3 DE VRIES, H. L. 1958. *Proc. Koninkl. Ned. Akad. Wetenschap. 61* no. 2, 1
4 WILLIS, E. H., MÜNNICH, K. O. and TAUBER, H. 1960. *Am. J. Sci. Radiocarbon Suppl. 2*, 1–4
5 STUIVER, M. 1961. *J. Geophys. Res. 66*, 273
6 CRAIG, H. 1957. *Tellus 9*, 1.
7 BROECKER, W. S. and OLSON, E. A. 1960. *Science 132*, 712
8 DE VRIES, H. L. 1958. *Proc. Koninkl. Ned. Akad. Wetenschap. 61*, no. 2, 1
9 BROECKER, W. S., GERARD, R., EWING, M. and HEEZEN, B. C. 1960. *J. Geophys. Res. 65*, 2903
10 KULP, J. L. *et al.* 1958. *Natl. Acad. Sci.—Natl. Research Council 573*, Nuclear Science Series no. 24
11 CRAIG, H. 1953. *Geochim. et Cosmochim. Acta 3*, 53
12 SUESS, H. 1954. *Science 120*, 5
13 RAFTER, T. A. 1954. *New Zealand J. Sci. Technol. 36*, 363
14 BRANNON, H. R., WILLIAMS, M., SIMONS, L. H., PERRY, D., DAUGHTY, A. C. and McFARLAN, E. 1957. *Science 125*, 919
15 DE VRIES, H. L., BARENDSEN, G. W. and WATERBOLK, H. T. 1958. *Science 127*, 129
16 BRANNON, H. R. *et al., op. cit.*
17 PUTNAM, P. C. 1953. *Energy in the Future*, New York
18 MÜNNICH, K. O. and VOGEL, J. C. 1950. In Godwin, H. *Nature 184*, 1365
19 WILLIS, E. H. 1960. *Nature 188*, 552
20 TAUBER, H. 1960. *Science 131*, 921
21 BROECKER, W. C. and WALTON, A. 1959. *Science 130*, 273
22 CRAIG, H. 1957. *Geochim. et Cosmochim. Acta 12*, 133
23 BROECKER, W. C. and OLSEN, E. 1961. *Radiocarbon 3*
24 CRAIG, H. 1961 *Radiocarbon 3*
25 BARGHORN, E. S. 1961. *J. Sediment. Petroc. 22*
26 GODWIN, H. 1951. *Am. J. Sci. 249*, 301
27 —— and WILLIS, E. H. 1959. *Proc. Roy. Soc. B. 150*, 199
28 DEEVEY, E. S., GROSS, M. S., HUTCHINSON, G. E., and KRAYBILL, H. L. 1954. *Proc. Natl. Acad. Sci. U.S. 40*, 285
29 MÜNNICH, K. O. 1957. *Naturwissenschaften. 44*, 32
30 ENGELKEIMER, A. G., HAMMIL, W. H., INGHRAM, M. G. and LIBBY, W. F. 1949. *Phys. Rev. 75*, 1825
31 JONES, W. M. 1949. *Phys. Rev. 76*, 885
32 MILLER, W. W., BALLENTINE, R., BERNSTEIN, W., FRIEDMAN, L., NIER, A. O. and EVANS, R. D. 1950. *Phys. Rev. 77*, 714
33 CASWELL, R. S., BRABANT, J. M. and SCHWEBEL, A. 1954. *J. Res. Natl. Bur. Standards 53*, 27

34 MANOR, G. G. and CURTISS, L. F. 1951. *Ibid., 46*, 328
35 RALPH, E. K. and STUCKENRATH, R. 1960. *Nature 188*, 185
36 CROWE, C. 1958. *Nature 182*, 470
37 LIBBY, W. 1955. *Radiocarbon Dating*, Chicago, 2nd ed.
38 EDITORIAL, *Radiocarbon 3*
39 LIBBY, W. F. 1952. *Phys. Rev. 86*, 128
40 CRANE, H. *Radiocarbon 3*
41 DE VRIES, H. L. and BARENDSEN, E. 1953. *Physica 19*, 987
42 FERGUSSON, G. J. 1955. *Nucleonics 13*, 18
43 BARKER, H. 1953. *Nature 172*, 631
44 CRATHORNE, A. R. 1953. *Nature 172*, 634
45 SUESS, H. E. 1954. *Science 120*, 5
46 MCAULAY, I. R. and DELANEY, C. F. G. 1959. *Proc. Roy. Dublin Soc.* Series A, *1*, 1
47 TAMERS, M. A. 1960. *Science 132*, 668
48 DE VRIES, H. L., DE VRIES, A. E. and HARRIS, A. 1958. *Science 128*, 472

4 Obsidian Dating

IRVING FRIEDMAN   ROBERT L. SMITH
DONOVAN CLARK

THE DATING OF OBSIDIAN ARTIFACTS is based upon the fact that a freshly made surface of obsidian, a variety of volcanic glass, will absorb water from its surroundings to form a measurable hydration layer.[1] This layer is not visible to the unaided eye and should not be confused with the patina that develops on many materials as a result of alteration or chemical weathering. The hydration begins the moment the surface is exposed by chipping or flaking and the penetration of water into the artifact continues at a known rate until the present time. Thus, when ancient man chipped or flaked a piece of obsidian he exposed fresh surfaces on which hydration then commenced. Measurement of the depth of penetration of hydration on the artifact should, then, provide a measure of the time that elapsed since the manufacture of the artifact.

This hydration process appears to be restricted to obsidian, and does not occur on other natural materials such as flint, jasper, quartz, chert, chalcedony and quartzite.

The development of this dating technique is very recent,[2] and although problems still remain to be worked out, the measurement of several thousand artifacts from archaeological sites all over the world has proven the method to be useful within the limitations to be discussed.[3]

The discovery that the hydration of obsidian was related, in part, to time, suggested that this fact could be utilized as a dating method. To accomplish this, however, required the following:

(1) Development of a technique for measuring hydration layers, that may vary from only a few tenths to perhaps 20 microns (10 to 1,000 millionths of an inch), and with a precision of about ± 0·2 micron (8 millionths of an inch).

(2) Determination of the rate at which the hydrated layer increased in thickness.

(3) Analysis of the factors that influence the rate of hydration.

(4) Analysis of the variability caused by alteration of the hydration layer by wear, etc.

(5) A determination of the archaeological factors that affect the correlation of the age of the artifact with the stratigraphic position in which it is found.

These factors will be considered in some detail in the sections to follow.

THE TECHNIQUE OF MEASUREMENT

The technique of measurement is fairly simple and quick. A thin platelike sample, which may be as small as 2 mm × 4 mm by 0·5 mm thick, is sawed from the artifact at right angles to the surface to be examined. This cutting is carried out, with the aid of an especially thin diamond-loaded metal saw blade, in a manner that causes little damage to the specimen. The cut slice is then cemented to a glass microscope slide and ground down, first with the aid of a motor-driven lap charged with a slurry of fine abrasive and water, and later by hand on a glass plate charged with the same abrasive, until the slice is about 0·05 mm (0·0025 in.) thick. The cutting and grinding of a typical sample requires about fifteen minutes.

This thin section is then examined under the microscope. Because the hydrated obsidian has a higher refractive index than does the non-hydrated obsidian and the interface between the hydrated and non-hydrated material is sharp, the division between the two can be seen under the microscope as a relatively sharp dividing line. Plate IVa is a photomicrograph of a typical sample taken with a 45 × objective and a 10 × ocular. The addition of water to the obsidian causes a change in volume that creates mechanical strain in the hydrated layer. This strain causes the hydrated layer to be seen as a bright band (strain birefringence) when viewed under crossed polarized light (Plate IVb). Strain birefringence is useful in detecting the hydrated layer, but the measurements to be described are usually made in plain light.

The measurements are made with the aid of a filar micrometer ocular, a special eye-piece containing a movable scale or hairline, the movement of which can be read on a drum on the side of the eyepiece. Layers thicker than 2 microns are measured using the 10 × or 12·5 × filar micrometer ocular and a 45 × objective (approx. 500 ×). Thinner layers are measured with a 100 × oil immersion objective with the filar micrometer eyepiece (approx. 1,000×) . Examination and measurement under the microscope require about ten minutes per slide.

In our first paper on the method[2] we assigned an error of ± 0·2 micron to our measurements. We found that on duplicate thin sections made from the same artifact, 90% of the time our repeat measurements would fall within this assigned error.

Recently one of us (D. Clark) has made a careful statistical analysis of the measuring technique. In a test involving four different persons, each measuring an identical series of slides, the results showed a standard error of the mean of ± 0·2 micron. However, since people differ somewhat in their placing of the hairline, it is suggested that future users of the method calibrate themselves by measuring a set of standard slides.

RATE OF HYDRATION OF OBSIDIAN

In order for the measurements of hydration layer thickness to be translatable into an age, it is necessary that the rate of increase in thickness of the hydrated layer with time be known. Because the rate is too slow to allow direct measurement in the laboratory, it was necessary to secure artifacts of known age and to use the thickness of the hydrated layer of these specimens to determine the hydration rate. The difficulty has been in securing obsidian artifacts of really 'known' and reliable age. The ideal sample for our use would be one made 2,000 or more years ago, inscribed with the date of manufacture, and kept in a known environment from date of manufacture to present. Since no such pieces are available, we are forced to approximate this ideal. One source of old well-dated material is to be found in obsidian used to decorate Egyptian mummies and burial containers. This material can be dated with sufficient accuracy both historically and by radiocarbon. Unfortunately few such samples have been available to us. Of the Egyptian samples that we have obtained, many are of a rather rare form of volcanic glass called

(a) The Radiocarbon Dating Laboratory, Cambridge University. The glass vacuum line is used in the purification of carbon dioxide gas for proportional counting.

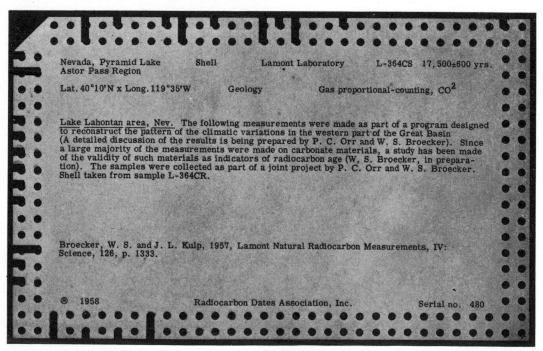

Nevada, Pyramid Lake   Shell   Lamont Laboratory   L-364CS 17,500±600 yrs.
Astor Pass Region

Lat. 40°10'N x Long. 119°35'W   Geology   Gas proportional-counting, CO_2

Lake Lahontan area, Nev. The following measurements were made as part of a program designed to reconstruct the pattern of the climatic variations in the western part of the Great Basin (A detailed discussion of the results is being prepared by P. C. Orr and W. S. Broecker). Since a large majority of the measurements were made on carbonate materials, a study has been made of the validity of such materials as indicators of radiocarbon age (W. S. Broecker, in preparation). The samples were collected as part of a joint project by P. C. Orr and W. S. Broecker. Shell taken from sample L-364CR.

Broecker, W. S. and J. L. Kulp, 1957, Lamont Natural Radiocarbon Measurements, IV: Science, 126, p. 1333.

® 1958   Radiocarbon Dates Association, Inc.   Serial no. 480

(b) A specimen of the punched–card index system published by 'Radiocarbon Dates Inc.' as a service to archaeology.

(see page 35) PLATE III

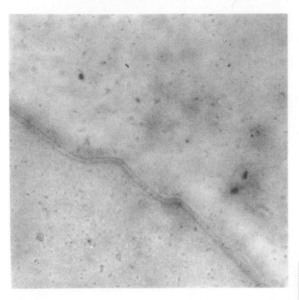

(a) Photomicrograph of a thin section of an obsidian artifact showing the hydration layer, as viewed in ordinary light. From Friedman and Smith.[2]

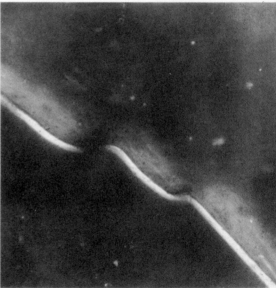

(b) Photomicrograph of the specimen shown in (a) viewed under crossed polarized light. The hydrated layer is bright because of strain birefringence. From Friedman and Smith.[2]

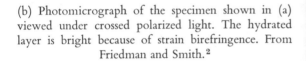

(c) Photomicrograph of a thin section of an obsidian artifact from Ecuador, showing a thick hydration layer along an original unworked surface (lower left) adjacent to a flaked area. Blows struck on the artifact introduced a series of short percussion cracks. The thickness of the hydration layer formed along these cracks is the same as on the remainder of the worked surfaces of the artifact. From Friedman and Smith.[2]

PLATE IV (see page 47)

trachytic obsidian that differs chemically from the usual rhyolitic obsidian. This chemical difference results in a more rapid rate of hydration than occurs with rhyolitic obsidian. The rate determined with the trachytic obsidian cannot therefore be applied to rhyolitic obsidian artifacts.

Another source is obsidian associated with material which can be dated by radiocarbon. The problems here are that not only must account be taken of the errors possible in C^{14} dating, but the material dated by C^{14}, because of uncertain stratigraphic correspondences, may prove to be of an age quite different from that of the obsidian. Thus, attempts were made to secure dated obsidian from stratigraphic horizons in excavations where the obsidian is associated with cultural material datable either historically, or by tree ring dating of associated wood, C^{14} dating of associated charcoal, etc. The correlations are not always valid. Even burials, where the obsidian artifacts were interred with the body, present problems of older obsidian being buried long after it was originally chipped.

However, bearing in mind these problems inherent in securing accurately dated obsidian in order to establish hydration rates, it was still possible to establish tentative hydration rates and to assess many of the factors that influence the rate of hydration. Work now in progress and proposed should help make the hydration rate data more precise.

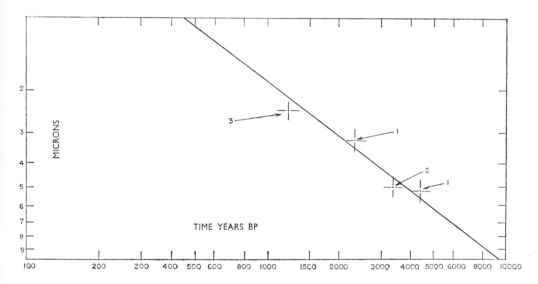

Fig. 2 Diagram showing the thickness of the hydration layer (microns) *vs.* time (years BP) on artifacts from Central California. From Clark[4]

On theoretical grounds it was thought that the penetration of water into the obsidian should follow the diffusion law $D = kt^{1/2}$, where D = thickness of hydration layer in microns, k = constant, t = time in years. The data first presented [5] fitted this equation within the precision of the data. Recent work by Clark [4] on a carefully selected group of obsidians from burial sites in Central California, where the relative dates of the burials are fairly well established and where there are several C[14] dates in sequence, suggest a hydration rate that may follow $D = kt^{3/4}$. Again, further work may help establish the equation of the hydration rate. We need more well-dated obsidian artifacts to settle this point. Whether the hydration follows $D = kt^{3/4}$ is not important for most artifacts under 4,000 years old. The differences become important when dating artifacts of much greater age, say 20,000 years old.

FACTORS THAT INFLUENCE THE RATE OF HYDRATION

Early in the research we recognized that while all surficially exposed obsidian hydrates, the rate at which a layer of hydration will thicken depends primarily on the temperature at which it has been exposed while hydrating. Thus, like most diffusion processes, the rate is faster in warmer, and slower in colder environments. Translated to specific examples, we have found that artifacts buried in coastal Ecuador will hydrate ten times as fast as those buried in the frozen arctic of the northern Alaska Arctic Coast. Therefore, dating material of a given site or area will ideally require a knowledge of the local climatology, past and present. This may mean data on the soil temperature at the depth where the sample was buried. Where this is lacking, approximations based on air temperature and soil conductivity estimates will usually suffice. The accuracy of these temperature estimates need not be great, and this information is now being collected for archaeological sites containing obsidian artifacts. In many cases the change of climate since the obsidian artifacts were made is small, and can be approximated from geological and climatological data.

The temperature coefficient of the rate of hydration, although probably the largest variable, does seem to be the easiest of the variables to assess and to correct for. We need but to construct hydration curves for different climatic zones as was done in Fig. 3. More closely defined zones will ultimately allow closer control of this variable. Indeed, we should soon know the temperature dependence of the 'constant' k in the hydration rate equations, and this will allow us to calculate a hydration rate curve for any given site.

It might appear that another possible variable would be the relative dryness of the environment where the obsidian is buried. We have shown that obsidian of the same chemical composition buried in wet tropical coastal Ecuador hydrates at about the same rate as does material buried in a tomb in Egypt. The relative humidity of the environment has no apparent effect, probably because in any natural environment there is enough water to saturate the outer surface of the obsidian with a molecular film of water, and keep it saturated throughout the hydration history of the obsidian, and it is this saturated outer surface that helps determine the rate of penetration of water into the interior of the obsidian.

The chemical composition of the obsidian also influences the hydration rate, and we know that gross differences in chemistry, such as that existing between rhyolitic and trachytic obsidian, will cause a major change in hydration rate. Fortunately, most obsidian used for artifacts does not differ very much in chemical composition. Little is known about the specific chemical differences that exist between obsidians obtained from different outcrops or quarries in one small area. Even less is known about the influence of such minor chemical differences, if they exist, on the rates of hydration of such obsidian. In the course of our research, we have found small anomalies in sets of data, that may be related to minor chemical differences among the artifacts.

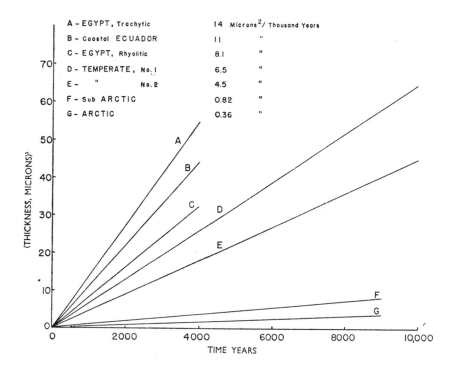

Fig. 3 Hydration rates A, B, C, D and E plotted on the same diagram to show the variation in the rate in different climatic regions. The rate of hydration of each scale is also stated as a mathematical expression of the slope of the corresponding line. From Friedman and Smith[2]

The Yayahuala site in the state of Hidalgo, Mexico furnishes us with such an anomalous set of data. Here artifacts made from grey obsidian are found mixed with artifacts made from a clear green obsidian. The two types of obsidian came from different quarries, and probably differ slightly chemically. The green objects have hydration rims greater than 3 microns, while the objects made from the grey obsidian all have rims less than 3 microns. Is this difference due to a variability in chemical composition between the obsidians, or is it a true age difference? In the latter case we may have a situation where the site was occupied for a time by people using obsidian and then abandoned. The people of a later occupancy then used obsidian from another quarry. In other words the two magnitudes of hydration in this site correlate with different coloured obsidian, and may reflect either a chemical difference in contemporary material, or the differences may express a change in cultural habits over time. Further work, both archaeological and chemical, will be necessary to further elucidate this problem.

CHANGES IN THICKNESS OF THE HYDRATION LAYER
BY MECHANICAL AND CHEMICAL PROCESSES

The hydration layer is extremely thin, and because it forms the outermost surface of the artifact it is subject to alteration by physical and chemical processes. For example, an artifact exposed to running water, wind, or sand for any length of time may lose part or all of the layer, at various locations, through abrasion. Commonly the abrasion will be obvious by inspection of the artifact. The edges, formerly sharp, are now rounded and the surface has a dull, matt appearance. However, it is unlikely that mechanical erosion can remove a uniform layer on all surfaces of the artifact. Often thin spots and chipped areas are seen on the thin sections. However, such effects can be caused during the grinding of the thin section, and may not be the result of natural abrasion. For these reasons, it is necessary to search the edges of the thin section thoroughly to locate the maximum and culturally representative thickness of hydration. We may stress, however, that typical thin section specimens present no measurement problems.

The hydrated layer consists of a glass containing about 3·5% water by weight, compared to less than 0·3% of water present in the main body of the non-hydrated obsidian. Diffusion of alkalis and other ions is very rapid in the high water content layer. Consequently, alteration and solution are speeded up in this layer as compared to the non-hydrated obsidian. Conceivably the chemical environment present in certain soils will speed up this chemical attack. Obsidian in areas of hydrothermal activity would seem especially prone to this vicissitude. Artifacts from sites near hot spring localities in Central California show a high degree of this form of alteration. This could account for the lack of any hydration on many of the artifacts examined from Jarmo, Iraq. However, except for a few sites, we have found little evidence for pronounced alteration of the hydrated layer by physical or chemical agents.

Because mechanical strain increases as the hydration layer becomes thicker a point is finally reached where the hydrated layer spalls off, and hydration begins again on the fresh surface that is created. Such spalling is not always complete and on some very old pieces of obsidian traces of a thicker layer can be found. We believe that spallation may occur when the layer is greater than about 40 microns. Therefore, on artifacts of supposedly great antiquity (over 50,000 years), it is well to cut several sections to look for such remnant layers.

Exposure of the artifact to fire, as, for example, when the obsidian is found in a cremation, affects the surface of the obsidian and makes it unsuitable for age determination. Such 'burned' artifacts are easily recognized by the fine, cross-hatched cracking or blistering of the surface.

CULTURAL FACTORS THAT AFFECT THE ARCHAEOLOGICAL
INTERPRETATION OF OBSIDIAN HYDRATION RESULTS

During the course of measuring and evaluating the results from thousands of obsidian artifacts, we have encountered occasional anomalous measurements, clearly not due to environmental factors or to laboratory error. The magnitude of the variability often indicates that these specimens are not contemporaneous with the provenience from

which they were collected. For example, in a lot of ten specimens from a given stratigraphic level, typically six or seven may yield measurements which cluster rather well
about the mode and mean. Three or four, however, may have a hydration layer
obviously too thin or too thick. Usually these erratic measurements may be explained
logically. Often, however, the archaeological grounds for so doing are less clear.
Attention has recently been drawn to the re-use of obsidian artifacts of an old culture by
peoples of a more recent culture. It is not, therefore, difficult to provide a plausible
reason for the presence in a given cultural level of specimens which are too thickly
hydrated, hence too old. It is rather the occasional presence of those specimens whose
hydration is too thin that is somewhat less amenable to simple explanation. We may
consider such factors as slight petrologic differences, post-cultural fracturing (thus
exposing fresh surfaces for hydration), or even differential wear on these specimens.
More plausible, perhaps, would be the chances of contamination of a given archaeological stratum by peoples of a later horizon and the intrusion of later obsidian artifacts
into this level. It seems equally possible that such a level can also be contaminated by
overlying material during excavation. Another, if less likely source of error could derive
from museum or laboratory mislabelling. Stratigraphic mixing is, of course, a chronic
problem in archaeology, and the problems encountered in obsidian dating will not provide us with the final solution. On the other hand, as we acquire more evidence, particularly typological, we can better explain the occurrence of anomalous measurements.
Meanwhile, we find it most feasible to measure five specimens or, if available, even ten
specimens from each burial, stratigraphic level or other cultural component to be dated.
We do not believe that reliance can be placed upon only one or two specimens with any
assurance of precise dating. In passing we can, however, note one rather special exception to this rule. In cases where the antiquity of manufacture is in question, it is a simple
matter by this method to test whether a single artifact or work of art made of obsidian
is authentically archaeological or a modern forgery. A lack of hydration safely implies
manufacture within the twentieth century, and we have had occasion to make this test
as a service to a few museums and collectors in the past few years.

We have discussed the method in some detail, and have stated that it is both reliable
and precise. It remains to support this claim with results. While this publication is not a
suitable medium for a detailed listing of hydration values, we hope that the following
three fairly typical examples will serve dual ends. First, to demonstrate the approaches
we have used in our research; and, secondly, to show the degree of confidence one may
place in the method when unfavourable conditions, such as cultural and stratigraphic
mixing, are not excessive.

The first illustration involves a study of fifty well-documented artifacts. These derived
from ten different burials in seven representative sites in Central California. For the most
part, associated artifacts, such as typological shell beads, permitted good relative placement of each burial lot. Since the obsidian artifacts in each lot clearly were associated
with the burial, it was assumed, a priori, that the members of each lot were contemporaneous. We shall observe that this assumption did not hold in a few cases because of re-use
and other factors which we have described. Incidentally, one aspect of the procedure,

we believe, added rigour to the test. This was the practice of making all the measurements on this series 'blind', that is, without the analysts making prior reference to the proveniences or assumed ages of the specimens. Table A lists the results of measurement on the entire series. The California sites represented are as follows:

(1) Kingsley Cave: A Late horizon (1,500 years BP to eighteenth-century site).
(2) Peterson 2: Another Late horizon site; two burials examined.
(3) Hotchkiss: A Late horizon site; two burials examined.
(4) Bodega Bay: A primarily Middle horizon (4,000 to 1,500 years BP) context, but containing an overlying Late horizon stratum.
(5) McClure: A Late horizon site.
(6) Goddard: A Late horizon site.
(7) Blossom: An Early horizon (c. 4,000 years BP) site; two burials examined.

It will be seen from these figures that, except for occasional anomalies, the within-burial variances are not great, and more importantly, the method readily discriminates between burials of different archaeological ages. It is unfortunate that a greater number of specimens for each burial were not available for testing; but we believe that, as they stand, the data are adequate.

A second example is that of Shanidar Cave, Iraq. The floor of the cave was partially excavated by Professor Ralph Solecki of Columbia University who submitted the obsidian samples for investigation. In excavating the cave, Professor Solecki made various cuts into the floor. Charcoal was found at certain depths in several of the cuts, and C^{14} dates were obtained on this charcoal. The obsidian was not usually associated with the charcoal and the correlation between the C^{14} dated layers and the obsidian was based on a comparison of cultural material found in the various strata. In Fig. 4 the thickness of the hydrated layer squared ($D = kt^{1/2}$) is plotted against the estimated age of the artifacts, as determined by the correlations mentioned above. In general there is good agreement between the thickness of the hydration layer and the estimated age of the artifacts. Additional samples secured by further excavation may clear up the few discrepancies.

The Chorrera site on the coast of Ecuador is an example of an archaeological site where obsidian artifacts made by an earlier culture have been re-used by later occupants of the site. The site consists of a habitation refuse deposit on the Rio Babahoyo, Guayas Province. Drs Clifford Evans and Betty Meggers[5] of the Smithsonian Institution excavated the site and studied the pottery found in the refuse deposit. Measurement of 62 obsidian pieces (see Fig. 5) from the site permitted us to group the artifacts into four groups as follows: (1) Hydration layers less than 2·0 microns. These, in view of their thinness and therefore late age, were classed as 'modern'. This checks with the fact that the site has been cultivated since the Spanish occupation and a banana plantation now occupies the site. (2) and (3). Two groups of artifacts found above the 285 cm layer. One group with hydration thickness from 2·9 to 3·9 microns and another from 3·9 to 4·9 microns. (4) Below 285 cm we find no artifacts with a hydration layer less than 5 microns. We conclude that artifacts having layers from 2·9 to 4·9 microns were made by

TABLE A

Thickness of hydration layer and approximate hydration age of artifacts associated with ten different burials from seven different sites in Central California.

Site and Burial	Measurements*	Hydration age approx.	Remarks
	μ	yrs BP	
Kingsley	1·4	700	Burial average 1·5±0·10 microns
Cave	1·5	750	Variance slight
Burial	1·6	850	Good agreement with archaeological
No. 93	1·6	850	estimate of age
	1·6	850	
Peterson 2	1·4	700	5th specimen contained two rims
Burial No.	1·5	750	of hydration. This condition
12/7697	1·5	750	ascribed to a case of reworking of
	1·7	900	an older artifact
	1·7/3·4	(omitted)	Burial average 1·5 ± 0·13
Peterson 2	1·6	850	6th specimen possibly reworked
Burial no.	1·6	850	Burial average: 1·7±0·13 microns
12/7696	1·7	900	
	1·8	1,000	
	1·9	1,050	
	2·0/4·1	omitted	
Hotchkiss	1·9	1,050	Burial average 2·1±0·14
Burial 52	2·0	1,100	Variance slight
	2·0	1,100	
	2·2	1,250	
	2·2	1,250	
Hotchkiss	2·1	1,150	Burial average 2·4±0·26 microns
Burial 22	2·5	1,500	
	2·5	1,500	
Bodega Bay	1·9	1,050	Burial average 2·5±0·50 microns
Burial 17	2·7	1,650	
	2·8	1,750	
McClure	2·3	1,300	Burial average 2·6±0·18 microns
Burial 13	2·6	1,550	
	2·6	1,550	
Goddard	2·6	1,550	4th and 5th specimens appear to be
Burial 7	2·9	1,800	cases of re-use
	3·0	1,850	Burial average 2·8±0·21 microns
	4·4	omitted	
	4·6	omitted	

TABLE A continued:

Site and Burial	Measurements*	Hydration age approx.	Remarks
	μ	yrs BP	
Blossom	4·3	3,100	Variance unexplained at present.
Burial 33	4·5	3,300	Burial av. 5·2±0·70 μ; av. of
	5·5	4,300	1st and 2nd, 4·6, of 3rd and 4th, 5·7.
	5·9	4,700	C¹⁴ composite dates on this site were
			4052±160, and 4100±250 BP
Blossom	4·8	3,600	Burial average 5·0±0·26 microns.
Burial 23	4·9	3,700	*See* remarks above
	5·3	4,000	

* Average of two analysts.
Hydration age estimates are based on the rate $D = kt^{3/4}$ (*see* Fig. 2, p. 49); samples submitted by Prof. R. F. Heizer, Univ. of California, Berkeley.

people who occupied the site subsequent to the first occupation. All the obsidian in the upper levels having hydration layers thicker than 5 microns could be interpreted as re-use and redeposition of older material.

On the basis of changes in pottery types Evans and Meggers [3] subdivided the Chorrera deposit into three parts:

'The Milagro period from o to 135 cm, the Tejar period from 135 to 300 cm; the Chorrera period from 300 cm to the bottom of the stratigraphic cut. The Chorrera period refuse coincides almost exactly with the earliest period distinguished on the basis of hydration thickness (greater than 5 microns). There is no clear demarcation in the thickness of the hydration layers at 135 cm that correlates with the Tejar-Milagro period subdivisions. However, the intermediate grouping of artifacts with hydration layers of 3·9 to 4·9 microns thickness gives a date that would be acceptable for the Tejar period, and the third group, with thicknesses of 2·9 to 3·9 microns, undoubtedly represents the Milagro period. If this interpretation is valid, then the artifacts, flakes, and chips of obsidian with hydration layers less than 3·9 microns in thickness in levels below 135 cm may be explained as mechanical mixture, either during occupation of the site, afterwards by rodent and small animal burrowing, or a specimen from an upper level in the walls of the stratigraphic cut accidentally falling into the excavation.

'The frequency of re-used material, which associates early objects with late levels; and the possibility of disturbance, which can move late material into earlier levels in habitation refuse, are two problems that the Chorrera stratigraphic excavation illustrates in an extreme way. The fact that the artifacts are chips or prismatic flakes used as blades or scrapers without shaping beyond the initial blows striking them from a

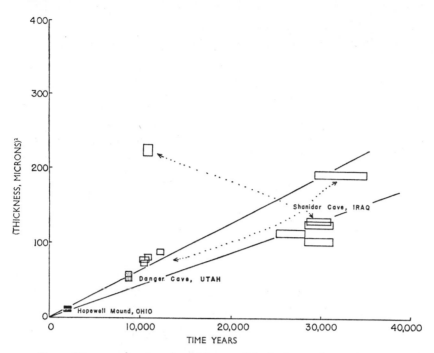

Fig. 4 Diagram showing the thickness of the hydration layer in microns squared on objects from Shanidar Cave, Iraq as well as from other sites in temperate zones. From Friedman and Smith[2]

core, rather than projectile points or carefully shaped artifacts, probably accounts for this extensive re-use. Comparable re-use might be predicted in other areas with similar rudimentary obsidian tools. However, with adequate knowledge of the cultural sequence and a sufficient number of samples per level, re-used objects can be readily distinguished from those of contemporary manufacture. Artifacts of too recent date can be recognized if a series of samples is secured for several sites of the same cultural period, and if the cultural sequence in the area is sufficiently well known. A good relative chronology is essential for evaluation of any absolute dates, whether they are derived from obsidian, radiocarbon, dendrochronology, or some other method.

CONCLUSIONS

The obsidian dating method is still in the developmental stage. In common with all dating techniques, it contains sources of error inherent in the technique. The authors have attempted to outline some of these sources of error. In addition to the technical errors, every dating technique contains archaeological problems related to the material used for dating. The re-use and stratigraphic mixing of obsidian is such a problem. In applying the obsidian dating technique, one must always keep in mind that the hydration thickness or 'date' represents the time from the moment of manufacture of the surface examined to the present time. This date may have little relationship to the time at

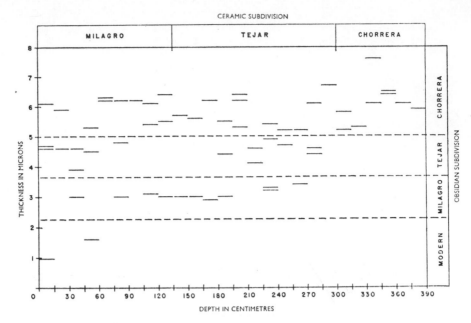

Fig. 5 The thickness of the hydration layers of the obsidian artifacts from various levels in Cut 1, Site R–B–1, Chorrera, on the coast of Ecuador. The cultural divisions derive from pottery classification and the levels at which they subdivide are shown at the top. The divisions suggested by differences in thickness of the hydration layers of the obsidian artifacts are shown at the right. From Evans and Meggers[3]

which it was buried, or to the provenience in which it is ultimately found. We have examined several thousand samples from archaeological sites which range geographically through most of the world areas where obsidian is known naturally or culturally, and which range in time from European contact to the Lower Palaeolithic. Some of our results, for one or more of the reasons outlined above, show disagreement with archaeological age estimates ascertained by other archaeological or geochronological methods. On the whole, the obsidian hydration results are quite concordant with chronological expectations. In not a few cases of apparent disagreement the reason has not been difficult to find. A large portion of these results has been published, and several series of obsidian dates from major excavations will accompany the respective excavation reports when these monographs are eventually published.

REFERENCES

1 ROSS, C. S. and SMITH, R. L. 1955. *American Mineralogist 40*, 1071–89
   FRIEDMAN, I. and SMITH, R. L. 1958. *Geochim. et Cosmochim. Acta 15*, 218–28
2 —— —— 1960. *Am. Antiq. 25*, 476–522
3 EVANS, C. and MEGGERS, B. J. 1960. *Ibid. 25*, 523–37
   CLARK, D. L. 1961a. *Curr. Anth. 2*, 111–14
4 —— 1961b. *The Obsidian Dating Method Applied to Central California Archaeology*. Ph.D. dissertation, Dept. of Anthropology, Stanford University
5 EVANS, C. and MEGGERS, B. J. 1957. *Am. Antiq. 22*, 235–47

R. M. COOK

ARCHAEOMAGNETISM—a term invented by its pioneer, Professor E. Thellier—is the study of the remanent magnetism of archaeological remains. It is distinguished from palaeomagnetism, which is the corresponding study of geological material, more for convenience than from principle. Both archaeomagnetism and palaeomagnetism are based on the facts that the magnetic field of the earth (of which the magnetic north of the compass presents the most familiar effect) is changing continually in direction and intensity and that these changes can leave natural records. Such records are said to have been observed in sedimentary rocks, where they result from the process of geological formation; but for archaeomagnetic studies it is the remanent magnetism caused through heat—and so named in full thermo-remanent magnetism—that is relevant.

GENERAL THEORY

General Statement. The process of thermo-remanent magnetization is, very simply, this. Many rocks contain magnetic oxides of iron. Above a certain temperature, known as the Curie point, the particles of these oxides lose their ability to retain magnetism; over a range of a few degrees between the Curie point and the so-called blocking temperature they are susceptible immediately to whatever magnetic field surrounds them—that is, they tend to acquire its direction and proportionately its intensity; below the blocking temperature they retain any magnetism they have acquired and are no longer affected by magnetic fields of low intensity, as in particular that of the earth. This general description needs some comments.

Curie Points. Different magnetic oxides have different Curie points. The highest, at 670°C, is that of haematite (α–Fe_2O_3). For magnetite (Fe_3O_4) it is 580°C. There are other oxides with lower Curie points, some within the range of ordinary atmospheric temperatures. It follows from the difference in Curie points that the different oxides in a rock may have different remanent magnetizations. If, for example, a rock containing magnetite and haematite is first heated to 670° and allowed to cool down and later is heated to 580° and again allowed to cool, the remanent magnetism of the haematite particles is that acquired during the first cooling and of the magnetite particles that acquired during the second cooling; if the surrounding fields during the first and second coolings were different, so too will be the remanent magnetisms of the two kinds of particles.

When a rock has two or more such magnetizations, its composite magnetization will be their mean. The components can be disentangled by reheating progressively to the appropriate Curie points, so that the magnetizations acquired at lower temperatures (and so more recently) are eliminated. In the example of the last paragraph, reheating to 580° would eliminate the later magnetization acquired by the particles of magnetite, but leave the haematite particles still undisturbed.

The magnetic constituents of rocks vary widely, but the proportion of oxides with low Curie points is inconsiderable in most of the well-fired clays encountered in archaeology.

Stability of Remanent Magnetism. Generally the remanent magnetism of a particle remains stable till it is heated beyond its blocking temperature. There are, though, some disturbing factors:

(1) Some rocks, because of their crystal structure, are unstable magnetically. This instability is very low in the commoner baked clays, but considerable in many volcanic rocks.

(2) In any rock some magnetic particles are likely to acquire a temporary magnetization from a low surrounding field. This viscous temporary magnetism seems to occur at temperatures in general not much below the blocking temperature, and so normally it affects only those particles which have a Curie point near atmospheric temperatures. Though the incidence of viscous magnetism increases with time, the rate of increase falls off quickly: as the Thelliers have shown, the number of particles affected after exposure of from 10 minutes to 14 days is as great as the number affected between 14 days and 90 years. So viscous magnetism can be detected and even calculated by reversing the position of a specimen for a few weeks and noting any changes in the magnetization. It can, of course, be eliminated by reheating to a convenient temperature, say 60°C.

(3) At temperatures below their blocking temperature the magnetic particles are not affected, viscosity apart, by other weak magnetic fields, such as that of the earth. But if the surrounding field is of higher intensity—for magnetite the resistance or coercive force is 20 oersted, for haematite 7,000 oersted—it can produce a new remanent magnetization. Such magnetization is described as isothermal or anhysteretic, according to the process by which it is induced. The only natural cause that is at all common is lightning. If isothermal or anhysteretic magnetization has not been complete and the particles of the more resistant oxides are unaffected, it can be eliminated or separated for calculation either by reheating to the temperature at which remagnetization took place or else by applying an alternating field equal in intensity to that which caused the new magnetization.

(4) After a rock has acquired a remanent magnetization chemical changes may occur, which convert a magnetic into a non-magnetic oxide or—more misleadingly—form new magnetic oxides. Such new oxides may acquire their remanent magnetism from the field surrounding them at the time of formation. Well-fired clays are not much subject to chemical changes, though experience suggests that prolonged waterlogging may have a considerable effect.

(5) Careless treatment in a laboratory may cause chemical changes or new magnetizations. If, for example, a sample is reheated to eliminate any remanent magnetism acquired at a low Curie point, it is obvious that, when the sample cools again through the critical range of temperature and is susceptible to remagnetization, cooling must be in a zero field (that is, in the absence of any effective magnetic field) or in a field of which the direction and intensity are known exactly.

Magnetic Fields. In normal conditions, when a rock is acquiring remanent magnetization, the principal field determining the magnetization is that of the earth. This field has several components, each of which varies more or less irregularly. The secular or long-term variation (that marked on the maps of the Ordnance Survey) is thought to be compounded of the main field of the earth, which has its North pole to the north of Hudson Bay and—at least for direction—is static over long periods, and of several regional disturbances, which are disposed erratically and have ranges of up to a thousand miles: these regional disturbances, recognized since the late seventeenth century, have a limited period of growth and decay (or of fluctuation) and move from east to west at a rate of about 1° in 5 years. For this reason the direction and intensity of the earth's field at one place does not necessarily (as far as is known) have a completely systematic relation to its direction and intensity at another place some hundreds of miles away, and so extrapolation for latitude and longitude is hazardous.

Besides the secular variation there are some minor, short-term variations, which fluctuate erratically in cycles of different lengths. Their contribution to the total field is small, very rarely exceeding 1° in direction and 1% in intensity and, considering the practicable limits of accuracy in archaeomagnetic work, they can usually be ignored.

Some other magnetic disturbances too must be considered. Deposits of magnetic minerals may produce local fields; usually these are already known and so can be discounted. A much more narrowly localized deflection may result from the proximity of some magnetized object, as for instance an iron crowbar leaning against the side of a cooling kiln; here with luck the investigator might be suspicious of his results, since the influence of a magnetic field decreases with the cube of its distance and so the further parts of the kiln would be noticeably less affected than the nearer. Further, when a potentially magnetic subject is cooling, those parts which first acquire a remanent magnetism may exert a weak magnetic effect on other parts as they in turn pass through their critical range of temperature; but since the magnetic intensity of archaeomagnetic subjects does not often exceed 10^{-2} e.m.u./cc or about one-fiftieth of the intensity of the earth's field, any errors so caused are not likely to be serious and may even be averaged out in the subject as a whole.

Unexplained Anomalies. Whenever specimens are taken from any sizeable archaeomagnetic subject, there are always appreciable differences between them in the direction and intensity of their remanent magnetism. If, for instance, eight samples are taken from a well-preserved kiln, the range in their respective declinations is rarely less than 5° (Table A). These differences, which do not seem to follow any logical pattern, are too great to be due to faults in collection or measurement; they are not regularly caused by accidental shifting of position, nor does it appear that they are completely explicable by any of the disturbing factors already mentioned. Whatever the reason or reasons, it is assumed that these differences can be discounted by taking a mean between them, and this assumption gives credible results.

Summary. The theory of remanent magnetism has not been worked out in complete detail, and the explanations of some phenomena are still tentative. For the practice of archaeomagnetism, what is most important is that most of the fired clays encountered have a very stable remanent magnetism, which records with fair accuracy the magnetic field of the earth at the time of magnetization: stones, unfortunately, are in general less stable, especially if they are of volcanic origin.

PURPOSES

The direction and intensity of the earth's magnetic field are, as has been said, changing continually, but observational records of these changes are very incomplete. For direction the first known observations of both inclination and declination were made in Rome in AD 1540, in London in 1586, and in some parts of the world not till the present century; the earlier of these observations made no allowance for short-term or local variations and are not precisely reliable. For intensity the first observations were made about 1830. So remanent magnetism offers geophysicists important evidence for the recent history of the earth's field, especially when the date of magnetization can be supplied by archaeological context, historical records, or (less accurately) by radio-carbon or some other natural chronometer. In this way it is practicable to plot approxi-mately the variations of the magnetic field of the earth for a few thousand years in a few parts of the world. As such plots are constructed, they become useful to archaeolo-gists for dating structures or objects of which the remanent magnetism is known but not the date: if, for example, a kiln of Roman-British type was found in Cambridge and the direction of its remanent magnetism gave values of 66° for declination and 1°W for inclination, its probable date (as Fig. 6 shows) would be the early third century AD. These are the major aims of archaeomagnetic study. There are also some minor applica-tions for archaeology, as regards both direction and intensity.

DIRECTION

No simple connection has yet been detected between the secular variations in direction and intensity of the earth's magnetic field and, since also the practical procedures of measuring them are different, it is easier to discuss them separately.

Definitions. The direction of a magnetic field is expressed most conveniently in terms of horizontal and vertical planes. For the horizontal component or declination (D), which is the direction shown by the ordinary compass, true North serves as the point of reference. The inclination or dip (I) is reckoned as the vertical angle between the direction of the field and the horizontal plane (that is, at a point of the earth's surface, the tangent plane). At London in 1956 the mean value of the earth's field for D was $8°36\cdot8'W$ and for I $66°37\cdot4'$, and in recent years the annual variation in D has been about $10'E$.

Specimens. In any archaeomagnetic specimen, if the direction of its remanent magnet-ism is to be intelligible, it must have a known external point of reference. In other words, the specimen's orientation (relative, if not absolute) at the time when it was magnetized must be ascertained. Archaeologists who find this concept hard to grasp may consider the analogy of a map or plan without any geographic bearing marked on it.

This means in the case of burnt structures that, to be useful, they must be strictly *in situ* and not have collapsed or shifted. Movable objects are generally worthless for the study of the direction of the earth's field, except under two conditions for inclination. The first condition is that the place of firing should be known to a hundred miles or so, since latitude and longitude partly determine the local direction of the earth's field. The second condition is that the position of the object during firing should be given; in particular, bricks are normally stacked level in kilns and some pots (especially if of glazed ware) set upright, so that in the first instance one of the faces and in the other the foot should be fairly horizontal and so allow an approximate measurement of dip (though not, of course, of declination).

Other requirements of archaeomagnetic specimens (which cannot be judged safely by eye) are that they contain a sufficient proportion of magnetic oxides—for present apparatus the minimum is about 10^{-6} e.m.u./cc^3—and that they have been fired well. It is an advantage too if they have not been exposed for long to weathering or water, and if they are not very fragmentary.

In practice the structures which provide the best material are kilns. They were generally sunk in the ground in open spaces, so that their lower part had an unusually good chance of surviving; more often than not their walls were made of clay or else lined with it, and they were fired to temperatures of not less than 800°C, that is well above the maximum Curie point. Hearths and cremation places as a rule were not so highly fired and the depth of magnetization is usually much less; further they are more liable than kilns to subsidence. The walls and floors of buildings that were burnt down can also give good results. Of structural materials clay (unfired at the time of construction) is best, stone more chancy, baked brick or tile difficult. In Roman hypocaust flues, for instance, the brick or tile already had a remanent magnetism when it was put in place and the subsequent heating may not have been high enough or penetrated far enough to replace that first magnetism completely.

For pots and other movable objects, if they are being considered for measurements of dip, there is a possible danger that they may have been remagnetized, whether wholly or partially, by accidental burning, during cooking or in a funeral pyre. This can sometimes be decided by discoloration or the circumstances of finding.

Collecting Samples. Since a portable magnetometer has not yet been produced to measure an archaeomagnetic structure *in situ*, samples must be removed for measurement in a fixed magnetometer in a laboratory. To compensate anomalies a number of samples—six or more—should be taken, preferably from different parts of the structure and in a symmetrical pattern. What is essential is that each sample should be marked with its present (that is, its original) orientation, to serve as a reference for the direction of its own remanent magnetism. The most satisfactory method, where it is practicable, is—before detaching the sample—to cap it with plaster, taking care that the top surface is horizontal; this gives a plane of reference for the dip. On this horizontal surface is inscribed a known horizontal bearing, to which the sample's declination can be related. For the magnetometers which are used at present it is convenient to have samples mounted in the form of cubes. Again it is convenient, though not necessary, to prepare the cube at the time of collection. This is done by first cutting round the sample, so that it projects as a boss, and next a collapsible form—4½ in. square has proved a convenient size—is set round the boss, levelled with a spirit level, and filled with plaster. The horizontal bearing is taken best from a theodolite sighted on the sample as well as on some known fixed point; failing that, a box compass can be laid on the sample and its position and bearing marked. After this the sample is cut away from below, and its bottom too may be plastered over. Since many specimens are fragile or friable, plastering has the advantage also of conserving them.

Measuring Apparatus. The magnetic fields of archaeomagnetic specimens are relatively very weak, and so when they are measured it is necessary to exclude the effects of the earth's field and of any local disturbances. Two types of measuring apparatus are in use.

The astatic magnetometer adapts the principle of the compass needle. Two bar magnets are fixed one above the other on a vertical rod, which is suspended so that it can revolve freely. The two magnets are of equal strength and set in diametrically opposite directions. Since the pull on the two parts of the magnet system is equal and opposite, the effect of the earth's field is cancelled. But if a magnetized sample is put a little below the magnet system, it will affect the lower magnet more strongly than the upper and the magnet system will swing towards the direction of the sample. The reason is that the strength of a field decreases according to the cube of the distance; with the earth's field and even quite local disturbances the difference in distance of the two magnets from the centre of the field is infinitesimal or anyhow unimportant, but with the sample the difference is considerable. To reduce interference and disturbance the magnet system and sample should be enclosed in Helmholz coils. By setting the sample on its top and bottom, its declination is measured directly; the dip is calculated from readings taken when the sample is set on each of its four sides. This large number of measurements is necessary to compensate for any eccentricity of the sample's field in relation to the axis of the magnet system. The astatic magnetometer is simple and sensitive to fields as low as 10^{-7} e.m.u./cc: on the other hand measuring and calculating are slowish, and it is liable to disturbance by, for instance, passing traffic. A simple version of this apparatus has been used in Tokyo: that in Cambridge is more elaborate.

The other type of magnetometer applies the principle of electromagnetic induction, that if a magnet (in this case an archaeomagnetic sample) is brought close to a coil of wire and there moved, an electrical voltage is set up between the ends of the coil. The voltage is greatest when the direction of the magnet's field is in alignment with the plane of the coil. The integrated voltage can be measured by attaching the coil to a galvanometer. Again disturbing fields are excluded by a system of Helmholz coils. For practical reasons samples are measured in three positions at right angles to each other, and their magnetic direction is ascertained from the three readings. The so-called ballistic magnetometer works by turning the sample quickly through half a circle, so producing a direct current. In the spinning magnetometer the sample is rotated continuously to produce an alternating current; unfortunately, the speed of rotation (on which the range of sensitivity depends) is often limited by the centrifugal momentum of the sample. The advantages of this type of magnetometer are that it is quicker in measuring and relatively immune to local disturbances; but it is more complex and less sensitive than the astatic type. Both the ballistic and the spinning magnetometers are used in Paris and Oxford.

Naturally each operator prefers his own type of apparatus; but if one compares the measurements of the same samples made in Paris, Oxford and Cambridge (Table A), it appears that in practice both rotating and astatic magnetometers can give equally satisfactory results.

TABLE A

Measurements made in Paris, Oxford and Cambridge of samples from a kiln at Grimstone End, Suffolk.

Sample No.	Declination			Inclination			Viscosity
	Paris	Oxford	Cambridge	Paris	Oxford	Cambridge	Paris
1	5·5W	1·2W	1·7W	66·4	65·6	63·5	0·9
2	6·0W	4·2W	4·0W	65·7	66·2	66·0	1·3
3	5·7W	3·2E	4·0W	67·9	67·5	67·0	0·7
4	4·25W	3·8W	3·0W	61·3	61·6	63·0	1·4
5	4·0W	2·8W	1·0W	62·7	60·7	65·0	0·4
6	2·6W	2·1W	2·5W	66·2	63·9	65·5	1·2
7	5·0W	1·9W	9·0W	66·4	65·4	68·0	0·4
8	1·8E	1·0W	0·0	67·9	68·4	67·0	0·6
9	9·5E	8·6E	10·5E	67·2	67·5	67·5	2·5
10	7·9W	5·5W	3·0W	63·9	63·6	65·5	1·1
average	3·0W	1·1W	1·8W	65·6	65·0	65·8	

Declination and inclination are given in degrees, the figure for viscosity is the percentage decrease in the vertical component after inversion.

Treatment of Measurements. The directions obtained by the magnetometer must first be related to the original orientation of the sample. If the sample has been made up into a cube in the way described on pp. 63–4, the reference for dip is to the top of the cube and for declination to the bearing marked on it. The result for dip is correct immediately; but the declination bearing must itself be related to true North.

The mean between the results from several samples of one structure may be plotted on a stereograph or computed. Fisher has developed a useful statistical treatment for the dispersion of the vectors. Where one sample of a set is very divergent from the others, it is probably fair to discard it, since few structures are completely homogeneous or perfectly preserved: in such cases it helps to have noted the position and state of each sample before collecting it.

Results for the Direction of the Earth's Field. For the past direction of the earth's field the present results are very limited in time and place. This is because good archaeo-magnetic material is not too easy to come by and little work has been done on it. Nor are the results in general precisely accurate, since most archaeomagnetic structures are

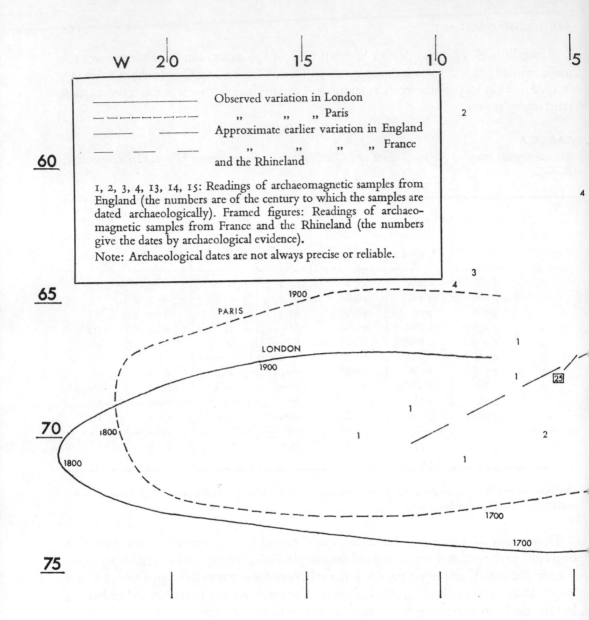

Fig. 6 Secular variation of the direction of the earth's magnetic field in England and in France and the Rhineland

not dated precisely; for kilns, which have provided so many of the specimens, the chronological evidence has usually been coarse pottery, on the dating of which archaeologists are not yet consistent with each other nor (I would guess) reliable to within fifty years.

Even so, the provisional values for declination and inclination are already useful. For Britain we have a fair idea of the direction of the earth's field from the first to the fourth century AD and for northern France and the Rhineland indications for a rather longer

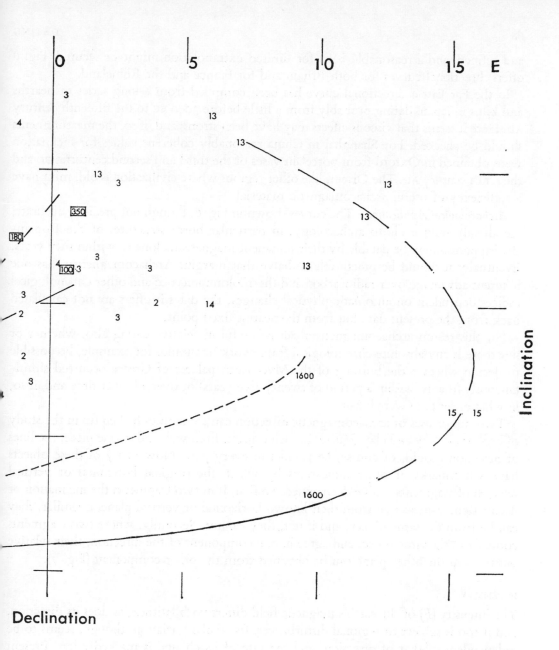

0   **5**   **10**   **15** **E**

3

4

13

13

13

13

13

3

350

180

3

100 3

3

13

3

2 14

3

2

3

2

3

1600

15 15

Inclination

1600

Declination

period. There is a little evidence for Tunisia in the second century BC and the third century AD. In Britain, France and the Rhineland the earlier medieval period is almost blank, the later rather sparsely represented. A scattered series of bricks offers further inclinations for France. Material in Cambridge not yet published adds a little information for Libya in the early Christian era and for Italy from the fifth to the first century BC and an unevenly distributed series for Greece from the third millennium BC to the eighth century AD. With time and patience these sets of results could be extended, linked and refined, and a reasonable basis for limited extrapolation might be secured. Fig. 6 offers directional curves for both Britain and for France and the Rhineland.

In the Far East a directional curve has been compiled from a long series of hearths and kilns in Japan, dating probably from a little before 3000 BC to the fifteenth century AD. Here it seems that viscous effects may have been strong and, if so, the measurements should be checked. For Shanghai in China reasonably coherent values for inclination were obtained in Oxford from porcelain vases of the third and second centuries BC and the tenth century AD. The Orient, like other regions where civilization is old, must have a sufficiency of useful archaeomagnetic material.

Archaeological Applications. The curves shown in Fig. 6, though not precisely accurate, are already serviceable to archaeology; in particular burnt structures of the Roman-British period may be datable by their remanent magnetism alone to within fifty years. Eventually it should be practicable to halve that margin. Archaeomagnetism has one inherent advantage over radiocarbon and thermoluminescence and other chronological indices dependent on automatic physical changes; the dates it offers are not calculated back from the present day, but from the nearest fixed point.

For this reason archaeomagnetism can be useful in relative dating also, whether or not there is any absolute chronological framework. It should, for example, be possible to decide whether the burning of the Mycenaean palaces of Greece occurred simultaneously (that is, within a period of twenty-five years) or over a longer time and, if so, in what order they were burnt.

Two minor uses of archaeomagnetic direction can sometimes be helpful in the study of broken pottery and clay figures. In such objects, fired well and in one piece, the lines of direction should, of course, be parallel in every part. Now many of these objects have wheelmarks or other indications by which the original horizontal or vertical relation of fragments can be determined. So first, if in two fragments the inclination or declination, as measured from their known horizontal or vertical plane, is similar, they can be from the same object; and if not, they cannot. Secondly, where two fragments come from the same object and agree in one component of the direction, their relative positions in the other plane can be obtained from the other component (Fig. 7).

INTENSITY

The intensity (*F*) of the earth's magnetic field differs with latitude, as does its direction, and it too is subject to regional disturbances. Its secular variation, though, seems to be independent of that of direction, and the rate of its change is markedly less. Present values for the intensity of the earth's field, measured on the surface of the earth, range from about 0·40 oersted at the magnetic equator to about 0·61 oersted at the magnetic poles.

Specimens. Specimens should, of course, be well fired and preferably, because of the methods of measurement, well oxidized and quite free from unfired or partially fired accretions. Since comparison is of intensity and not of direction, the orientation at the time of magnetization has no relevance here and so specimens can be taken freely from movable objects, such as pottery, as well as from structures. This means that there is available already a very large supply of usefully dated specimens which cover many parts of the world as far back as their Neolithic periods, when the making of pottery began. The main proviso is that, because of latitudinal and regional differences in the intensity of the earth's magnetic field, the place of firing (and not of finding) should be known. It is also worth repeating that if specimens have been reheated—in cooking, accidental fires or cremations—the original remanent magnetism may have been replaced in whole or part.

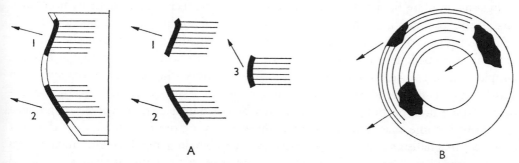

Fig. 7 Simplified diagram showing use of magnetic direction to determine (A) if sherds can be from the same pot, (B) the relative positions radially of sherds from the same pot. (In A, which is sectional, the horizontal lines represent wheelmarks and the arrows the magnetic inclination: so 1 and 2 can be from the same pot, but 3 cannot. In B, which is a schematic view from above, the arrows represent the magnetic declination.)

Measurement. The intensity of the remanent magnetism of a specimen depends on two factors. One is its magnetic constitution—what magnetic oxides it contains and in what abundance; this sets a limit to the maximum possible intensity, though in practice the limit is irrelevant for a field as weak as that of the earth. The other factor is the intensity of the field which caused the magnetization; the effect, up to the possible maximum, is proportionate to the cause. Since the aim of measuring is to determine the intensity of the magnetizing field, it is this proportion that must be determined. The one practicable method is first to measure the original remanent intensity of the specimen, then to eliminate that intensity by heat and remagnetize the specimen in some magnetic field of known intensity (for instance, the present field of the earth) and finally to measure the new remanent intensity. The ratio of the new to the old remanent intensity of the specimen should be the same as the ratio between the surrounding field now and at the time of the original magnetization: this statement is perhaps more clearly expressed by

the formula $\frac{M_L}{M_o} = \frac{F_L}{F_o}$, where M_L is the sample's new and M_o its original remanent

intensity and F_L and F_o the intensity of the surrounding field at the times of the second and the original magnetization. It is here assumed that the surrounding field at the time of original magnetization was that of the earth; for archaeomagnetic specimens the assumption is in general likely.

Both the types of magnetometer described on pp. 64–5 measure intensity as well as direction. In the rotating type readings are taken directly from the galvanometer. With the astatic type it is anyhow convenient to restrict the swing of the magnet system by suspending it on a torsion fibre, and so the intensity of a specimen can be calculated from the degree to which it can deflect the magnet system when at a given distance from the specimen.

Remagnetization is more troublesome. The specimen must be heated to eliminate its original remanent magnetism and then let cool to acquire a new remanent magnetism from a surrounding field of known intensity; here two special precautions are necessary. First, if the specimen is to cool in the oven in which it was heated, that oven must itself be non-magnetic or else there are likely to be unpremeditated changes in the intensity of the field immediately surrounding the sample: if some such accident is suspected, the sample can, of course, be remagnetized again. Secondly, the heating of the specimen may change its magnetic constitution—new magnetic oxides may be formed, and un-fired or underfired portions of the specimen which had little or no remanent magnetism may now become magnetized—so that the intensity of the original and of the new remanent magnetisms may not be properly comparable. In general, well-cleaned objects of well-fired clay, if well oxidized, are immune from such chemical changes; reduced specimens may need to be remagnetized in an atmosphere of nitrogen, to prevent oxidation and its magnetic consequences.

Results for the Intensity of the Earth's Field. Relatively few measurements have been made of the remanent intensity of archaeomagnetic specimens. The only area for which

TABLE B

Intensity of the remanent magnetism of French and other specimens.

Place	Date	Intensity (actual)	Intensity (adjusted)
		oersteds	oersteds
Paris	AD 1955	0·464	0·466
Paris	1930	0·459	0·461
Paris	1885	0·463	0·462
Paris	1848	0·471	0·460
Versailles	1750	>0·48	>0·43
Lille	1460	0·56	0·57
Paris	c. 300	0·70	0·73
Basle	c. 175	0·73	0·74
Fréjus	c. 0	0·65	0·69
Carthage	BC 146	0·71	0·78

The adjusted figures in the fourth column are based on the assumption that intensity is related to inclination; a value of 65°, close to the present value for Paris, has been taken as a norm.

coherent results have been published is France, so that we cannot yet say how far the variation is regional or secular. But it appears from the examination of bricks of known date that at Paris the intensity of the earth's field has decreased by about a third in the last 1,750 years. This fits with a general decrease of more than 5% since 1830, when direct observations began. The French results are shown in Table B.

Archaeological Applications. For obtaining dates the intensity of remanent magnetism is much less exact than is its direction, perhaps eight or ten times less. Even so, it may be helpful in distinguishing between two dates at which the direction was the same. An application that might be important is the detection of forgeries of terracotta figures and pottery, if it proves that there was an appreciable difference between ancient and modern intensities. Here, though, there is another complication; ancient kilns were of clay or stone, but since the adoption of the electric kiln very recent forgeries may have intensities markedly different from those of the contemporary field of the earth. Again, if regional variations are large enough, it may be practicable to suggest the place of firing (or manufacture) for objects of which the date is known approximately. The ingenious reader can no doubt discover other applications.

CONCLUSION

The study of archaeomagnetism has not advanced far, more from shortage of students than of materials. There are still important theoretical problems to solve and very many more routine measurements must be made before a reasonably complete set of plots of variation can be produced. But it offers both geophysicists and archaeologists some information of kinds they cannot, anyhow yet, obtain elsewhere.

ACKNOWLEDGMENT

I am very grateful to my geophysical colleague Dr J. C. Belshé for reading and improving this account.

REFERENCES

1 THELLIER, E. 1938. *Annales de l'Inst. de Phys. du Globe* 16, 157–302. (A detailed general study of methods and principles.)
2 THELLIER, E. and O. 1959. *Annales de Géophysique* 15, 285–376. (A comprehensive account of the study of intensity.)
3 AITKEN, M. J. 1961. *Physics and Archaeology*. London and New York, pp. 8–11, 18–19, 121–55. (A good general account with long bibliography.)
4 COOK, R. M. and BELSHÉ, J. C. 1958. *Antiquity* 32, 167–78. (Results for direction in Britain.)
5 WATANABE, N. 1959. *Journal of the Faculty of Science, University of Tokyo*, sec. 5, 2, 1–188. (Results for direction in Japan.)

6 The Potassium–Argon Dating of Upper Tertiary and Pleistocene Deposits

W. GENTNER and H. J. LIPPOLT

AFTER THE DISCOVERY OF RADIOACTIVITY, Rutherford proved the possibility of dating geological events by showing that at least 500 million years must have elapsed since the formation of a fergusonite crystal which contained 7% uranium and 1·8 cc helium. By measuring the ratio of U/Pb in uranium minerals and the ratio of U/He, Boltwood[10] and Strutt[42] respectively put geological chronology on an absolute basis which was especially important for the Pre-Cambrian.

In the last decade all long-life isotopes have been examined for their suitability for absolute age determination, the Rb–Sr method and the K–A method becoming ever more important. The K–A method can be applied particularly for the dating of lower geological ages by virtue of the abundance of potassium and the improvements in high vacuum technique and sensitivity for measuring very small quantities of rare gases. However, there is at present considerable interest in applying the method to Quaternary problems. The following comments deal with this development.

THE DECAY OF K^{40}

Potassium as we find it in nature contains 93·2% K^{39}, 6·8% K^{41} and 0·0118% radioactive K^{40}. At the time of the formation of the earth the abundance of K^{40} was about 0·2%. Most of the K^{40} decayed into the isotopes Ca^{40} and A^{40}. Since the high half-life, of K^{40}, $1·30\pm0·04 . 10^9$y, is comparable to the age of earth, a small amount of K^{40} is still present, whereas the nuclides palladium 107 and iodine 129, with shorter half-lives, have decayed some billion years ago.

For each 100 K^{40} atoms which decay, 89% become Ca^{40} by β decay and 11% become A^{40} by K-capture. This branching ratio of $0·123\pm0·004$ is usually mentioned in addition to the half-life when giving age data. The K-capture of K^{40} is the reason for the large abundance of A^{40} in the atmosphere. The atmosphere con-

TABLE A
Amounts of rare gases in the atmosphere.

Rare gas	Volume %
Helium	$5·2 . 10^{-4}$
Argon $^{38+36}$	$3·7 . 10^{-3}$
Argon^{40}	0·93
Neon	$1·8 . 10^{-3}$
Krypton	$1·1 . 10^{-4}$
Xenon	$8·6 . 10^{-6}$

tains about 1% argon which is 100 times more abundant than the other rare gases. This explanation of the A⁴⁰ in the atmosphere was made in 1937 by von Weizsäcker; it was proved to be the case by the measurement of A⁴⁰ in minerals by Aldrich and Nier.[8] Fig. 8 shows the decay scheme of K⁴⁰ as it has been confirmed by extensive investigations of various authors in the field of nuclear physics.

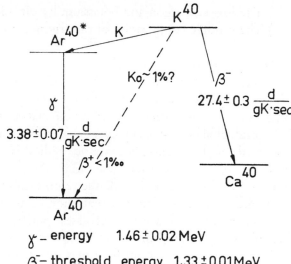

γ – energy   1.46 ± 0.02 MeV

Fig. 8 Decay scheme of K⁴⁰ β^- – threshold energy 1.33 ± 0.01 MeV

Ever since it was discovered that A⁴⁰ is produced by the decay of K⁴⁰ the use of this method has found ever more applications for the following reasons:

(1) Potassium with about 2·8 weight per cent is one of the most abundant elements in the earth's crust and is contained in practically all minerals.

(2) A⁴⁰ can be measured more easily than most other elements even in very small concentrations.

(3) The half-life of potassium⁻⁴⁰, 1·30 . 10⁹y, is long enough for appreciable A⁴⁰ to be formed in potassium minerals within geologically interesting periods. By measuring the radiogenic A⁴⁰-concentration and the total content of potassium of a mineral one may determine the time which is necessary to produce the radiogenic A⁴⁰-concentration by radioactive decay.

$$A^{40}/K^{40} = (R/1+R) \cdot (e^{\lambda t} - 1)$$ R = branching ratio
λ = decay . constant

This period is designated as the potassium–argon age of the sample under the following assumptions:

(1) At time $t = 0$ the crystal contains only argon with an isotopic ratio the same as atmospheric argon, that is, no radiogenic argon is present.

(2) During the measured time the K–A ratio is not changed by any chemical or physical process except by the radioactive decay of K^{40}.

(3) The period of the formation of the mineral must be much shorter than the age of the mineral.

These prerequisites however are not always completely fulfilled. There are two difficulties that require discussion:

(1) The losses of argon and potassium by diffusion and metamorphic changes.

(2) The isotopic composition of the argon in the mineral when it was formed.

POTASSIUM AND ARGON ANALYSIS

The content of potassium is usually determined by a flame-photometer. For small concentrations isotopic dilution analysis is used ($< 10^{-3}$ g/g). For even smaller potassium contents ($< 10^{-5}$ g/g), neutron activation analysis is required. An interesting survey of the reproducibility and accuracy of the different methods was made by Pinson.[35] He concluded that the flame-photometric method is very reliable. For example the results agree with gravimetric determinations by the J. L. Smith method. Systematic errors of about 6% are encountered while the reproducibility is about 2%.

The determination of the concentration of argon is made in three steps: melting of the samples for the extraction of gases, purification of the extracted rare gases and determination of the quantities by an isotopic analysis.

The last step is carried out by a mass-spectrometer. The measurement of the argon by a McLeod manometer without the isotopic analysis gives reliable values only for concentrations over 10^{-4} cc A/g material. Measurements with neutron activation become unreliable for high atmospheric argon content.

Of the possible extraction methods, it is preferable to extract the gas by direct heating without the addition of auxiliary material to lower the melting point. The material can be melted in high vacuum by induction or by resistance heating in either a graphite or molybdenum crucible. In this way one can obtain temperatures considerably above the melting point of the minerals being investigated (mica 1,000°, feldspar 1,200°, quartz 1,700°C). All of the impurities which one obtains by such a melting procedure can be removed by getter-materials (Ca–Cu–CuO, Zr, Ti-sponge).

In addition to the radiogenic A^{40} the material to be dated also contains argon from the atmosphere with an isotopic ratio $A^{40} : A^{38} : A^{36} = 296 : 0.19 : 1$. During the measurement atmospheric argon is added from small leaks, from diffusion through the walls of the apparatus, from the getter-materials and from the hot crucible and its surroundings. By measurement of the A^{36} and A^{38} concentrations one can determine the radiogenic A^{40}. If one has for example 1% atmospheric argon in addition to the radiogenic argon, the amount of A^{36} is quite small, only about 3.4×10^{-5} of the A^{40}. The mass-spectrometer used must therefore have sufficient resolution and with the tendency to smaller and smaller samples be suitable for high and ultra-high vacuum. A 60° glass sector spectrometer has proved successful for this application.[37] The cycloidal spectrometer and the omegatron can also be used in this way.

In general the potassium and the radiogenic argon are not distributed homogeneously through the sample. The ideal solution is to determine argon and potassium in the same sample but this is only useful in special cases, as then it is only possible to make one determination. If one wished to measure several samples one after the other, it is better to use pulverized homogeneous material. The argon and potassium determination can then be made independently. If the grain size is too large one obtains a large variation from sample to sample. By the use of a grain size from 0·6 to 1·0 mm one has in a 0·5 to 1·0 g sample approximately 300 to 600 grains and therefore a representative sample. If one uses substantially smaller samples, then one must make the grain size still smaller. Gentner and Kley[21] have shown however that it is not advisable to have a grain size less than 100μ as then one must contend with substantial loss of argon.

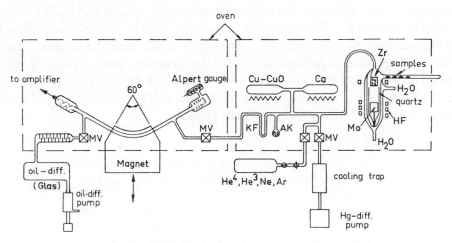

Fig. 9 Schematic diagram of an apparatus for measuring small amounts of argon

MINERALS SUITABLE FOR DATING

Potassium–argon ages have been determined for the igneous minerals muscovite, biotite, phlogopite, orthoclase, sanidine, microcline, and leucite, as well as volcanic glass and the sedimentary minerals glauconite, illite, carnallite and sylvite.

A number of these minerals are easily altered by metamorphism or can lose argon through diffusion. As a result one usually restricts the dating to biotite, muscovite and sanidine.

In addition to these minerals, because of the increased sensitivity of the procedures for determining argon and potassium, it is possible to use minerals which only have trace amounts of potassium. Indeed good results have been obtained for anorthoclase, oligoclase, augite, calcite and hornblende.

It is possible to have processes which alter the argon-40 to potassium ratio in the dated material. For example one can have a recrystallization of a potassium salt, or alteration of a feldspar into kaolin and sericite or chloritization of pyroxene; deposition of calcite or chlorite in the pores, or anion-exchange in clay minerals which alters the potassium content. A number of these changes can be recognized microscopically and the corresponding samples left aside. The loss of argon through diffusion from the crystal lattice is usually not recognizable.

From the standpoint of the measurements one prefers to date unaltered minerals. In view of the geological or archaeological problems however it is often desirable to date whole rock samples, which are easier to obtain and for which one does not require the labour of separating the minerals.

One must consider that whole rock samples contain in addition to large biotite and sanidine crystals other minerals which lose argon. Very small biotite and sanidine crystals lose argon too because of diffusion from the small grains. For this reason in dating complicated strata one rarely uses whole rock samples.

On the other hand such samples can be used for relative age determinations. The relationship between the grain size and the potassium argon age is given by two examples. Hart[25] measured a Pre-Cambrian muscovite which was metamorphosed and found the results shown in Table B(i). The two samples with the smallest grain sizes give the same age which is perhaps the time of the metamorphism. A similar result (here recalculated) was found with sylvite by Gentner *et al.* (Table B (ii)). The true age was taken as the age for a very large grain size obtained by extrapolating the samples measured. For stones this is in most cases not possible.

TABLE B

Relationship between grain sizes of rock samples and potassium–argon age, after Hart (i) and Gentner et al. (ii).

(i) Radius	K–A Age
muscovite μ	million yrs.
1,000	700
690	555
250	440
110	350
55	360

(ii) Radius	K–A Age
sylvite *mm*	million yrs
2·0	17·5
1·3	16·3
0·8	14·3
0·4	11·3

COMPARISON OF POTASSIUM–ARGON AGES WITH OTHER METHODS

The different ways in which the radioactive ages of minerals are altered by metamorphic processes make it desirable to use two independent methods such as the K–A and the Rb[87]–Sr[87]. Age-determinations obtained from both methods for mica have about the same reliability as concordant lead ages. The results of the Rb–Sr and K–A methods agree well except for the cases of metamorphic rocks. This is shown by the histogram of Aldrich and Wetherill.[2] In Fig. 10 the abscissa has been changed to correspond to the newly determined half-life of Rb[87] of $4·7.10^{10}$y.[24] As the lowest published Rb–Sr age is 16 million years no other comparison is possible than the dating of an Upper Tertiary biotite obtained from a gneiss from Brione by Jäger and Faul.[28] (Rb–Sr 16.10^6y, K–A 18.10^6y.) Basset et al.[9] found a potassium–argon age of $13·5.10^6$y for a sericite from a lead-zinc-silver-mine while Miller[34] found a uranium–lead age of 13.10^6y for a cogenetic uraninite. This is an example of the agreement of these two methods in the low age range.

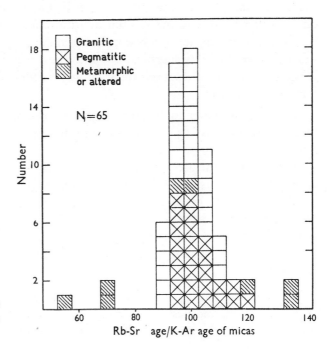

Fig. 10 Histogram of the ratio of the Rb–Sr age to the K–A age for micas from a number of rocks

THE POSSIBILITY OF DATING MORE RECENT PERIODS

The absolute age-determination of Tertiary and Pleistocene samples is difficult since the half-lives for the isotopes available are either too long or too short for the time involved. The lowest lead ages and the lowest Rb–Sr ages are about 20 million years while the highest C[14] ages are some 70,000 years. Only the ionium or the Th[230]–Pa[231] method is reliable for most of the Pleistocene. It is, however, restricted to deep-sea sediments. There remains a long time between 10^5y and 10^7y which can nowadays only be dated by the potassium–argon method. According to new results obtained by Pinson et al. the Rb–Sr method too will be extremely sensitive, and will be practicable down to Pleistocene ages when applied to obsidians and acid volcanic rocks.[36]

In this connection it is interesting to remember that one of the first potassium–argon determinations was made on a sample whose mineral age was Lower Miocene, namely 20 ± 1 million years, but for this determination 200g of potassium-rich sylvite was used.[40]

For ages in the Lower Tertiary the radioactive formula for potassium decay can be simplified to the form:

$$A^{40} = (\lambda . R/1 + R).t.K^{40}$$

It can be clearly seen that with comparatively young ages the amount of measured argon also becomes small, so that in order to extend the method to recent periods it is necessary, as was also the case for very small samples, to develop the technique of the mass-spectrometric determination of small amounts of rare gases. One must find out which factors restrict the method. One is concerned on the one hand with the apparatus used, for example, the amount of argon degassed during a blank determination, and on the other hand with the amount of atmospheric argon in the sample material.

With modern apparatus a blank determination yield of approximately 10^{-8}cc atmospheric argon (STP) is possible. This amount can probably be made smaller so that it is not necessary to discuss this question any further. For the second question however one must consider:

(1) What is the ratio of atmospheric to radiogenic argon in the potassium-rich material used for dating, for example biotite, muscovite or sanidine, as well as the rock samples?

(2) Must the same precautions against the diffusion loss of argon be used for the young ages as for the older ages? That the mineral must be fresh is out of question.

(3) Is the basic prerequisite satisfied that the samples did not contain radiogenic argon when they were formed but that all was expelled through melting? In other words: was the K–A clock set back to zero? Connected with this is the question whether in addition to the young minerals one has also trace amounts of older minerals with higher A^{40}.

To clarify question (1) Table C gives the radiogenic and atmospheric content of argon in several biotites. The atmospheric argon does not come from the apparatus but comes from the sample itself. One sees that the ratios are unfavourable for young

TABLE C
Radiogenic and atmospheric content of argon in different biotites.

Sample	Age	Material	A^{rad}	A^{at}	ratio A^{rad}/A^{at}
	million yrs		10^{-7}cc/g Mat	10^{-7}cc/g Mat	
Katzenbuckel	66 ± 3	biotite	97·6	9·9	10
Eifel S	$0·27 \pm 0·10$	biotite	0·77	10·2	0·08
Bürzeln	$20·4 \pm 0.·8$	tuff biotite	48·3	24·8	2
Eifel L	$1·5 \pm 0·3$	tuff biotite	4·4	62·4	0·07

ages because the atmospheric argon requires a large correction. A small error, 1%, in the determination of argon-36 causes a 10% error in the radiogenic A^{40} when one has 90% atmospheric argon. From these results we conclude that it is not advisable to use tuff biotite for ages less than 1 million years. But it is easier to obtain results from rock biotites.

Reynolds[38] attempted to separate the air argon under the assumption that it was all adsorbed on the surface. In this case heating at 300–400°C should improve the ratio, in the same way that the inside walls of the high vacuum system are outgassed. As Fig. 11 shows, however, only a small fraction of the atmospheric argon is on the surface, most of it is within the crystal. One sees that in all cases when 60% of the argon is removed by heating also 10% of the radiogenic gas is lost. This is not a favourable situation. If the atmospheric argon is contained in a thin layer under the surface, the distribution is changed by heating so that only a part is pumped away.

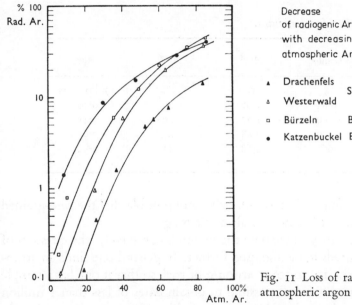

Decrease
of radiogenic Ar
with decreasing
atmospheric Ar.

▲ Drachenfels
                    Sanidine
△ Westerwald

□ Bürzeln   Biotite

● Katzenbuckel Basalt

Fig. 11 Loss of radiogenic argon as a function of atmospheric argon loss

One therefore requires minerals with a high potassium content and with a small content of atmospheric argon. Gentner and Zähringer[22] found this to be the case for the Australian-Indonesian tektites. They were able to determine an average age of 610,000 years. Sanidine, a volcanic glassy feldspar found in tuff, bentonite or other volcanic rocks, behaves similar to tektites. J. Frechen (Bonn) together with Gentner and Lippolt[19] has investigated sanidine crystals from different locations in the Pleistocene volcanic region of Germany. Table D shows several results which illustrate question (3).

Sample D was obtained from a large sanidine bomb. Samples E, M and O were sanidine grains of mm size obtained from tuffs. The percentage of atmospheric argon is quite low so that the ages are reliable. Unfortunately the ages from E, M and O do not agree with the stratigraphy. Geologically the ages should decrease in the sequence E, M, O, however the potassium–argon ages show the inverse tendency.

For biotites similar errors can be shown. It follows that these ages which should be under 300,000 years are not usable. The question arises whether one must contend with excess argon in all tuff minerals, as was also the case for one of the biotite samples obtained from Hegau tuffs. According to encouraging results obtained by Curtis and Evernden this is not the case in all regions. These authors state that their volcanic sanidines of historic, Post- or Late-Pleistocene age yielded ages consistent with the concept of zero radiogenic argon content at the time of eruption.[11]

The danger that the age is too high because of the presence of old minerals is illustrated by the following example. The potassium–argon age of a sanidine and biotite sample obtained from the bentonite of Bischofszell in Hegau should show a sarmat–torton age in the Upper Miocene. As they show ages of 14·6 and 18·4 million years respectively the

TABLE D
Argon contents of Pleistocene sanidines.

Sample	Potassium	A^{rad}	A^{atm}	Age
	%	cc	%	million yrs
Eifel D	10·85	1·66	27	0·39
Eifel E	10·69	1·71	16	0·41
Eifel M	10·00	2·48	23	0·63
Eifel O	5·66	5·68	13	2·54

first may be right but the second 25% too old. It is quite possible that the fine-grained material contains tiny sanidine or biotite crystals of older age.

As it is certainly not always easy to separate the minerals completely, the question of dating whole rock samples needs to be discussed further. In general one finds an atmospheric argon content of about 10^7 to 10^6 cc argon/g of rock so that if one has a sample with a high potassium content it is still possible to obtain dates of less than 1 million years. If the samples have not been altered by metamorphic processes one can certainly use them for dating as the loss of gas by volume diffusion for young ages is lessening.

DATES OF YOUNG SAMPLES

The problems which can be solved with the help of potassium–argon age-determinations of the Pliocene and Pleistocene periods include the determination of an absolute time-scale, dating the origin of Man, the coincidence in time of the fossils in the different continents, the constancy of the earth's magnetic field, the origin of tektites, as well as other special geological problems. These problems are usually interrelated. At present, because of the few measurements, most questions are unanswered. The results to date are presented in Table E.

TABLE E

Potassium–Argon ages of Plio-Pleistocene samples from various authors.

K–Ar/Age	Locality	Material	Geological age	Authors
million yrs				
12·5 ± 0·4	Hohenstoffeln, Germany	Sanidine from tuff	Sarmat, late Miocene	Lippolt, Gentner, Wimmenauer [33]
12·0 ± 0·5	Coal Valley, Nevada		Clarendonian, near Miocene–Pliocene boundary	Curtis, Savage, Evernden (1960)[13]
11·2 ± 0·5	— Nevada		Clarendonian, Lower Pliocene	Curtis, Savage, Evernden (1960)[13]
11·1 ± 0·5		Biotites from tuffs		
10·7 ± 0·4	West Walk River Canyon, California			Evernden, Curtis, Obradovich, Kistler (1961)[17]
9·1 ± 0·4	Western Nevada		Lower Hemphillian, Pliocene	Curtis, Savage, Evernden (1960)[13]
7 ± 1	Kruisschans, Belgium	Glauconite	Scaldisian, Middle Pliocene	Hurley (1960)[26]
6·0 ± 0·3	Höwenegg, Germany	Whole rock basalt	Pontian, Lower Pliocene	Lippolt, Gentner, Wimmenauer[33]
5·2 ± 0·5	Mendoco County, California	Glauconite	Upper Pliocene	Evernden, Curtis, Obradovich, Kistler (1961)[17]
4·2	Valle Grande, New Mexico	Sanidine from tuff		Evernden (1958)[15]
2.4	Tolfa, Italy		Upper Pliocene	
3·3 ± 0·5	Grants, New Mexico	Obsidians	—	Basset, Kerr, Schaeffer, Stoenner (1962)[9]
1·6 ± 0·5	Sutter Buttes, California	Biotites from rhyolite and andesite	Blancan, Late Pliocene	Curtis, Lipson, Evernden (1956)[12]
1·7				
1·75 ± 0·10	Olduvai, E. Africa Bed I	Biotite, oligoklase and anortho-clase from tuffs	Villafranchian	Leakey, Evernden, Curtis (1961)[31]
1·23 ± 0·10				
4·2 ± 0·2	Olduvai, E. Africa	Whole rock basalts	Villafranchian	Curtis and Evernden (1962)[11]
1·7 ± 0·2				v. Koenigswald, Gentner, Lippolt (1961)[30]
1·3 ± 0·1				
1·4 ± 0·1				
1·0 ± 0·2	Bishop Tuff, Sierra Nevada	Sanidine	Early Pleistocene	Evernden, Curtis, Kistler (1957)[16]
0·61 ± 0·09	Different localities between Indo-China and Australia	Tektites	Upper Trinil	Gentner and Zähringer (1960)[22]
0·50 ± 0·06	Muriah volcano, Java	Whole rock basalt	Late or Post Trinil	v. Koenigswald, Gentner, Lippolt (1961)[30]
0·39 ± 0·02	River Terraces of Rhine, Germany	Sanidine	Waal-interglacial	Frechen, Gentner, Lippolt (unp.)[19]
0·35 ± 0·02		Sanidine	Günz glaciation	
0·36	Olduvai, E. Africa, Bed II	Minerals from tuff	Post Chellean II	Leakey, Evernden, Curtis (1961)[31]

Evernden *et al.*[17] in their paper on the utilization of glauconites and illites present some biotite ages from which the border between the Miocene and Pliocene can be estimated. The biotite from Coal Valley tuff in Nevada has an age at this border of 12 million years. An age of 12·5 million years measured by Gentner *et al.* for a sanidine from a sarmat Hegau tuff is a good confirmation of this date since sarmat is late Miocene.[33] An age of 9·1 million years determined by Curtis *et al.*[13] for a Lower Hemphillian biotite is only a little older than a Scaldisian glauconite from Belgium dated by Hurley *et al.* as 7 million years.[27]

By means of a whole rock analysis Lippolt *et al.* determined the age of the fossil-rich Pontian (that is Lower Pliocene) Höwenegg-layer to be 7 million years while Evernden *et al.* find for an Upper Pliocene glauconite from California an age of 5·2 million years which is close to this value. Early in 1956 Curtis *et al.*[12] measured two very young biotite samples which, because of the large amount of air argon yield, gave the rather approximate age of about 1·7 million years. This could be a measurement for the late Pliocene.

The age determined by Evernden *et al.*[17] of 1 million years for a sanidine-containing tuff of the Sierra Nevada appears to be a more accurate young age. This tuff lies under the oldest widespread moraine but on an older moraine which is not well known. It was concluded to be an early Pleistocene montane glaciation and perhaps contemporaneous with the European Donau glaciation. In the same investigation it was shown by the use of a sanidine sample from the young volcanic Eifel that it is possible to measure potassium–argon ages younger than 1 million years. This sanidine sample together with other samples from the same area was investigated by Gentner *et al.*[19] Their results showed that the previously used Milankovitch time scale for the Pleistocene is not correct but that for the four major glaciations the periods of Emiliani[14] are probably better (with the Günz glaciation at about 350,000 years).

Tektites, strange natural glassy objects which are found at different places on the earth and are apparently not of volcanic origin, can be divided by potassium–argon dating into three age groups: an old Tertiary group in North America, a young Tertiary group in Europe and a Pleistocene group in Indo-China, Indonesia and Australia. For the latter Gentner and Zähringer[22] find an average age of 610,000 years ±15%. Measurements of Reynolds[39] agree, within the error, with this value. An important result of these two investigations is that the material has an astonishingly small air argon content. One can consider these tektites as fossils for the upper Trinil Beds in Indonesia. Curtis and Evernden, and independently von Koenigswald and the present authors, have determined the potassium–argon age of a post or late Trinil basalt from the Muriah volcano in Central Java to be 500,000 years. This confirms indirectly the Pleistocene tektite ages and furnishes an age estimate for *Pithecanthropus*.[29]

Further investigations were made to determine the absolute age of *Zinjanthropus* which Leakey found to belong to the upper half of the Lower Pleistocene. Leakey, Evernden and Curtis[31] obtained a potassium–argon age of 1·23 and 1·75 million years for different tuff minerals from the top and the bottom of Bed I at Olduvai. The *Zinjanthropus* remains were found near the bottom of Bed I.

From the above-mentioned potassium–argon dates of the Günz glaciation it appears that the stratigraphic division and the potassium–argon age of this discovery are contradictory. However this is perhaps not so astonishing since up to now no indisputable correlation has been found between the geological and palaeontological sequence in Africa and that in the Mediterranean area or in Europe. Von Koenigswald and the present authors[30] determined the potassium–argon age of three whole rock samples from Olduvai which contradict the result of Leakey et al. without denying a high age for Zinjanthropus. A basalt under Bed I gives an age of 1·3 million years, a stone tool from Bed I 1·4 million years and a second pebble tool 2·25 million years. An age discrepancy of 0·5 million years is found between the basalt and the geologically younger tuff minerals. The questions raised herewith were discussed by Straus and Hunt.[41] Inherited argon or eroded debris of older minerals could explain the older age, or the low results of von Koenigswald et al. could be explained by metamorphism of their samples. Meanwhile, Curtis and Evernden determined the ages of two basalt samples from Olduvai, selected specially for dating purposes, as 1·7 million and 4·2 million years.[11] They conclude that the basalts at Olduvai are at least 4 million years old, but are unreliable for dating purposes because of chemical alterations visible in the thin sections of all dated Olduvai basalts except those associated with the older pebble-tool industry. As no further inconsistency exists between the dates of the overlying tuff and the basalts, an age of 2 million years for Zinjanthropus seems to be possible.

It is clear, however, that only further measurements of Pleistocene samples will solve the question of the duration of the Lower Pleistocene and related topics.

CONCLUSIONS

The errors given with the potassium–argon dates are usually the statistical errors, denoting the reproducibility of the potassium and argon determinations. Possible systematic errors are often not considered. In addition the errors introduced by the decay constants are not included, but these are noted in the text and tables.

Errors introduced by diffusion or metamorphic processes which alter the potassium and argon contents of the samples are not considered so long as one cannot discern a change by microscopic examination of the samples.

The selection of suitable material for dating is indeed the main problem before undertaking potassium–argon measurements on a comparatively recent period. By the use of large samples it is possible to overlap with C^{14} results. It is only necessary to have a substance with little atmospheric argon and which meets the conditions outlined above. The method can be extended if the accuracy of the isotopic measurements of argon is improved.

In this connection it is interesting to ask if it is possible to measure the potassium–argon age directly on fossil materials. The authors have tried to date early Tertiary bones and teeth.[23] Their material had considerable air argon and because of the low potassium content ($< 1°/_{oo}$) the small amount of radiogenic argon was not measurable. Furthermore a high diffusion rate was found. So for this reason it does not seem possible to date young fossil material.

REFERENCES

A: Review articles

1 AHRENS, L. H. 1956. Radioactive methods for determining geological age. *Reports on Progress in Physics 19*, 80
2 ALDRICH, L. T. and WETHERILL, G. W. 1958. *Ann. Rev. Nuclear Sci. 8*, 257
3 CARR, D. R. and KULP, J. L. 1957. *Bull. Geol. Soc. Am. 68*, 763
4 TILTON, G. R. and DAVIS, G. L. 1959. Geochronology. *Researches in Geochemistry*, New York, 190
5 WASSERBURG, G. J. 1954. Potassium-argon dating in FAUL, H. (ed.) *Nuclear Geology*, New York, 341
6 WETHERILL, G. W. 1957. *Science 126*, 545
7 ZÄHRINGER, J. 1960. *Geologische Rundschau 49* (1), 224

B: General references and notes

8 ALDRICH, L. T. and NIER, A. O. 1948. *Phys. Rev. 74*, 876
9 BASSET, W. A., KERR, P. F., SCHAEFFER, O. A. and STOENNER, R. W. 1962. In *Bull. Geol. Soc. Am.*
10 BOLTWOOD, B. B. 1904. *Am. J. Sci. 23*, 77
11 CURTIS, G. H. and EVERNDEN, J. F. 1962. *Nature 194*, 611
12 —— LIPSON, J. and EVERNDEN, J. F. 1956. *Nature 178*, 1360
13 —— SAVAGE, D. E. and EVERNDEN, J. F. 1960. *Ann. N.Y. Acad. Sci. 91*, 342
14 EMILIANI, C. 1955. *J. Geol. 63*, 538
15 EVERNDEN, J. F. 1958. Report given in Hamburg
16 —— CURTIS, G. H. and KISTLER, R. 1957. *Quarternaria 4*, 1
17 —— —— OBRADOVICH, J. and KISTLER, R. 1961. *Geochim. et Cosmochim. Acta 23*, 78
18 FECHTIG, H., GENTNER, W. and ZÄHRINGER, J. 1960. *Ibid. 19*, 70
19 FRECHEN, J., GENTNER, W. and LIPPOLT, H. J. 1963. In *Geochim. Acta*
20 GENTNER, W., PRÄG, R. and SMITS, F. 1953. *Geochim. et Cosmochim. Acta, 4*, 11
21 —— and KLEY, W. 1958. *Ibid. 14*, 98
22 —— and ZÄHRINGER, J. Z. 1960. *Naturforschg. 15a*, 93
23 —— and LIPPOLT, H. J. 1962. *Geochim. et Cosmochim. Acta, 26*, 1247
24 GLENDENIN, L. E. 1960. *Ann. N.Y. Acad. Sci. 91*, 166
25 HART, S. R. 1960. *Ibid. 91*, 192
26 HURLEY, P. M. 1960. *Ibid. 91*, 294
27 —— CORMIER, R. F., HOWER, J., FAIRBAIRN, H. W. and PINSON, W. H. JR 1960. *Bull. Am. Ass. Pet. Geol. 43*, 654
28 JÄGER, E. and FAUL, H. 1959. *Bull. Geol. Soc. Am. 70*, 1553
29 KOENIGSWALD, G. H. R. VON 1962. In KURTH, G. *Evolution und Hominisation*, Stuttgart, 112
30 —— GENTNER, W. and LIPPOLT, H. J. 1961. *Nature 192*, 720
31 LEAKEY, L. S. B., EVERNDEN, J. F. and CURTIS, G. H. 1961. *Ibid. 191*, 478
32 LIPPOLT, H. J. 1961. Title Thesis, Univ. of Heidelberg
33 —— GENTNER W. and WIMMENAUER, W. 1962. In *Jahreshefte des Geolog. Landesamt Freiburg*
34 MILLER, D. 1959. Title Thesis, Columbia Univ.
35 PINSON, W. H. JR 1960. *Ann. N.Y. Acad. Sci. 91*, 221
36 —— BOTTINO, M. L., FAIRBAIRN, H. W. and FAURE, G. 1961. NYO 3942, *Ninth Ann. Progress Rep. for 1961*, Cambridge, 117
37 REYNOLDS, J. H. 1956. *Rev. Sci. Instrum. 27*, 928
38 —— 1957. *Geochim. et Cosmochim. Acta 12*, 177
39 —— 1960. *Ibid. 20*, 101
40 SMITS, F. and GENTNER, W. 1950. *Ibid. 1*, 22
41 STRAUS, W. L. and HUNT, C. B. 1962. *Science 136*, 293
42 STRUTT, R. J. 1910. *Proc. Roy. Soc. Lond. 83* (A), 298
43 WEIZSÄCKER, C. F. V. 1937. *Phys. Z. 38*, 623

J. A. MILLER

THE TECHNIQUE OF POTASSIUM–ARGON DATING* has so far been applied mainly to geological problems concerning the chronology of plutonic and metamorphic rocks. Both these rock types are often rich in mica or hornblende and consequently present little difficulty.

Unfortunately, neither metamorphic or granitic rocks have any significance from a chronological viewpoint in the period of time of interest to the archaeologist. Clearly only those rocks which are closely associated in time with archaeological remains will be satisfactory.

Sedimentary rocks are the most obvious choice, and quite a number of successful measurements have been made on them. The other alternative is to use basalts which commonly provide precise markers of time.

SUITABILITY

Micas occur in basalts comparatively rarely. The lavas of Killerton Park, near Exeter in Devon, and the Palisades Sill, New Jersey, contain some biotite, but they are the exception rather than the rule.

In basalts the potassium is situated mainly in the feldspars, and it is frequently ten times less abundant per unit weight in the rock as a whole than in mica. Consequently problems of argon loss from the feldspars and accurate potassium determination at low concentrations must be solved.

It has already been shown that very fine-grained minerals when separated from their parent rock yield low apparent ages owing to the diffusion of argon from their lattices. Apart from sanidine, feldspars lose argon irrespective of grain size. Therefore little can be gained by using a coarse-grained basalt in the hope that diffusion will be minimized. The other possibility is that even though argon loss from discrete mineral grains does take place, it might under suitable conditions be retained in the rock as a whole. After diffusing from the crystal lattice, the argon undoubtedly migrates along the cracks between grain boundaries and escapes to the atmosphere. Should the percentage of cracks which extend from the outside into the body of the rock be low, then one would expect the amount of argon lost in this manner to be low also.

A very fine-grained basalt would be most likely to fulfil this condition, and a number of preliminary measurements were made on an Upper Carboniferous basalt from the north of England. The results obtained showed clearly that there is some form of inverse relationship between grain size and retentivity. Very fine-grained material taken from a few inches away from the contact yielded an age of 300 ± 14 million years

---

* Because of the importance of the relatively new potassium–argon dating method, we make no excuse for this further note—concerned especially with basalts. EDS.

(Upper Carboniferous) while more coarsely grained rock from the interior of the body yielded apparent ages ranging from 135 to 190 million years (Jurassic and Triassic).

Erickson and Kulp[1] have made a detailed study of the Palisades Sill, New Jersey. This body has a wide range of textural and mineralogical variations which have been described by Walker[2] and includes the presence of a small amount of biotite. By carrying out age determinations on the biotite it was possible to ascertain the true age of intrusion of the sill. Measurements were then made on whole rock samples of diabase which had been ground and sieved to between 20 and 80 mesh. Very fine-grained diabase from the chilled contact which contained plagioclase feldspars less than 0·1 mm in length showed a retentivity of 100%. Samples containing larger feldspars were shown to have lost a proportion of their radiogenic argon. It was also demonstrated that fine-grained hornfels formed by the thermal effect of the hot intrusion on the sediment had also retained all its radiogenic argon. It yielded a similar age to that of the biotite.

A similar study carried out in Cambridge in collaboration with Dr A. E. Musset of Imperial College, London, on dolerite from the Whin Sill, has shown why deviations from the ideal grain size-apparent age relationship exist. Although, in general, coarse-grained basalts gave low apparent ages, this is by no means the rule.

A careful examination of the rocks showed that age was closely related to the freshness of the fine interstitial material between the feldspar laths. Measurements using an electron probe microanalyser showed conclusively that most of the potassium lay in the interstitial material, and little in the laths of the plagioclase feldspar. Coarse varieties of this rock were presumably more susceptible to alteration than the finer-grained types. In basalts, where the fine-grained matrix, which probably contains late stage potash feldspars, is in an unaltered condition, the rock will yield the correct age.

It is clear that basalts can be used in geological problems and consequently are potentially suitable for work in the time period of archaeological interest.

ATMOSPHERIC CONTAMINATION

The main difficulty that must be overcome when working with very young samples is the presence of atmospheric argon. Atmospheric argon arises from four main sources:

(1) Small leaks.
(2) Outgassing of argon extraction apparatus.
(3) From air occluded on to the crucible and crucible support.
(4) From air occluded on to the surface of the sample.

The mass spectrometer is an extremely efficient leak detector and by having it connected directly to the argon extraction line very small leaks can be detected and then repaired.

Outgassing of the argon line itself can be reduced by baking the whole of the apparatus to a temperature of the order of 200°C for about a day.

It is difficult to remove air occluded on to the surface of the crucible and its support as the application of heat might result in loss of argon from the sample. Contributions of atmospheric argon from this source can be kept to a minimum by using a crucible having a low surface area. Molybdenum crucibles are used in preference to carbon crucibles, and yield blanks of the order of 10^{-8} cc of argon at normal temperature and pressure.

By far the larger part of atmospheric argon arises from air adsorbed on to the surface of the sample. Experiments were made with different size fractions of various micas and yielded the results shown in Table A, which suggest that in a general way the higher the total surface area, the higher the atmospheric contamination.

TABLE A

Variations in atmospheric contamination with grain size of sample.

Sample	Mesh size	Atmospheric contamination %
R 260 biotite from Moine schist	70–140	4·4
	70–140	4·7
	50– 70	1·8
U 2681 biotite from Moine schist	70–140	8·6
	50– 70	4·0
Biotite from Mount Sorrel granite	70–140	4·6
	70–140	5·5
	50– 70	4·1
A/1 biotite from Eskdale granite	70–140	6·0
	50– 70	2·8
A/13 biotite from Rannoch Moor granite	70–140	3·3
	50– 70	2·8
A/21 biotite from Strontian granite	70–140	2·7
	50– 70	2·3
A/38 biotite from Carn Chuinneag	70–140	3·8
	50– 70	2·4
A/19 biotite from Moine schist	70–140	2·5
	50– 70	2·0
A/14 biotite from Cruachan granite	70–140	3·9
	50– 70	1·7
Mica from Conger Township, Ontario	Solid block	0·1

Clearly there is advantage in keeping the surface area of the samples to a minimum. In work on basalts larger chips of material have been used in preference to ground and sieved samples. This minimizes the chances of argon loss by diffusion and argon gain from occluded air. Table B shows some results obtained from fine-grained oceanic basalts using this technique. In none of the cases was either the crucible or sample outgassed in any way previous to fusion.

Problems of accurate isotope analysis are mentioned elsewhere in this book and therefore do not demand further comment. Using modern mass spectrometers they should not be an insuperable difficulty.

The overall experimental accuracy of any potassium–argon age determination depends upon the accuracy with which the volume of radiogenic argon and potassium content can be obtained. Volume is calculated either from the isotope ratio of the argon from the rock sample mixed with a known amount of argon-38 spike, or from the relative peak heights produced by the mass spectrometer for the argon sample from the rock and an argon sample of known volume when measured separately.

In general a 1% error in either the proportion of potassium oxide or the volume of radiogenic argon will give rise to approximately a 1% error in the age.

TABLE B

Potassium–Argon age determinations on samples of fine-grained oceanic basalt ($\lambda\beta = 4\cdot72\cdot10^{-10}$ *yr.*$^{-1}$; $\lambda e = 0\cdot584\cdot10^{-10}$ *yr.*$^{-1}$).

Sample	Reference	Volume of radiogenic A^{40} (mm^3 N.T.P.) / Weight of sample (gm)	K_2O	Atmospheric Argon	Age to nearest million yrs
			%	%	
Basalt, Settlement Plain Tristan da Cunha	0/11	0·000279	2·79	54·1	3
Basalt from edge of Lake, Tristan da Cunha	0/14	0·000330	3·3	37·5	3
Plug at head of Deep Glen, Gough Island	0/9	0·000550	5·5	78·2	3
Basalt, near sea level, Waterfall Point, Gough Island	0/10	0·000386	5·8	44·7	2
Basalt from Inaccessible Island	0/13	0·000380	1·9	43·2	6

DETERMINATION OF POTASSIUM

The difficulties involved in determining the potassium contents of rocks or minerals are not great provided that the concentration of potassium is greater than 1%.

− Flame photometry is the most common technique used. About 0·1 g. of mineral is needed to make one determination provided that it contains more than 1% of potassium.

The mineral is dissolved in hydrofluoric and sulphuric acids and evaporated to dryness. After cooling, the salts are redissolved in distilled water containing one drop of sulphuric acid and then transferred to standard flasks where they are made up to the correct volume with ammonium carbonate-ammonium hydroxide solution and distilled water.

This causes heavy metals to be precipitated which, after being allowed to settle, are filtered off. The solution is then measured in the flame photometer, previously calibrated using solutions of known potassium content.

To make a reliable measurement of the potassium content of a mineral, at least six separate determinations should be made. This means that at least 0·6 gm of mineral would be required. In dealing with basalts this would present no problem.

Difficulties do arise when the amount of potassium present is very low. Under such conditions, potassium would be determined either by isotope dilution using a solid source mass spectrometer or by the process of neutron activation.

CONCLUSION

Both practically and theoretically the dating of basalts is possible. Basalts have certain advantages over sediments in this work inasmuch that there is no shortage of material once a suitable flow has been located. The minerals used in dating sediments are often quite rare and a considerable amount of sediment might have to be processed before a gram of the right mineral could be isolated.

In the case of basalts, there is less chance that the rock contains argon which originated before the date of eruption. It is possible for sedimentary minerals known to be of authigenic origin to contain minute inclusions of sedimentary material which would give rise to incorrect ages.

It is possible that secondary effects could take place within the sediment that would result in potassium being either added or subtracted from the mineral. Both these processes would give rise to spurious results. Such changes are much less likely to take place in a hard fine-grained basalt.

From an archaeological viewpoint there are certain advantages in dating basalts rather than sediments. It is often possible to correlate periods of volcanic extrusion or eruption with archaeological events. By using potassium–argon age measurements on the lavas it would be possible to fix these events in time.

A further problem facing the archaeologist is the low efficiency of radiocarbon dating at high ages. There is no theoretical reason why potassium–argon dating should not be used to close this gap. In many places, such as on Tristan da Cunha, bands of lava and tuff have been extruded into bogs and have been quickly overgrown with peat. Using material such as this, both radiocarbon and potassium–argon ages could be used to date the event and their relative accuracies checked.

REFERENCES

1 ERICKSON, G. P. and KULP, J. L. 1961. *Bull. Geol. Soc. Am.* 72, 649
2 WALKER, F. 1940. *Ibid.* 51, 1059

8 Dating Pottery by Thermoluminescence

E. T. HALL

ONE OF THE ARCHAEOLOGIST's most important sources of information is his pottery. On this much of his stratigraphy and indeed his conclusions will depend. Perhaps the most valuable contribution the scientist could make to helping the archaeologist would be to provide a *reliable* and universal dating method for pottery sherds. Thermoremanent magnetic dating provides us potentially with a direct method of dating kilns; however, but for exceptional instances, this method will not help us with the dating of the pottery itself. The technique of thermoluminescence has, however, given at least a glimmer of hope that we may be able to date isolated finds of pottery found in all places and conditions.

A word of warning must be given at once. The amount of work published or indeed so far undertaken has been small and the validity of the method has been far from proved. Work from the archaeological point of view is being undertaken at three universities at the present time: California,[1] Oxford,[2] and Bern.[3] This note is intended to give a brief outline of some of the principles involved but is in no way complete.

PRINCIPLES

Careful – compare with LIB

If we grind up a small quantity of ceramic which will always contain some crystalline material and then heat it up, visible light will be emitted. This effect was first noted with geological minerals and was indeed used in investigations of single crystals as long ago as 1927.[4] Since then several workers have attempted to use the method for dating rocks, in particular at the University of Wisconsin.[5–7] This property of light emission is called thermoluminescence and is the result of the release of energy stored as electron displacements. The mechanism is still somewhat uncertain and there appear to be differing views as to what is happening. It will be sufficient for the purposes of this short article to outline one approach.

All ceramics will contain certain amounts of radioactive impurities (e.g. uranium and thorium) although only in the parts per million concentration range. These elements will emit α particles at a definite rate which will only depend on the impurity content of the sample. These α particles will cause ionization within the sample and electrons will result. Now also within the sample will be crystal imperfections or 'holes' which were formed during and after crystallization. The released electrons will tend to be trapped in these 'holes' at ordinary ambient temperatures. When the ceramic is heated these electrons will be released from their traps at definite temperatures and on release a photon of light is ejected. The longer the ceramic has been crystallized the more ionizing radiation will have resulted and the more trapped electrons will be held in the crystal structure.

In dating a ceramic, therefore, we must make the following essential measurements:

(a) Measure the light output of the ceramic when heated up.
(b) Measure the intensity of α activity of the ceramic.
(c) Measure by artificial irradiation the susceptibility of the ceramic to bombardment with α rays.

By a combination of these results with those obtained from ceramics of known date it should be possible to estimate the age of an unknown sample.

ACCURACY

There are of course inevitably many disturbing factors which may reduce the accuracy of the results, although at first sight these should not be so serious as those encountered with geological samples. Archaeological specimens have not been subjected to unknown conditions of temperature, pressure and recrystallization, all of which may disturb geological results.[7,8] Moreover, the measurement of a large number of samples from the same source should minimize the experimental error, provided of course that the archaeologically dated specimens which are used as standards are correctly assessed. It is very hard at this stage to give an estimate of the likely absolute accuracy of age determination: one might reasonably expect, however, an accuracy of ±100 years; in exceptional circumstances this might be divided by three provided several specimens were available. I should emphasize again, however, that as yet the physical mechanism is little understood and the best experimental procedure has yet to be determined.

APPARATUS

Thermoluminescence from certain minerals may be demonstrated by pounding a few lumps and putting them in a heated frying-pan in a dark room; they will then glow for several seconds brightly enough to read a newspaper. Unfortunately ceramics have not been made for long enough periods, nor contain sufficient radioactive material, to produce such spectacular and easily measured results. Very special apparatus must be constructed. The powdered material is mounted on a suitable thin plate (both graphite[1] and steel[3] have been used) which may be heated quickly by passing a large current through it. Quick heating (up to 100°C/sec.) is essential in order that the light intensity is as great as possible. The light output from the ceramic is measured by a very low background photo-multiplier and the intensity plotted against temperature on a recorder or oscilloscope. The recorded curve is compared with that produced during a second heating cycle when all thermoluminescence has been displaced and only the background emission from the heated plate is measured. The difference of the two recorded areas will be a measure of the thermoluminescence of the sample.

The α activity of the specimen may be measured with standard low-level α counting equipment and should present no difficulty.

The estimation of susceptibility to α radiation 'damage' is more difficult since comparable damage to that produced in thousands of years by uranium and thorium must be achieved in hours by different means. 20 MeV proton beams and polonium sources have been used to cause the effects, but more evidence is required to evaluate the best procedure.

CONCLUSION

Archaeologically the possibilities of the use of thermoluminescence are exciting and could have far-reaching consequences. Scientifically the problems are intriguing and create an interesting challenge, although their solution may prove more difficult than was at first thought likely. Only time will tell us whether we have here a technique which is any better than existing time-honoured stratigraphic methods.

REFERENCES

1 KENNEDY, G. 1960. *Arch. News 13*, 147
2 Research Laboratory for Archaeology and the History of Art, Oxford University, *Archaeometry 4*
3 HOUTERMANS, F. G. 1961. *Helv. Phys. Act. 33*, vi/vii, 595
4 FRISCH, O. R. 1927. *Wien. Ber.* 11a *136*, 57
5 FAUL, H. (ED.) 1954. *Nuclear Geology*, New York
6 ZELLER, E. J. 1957. *Bull. Am. Ass. Pet. Geol. 41*, 121
7 DANIELS, F., BOYD, C. A. and SAUNDERS, D. F. 1953. *Science 117*, 343
8 ARGINO, E. E. 1959. *J. Geophys. Res. 64*, 1638

SECTION II ENVIRONMENT

9 *Environmental Studies and Archaeology*

J. M. COLES

ARCHAEOLOGY AT THE PRESENT TIME has moved from a phase of preoccupation with the material equipment of early man to an expanded study of man in his prehistoric setting —the material equipment as it relates to the natural environment. Environment, as used by archaeology, means a number of factors interrelated, a combination of climate, soil, fauna and flora, topography, and it is the study of these factors as determining or influencing the activities of prehistoric man that concerns us.

Geological and pedological studies, and analysis of animal and vegetable matter, have brought about a transformation in the knowledge we can obtain about environmental conditions, especially so in certain areas such as northern Europe. This knowledge of the development of vegetation and fauna in response to topographical and climatic agencies can be used by the archaeologist in two ways. First, by establishing a sequence of climatic, floral and faunal stages, and by correlating these with prehistoric remains, a reliable dating method is gained, and in the majority of archaeological reports these scientific studies are pursued for this chronological purpose. Of equal importance is the interpretation of these same scientific reports into a reconstruction, as far as is possible, of the former environment.

Apart from the traces of industrial activity, soils and remains of animals and plants are the principal witnesses of the extent of man's activity at a particular site. The scientific study of these remains will tell us something of his prehistoric environment only if correctly interpreted by the archaeologist, and with the realization that a complete reconstruction of the habitat can never be made, because the evidence available will be conditioned by natural destructive agencies as well as by the type of human activity represented at the site.

Especially for the earliest periods, the archaeologist relies to a great extent on the sciences of geology and pedology for information about environment. These have been concentrated mainly upon the events of the Pleistocene, extending into the early Holocene, and up to the present have been turned more upon chronological problems than upon the related environmental studies. This is understandable, because one of the first necessities of archaeological investigations is to establish some sort of relative time-scale, and during the Pleistocene of course a good many of the deposits studied by geology and pedology are by their nature rarely productive of archaeological material *in situ*.

These include such glacial phenomena as till or boulder clay, glacifluvial deposits, and more local solifluction. Loessic deposits however, generally brickearths of the silt grade, while denoting glacial phases in continental Europe, have in some cases preserved archaeological remains. They show the adaptation of prehistoric man to meet the limiting and rigorous living conditions at that time. The main area of loess deposition is generally thought to lie at a distance from the ice margins sufficient to be tolerable to prehistoric hunters and the game on which they lived. Comparatively recent finds in European Russia show well how early man existed in these glacial periods, utilizing as best he could the loess land with its attendant vegetation and animal life. The first known house was found in Russia at Gagarino in 1927,[1] and consisted of an oval depression about 17 × 14 feet scooped in the earth; limestone slabs paved the floor and it is probable that the roof was supported on poles covered with skins or boughs. Five of these Palaeolithic earth-houses formed a small settlement at Timonovka on the Desna, while a communal house at Pushkari I had three separate hearths and was over 36 feet long. At Pushkari evidence was also recovered suggesting that during mild seasons of the year the Upper Palaeolithic folk had worked and taken meals outside a large tent-like structure. As far east as Siberia traces of settlements of this date have been found. At Mal'ta and Buret, for instance, bone was used extensively in the building of the huts: the femurs of mammoths as posts and supports, skulls of the same animal and of the woolly rhinoceros as a backing and base for the walls.

Work on other Pleistocene deposits includes the geological study of raised beaches and river gravels, both of which can provide evidence not only of date but also of environment. At Slindon,[2] Sussex, occupation by Acheulean man apparently took place directly on a beach, now 100 feet above sea level, during an interglacial period. His way of life may not have been much different from that of the Mesolithic strand-loopers of northern Europe. Work on beach and other gravel and sand deposits by Hey[3] in Cyrenaica has demonstrated the value of such studies in the determination of climatic phases. For river gravels, recent work[4] has shown that size and shape can be used to indicate climatic temperatures, but generally such terrace deposits are dated by their climatic or thalassostatic character, aided by associated fauna wherever possible.

Another field of soil science of great potential value to the archaeologist is the recently developed study of cave sediments. These deposits are often complex, but work in the last few decades has clarified and explained the various natural processes which account for the great variety of sediments in caves, limestone rubble from percolating water or from insolation and frost-weathering, wind-blown and hill-washed silts and clays, and travertines. Clearly the information about climatic phases represented in cave sediments will be of extreme value to workers attempting to place archaeological material, especially of Upper Palaeolithic age, into its proper setting.

The work of Lais[5] on cave sediments of the Isteiner Klotz in Baden combined physical and chemical investigation of the deposits with statistical analyses of various species of snail. He was able to relate the climatic phases represented in the cave with pollen zones of Postglacial vegetation, with its attendant value for environmental studies. Schmid has continued this work. More recently, pollen analysis of cave deposits[6] has been shown to be possible through concentration of the material, so direct correlations should be obtained between the cave sediments and the outside vegetational changes.

Both of interglacial and Postglacial date, fossil lake and peat-bog deposits can be employed by the archaeologist to reveal the development of climatic phases through the technique of pollen analysis, but pedological work too can show the stages of silting and bog-formation. The combination of the two sciences should enable the archaeologist to deduce the exact type of swamp, marsh or bog in existence during any prehistoric occupation of the immediate area. The preservative qualities of this type of deposit have also contributed a great deal of information about early man and his equipment. The yew spear from the Lehringen brickearths,[7] and the Mesolithic equipment from Star Carr, enable us to get glimpses, some more complete than others, of the materials early man adapted to fit into his environmental conditions, and emphasize the potential value of examination of comparable deposits.

In effect opposed to these deposits are sands and heath formations which do not often allow the preservation of material equipment other than stone. Yet in these areas the interrelations between soil and topography on the one hand and prehistoric settlement on the other is great not only in early Postglacial times when some Mesolithic people shunned the forests and settled on acid sandy soils, but in the later periods too. The loess lands, of light calcareous soil, are another example of environmental effect upon prehistoric man, in this case the initial Neolithic colonization of central Europe.

With the development of technology and widespread settlement during the Neolithic and later periods, natural environmental conditions will be altered to a much greater degree than during a purely hunting and gathering economy, and so it becomes increasingly difficult to find sufficient evidence to reconstruct the regional conditions under which this later settlement took place. The soil scientist here is more concerned with artificial structures, postholes, ditch infillings, banks and discolorations of soil, than with purely natural deposits. The fact that climate, fauna and flora were not unlike that of the present day increases the difficulty of determining exact environmental conditions through fossil evidence, and here the emphasis is placed more upon scientific study of flora and fauna than upon topographical and geological work.

A second major source of information about environmental conditions comes to the archaeologist through the study of faunal remains associated with industrial material. Lartet[9] was among the first prehistorians to point out, in his mid-nineteenth-century classificatory system for the Palaeolithic, this relationship between the archaeological material and the associated fauna. When this evidence is combined with studies of vegetation and soil deposits, the archaeologist can reconstruct to a certain degree the prehistoric environment into which the cultural remains were originally designed to fit.

As much for the earliest periods in man's prehistory as for the latest, faunal assemblages studied in their entirety can reveal important evidence for environmental studies.[10] For the Palaeolithic and Mesolithic periods this evidence can be used in two ways, first as providing climatic dating so vital to these early periods, second as showing some elements of the organization of hunting activity. In the first instance, the animals represented on a site provide climatic dating dependent upon their preference for different temperature ranges and type of landscape, varying from tundra, subarctic forest and loess steppe to temperate forest and warm continental parklands or grasslands. Within these regions, not static during the Pleistocene, certain characteristic faunal assemblies can be identified, and the emphasis surely must now be placed upon the total range of animals rather than upon one or two individual species as has been done in the past, for example in the dating of certain deposits of the Somme River terraces.[11]

It is necessary also to limit to a certain extent the genera used in this climatic work. Herbivores may be more intimately connected with climatic fluctuations than carnivores, because of the former's direct dependence upon vegetation. The recognition of faunal relict areas, such as regions of north Spain and the Riviera, should also be considered as showing rates of environmental change. The biological interest in the evolutionary aspects of such animals as the elephant, rhinoceros and horse can provide the archaeologist with firm climatic and environmental evidence, such as that obtained at Brundon,[12] but more detailed knowledge of the development of the reindeer, with its corollary improvement in our understanding of the late glacial phases, will not be acquired until the archaeologist stops making only generic identifications of a selective group of remains; total collection with precise and detailed stratigraphical positioning is necessary if determination of subspecies, and then regional types, is to be made.

However, even if statistically sufficient numbers can be obtained, this aspect of environmental studies will be incomplete, because nothing will be known of the types not represented in the collection, not represented because of destruction by natural agencies, carnivores or selective hunting methods, a point first made by Boyd Dawkins[13] in his criticism of Lartet's scheme. The fauna recovered at an archaeological site may only represent preferential hunting methods, the animals best suited for food or raw materials, the animals obtainable in the area at any particular period, the animals most easily killed by the hunting weapons and methods available. And these periods may be extremely short, with seasonal migration causing temporary faunal displacement.

For later periods, the development of studies concerning the degree of domestication of animals has only recently reached a high standard, with attendant statistical work on mortality rates of animals found in archaeological deposits.[14] This clearly has an important bearing on the organization of Neolithic communities, and reflects the environmental conditions that prompted such organization. For the earlier periods the evidence will not be as complete, but with proper statistical work on faunal assemblages, the scientist will be able not only to establish a climatic dating but also to assist the reconstruction of the former environmental conditions under which early man struggled to survive.

Equally as important as soil and faunal studies is the work of the pollen analyst who, through the identification and counting of fossil pollen grains incorporated in certain deposits, can aid in reconstructing the prehistoric habitat. Macroscopic studies of vegetation debris also serve the same purpose. This work has in the main been limited to temperate zones, initiated by von Post,[15] and as yet we know relatively little about the fluctuations of climate in the present subtropical zones with their corresponding implications for the emergence of animal domestication and cereal cultivation. The difficulties encountered by the pollen analyst are not however easily overcome in his attempt to determine phases of vegetational change in specific areas. Over-representation of plants such as hazel is well understood, but varying degrees of wind and water flotation, differences in preservative qualities of different pollen grains, the possibility of bog growth interruption with resulting losses of vegetational phase representatives, all these contribute to the palynologist's problems. In Britain and Ireland the work of Godwin[16] and Mitchell[17] has shown the great importance of scientifically controlled pollen analysis to environmental studies.

Allied to this, the study of woods and charcoals can also throw some light on conditions of economy and environment. In some cases, wooden objects such as the Somerset trackways will be preserved in waterlogged and airless soils, others such as furniture in Egyptian tombs will be preserved in dry and desertic conditions. But such finds are comparatively rare, and it is the work on wood charcoal so commonly found on archaeological sites that is particularly important. Knowledge of industrial organization as well as environmental conditions can be obtained from the identification of wood used in buildings, or as firewood, or for the production of small objects.

A century ago, the fauna and flora recovered from the Swiss lake dwellings were subject to a detailed study by Rutimeyer and Heer, and the information obtained about the prehistoric economy and environmental conditions showed the value of such work. Since this time, specialist studies have become common, including work on soils, fauna and flora. Allied to these scientific aids is the interpretive analysis of objects in relation to their geographical background. This environmental method was developed in Britain by field workers such as Guest[18] and Freeman, and later carried to fruition by Crawford and Fox. In Germany, Gradmann[19] and Wahle[20] also pioneered. Crawford[21] as early as 1912 showed the correlations between distributional patterns of early metal objects and the geography of Britain. He realized that complete patterns had to be seen against the prehistoric landscape, and emphasized vegetation cover as being the most important factor in the prehistoric environment.

This work was carried into greater detail by Fox[22] in 1923 with his examination of prehistoric distributions in the Cambridge region compared with the background of soil types and their allied vegetation. He was able to show how the patterns of distribution were related to the contemporary landscape rather than the modern one. Fox's *Personality of Britain*, first published in 1932, combined distributional and geographical notions previously developed by himself and Crawford and MacKinder to show how the prehistoric environment, landscape and vegetation controlled or influenced early settlement. This idea of geographical determinism has recently been criticized as too drastic and rigid, but its effects at the time were widespread and striking. Since this time, of course, recognition of fundamental as well as minor changes in the prehistoric environmental phases over even a short period of time has been made, by the improved techniques of pollen analysis and soil studies, adding to our knowledge of changing prehistoric settlement within changing environmental conditions. But this geographical approach to archaeology was nevertheless a major step towards the recognition that environmental studies, using a number of scientific disciplines, are the only justifiable way with which to treat archaeological material.

REFERENCES

1 MONGAIT, A. L. 1961. *Archaeology in the U.S.S.R.* London
   GOLOMSHTOK, E. A. 1938. *Trans. Am. Phil. Soc. N.S. 29,* Pt. 2, Art. 3.
2 PYDDOKE, E. 1950. *Inst. Arch. Univ. London,* no. 6, with references
3 McBURNEY, C. B. M. and HEY, R. H. 1955. *Prehistory and Pleistocene Geology in Cyrenaican Libya,*
   Cambridge.
4 CAILLEUX, A. 1945. *Bull. Soc. géol. de France 15,* 375
   —— 1947. La géologie des terrains récents dans l'ouest de l'Europe, 91, in *Rep. extraord. Sess. Socs.
   belges de Géol.,* Brussels
5 LAIS, R. 1932. *Fortsch. der Geol. und Paläont.* no. 11
   —— 1941. *Quartär 3,* 56
6 LEROI-GOURHAN, A. 1959. *C.R. Congr. préhist. de France,* Monaco
7 JACOB-FRIESEN, K. H. 1956. *Jahrbuch des Röm.-Germ. Zentralmuseums Mainz 3,* 1
8 CLARK, J. G. D. 1954. *Excavations at Star Carr,* Cambridge
9 LARTET, E. 1875. *Reliquiae Aquitanicae,* London, 4th ed.
10 DONNFR, J. J. and KURTÉN, B. 1958. *Eiszeitalter und Gegenwart 9,* 72
11 BREUIL, H. and KOSLOWSKI, L. 1931–2. *L'Anthropologie 41,* 449; *42,* 27 and 291
12 MOIR, J. and TINDELL HOPWOOD, A. 1939. *Proc. Prehist. Soc. 5,* 1
13 BOYD DAWKINS, W. 1874. *Cave Hunting,* London
14 REED, C. A. 1961. *Zeitschrift für Tierzüchtung und Züchtungs biologie 76,* I, 31–8
15 POST, L. v. 1916. *Geol. Fören. Stockh. Förh 38*
   ERDTMAN, G. 1943. *An Introduction to Pollen Analysis*
16 GODWIN, H. 1956. *The History of the British Flora,* Cambridge
   —— 1960. *Proc. Prehist. Soc. 26,* 1
17 MITCHELL, G. F. 1940–1, 1945, 1951–3. *Proc. Royal Irish Acad. 46B* (13–14); *50C* (1); *53B* (11); *55B* (12)
18 GUEST, E. 1883. Origines Celticae (a fragment) and other contributions to the *History of Britain,* London
19 GRADMANN, R. 1898. *Das Pflanzenleben der Schwäbischen Alb*
20 WAHLE, E. 1918. *Mannus Biblio.* 15
21 CRAWFORD, O. G. S. 1912. *Geog. J. 40,* 184
22 FOX, C. 1923. *The Archaeology of the Cambridge Region,* Cambridge

IIa CLIMATE

10 The Significance of Deep-sea Cores

CESARE EMILIANI

THE UNUSUAL IMPORTANCE AND INTEREST of deep-sea cores among Pleistocene studies stems from the fact that by using such cores it is possible to reconstruct a continuous, time-calibrated record of the temperature variations of the surface water of the ocean during the Pleistocene. The surface temperature of the ocean, especially in the Atlantic and adjacent seas, is known or inferred to be closely related to the amount of ice on the northern lands. The oceanic temperature curve obtained from the deep-sea cores is thus a representation of continental glaciation, with temperature valleys and peaks corresponding, respectively, to glacial and interglacial ages. It is therefore possible, by correlation, to estimate the ages and durations of continental Pleistocene stages beyond the range of C^{14} dating. Deep-sea cores consisting of undisturbed sections of *Globigerina*-ooze sediment are most useful for this type of studies.

Globigerina-ooze, covering approximately 40% of the ocean floor, consists essentially of clay and a substantial amount (from 30% to more than 90%) of calcium carbonate. The clay component consists of the finest detritus brought to the ocean by rivers and winds and distributed widely by ocean currents. The carbonate component consists largely of the shells of pelagic Foraminifera living in the euphotic zone. These shells are emptied upon reproduction and fall to the bottom. Other elements of the carbonate component are coccoliths and the shells of benthonic Foraminifera. Accessory elements in the sediment include shells of Radiolaria and diatoms, Fe-Ni spherules of cosmic origin, volcanic ash, water-, wind- and ice-borne mineral particles of terrestrial origin, fish teeth and otoliths, holothurian sclerites, and some precipitates (largely Fe and Mn compounds).

Calcium carbonate elements are dissolved to varying extents both during sinking through the water and on the ocean floor. The dimensionally smaller elements, such as foraminiferal spicules and coccoliths, are especially affected. Solution becomes conspicuous at depths greater than about 4,000 m., leaving red clay as the predominant sediment.

Mechanically, accumulation of deep-sea sediments occurs mainly in two ways: (a) by settling of particles from the water column above, and (b) by lateral influx of material along the ocean floor. Lateral influx ranges from the addition of micron-sized particles (clay and coccoliths) reworked from adjacent areas by gentle bottom currents, to catastrophic floods introduced by turbidity currents originating on continental and island slopes, sometimes hundreds of miles away. In addition, sections of deep-sea sediments ranging in thickness from centimetres to perhaps tens of metres may be removed by sudden slumps caused by earthquake waves or other natural agencies.

Bottom topography exerts an important effect on the pattern of deep-sea sedimentation. Thus, little or no sediment may accumulate on the tops of seamounts; elisions are frequent on the slopes bordering continents, islands and seamounts; and lateral influx of sediments by turbidity currents is common in basins draining slopes on which sufficient sediment accumulation occurs. As a result of the great amount of sediments contributed from land and the strong erosion of shelf sediments by the sea during times of low sea level, the deposition of sediment layers transported by turbidity currents has been conspicuous and widespread during the glacial ages in both the North Atlantic and the North Pacific. Indeed, the majority of the 221 deep-sea cores recently surveyed by Ericson et al.[16] contain sediment layers deposited by turbidity currents.

Deep-sea sediments are easily sampled using the piston corer, a device invented by Kullenberg [22] and further developed by Ewing and associates.[17] This device permits the recovery of cylindrical sedimentary sections 5 cm. in diameter and up to 25 m. long. A few thousand deep-sea cores of various lengths have been recovered during the past 15 years by various expeditions at sea, notably the Swedish Deep-Sea Expedition of 1947–1948 and the numerous expeditions of the Lamont Geological Observatory, the Scripps Institution of Oceanography, and the Soviet Institute of Oceanology. Only a small minority of these cores have been found free of both elisions by slumping and additions by turbidity current deposition. These undisturbed cores provide continuous stratigraphic records, covering in continuity the time during which the sediments were deposited.

Globigerina-ooze accumulates at rates ranging from one to several centimetres per thousand years, depending upon geographic location, depth of the water, and the local topography of the ocean floor. Thus, undisturbed Globigerina-ooze cores 10 m. to 20 m. in length may contain continuous stratigraphic records ranging in time from the present to more than a million years ago. At least two of the cores thus far described are believed to contain sediments representing the whole Pleistocene and part of the Late Pliocene.[1,5]

Probably the most significant geophysical parameter of the Pleistocene is temperature. In fact, temperature is known to have changed markedly, repeatedly, and on a world-wide basis, in response to the various continental glaciations. The temperature variations of the surface waters of the oceans can be reconstructed from suitable deep-sea cores of Globigerina-ooze facies by using a variety of methods. Most important among these are the studies of relative abundances of different species of pelagic Foraminifera which have different temperature tolerances, and the measurement of the ratio of the two stable oxygen isotopes, O^{18} and O^{16}, in the calcium carbonate of the foraminiferal shells. The former method was first proposed by Philippi [24] while the latter was proposed by Urey [38] and developed by Urey, Epstein, and associates.[39, 11, 12] The percentage of $CaCO_3$ and the weight percentage of the foraminiferal shells are two additional parameters which have been found to be temperature dependent under special conditions.

Globigerina-ooze is commonly reworked by bottom animals to a depth of several centimetres below the sediment surface. Consequently, the time resolution of the deep-sea cores of *Globigerina*-ooze facies is generally not better than a few thousand years, and events closely spaced in time cannot be recognized as separate in the cores. As an example

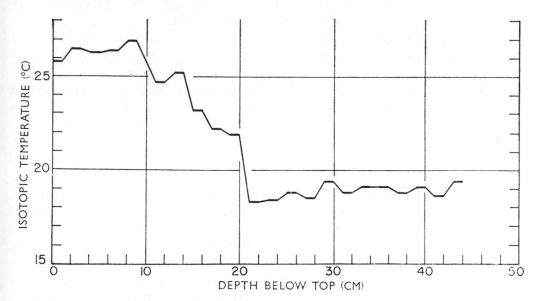

Fig. 12 Core 234A (equatorial Atlantic): isotopic temperatures obtained from *Globigerinoides sacculifera*. From Emiliani.[5]

the temperature fluctuations which are likely to have accompanied the various pulsations of the continental glaciers during the last deglaciation are represented in the deep-sea cores by a relatively smoothly rising temperature curve (Fig. 12). *Globigerina*-ooze cores, therefore, are most useful in the reconstruction of the major temperature variations of the Pleistocene, but are of little use for the study of the minor ones.

The stratigraphically longest deep-sea core of *Globigerina*-ooze facies so far described is core 58 of the Swedish Deep-Sea Expedition of 1947–1948, raised in the eastern equatorial Pacific from a depth of 4,400 m. This core is believed to contain an essentially continuous sedimentary section extending from the present to about one million years ago. Chemical analyses on this and other cores from the same general area[1] have revealed numerous, approximately periodical variations of the carbonate percentages, which are

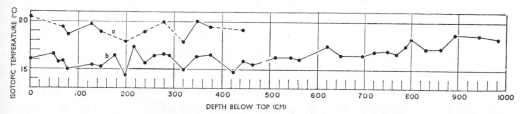

Fig. 13 Core 58 (eastern equatorial Pacific): isotopic temperatures obtained from (a) *Pulleniatina obliquiloculata* and (b) *Globorotalia tumida*. From Emiliani.[5]

believed to have occurred in response to climatic changes. O^{18}/O^{16} analysis of core 58 (Fig. 13) showed a temperature decrease from the bottom of the core to its midpoint, followed by small temperature fluctuations in the upper half. Although the core may well penetrate the Pliocene, the position of the Plio–Pleistocene boundary cannot be established as this boundary is defined on the basis of the Plio–Pleistocene sections of southern Italy,[21] and no correlation between the two stratigraphies has yet been made.[10]

The temperature fluctuations in the upper portion of core 58 are of only 2° to 3°C. This small amplitude is probably due to the geographic location, the local pattern of vertical circulation of the ocean water, and the fact that only pelagic foraminiferal species of the relatively deeper growth habitats were available for isotopic analysis.[5] The temperature record is therefore not very clear.

A far clearer temperature record is provided by deep-sea cores from the Atlantic and adjacent seas, although none of the cores thus far described appears to represent the whole Pleistocene. This greater clarity probably results from the greater heat exchange between the water masses of the Atlantic and adjacent seas on one side and the northern ice caps on the other, producing temperature fluctuations greater than those of the equatorial Pacific. The more recent fluctuations were already rather clearly shown by the early works of Schott,[36] Bramlette and Bradley,[2] Cushman and Henbest,[4] Cushman,[3] Phleger[25, 26] and Phleger and Hamilton.[29] These investigations were based on the distribution of pelagic Foraminifera through relatively short cores from the equatorial and North Atlantic and the Caribbean. Similar work on the longer cores which have become available since the invention of the piston corer[27, 28, 30, 14, 17, 19, 23, 37, 16] has confirmed the early observations and extended the temperature record further back in time.

Estimates of temperature variation through deep-sea cores which are based on the relative abundances of pelagic Foraminifera are dependent upon the significance of different species as temperature indicators. Since the present latitudinal distribution is reasonably well known, especially in the Atlantic, the method is well founded in principle. In practice, however, different species may give different temperature estimates, as shown in Emiliani,[7] Figs 1 and 2. In fact, temperature may not be the only factor controlling the relative abundances of pelagic Foraminifera, and temperature estimates based exclusively or predominantly on a single species are open to question. Furthermore, the relative abundances of pelagic Foraminifera in *Globigerina*-ooze, which characteristically includes a large number of specimens belonging to a few common species and fewer specimens belonging to a number of less common species, form a close statistical system in which the relative abundance of any given common species is affected or controlled by the abundances of the other common species. Thus the relative abundance of *Globorotalia menardii*, extensively used by Ericson,[14] Ericson and Wollin,[17, 18] Ewing et al.[19] and Ericson et al.,[16] is controlled not only by temperature and other ecological factors but also by the relative abundances of other common species, some of which are markedly eurythermal. If the relative abundances of less common species are chosen for temperature estimates, the restriction imposed by the close statistical system is reduced. Indeed, the relative abundances of *Pulleniatina obliquiloculata* and *Sphaeroidinella dehiscens* in two Caribbean cores, as determined by Ericson and Wollin,[17] give

temperature estimates which are in much closer agreement with the isotopic temperature determinations than similar estimates based on *Globorotalia menardii*.[7] If groups of
species rather than single species are used for temperature estimates, a close agreement
with the isotopic temperatures is also observed (Parker,[23] p. 236 and Fig. 2).

A number of deep-sea cores from the Atlantic and adjacent seas have been analysed
by the oxygen isotopic method (Fig. 14).[5,8,33] The isotopic temperatures thus obtained are
not unequivocally determined because the O^{18}/O^{16} ratio in carbonates deposited from
water solutions is dependent upon not only the environmental temperature at the time
of deposition but also the oxygen isotopic composition of the water. The present oxygen
isotopic composition of the open oceanic water is reasonably well known or may be
closely estimated from salinity data.[13] The assumption made in working with deep-sea

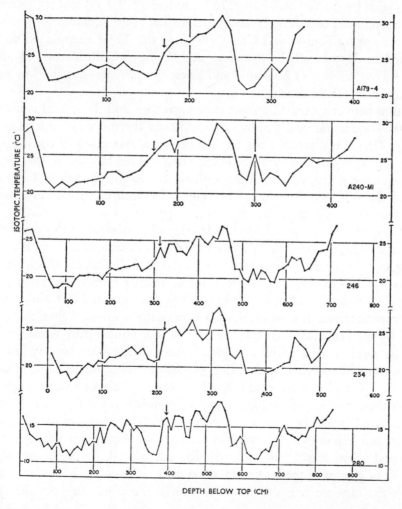

DEPTH BELOW TOP (CM)

Fig. 14 Isotopic temperature curves of various cores (core numbers to the right); core 280: North
Atlantic; cores 234 and 246: equatorial Atlantic; cores A240–M1 and A179–4: Caribbean. Arrows indicate
the last occurrence of the subspecies *Globorotalia menardii flexuosa*. From Rosholt *et al.*[33]

cores is that the present oxygen isotopic composition of the open oceanic waters obtains also for the past. Corrections have been made for the isotopic effects caused by formation of the ice sheets during glacial ages.[5] While the oxygen isotopic temperatures obtained from deep-sea cores may not be identical to the natural temperatures, they are believed to be a fairly close representation.

The temperature curves of the various cores (Fig. 14) show an appreciable background noise, which can be estimated at about 2°C. This noise arises from imperfect mixing of the sediment by bottom animals, sampling statistics, and an analytical error of $\pm$ 0·5°C. The various temperature curves can be correlated easily and may be combined into a single, generalized temperature curve, thus filtering out much of the noise (Fig. 15).

The time scale shown in Fig. 15 has been obtained by absolute dating of deep-sea cores to 150,000 years by the C^{14} and Pa^{231}/Th^{230} methods,[34, 35, 15, 33] and by a simple extrapolation beyond that point. It is of interest to note that a similar chronology was obtained twenty years ago by Piggott and Urry[31, 32] using the Th^{230} method on cores which were studied stratigraphically by Bramlette and Bradley,[2] Cushman and Henbest[4] and Cushman.[3] The estimates of Emiliani[5] and Ericson et al.[16] are also in close agreement with the C^{14}-Pa^{231}/Th^{230} time scale.

Correlation between oceanic temperature variations and the glacial and interglacial stages of the continental stratigraphy is assured only for the time interval covered by C^{14} dating. Thus it is clear that the last temperature maximum of the deep-sea cores (stage 1 in Fig. 15) correlates with the Postglacial, and the last major low-temperature section (stages 2–4 in Fig. 15) correlates with the last major glaciation (Early and Main Würm) (cf. the evidence summarized by Flint and Brandtner[20]). No sure dates of continental Pleistocene events earlier than 60,000 years ago are yet available, although K^{40}/A^{40} dating of Pleistocene volcanics and dating of continental carbonates by uranium isotopes and daughter products may make such dates available in the near future. For the time being, correlation between oceanic and continental Pleistocene stratigraphy for the time preceding the last major glaciation must necessarily remain uncertain.

The correlation shown in Fig. 15 (Emiliani[5, 6, 8]) was suggested by the observation that isotopic temperature minima of the deep-sea cores attain similar values throughout the cores, and by the deduction that because the last low-temperature section of the cores correlates by absolute dating with a major glaciation, the earlier, equally low-temperature sections should correlate with earlier glaciations of equivalent magnitude. If this is correct, the Günz glaciation would then have occurred about 300,000 years ago, that is long after the beginning of the Pleistocene (cf. Emiliani[5]). On the basis of temperature estimates derived from the relative abundance of Globorotalia menardii, Ericson and Wollin[17, 18] and Ericson et al.[16] consider stage 5 (see Fig. 15) a substage of the last glaciation and assign stages 7 to 10 to the last interglacial. As previously mentioned, other species or groups of species yield temperature estimates which are in closer agreement with the isotopic temperatures and which, therefore, support the correlation

Fig. 15 The Glacial Pleistocene: generalized chronology (by absolute dating to about 15,000 years ago, and by extrapolation beyond); temperature variations in the low latitudes; the standard stratigraphies of Europe and North America; and selected fossil hominids.

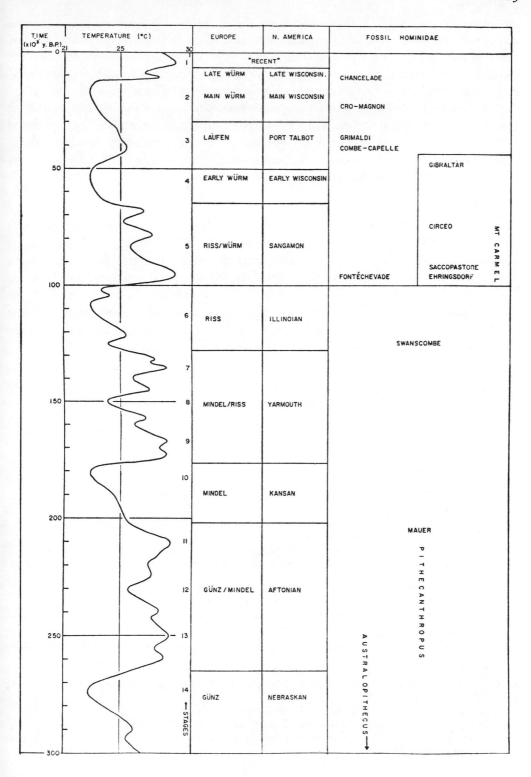

shown in Fig. 15. While a final solution of the problem will come only by absolute dating of continental materials significantly related to climatic events preceding the last major glaciation, the correlation shown in Fig. 15 seems at present the most probable. Using this correlation, Emiliani[6, 9] estimated the ages of various fossil hominids found in deposits of reasonably well-known stratigraphic position. The estimates thus obtained (Fig. 15) suggest that *Pithecanthropus* may have become extinct about 200,000 years ago; that both *Homo sapiens sapiens* and *Homo sapiens neanderthalensis* may have speciated between 125,000 and 100,000 years ago; and that the Neanderthals became extinct about 50,000 years ago.[6, 9] These figures will need revision if the correlation for the time preceding the Early Würm should prove incorrect.

SUMMARY

Deep-sea cores have provided a continuous, time-calibrated record of the temperature variations of the surface water of the ocean during the Pleistocene. This record is believed to reflect closely the continental glaciations, making it possible to estimate, by correlation, the ages and durations of continental Pleistocene stages too old to be dated by C^{14}. As a result, estimates for the ages of fossil hominids found in deposits of known stratigraphic position are also obtained. These estimates rest on the validity of the correlations between oceanic temperatures and continental stages, and between the source beds of the fossils and the standard continental stratigraphy.

REFERENCES

1 ARRHENIUS, G. 1952. *Swedish Deep-Sea Exped. 1947–1948, Repts.* 5 (1)
2 BRAMLETTE, M. N. and BRADLEY, W. H. 1940. *US Geol. Survey Prof. Paper 196*, 1–34
3 CUSHMAN, J. A. 1941. *Am. J. Sci. 239*, 128–47
4 —— and HENBEST L. G. 1940. *US Geol. Survey Prof. Paper 196*, 35–50
5 EMILIANI, C. 1955. *J. Geol. 63*, 538–78
6 —— 1956. *Science 123*, 924–6
7 —— 1957. *Ibid. 125*, 383–7
8 —— 1958 *J. Geol. 66*, 264–75
9 —— 1960. Dating human evolution, in TAX, S. (ed.), *Evolution after Darwin*, Chicago, vol. 2, 57–66
10 —— MAYEDA, T. and SELLI, R. 1961. *Bull. Geol. Soc. Am. 72*, 679–88
11 EPSTEIN, S., BUCHSBAUM, R., LOWENSTAM, H. and UREY, H. C. 1951. *Ibid. 62*, 417–25
12 —— —— —— —— 1953. *Ibid. 64*, 1315–25
13 —— and MAYEDA, T. 1953. *Geochim. et Cosmochim. Acta 4*, 213–24
14 ERICSON, D. B. 1953. *Columbia University, Lamont Geol. Observatory Tech. Rept. on Submarine Geology*, no. 1
15 —— BROECKER, W. S., KULP, J. L. and WOLLIN, G. 1956. *Science 124*, 385–9
16 —— EWING, M., WOLLIN, G. and HEEZEN, B. C. 1961. *Bull. Geol. Soc. Am. 72*, 193–286
17 —— and WOLLIN, G. 1956. *Deep-Sea Research 3*, 104–25
18 —— —— 1956a. *Micropaleontology 2*, 257–70
19 EWING, M., ERICSON, D. B. and HEEZEN, B. C. 1958. Sediments and topography of the Gulf of Mexico, in 'Habitat of Oil', *Am. Assoc. Petrol. Geol.* 995–1053
20 FLINT, R. F. and BRANDTNER, F. 1961. *Am. J. Sci. 259*, 321–8
21 International Geological Congress 1948. *Recommendations of Commission on Pliocene-Pleistocene boundary*, London, 1950, report, Pt. 9, p. 6
22 KULLENBERG, B. 1947. *Svenska Hydr.-biol. Komm., Skr., Tredje Ser., Hydr. 1*, H. 2
23 PARKER, F. L. 1958. *Swedish Deep-Sea Exped. 1947–1948, Repts. 8* (4), 217–83
24 PHILIPPI, E. 1910. *Die Grundproben der deutschen Südpolar-Expedition, 1901–1903. II, Geographie und Geologie 6*, 411–616

25 PHLEGER, F. B. JR. 1939. *Bull. Geol. Soc. Am. 50*, 1395–1422
26 ——1942. *Ibid., 53*, 1073–98
27 —— 1947. *Göteborgs K. Vetensk. Vit. Samh. Handl., Sjätte Följden*, Ser. B, 5, 5
28 —— 1948. *Ibid.*, 14
29 —— and HAMILTON, W. A. 1946. *Bull. Geol. Soc. Am. 57*, 951–66
30 —— PARKER, F. L. and PEIRSON, J. F. 1953. *Swedish Deep–Sea Exped. 1947–1948, Repts. 7*, no. 1
31 PIGGOTT, C. S. and URRY, W. D. 1942a. *Am. J. Sci. 240*, 1–12
32 —— —— 1942b. *Bull. Geol. Soc. Am. 53*, 1187–1210
33 ROSHOLT, J. N., EMILIANI, C., GEISS, J., KOCZY, F. F. and WANGERSKY, P. J. 1961. *J. Geol. 69*, 162–85
34 RUBIN, M. and SUESS, H. E. 1955. *Science 121*, 481–88
35 —— —— 1956. *Ibid. 123*, 442–448
36 SCHOTT, W. 1935. *Wiss. Ergeb. deutsch. Atlant. Exped. Forsch. u. Vern.. 'Meteor' 1925–1927 3*, no. 3, 43–134
37 TODD, R. 1958. *Swedish Deep–Sea Exped. 1947–1948, Repts. 8*, no. 3, 167–215
38 UREY, H. C. 1947. *J. Chem. Soc.* 562–81
39 —— LOWENSTAM, H. A., EPSTEIN, S. and McKINNEY, C. R. 1951. *Bull. Geol. Soc. Am. 62*, 399–416

IIb SOILS

11 Soil Silhouettes

L. BIEK

FOR EVERY MATERIAL and environment there is a (different) range between what is
scientifically just recognizable and an apparent 'total absence' of indications. Over this
range, evidence persists in soils in a reflected or even refracted form—usually as a colour
contrast ('stain') with the ambient medium ('soil'), or sometimes by retaining some
textural quality ('grain'), with or without staining. 'Silhouette' usefully describes this
phenomenon as a whole, especially when (as often) there is a dark stain against a lighter
background, and as it appears in a given plan or section. But the word has a two-
dimensional connotation which may be misleading, and better designations might be
'altered feature', and, where appropriate, perhaps 'pseudomorph'.

During burial there is interaction between any man-deposited assemblage and the
'natural' environment, tending towards thermodynamical equilibrium. Strictly speaking,
matter is always conserved, but in practice the results will vary widely. The significant
criterion for archaeological work is persistence of either material or organization 'close
enough' in nature or space for confidence in relating it back to the original. This
approach is theoretically insecure because one cannot make comparisons except with
better-preserved material elsewhere on typological grounds; and in the limit, when, and
only when infinite dilution of significant characters has been reached, there can clearly
be no certainty in *any* conceivable instance (for the next three or four millennia) that
anything prehistoric was in fact ever buried at the given spot (e.g. bone[1]).

One should distinguish between 'typed' and 'untyped' altered features, on the one
hand, and between 'pragmatic' and 'supported' ones on the other. Clearly, where such
a feature 'fits' into some preconceived typological pattern it must for the moment be
accepted on that basis alone—as a pragmatic feature, such as a 'post hole', for which
there may be no material proof. Where opportunity offered, some scientific work may
have been done to support a hypothesis, such as a 'skeleton in coffin'.

The most difficult and important cases arise with untyped features, where scientific
examination must suggest an origin for a stain, or even develop some pattern where
none may be visible.

The study ranges over the whole spectrum of materials; yet by definition the appropriate specialists are not normally equipped to deal with their own materials owing to
the alteration. It thus usually falls to the soil scientist or surface geologist to attempt
an interpretation of the altered remains, mainly by contrast with what they know could

be 'natural'. At the same time it is clearly important that contact should be maintained as closely as possible with the specialist concerned.

For example, it is conceivable that a calcareous sandstone buried in acid soil might leave only an amorphous mass of the siliceous particles, petrologically characteristic in the same way as windblown deposits.[2] A collapsed cob-type wall built of gravel and sand strengthened with lime, from which the lime had been leached completely during burial, might be indistinguishable from the subsoil unless it contained 'foreign' material or showed an anomalous oxidation state.[3] Lightly burnt clay, perhaps completely rehydrated during burial, might nevertheless show some significant difference from the unburnt state, both structurally[4] and (hence) magnetically.[5] Indeed, changes in magnetic properties have been shown to occur without application of heat, presumably owing to oxidation-reduction phenomena in presence of much residual organic matter,[6] and hence relevant in connection with occupational altered features.[7]

Other silhouettes may appear as a regular pattern of ferruginous concretions resulting from iron nails in wood that has itself been completely altered;[8] a trail or jumble of green spots due to copper or copper alloy working;[9] or some white or (on exposure) pale violet spreads of lead or silver salts, respectively.

But by far the most numerous and important altered features result (presumably) from the decay of organic material. 'Wood' in the form of 'post holes', 'timber slots', 'sleeper trenches' and other 'structural members' is too common to deserve more than a mention, except in two respects: First, interaction may be fairly rapid and intense, so that a presumably permanent 'micropodzol' may be produced even horizontally around a ship[10] or coffin[11-13] in acid, sandy subsoil; or extensive 'shadowing' in blue-grey (? *vivianite*) may occur around even medieval 'trellis paths' under anaerobic, water-logged conditions[14]—here the wood itself is also preserved, but the shadows might remain even if the wood were subsequently removed. Secondly, extensive mineralization may occur quite rapidly, too—both by calcium[15] under neutral or alkaline conditions, and by iron and manganese[11, 13, 16-18] in more acid soils, although a very similar appearance may be due largely to organic residues.[19] This in itself does not affect the interpretation of a feature. But great care is necessary in working back from supported but untyped deposits: even a regular feature 'in manganese' may be misleading until full excavation shows, for instance, that accumulation must have resulted from impedance of drainage—as at the bottom of a silted ditch.[20]

Smaller fragments, and parts of the lower plants, are similarly affected[15,16,21,22] but are less obvious unless present in quantity. Throughout, calcium-rich pseudomorphs are more likely to be interpretable than others. Animal remains, being more varied, give more complex results. (Presumed) skeletal silhouettes (Pl. V) are the most common,[12,16,23] the mineral component of bone having the greatest resistance under most conditions, as might be expected, although such resistance is often modified by the close juxtaposition of organic matter which is subject to rapid biological attack. Keratinous material, such as animal hair in its natural state, comes next in resistance, followed by leather and then dressed and finally undressed skin. In all these cases coherent persistence is relatively shortlived (p. 529), although there was refracted evidence of leather tyres after some six millennia, in the form of alum residues from the tawing.[24]

The position becomes really complex when in a typed feature all kinds of material are presumed to occur together. Phosphate analysis had been found useful in some cases in the characterization of 'body stains'[25] and was thus employed in another case[16] in an attempt to localize a 'skeleton' in a 'coffin' but failed to reveal significant differences. Instead, the visible stains appeared to be due mainly to manganese, exceeding ambient 'grave fill' controls by *one* order of magnitude in the 'skeleton', and by up to *two* in the 'wooden coffin', where closer examination further deduced remains of cereal or grass. Mineral accumulation in cellular tissue—preferentially on vegetable material, and possibly in the main an adsorption phenomenon—had evidently formed fair pseudomorphs before the organic structure was destroyed. 'Micropodzols' have been seen around an extant cremation bundle in a presumed 'cloth bag'.[26]

Similar mineralization is, of course, common for both vegetable and animal remains in contact with corroding iron objects; and a related but different mechanism acts even better by inhibiting microbiological activity to 'preserve' such material buried near enough to corroding copper (alloy) artifacts. In one case pseudomorphism was virtually complete, the weave of a textile fragment being preserved but the fibre altered beyond scientific recognition. In another, exactly comparable, case the fibre was just determinable as animal, probably wool, though part of it was found encased in a (modern) root.[27]

Throughout, only unburnt material has been considered; and the states described are implicit evidence that unburnt material was buried. If not too distorted by firing or burial, organic matter is normally more useful charred rather than altered. Chemically, the residual carbon is virtually indestructible and the pseudomorphs so formed are usually faithful enough for quite close interpretation. Similar considerations apply to charred, and even calcined, bone—presumably because viable organic matter is removed from the sphere of microbiological attack which normally will not affect very seriously what amounts to the 'mineral ash'.

In general, it will be clear that a detailed knowledge of the basic geological and pedological background is essential if uncertainty is to be reduced to the minimum. If the specialist cannot visit the site, adequate control samples of such background material must be taken, on his instructions, to ensure that differentiation is statistically significant, if necessary. The alteration takes place in moist and aerated soils and would appear to produce more important evidence from acid, sandy environments. This may be due partly to the better preservation of bone in chalky soils, and to the greater clarity of dark organic residues in them, making the establishment of pragmatic features a commonplace. On the other hand, the marked prominence of iron and manganese movement draws attention to both natural and altered features in siliceous sandy and gravelly soils; yet differentiation is more difficult, and hence there are more cases of supported, typed features, even though support must remain ambivalent.

Almost the only examples of systematic surveys of untyped features have come in the search for limits of occupation;[28] geochemical reconnaissance[29] should, however, rank with aerial and geophysical surveys, in due course, wherever it can usefully complement them, as, for example, in developing features where no physical contrast shows. One might envisage the spraying of selected sections, or even large areas of scraped ground from helicopters (as with weedkillers), with suitable reagents, followed by aerial or other photographic survey. Alternatively, comparatively rapid 'statistical gridding' surveys are now a definite possibility, thanks to X-ray fluorescence spectrometry.[30] But underlying all this work, as in other geo-surveys, the subsoil drainage pattern is decisive and, if very irregular, may produce anomalous or spurious effects that will obscure any altered feature unless they are properly taken into account.

From the specialist angle, all such evidence is inclined to be patchy and makes total investigation of the suspected area or section necessary. Research is needed into the exact material state of the just recognizable, coupled with the study of successively degraded material, to make extrapolation safer and to delimit the area within which altered features can usefully be supported by scientific analysis. If the present review is largely chemical in outlook, that is mainly because hardly any physical data—for instance, on the effects of compression and distortion, and other changes in morphological or even electrical properties—exist as yet. The British Association Committee's experimental earthworks[31] will provide many valuable pointers, but only much detailed specialist study and increased interest on the part of the excavator will accelerate development in this field. Ultimately, a new kind of specialism, primarily concerned with subsoil pedology and/or subsurface geomorphology, will have to be recognized and take its proper place alongside the others.

REFERENCES

1 THOMPSON, M. W. and DIMBLEBY, G. W. 1957. *Proc. Prehist. Soc. 23*, 126
 PIGGOTT, C. M. 1943. *Proc. Prehist. Soc. 9*, 3; also in[13] p. 6
 E.g., at Sutton Hoo: ZEUNER, F. E. 1940. *Ant. J. 20*, 201–2, describes the environment, and the point was argued in detail at a later lecture (private communication); here, only *c.* 1300 years of burial are involved.
2 E.g., PERRIN, R. M. S. 1956. *Nature 178*, 31–2: heavy-mineral assemblage in windblown sand
3 BIEK, L. 196-. In HURST, D. G. and J. G., *Excavations at Milton, Hants., 1957* (forthcoming)
4 BROWN, D. W. 196-. In GREENFIELD, E. *Excavations at Holbeach St. John's, Lincs., 1961* (forthcoming)
5 LE BORGNE, E. 1960. *Ann. Géophys. 16*, 159–95
6 —— 1955. *Ibid. 11*, 399–419
 HAIGH, G. 1958. *Phil. Mag. 3*, 267–86
7 AITKEN, M. J. 1961. *Physics and Archaeology*, London and New York, 25–30
8 E.g., at Sutton Hoo: PHILLIPS, C. W. 1956. In BRUCE-MITFORD, R. L. S. (ed.) *Recent Archaeological Excavations in Britain*, London, 162–3 and Pl. XXIX
9 BIEK, L. 196-. In WACHER, J. S. *Excavations at Catterick, Yorks., 1958–9*
10 PHILLIPS, C. W. 1940. *Ant. J. 20*, 101 and Fig. 5
11 BIEK, L. 196-. In RAHTZ, P. A. *Excavations at Little Ouseburn, Yorks., 1959* (forthcoming)
12 VAN GIFFEN, A. E. 1945. *Nieuwe Drentsche Volksalmanak 63*, Pl. 7⎱ visual appraisal only;
 KRAMER, W. 1951. *Germania 29*, 135–6 and Fig. 2; 137 and Fig. 4⎰ no details given.
13 BIEK, L. 1956. (Unpublished field notes on feature described in:) GREENFIELD, E. 1960. *J. Derbys. Arch. N.H. Soc. 80*, 4–6 and Fig. 4
14 THOMPSON, M. W. 1956. *Arch. Cant. 70*, 52
15 LEVY, J. F. 196-. In MACKAY, R. R. *Excavations at Winklebury Camp, Hants., 1959* (forthcoming)
16 BASCOMB, C. L. and LEVY, J. F. 1957. In ASHBEE, P.: *Proc. Prehist. Soc. 23*, 162–3 and Fig. 7
17 FARMER, R. H. 1958. In RAHTZ, P. A., *Arch. Cant. 72*, 135

18 GOVERNMENT CHEMIST'S LABORATORY. 196–. In BIDDLE, M. *Nonsuch Palace*, Soc. Antiqs. Res. Rept. (forthcoming)

19 ——— ——— ———. 196–. In BIDDLE, M. *Excavations at Dover Castle, 1961–3, Arch. J.* CXX (forthcoming)

20 BIEK, L. 196–. In RAHTZ, P. A. *Excavations at Cheddar, 1960–2* (forthcoming)

21 FARMER, R. H. 1957 (unpublished). *Report on wooden remains in iron pick head from White Castle, Mon.*
—— 1960. In Greenfield, E., *Arch. Cant. 74*, 67–8
—— 1961 (unpublished). *Report on charred wooden fragment from Downing Street site.* (A.M. no. 610141)

22 MONTGOMERY, G. W. 196–. In WEBSTER, G. *Excavations in Chesterton-on-Fosse, 1961* (forthcoming)
METCALFE, C. R. 196–. In BIDDLE, M. *Excavations in Winchester, 1961ff.* (forthcoming)

23 VAN GIFFEN, A. E. 1941. *Nieuwe Drentsche Volksalmanak 59*, 7–12 and Pl. 5
—— 1943. *Ibid. 61*, 9–10 and Pl. 14

24 WOOLLEY, SIR LEONARD. 1929. *Ur of the Chaldees*, London, 50 and 55; additional information kindly supplied by J. W. Waterer.

25 JOHNSON, A. 1954. In PIGGOTT, S. *Proc. Soc. Ant. Scot. 88*, 200–4
—— 1955. In SCOTT, J. G. *Ibid. 89*, 53

26 BIEK, L. 196–. In DUDLEY, D. *Excavations at Carvinack, Cornwall, 1959* (forthcoming)

27 HAIGH, D. 196–. In GILYARD BEER, R., and KNOCKER, G. M. *Excavations on the site of Chertsey Abbey, Surrey, 1954* (forthcoming)

28 DAUNCEY, K. D. M. 1952. *Adv. Sci. 9*, 33–6
LUTZ, H. G. 1951. *Am. J. Sci. 249*, 925–8
SOKOLOFF, V. P. and CARTER, G. F. 1952. *Science 116*, 1–5

29 NORTH, A. A. and WELLS, R. A. 1959. *Symposium de Exploración Geoquimica II*, 347–62

30 BELFORD, D. S. 1961. *Record of Brit. Wood Pres. Assocn. Convention*

31 JEWELL, P. A. 196–. *The Experimental Earthwork on Overton Down, Wilts., 1960* (forthcoming); a second earthwork is to be built on sandy heathland near Wareham, Dorset, in 1963

12 Soil, Stratification and Environment

I. W. CORNWALL

THE TERM 'UNSTRATIFIED', as applied to archaeological finds, has today become an epithet of opprobrium in the vocabulary of trained excavators, the implication being that any object, to be of much service in adding to our knowledge, should be relatable to the context in which it lay buried, so that no relevant information may be overlooked. Without this authentication, it is just another object, which, unless unique, or at least unusual among its kind, has nothing new to tell us.

Stratification, then, is the key to interpretation of a sequence of long-past events, whether affecting buildings with walls and floors, repairs, replannings, destructions and additions of different periods of occupation, or the substantially contemporaneous successive stages in the construction of a simple earthen barrow over a burial in open country. In the one case, the excavator is, most of the time, concerned with purposeful artifacts and modifications of them, which he, as an archaeologist, has been taught to recognize. In the other, the work, originally composed of natural materials, has frequently been left, ever since the time of its erection, to the forces of Nature, without further human interference, so that the sequence of events in the filling of the ditch, for instance, demands rather the eye of the natural scientist than of an archaeologist for its elucidation. The distinctions, here, between 'natural' and 'artificial' become rather fine, so that an excavator is often glad to seek the advice of a specialist to help in the explanation of his stratigraphy.

This is, perhaps, the prime function of the 'soil'-investigator from the prehistorian's point of view—to answer detailed questions such as: 'Is this black layer due to burning?', 'How was this pit-filling formed?' and so on. The consultant, for his part, has to be somewhat conversant not only with the science of the soil, in the narrow sense of pedology, but to some extent also with geology, geomorphology, climatology, mineralogy and petrology—the study, in fact, of the whole inanimate environment of the site, from the atmosphere above it to the geological 'solid' beneath and around it, both today and in times past, and of the materials at all periods available to the ancient inhabitants.

This aspect of the investigation of archaeological deposits is chiefly a matter of exercising the techniques of the sedimentary petrographer, combined with some fairly simple inorganic chemical procedures for the identification of common mineral substances, some of them perhaps artificial.

An approach of rather wider interest, however, is that of the environmentalist, the student of the natural settings of human cultures and of the relation of communities to their surroundings. The biological environment of early man has received considerable attention—as witness the important advances made through the study of floras and faunas of various periods. Of the inanimate environment, the important climatic part has mainly attracted interest, its direct influence on flora, fauna and human communities being obvious. The mineral environment ('mineral' being taken in the widest sense of the word, to include earth, air and water) has been studied mainly as the source of supply of industrial materials: stone, metals and building materials. This is certainly an important aspect of ancient economy, but scarcely touches the main theme.

Natural soils of today reflect the effects of climate on the local geological deposits and where, as beneath barrow-mounds and other earthworks, soils of earlier times have been preserved, their study may yield information about past climates to compare with that obtained (say) from pollen-analysis. Not only buried soils, but sediments in general, as, for example, those forming part of ditch-fillings or the overall mantling of a site, probably consist largely of redeposited contemporary soil-materials, so that even these 'colluvial' deposits may be of considerable interest.

Combining these two functions—helping to explain archaeological stratification and independently inquiring into the details of contemporary environment—the soil-investigator has become a recognized collaborator, so that such information as can be gained from the deposits themselves, which contain and cover archaeological finds and structures, is nowadays frequently with advantage added to that obtained by the study of the archaeological material proper. Recognition is thus practically accorded to the idea that archaeology is only one part of the whole study of ancient communities, in which the natural sciences also have a large role to play.

The further back in time that we carry our inquiry into the ways of life of ancient man, the more important become the relevant environmental studies. From Palaeolithic times we have, for the most part, only the worked stone and bone implements and the rare human fossils to guide us. Environmental evidences—animal bones, shells and plant-remains, geology, geomorphology, spelaeology, soil-studies—all can give us some glimpses of the climate and conditions of life of the time. They are necessary tools in the armoury of the Palaeolithic archaeologist, for without them he is relatively helpless, a mere typologist and technologist, bereft of any natural frame within which to comprehend the lives of the makers of his finds.

Glacial, river and lake deposits, marine and desert sediments, cave-fillings, volcanic ashes, dune-sands and, especially on the continent of Europe, the fossil soils represented by loess-loams, give to the student of archaeological deposits and soils an enormous variety of chiefly mineral materials with which to work out the environments of remote times past, which often differed enormously from those of today. Beyond the sand-grains or the soil thin-section under the narrow circle of his microscope-objective, he needs wide-angle geological and geographical insight to visualize landscapes unrecognizable now, owing to sea-level changes and later valley-cutting which have resulted in our existing topography. How did the beach-pebbles on the Chalk summits of the North Downs [1] come to be formed, seeing that the present watercourses and sea-beaches lie at so comparatively low a level? Evidently, when they were laid down the present Wealden basin did not exist. A long-enduring warm-temperate climate has rendered almost unrecognizable a once almost certainly chalky boulder-clay overlying the Hertfordshire Pebble Gravel [2] on the 400-foot contour, far above the Vale of St Albans, on the floor of which the later Chalky Boulder-Clay glaciation advanced. On this land-surface perhaps walked the contemporaries of Swanscombe Man, but of it remains only a few patches, capping what are now hill-tops, dissected remains of the wide, level forest floor of 200,000 years ago. Thin sections of the material show parabraunerde,*³ or even braunlehm, soil-types, indicating much warmer summers than we have today.

The late S. Hazzledine Warren, reinterpreting the Clacton flint industry in 1951,⁴ made an obvious, but all too often forgotten, observation: that though we find the tools of Lower Palaeolithic man in the former channel-deposits of the river, he did not live in the river-bed, but on its banks! One may straightway conclude from this that *none* of the river-gravel implements is archaeologically *in situ*. The living floors may once have resembled those of Olorgesailie⁵ or Olduvai,⁶ more fortunately preserved in East Africa, but here the meandering river has re-worked its own old flood-plain materials, sorting out the hand-axes and flakes with the coarser ballast and washing away the rest of the evidence. One must visualize the Great-Interglacial Thames flood-plain extending at about the 100-foot level above the present river, from Boyn Hill and far upstream down to Swanscombe, and a North Sea much more extensive than it is at present, the existing coasts being at about the 15-fathom line of soundings! Small wonder that we have not yet chanced on any 'floors' in the few vestiges left of that almost-vanished landscape!

Volcanic deposits present both problems and facilities unknown to British pre-historians, seeing that none as late in date as the Pleistocene exists here. Having had the opportunity, recently, to visit Mexico, this branch of sedimentary investigation is fresh in mind. The centre of that country is traversed from east to west by a major axis of crustal weakness, known as the Clarion Line, from its connection, to the west, with Clarion Island, far out in the Pacific. It appears to have originated in the later part of the Tertiary, but is still active today, as witness the first outburst of a new volcano, Parícutin, in the late 1940's, while Popocatépetl is still in the fumarolic stage and hot mineral springs are not uncommon. During the Pleistocene and Postglacial there were repeated eruptions, which mantled whole countrysides with pumice and ashes, chiefly andesitic in character. Between these, there were longish quiet phases, when the surface of such fresh deposits underwent some chemical weathering and soil-formation. Each soil formed was sometimes perfectly preserved in its entirety by the succeeding fall of freshly-ejected ash.

Thus, near the town of Puebla, a single gully, eroded under modern semi-arid conditions, with torrential downpours during a short wet season, exposed more than half a dozen such weatherings, some of considerable thickness, within a vertical compass of some 100 feet. The accumulation of andesite ashes overlay a fluviatile bone-bed, yielding a fauna with *Mastodon* and *Glyptodon*. This almost certainly antedates the great volcanoes which emitted the ashes and may be perhaps Late Tertiary in age. No andesite pebbles occur in the bone-bed, while more than 90 per cent of present-day river gravels nearby consist of that rock. This gully, therefore, showing alternating

* Some account of the principal soil-types and their environmental significance may be found in Cornwall,³ pp. 85–112.

vulcanism and soil-formation, may expose the entire local environmental sequence from the Late Tertiary to the present day, as far as can be seen without a break. This conclusion is only provisional and based on a brief field-survey. The confirmatory detailed stratigraphical fieldwork, petrological, palaeontological and pedological laboratory investigations are still to be done by the new Laboratory of Prehistory in Mexico City.

The importance to Mexican prehistory of this discovery lies in the fact that several archaeological horizons in the Basin of Mexico occur in Pleistocene and Recent lake-deposits, or are correlatable with them by their relation to fossil beaches, indicating former higher levels of Lake Texcoco. Among these is the hitherto not firmly datable Tepexpan [7] human skeleton, with fossil pollen, mammoth-bones and implements of Palaeo-eastern type, as found in the south-western United States, occurring at the same horizon nearby. These same lake-deposits contain, at frequent intervals, layers of volcanic pumice, marking a series of ash-explosions which took place during their formation. It is more than likely that these correspond to, and may be petrologically correlatable with, some of the various ash-layers surmounted by soils in the state of Puebla, so that eventually the lacustrine sequence with pollen, the volcanic sequence and the included soil-sequence may be inter-correlatable with the archaeological sequence over the wide area affected by the volcanoes.

It can be seen that this problem involves the close co-operation of several scientific specialists. All stand to gain by working out a joint system of relative dates. Though archaeology may seem to be the principal beneficiary, the most recent lava-flow from the Xitli volcano in the Mexico Basin took place at about the beginning of the Christian Era and the vulcanologists have been glad enough to accept the *terminus post quem* given by the radiocarbon date of the Late Pre-Classic cemetery which it covered at Copilco, [8] in the Federal District of Mexico.

Environmentally, the buried soils exposed in the Puebla gully promise to be extremely interesting. At least one, of rotlehm character, some halfway down the series and several feet thick, indicates a long-enduring warm-moist climate, perhaps with forest vegetation, completely different from the almost arid conditions of modern times. Such a prominent feature should readily be recognizable everywhere in the region and so afford a valuable stratigraphical datum.

Stratified Mesolithic sites in north-western Europe, save those discovered in peat-bogs and lake-deposits, are not very numerous. Where there is peat, pollen-analysis obviously provides the best environmental and stratigraphical tool. Since the mineral content of such humic materials is generally low, the evidence from it in these circumstances is relatively unimportant.

One recent exception was a thick calcareous marl seen in sections at a prolific site at Thatcham, Berkshire. [9] This certainly indicated a lake and a long phase of open water with a minimum of vegetation, for the material often contained very little organic matter. This indicates deep water, 6 ft to 8 ft at least, for plants with floating leaves, such as water-lilies, will crowd lesser depths and give rise to a muddy or peaty bottom. Marls consist, in part, of chemically-precipitated calcium carbonate with such other mineral sediment, mainly of the finest silt and clay grades, as may be available. Limy crusts, formed on growing submerged weeds by withdrawal of CO_2 from the lime-bearing water, shells and the skeletons of planktonic plants and animals account for the rest.

Now, a mere study of the map will suggest that water of this depth covering the marl at Thatcham would drown the present Kennet floodplain, perhaps as far upstream as Newbury racecourse, so that the lake, at that stage, must have been very extensive. The extent of the former deep water could probably be mapped without great difficulty by numbers of auger-holes of no great depth, strategically sited with regard to the present contours, to locate the shoreward margins of the marl deposit. Archaeologically speaking, this conclusion is not without significance, for it suggests that the Thatcham site is perhaps only one of many such in the vicinity, of which the remainder still await discovery.

The reason for the very existence of a Thatcham Lake has not yet been fully explained. At such a comparatively late date, any major geomorphological difference in the drainage-pattern of the Kennet valley from that of today can probably be discounted. Zeuner has suggested that a beaver-dam some way downstream towards Reading may have been responsible, for beavers figured in a small way in the Thatcham fauna. If so, prospecting for the likeliest site, and even for preserved remains, of such a dam might be rewarding.

With the arrival of Neolithic farmers and herdsmen, archaeology becomes at once more concerned with settlement-sites, communal tombs and other evidence of man-made structures. Clearance of forest or scrub for the establishment of fields and pastures represented man's first major intervention in Nature, not merely accepting the natural environment as he found it, but adapting it to his own purposes. Slash-and-burn with hoe-culture and the maintenance of clearings as grassland by grazing and browsing domestic stock are not now reflected with any clarity in our more recently disturbed soils. The best hope of discerning something of such activities is in soils of the period buried under earthworks—banks and barrow-mounds.

Especially on Chalk, and other limestones, any long period without mechanical disturbance of the surface results in the formation of a more or less thick layer of stone-less humic soil. Cast-forming earthworms are chiefly responsible for this, for their activities in throwing up fine material at the surface result in the gradual sinking of stones and other solid bodies too large for them to swallow. The uppermost few inches, where they are chiefly active, consist of distinct crumbs composed largely of broken castings (rendsina). On silicate-soils of adequate base-status (e.g. the richer brownearths) this is also often the case, though the crumb-structure may be less marked. It is clear, therefore, that if the ancient soil beneath a Neolithic structure shows this typical 'worm-layer', it was not cultivated for some time before the erection of the earthwork, save, perhaps, by the most superficial scratching. If, however, the buried soil is not excessively acid, precluding habitation by cast-forming worms, and is found to be uniformly chalky or stony, it must have been disturbed, possibly by primitive tillage, at most within a decade or so before being covered. This consideration of course applies also to suitable buried soils of any age, though with the introduction of improved tools and deeper cultivation, an even longer period of quiescence is needed, after disturbance, to re-establish the 'worm-layer' so that land only intermittently occupied is unlikely to show it.

Ploughing, as such, is very difficult to prove, unless the bedrock, as possibly in shallow soils on Chalk, retains clear marks of the share. This is a question regularly posed to the soil-consultant, but no unmistakable affirmative case is known to the writer in this country. Flints, especially those with a white patina, and other hard stones are sometimes found spotted and streaked with rust. These are a permanent mark of cultivation with iron tools. Most must be attributed to contact with comparatively modern farm implements.

The fillings of ditches have, from time to time, provided interesting environmental evidence. The cursus-ditches covered by the bank of the Thornborough Middle Rings [10] showed such a concentration of organic matter that it seems likely that the area was forested while they were open. Similar evidence of forest environments has been adduced for earthworks (round barrows and hill-forts) of later periods also. It may well be that when many such structures were originally erected the country was wooded, so that they would not have been seen in the comparatively open situations which they now occupy. It is known from Roman sources, of course, that some Iron Age peoples deliberately chose wooded sites for their defensive earthworks. Missile weapons of the time having only a comparatively short effective range, a clear field of fire, such as has been desirable to static defence in later times, was not then so necessary. We tend to regard these things too much through modern eyes and to make unnecessary difficulties for ourselves in comprehending the ancients. Doubtless thick cover for attackers was not allowed to develop too close to the ramparts, but forest not only conceals defensive works and puzzles the stranger; it makes impossible any assault in formation and favours guerrilla tactics by the defenders.

The ditch of a Neolithic long barrow at Nutbane [11] showed a lens of distinctly wind-sorted sediment well up in the filling, that is formed some longish time after the erection of the monument, when it was already grassed over. The stratigraphical discontinuity of this lens with any body of material on the banks, from which it could have been washed in, led to a closer examination and, though somewhat cemented with calcium carbonate since its deposition, the well-graded quartz-grains suggested wind as the depositing agency. The insolubles, after acid-treatment, gave a mechanical analysis typical of wind-sorted sediment.

This material might have been deposited at the same time as the filling of one of the Y-Holes at Stonehenge,[12] previously shown to have a similar grading and probable mode of accumulation.

The same phenomenon was observed in some natural soils in Oxfordshire, buried under round barrows near Cassington,[13] of presumed Early-Bronze-Age date, the wind-action (if the same event) therefore having taken place *since* the building of the Nutbane long mound and *before* that of the round barrows at Cassington. No appreciable accumulation of wind-blown dust could happen in Wessex under present-day conditions of moisture all the year round and close vegetation-cover. Its occurrence during prehistoric times, therefore, is likely to be due to a period of somewhat warmer and drier summers (that is, a more continental climate), with at least seasonally and locally bare soil to provide a source of airborne dust. The palaeoclimatologists, on pollen evidence, have recognized such a phase, called the Sub-boreal, coincident in Britain with some part of the Early Bronze Age. If such wind-sorted sediments are attributable to the Sub-boreal climatic oscillation, they should be widespread in the southern counties in suitable situations and a watch is being kept for further examples.

Not long since, samples were examined from the section of a ditch associated with a Neolithic long mortuary enclosure at Normanton Down.[14, 15] Nothing resembling the Nutbane silt-lens was found, though this site was regarded as approximately of the same age as Nutbane. The only disturbance in the section was the modern ploughing of the surface, extending no more than 8 or 9 inches in depth. If a windborne silt had ever existed there, it could only have been obliterated by the plough if it lay high enough in the ditch-filling, that is, having been formed at a late enough stage, after the ditch had been almost completely filled. Without abandoning the above conclusions about wind-action, which seem to be justifiable in their own context, since the evidence is hard to explain by any other theory, one is inclined to suggest that the mortuary enclosure was perhaps distinctly earlier in date than the Nutbane barrow, so that any silty wind-blown deposit was either never accumulated in the already only shallow ditch-depression, or has since been ploughed up. It is perhaps risky to suggest even a relative date on such merely negative evidence. Only further independently dated examples will show whether this conclusion can be sustained. For another case of possibly early date, one may perhaps point again to the fillings of the cursus-ditches at Thornborough, which gave no hint of any phase of wind-action in that part of Yorkshire before they were naturally obliterated and the henge-banks raised over parts of them.

As more sophisticated cultures than those of semi-sedentary Neolithic cultivators and Bronze-Age stockmen developed or intruded, structures due to man's activities become larger and more complex. Since the climate of the Early Iron Age apparently differed scarcely at all from that of the present day, the environmental aspect of soil-investigations becomes less important than the purely stratigraphical. Buried soils under ramparts of hill-forts are almost invariably identical in type with their modern counterparts on the same bedrock. Nevertheless, a knowledge of soils sometimes enables a consultant to assist materially in the interpretation of stratification. Defensive earthworks and their ditches, for example, include evidences of natural denudation, silting and soil-formation along with the artificial features of their structures and fillings.

At Caesar's Camp, Holwood Park, Keston,[16] it was possible, from soil-evidence, to distinguish two clear phases of building of the inner bank, separated by a period long enough for natural weathering to have formed an immature soil on the sandy material of the first construction, before it was covered by the freshly-dug ditch-spoil of the second. Three podzol-soils clearly appeared in the rampart-section—the original soil before there was any occupation of the site, that formed on the first bank before its reconstruction, and the modern profile, developed since the abandonment of the site on the make-up of the enlarged rampart.

The relative immaturity of the second suggested that not more than a few decades had elapsed between the phases. This last not very precise conclusion was borne out by the archaeological material of the two phases, which, when fully studied, will probably yield more exact limiting dates for the intervening lapse of time. This, added to similar information from other sites, will eventually enable us to make better estimates of soil-maturity in future cases, under similar soil-conditions, where corroboration from external evidence may be lacking. Much more work on well-dated sites will be needed before any useful degree of precision can be expected in this sort of comparative dating.

A further extremely immature buried soil was detected within a single phase of addition to the rampart in another section at Keston, but was unsupported by any archaeological evidence for a break in the reconstruction. A possible explanation suggested for this was that the enlargement of the bank took place in partial stages over a considerable number of years. In view of the large area enclosed by the defences and the imposing dimensions of the rampart, this reconstruction represented a very considerable undertaking of earth-moving. Using only the primitive methods then available, this would either have involved literally thousands of full-time workers or, with a lesser labour-force, a proportionately longer time. The soil-evidence suggested that a number of years passed, at this particular point, between the beginning of enlargement of the rampart and its completion to the desired height.

While on sites of the Roman and later periods, up to quite late historical times, the stratigraphical method of excavation remains a valid tool to investigate those aspects of the life of societies which are incompletely, or not at all, known from literary sources, opportunities to use soil-investigations proper to supplement them become fewer and fewer. The consultant is, on the other hand, more and more called on to explain the nature and, if possible, to suggest the provenance of artifacts, in the shape of building materials, imported stones (such as tesserae), pigments, ornamental substances and evidences of technological activities such as tanning, metal- and glass-working, from floors, pits, hearths and drainage-gullies. A few instances may be quoted by way of illustration.

A sample from Verulamium formed part of a deposit found on the floor of a building. Black in colour, it was seen under the microscope to contain numerous small, dull-black, heavy, scale-like bodies, together with the usual debris of fallen buildings—quartz sand, lime-plaster or mortar, chips of flint, tile or pottery, bone and charcoal. The visual aspect of the scales not being very informative, save that they were clearly not natural objects, a qualitative analysis of a washed portion showed only iron present in quantity, among the metals, and no corresponding cations such as sulphide, which might have accounted for the black appearance. The material was evidently black iron oxide. A test with a magnet proved it to be, mineralogically, magnetite and its occurrence was thus easily explained as an accumulation of 'blacksmith's scales', the flakes of oxide forming on red-hot iron exposed to the air and falling from the anvil under the hammer. The room was thus shown to have been a smithy.

Charred grain and Purbeck 'Marble' from Dorset, used as an ornamental stone in buildings, were other interesting finds recorded from this site.

Anglo-Saxon Thetford [17] yielded a lump of crude glass, still retaining the form of the crucible in which it had been melted, bronze- and iron-slag, masses of wood-ash from industrial furnaces and fragments of Niedermendig (Eifel, Germany) lava, imported as quern-stones.

In every department of this work, though a beginning has been made, it is evident that we still have far to go. One of the most frequently recurring (and so far, generally insoluble) problems concerns organic matter. The humus of soils and archaeological deposits is an amorphous nitrogen-containing acidic complex of, at present, almost unknown composition and chemical constitution. Though, in most cases, obviously predominantly vegetable in origin, it must nearly always contain animal residues also, yet we have as yet no way, certainly no simple, practical way, of distinguishing the one from the other, or of estimating their proportions.

Archaeologists submitting samples often want to know, specifically: 'Was this wood or leather?' Unless some recognizable microscopic structure survives, this is, so far, unanswerable in most cases. Other typical queries are: 'Is this deposit in a pot remains of food? If so, what sort of food?', 'Did this vessel contain milk or beer?' Search for surviving fats, starch-grains, proteins or yeast-cells has not yet been successful in the case of most British samples, or for tannins in supposed leather, though interesting and suggestive results have been obtained from Egyptian and other samples from arid climates.

It seems, however, that possibility of advance in these directions must exist could only specialist organic chemists be found having the skill, the time and the interest to devote to such problems. Little attention seems, as yet, to have been directed to them, perhaps because the results seem not to be economically valuable. It is, however, known [18] on the environmental side, for instance, that, today, holly (*Ilex aquifolia*), marching before the edge of a wood, is able, by the humus formed from its fallen leaves, so to improve podzolic heath-soils that deciduous trees, such as oak, may eventually spread in its wake and regenerate forest brownearth on relatively barren sands. Exactly how holly-humus differs from that of any other broad-leaved tree seems to be unknown, but the knowledge should be worth gaining for the forester.

On the chronological side, soils have been scientifically observed and investigated for little more than half a century. Their formation and growth are, on the other hand, extremely slow—a matter of thousands, rather than hundreds, of years in attaining a degree of maturity. Their rates of development under the infinitely variable conditions of Nature in different situations can only roughly and precariously be estimated. Here, archaeology, by affording evidence of soil-development on monuments and works well dated by other means, may, in due course, provide some sort of a time-scale, which could later be applied in its own favour, where other dating evidence was lacking. We have, so far, scarcely laid the foundations of this work.

There is, at the time of writing, a single long-term experiment under way with just this object (among others of archaeological interest) in view. In the summer of 1960, a British Association Sub-Committee on Field Experiments,[19] set up in the Nature Reserve on the Chalk of Overton Down, Wiltshire, a 100-foot length of earthwork (linear bank and ditch) to investigate practically, over the next century or so, the processes and rates of denudation, ditch-filling, compaction, slumping, soil-formation, etc., in and on this 'monument' and the preservation of various materials incorporated in its structure during erection. The work was carried out by volunteer labour to exact specifications and dimensions, planned in advance and duly recorded. It is intended to section the bank and ditch at increasingly long intervals in the future, to determine, by the techniques of archaeological excavation, exactly how the original structures and materials have been altered or displaced during the known passage of time. Other, similar, experiments will, it is hoped, be set up on different soils and in different places, to afford information on the influence of particular, varied environments on the processes and rates to be studied. Several branches of Natural Science, as well as archaeology, are expected to benefit from the exact quantitative knowledge gained. All have co-operated closely in the planning and will continue to do so at each future 'sampling'.

REFERENCES

1 WOOLDRIDGE, S. W. 1927. *Proc. Geol. Assoc. 38*, 49–132
2 ── 1960. *Proc. Geol. Assoc. 71*, 119
3 CORNWALL, I. W. 1958. *Soils for the Archaeologist*, London
4 WARREN, S. H. 1951. *Proc. Geol. Assoc. 62*, 107–35
5 LEAKEY, L. S. B. 1952. *Proc. 1st Pan-Afr. Cong. Prehist.*, Oxford
   COLE, S. 1954. *Prehistory of E. Africa*, London, 138
6 LEAKEY, L. S. B. 1961. *Nature 189*, 649
7 DE TERRA, M., ROMERO, J. and STEWART, T. 1949. Tepexpan Man. *Viking Fund publications in Anthropology*, no. 11, New York.
8 GAMIO, M. *c.* 1917. Las excavaciones del Pedregal de San Angel y la cultura arcáica del Valle de México, quoted in MARQUINA I., 1951, *Arquitectura prehispánica*, Inst. Nac. de Antr. e Hist. Mexico D.F., 20–21
9 WYMER, J. 1958, 1960. *Berks. Arch. J. 57*, 1–33; *Proc. Prehist. Soc. 26*, 342
10 THOMAS, N. 1956. *Yorks. Arch. J. 38*, 425–45
   CORNWALL, I. W. 1954. *Proc. Prehist. Soc.* (1953) *19*, 144 ff.
11 VACHER (*née* MORGAN), F. DE M. 1959. *Proc. Prehist. Soc. 25*, 15–51
12 CORNWALL, I. W. 1954. *Ibid.*
13 *Ibid.*
14 VACHER, F. DE M. 1960. *Proc. Prehist. Soc. 26*, 342
15 ── 1961. *Ibid. 27*, 160–73
16 PIERCY FOX, E. V. 1951. *Arch. Cant. 71*, 243–5
17 DUNNING, G. C. 1949. *Arch. J. 106*, 72 ff.
18 DIMBLEBY, G. W. and GILL, J. M. 1955. *Forestry 28*, 95–106
19 JEWELL, P. 1961. *Advancement of Science*, 106–9
   PROUDFOOT, V. B. 1961. *New Scientist 11*, 596–8
   ASHBY, P. and CORNWALL, I. W. 1961. *Antiquity 35*, 129–34

13 Cave Sediments and Prehistory

ELISABETH SCHMID

CAVE EXCAVATIONS DEMAND not only a knowledge of prehistory, but a considerable amount of geological observation and research. This is because caves are places of mani-fold geological occurrences, the results of which are preserved in and as sediments. Where these sediments are sheltered inside a mountain they are more easily preserved than those at the surface. From an exact analysis of sedimentary accumulation in a cave it is possible to deduce the sequence and causes of the geological events, which are due mostly to climatic change and its consequences. As nearly all caves and cave sediments date from the later Quaternary period (the Upper Pleistocene and Holocene) their study comprises the most recent history of the earth. At the beginning of this period man was already in existence and during it he developed into his modern form.

Man has frequented caves and rock shelters at all times and in many areas of the world. In the earlier cultural periods caves were commonly used as living sites just as in later times; in addition they served as burial sites or places of ritual.

So long as the evidence of human activity lies directly on the surface of a cave floor, a straight study can be made of the individual objects. But geological questions arise with the excavation of cultural evidence when stony layers, earth or cave travertine have been deposited during or after the appearance of man. The sediments should be closely examined not merely for the purpose of answering geological questions: their analysis helps to answer many questions to do with culture. For instance an assessment can be made of the date of a cultural layer, the time interval between two excavated layers and contemporary conditions of landscape and climate. Moreover a detailed knowledge of the natural phenomena associated with caves allows conclusions to be drawn about the degree of human influence on the cave deposits.

Caves and shelters have provided refuge to animals as well as men. Wild and dom-estic animals like to escape from the sun into the shade of caves and to take shelter there from rain, snow and storms. Frequent visits of large groups of animals over a prolonged time may change the floor with their droppings and trampling. But as these animals use only the entrance, the floor in the interior of deep caves will remain undisturbed by them.

Carnivores like to use caves in order to devour their prey in peace. Gnawed bones often bear witness to this, and the eating places of the Ice Age cave hyaena are spectacu-lar examples.

The caves of cave bears were of special significance in the Pleistocene. In the mountain interior the bear hibernated in the uniform, though often low temperature. The female bore her young in the middle of winter and suckled them through the first months of their lives. Individuals died there—newly born weaklings, young animals which had not gained sufficient strength during the summer to stand the lack of food during the long hibernation, female bears at whelping time and wounded or aged adults. The carcasses having rotted, the skeletons, covered by stone rubble and earth, remained preserved in the caves of calcareous hills..

Thus there are two natural ways to account for animal bones found in cave sediments; as the remains of prey and as the remains of animals that died a natural death. Bones of small mammals are also found at the roosting places of birds of prey. Bat bones occur underneath their own sleeping places.

There is a third important cause of animal bones being found in cave sediments— the remains of human meals. However, the association of cultural remains and animal bones in one layer is not sufficient proof that the animal remains are due to human activity. For the occupation of the cave by man could have been followed by intervals during which animals frequented the cave, bearing their own traces. Short periods of time between these various visits are often undefined in cave sediments. It is thus all the more important to distinguish natural and 'artificial' deposits. The only way to accomplish this is with the help of the natural sciences.

All these aspects of cave excavation emphasize how closely linked prehistoric problems are with those of mammalian palaeontology and geology.

CAVES AND CAVE SEDIMENTS

The character of a cave sediment is dependent on various influences, which must be discussed systematically. It is impossible to enter into every aspect, but any classification should consider the manifold geological and morphological conditions. These enable a recognition of contemporary events within one cave and provide correlations between different ones.

Origins and forms of caves. The processes of sedimentation are to a marked degree determined by the shape of the cave. Rather than give a detailed classification of caves we will confine ourselves to a division relative to sedimentary conditions, since these are important especially in relation to prehistory.

From the shape of a cave we can often deduce what material we can expect to find in it. From the sediments two types of caves can be distinguished:

inner ('endogene') caves—mostly passages and chambers;
outer ('exogene') caves—mostly shallow caves, shelters and niches.

Endogene caves are those which penetrate deep into a hill. Varied causes may produce such a cave formation. It may be the remains of a subterranean river course which ran through the hill before the valleys were carved into the present landscape, that is, a *karst* cave. Owing to the intensive subterranean activity of water a hill can be sponge-like, intersected by passages meeting in a chamber. Then follows an enlargement of the rounded passages by erosion. The water running in them deposits locally derived material and also some from greater distances. These local and foreign materials, carried along for deposition, have been moved on in a more or less horizontal direction. As soon as water ceases to flow through the passage, corrosion (solution processes of percolating water) sets in on the walls.

Long passages can also be formed by corrosion along lines of tectonic disturbance—the enlargement of a crack. This may occur at a particular depth when a constriction or the damming up of sediment prevents further downward erosion, so that this type of cave is often shaped like a horizontal tube. The ceiling is vaulted like an inverted 'V', and generally stretches up to a scarcely visible crack. Into such caves the water carries either fine material from the surface or dissolved calcium carbonate and freed residue from the rock in which the cave is situated. Often materials of both kinds are deposited together. The transportation of the descending material occurs in a more or less vertical direction. In smaller folds and faults dams also occur, occasionally initiating corrosion and cave formation. Here the percolating water transports dissolved calcium carbonate and freed residue along the line of the tectonic disturbance.

Endogene caves can also form at the contact surfaces of distinct rocks, where an underlying rock forms an impermeable dam. The combination of a vertical crack above a horizontally bedded rock of different composition is the most favourable condition for the formation of endogene caves. The most active process here is corrosion.

If endogene caves do not open onto a clear hillside or rock face, but onto the top edge of a rubble slope cloaking the foot of a hillside, then a damming of the water is caused by this material, which is mainly earthy. Groundwater overflows at the top edge of the rubble slope and can thus form caves by corrosion at the varying water levels.

Thermal waters and waters charged with minerals ascending from a considerable depth dissolve out many a cave passage by their corrosive activity.

Many endogene caves originally had no exits to the outside, until they were exposed by erosion from outside, or until the wall between the cave and the hillside got thinner and thinner, owing to internal corrosion, and then collapsed. Both processes can take place simultaneously. Only after such an exposure of the cave passage can the outside climate work directly on the cave walls and thereby on sedimentation.

Exogene caves are all those that do not penetrate into a hill as deep passages but which are formed from outside in the nature of niches, shallow caves and shelters. They are often eroded out either by a river, or on a lake- or sea-shore. They are situated at the height of a past water level, singly or side by side along a cliff. If they contain water-laid sediments these must have been carried into the cave from outside.

Similar caves can also be formed on isolated rock walls by the corrosion of less resistant parts of the stone. The floor of these corrosion caves generally slopes down towards the outside. The broken-off rubble falls outside in the initial stage. When the cavity has reached a sufficient depth the rubble accumulates at the entrance. In the case of rock shelters on a less sheer slope it piles up in front of the cave, so that a more horizontal floor is gradually formed. At this stage man has a use for the cave. In the course of time the floor at the back of the cave also gets covered. As soon as this happens the rock floor is protected against weathering and sedimentation takes its course as in any other cave with an originally horizontal floor.

Exogene caves do not penetrate deep into a hill. Only when several causes combine in cave formation do other forms arise, for example angular or displaced passage caves, which open out in front with a wide mouth.

Topographical positions of caves. Caves can occur in various positions on a hill, mountain or mountain range and show the processes of formation discussed in the previous section. Their topographical position is of importance with regard to sedimentation, because the effect of daily, seasonal or long-term changes in temperature and precipitation can vary considerably in different places.

If a cave is situated just beneath the surface on the slopes of a mountain, then daily precipitation has a direct effect on the cave climate. Seasonal changes of climate can also influence processes in the inner part of the cave. It is however essential that there should be a link with the surface by means of crevices, passages or chimneys.

But if a mountain range is high over the cave such a direct influence is not to be expected. Only in the case of low-lying caves can much decomposed rubble from the hill accumulate, enough sometimes to block up the entrance from the outside. In caves situated high up a mountain there tends to be a steady decomposition of the entrance area and thus a retreat of the mouth of the cave.

When a cave lies at the bottom of a valley, or a one-time valley, sediments are usually carried there by a river or stream either at the time when the stream channel is being shaped or by later flooding. These deposits can assist in the dating of the cave. The same holds with caves on lake- and sea-shores.

The direction in which a cave faces is important to the effect of the outer climate on sedimentation, especially at the entrance. Some situations can be quoted to illustrate this. If a cave faces south the sun can shine on the mouth for a long time and thereby have a direct effect on the front part of the cave's climate; but in a shaded position facing north only the air temperature has any effect. If it faces east a cave receives the warmth of the sun directly after the cool of the night, whereas if it faces west it catches the sun's rays after the air has warmed up for many hours.

Position of sediments within the cave. To interpret a cave sediment it is vital to examine the position within the cave where deposition has taken place (Fig. 16).

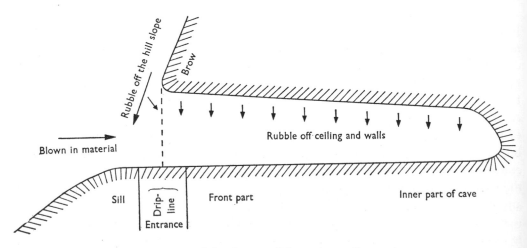

Fig. 16 Sources and distribution of the various sediments in a cave.

In a cave which does not lie in the flooding area of a stream, lake or the sea and cannot be flooded by water from inside the hill, we can expect the various parts of the cave to have accumulated the following materials:

Caves possessing a *sill* will collect there scree material from the brow of the cave. The scree can contain stones, soil and plants and animal remains from the entire area of the hill above the cave. In times of strong winds, during loess formation for example, there will also be present a considerable amount of aeolian deposit. The sediment, in other words scree plus material blown in, is then subjected to immediate processes of soil formation, to which plants contribute. Animal life appears, most clearly evidenced by snails. The swifter the process of deposition, the less the intensity of soil formation. Marked accumulation of scree, which in itself has been exposed to several processes of decomposition, prejudices a direct climatic interpretation of the sequence of layers. Another difficulty is the likelihood of part of the sediments having been washed away.

The area under the brow of the cave is called the *entrance*. At the entrance is the drip-line of rain or melted water running off the brow of the cave. Scree from above falls on this entrance area, as well as on the sill, in varying amounts. Material is also blown in this far. To these items are added decomposition products from the front of the roof of the cave. Since this area is under the unimpeded influence of climate, we can, by means of the deposited material, directly deduce the climatic causes of decomposition. During undisturbed sedimentation, material is in the main accumulated in the entrance area, because here scree plus blown-in material and decomposition products unite, and above all the influence of the weather is most active. In the event of sedimentation being not too rapid, plant and animal life develops as well. Inclusion of soil particles and organic remains from the scree is also a possibility.

Sediments thus reveal the climatic influences which create decomposition, together with those influences which produce soil formation. This being a contemporary occurrence, we are provided with a basis for reading climatic conditions by means of sedimentary processes and thereby both deducing relative dates and reconstructing environment.

A *drip-line* is only formed when the brow of the cave is of such a shape that rain and melted water can run along it. The drip starts where the brow meets the roof of the cave. Most caves possess such a drip-line. The water which drips or sometimes pours onto the floor of the cave loosens all fine particles and carries them away. This results in a strip of washed-off coarse material being exposed. If loosely packed stone material lies underneath then the water carries the fine material into the interstices. Thereby coarse and splintered rubble lower down receives 'secondary' earth. More frequently, however, the fine materials are deposited in front of and behind the drip-line. If the water dripping from the brow of the hill contains calcium carbonate, which it most commonly does, then this is deposited on the floor as sinter. On the other hand water containing CO_2 can also dissolve calcium carbonate, which it deposits immediately adjacent to or underneath as sinter; the more hollow spaces the percolating water finds, the deeper the calcification of the sediments. Both processes generally occur together. In caves whose brow is eroded back we can deduce the one-time position of the entrance from a similar calcification of sediments in front of the present brow of the cave.

In short, wherever the structure of a sediment makes washing a possibility we must examine minutely whether earth and travertine are primarily or secondarily deposited. On the sill, washing of this kind is caused by rainfall; at the entrance and further inside by dripping water.

In the *front part of the cave* sedimentation is directly influenced by the weather outside. But little light enters. There is a lack of vegetation, snails and soil formation. The rubble from the roof and walls settles down on the cave floor and is subjected to the same climatic influences as at the entrance, though the effect is less. There is, however, no extraneous material. For that reason the climatic conditions of sedimentation can generally be easily read in the front part of the cave.

In the *interior of the cave* sedimentation is subject to different laws. Daily and seasonal changes in climate do not penetrate or at least not directly. Therefore only important long-term changes can alter the mode of sedimentation. Earth and rubble can be included here, as evidence of marked changes in the course of major climatic events.

If we find materials in the lower sediments of the cave entrance which could only have been created in the front part, or even the interior of the cave, then they must have been secondarily carried to the entrance, in which case we must examine whether water activity or solifluction is responsible. Alternatively, if their creation can be proved as autochthonous, then we have proof that the mouth of the cave has been shifted back by weathering of the hillside. Thus we are now looking at what was once an inner section of a longer cave.

The nature of cave rock. The cave rock will play an important part in the process of sedimentation and in the type of sediments produced. If the cave lies in compact limestone the pieces that break off are different from those in the case of lumpy, shattered, laminated or fissile limestone. Also the mineral composition of the cave rock and the included substances must be considered in an examination of cave sediments—for example parts with a high content of quartz sand, oolite or fossils. An exact knowledge of cave rock allows a recognition of alien constituents in the sediments. Observation of the geological conditions in the neighbourhood of the cave enables one to judge from where and how alien substances got into the cave: because a cave impinged upon another rock formation inside the hill or because particles reached the cave floor through crevices and in percolating water from an overlying rock formation, or when gravel, erratic pieces, loess or soil were washed in from the hillside through cracks in the walls of the cave. In addition, a layer which once covered the hillside but is now weathered away may be represented in cave sediments.

Only if all natural explanations fail can foreign stone testify to the past presence of man.

Non-geological contributions to sediments. Many sediments contain inclusions which cannot be put down to any geological cause. They are brought in by either man or animals.

Material imported by man can be: tools and waste pieces of stone, bone, and in later cultures baked clay and metal. Stones can be included here which served as pot-boilers, hearths, punches, hammer-stones, anvils, grindstones and paving-stones, etc. In addition there are the minerals and fossils used by man as ornaments, and above all animal bones and their fragments with or without traces of cutting and burning. Often charcoal from wood fuel proves human activity. Collected foliage, plants and earth clinging to feet and clothes were likewise imported. Fire in a hearth affected by its heat the character of the cultural layer in the area. The climatic significance of the sediments is strongly prejudiced by human influence, if a direct interpretation cannot be made from the plant and animal remains themselves.

When a burial is made in the cave the layers, at least around the skeleton, are jumbled up by the digging and filling of the grave. We thus have a later disturbance.

The influences on a sediment which are attributed to man can be wiped out in the course of time after deposition. The older the layer the more the small distinguishing features disappear; this must also be taken into consideration when assessing sediments.

Caves are often visited by *animals*. The material brought in by them can be small stones, sand and soil stuck to their feet and fur. Deposited faeces also introduce foreign matter into the sediment, as does the decomposition of carcasses. The various origins of animal bones were mentioned on pp. 123–4. Great masses of almost homogeneous snail shells are brought in by rodents and birds and in Mesolithic stations by man as well.

In order to imply by nomenclature the mode of formation of a layer, I consider the following definitions useful:

geological layer	a natural accumulation of stones, earth, clay, etc., defined in more detail according to predominating components
fossil layer	animal remains included naturally in a sediment
archaeological layer	the occurrence of individual proofs of human presence, with or without fossil remains, and no noticeable alteration in the sediment
cultural layer	a sediment strongly influenced by human activity (fire, tool production, etc.), with many imported objects (stones, earth, bones, mollusc shells, plants, etc.)

Types of sediment and methods of interpretation. The most important cave sediments are limestone rubble, earth and cave travertine (sinter).

(a) Limestone rubble. There are two causes of limestone rubble breaking off from the walls and roof of a cave: one cause is water escaping through cracks, clefts and breakages in the limestone and carrying with it calcium carbonate together with loosened clay and sandy substances, which limestone contains in varying quantities; these are deposited on the floor of the cave. In this way the stone pieces surrounded by cracks lose their adhesion and fall to the floor. Evidence of corrosion, leaching of superficial alkalis, eroded and rounded edges are the indication of this on stone fragments of all sizes, which are embedded in an earth or travertine matrix. Such weathering is only possible in a temperate or warm climate with considerable precipitation.

A second cause of the formation of coarse limestone rubble is freezing and thawing. The increase in volume of water in the cracks during freezing loosens the stone pieces from their matrix, but the ice for the time being acts as a bond. It is only after thawing that the fragments fall out. Only a little water is necessary for this, but what is very necessary is frequent freezing and thawing, that is, temperature oscillations round about freezing point. Thus in the entrance and front part of the cave daily and seasonal variations influence sedimentation, which is also affected by rubble from the slopes of the hill above.

The inner part of the cave however is only affected by long-term changes of temperature. In cold times, that is in an ice age, such regular happenings occur in the great periglacial areas, their influence penetrating into caves. Above all, the times of transition, representing the advance and retreat stages of the ice sheets, bring fluctuating temperatures around freezing point deep into the inner cave. Deep perma-frost prevalent at peak phases of glaciation meant a cessation of sedimentation. In proportion to the penetration of the stone by water, which above all depends on the porosity of the rock, and in proportion to the frequency of freezing and thawing, coarse or fine-grained rubble is fractured off and deposited on the floor. The fact that this frost-fractured rubble shows marked variations in the various parts of the cave, even in contemporary deposits, is explained by the different degrees of influence by the outside climate. We can also expect that at the same place in the cave during different phases of a cold period the material will be reduced to different sizes. The frost-fractured fragments are weathered a little or not at all in most cases. The edges exhibit a fresh surface. Earth and travertine only play a small part in such sediments. However in the entrance or where water percolates an admixture with small loess particles or earth is possible.

The larger the stone fragments in the frost rubble are, the greater are the interstices likely to be. In these the earth masses remain mostly loose because the blocks continue to support one another afterwards by a diagenetic clinging together of the sediments and by the pressure of more recent layers above the blocks. Therefore in layers with large tabular stones and blocks the fossil remains can be larger and less compressed than in layers with small stones. Sometimes fine material trickles down later into the interstices, so in sediments with large stones we must consider whether the earth is contemporary or later than the stones. In small stony layers large bones can be broken up by pressure of the sediments.

Such considerations are therefore very important as on them must be decided whether bones occurring between large stones are intrusive or indigenous and whether fractures in the bones are due to human or other processes.

(b) Earth. Silt and clay-like components are almost exclusively blown or washed into the front part of the cave during cold periods. In warm times however there is an important addition of earth washed by rainwater from the brow of the cave or the hill rising above. Fine material can also run off the rubble cone on the sill. In addition the atmosphere and plants in the entrance area make an additional attack on the rubble by a soil-forming process. Here also the loosening power of percolating water can be increased by the outer climate, so that more residues are freed from the stone.

With the separating of the calcium carbonate content from dripping water by evaporation, the newly created travertine often receives all the components of the cave stone which had remained stuck together up till then. In this process only the material from the native stone is laid down on the floor of the cave, without the earth content being increased.

Earthy deposits in cave interiors have neither blown in, nor in there turned to soil. But the trickling in of fine materials from the surface (loess, soil, etc.) particularly in caves very near a summit is highly likely. Then a sediment can survive in a cave, which has long ago been eroded from the surface or been recently weathered. Besides these fine components derived from the surface there are, in particular, residues freed from the native stone which can be piled up on the cave floor and form a complete earth coverage. Change of intensity in the water flow can cause bands varying between coarse and fine-grained sands and clays. A difference in mineral content can likewise cause banding which is in the main evidenced by fine layers of clay, iron or mineral efflorescences in the sequence of sedimentation. A yellow or brown colour in an earth complex depends primarily on iron content.

In the interior of the cave, sediments can change if there is a frequent occurrence of faeces and the decomposition of animal carcasses. The phosphate of bat guano is mostly coloured red or red-brown, without climate or soil development having had any share in this. Those cave bear layers which contain bones in a good quantity are mostly red-brown. Phosphate and the products of the decomposition of animal material cause the brown colour, or varying shades of red, yellow or black.

The earth carried in by cave bears on their fur and paws can never make a decisive contribution to accumulation in the interior of caves. A direct climatic interpretation of warm climate cannot be made from this red-brown colour of a cave bear layer, which always contains stone rubble. All that can be said about climate is that at the time of the formation of the sediment cave bear life was possible within reach of the cave and that ceiling rubble was being fractured off. A warm climate during the formation of a red-brown cave bear layer is therefore not an essential postulate.

(c) Travertine. In nearly all caves travertine plays a great part. It can have varied appearances: hard, crystalline and translucent, or a soft, crumbly, chalky or clay-like accumulation. With a heavy intake of water, this last type of travertine can become a slippery dough-like mass (*Montmilch*). Compact travertine masses mixed with earth can also occur in the caves.

In the *interior* of caves a clay-like travertine sinter is deposited by the percolating water. Evaporation and temperature oscillations play only a subordinate part. The decisive factor is the CO_2 content of the percolating water. This is originally rainwater which by trickling through soil on the hill absorbs CO_2 with which it can dissolve considerable quantities of calcium carbonate in the cracks of the stone. By means of the differential pressure when the water reaches the open cave large quantities of calcium carbonate are precipitated as stalactites. Therefore a high travertine content in a cave layer can only give a climatic clue in so far as during the time of its formation the hill must have carried vegetation. In the *entrance area* of the cave, however, the conditions resemble those of the surface. Here a warm climate encourages travertine formation, while strong air movement can also increase evaporation.

A special formation is 'clay travertine', consisting of dissolved cave stone; the dissolved components of the stone are transported by water and redeposited in a fine-grained form. In most cases this material with a high carbonate content is uniformly distributed throughout the clay, so that one can speak of a *white clay*. This does not demand an extremely warm climate, merely vegetation on the mountain surface.

(d) Humus content. The humus content in cave sediments is formed by vegetation or the decay of plant parts (grass, leaves and ferns) carried in by man or animals for the purpose of bedding or litter. If this humus content is once included in the soil it rarely disappears, so it can even be traced in very old layers. Washed-in soil can also be added to this. From the humus content the only deduction concerning the climate that can be made is that vegetation must have existed in the vicinity of the cave.

Acid humus can also be formed of disintegrated animal excreta and carcasses. The mineral arising from this is *Scharizerit*, related to phosphate earths. Thus a humus content may well be found in much frequented cave bear layers. All we can say about climate from this is that animal life was possible.

(e) Phosphate content. Stone and soil possess a natural amount of phosphate, which is not removed by circulating water. Also the phosphate contributions, which arise from decay of human meals (kitchen refuse) or of the excreta of cave bears as well as their carcasses, are preserved for tens of thousands of years in sediments. This observation has given rise to the 'phosphate method'. This is an analysis of the distribution of the phosphate content on a surface in order to discover the past presence of settlements, paths, burials, animal folds and such-like, which are indicated by high phosphate values. The measuring of phosphate content in a layered sequence can also help to trace the presence of man or animals at a particular horizon. Of course it must be borne in mind that while there is a concentration of phosphate on the surface, percolating water absorbs a certain amount and infiltrates the layers. It then happens that the phosphate content decreases uniformly downwards, until it reaches the permanent value of the sediments which are free from organic influences. In such layers nothing can be said about the measure of indigenous or infiltrated phosphate content. But a sudden decrease of the phosphate content in overlying strata indicates that then man or animals no longer frequented the cave.

But phosphates supply no evidence of climatic conditions. Their appearance is possible in cold as well as warm times. However in a cave bear layer, in the case of a uniform occupation, the phosphate content is higher if the breaking off of the ceiling rubble and the washing in of fine material decrease; this is because the changing ratio of intensity of sedimentation to the number of dead animals causes changes in phosphate content. Therefore the composition of a sequence must be examined in this light, because few bears plus little sediment can supply the same phosphate content as many bears plus much sediment. But likewise fewer bears and more sediment can cause a lessening of phosphate content. Therefore conclusions on climate must come much more readily from stone rubble or earth than from the strength of phosphate content.

(f) Disturbances. All these physical and chemical phenomena only supply indications of the primary sedimentation process if no later events have caused disturbances, such as that made by an intrusive stream of water, rolling or transporting bodily the assorted particles; distinct layers can also be mixed, while percolating and dripping water may carry clay down into a loosely packed rubble so that in hollow places travertine especially develops (secondary travertine on the undersides of stones). Clay particles can swell up so much when saturated with water that at a slight inclination of the layer the material can start flowing gradually, and at the cave entrance this phenomenon can be enhanced by cryoturbation during cold times. Prehistoric man was also able to cause considerable disturbance by digging in caves, and burrowing animals may do likewise. Thus in the study of sediments in a cave we must first examine whether any sort of disturbance has subsequently altered the deposits.

RESEARCH METHODS

To recognize the various characteristics of the sediments described and to compare them quantitatively, they must not only be closely examined by excavation on the spot but a succession of analytical tests on the material must be made in the laboratory. When the samples are collected the following rules must be observed.

A series of samples should be taken if possible at various places in the cave—sill, entrance, front part of the cave, interior of the cave—from the rock floor right up to the surface of the deposits. The sedimentary process under the varied action of daily, seasonal or long-term changes of climate can be better followed using this method than if these influences are reconstructed only at one place.

The samples should be cut out of the section in a compact area and in a vertical line one on top of the other. By doing this the distance between the individual samples in fine-grained layers is narrowed; in layers with coarse stones however the distance apart can be very much greater. This is not only a requirement of technique but is more in keeping with the sedimentary process, since coarse material raises a sediment quicker than fine earth. It is advisable to take several samples even out of thicker layers which look homogeneous because experience has shown in many cases that important differences are only brought out by analysis.

Furthermore it is advisable, on a clean-cut section, to begin the extraction of the samples at the bottom. In this way only the portions that have already been sampled are contaminated by the loosened particles which are bound to fall down during the work. For analyses in the laboratory nothing must be removed in the way of artifacts, bones, stones and charcoal, otherwise the character of the deposits would be altered. Only where especially large stones or artifacts make the sample unnecessarily heavy can one leave them out, but this must be noted on the label of the samples. For any other technical details in the collection of samples reference can be made to a detailed account by the author (1958; pp. 26–29).

The object of analysis in the laboratory is to express the make-up of the scree by the distribution of grain-size in a sieving analysis, to discover the character of the fine material by its grain-size distribution in a washing analysis, and to define the most important chemical characteristics such as calcium carbonate content, humus content, and phosphate content. For techniques see the above-mentioned account, pp. 29–36.

Sieving analysis supplies quantitative values for the decrease in size of the limestone rubble. Thus the characteristics described on page 130 can be more exactly compared within the sediment, the cave and between various caves. Since stones are cleaned by such an analysis, their freshness or erosion, the sharp or rounded edges, and rolled and foreign materials can be more easily recognized. Washing analysis supplies quantitative values for earth and clay. Besides the help which it provides in the recognition of differences and similarities not visible to the naked eye, it also makes it possible to recognize when loess is a major component—in this way climatic readings can be made. Soil from fields can be recognized in a washing analysis by its characteristic grain-size distribution. Under a binocular microscope of 10–20 times magnification the components of the separate groups can be ascertained.

Simple chemical analyses to determine calcium carbonate, humus and phosphate contents make for an easy recognition of their origin and for their comparison with other caves. The values obtained from sieving and washing analyses and the determination of calcium carbonate content are values of weight which are best recalculated as percentages. Humus and phosphate contents are given in colour values. To provide a better impression than with rows of figures, all the values obtained should be drawn as *diagrams* and these are presented most clearly if the columns for the separate analyses are put side by side and the samples one on top of the other, in accordance with the profile. However the intervals can be small and regular because the size of the intervals in the profile does not imply time, but is merely dependent on the size of the rubble or the rapid change of unimportant more homogeneous sediments.

As every excavation means disturbance of the deposits, scaled drawings and photographs of important profiles should be made as well as possible. In addition there should be taken from at least one characteristic spot a lacquered strip so that the original full sequence of layers can be observed later. Where this is not possible one must be content with 'colour stripes', which at any rate preserve the colour impression of the separate layers in a small space. For these lacquered strips the method developed by Voigt has proved of value, but nowadays the so-called 'Capaplex' method of Herrnbrodt can be recommended which has the advantage that the profile need not be pre-dried. A simple method of producing colour stripes is described in detail by the author (*op. cit.*, pp. 37–39).

CAVE SEDIMENTS AND QUATERNARY GEOLOGY

The clearest time indicator for a chronological assessment of cave sediments is the last glaciation—the Würm ice age. Its effects were so penetrating and the deposits formed so recently that it is of advantage to deal first of all with the influence of this cold phase on sedimentation. From this point we can assess deposition in earlier and later phases.

The most striking glacial factors influencing sedimentation in caves are: an alteration of the snow line (the edge of the permanent snow field), the vegetation, tree and forest lines, the surface of ice streams, the boundaries of the ice caps, precipitation and the maximum penetration of perma-frost.

During the ice age, in all regions not covered by glaciers between the northern ice cap and the Alps, as well as far beyond, the water in ground and rock was locked up by *perma-frost* to great depths. Its effect on sedimentation in the interior part of a cave has already been discussed in the section on limestone rubble. We concluded there that the peak of a cold phase can be bordered by the coarse rubble of the advance phase of the glacier and the coarse rubble of the thaw, and itself leave no trace.

The *surfaces of the ice streams* allow us to recognize the mountains, peaks and the ranges which were free of ice and on which vegetation and animal life (within the zones of vegetation) were also possible side by side with glaciers. Caves which had been reached by glaciers were no longer visited by man or beast. Heavy precipitation, which is characteristic of the first part of a glacial advance and which possibly appears again later with the coming of a warmer oscillation, had both a direct and an indirect effect on sedimentation in caves. It provided the material necessary for glaciation and the descent of the snow line.

Figs. 17 and 18 provide information about the great significance of times of transition with their changes in the position of the snow, tree and forest lines. The columns in Fig. 17 signify the change in average height of the permanent snow line as well as the tree and forest boundaries in the central Alpine region from the Riss-Würm Interglacial through the Würm Glaciation to the present day. The names of the caves are put down in order of their heights above sea-level. The dotted and barred lines, which begin at the names of the caves and link up the columns, show their position in the landscape during the three periods of time. It must be stressed that maximum conditions are indicated. From this figure we can gauge the significance of the long transition times with their associated changes.

The case of the snow line is illustrated in Fig. 18. Every cave has its own column, which shows the extent by which the boundary of the permanent snow line must have descended, from its peak during the Riss-Würm Interglacial until it reached the cave. For the snow line to descend a thousand or more metres much precipitation and a long time were required. Much might have happened in the cave during this time. Man and beast could have visited it long after the start of the cold phase and also several changes could have left their marks. Thus one can see quite clearly that the duration of sediment-ation and the point in time of its cessation under deep frost conditions could be different in every cave according to its situation. Caution must be advised when a chronological correlation is made between the fossil, cultural and archaeological layers of different caves. The beginning, duration and end of such layers must be specially examined in each cave. An uncritical correlation of the results from one cave can lead to erroneous deductions.

The examples illustrated in Figs. 17 and 18 come from the Alps and Jura. In other land-scapes snow, tree and forest lines have different values, but they were always of con-sequence in some way or another. In the region of the great ice caps there were added the effects of these reserves of cold, and at sea coasts there was a possible amelioration of the climate and its extremes, in addition to glacial eustatic changes of sea-level.

As man and beast can also hunt and live above the forest line—at least in summer—their traces in caves are of little climatic significance. The cave is only uninhabitable in summer when the snow line reaches the cave and perma-frost penetrates the

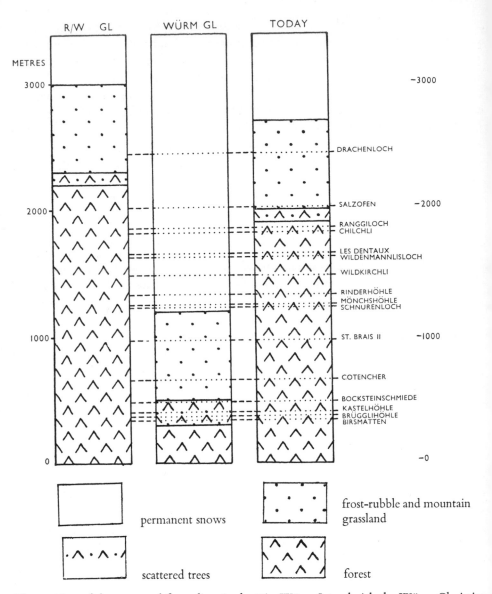

Fig. 17 The position of the snow and forest lines in the Riss-Würm Interglacial, the Würm Glaciation and today, in heights above sea-level, and the positions of caves within the region of the Alps and Jura.

mountain. On the other hand caves below the snow line remained open the whole year round. But there the frost was also an effective deterrent, so that in wide regions of central Europe during the main cold phases man did not necessarily inhabit caves. But the increasing warmth at the end of the ice age again offered hunters caves to occupy in many places, which certainly made migrations and an expansion of population easier.

Postglacial sediments were directly imprinted by climate. The renewed vegetation of grasses and plants (and later of forests) on the hillside markedly changed the balance of

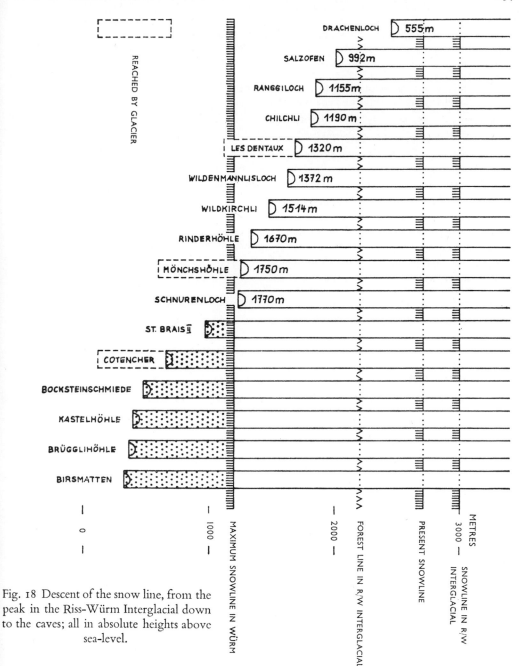

Fig. 18 Descent of the snow line, from the peak in the Riss-Würm Interglacial down to the caves; all in absolute heights above sea-level.

water in the hill. Then was the time of travertine formation as described above. Soil formation was possible in the entrance areas of caves, which enabled the nuances of Holocene climatic changes to register and hence permits the reconstruction of the environment of the prehistoric men whose presence is revealed in their cultural remains.

REFERENCES
In order to recognize the age and duration of a culture layer within cave sediments, as well as the environment and behaviour of prehistoric man, a good knowledge of natural history and an exact analysis of sediments are essential. This article, therefore, is intended to provide a guide to this. Specialized literature provides an abundance of detail. The author has confined herself here to a few new basic works out of which further details can be obtained from bibliographical lists.

A full discussion of glacial phenomena is given in:

WOLDSTEDT, P. 1954 and 1958. *Das Eiszeitalter*, I and II

ZEUNER, F. E. 1959. *The Pleistocene Period*, London

The application of geological and pedological methods in various combinations to the interpretation of cave sediments was worked out by Robert Lais and was initially published by him in detail in:

LAIS, R. 1941. Über Höhlensedimente. *Quartär* 3, 1940, Berlin 1, 56–108

The work of the author, especially in Swiss caves, has been carried out for many years and arose as a continuation of the work of Lais:

SCHMID, E. 1958. Höhlenforschung und Sedimentanalyse. Ein Beitrag zur Datierung des alpinen Paläolithikums. *Schriften des Instituts für Ur- und Frühgeschichte der Schweiz*, no. 13, Basel.

In this work the techniques of the different analyses are described in detail as well as an account of the analyses and interpretation of the sediments of all the caves named in Figs. 2 and 3. There is a full list of references to similar caves.

Shortly after appeared a work on the caves of Hungary, also based on the work of Lais:

VERTÉS, L., 1959. Untersuchungen an Hölensedimenten. Methode und Eegebuisse. *Régészeté Füzetebs*, ser. II, 7

With their new research methods and bibliographies the above works present the point now reached in the study of Pleistocene and Holocene cave sediments. They provide the necessary tools for dating cultural layers in caves.

IIc PLANTS

14 *Pollen Analysis*

G. W. DIMBLEBY

SAMPLES TAKEN FOR POLLEN ANALYSIS may range from long series covering a span of thousands of years to the single sample for a spot determination of date. Basically the analysis consists of the identification and enumeration of the various types of pollen present in each sample; in other words, the preparation of a pollen spectrum for each sample. This in itself is not always a simple matter, especially in certain types of material, but the techniques are now well established and the inherent limitations of the method understood. As this aspect of the subject is fully covered in textbooks (e.g. Faegri and Iversen[4]) it is not proposed to deal with it here. What is of more concern is the interpretation of the pollen spectra so obtained.

Pollen analysis is often thought of as a technique for dating, but it only serves this purpose if the pollen spectra can be tied in to a time scale based on some direct dating method, such as radiocarbon dating. In fact there are many occasions when pollen analysis can give valuable information about the archaeological environment and yet be of little or no use for dating.

For many parts of the world a pattern of change has now been established in the pollen rain over a long period of the past, so that even isolated analyses may be fitted into their appropriate position in the sequence. Thus in Europe the Postglacial period has been divided up into zones, each having a characteristic tree pollen spectrum, reflecting the sequence of climatic changes which have taken place as the Postglacial developed. Knowing the present ecological tolerances of these tree species, it is possible within limits to assess the climatic features of each zone. However, each of these zones may cover two or three millennia, so their value for dating is restricted, though in some cases subdivision is possible, based on the behaviour of certain critical species. In Europe and elsewhere the zone and sub-zone boundaries have now been tied in with considerable accuracy to an absolute time scale, principally by C[14] determinations on organic matter stratified immediately adjacent to these boundaries (Godwin, Walker and Willis[6]). Where such a system of absolute dating has not yet been worked out, pollen analysis is only capable of establishing relative chronology. For pollen analysis to be of value in dating it is not necessary to interpret the pollen spectra in terms of the plant communities on the ground; many correlations are based only on the percentages of the different pollen types, in particular the tree species, without any consideration of the ecological structure of the forests producing the pollen. In fact, as we shall see in the following pages, it may not always be possible to arrive at such ecological conclusions.

For the archaeologist, however, pollen analysis is potentially of much greater value than just as an indirect instrument for dating, important though this is. It can also give information of the ecological environment in which human remains and artifacts were situated, and a knowledge of the ecological environment may in turn point to the use— or misuse—of the land at that time.

Thus pollen analysis is of potential value in archaeology in three ways: (a) as a means of dating, (b) to provide evidence of the contemporary environment, and (c) as an indication of what man was doing to that environment. It is rare for these different facets to emerge equally from any one investigation and indeed sometimes one or more of them may be impossible of interpretation. Generally it may be said that a site which gives first-class material for dating tends to give only limited ecological information, and vice versa.

The Postglacial forest sequence in Europe has been worked out in detail from a large number of palynological investigations; the entry or disappearance of the different tree genera, together with the relative abundance of their pollen, characterizes the various pollen zones and sub-zones. For such information the ideal material is an unbroken sequence of stratified deposits in conditions which favour the preservation of pollen. Anaerobic peat deposits or lake sediments are therefore usual subjects for study. The information they provide, however, is not relevant to any particular piece of ground or plant community. It reflects the forest sequence of the district as a whole, which is what is required for dating purposes. Clearly, therefore, the ecological value of such information is limited. Nevertheless, the impact of man on the forest can be seen in such analyses, and, when seen, can be dated with some precision, but its expression will only be in general terms and will not be related to any given place. This is well illustrated by the work of Pearsall and Pennington[12] on the Windermere muds, in which they were able to show the increased grass pollen and the correspondingly decreased tree pollen percentages as the result of prehistoric occupation. The pollen analyses alone, however, could not tell them where in the district the main forest destruction had taken place, though by bringing other facts to bear, a definite conclusion was reached.

The ratio of non-tree pollen to tree pollen is a good guide to the density of the forest and the density is often dependent on man's activity. A marked increase in this ratio, due to an increase in the pollen of light-demanding herbs, is a usual indication of human influence. It is important to realize that in order to diminish the forest cover it is not necessary to cut trees down. Fire is a potent factor, damaging standing timber and destroying regeneration: at the same time it often has the incidental but cumulative effect of increasing the fire hazard. Grazing, too, can in the course of time destroy or mutilate a forest by constant attack on the next generation of trees. One need not hesitate, therefore, to attribute observed changes in the pollen spectra to human agency solely because that culture had not the mechanical means to clear forest. As far as we know fire was always available and it is significant that West[17] suggested that an episode of deforestation in the Hoxne interglacial deposits might be attributable to the influence of Palaeolithic man.

In every complete pollen sequence through the Postglacial period evidence will

appear sooner or later of the effect of man in the environment. In Europe this usually
starts in the Neolithic period, though, as we shall see later, Mesolithic man could cause
local modification of his environment. But it was when some sort of husbandry,
whether of stock or crops, became part of everyday life that the forest became an undesirable nuisance to man rather than just the setting in which he found himself and
from which he won the necessities of life. Then the effects of deliberate clearance became
sufficiently widespread to affect the pollen rain from a whole district and so show in the
bog or lake analyses. Iversen[8] in Denmark has shown with great clarity the sequence

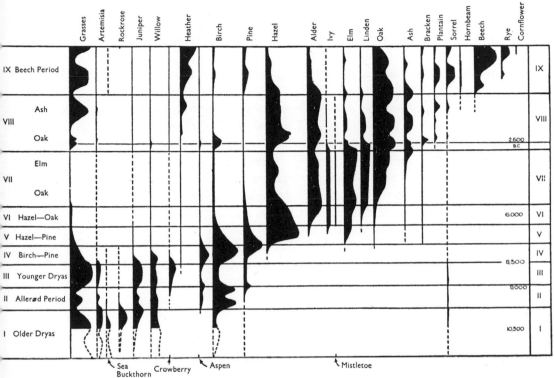

Fig. 19 Idealized diagram illustrating the Postglacial pollen sequence in Jutland. By kind permission
of Dr Johs. Iversen.

of forest destruction (in which fire was the chief implement), cultivation and forest re-
growth, which he calls *Landnam* (= land taking) and which is now widely recognized
all over Europe. Fig. 19 is an idealized diagram of his showing the sequence for Jutland;
the spread of heather, grasses and weeds of cultivation from the Neolithic onwards
(zones VIII and IX of his classification) can clearly be seen. The non-tree pollen often
gives some guide to the use being made of the land; the appearance of cereal pollen,
distinguishable from that of other grasses, together with the pollen of weeds of cultivation such as plantain and goosefoot, is conclusive proof of the onset of cultivation. There
will be differences in detail, of course, in regions of different plant geography, topography
or soil.

Now, whilst all such changes in a peat bog sequence may be datable—within the precision of the pollen zonation—they cannot be related to particular sites or to particular cultures without complementary evidence from another source. For instance, an artifact typologically characteristic of a certain culture may be found associated with the *Landnam* horizon, thus equating culture with environment and land use. Adventitious finds of this sort may, however, be of great value to the archaeologist when the artifact itself is not datable by type; e.g. ploughs, skis, boats, and other wooden objects not preserved in land sites. In such cases the period can be established by pollen analysis of the layer in which it is found (assuming that it is properly stratified—*see* Faegri and Iversen,[4] p. 116). Objects from museums have been dated by analysis of peat still clinging to them—a reminder that cleanliness is not necessarily righteous in archaeology. It should also be said that the chances of determining the exact stratification of an object are greatly reduced if that object is removed before appropriate sampling has been carried out.

A special case of adventitious bog finds which captures the imagination is the bog burial; examples of the value of pollen analysis in such circumstances are given by Schütrumpf.[13] The anthropological as well as archaeological significance of such rare occurrences is so great that a reliable dating is of first importance, though today C^{14} dating would be used in addition to pollen analysis.

As the potentialities opened up by pollen analysis of peats are now so widely realized, in conjunction with the remarkable preservation of remains so often associated with such material, it is natural that there has been intensified research in regions where peat abounds. The working together of archaeologists and pollen analysts in such areas has been very fruitful; Denmark and Ireland have made great progress, both countries owing a great deal to the Danish palynologist, Knud Jessen. Moreover, the importance of peat investigations in many other aspects of Quaternary research has been recognized and the appropriate experts brought in. Such intensified work has led not only to more detailed knowledge of existing sites but the recognition of many new sites. Most important is the increasing number of actual occupation sites which has become known. Occupation sites of this sort—even though they may be the ephemeral settlements of nomadic people—make it possible more fully than before to correlate a culture with its environment and at the same time to give it a reliable dating. Again, for typologically important sites a C^{14} dating will probably be sought, but for many others reliance will still be placed on the pollen analysis alone. In some cases the date may be rendered more precise if the occupation can be related to one or more 'recurrence surfaces'—recognizable changes in the nature of the peat due to resurgence of bog growth as a result of the increased wetness of the bog surface. The ages of these surfaces may be known with reasonable accuracy, but it is often difficult to identify individual ones with certainty.

The Maglemosian site at Star Carr[1] is a fine example of how an actual occupation site well stratified in peat can be made to yield up a very comprehensive mass of evidence concerning the people, their environment and their way of life, to a degree that would not be possible either from isolated finds or from an archaeologically sterile bog profile. From a later period may be quoted Troels-Smith's investigation of the Neolithic

Ertebølle culture in Denmark and his comparison of it with the Egolzwil lake-dwelling culture in Switzerland.[14] These are occupation sites preserved in stratified deposits, one in peat and the other in lake mud, but both providing material for pollen analysis (and for C^{14} tests). In fact both proved to be of virtually the same date and both showed the clearing of the forest in preparation for agriculture; but whilst in Denmark it was the elm which suffered most by the clearance, in Switzerland it was the beech. Here then were similar and contemporary cultures producing similar effects in floristically different environments. The nature of the actual settlements was, of course, very different in the two cases, but this is not our concern here.

Though not strictly occupation levels, and yet not adventitious finds either, are the trackways sometimes found embedded in peat bogs. Recently Godwin[5] has made a detailed study of the trackways of the Somerset Levels, using pollen analysis not only to confirm dating—mainly based on the C^{14} date—but to demonstrate the ecological conditions of the Neolithic or of the Late Bronze Age when these tracks were constructed. He sees them as an attempt to keep communications open over land that was becoming increasingly swampy, an attempt which ultimately failed as peat growth relentlessly continued.

So far discussion has centred on sites associated with deposits formed under waterlogged conditions, but it must be recognized that in such places archaeological sites cannot give a complete picture of the total effect of man on his environment. Occupation sites embedded in peat were probably only occupied during the summer; during the winter the people must have moved away above the high water-table to influence another environment. In the case of the Swiss lake-dwellings, it is obvious that the occupation layer was not itself on the site of forest clearance. The pollen record of forest clearance refers to the dry land, to sites which cannot be precisely identified. In such cases, then, the ecological picture is either blurred or incomplete, and it must be recognized that this is an inherent limitation in the study of all sites liable to waterlogging (and hence to peat formation), particularly in the later prehistoric cultures. Contemporary with such occupations other people were living on the dry land and sometimes the wealth of information which can be obtained from peat sites blinds us to this fact. In a country such as Britain, in which the bulk of the land is well above the water-table at all times of the year, even in this damp Sub-atlantic climate, the conditions exemplified by the bog or water-side sites cannot be regarded as typical for the country as a whole. The fact is, of course, that normal terrestrial sites do not lend themselves to the same methods of study, though, as we shall see below, pollen analysis may still yield unexpected results.

Before turning to purely terrestrial sites, however, we must look at that very large group of sites which in their day were terrestrial but which are now buried beneath peat. This is most commonly the case where the onset of the wetter Sub-atlantic period, about 500 BC, resulted in the initiation of peat formation in many places where it had not taken place before. Thus in Ireland Jessen[10] found that the onset of Sub-atlantic peat formation generally followed the Late Bronze Age, and proof of the original normal terrestrial nature of some sites may still persist in the form of old field systems beneath several feet of peat. Sites in such a situation offer a very different problem from those we have discussed so far. As with all sites covered by peat, of course, the peat above the occupation is only relevant for the dating of the site in so far as the very lowest layer gives a latest possible date for the site, but there may be a long interval between the occupation of the site and the onset of peat formation.

To put this in its correct perspective it is necessary to introduce here a rather different principle, namely the analysis of the pollen in normal soils. It was pointed out at the beginning of this chapter that pollen analysis is ideally carried out in anaerobic stratified deposits. Under such conditions microbiological activity is excluded, though if a peat becomes drained intense microbiological activity may start up in the peat, destroying both the peat itself and the pollen in it. This is especially true of fen peats, which are of high base status. It might be expected, therefore, that pollen falling on the surface of a freely drained soil would be exposed to the same processes and rapidly be destroyed. On calcareous and circumneutral soils this is so, such pollen as they do contain being so corroded as to be largely unrecognizable. But with soils of greater acidity, especially those with a pH less than 5·5, pollen may be found in very large quantities. This pollen is not lying free in the soil, but is apparently stabilized in humic material; if soil is shaken up with water the pollen will not be extracted, but if the humus is broken down with caustic potash large quantities of pollen may be set free. For this reason, the pollen does not wash freely through the soil profile. It does move downwards, presumably in association with the movement of the humus, but the process is slow and, incidentally, independent of the size of the pollen grains. Thus a crude stratification is produced which reflects broadly the history of vegetation as long as the pollen has been accumulating.[2]

Now soils are not static but are maturing. Many of the soils of Europe, forming on material exposed during the Ice Age, were initially more or less calcareous, gradually becoming leached and more acid as time went on. This leaching process appears to have been more rapid in the higher rainfall areas, and, in soils of low base status particularly, to have accelerated following deforestation. Consequently, the pollen record seldom goes back as far as the primeval forest stage, but usually starts in the transition from forest to open country. This progressive acidification of soil has one other important effect, namely to bring about the elimination of those members of the soil fauna which are responsible for soil mixing: these animals, in particular certain earthworms, are intolerant of acidity. In cases where they do occur together with pollen they wreck any pollen stratification. Stratification may be as much a matter of actual quantities of pollen as of percentages. The usual pattern is that the highest concentration is at the surface and that it falls with depth until at 18 in. to 2 ft it peters out altogether. The high concentration at the surface is very important in recognizing buried surfaces (*infra*).

The interpretation of soil pollen analyses differs in one important manner from that of peat or lake deposits. The bulk of the pollen falling on a soil comes from the vegetation on the spot; the influence of more distant vegetation, particularly if the site is forested, is largely masked. In other words, a soil pollen spectrum is of much more use for the interpretation of the ecology of the site itself but is of correspondingly less use for dating purposes, because critical species (e.g. the calcicolous elm) may not occur in the local

Silhouette skeleton in Tumulus II, Elp (municipality of Westerbolk), Drenthe, Netherlands. Excavated by A. E. van Giffen, 1932.[23] Photo courtesy Institute for Biological Archaeology, State University, Groningen

(see page 108) PLATE V

(a) Cook's Study. The zone of greater fissuring at the base of the peat marks the raw humus layer overlying the Mesolithic artifacts (see Fig. 20, p. 146).

(b) Bickley Moor Barrow. Section of the top soil mound. The thin dark line below the pale zone in the centre of the photograph is shown by pollen analysis to be the primary surface. The present soil contrasts markedly in type with that of the Bronze Age (see Fig. 22, p. 148).

PLATE VI (see page 139)

forest type. This drawback becomes most serious in deforested country when the re-presentation of tree pollen, the essential basis for dating, may be so low that an adequate count cannot be obtained. On the other hand, if dating is not possible, at least there is a better chance of obtaining precise information about the environment and man's effect on it.

An effect of soil development which is of importance in the present context is the formation of a raw humus layer. Once such a layer has formed it tends to build up and it has been shown that for palynological purposes it may be treated like a peat. In other words, it collects the pollen, but does not transmit it to the underlying layers. Such a raw humus layer is susceptible to burning, and it is a feature of heathlands, for example, that the raw humus is repeatedly consumed by fire. Consequently, a marked 'uncon-formity' builds up between the pollen spectra of the contemporary raw humus and the underlying mineral soil, an 'unconformity' which can span a thousand or two years.

This has particular relevance to occupation sites which though once terrestrial, are now peat-covered. On the Pennines, Mesolithic, Neolithic and Bronze Age flints lie beneath the peat. Many examples are known of microliths emerging from the base of the peat as it erodes; they apparently lie on the mineral soil beneath the peat. Hallam[7] has recently investigated such a site in order to determine the environmental setting of the Mesolithic culture, Plate VIa shows a section of the peat and underlying soil of this site, at Cook's Study, near Holmfirth, Yorks. This photograph was taken during the dry summer of 1959, before the face was trimmed for sampling. At the base of the peat (c. 30 in. thick) there is a narrow band of humic material showing distinctive cracking; therefore it is distinct colloidally. The microliths occurred below this and on top of the slightly bleached mineral soil. Fig. 20 shows the pollen analysis of the whole section. Except at its surface the mineral soil contains predominantly tree and hazel pollen, and is attributable to zone VII, though owing to the absence of elm, which may have been ecologically unsuited to this site, the forest phase cannot be allocated to a sub-zone, so that dating is imprecise. At the soil surface, heather and grass preponderate—perhaps an expression of Mesolithic influence on the environment.

The distinct humus layer at the base of the peat contains much smaller amounts of the pollen of woody species, but has high values for heather and grasses. It can be interpreted, in fact, as a raw humus layer. It is to be noticed that this layer contains cereal and weed pollen, which on the face of it seems to indicate that as soon as the Mesolithic forest was cleared the pollen rain from the surrounding landscape brought evidence of cultivation. Whilst this may imply some reappraisal of the relationship between the Mesolithic and the farming cultures in a region like this, it does not necessarily do violence to accepted views, because a raw humus layer, as mentioned above, may not be chrono-logically contiguous with the soil beneath. In this instance the difference between the pollen spectra from the base of the raw humus and the top of the mineral soil is not as great as in many modern soils. Whilst this may suggest a relatively short passage of time, any estimate would be guesswork in our present inadequate state of knowledge. The peat covering the raw humus is wholly Sub-atlantic in date and may be seen as the result of a climatic change on a land surface already seriously influenced by man.

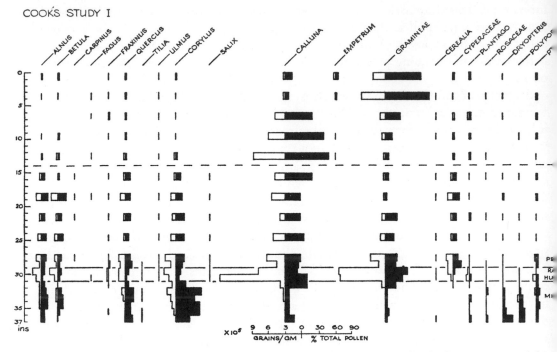

Fig. 20 Cook's Study. Pollen analysis through peat, raw humus and mineral soil of a Pennine Mesolithic site. Microliths occurred on the surface of the mineral soil.★

Even in areas where peat has never formed pollen analysis can give valuable information about ancient man's environment and his influence on it. Wherever a soil surface has been sealed it is possible that pollen will be preserved, particularly if the soil is acid. It is fortunate that from the Neolithic onwards the habit of constructing earthworks has brought about the preservation of many surfaces contemporary with the particular culture. In Holland Waterbolk[16] has drawn attention to the difference of environment in the Neolithic and Bronze Ages, with particular reference to the spread of heathland, basing his conclusions on the pollen content of surfaces buried beneath barrows. Similar work in this country has shown the gradual retreat of the forest and the differing types of land use practised at high and low altitudes. Thus cultivation was widespread in the lowlands, but at higher altitudes final deforestation came about through forest pasture.[3]

It is not always easy to interpret the analyses of such buried surfaces. There is usually a mixture of pollen of trees and shrubs with that from grasses and herbs. Bearing in mind that under a tree cover many species, even if able to survive, flower much less profusely, it is clear that these grasses and herbs must have been growing in full light. Yet the woody species were sufficiently close at hand to contribute to the pollen rain. The only feasible interpretation is one of clearings within a generally forested area. Through comparative

★ In Figs 20, 21 and 22 the histograms are double, the left-hand side representing the absolute pollen frequency in grains/gm and the right-hand side the percentages of total pollen plus fern spores.

analyses the extension of such clearings can sometimes be traced until the condition is reached where the landscape is no longer forested.

It was said earlier that the surface of a soil contains the highest pollen content, and it is sometimes obvious that the soils buried underneath earthworks show a truncated pollen profile; that is, they have been stripped. This in itself is a point of interest, but it seriously restricts the value of such an earthwork for pollen analysis. However, it may happen that such a mound is made up of recognizable turves, and Waterbolk has used such turves for pollen analysis when the soil surface is disturbed. At the same time there is no proof that the turves came from the immediate vicinity of the earthwork and in one case where a buried surface was also present I have found that they did not. Even where a mound is not obviously built of turves, a pollen profile through it can give interesting information about the structure. Thus it is sometimes found that barrows are constructed entirely of subsoil, since they contain little pollen except that which has demonstrably washed down from the new surface (Fig. 21). In other cases (Plate VIb; Fig. 22) the pollen content is high throughout, showing that they are built up of topsoil. Sometimes it can be shown that the mound is heterogeneous, and that some of the material did not come from the neighbourhood of the monument; likewise, it can also be shown that some, at any rate, of the material came from a surrounding ditch. Each case must be

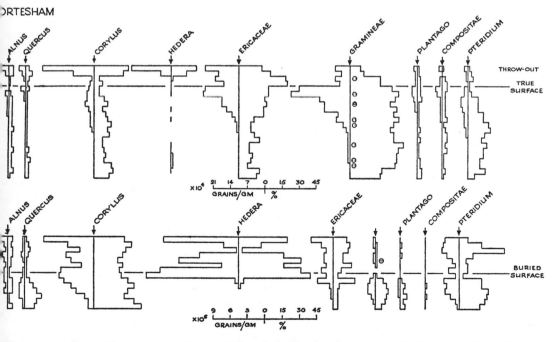

Fig. 21 Portesham. The upper set of curves shows the pollen distribution in and below the surface of a Bronze Age barrow. Pollen is only abundant near the surface, indicating that the mound itself was constructed of subsoil material. The lower set of curves shows the pollen spectra from the turf core down into the soil underlying the primary surface. The high proportion of ivy pollen is puzzling but may be due to the use of ivy for fodder. The barred circle indicates the presence of cereal pollen.

BICKLEY MOOR- BARROW
(COMPLETE SECTION)

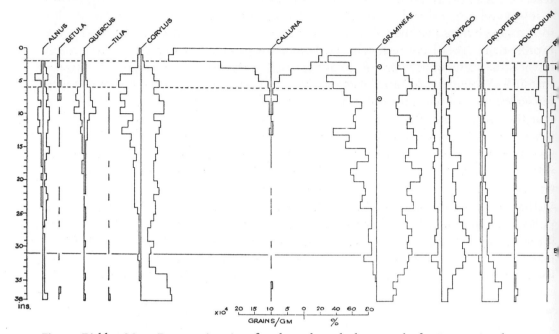

Fig. 22 Bickley Moor Barrow. A series of analyses through the mound of a Bronze Age barrow on heathland. There is abundant pollen throughout the mound, showing that it was built of topsoil. The present heathland surface contrasts with the agricultural condition in Bronze Age time, as indicated by the pollen analyses.

examined on its merits, but a complete profile through an earthwork, though laborious to analyse, can cast unexpected light on the mode of construction.

The applications of pollen analysis to archaeological material will doubtless extend even beyond the scope indicated here. We know that pollen can be found in various biologically inactive materials, and if these happen to be associated with human remains or artifacts they offer scope for investigation by this technique. It is often easier, however, to make an analysis than to interpret it.

It can be seen from what has been said that pollen analysis has already contributed greatly—and will continue to do so—to our knowledge of our distant ancestors and their way of life, but before closing this chapter it must be said that what has been discovered has recently led to some re-examination of the method itself. The different pollen zones of the Postglacial are characterized by the occurrence or abundance of certain pollen types which have been found to be critical; this applies particularly to the division into sub-zones. It has been generally assumed that because such differences were general over a wide area, they were climatically induced. Recently, however, several workers have questioned this, suggesting that man himself influenced some species more than others, and it so happens that the critical species are the ones most in question. Elm, for instance, was a tree particularly useful to primitive man, for cattle fodder and for making of bark bread. It is the species which best separates the Atlantic (zone VIIa) from the Sub-boreal (zone VIIb), being much less abundant in the latter. In Ireland, according to Mitchell,[11] elm declined at a later date than on the Continent or in the rest of the British Isles. Its disappearance therefore was not climatically determined. In the same way, Iversen[9] has shown that the decline of lime, another indicator species, was to be correlated with early agriculture rather than with time. Other important species similarly affected are ivy and mistletoe, which Troels-Smith[15] believes were used as fodder plants for stalled animals, especially in the winter, whilst birch, whose spread may indicate cooler conditions in the Sub-atlantic period, may also have been favoured by an increase in the practice of burning, after which it is a common colonizer.

It is impossible at present to say to what degree human influence has affected such species: no doubt it varied from place to place according to culture, climate and local ecology. We have seen that from earliest times man has had the power to influence his surroundings and it would be ecologically irrational to expect that his effects would not modify the floristic composition of the flora, particularly of the forest flora. Indeed, it is possible that his effects locally went beyond that; thus it is common to find from soil pollen profiles that mass movement of soil has taken place, which appears to be associated in many cases with early forest clearance. If such deforestation were general over a catchment area it is conceivable that flooding might increase, resulting in increased wetness of swampy land and so to increased peat growth in topogenous mires. Whether false recurrence surfaces have originated in this way I do not know, but we are only beginning to recognize how drastic were the effects early man had on his environment, in spite of the smallness of the populations. It is pollen analysis that is opening this field of knowledge to us, but we must not be surprised if some of our earlier beliefs and assumptions themselves come in for some re-examination.

REFERENCES

1 CLARK, J. G. D. 1954. *Excavations at Star Carr*, Cambridge
2 DIMBLEBY, G. W. 1961. *J. Soil Sci. 12*, 1–11
3 —— 1961. *Antiquity 35*, 123–8
4 FAEGRI, K. and IVERSEN, J. 1950. *An Introduction to Pollen Analysis*, Copenhagen
5 GODWIN, H. 1960. *Proc. Prehist. Soc. 26*, 1–36
6 —— WALKER, D. and WILLIS, E. H. 1957. *Proc. Roy. Soc. Ser. B. 147* (928), 352–66
7 HALLAM, J. S. 1960. *The Mesolithic of the Central Pennines* (M.A. Thesis, Liverpool University)
8 IVERSEN, J. 1949. *Danm. Geol. Unders. 4* (3), no. 6
9 —— 1958. *Veröff. Geobot. Inst. Rübel Zürich 33*, 137–44
10 JESSEN, K. 1934. *Irish Nat. J. 5*, 130–4
11 MITCHELL, G. F. 1956. *Proc. Roy. Irish Acad. 57B*, 185–251
12 PEARSALL, W. H. and PENNINGTON, W. 1947. *J. Ecol. 34*, 137–48
13 SCHÜTRUMPF, R. 1958. *Praeh. Zeits. 36*, 156–66
14 TROELS-SMITH, J. 1956. *Science 124*, 876–9
15 —— 1960. *Danm. Geol. Unders 4* (4), no. 4
16 WATERBOLK, H. T. 1954. *De Praehistorische Mens en zijn Milieu*, Groningen
17 WEST, R. G. and McBURNEY, C. B. M. 1955. *Proc. Prehist. Soc. 20*, 131–54

15 Wood and Charcoal in Archaeology

A. CECILIA WESTERN

PLANT REMAINS ARE VERY COMMONLY found on archaeological sites of all periods, and the most usual form in which they survive is as wood charcoal. On very dry or completely waterlogged sites, parts of plants, twigs and branches, nuts and seeds, pollen, and even leaves or flowers, may survive in a recognizable condition, but in normal circumstances vegetable matter decays by the action of bacteria in the soil and can only survive when completely carbonized. Wood burned in an inadequate supply of oxygen forms charcoal, consisting of carbon which does not decay in the soil, and these fragments may be found by archaeologists upon ancient hearth sites. Wooden posts, beams or planks used in the construction of defensive structures, huts or other buildings may also be carbonized if destroyed by fire in too little air. In wells, lakes, rivers and bogs, where the soil is completely waterlogged and airless, wood and other organic matter survive for thousands of years. Examples of this are the Roman writing tablet from Chew Stoke, Somerset,[1] trackways of Neolithic and Bronze Age date from Somerset peat-bogs,[2] the brushwood flooring at Star Carr, Yorkshire,[3] and the mass of brushwood from the lake at Thatcham, Berkshire,[4] both Mesolithic, dug-out canoes of oak and ash in the estuary of the Humber at North Ferriby[5] probably from the late Iron Age or Roman period, boat-shaped coffins at Loose Howe, Yorkshire,[6] medieval wooden spoons, knife-handles and a casket from York,[7] and the various remains of wooden structures and objects from the Swiss lake-villages,[8] of which some hundreds from the Neolithic to late Iron Age periods are known. Where the soil is completely dry, as in desert countries for example, wood can remain undecayed for thousands of years, and numerous wooden objects, coffins, furniture, figurines, combs, and so on, dating from 3000 BC onwards have been found in Egypt. Other examples of relatively dry preservation are the tomb chamber constructed of juniper or cedar logs inside a large Phrygian tumulus at Gordion, Anatolia,[9] dating from the eighth century BC and containing remains of ornate wooden furniture, and the large numbers of wooden domestic articles and pieces of furniture found in the Middle Bronze Age tombs at Jericho.[10] In these cases preservation appears to be due, not to lack of moisture, although the objects seem to be dry when found, but to circumstances not yet completely understood preventing the survival of the bacteria causing decay.

It is of interest to the archaeologist to know what kinds of trees and shrubs have been used by ancient peoples for firewood, for building, and for the making of objects required in daily life or religious ritual. Such information may throw light on climatic differences at distant periods of time, on local vegetation and whether a district was forested, or merely supported grassland or scrub. It may also show whether local woods only were used or if timber was imported from elsewhere for special purposes, and to what extent craftsmen had discovered and appreciated the qualities of different timbers for specific purposes. Wood and charcoal remains also provide very suitable material for radiocarbon dating.

The standard work on the whole subject of the flora of the past in Britain is *History of the British Flora* by H. Godwin (1956). There is unfortunately nothing comparable to it at present for the Mediterranean and Middle East region, although much work is now being done on plant remains from these areas. For the anatomy of wood and its determination *The Structure of Timber* by F. W. Jane (1956) should be consulted.

Most trees and shrubs can be distinguished by the structure of the wood. This statement does not generally apply to species, but on the whole it is true to say that one genus can be distinguished from another by wood anatomy. Apart from the tree ferns all the trees and shrubs of the world can be divided into two groups, the gymnosperms or softwoods, which are cone-bearing trees such as pine and cedar, and the angiosperms or hardwoods, such as oak and poplar. The latter group also includes the palms, but these have a different structure from either softwoods or hardwoods. Fig. 23 illustrates

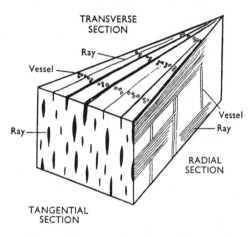

Fig. 23 Diagram showing sections and
main features of wood

diagrammatically the basic structure of a piece of the trunk of a tree, and the three sections cut by the wood-anatomist to show three-dimensionally the structure of each kind of cell. The transverse section is the most important in identifying hardwoods and is cut straight across the trunk or branch. It shows the rays like the spokes of a wheel, and growth rings as concentric circles normally defined in hardwoods from a temperate climate by a band of denser tissue at the end of one growing season and by an increase in the size or number of the vessels of the new season's growth. Woods grown outside the temperate zone may not show distinct growth rings, owing to lack of definite periods of growth and of rest, or may show more than one period of growth during the year. Therefore it is better not to use the less accurate term, annual rings.

Most types of cells in wood are aligned longitudinally so they are cut through their shorter axis by a transverse section, and from an examination of this section temperate hardwoods may be divided into ring-porous and diffuse-porous woods. In a ring-porous wood (Plate VIIa) the vessels formed early in the growing season are considerably larger than those formed later; there may be from one to four or even five rows of large early vessels, and normally the change from these to smaller late vessels is fairly sudden. The latter may be numerous or sparse, and solitary or in groups or strings variously arranged (Plate VIIb), according to the genus or species of the wood. In a diffuse-porous wood (Plate VIIc), on the other hand, there may or may not be a ring of vessels at the beginning of the season of growth, but there will be only a gradual reduction in the size of the vessels produced as the season advances. Here again the vessels may be numerous or sparse, solitary or in groups, clusters or strings, which may be arranged in a radial, obliquely radial or tangential direction. Ray cells are the only cells which have their longer axis at right angles to the direction of the trunk or branch, and grow in a radial or horizontal direction, so they appear in both ring-porous and diffuse-porous woods similar to the spokes of a wheel. They may be only one cell wide (uniseriate), two cells wide (biseriate), or any number up to about thirty or more cells wide (multiseriate), although in the majority of timbers with multiseriate rays they will be something between three and seven or eight cells in width. The rest of the wood consists of various other kinds of cells which are rather less important in the identification of the timber. All wood cells have one or more functions, conduction or storage of food or water, or mechanical support of the tree.

The other two sections used in identifying timbers are both longitudinal cuts, one along the radius of the trunk, the radial longitudinal, and the other at right angles to the radius, the tangential longitudinal section. The radial longitudinal section shows the vessels as vertical chains of cells or vertical channels where the ends of the cells have broken down in the heartwood and the vessel has become a long tube, and the rays as horizontal bands. The tangential longitudinal section also shows the vessels as vertical chains or channels, and the rays as vertical chains of cells (uniseriate rays) or boat-shaped groups of rounded or irregularly shaped cells if the rays are biseriate or multiseriate. The shape of the rays in tangential sections varies considerably and ray width is a valuable diagnostic feature.

The two longitudinal sections also show three other minute features useful in identification, vessel pitting, perforations, and spiral thickening. Each cell of which a vessel is composed, known as a vessel element, has secondary material laid down upon the inner sides of the walls, but this material is laid down unevenly, leaving thin areas, called pits, which usually coincide with pits of neighbouring vessel elements, and vary between genera in shape, size and arrangement. Details of pit shape are often invisible in charcoals, but the pits themselves are usually clearly in an 'opposite' arrangement where they are in vertical rows with one row of pits beside or opposite to those of the next row, or 'alternate' where the pits are fitted in alternately with those of the next row. The end walls of each element in heartwood may be broken down altogether, leaving merely a rim round the edge when the vessel becomes simply a tube, and this is known as simple perforation. Sometimes the end walls disappear in part, leaving a grid or ladder-like structure, scalariform perforation, or a network, reticulate perforation. Scalariform perforations may be further differentiated by whether there are few or many bars. The vessels of certain kinds of wood can also be distinguished by the presence of spiral thickening, an extra layer of material laid down spirally upon the cell wall.

Softwoods are examined in much the same way as hardwoods, except that in the transverse section almost all conifers are basically much alike, being composed of regularly arranged vertical tracheids which both provide support and conduct water (Plate VIId). There are no vessels, and the most noticeable feature on this section is the much denser appearance of the late wood, where the tracheid walls are much thicker than in that formed earlier, and the dense late wood may in some timbers amount to as much as half of the total growth of one season. The change from thin to thick walls may be sudden or gradual, and this again is a generic or specific feature. The rays of a coniferous wood are uniseriate, except in rare instances when a small part of a ray may be biseriate. Resin canals, which appear as very large cells, are found in a few coniferous genera, but not in the majority. They are infrequently and irregularly spaced so that a very small section may not include any. In the tangential longitudinal section the same genera may have irregularly spaced resin canals included in the centre of some of the rays, which then appear boat-shaped and biseriate above and below the resin canals, although the other rays in the section will be uniseriate and straight-sided. The radial longitudinal section is very important in softwoods for a very minute feature known as crossfield pitting. These pits occur in the walls of the ray cells adjacent to vertical tracheids. Pits may be of various shapes, simple or with round, oval or slit-like openings, and borders of various widths, and these variations are constant in a genus. They are only visible for study at fairly high magnifications (about × 120).

The quantity of charcoals found on many archaeological sites makes it imperative that rapid methods of preparation for identification should be employed, since a fragment of charcoal of an indeterminate wood, perhaps distorted by heat, may require some hours for its identification. Ideally every fragment large enough should be examined, but in practice there is usually insufficient time to be so thorough, and a preliminary sorting can be quickly made with a × 10 hand lens, grouping the fragments into kinds that appear to be alike. This magnification may, with experience, suffice to determine the British ring-porous woods, but is usually inadequate for more than a rough grouping into types of wood for the diffuse-porous species, into those with numerous vessels evenly dispersed, those with fewer vessels arranged in strings or clusters, those with some very broad and conspicuous rays, and so on. Oak, a ring-porous timber, is normally fairly easy to distinguish, and much time could be saved if specimens of it were picked out from the rest by the archaeologist before submitting the whole group to the wood-anatomist. A quick check would then probably be enough to confirm the oak determinations. The first sorting out is done almost entirely on the transverse section, because a × 10 hand lens is of relatively little use on the longitudinal sections of charcoals, which are particularly hard to see. A detailed examination has then to be made using a microscope, and good detail can be observed at magnifications of about 40–50 and 100–120. Magnification above 120 is of limited use, except for special details, because a charcoal section is seldom flat, although this depends upon the preparation of the specimen.

Charcoals can be prepared in two main ways. The simplest and quickest way, which is obviously preferable if it gives adequate results, is to make fresh breaks in the charcoal in the three planes already described, to give a transverse section and radial and tangential longitudinal sections. Charcoal normally breaks quite cleanly, though not always exactly in the desired plane, but any unevenness leads to difficulties at higher magnifications because the depth of focus decreases proportionately as the magnification increases and therefore throws out of focus any part of the section that is in a different plane from any other. The charcoal fragment is broken into at least three small pieces, each presenting a clean, newly-broken face in the transverse, radial or tangential plane, and they are mounted on small lumps of plasticine on a glass slide for examination in turn under the microscope. If this method does not reveal enough, or accurate enough, detail the charcoal fragments, already broken to show the required sections, can be impregnated in a synthetic resin such as Lakeside 70C, ground down with grades of carborundum, and mounted on a microscope slide by the same technique as is used for making sections of rocks and soil samples. This is a slow and laborious process, requiring a certain amount of apparatus, and is impracticable where large numbers of specimens are involved. The heat needed for impregnation sometimes causes cracking and warping, and it would be advantageous if the method could be improved by employing an impregnating medium applied cold, which could be sectioned when set instead of ground, but such a medium is not available at present.

A quicker and easier method of producing thin sections of charcoal would be of assistance where microphotography is necessary. A fresh break on a piece of charcoal does not remain clean and bright indefinitely. It becomes dusty and smudged after a while, and though it may be kept as a piece of evidence, if it is to be re-examined in after-years it will probably have to be broken again. It is therefore valuable to be able to record the section permanently by means of a microphotograph, but it has already been noted that charcoals very seldom break perfectly flat, and it is therefore difficult, especially at magnifications of 100 or more, to get a photograph which is in focus all over the field. This difficulty should not be experienced when dealing with thin sections, either cut or ground, and so the practical detail of recording evidence is simplified where thin sections of charcoal can be used.

One of the difficulties in identifying charcoals is that of lighting the specimen. Charcoal is always dense and black, and often has smooth, highly reflecting surfaces. It is therefore important that the light should fall on the surface at a fairly high oblique angle, which can be achieved by having an internally lit microscope, so arranged that the light passes down the microscope tube as a hollow cylinder, which is then reflected on to the point upon which the objective is focused. Other forms of top lighting can also be used very well, but they become less efficient at very high magnifications when the objective is almost touching the specimen. The best angle of light varies between one specimen and another, and the disadvantage of the internal vertical illuminator is that the angle cannot be altered.

Dry wood from desert sites can vary considerably in condition, from very hard and solid to brittle and powdery, and is often heavily impregnated with crystals of gypsum and other minerals. It is frequently found in the form of an object which cannot be broken to provide a sample, but if it is merely the remains of beams or unidentifiable fragments of furniture or other objects it can often be treated as charcoal and examined on a fresh break, or impregnated, ground and mounted on a slide. Dry wood of this kind will only break to give a flat section if the wood is considerably decayed, but yet retains its form, otherwise it will break unevenly on the transverse section, leaving a torn end which shows nothing, and in this state it will have to be treated as a piece of modern wood, by sectioning on a microtome. But this leads to further difficulties, since it cannot be cut dry without tearing the cell walls, and boiling the specimen in water or caustic soda, as modern wood is prepared, may cause it to collapse. The wooden furniture and objects found in the tombs at Jericho appeared to be very dry when the tombs were first opened, but within minutes of the air being admitted were covered with drops of moisture. The wood mainly retained its shape, though it was calculated that it had shrunk as much as 25% in a radial and tangential direction, and somewhat less in length, but it was completely 'denatured', being apparently composed of tiny particles, probably of lignin, which retained their relative positions until they were disturbed, and the whole resembled cocoa powder gone into lumps. It is not known why this wood survived at all in this condition, and it has been found extremely difficult to deal with. It can, to a certain extent, be impregnated with synthetic resins, but not without causing considerable deformity, and so far the best way of identifying many of the specimens appears to be by examination of a fresh break. It is thus clear that ancient wood preserved in dry, or apparently dry, conditions presents a number of problems which are not yet solved, and further experiment is needed in the hope of finding an impregnating medium which would preserve objects without altering their external appearance and yet could be easily sectioned, as we already have for the treatment of waterlogged wood.

Wet wood may come from lakes, swamps, bogs, wells, river-banks or estuaries, ancient forests submerged by the sea or shipwrecks, when further problems may be presented because of the presence of salt or other minerals. Large branches of oak from between high- and low-water marks in the Lyonesse surface at Clacton, Essex, dating from the Mesolithic period, were impossible to section with a razor because all the large vessels were lined with a deposit of pyrite. This was hard and tore the surrounding tissue when compressed by the action of cutting, although specimens of diffuse-porous woods (maple, etc.) from the same conditions were easily sectioned by hand while still wet. It is most important that excavated wood should be kept in the same state of humidity that it was in before excavation. Wood from under the sea can therefore be kept immersed in changes of fresh water until examination, thus helping to reduce its salinity.

Impregnation of wet wood to prevent deformation and to preserve it in a condition fit for handling can be carried out by immersing it over a period in a water-miscible synthetic wax, polyethylene glycol. When thoroughly impregnated the specimens are removed from the wax bath, drained, when the wax hardens, and the surplus is removed by gentle wiping with a cloth damped in cold water. The wood then has the appearance of damp wood newly excavated, but the main advantage for the wood-anatomist is that it is soft enough for sections to be cut from it in the hand with a razor, and although these are apt to curl, as is frequently the trouble with tissues sectioned in wax, they uncurl rapidly in water, and can be floated off on to a slide for thorough examination. Unfortunately this method has, so far, been unsuccessful for dry wood, but wood excavated damp, but not thoroughly wet, can be kept damp and usually contains enough water to take up the wax without further wetting.

The specimens or sections being set up, their structure can be studied three-dimensionally, and grouped and identified by means of suitable keys. These are either dichotomous, when one of two alternative features is selected which leads on to another pair of alternatives, gradually eliminating all but the correct genus, or a punched card or table key. The advantage of the latter keys is that for material in poor condition features can be picked out in any order and there is less risk of being unable to determine an identity because a feature in the middle of the series is invisible. Finally, the identity being reduced to a few possibles, the specimen is compared with sections, and if necessary charcoal specimens, of known woods. A good representative collection of named modern specimens is thus a vital tool in the work of identifying ancient wood and charcoal.

In common with some other specialist studies of which archaeologists are making increasing use, the identification of timbers is mainly valuable as an aid to interpretation in conjunction with all the other evidence. First and foremost, this consists of the archaeological evidence of the site, the plan and the stratification, combined usually with that from parallel or archaeologically associated sites, and also the pottery and small finds of all kinds. Of the more specialized studies of material from an excavation only a few need be mentioned. Pollen analysis can, in some circumstances, give a more accurate environmental picture than some other studies, since it indicates the presence of certain plants in the area, which may reveal climatic and other factors, although it must be remembered that many plants are pollinated by insects and not by wind, which leads to under-representation of the former. Furthermore, pollen is often carried very long distances by wind, so the presence of a kind of pollen in a sample may not necessarily mean the presence of that plant in the immediate vicinity. However, the pollen itself has not been interfered with by man, although man may have had some influence on the pollen represented by his activities in clearing forest or scrub for settlements and cultivation. A study of animal bones and of shells also contributes to the environmental evidence.

Similarly, timber for structures, tools and weapons was probably selected for its purpose, to some extent at least, because of certain qualities, as well as for ease in felling and working with the tools available. Builders or craftsmen probably travelled some distance to find the timbers they required for their houses or their tools, and would certainly have taken trouble to make the hafts and shafts of their weapons of the best material available. Firewood is more likely to have been supplied from near at hand, since in few areas of north-western Europe, at least, except in very cold areas or periods, can there have been a great shortage of fuel until a comparatively late date. In desert conditions, of course, it must have been necessary to fetch firewood from a distance, as Arab women do today, going as much as ten miles from their homes to collect huge bundles of scrub and thorn. The fuel would also have been augmented by the waste material from timber collected for other purposes, and also probably by broken and discarded domestic objects.

Sometimes the wood from which an object is made is found to be an alien, that is, a species which either does not at present grow anywhere near the area concerned, or, it may be, never could possibly have grown anywhere near it because of what is already known of soil conditions, climate or altitude. In such case great caution is needed. It may be that the object as such was imported from elsewhere, either in course of trade or as a personal possession by a migrant or traveller, or it may indicate trade in timber in bulk, such as is known from literary evidence to have taken place from Syria to Egypt. But another factor to be taken into account is that ancient wood, and particularly charcoal, is often very difficult to identify with certainty. A determination of this kind may need to be supported by other evidence, perhaps of other macroscopic plant remains, of objects such as pottery, weapons or jewellery which can be paralleled with objects in the area where the suspected timber is known to grow or to have grown, or of written evidence of trade between the two places, as already stated. The horse chestnut, *Aesculus hippocastanum*, is a case in point. For various reasons this species is believed to be an introduction to this country, probably as late as the sixteenth century, and it is certainly native to the Balkans, but a number of identifications of this tree have been made, dating between the Neolithic and Romano-British periods, and it is interesting to note that they are nearly all of specimens of charcoal. These determinations have not upset the established belief, because *Aesculus* may easily be confused with *Populus* and *Salix*, unless the specimen is so good that it is possible to see very minute features, and this is frequently not the case. Thus the specimens may have been wrongly identified, or may possibly be intrusive. Points like these have to be borne in mind when endeavouring to interpret the meaning of a list of timbers represented among the wood and charcoal fragments from a site.

Present knowledge of the vegetation of Britain, Ireland and Scandinavia at different periods is fairly extensive, a large amount of work having been done on pollen and macroscopic plant remains from bogs, and therefore the identification of wood from sites in these areas contributes chiefly material to fill in a picture of which the main outlines and considerable details are already known. But it may be that evidence will be found for certain trees having returned to these islands, or having become widespread, earlier than is at present thought. The discovery of beech, *Fagus sylvatica*, in South Wales in the Iron Age proves an earlier and wider distribution for this tree than had been believed previously. The flora of the Mediterranean basin and the Middle East in the past is not so well known, although a good deal of work has been done on modern floras of the countries concerned, particularly since the Second World War. This problem is complicated by the facts of millennia of civilized life, constant movements of peoples and trade from early times, with consequent introductions of new plants and destruction of indigenous floras. Trees and plants valued for their timber, fruits or other products have probably been transported from one area to another by man, so that it is difficult in many cases to prove whether a plant is spontaneous or naturalized so long ago as to have escaped from cultivation and appear to be native. Some plants have certainly been greatly altered by selection and cultivation, and possibly grafting also, and it may conceivably be possible in the future, from investigation of grafted and natural samples, to discover when and where this practice began. These problems require much further study, including that from the linguistic angle, since some guidance can be obtained from the fact of an ancient language having names for certain plants.

Much more information of value might be discovered from the identification of timbers used for known purposes, for structures, for handles of tools and weapons, for domestic equipment, and so on, and this requires co-operation between excavator and wood-anatomist. The latter usually receives boxes or bags of samples marked with some such legend as 'PK 47/109' or 'Mer 15a NW Black Fill', which is meaningless to anyone not knowing the site or method of excavation, and this is where help can be given to the wood-anatomist by the excavator, to the advantage of both. If the specialist can be given some idea of what is expected, or hoped for, from the identification of the various samples submitted—'This may be a sleeper beam from a dwelling'; 'These were found associated with three axe-heads: could they be the remains of axe-handles?' —he is more likely to be able to make useful comments on his findings. It is his business to give any environmental and botanical information he can in his report, and to interpret his identifications in the light of such information. All this must then be interpreted and weighed by the archaeologist with all his other archaeological and environmental evidence, if specialist studies of various groups of material such as wood and charcoal are to play their full part in building up our knowledge of ancient times and peoples.

REFERENCES

 1 TURNER, E. G. 1956. *J. Rom. Studies 46*, 115
 2 GODWIN, H. 1960. *Proc. Prehist. Soc. 26*, 1
 3 CLARK, J. G. D. 1950. *Ibid. 16*, 109–13
 4 Unpublished
 5 WRIGHT, E. V. and WRIGHT, C. W. 1947. *Ibid. 13*, 114
 6 WARD, H. and ELGEE, F. 1940. *Ibid. 6*, 90–95
 7 WATERMAN, D. M. 1959. *Arch. 97*, 85–87
 8 KELLER, F. 1866. *Lake Dwellings of Switzerland*, London
 9 YOUNG, R. 1958. *Am. J. Arch. 62*, 148–50
10 KENYON, K. M. 1960. *Excavations at Jericho*, London, vol. 1

16 The Condition of 'Wood' from Archaeological Sites

J. F. LEVY

WOOD CAN SURVIVE the centuries in a great variety of conditions and may be found hard or soft, brittle or tough, heavily impregnated with other materials or thoroughly leached. It often exhibits some facet of degrade by biological or chemical agencies with which is associated a very high moisture content. On the other hand, when incomplete combustion has occurred and the wood has been converted to charcoal, this charcoal will persist with little or no visible alteration unless it has been subject to very wet situations and distorted by pressure.

After the bombing of Rotterdam in 1940, the timber piles on which a large part of the city had been built attracted the attention of Varossieau[1] who made an anatomical investigation of the wood. His observations formed part of the evidence that certain fungi will decay wood by growing through the middle layer of the secondary cell wall and cause a degrade of wood termed 'soft rot'.[2-4]

There are many instances in which one suspects that biological or chemical degrade, or both, have taken place, yet no conclusive evidence has remained. The problem resolves itself into examining site conditions, observing the state of the wood before and after its removal from the place of burial, and studying the nature of the material in which it is buried. For example, under the Jewel Tower, Westminster, elm piles some six feet in length and pointed at one end formed the foundation for the fourteenth-century building. During repair work it was noted that some of the piling was in a decayed condition. The subsoil in one area consisted of a disturbed upper layer about a foot deep, fine green-grey clay some four feet thick, and a layer of sandy gravel beneath. Piles driven through the clay and projecting some six inches to a foot into the sandy gravel showed interesting differences in the process of decay. The tip in the sand was little more than a stain and had apparently been thoroughly decayed by wood-rotting fungi. The upper region in the disturbed topsoil layer and much of the heartwood lower down was also decayed. But the outer portion (about 1-2 in. in from the surface) of the middle section, in the anaerobic clay, was relatively sound and no traces of fungi could be detected. Thus there appear to be soil conditions under which the decaying organisms will not flourish whereas at quite close quarters decay is active.

In Dover,[5] oak piling from Roman harbour works was again found in two distinct sets. The timber as a whole had retained its shape, and presumably size, quite well and tool marks were still sharp. One set of piles had been considerably softened so that a finger could be pushed into the surface with little difficulty, and when cut up the wood broke cleanly across the grain, showing that the strength properties were greatly reduced. Other piles very closely associated with these were, however, found in a much tougher condition. The surface in some cases was softened, but the wood was extremely difficult to break across the grain and in part at least it retained a very considerable tensile strength. The chemical analysis[6] showed that the ash content in both sets was abnormally high; in addition the tougher wood in fact came from slow-grown timber which (in its natural state) one would have expected to be weaker. The reasons for such differences would be important to discover.

The most common feature of buried wood found in a well-preserved, recognizably 'woody' state is its so-called 'waterlogged' condition. This is distinct from the use of the term for wood that has become saturated with water and sunk. Softwood logs recently raised from Norwegian rivers after lying submerged for about a century show little change apart from an increased permeability, although the effect of the presumably low temperature in this case is difficult to assess. The outstanding characteristics of ancient 'waterlogged' wood, on the other hand, appear to be a very high moisture content (up to 700% on the oven-dry weight) allied to an extremely high shrinkage on drying, particularly in the tangential direction, and when dry the distorted timber is extremely hard and tough. Some botanical and chemical data are available,[7] and recent investigations[8,9] have been concerned with the mechanics of conserving woody material found in this condition. One is left with the thought that micro-organisms, including, perhaps, bacteria, may be responsible; or that continued subjection to the chemical effects of anaerobic waterlogged media might be sufficient—the results in both cases being similar: hydrolytic breakdown of the cell wall material.[10] Any attempt at isolating the micro-organisms present in such material is likely to be some centuries too late to find the original causal organisms still active. Nevertheless, accurate field observations could make an immediate contribution, especially where backed by anatomical and chemical laboratory work.

Accurate observations of the state of the wood and the conditions of burial could be important to fundamental research into the nature of the plant cell wall and the physiology of decay by micro-organisms. Analysis of a particular tree species on similar site conditions at progressive stages of degrade might well yield information as to the chemical and physical nature of the cell wall, which is not readily seen in the undegraded state. This in turn could yield information as to the mode of action of the micro-organism causing the degrade.

From the archaeological point of view, such studies might make it possible to identify not only the recognizable wood remains, but also the various 'fibrous residues' and stains in so-called post holes, sleeper trenches and coffins where little or no botanical evidence remains. Even if the identification went no further than 'wood', it could, in many cases, be of considerable importance to be sure of this fact. At the same time it might be possible to interpret conditions under which the degrade occurred and this might well have an important bearing on other archaeological evidence.

REFERENCES

1 VAROSSIEAU, W. W. 1949. *Houte in alle Tijden* 1 (5), 331–87
2 BAILEY, I. W. and VESTAL, M. R. 1937. *J. Arnold Arboretumn* 18, 193–205
3 BARGHOORN, E. S. and LINDER, D. H. 1944. *Farlowia* 1, 395–467

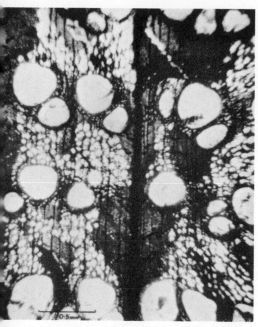

(a) Transverse section of oak (*Quercus* sp.), showing early and later vessels, and one broad and many narrow rays. Ring-porous.

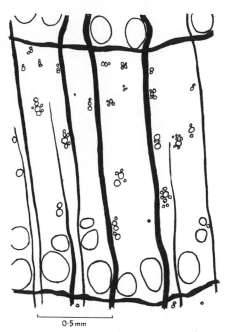

(b) Transverse section of ash (*Fraxinus excelsior*), showing 1–3 rows of large early vessels, later vessels in small clusters, and uniseriate and multiseriate rays. Ring-porous.

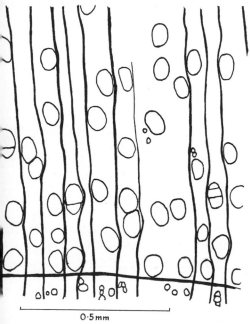

(c) Diagram of transverse section of willow (*Salix caprea*), showing scattered vessels, sometimes grouped, and uniseriate rays. Diffuse-porous.

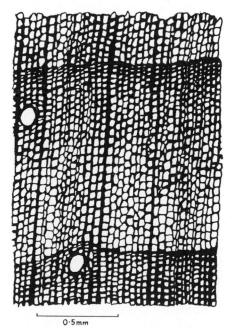

(d) Diagram of transverse section of pine (*Pinus cembra*) showing tracheid, rays, and resin-canals.

(see page 150) PLATE VII

a

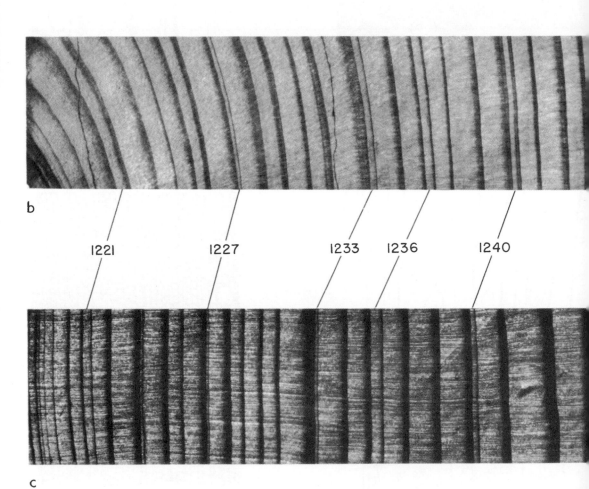

b

1221   1227   1233 1236   1240

c

Cross-dating and types of tree-ring series: (a) a complacent record lacking ring character; (b) and (c) sensitive tree-ring series which cross-date; (b) and (c) are from the thirteenth-century ruin Betatakin in northern Arizona.

PLATE VIII (see page 162)

4 SAVORY, J. G. 1954. *Ann. appl. Biol. 41*, 336–47
5 RAHTZ, P. A. 1958. *Archaeologia Cantiana 72*, 111–37
6 FARMER, R. H. 1955. Private communication from Forest Products Research Laboratory, D.S.I.R.
7 BARGHOORN, E. S. 1949. *Papers of R. S. Peabody Found. for Archaeol. 4*, 49–83
8 ORGAN, R. M. 1954. *Studies in Conservation 4*, 96–105
9 ROSENQUIST, A. M. 1954. *Ibid.* 13–21 and 62–72
10 BARGHOORN, E. S. 1949. *Harvard Bot. Mus. Leaflets 14*, 1–20

17 Dendrochronology

BRYANT BANNISTER

THE EMERGENCE OF DENDROCHRONOLOGY as a significant archaeological dating tool can be precisely determined in both time and space—June 22, 1929; Showlow, Arizona. To be sure, speculation on the nature of tree-rings can be traced back to the third-century BC writings of Theophrastus, and certainly the detailed observations of a long succession of botanists and naturalists have been instrumental in our understanding of growth rings and their implications.[85] But it remained for the astronomer A. E. Douglass, the recognized pioneer of the science of dendrochronology, to apply tree-ring phenomena in a systematic attack on the chronological problems of archaeology.

Douglass began his examination of tree-rings in 1901 while searching for a tool to be used in the study of sunspot cycles. He first became aware of the potential archaeological applications of his work some two decades later, at which time he commenced a ten-year investigation into the dating of the spectacular American Indian ruin Pueblo Bonito. This project stands out as a model of inter-disciplinary co-operation and culminated in the establishment of construction dates not only for Pueblo Bonito but for more than forty additional major ruins in the American South-West as well.[13,60] The dramatic conclusion to this historically important project took place on a summer night in the small town of Showlow where Douglass, after carefully studying the day's collection of tree-ring specimens excavated from a nearby ruin, realized that he had finally spanned the gap between a centuries-long floating chronology, made up from ancient construction beams, and a dated tree-ring record extending backwards from modern times.[14] The gap was bridged, scores of prehistoric ruins were immediately assigned absolute dates, and archaeological tree-ring dating became of age!

BASIC PRINCIPLES

The term dendrochronology refers both to the method of employing tree-rings as a measurement of time, wherein the principal application is to archaeology, and to the process of inferring past environmental conditions that existed when the rings were being formed, mainly applicable to climatology. While some would prefer to restrict the appellation to the former usage, it matters little to the archaeologist, for he stands to benefit from all aspects of tree-ring research.

The basic principles involved in dendrochronology are deceptively simple. Tree-rings, which are so obvious on the cross-sections of most trees, can be more accurately described as the transverse sections of successive layers of xylem growth—each layer having been formed by the tree in response to some environmental fluctuation, normally of an annual nature in seasonal climates. In conifers, the annual ring is composed of two parts: an inner band of large light-coloured cells that merges, sometimes very gradually, with an outer band of thicker-walled, dark-coloured cells which in turn usually terminates abruptly, leaving a sharply defined outer edge. A number of angiosperms and shrubs have annual rings of somewhat similar gross characteristics, but tree-rings of considerable complexity are also known to exist.[44]

In those regions where dendrochronology has successfully been applied to archaeological specimens there are basically two types of tree-ring series commonly found (Plate VIII); or perhaps the two types should best be termed end points along a continuum of variation. In the first type, the rings are of relatively uniform thickness, as measured along a radius, and often exhibit a slow algebraic decrease in width as the tree approaches maturity. Such ring series lacking in distinctive character are termed complacent (Plate VIIIa). In contrast, the second type of ring record is distinguished by variability of individual ring widths, even though there may be a gradual decrease in the relative size of rings as the tree grows older. These series (Plate VIIIb, c) are called sensitive and are far more suitable for dendrochronological purposes.

Under certain conditions, contemporaneous ring records formed by sensitive trees will show remarkable similarity when compared with each other. The patterns of narrow and broad rings in one tree will closely match the patterns found in other trees (Plate VIIIb, c). Cross-dating, which is based on this phenomenon, can be defined as the identification in different trees of the same ring patterns, each series of rings representing exactly the same period of years. It is cross-dating that stands as the fundamental principle underlying tree-ring dating, and it must be present before either absolute or relative dates can be derived.

The cross-dating principle gives rise to the two most important facets of tree-ring research. First, in regions that contain modern cross-datable trees which can serve as controls, proper application will permit the assignment of calendar years to each of the individual rings within a specimen. It is this feature, of course, which has been responsible for archaeological tree-ring dating in the absolute sense. Even where modern tree-ring controls are not available, relative dating is still possible. Second, the very fact that ring patterns which lead to cross-dating are present in trees at all implies the existence of some environmental factor, or complex of factors, which not only fluctuates itself on a year-to-year basis (when dealing with annual rings) but also has the capacity to induce similar and simultaneous growth responses on the part of trees over a given geographical area. The isolation and understanding of such controlling factors has been of interest to tree physiologists and dendrochronologists alike.

It should not be assumed that the conditions responsible for cross-dating are the same wherever the phenomenon occurs. For example, in the semi-arid regions of south-western United States, soil moisture is apparently the dominant controlling factor, whereas in Alaska and other northern latitudes temperature seems to be the chief determinant. Nor should it be assumed that cross-dating is universally present, for, in fact, only certain trees in an area cross-date with each other, only certain areas in the world contain cross-datable trees, and cross-dating between separated areas is usually non-existent.

A considerable body of literature pertaining to the basic principles of tree-growth and its dendrochronological implications has been produced. In the American South-West a few of the more important works are by Douglass;[11,12,15] Ferguson;[24] Glock;[41] Glock,

Studhalter, and Agerter;[44] and Schulman,[80] Bell,[3] Hawley,[47] Schulman,[77] and Willey[96] have treated the Mississippi drainage, while Weakly[91,92] and Will[94,95] have carried out investigations in the Great Plains of the United States. Lyon[57-59] has reported on New England tree-ring studies. The basic contribution to Alaskan dendrochronology is by Giddings,[28] although additional pertinent studies have been made by Giddings[30,31,33,35] and Oswalt.[68,69] Other treated regions in the Western Hemisphere include parts of Canada, western America, Mexico, and South America.[80]

Scandinavian scientists have produced a number of excellent studies. Some English-language summaries are Eklund[23] for Sweden, Høeg[48] for Norway, Holmsgaard[49] for Denmark, and Mikola[62] for Finland. Hustich[52,53] has dealt with trees throughout the northern latitudes. The works of Huber and Jazewitsch[50] of the Forestry-Botany Institutes of Tharandt and Munich are outstanding. Dobbs[9, 10] and Schove[72, 73] have been active in reporting tree-ring studies carried out both in the British Isles and in Scandinavia, and Messeri[61] has published on tree growth in Italy. To date little work has been done in Africa, although a few investigations have been made in Asia—Rudakov[70] in Russia, Gindel[37] in Israel, DeBoer[8] in Java, and Kohara[55] and Nishioka[63] in Japan. Bell and Bell[5] have provided a rather pessimistic view of the situation in New Zealand.

It should be emphasized that the above citations by no means constitute a complete list of tree-ring publications, although they are reasonably representative of the basic work being done in the designated regions. For the most part, these citations have been chosen because they deal with fundamentals and reflect the potentialities of tree-ring dating rather than merely recording archaeological results. Wherever possible, the more recent publications with bibliographies have been given so that the reader may investigate further if he wishes. A much more comprehensive review of tree-growth studies is presented by Glock,[42] with a highly critical assessment of dendrochronology in general.

REQUISITES OF ARCHAEOLOGICAL TREE-RING DATING

Before the tree-ring method can be applied to archaeological problems in any given region, there are several favouring circumstances that must exist and, unfortunately, these necessary conditions are by no means universal in nature. The first requirement is an ample supply of wood or charcoal tree-ring specimens in association with the archaeological environment to be dated. Not only must the prehistoric inhabitants of an area have used wood extensively, preferably for construction purposes, but the wood must be preserved so that both cellular and ring structure remain evident. Large areas of the world are immediately ruled out because either wood was not used extensively in ancient times or what was used has long since rotted away. On the other hand, certain regions are particularly favourable: the American South-West, northern Mexico, some arctic areas, Turkey, Egypt and various places in Europe and Asia where local conditions have ensured preservation. Charcoal, one of the most indestructible of materials as long as it remains uncrushed, is an excellent source of tree-ring records but its presence in quantity in archaeological sites is in part related to the cultural practices of the original inhabitants.[2]

The second major requirement for the establishment of tree-ring dating is that the specimens cross-date. As indicated previously, for cross-dating to occur the samples must contain clearly defined rings that show fluctuations of thickness throughout the series. The rings whether annual or multiple must be the result of a periodicity in growth factors which induces similar responses (measurable in variable ring widths) in trees within the region, and the specimens must contain enough rings to permit positive identification of like patterns in different pieces.

As long as tree-ring samples are available from a particular site and the specimens cross-date with each other, relative dates are possible. The establishment of absolute dates, however, is another matter. Even though contemporaneous relative dated specimens may be merged into a composite whole, forming a floating chronology, it is still necessary to build a known tree-ring chronology back far enough to overlap and cross-date with the unknown segment in order to achieve absolute dating. This is known as chronology building (Fig. 24) and although simple in concept usually requires considerable time and effort to accomplish. Starting with modern samples of known date, successively older and older specimens are cross-dated and incorporated into the matrix until a long-range tree-ring chronology is established. Depending on the materials available, this procedure may take many years to perform if, indeed, it is possible at all. Once a precisely dated master chronology is produced, however, the ring patterns contained in samples of unknown age may be cross-dated with the master chronology and assigned absolute dates.

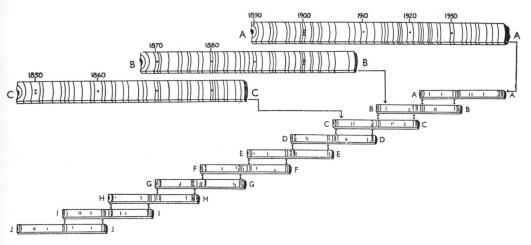

Fig. 24 Chronology building. A: radial sample from a living tree cut after the 1939 growing season; B–J: specimens taken from old houses and successively older ruins. The ring patterns match and overlap back into prehistoric times. After Stallings.[84]

COLLECTION AND ANALYSIS

The collection of tree-ring specimens is guided by the basic aim of preserving as complete a record of the ring series as possible. A full cross-section is preferable to a core or radial sample, although it often is not practical to obtain a complete transect when dealing with living trees or archaeological structures which are to be preserved. Various types of coring tools have been developed: among others, the Swedish increment borer which is designed for sampling living softwood trees, the brace-driven tubular borer with circular saw teeth which has proved effective on prehistoric beams,[12] and the power-driven long-core extractor developed by Bowers.[6] New type tools for sampling museum pieces and archaeological timbers are currently being tested.

Specialized techniques for collecting wood and charcoal from excavations are so closely related to particular field conditions that it is impracticable to describe them all. In general, however, special care must be exercised to prevent damage or loss of outside rings. Charcoal and certain types of wood usually need immediate application of some preservative. A solution of gasoline saturated with paraffin wax is both economical and effective but other preservatives may be equally useful. The standard archaeological procedures for handling any delicate and valuable artifact are called for, and detailed notes on provenience, physiology, and ecology of the collection area are vital.[41,2]

Before actual study can begin, specimens must be surfaced so that cellular structure is visible and the ring series may be examined with clarity. The importance of this step cannot be overemphasized since adequate surfaces are absolutely essential in the process of achieving precise dates. Charcoal and soft or rotten wood can readily be prepared with a razor blade, a technique that is rapid but fairly difficult to master. Excellent surfaces on small sections can be obtained with a sliding microtome, but for large cross-sections sanding is highly recommended. Although small hand-held belt sanders utilizing a series of graded sandpapers will do a presentable job, there now exist specially designed sanding devices which are capable of producing full transect surfaces that satisfy the most stringent requirements. One such device, the Bowers-Vossbrinck sanding machine, employs the 'abrasion along a line' principle and uses metal cutting belts 12 inches wide.

Noteworthy discussions of collection and sample preparation practices are to be found in Douglass,[16-20] Glock,[41] Hall,[45] Scantling,[71] and Smiley.[81]

In the analysis of tree-ring specimens for archaeological dating purposes the first objective is the establishment of cross-dating between samples. When absolute dating is involved, the process is carried one step further and cross-dated specimens are matched against a master chronology which itself is a product of previously cross-dated pieces. In its simplest form, therefore, the problem is reduced to recording individual ring series and comparing them with other series. Consequently, the initial requirement is the positive identification of each of the visible growth increments within the sample. Rings that are present on only a portion of their circumference, so-called 'false rings' or 'lines' which do not represent a full season's growth, microscopic rings—these and other anomalies must be recognized before cross-dating can be attempted. The subject of ring 'reading' is treated in detail by Douglass,[20] Glock,[41] and Schulman.[80] Additional problems such as completely absent rings (see references above) can only be solved through the process of cross-dating itself.

All of the different systems of tree-ring dating, and there are several currently being used throughout the world, are nothing more than alternate ways of representing growth patterns and establishing cross-dating. For the most part, the various techniques have been adopted because they are particularly suited to certain local conditions of tree growth and certain types of ring chronologies. Since the best known of these, the Douglass System, is basic to most subsequently developed methods, it alone will be discussed here. Further explanations of this system are to be found in Bannister and Smiley,[2] Douglass,[11,12,20] Glock,[40,41] Schulman,[80] and Stallings.[84]

The Douglass method, which has been most successfully applied in the American South-West, is primarily useful where highly sensitive trees constitute the main source of datable specimens and the amount of correlation between ring records is often of a very high degree. The technique emphasizes, first, those rings which deviate from the normal—noticeably narrow or broad rings—and, second, the internal relationship of these rings within the overall series. Comparison of one ring record with another is accomplished in three ways: the memory method, skeleton plots, and precisely measured ring widths. The memory method simply entails memorizing all of the ring patterns encountered. It is, of course, a very rapid and convenient way of comparing specimens but it does require a thorough knowledge of the local chronology. For the experienced investigator, however, the memory method supplemented by comparative wood samples is perhaps the most satisfactory way of verifying cross-dating.

When one is working with large quantities of materials or in unfamiliar areas, either temporally or geographically, the skeleton plot has proved to be an exceedingly useful tool.[41,84] Basically a specialized graph depicting the relative widths of diagnostic rings (Fig. 25), the skeleton plot has the advantage of being free of any age trend within the specimen since the size of each ring is judged in relation to neighbouring rings (compare Fig. 25A, B, with Fig. 26A, B). Thus skeleton plots of a standard scale can rapidly be compared with each other and, if cross-dating is found to exist, the plots may be merged to provide an easily understood representation of the site or local chronology (Fig. 25A). The skeleton plot method is considered only a preliminary step in the dating process, however, and it must be used with caution since it records only the most striking characteristics of a ring series rather than the totality of traits upon which dating must depend.

Various measuring devices designed to accurately record widths along a radius have been developed. The Craighead-Douglass measuring instrument,[19] the De Rouen Dendro-Chronograph, the Addo-X designed by the Swedish Forestry Research Institute,[22] and the German machine developed at the Forestry-Botany Institute in Munich[54] are but a few. After the measured values are translated into plotted graphs (Fig. 26) both visual and statistical comparisons can readily be made. Since absolute values are involved, however, standardization or correction for the effect of age is frequently necessary before the material can be used for the study of the relation between climate and growth. Age trend line introduction and standardization processes employed in the Douglass System are discussed by Schulman[79,80] and by Smiley, Stubbs and Bannister.[83] After standardization, the plotted curves express yearly values as percentage departures from average growth. Fritts (personal communication) is currently engaged in adapting standardizing processes to electronic computor techniques.

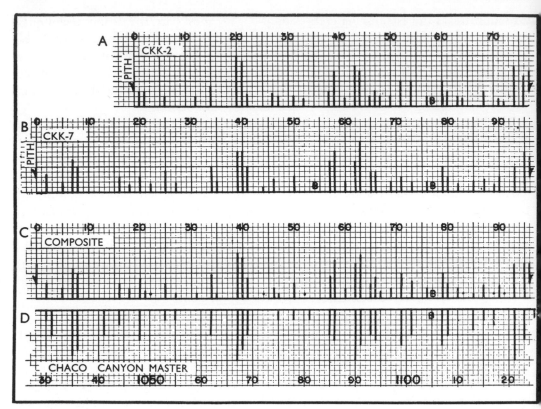

Fig. 25 Comparison of skeleton plots. A and B: skeleton plots of the ring series in two beams from the prehistoric ruin Kin Kletso, Chaco Canyon, New Mexico; C: composite plot of A and B; D: regional master chronology for Chaco Canyon. Matching of C with D establishes tentative dating of specimens (see text). The length of each vertical bar on the graph is inversely proportional to the relative width of the ring; average width rings are not recorded, and extra large rings are indicated by the letter B.

Another tree-ring dating method once used in south-western United States was developed by Gladwin.[38],[39] This system depended upon a statistically constructed variation of the skeleton plot which recorded all rings. In Alaska, Turkey, Egypt, and New Zealand the Douglass System has been employed. In the wetter climates of Europe and in Scandinavia, the lack of highly sensitive trees with strong cross-dating tendencies precludes the use of the Douglass System. Various methods of statistical analysis involving coefficients of parallel and opposite variation, logarithmic plotting, special mechanical devices for automatically comparing series, and other innovations have been devised.

No matter what system of tree-ring dating is used, the validity of the results depends upon the preciseness with which cross-dating can be accomplished. Absolute identification can be secured by means of the forecast-and-verification method, wherein additional ring characteristics are sought and compared after test correlations have been made. When a sufficient number of positive verifications are found, the probability of chance correlations becomes increasingly remote and accurate cross-dating is assured.

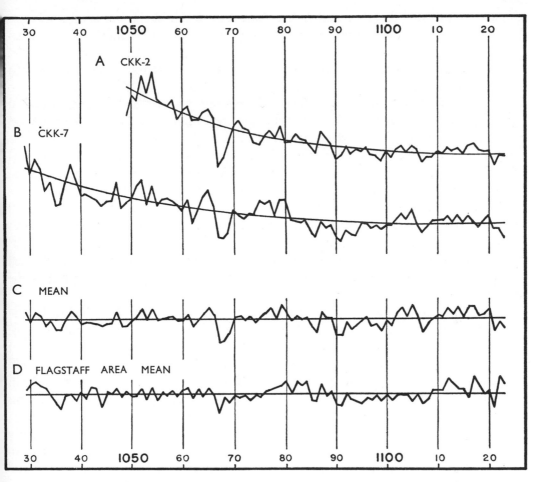

Fig. 26 Comparison of measured curves. A and B: measured ring widths (with standardizing lines superimposed) of the ring series in two beams from the prehistoric ruin Kin Kletso, Chaco Canyon, New Mexico; C: standardized mean of A and B with ring widths expressed as percentage departures from average growth; D: Flagstaff Area Mean in standardized form. Comparison of C with D leads to absolute dating of specimens (see text).

THE INTERPRETATION OF TREE-RING DATES

Once a tree-ring date has been established, its archaeological significance can vary greatly. After all, a tree-ring date can only be applied with authority to the specimen itself, and it may or may not be directly related to the archaeological context from which the specimen originated. There is a basic problem, consequently, of the time relationship that exists between the date of the specimen and the archaeological manifestation being dated.

Where the tree-ring dating method has been used extensively, as in Alaska and in the south-western United States, refined techniques of date interpretation have become increasingly necessary. The scheme that follows, therefore, is for the most part based on archaeological conditions as found in the American South-West, but because of their general nature the implied rules of interpretation should have relevancy wherever tree-ring dating is feasible.

The usual errors of interpretation that confront the archaeologist can be classified into four general categories:

Type 1. The association between the dated tree-ring specimen and the archaeological manifestation being dated is direct, but the specimen itself came from a tree that died or was cut prior to its use in the situation in question.

Type 2. The association between the dated tree-ring specimen and the archaeological manifestation being dated is not direct, the specimen having been used prior to the feature being dated.

Type 3. The association between the dated tree-ring specimen and the archaeological manifestation being dated is direct, but the specimen itself represents a later incorporation into an already existing feature.

Type 4. The association between the dated tree-ring specimen and the archaeological manifestation being dated is not direct, the specimen having been used later than the feature being dated.

If, for instance, a tree-ring date derived from a roofing timber were used to fix the time of construction of the roof, it would be an example of direct association; whereas, if the same date were used to determine the age of the contents of the roofed room, it would constitute an indirect application. It is quite possible, of course, to be confronted with a fifth type of general error, actually a variety of Types 2 and 4, which stems from the presence of intrusive specimens in unrelated archaeological environments. Since this problem is strictly an archaeological matter, however, it will not be discussed here.

The Type 1 error, wherein the association is direct but the dating is early, is usually caused by the presence of re-used beams. Judging from the situation in the American South-West, the re-use of construction timbers was an extremely common practice and hardly surprising when one considers that it was often far easier to salvage old logs from nearby abandoned structures than it was to fell growing trees with a stone axe. Obviously, the re-use of timbers in later structures can result in erroneous interpretation. Although the tree-ring date derived for the specimen may be perfectly correct, its application to the structure from which the specimen came would result in the assignment of too early a construction date. The aboriginal use of wind-fallen trees and driftwood logs, if not recognized as such, would introduce a similar tendency to overestimate the age of a feature incorporating this kind of wood. Even the stockpiling of beams before use would introduce a slight but consistent error of the same type.

In regions where wood was relatively scarce it is easy to envisage the problems caused by the re-use of old wood. Any wooden artifact might well tend to acquire heirloom status, and consequently any dates obtained would be subject to the Type 1 error. If a worked artifact were involved, even the process of shaping the wood could contribute to the magnitude of the error.

When the association is not direct but the dating is early, we are dealing with the Type 2 error. This usually comes about as a result of attempting to date artifacts within a room through the application of tree-ring dates derived from logs used in the construction of the room. The problem is basically archaeological in nature and resolves itself into the question of the temporal relationship between a room and its included contents. In short occupation sites the problem may be of only minor significance, whereas in sites of long occupation the problem can be critical. All too often there have been attempts to assign tree-ring dates to a particular item (pottery type for example) on the basis of dated beams in a room which might well have been constructed several centuries before the item in question was manufactured. Again, the tree-ring dates may be correct, their application to the construction of the room may be equally correct, but their assignment to the contents of the room could lead to highly fallacious interpretations. It is also theoretically possible to encounter Type 2 error when non-construction tree-ring dates derived from specimens in old trash are erroneously applied to later constructive features.

In the Type 3 error the association is direct but the dating is late. Over the course of years a prehistoric structure may well become weakened and in need of repair. If a particular roofing timber is replaced, perhaps centuries after the original roof was built, a tree-ring date derived from that timber would represent the time of repair and not the time of construction of the room. In some cases such dates, if recognized, are an advantage since they may give insight into the length of occupation of a particular structure. Dates from buildings that have been abandoned and then reoccupied and re-modelled are subject to similar errors.

Finally, the Type 4 error occurs when the association is not direct but the dating is late. For the most part, this type of error is a result of applying dates from non-construction specimens to construction features. For example, firepit charcoal and wood or charcoal specimens found in room fill or trash mounds could conceivably give far more recent dates than the architectural features they are loosely associated with. On the other hand, non-construction dates used judiciously with construction dates from a single ruin may well indicate at least a minimum period of occupation.

Although the usual errors of interpretation can be identified with one or more of the four general types of error enumerated, it is not to be supposed that the specific error-producing situations mentioned are all that can be encountered. For one thing, these four types of chronological error can occur either independently or in combination with each other, and in the latter case the amount of error involved will either be increased or will tend to cancel out. Each dating problem, therefore, presents its own unique set of circumstances, and an understanding of both the dendrochronological and archaeological conditions involved is necessary for a satisfactory solution.

If it appears from the foregoing discussion that the chances of error associated with the time relationship problem are so high as to cast doubt on the interpretation of all tree-ring dates, it should be remembered that the extent of the danger involved is inversely proportional to the number of dated specimens from any given feature. If a single structure, for example, yields only one date, its interpretation is definitely subject to the types of error enumerated. If this same structure yielded 100 dated specimens the chances of fallacious interpretation would be greatly reduced. Errors of the Type 1 and

Type 3 varieties are particularly amenable to correction through the use of tree-ring date clusters. The fundamental premise is that if there are a number of tree-ring dates from a single structure or architectural feature which cluster about a single point in time, then dates that deviate from the cluster represent re-used or repair timbers, depending upon whether they are earlier or later than the majority. The same reasoning, with modification, would apply to groups of non-construction dates. In similar fashion, the clustering of archaeological traits or characteristics is useful when dealing with errors of the Type 2 and Type 4 varieties. Properly applied, the clustering techniques are powerful problem-solving tools, but they have limited use in those cases where there is an insufficiency of data.

A further complication in the interpretation of tree-ring dates is introduced when the condition of the outside of the dated specimen indicates that exterior rings have been lost through shaping, rot, burning, or some other eroding force. Again various techniques have been developed which tend to minimize this potential source of error. Both the time relationship problem and the problem of outside rings are discussed in detail by the author elsewhere.[1]

THE THREE MAJOR ARCHAEOLOGICAL APPLICATIONS OF TREE-RING DATA

A review of the archaeological applications of tree-ring data leads to a convenient threefold classification scheme. First, there are those applications wherein chronology, either relative or absolute, is the chief consideration. Second, there are those interpretations which depend upon the environmental histories recorded in the ring series themselves. And third, there is that class of fundamentally non-chronological information which stems from the juxtaposition of related dates and which gives rise to inferences of a cultural nature.

By far the most common use of archaeological tree-ring data has been in the field of chronology and the best example of this use is in the American South-West. Today in this area of heavy concentration of archaeological sites there exist a number of regional dendrochronologies which have relevance to fairly broad geographical areas, the longest extending back to the year 59 BC. In addition, more localized chronologies have been developed to aid in dating materials from specific locations.

The Laboratory of Tree-Ring Research at the University of Arizona in Tucson serves as a central repository for the major South-Western tree-ring collections and currently houses an estimated 125,000 individual archaeological specimens. These pieces come from about 2,000 prehistoric sites, some 800 of which have yielded at least one dated sample. Although precise numbers are difficult to determine, roughly 10,000 separate archaeological specimens from the South-West and adjacent regions have been dated.

A chronological history of the development of archaeological tree-ring dating in the South-West is given by Schulman,[80] and a more comprehensive view is to be found throughout the pages of the *Tree-Ring Bulletin* (1934 and following issues).[86] It would be impracticable to list all papers dealing with tree-ring dates in the region but recent summaries of dates have been published by Smiley;[82] Smiley, Stubbs, and Bannister;[83] and Bannister.[1]

As a result of the intensive tree-ring research carried out in the South-West, the pre-history of this area is better understood from the chronological point of view than it is in any other place in the world. Glock,[43] however, has questioned the accuracy of the South-West archaeological tree-ring calendars and has estimated that they may be 5% in error. Other workers, including the author, have confidence in the essential correct-ness of South-Western dendrochronologies, and this view is being continually confirmed by the cross-dating process and present-day research.

Outside the South-West there are numerous localities where the tree-ring dating method has been applied. Results range from the well-substantiated absolute dates of Alaska and Germany to the very preliminary analyses carried out on Turkish and Egyptian specimens. Not all of the studies here reported, however, have received un-qualified acceptance by other workers. Bell[3] has established dates for the Kincaid Site in Illinois; five log cabins in the Mississippi Drainage have been dated by Hawley;[47] Will[93-95] has derived dates from a number of sites in North and South Dakota; three dated sites in the Great Plains have been reported by Weakly;[89,90] and preserved wood in New England has been dated by Lyon.[56] Present efforts in the Missouri River Basin are summarized by Caldwell;[7] a summary for the Mississippi Valley is given by Bell[4] and for Nebraska by Weakly.[91] A current and as yet unreported project by the author on specimens from the Casas Grandes Site of Chihuahua, Mexico, has resulted in the establishment of a 500-year floating chronology.

The many dated sites in Alaska and the tracing of driftwood origins are largely the work of Giddings,[26-29,32,34,36] Oswalt,[65-67] and VanStone.[87,88] Schulman[78] describes dating work carried out by Aandstad in Norway on six late structures whose approximate ages were already known. Ording[64] reports a floating chronology based on a hundred logs from Raknehaugen in south-eastern Norway, and Eidem[21] dated beams from eight houses in Flesberg. Høeg[48] has made a summary of Norwegian dating work.

Dendrochronological dating in Great Britain is documented by Schove[74,75] and Schove and Lowther,[76] while Zeuner[98] reports work on seventeenth-century wood from the City of London and on Beaker age stumps located near Clacton-on-Sea. Huber and his associates in Germany have succeeded in developing a relative chronology based on log palisades at the Bronze Age fort at Wasserburg or Bachau.[50, 51] Other floating chronologies have been derived for the Neolithic sites of Thaingen Weier and Egolzwil III in Switzerland and Ehrenstein near Ulm in south Germany and for the Bronze Age site of Zug-Sumph in Switzerland.[51] Absolute dating was accomplished on beams from the medieval town of Zeigenhain near Kassel, Germany.[50] Two recent summaries of European tree-ring work are Dobbs[10] and Zeuner.[98]

A prehistoric floating tree-ring chronology in Russia is reported by Zamotorin[97] while Kohara[55] documents an attempt to date a five-storied pagoda in Japan. The Middle East would appear to be potentially an excellent area for the development of at least relative chronologies. Although problems of importation and re-use of wood are associa-ted with Egypt, current research by the author on archaeological tree-ring specimens from Turkey and Egypt indicates that cross-dating exists in specific regions and that long relative chronologies are a definite possibility. Tree-ring dating in New Zealand is apparently not feasible because of the lack of cross–dating.[5]

The relationship of tree growth to climate has been the subject of many dendro-chronological studies, and certainly information of past environmental conditions as estimated from tree-rings constitutes a major contribution to archaeological knowledge. On the whole, however, the present state of tree-ring research indicates that caution should be exercised in making such interpretations. Tree growth itself is an immensely complex mechanism, and the various external and internal factors that influence growth and are responsible for the existence of cross-dating between trees are as yet imperfectly understood. Certain dominant controls such as temperature and soil moisture may be isolated, but quantitative evaluations of even these factors in ancient times are presently unobtainable. On a relative basis it may be possible to speak of droughts and other climatic fluctuations, but all too often the archaeologist has seized on such relative indications and has used them to explain away highly intricate archaeological situations and cultural behaviour. Great strides in understanding the significance of dendrochronologies have been made,[80] but still the newest mathematical techniques of analysis continue to demonstrate that the final answers have not yet been reached.[25]

A third application of tree-ring data is concerned with the internal relationships of associated dates rather than their placement in time. For example, Haury,[46] among others, demonstrated the exact developmental process of a multi-roomed pueblo in Arizona. If enough comparable data were available, it might be possible to identify culturally motivated construction practices among primitive peoples. Similarly, Huber found frequent building periods in the houses of Ehrenstein near Ulm and gained insight into the technology and economic conditions of the time. From a study of cutting dates derived for beams from a single roof, Bannister[1] was able to conclude that the prehistoric population of Chaco Canyon in north-western New Mexico practised stockpiling of their timbers before use. Also, by means of the clustering of dates derived from beams re-used in a later structure he[1] was able to infer the prior existence of a building which had not been discovered through usual archaeological techniques. These are but a few of the many cases of this type of application and by no means represent the range of possibilities along this line.

There is no doubt that the results of tree-ring research will continue to be important within the field of archaeology. The expansion of the method into as yet untested regions, the improvement of our knowledge of the meaning of rings as climatic indicators, and the application of tree-ring dates to problems of culture stability and change—these are the areas in which rapid future progress can be expected to occur.

REFERENCES
1 BANNISTER, B. 1959. Tree-Ring Dating of Archaeological Sites in the Chaco Canyon Region, New Mexico; MS, doctoral dissertation, Univ. of Arizona
2 —— and SMILEY, T. L. 1955. Dendrochronology, in SMILEY, T. L. (ed.) 'Geochronology, with Special Reference to Southwestern United States', Univ. of Arizona Phys. Sci. Bull. 2, 177–95
3 BELL, R. E. 1951. Dendrochronology at the Kincaid Site, in COLE, F. C., Kincaid, A Prehistoric Illinois Metropolis, Appendix I. Chicago

4 BELL, R. E. 1952. Dendrochronology in the Mississippi Valley, in GRIFFIN, J. B. (ed.) *Archaeology of Eastern United States*, Chicago, 345–51

5 BELL, V. and BELL, R. E. 1958. *Tree-Ring Bulletin 22*, nos. 1–4, 7–11

6 BOWERS, N. A. 1960. *Ibid. 23*, nos. 1–4, 10–13

7 CALDWELL, W. W. 1960. *Ibid. 23*, nos. 1–4, 14–17

8 DEBOER, H. J. 1951. *Proc. Koninkl. Nederl. Akademie Van Wetenshappen*, Ser. B, no. 54, 194–209

9 DOBBS, C. G. 1951. *Forestry 24*, no. 1, 22–35

10 —— 1960. *New Scientist, 182*, 1213

11 DOUGLASS, A. E. 1919. Climatic Cycles and Tree-Growth, vol. 1; *Carnegie Inst. of Washington Pub. 289*

12 —— 1928. *Ibid.* vol. 2

13 —— 1929. *Nat. Geog. Mag. 56*, 736–70

14 —— 1935. *Nat. Geog. Soc., Contributed Papers, Pueblo Bonito Series* no. 1

15 —— 1936. Climatic Cycles and Tree-Growth, vol. 3; *Carnegie Inst. of Washington Pub. 289*

16 —— 1940. *Tree-Ring Bulletin 7*, no. 1

17 —— 1941a. *Ibid. 7*, no. 4

18 —— 1941b. *Ibid. 8*, no. 2

19 —— 1943. *Ibid. 10*, no. 1

20 —— 1946. *Laboratory of Tree-Ring Research Bull.* no. 3, Univ. of Arizona

21 EIDEM, P. 1956. *Tidsskrift for Skogbruk 64*, no. 2, 96–116

22 EKLUND, B. 1949. *Meddelanden Statens Skogsforskningsinstitut 38*, no. 5, 1–77

23 —— 1956. *Tree-Ring Bulletin 21*, nos. 1–4, 21–24

24 FERGUSON, C. W. 1959. *Kiva 25*, no. 2, 24–30

25 FRITTS, H. C. 1960. *Forest Science 6*, no. 4, 334–49

26 GIDDINGS, J. L., Jr. 1938. *Tree-Ring Bulletin 5*, no. 2, 16

27 —— 1940. *Ibid. 7*, no. 2, 10–14

28 —— 1941. *Laboratory of Tree-Ring Research Bull.* no. 1, Univ. of Arizona

29 —— 1942. *Tree-Ring Bulletin 9*, no. 1, 2–8

30 —— 1943. *Ibid. 9*, no. 4, 26–32

31 —— 1947. *Ibid. 13*, no. 4, 26–29

32 —— 1948. *Ibid. 14*, no. 4, 26–32

33 —— 1951. *Ibid. 18*, no. 1, 2–6

34 —— 1952. *Proc. Am. Phil. Soc. 96*, no. 2, 129–42

35 —— 1953. *Tree-Ring Bulletin 20*, no. 1, 2–5

36 —— 1954. *Ibid. 20*, nos. 3–4, 23–25

37 GINDEL, J. 1944. *Ibid. 11*, no. 1, 6–8

38 GLADWIN, H. S. 1940a. Methods and Instruments for Use in Measuring Tree-Rings, *Medallion Papers*, no. 27

39 —— 1940b. Tree-Rings Analysis, Methods of Correlation, *Medallion Papers*, no. 28

40 GLOCK, W. S. 1933. *Pan-American Geologist 60*, 1–14

41 —— 1937. Principles and Methods of Tree-Ring Analysis. *Carnegie Inst. of Washington Pub. 486*

42 —— 1955. *Botanical Review 21*, nos. 1–3, 73–188

43 —— 1960. Dendrochronology, in *McGraw-Hill Encyclopedia of Science and Technology*, New York, 58

44 —— STUDHALTER, R. A. and AGERTER, S. R. 1960. Classification and Multiplicity of Growth Layers in the Branches of Trees at the Extreme Lower Forest Border. *Smithsonian Miscellaneous Collections 140*, no. 1

45 HALL, E. T., Jr. 1946. *Tree-Ring Bulletin 12*, no. 4, 26–27

46 HAURY, E. W. 1934. The Canyon Creek Ruin and the Cliff Dwellings of the Sierra Ancha, *Medallion Papers*, no. 14

47 HAWLEY, F. M. 1941. *Tree-Ring Analysis and Dating in the Mississippi Drainage*, Chicago

48 HØEG, O. A. 1956. *Tree-Ring Bulletin 21*, nos. 1–4, 2–15

49 HOLMSGAARD, E. 1956. *Ibid. 21*, nos. 1–4, 25–27

50 HUBER. B., and JAZEWITSCH, W. VON, 1956. *Ibid. 21*, nos. 1–4, 28–30

51 —— 1958. *Flora 146*, no. 3, 445–71

52 HUSTICH, I. 1948. *Acta Botanica Fennica 42*

53 —— 1956. *Acta Geographica 15*, no. 3

54 JAZEWITSCH, W. VON, BETTAG, G. and SIEBENLIST, H. 1957. *Holz als Roh- und Werkstoff 15*, 241–4

55 KOHARA, J. 1958. *Kobunkazai no Kagaku 15*, 12–17
56 LYON, C. J. 1939. *Science 90*, 419–20
57 —— 1946. *Tree-Ring Bulletin 13*, no. 1, 2–4
58 —— 1949. *Ecology 30*, no. 4, 549–52
59 —— 1953. *Tree-Ring Bulletin 20*, no. 2, 10–16
60 McGRGEOR, J. C. 1938. *Museum of Northern Arizona Bulletin* no. 13
61 MESSERI, A. 1953. *Nuovo Giornale Botanico Italiano 60*, nos. 1–2, 251–86
62 MIKOLA, P. 1956. *Tree-Ring Bulletin 21*, nos. 1–4, 16–20
63 NISHIOKA, H. 1952. *Proceedings of the Seventh Pacific Science Congress 3*, 118–21
64 ORDING, A. 1941. *Meddelanden Norske Skogforsøksvesen 8*, no. 27, 91–130
65 OSWALT, W. H. 1949. *Tree-Ring Bulletin 16*, no. 1, 7–8
66 —— 1951. *Ibid. 18*, no. 1, 6–8
67 —— 1952. *Anthropological Papers of the University of Alaska 1*, no. 1, 47–91
68 —— 1958. *Tree-Ring Bulletin 22*, nos. 1–4, 16–22
69 —— 1960. *Ibid. 23*, nos. 1–4, 3–9
70 RUDAKOV, V. E. 1958. *Botanicheskiy Zhurnal 43*, no. 12, 1708–12
71 SCANTLING, F. H. 1946. *Tree-Ring Bulletin 12*, no. 4, 27–32
72 SCHOVE, D. J. 1950. *The Scottish Geographical Magazine 66*, no. 1, 37–42
73 —— 1954. *Geografiska Annaler 36*, nos. 1–2, 40–80
74 —— 1955. *Weather 10*, no. 11, 368–371, 395
75 —— 1959. *Medieval Archaeology 3*, 288–90
76 —— and LOWTHER, A. W. G. 1957. *Ibid. 1*, 78–95
77 SCHULMAN, E. 1942. *Ecology 23*, 309–18
78 —— 1944. *Tree-Ring Bulletin 11*, no. 1, 2–6
79 —— 1953. *Ibid. 19*, Nos. 3–4.
80 —— 1956. *Dendroclimatic Changes in Semiarid America*, Tucson
81 SMILEY, T. L. 1951a. *Archaeological Field Practices Regarding Tree-Ring Specimens*. Mimeographed paper, Laboratory of Tree-Ring Research, Univ. of Arizona
82 —— 1951b. *Laboratory of Tree-Ring Research Bull*. no. 5, Univ. of Arizona
83 —— STUBBS, S. A. and BANNISTER, B. 1953. *Laboratory of Tree-Ring Research Bull*. no. 6, Univ. of Arizona
84 STALLINGS, W. S., Jr. 1949. *Dating Prehistoric Ruins by Tree-Rings*. Laboratory of Tree-Ring Research, Univ. of Arizona, revised ed.
85 STUDHALTER, R. A. 1955. *Botanical Review 21*, nos. 1–3, 1–72
86 TREE-RING BULLETIN. 1934–. Published by the Tree-Ring Society with the co-operation of the Laboratory of Tree-Ring Research, Univ. of Arizona, Tucson
87 VANSTONE, J. W. 1953. *Tree-Ring Bulletin 20*, no. 1, 6–8
88 —— 1958. *Ibid. 22*, nos. 1–4, 12–15
89 WEAKLY, H. E. 1941. Letter to A. T. Hill, in (p. 205) HILL, A. T. and METCALF, G., *Nebraska History 22*, no. 2
90 —— 1946. A Preliminary Report on the Ash Hollow Charcoal, in CHAMPE, J. L., 'Ash Hollow Cave', *Univ. of Nebraska Studies N.S.* no. 1, appendix I
91 —— 1949. *Proc. Fifth Plains Conf. for Arch., Note Book* no. 1, 111–14
92 —— 1950. *Proc. Sixth Plains Arch. Conf., Anth. Papers* no. 11, 90–94
93 WILL, G. F. 1946. *North Dakota Agricultural College Bulletin* 338
94 —— 1949. *Proc. Fifth Plains Conf. for Arch., Note Book* no. 1, 114–16
95 —— 1950. *Proc. Sixth Plains Arch. Conf., Anth. Papers* no. 11, 95–97
96 WILLEY, G. R. 1937. *Tree-Ring Bulletin 4*, no. 2, 6–8
97 ZAMOTORIN, I. M. 1959. *Sovetskaya Arkheologiya 1959*, no. 1, 21–30
98 ZEUNER, F. E. 1960. Advances in Chronological Research, in HEIZER, R. F. and COOK, S. F. (eds.), 'The Application of Quantitative Methods in Archaeology', *Viking Fund Publications in Anthropology* no. 28, 325–43

18 Palaeo-Ethnobotany

HANS HELBAEK

IN THE NEOLITHIC several cereals were cultivated which are unknown to the modern farmer, for instance naked barley, Einkorn, and Emmer. This is common knowledge— but what are our sources? For grain is very perishable: it either sprouts or decays (it can keep for millennia only in deserts). What foundations have the statements and descriptions we read of plants which died many thousands of years ago and which were the indispensable basis for the existence of the ancient cultures? In many museums no evidence of a vegetable diet is exhibited and the visitor has little opportunity to form an opinion of the basis for statements on plants as food in prehistory. This chapter is concerned with demonstrating the nature of the archaeological plant material, and how this material is examined and interpreted in the laboratory. Discussion is confined to the Old World where wheat and barley were the established qualifications for human existence. It will appear that the evidence is abundant although some of it may seem remote and intangible.

Some kinds of material occur everywhere, others are limited to certain climatic regions. Thus mummy wheat is only found in Egypt, and the ritually murdered Iron Agers, whose stomach contents are such a valuable and rare source of information on prehistoric diets, have been found only in bogs within a restricted area in north-western Europe. Silica skeletons are commonest in the Arid Zone, while the two most important categories, carbonized grain and seeds, and the imprints of such, may be met with in any excavation all over the world except the Arctics.

The result of this particular study is a long story which has recently been touched upon in a series of brief surveys;[17,18,20,22] here it is proposed to give the reader an idea of the evidence itself and the technique by which results have been attained.

MUMMY WHEAT

The so-called mummified grain from Egyptian tombs is the nearest we can get to the original state of the food plants of antiquity. Because of the severe aridity, agriculture in Egypt is wholly dependent upon irrigation, either from small wells or, more important, by the distribution of the waters of the Nile through canals to the low-lying lands in the delta and to narrow strips along the banks further up the river. In the passages beneath the pyramids as well as in pits in the open desert, stores of grain may be found which have kept almost completely fresh for sometimes as long as five to six millennia. Indeed the husk may be a little darker than contemporary grain and it will oxidize like wood, but all the details, the tiny hairs on kernels, husks, internodes, etc., still remain and the cell structure is rather more easily observed than in fresh cereals.[10,13,28] Even the starch will still react to the iodine test and stain a deep violet. It might be expedient to point out that the very common belief is unfounded that mummy wheat is still viable. Even in its dormant state a seed is alive, so that assimilation and respiration must go on, and for this purpose moisture is necessary. Thus the complete desiccation which is the reason for the preservation of the grain is the very instrument by which it was killed—and indeed long ago. Although the microscope reveals the normal pattern of cells in the grain shell (seed case) numerous ruptures disturb the order in this vital protective organ. A few years after deposition the grain died from desiccation, and no superstition can revive it. (The belief that wheat found in ancient tombs can still be made to sprout and propagate is supported by the tales of the guides in the Egyptian Museum in Cairo, who repeat it daily to visitors from all over the world.) Incidentally, that particular species has not been grown in Egypt since the time of the Romans and nowhere can an authentic example of the live progeny of genuine mummy wheat be demonstrated.[29] However, before it became extinct in Egypt it was taken to Abyssinia where it has been grown ever since under the Ethiopian name of *Adaz*. Other races of the same species are grown in more remote mountainous districts in Europe and elsewhere, relics of local prehistoric strains. In Germanic languages it is called *Emmer*. Though wheat alone is reputed to be immortal, barley also was a very important cereal in ancient Egypt, used for bread and beer alike.[1] Many other plants were cultivated, particularly flax and a number of species of the pea family, but they still grow there and do not cause exaggerated speculation.

EVIDENCE PRESERVED IN BOGS

Generally speaking, a combination of moisture and oxygen is a prerequisite for the activity of putrefactive microbes. In Egypt there is little moisture; hence the plants may keep for ever. On the other hand, in peat bogs we find many categories of vegetable matter preserved because no fresh air is available and further because of the long-term action of humic acid. These circumstances afford us unlimited material for the study of the vegetational history of those regions where peat deposits are preserved, both in the form of wood, leaf, and fruit samples and in the form of pollen,[3] but as a source of the study of plant husbandry and past human diet the possibilities are somewhat limited. Starch is not preserved and even such plant parts as husks and grain shells are rarely reported from peat analyses. However, many seeds and fruits have such a tough shell that they will never disappear unless the bog dries up.

In the excavation of prehistoric marsh-dwelling sites in the foothills of the Alps large deposits of stones and seeds of berries may be encountered which have preserved their shape and sometimes even their characteristic colours. Most often they prove to come from juicy and more or less sugary fruits while carbonized plant remains seldom occur in such context. Such remains are the refuse from wine-making; already in the beginning of the second millennium BC—or maybe even earlier—people had discovered how to make attractive drinks of the berries which grew wild on the lower slopes of the Alps. They used mainly grapes of the wild forest vine which at that time grew in these areas, also blackberries, raspberries, elderberries, the fruits of the bittersweet nightshade, and cornelian cherry which is very common in the open forests in the southern foothills and which in certain tracts in northern Italy is still collected by the peasants and used for the same purpose. Some authors have suggested that these accumulations are human excrement, a suggestion which is contradicted by the massive occurrences of the stones of the cornelian cherry which are up to 1·5 cm long and certainly must be awkward eating on a large scale.

In northern Holland, north-west Germany, and in the Danish peninsula, human corpses of Iron Age date have sometimes been found in peat deposits. Peat is known to have been used for fuel in this region since the Neolithic, and the corpses seem to have been thrown into the small ponds left open by the peat cutters some two thousand years ago.[2,27] The corpses from Tollund and Grauballe have received particularly widespread publicity.

The conditions for preservation of vegetable matter seem to differ if it has been enclosed in the intestinal canal; it is, at any rate, a fact that husks and seeds of grass removed from the stomachs of bog-found corpses may prove to be quite extraordinarily well preserved. Thus starch may be found which has kept its specific agglomerate structure and the ability to stain with iodine, while husks may have kept their otherwise easily perishable surface (epidermis). Many fragments of the inner integument (seed coat) of cereals may be encountered and even the protein cells which would not seem to be very resistant may cover the inner surface of the seed coat. These delicate pellicles are identified in part by their specific cell formations, in part by the microscopic hairs which may occur still attached to fragments of seed coat. The hairs from the grains of wheat, barley, rye, and oats are different and of good diagnostic value.

Sometimes many whole seeds and fruits are found in the remains of a meal, specially those that have a strong shell and have avoided grinding and chewing. Thus many fruits of willow weed and goosefoot made up considerable proportions of the meals and many were intact and macroscopically determinable. Apart from that, the stomach contents consist of a mud-like matter from which particles are selected by low magnification for examination by the high-power microscope. Very small fragments may suffice for an identification—in some cases half a square millimetre of tissue may be plenty. Under the microscope these mud particles present an inexhaustible variety of shape and colour, sometimes fragments consisting of a series of layers of different structure, at others bits of a single layer of tissue with its cells clearly exposed to observation and measuring, such as the corn spurrey seed coat shown in Plate IXd.

These 'Bog Men' subsisted on a highly mixed diet. For instance, Grauballe Man had in his intestinal duct the remains of 66 species of plants only seven of which were cultivated. Various plant diseases were established, such as ergot and smut, and the man himself must have suffered from more or less continuous stomach-ache caused by an intestinal worm (Trichuris), the eggs of which occurred literally by the million. All the non-cultivated plants were species the seeds of which were collected on the fallow field or in the meadow and forest, and they tend to show that life on the basis of agriculture was anything but carefree in those days, at least in that part of Denmark, which is mostly rather poor moorland. It should, however, be added that, as opposed to Tollund Man, he had had some meat also, judging by small splinters of animal bone among the plant remains.[7,16]

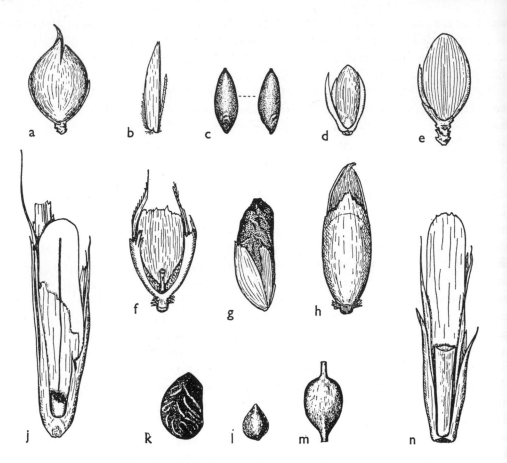

Fig. 27 Grasses, seed and fruits from the stomach of Grauballe Man ($\times$ 20): (a) Spikelet of *Echinochloa crus-galli*, dorsal view (the sterile floret is visible behind the fertile one); (b) floret of *Poa nemoralis*, lateral view; (c) grain of *Deschampsia caespitosa*, dorsal and lateral views; (d) palea and margins of lemma of *Setaria viridis*, distal view; (e) palea with remains of lemma of *Echinochloa crus-galli*, distal view; (f) palea with portion of lemma of *Sieglingia decumbens*, distal view; (g) floret of *Holcus* containing an *Ergot sclerotium*; (h) floret of *Sieglingia decumbens*, dorsal view; (j) floret with caryopsis of *Agropyron caninum*; (k) fruit of *Potentilla erecta*; (l) fruit of *Alchemilla*; (m) fruit of *Carex*; (n) floret of *Lolium perenne*, ventral view (this is an unusually long rachilla).

CARBONIZED MATERIAL

Charcoal is an extremely durable matter; if not exposed to high temperature or mechanical action it may keep and stay determinable indefinitely whether deposited under wet or dry conditions. The same applies to other forms of carbonized vegetable matter, and to the student of the dietary practice of the remote past this circumstance is of the greatest value.

Now and again one may meet in literature the expression 'spontaneous carbonization' in connection with deposits of prehistoric grain. The term serves to indicate that grain may turn into charcoal at ordinary temperatures if only kept underground long enough. This, in fact, is an invention; carbonization requires heat, and deposition of grain under conditions such as are met with in excavations would very soon result in putrefaction and complete destruction if the grain was not heated beyond roasting point.[4,9] There is too little cellulose and too much easily decaying starch in a cereal grain for the fermentation heat to turn it into charcoal. We may take it for granted that the carbonized food remains found in archaeological context have always been exposed to direct or indirect fire. It may have happened by an accidental house fire or it may be the consequence of miscarried parching.

From the earliest times it was customary to dry the grain artificially, the purpose varying with the circumstances. The primitive wheat species, Einkorn, Emmer, and Spelt, have a very tough and sturdy spikelet which does not release the grains in ordinary threshing; the spikes are beaten to pieces, but the grains are still enclosed in their individual husks. If the spikes are heated, however, the solid portion of the spikelet becomes dry and brittle and then it is possible to crush them. Therefore grain drying was used in all regions where these three species were grown. It was also employed in cool and rainy regions, such as the Hebrides, but here simply in order to store the harvest without risk of fungus attack and other damage, whichever species was involved. In hot and humid climate the drying aimed at preventing ill-timed sprouting. Of course the seed grain for the next season had to be put aside and preserved by other means since the germinating power is destroyed at a comparatively low temperature. This is expressly mentioned by Pliny in his *Historia Naturalis*. Our finds show clearly that no proper temperature control was possible in the primitive drying plants, even the comparatively sophisticated Roman kilns the ruins of which abound in southern England.

Thus it often happened that the grain was overdone, scorched or wholly carbonized. Then it was thrown on the midden—and was preserved for ever. In case of datable artifacts being found in the same strata the grain constitutes most valuable material for our study. And it is by no means always just small quantities we find; a pint is common, a gallon not unusual, and several finds of up to ten gallons are recorded in the annals of archaeology. Such large quantities mostly come from burnt houses; much useful information may be acquired for instance about the relative importance of the several cereals and legumes and about the weed flora of the fields, items that may reveal the economic status of a prehistoric community and of its contacts with the world abroad.[12,14,15,24]

The technique of identifying carbonized plant remains is based upon the same principles as in the case of other types of material, viz. comparison with fresh homologous plant parts. The examiner must, however, be intimately acquainted with the specific changes of shape, size, and proportions caused by heat in order to visualize the original appearance of the deformed and often mutilated carbonized matter and to put a name to it.

Complete carbonization turns the cereal grain into an amorphous mass almost devoid of traces of structure. It does, however, happen that some kernels are but imperfectly carbonized and then it may be possible to study the microscopic details of husks and grain shells. Even carrier tissue of starch bodies or the branching system of the fungi which attack grain left too long in wet condition (*Dematiaceae*) may occasionally be observed.

These exceptions come in handy to the study of crushed remains of carbonized foods such as bread and buns. It is sometimes possible to find evidence of the species from which the buns were made which occur in Bronze Age sites in central and southern Europe (and the Iron Age site of Meare in Somerset), and other similar material.⁴ When plant matter carbonizes a lot of tar is formed, and this old and cindery tar is actually the main obstacle to identification as it is largely insoluble in agents which leave the cell tissues undamaged.

By and large carbonized grain is in a rather poor state as regards morphological detail, but now and again it happens that it passes through the process surprisingly unscathed. Thus for instance a collection of grains and spike parts got overheated in a pot in an Assyrian palace in northern Mesopotamia some 2,600 years ago; the remains are as good for determining the exact spike form as freshly harvested barley. The kernel may be precisely described: the wrinkling of the husks, the serration of the veins, the specific shape of the bases, the rachilla and the internodes with the remains of the lateral florets enable the classification of the race. One problem only eludes us: the colour of the grain. A great variety of grain colour is met with beyond Europe: the kernels and husks may be white, yellow, purple, violet, grey or black. Thus in the country where this old barley was grown, the modern product is yellow or purplish-black.

As a rule, carbonized plant remains from regions with little or no frost and a dry soil are much better preserved than those coming from northern latitudes. In frost and thaw the soil particles will move and eventually grind off the finer details of the fragile plant bodies. Even though most grain is fetched from some depth beneath the present surface, there will have been a time when it lay scattered among other debris on the ground before erosion, sand drift, and renewed human activity covered up the traces of the habitation site and kept the frost at arm's length; that is when the damage was done. One very attractive exception is shown in Plate IXb. It is part of a large heap of linseed, and the seeds of a weed which occurs in flax fields, Gold-of-Pleasure. The two plants were grown together in the Danish Iron Age and both kinds of seed were used for food because of their considerable oil content. On top of the seeds is seen the pear-shaped pod valve of Gold-of-Pleasure. These and many other food remains were found in Jutland in a house burnt down some time in the first century AD. Also in that house was a large vessel filled with malt (sprouted barley), the only example hitherto of prehistoric brewing encountered in Denmark.⁵

SILICA SKELETONS

In most excavations in arid zones, e.g. in Egypt and Mesopotamia, one comes across heaps or extensive strata of ash. It is of course desirable to find out what the fuel was since very often it has a bearing upon the common vegetable food of that time. Usually the ash will prove to consist of an amorphous powder mixed with small bits of structurally highly organized glass matter. These fragments are the silicious elements of the epidermis of the vegetative parts of grasses. During its growth the epidermis cell of grasses and some other families undergoes a 'mineralization'. The minute interstices of the fundamental cellulose framework of the cell wall will eventually be filled up with other organic substances as also quite prominently by silica. When the plant burns or decays this element of silica will remain, and if the plant part is protected against mechanical action, as for instance in the wall of a clay vessel, it will today represent a true copy of the cells exhibiting all their specific structural details.[21] The difference in dimensions and design in the epidermis of the various grasses may be very pronounced and thus it is possible to distinguish between the cultivated species by means of these glass-like objects when they are properly magnified. The attractive design of millet ash (husk) from an Assyrian palace is illustrated in Plate IXc.

There would seem to be two reasons why silica skeletons figure less prominently in palaeo-ethnobotanical material from northern regions: the silica solidification in the epidermis is conspicuously heavier in hot and arid climates; and the formation of ice crystals in such delicate and unelastic structures is bound to prohibit their preservation.

GRAIN IMPRINTS

In areas in the Near East and elsewhere where no suitable building stone is available and where timber belongs to the imported luxuries, common houses are built of clay or mud mixed with straw, stubble or chaff. This was the technique ever since man became settled with the invention of agriculture. Such prehistoric houses are encountered in excavations, and in the chunks of wall and floor material there may be a multitude of imprints of plant parts yielding highly important information on the plants being cultivated when the house was occupied. Sometimes silica skeletons also are preserved even if no fire was involved.

The ceramic too, which was made at the fireplace in the house, very often contains imprints because the food was prepared at the same place and the grain and seeds spilled on the floor got stuck to the lumps of wet pottery material and were eventually kneaded into the clay. Grain imprints may occur in hand-made pottery from all agricultural regions of the world, and in Denmark they are particularly common. There are Bronze and Iron Age vessels of a moderate size which on their surface bear as many as 200 imprints of seeds and grains.[6,9,11,18,25]

If a dry seed is kneaded into the wet clay at the shaping of a vessel it will absorb moisture from its surroundings. Together with the water it will attract the finest particles of the clay which will form a fine-grain coat all over the surface of the seed. When the vessel is fired the seed will burn away, but the cavity left in the now hardened clay is lined with this fine-grain material in which minute morphological features of the plant body may be moulded. A cast of the cavity will show the seed in sufficient detail for an exact description and identification. Even small seeds may in this way leave determinable traces, for instance the seed of corn spurrey which is less than one millimeter in diameter.

As a rule, large particles of plants were picked off the clay by the potter, but in the large bricks from Mesopotamian monumental buildings one may come across more or less whole spikes. One of the best possible examples of this kind is illustrated in Plate IXa. In it is represented all necessary detail for a systematic classification of the type of two-row barley. Incidentally, these bricks which are upwards from 12 in. square may bear hundreds of determinable imprints of chaff and grains.

APPENDIX

Recently an attempt was made to throw light on the evolution of plant husbandry in Iraq.[26] This country, which consists of a mountainous region in the north (Kurdistan) and a southern alluvial plain (Mesopotamia), is within the general area where agriculture is believed to have originated. In the uplands the prototypes of the most important cultivated plants are still to be found, and the adjoining low-lying river plain would have been a natural area of development for the intensive irrigation agriculture which was the fundamental qualification for the rise of the vigorous Mesopotamian cultures of the fourth and subsequent millennia.

This project was carried out by a systematic tracking and determination of imprints in well-dated pottery and bricks from ancient habitation sites, palaces, and ziggurats, as also by examination of carbonized material and ash from the area in question. The investigator visited museums in Europe and Iraq; the ruins of numerous ancient cities in Mesopotamia, from Nimrud and Babylon in the north to Ur and Warka in the south, were examined from this particular point of view. The result was a quite coherent picture of plant husbandry stretching from the seventh millennium BC to the time of Harun-al-Rashid, c. AD 800.

In the beginning man had domesticated the wild Emmer and the wild two-row barley of the northern mountains and he also took up the cultivation of the wild flax. Presumably during the fifth millennium farmers migrated into the river plain in the south with its fertile alluvial soil, and there they eventually developed irrigation agriculture. This forcible change of environment led by mutation to the transformation of the two-row barley into the six-row form, and Emmer and flax attained a higher state of efficiency. The general expansion of the fifth millennium brought agriculture to Egypt, and from Asia Minor to Europe.[20,22,23]

The small-grain wild wheat, Einkorn, which was domesticated together with the wild Emmer attained a high state of development in Asia Minor and became the third member of the group of important cereals which were taken to Europe and, presumably via the Danube basin and the western Black Sea coastlands, spread all over that continent in the course of two millennia. Flax and some of the Oriental legumes, such as pea, lentil, and vetchling, accompanied the cereals as secondary cultivars. Millet turns up in Mesopotamia about 3000 BC, but the traces of that plant are not consistent in the Near East. Whereas during the third and second millennia it was widely grown in southern Europe, in Iraq we do not encounter it again until the middle of the first millennium, and in Egypt it does not seem ever to have been grown in antiquity. Certain interesting developments took place in Asia Minor at an early time, concerning naked barley and the free-threshing wheat (e.g. bread wheat), but the evidence is only just emerging and its interpretation is sketchy.

This field of research is but one of numerous auxiliaries to modern archaeology. If we aim at the whole truth and nothing but the truth regarding the life and achievement of our remote ancestors, this study is as indispensable as the excavation and interpretation of the more conspicuous remains of ancient cultures, and it need not be emphasized that without correct dating of the plant remains all the endeavours of the palaeo-ethnobotanist are utterly futile. This applies to the corresponding fields within other natural sciences as well. The excavator must be informed and interested in these problems and he must give considerable attention to the recovery of the pertinent material. If he is alert, treasures of information may be acquired. The interpretation is comparatively simple; it requires only the prerequisites of all scientific research: special training, patience, and luck.

REFERENCES

1 ABERG, E. 1950. In LAUER, J. P., LAURENT-TACKHOLM, V. and ABERG, E. *Bull. Inst. d'Egypte 32*, 153

2 BECKER, C. J. 1948. Torvegraning i aeldre Jernalder. *Nationalmuseets Arbejdsmark 1948*, 92

3 GODWIN, H. 1956. *The History of the British Flora*, Cambridge

4 HARRIS, T. M. 1958. *J. Ecol. 46*, 447

5 HELBAEK, H. 1938. Planteavl. *Aarbøger 1938*

6 —— 1948. Les impreintes de céréals, in RIIS, P. J. *Fouilles et Recherches de la Fondation Carlsberg 2*, 3

7 —— 1950. *Aarbøger 1950*, 311

8 —— 1952a. *Acta Archaeologica 23*, 97

9 —— 1952b. *Proc. Prehist. Soc. 18*, 194

10 —— 1953. *Dan. Biol. Medd. 21*, 8

11 —— 1954. *Aarbøger 1954*, 202

12 —— 1955a. The Botany of the Iron Age Vallhager Field, in STENBERGER, M. *et al.*, *Vallhagar, a Migration Period Site on Gotland, Sweden*, Stockholm

13 —— 1955b. *Proc. Prehist. Soc. 21*, 93

14 —— 1956. In GJERSTAD, E. *Acta Inst. Romani Sueciae*, ser. 4, 27:2

15 —— 1957. In KLINDT-JENSEN, O. *Nat. Mus. Skr. St. Ber. 2*

16 —— 1958. *Kuml 1958*, 83

17 —— 1959a. Die Paläoethnobotanik des Nahen Ostens und Europas. *Opusc. Ethnol. Mem. L. Biro Sacra. Akademiai Kiado*, Budapest

18 —— 1959b. *Science 130*, 365

19 —— 1959c. *Archaeology 12*, 183

20 —— 1959d. *Kuml 1959*, 103

21 —— 1960a. Cereals and weeds in Phase A, in BRAIDWOOD, R. J. and BRAIDWOOD, L. *Excavations in the Plain of Antioch*, vol. 1, Chicago

22 —— 1960b. The Paleo-Ethnobotany of the Near East and Europe, in BRAIDWOOD, R. J. and HOWE, B. *Prehistoric Investigations in Iraqi Kurdistan* (*Studies in Ancient Oriental Civilizations, no 31*), Chicago ch. 8

23 —— 1960c. *Iraq 22*, 186

24 —— 1961. *Anatolian Studies 11*, 77

25 JESSEN, K. and HELBAEK, H. 1944. *Dan. Biol. Skr. 3* (2)

26 JACOBSEN, T. and ADAMS, R. 1958. *Science 128*, 1251

27 JORGENSEN, S. 1956. *Kuml 1956*, 128

28 LAURENT-TACKHOLM, V. 1952. *Faraos Blomster*, Copenhagen

29 TACKHOLM, V., TACKHOLM, G. and DRAR, M. 1941. *Flora of Egypt*, Cairo

19 Diet as Revealed by Coprolites

E. O. CALLEN

UNTIL RECENTLY THE BRITTLE NATURE of any coprolites recovered from cave or campsite precluded a careful examination being made of them. MacNeish[1] records breaking open eleven coprolites from Mexico, revealing two containing wings and legs of grasshoppers, three with *Agave* fibres, one with a possible squash seed, and two others peppered with snail shell fragments. No doubt there have been other attempts, but none happens to be known to the writer.

The first successful examination of the contents of coprolites was made by Callen and Cameron,[2] who discovered a method of softening them that practically re-constituted the coprolites to their original consistency. They soaked the coprolites in a 0·5% aqueous solution of trisodium phosphate* for 72 hours or longer, which in addition to softening the material, extracts much of the bile pigment. The removal of that pigment makes the examination easier, so that soaking for a period in excess of 72 hours is preferable. The trisodium phosphate itself does not have any apparent smell at that dilution, but after the coprolite has been soaked in it for several days, there is usually a fusty or earthy smell. In only a few cases has a faecal smell developed, but when present, it has been overpoweringly strong.

The above authors[2] worked out their method on coprolites from the Huaca Prieta, Peru, which they had obtained through the courtesy of Mr Junius Bird, of the American Museum of Natural History in New York. According to Bird,[3] who had excavated the site, the economy of these peoples was based on farming combined with fishing. Their culture was quite primitive, the only artifacts being unworked stone flakes, with no trace of pressure flaking. This was a definite pre-pottery and pre-maize culture, which lasted from about 3000 BC to 1000 BC, when pottery and maize were introduced. The Huaca Prieta was abandoned as a habitation around 500 BC (Fig. 28).

The plant remains sifted from the refuse show that the diet mainly consisted of squash, chili peppers, beans of possibly four varieties and *Canna* lily rhizomes, as well as sundry rhizomes of cattails, rushes and sedges. The presence of a few fruit seeds indicates that several fruits had been eaten in season.

Examination of the actual coprolites brought to light only one type of seed, that of *Capsicum*, the chili pepper, and there were never more than two or three per coprolite. The absence of anything that could be described as epidermis and cuticle of the fruit, and the almost complete absence of seed fragments, all tend to suggest the consumption of immature fruits. Ripe seeds of *Capsicum* are very 'hot' to the taste, which might be further confirmation that the fruit was consumed when young, before the seeds became 'hot'.

Surprisingly enough, no *Cucurbita* (pumpkin) seeds were found. Whitaker and Bird[4]

* In their original paper, Callen and Cameron[2] inadvertently wrote sodium triphosphate.

recorded over 30 seeds from the HP3-M level of the Huaca Prieta, a very small number
of seeds in relation to the 81 stems and 73 shells with stem scars from the same level,
and 1,300 seeds, 11,000 shell fragments and 550 stalk fragments from the whole excavation. In view of this, and the present–day Indian habit of roasting and eating cucurbit
seeds, Whitaker postulated that the early inhabitants of the Huaca Prieta must have done

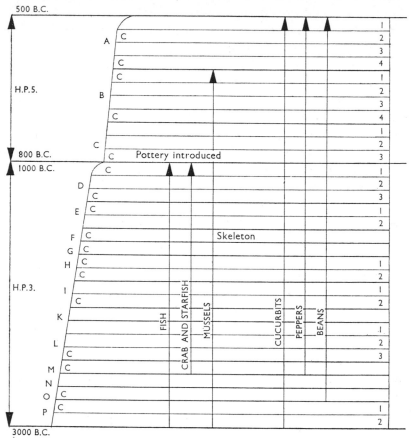

Fig. 28 Diagrammatic section of two pits, Huaca Prieta 3 and Huaca Prieta 5,
showing occupation levels from which coprolites were examined.

so as well. However, their total absence in the coprolites seems to contradict this, and
led Callen and Cameron to the conclusion that *Cucurbita* was mostly eaten young,
like summer squash, before the seeds had formed their tough and distinctively patterned
seed coats. The presence of small stout hairs in the coprolites, such as are found all over
cucurbit plants including the fruits, especially when young, seems to lend credence to
this suggestion. In subsequent work by Callen, Marsh and Cameron, unpublished
as yet, but summarized in the second half of this paper, cucurbit seeds have been
recovered from much older coprolites excavated in Mexico, showing that if and when
reasonably mature seeds are eaten, some come through relatively intact. The Huaca
Prieta material also contained a good deal of tissue with parallel vascular or fibro-vascular

strands, which could be cucurbit flesh, but as there is no distinctive feature by which fragments of this material can be identified, no absolute determination could be made.

Bird[3] had tentatively been able to identify three or possibly four bean varieties from the dried plant remains of the huaca, all referable to the genus *Canavalia*, the Jack bean. In the coprolites, the presence of strong hooked hairs and crystalline druses seemed to confirm this, but it could equally well apply to *Phaseolus*, the green or French bean, known to have occurred on the huaca at a much later date along with pottery and maize. Several pieces of epidermis were found in the same coprolite, some of which possessed the rubiaceous type of stoma found in *Phaseolus*, clearly showing this bean occurred on the huaca at the same time as *Canavalia*, which possesses the rosette type of stoma in the epidermis. Subsequently *Phaseolus* plant remains, which had previously been unrecognized, were identified amongst the plant remains recovered from the pre-pottery phase of the Huaca Prieta.

No other plant remains could be identified with any certainty, as the cells and scraps of tissue were not distinctive enough. Some could have come from fleshy roots (rhizomes), others from fleshy fruits, including peppers.

The balance of the diet appears to have come exclusively from the sea. According to Bird[3] no land animals appear to have been eaten, and only occasionally a sealion or porpoise. He suggested that a good deal of fish was consumed, in view of the nets and floats recovered from the diggings. On the other hand, there was no evidence of fish in the coprolites, probably due to the small sample examined. However, as the delicate tissues of mussel survived in the coprolites, there is no reason why fish tissue, being firmer, should not be present too. In addition, fish bones should have survived, since pieces of mussel shell occurred frequently.

There was apparently an offshore reef at the huaca, from which large mussels, seaurchins, crabs, clams and even starfish were harvested. Remains of all these were found in the huaca, and all except starfish were found in the coprolites. They were eaten uncooked, and with very little chewing, as surprisingly large pieces of mussel and seaurchin shell and small crab claws negotiated the digestive tract successfully. Small mussel shells even came through intact. In surveying the list of materials obtained from the coprolites of each occupation level, it was very noticeable that seafood suddenly ceased to be present. Junius Bird explained (personal communication) that there had been a cataclysm some time during the occupation of the Huaca Prieta, and that the sea had advanced to the base of the huaca. At this time the reef must have sunk, and the disappearance of seashells from the refuse could just as clearly be demonstrated in the coprolites.

Bird[3] concludes that cooking must have been of the roasting type, as no blackened cucurbit fragments were found. Judging from the coprolites, this roasting seems to have caused charring on the outside of the material, though often still leaving it raw in the centre. The coprolites obtained from the different levels can be classified as follows: (1) Entirely fresh: G, H2 and M. (2) Mixed fresh and roasted: (a) Predominantly fresh: A2, A4, B4, D1/D3,* E1 and P1. (b) In equal proportions: F, H1 and L3. (3) Entirely fresh material: B1, D1/D3 and O.

* The D1 and D3 labels are believed to have been switched.

When just a few charred fragments could be detected in a coprolite, this may have been the remains of a previous meal, as all food does not pass down the digestive tract at the same rate. On the other hand, the human stomach empties in from two to four hours, so that a single coprolite should represent the materials mixed together in the stomach. From the coprolites it was therefore possible to determine that a 'meal' generally consisted of mixed plant and animal material.

Bird found the remains of a mummy buried in the rubbish of layer F of HP-3. From the abdomen he was able to collect 28 small packets of material, but was unable to number them in any way to indicate a relationship one to another, nor from which part of the digestive tract they had originated. They probably represent the food consumed during the 48 hours prior to death.

Upon examination of the packets, 16 were found to contain some evidence of seafood or fish, and 18 contained some vegetable material (including *Phaseolus vulgaris* and *Capsicum*). Of these 18, seven contained plentiful plant remains, suggesting recent consumption, and probably originating from the stomach and/or duodenum. The contents of 12 packets consisted almost entirely of sand. Whether this had just filtered in, or been carried in by coprozoic insects, or whether it had been accidentally swallowed, or administered as a cure for hookworm or other disease, we shall never know. In three of these 12 packets unrecognizable charred remains were mixed with the sand.

The presence of fairly plentiful food remains in a large part of the digestive tract suggests that the subject had died rather unexpectedly, and the fact that much of the food was *Capsicum* suggests that death occurred in February or March, when these fruits are obtainable. The packets clearly show that this individual had eaten two, and sometimes three kinds of fruits at one sitting, not one alone, and that a mixed diet of fruit and sea-food had probably been consumed at the same time.

Judging from the coprolites, the diet of these Huaca Prieta inhabitants seems to have consisted mainly of beans, cucurbits, peppers, various roots, mussels, and other sea organisms. Fish did not apparently form a large part of the diet at this time. Clams, snails, sea-urchins and crabs, as well as sundry fruits in season, seem to have been more in the nature of delicacies, rather than staple foods. Traces of meat were found in the coprolites, probably also a delicacy, as Bird concluded from the absence of land animal bones in the refuse.[3]

A further opportunity to study coprolites occurred through the courtesy of Dr R. S. MacNeish, of the National Museum of Canada in Ottawa, who had excavated them from two neighbouring caves of the Sierra Madre, in south-western Tamaulipas, Mexico, and designated them Tmc 247 and Tmc 248. This material covers the period between 7000 BC and 400 BC, the older cultures being pre-pottery and pre-maize, thus dating from the time of domestication of plants, and in fact, according to Willey,[5] this area is believed to be one of the centres of domestication of plants in the Western Hemisphere.

As before, the coprolites were soaked for 72 hours or more in trisodium phosphate, but certain refinements were introduced, notably benzene and salt (NaCl) flotation tests. These allow a much more detailed examination to be made. In the benzene tests, chitinous (i.e. insect) material floats to the surface. However, scraps of plant epidermis, grass seeds and glumes and other plant debris tend to come to the surface also. The salt tests are intended to bring parasite eggs to the top, but the same scraps of plant tissue as had appeared on the surface of the benzene generally floated to the surface of the salt solution as well. Details of these tests will be published elsewhere.

The coprolites from caves Tmc 247 and Tmc 248 (Table A) between them span eight cultural phases, the oldest, Infiernillo, covering the period from 7000 to 5500 BC. From the refuse on the cave floor there have been recovered *Opuntia* (prickly pear),[1] *Lagenaria siceraria* (domestic gourd) and *Cucurbita pepo* (pumpkin),[6] and *Phaseolus coccineus* (runner bean).[7] From the coprolites *Opuntia* seeds and *Phaseolus* have been recovered, and in addition, plentiful *Capsicum* (chili pepper), represented by seeds with their characteristic seedcoat pattern. No *Lagenaria* seeds were recovered—suggesting that although gourds were hollowed out for use, the seeds were not eaten. As yet no *Cucurbita pepo* has been found.

The following culture, Ocampo, covering the period from 4000 to 2300 BC, contained the same plants in the refuse as the Infiernillo phase, with the addition of *Phaseolus vulgaris*, the French or green bean.[7] From the coprolites, *Opuntia*, *Capsicum* and *Phaseolus* were obtained as before, but with the addition of *Cucurbita pepo*. The presence of *Agave* epidermis indicates a widening food horizon. The remains of what the authorities at Kew Botanic Gardens believe to be *Carthamnus* seeds are of special interest, as

TABLE A

Materials identified from Sierra Madre coprolites.

Culture	Level	Tmc 247	Level	Tmc 248	
Infiernillo			7	Opuntia Capsicum Agave	'golden ball' fruit bone bean
			6	Opuntia Capsicum bean	
Ocampo			5	Opuntia Capsicum Cucurbita Setaria	'golden ball' fruit bone Carthamnus pygmy mouse
			4a	Opuntia Capsicum Cucurbita bean	
			4	Opuntia Capsicum Cucurbita Agave bean	'golden ball' fruit bone lizard

TABLE A continued:

Culture	Level	Tmc 247		Level	Tmc 248	
Ocampo (continued)	9	Opuntia Capsicum Cucurbita Setaria Agave	bean bone 'golden ball' fruit Carthamnus			
Flacco				3	Opuntia Capsicum Cucurbita Setaria Agave Aloë bean	'golden ball' fruit bone Helianthus Carthamnus small mammals
Guerra	4b	Opuntia Capsicum Cucurbita Setaria Agave	'golden ball' fruit bone bean			
	4	Opuntia Cucurbita Setaria Agave Aloë	'golden ball' fruit bone Carthamnus rodent bean			
Mesa de Guaje	4a	Opuntia Capsicum Cucurbita Setaria Agave bean	bone Carthamnus rodent Peromyscus Mazama eggshell feathers			

this is a member of the sunflower family from which Indians are known to have obtained a red dye.

Of even greater interest is *Setaria* (foxtail grass), seeds of which were obtained from the lowest level of the Ocampo phase. This has proved to be *Setaria geniculata* (*fide* C. E. Hubbard). It was consumed in large quantities when eaten, and does not appear to have been ground into flour, though some seeds, by their colour, suggest roasting.

Another plant of interest in both the Infiernillo and Ocampo phases has been called 'golden ball' fruit at present, for lack of correct identification. The epidermis and tissue have many golden or orange rounded bodies embedded in them. Actually, as will be seen from Table B, this fruit formed a quite substantial part of the diet.

TABLE B

Percentage of Sierra Madre coprolites containing the materials identified.

Tmc 247 & 248	Agave	Bean	Capsicum	Cucurbita	*Golden ball*	Opuntia	Setaria	*Bone*
Infiernillo	40	60	40	0	20	60	0	20
Ocampo	49	20	53	7	20	65	32	20
Flacco	62	12	61	23	41	75	40	20
Guerra	50	17	25	33	37	8	42	8
Mesa de Guaje	44	11	22	29	2	24	17	26

The next younger culture is Flacco (2300–1800 BC), developed directly from Ocampo,[7] and in the coprolites, the 'new' plants to appear are *Aloë* and *Helianthus*, the sunflower. The Aloe probably supplied water. The sunflower proved to be *Helianthus annuus* var. *lenticularis*, of which two complete seeds and a number of fragments have been recovered. They have been found in only two coprolites of 68 examined in this culture, and they are the only two in the 221 coprolites from the Sierra Madre that have been examined so far. No sunflower seeds appear to have been recovered from the refuse. What is believed to be *Yucca*, *Amaranthus* and possibly even cassava (*Manihot*) have also been found in this culture.

According to MacNeish[7] there was a fundamental shift in diet with the advent of the Guerra culture (1800–1400 BC). This is not evident from Table A, but Table B does show that there was a change, and of the plants mentioned so far, the consumption of the foxtail grass, *Setaria*, has increased, whilst that of *Opuntia* and *Capsicum* has dropped, which can no doubt be explained by the appearance of maize (*Zea mays*), cobs of which have been recovered from this level.[7]

In the fifth cultural phase, Mesa de Guaje, covering the period from 1400 to 400 BC, the most notable change is the almost complete absence of 'golden ball' fruit remains. On the other hand, quite a number of additional fruits, seeds and fleshy roots were consumed. *Dioon* and *Lonchocarpus* have been tentatively identified, both also recovered from the refuse.[7] The most outstanding 'absentee' plant from the coprolites, however, is *Zea mays*. If the grains had been eaten when reasonably mature, some trace of the maize pericarp should be present—but careful inspection has failed to reveal them as yet. It therefore seems possible that the whole maize cob was eaten young, soon after pollination, when it is very sweet, as has also been suggested by MacNeish, who found many quids of fibres, apparently young ears chewed, husks and all, which had been expectorated after the sweet juice had been sucked out.[7] The three most recent cultural phases, Palmillas, San Lorenzo and San Antonio, have not as yet been examined.

Summarizing the plant materials so far identified from the coprolites of the Sierra

One of the most perfect imprints of grain
er encountered. Two-row barley from a
ick which was used about AD 800 in building
huge weir in the ancient Nahrwan Canal east
of Baghdad ($\times 4$).

(b) Portion of a carbonized heap of the olea-
ginous seeds of flax and Gold-of-Pleasure,
from a burnt Iron Age house in Denmark.
The pear-shaped object on top of the seeds is
the pod-valve of the Gold-of-Pleasure ($\times 4$).

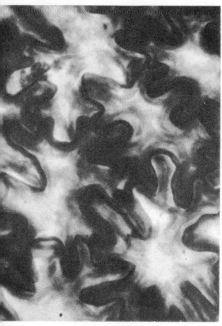

) Silica skeleton of millet husk found in an
ssyrian palace in Iraq which was sacked
shortly before 600 BC ($\times 675$).

(d) The stellate epidermis cells in the seed coat
of corn spurrey (*Spergula arvensis*) from the
stomach of the Iron Age man from Grauballe,
Denmark ($\times 400$).

(see page 177) PLATE IX

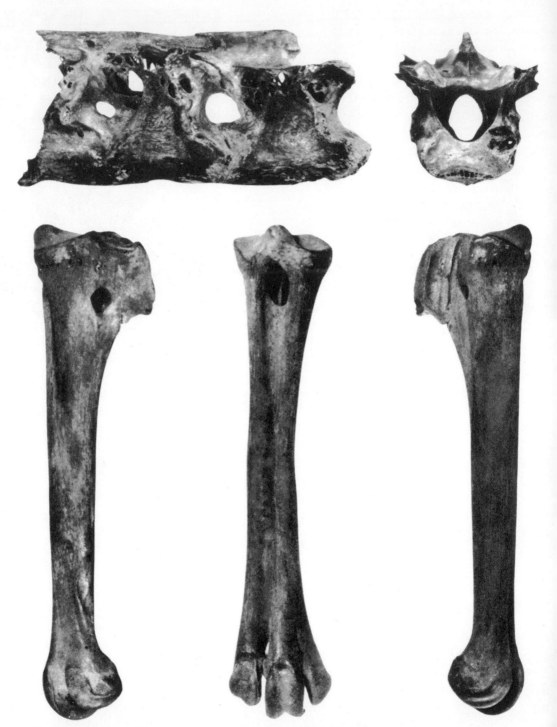

Pelican bones from Britain. Upper row: right and anterior views of fused thoracic vertebrae from the anterior e1
of the synsacrum of a pelican (species indeterminable), from the peat of Saddlebow, King's Lynn, Norfolk (Sedgwic
Museum, D.5762). Lower row: left, anterior and right views of the tarso-metatarsus of a Dalmatian Pelican (*Pel*
canus crispus), from the peat of Cambridgeshire (Sedgwick Museum, D.5761).

PLATE X (see page 197)

Madre, we can clearly see certain trends, even though the figures are based on as yet incomplete work, and in some cases on only a very few coprolites. Table B shows that in Infiernillo, the earliest culture found in these caves, *Opuntia*, the prickly pear, formed a very large part of the diet. This plant was almost certainly not cultivated, and reinforces the conclusion of MacNeish[7] that these were nomadic bands of wild-plant collectors rather than incipient cultivators as suggested by Willey.[5]

On the other hand, *Capsicum* and bean, the two next most frequently consumed plants (fruits), might suggest incipient cultivation. True, these fruits were apparently consumed in a young unripe condition, rather than mature and ripe, hinting at a borderline existence in keeping with plant collecting. This is further borne out by the animal remains of the coprolites—any small animal, even mice, grasshoppers and beetles. The *Capsicum* remains in the coprolites are of special interest, as there was no trace of them in the refuse, and strangely enough the thick cuticle and epidermis have not as yet been identified from the coprolites.*

Studying Table B, we find that further plants were introduced into the diet in the Ocampo phase when incipient cultivation was definitely practised. The amounts of *Opuntia*, *Agave* and *Capsicum* show an increase, but bean a decrease. The most notable addition to the plant list is *Setaria*, identified by C. E. Hubbard as *Setaria geniculata* (*Chaetochloa imberbis* in Hitchcock's Mexican Grasses) which appears in the oldest level of Ocampo. Another grass which appears in the younger levels of Ocampo and in subsequent culture was tentatively identified as *Panicum*, and was referred to by MacNeish under that name.[7] However, C. E. Hubbard is quite positive that this is a *Setaria* as well, though he is unable to identify the species. In a private communication he states: 'The nearest species appears to be *Setaria macrostachya* (*sensu lato*) (*sub Chaetochloa macrostachya* in Hitchcock's Mexican Grasses). It may be that this grass was selected from a large seeded wild grass for use as a cereal, and that it has been lost due to an unsuitable habitat. *Setaria glauca* in N. India has a comparable large seeded strain collected on but few occasions and very imperfectly known.' No trace of the *Setaria* species had been found in the Sierra Madre caves, except in the coprolites, but one or more of them is known from the La Perra phase of the Sierra de Tamaulipas horizon.[1]

Of the *Cucurbita* species, only *C. pepo* (the pumpkin) has been found, and there has been no trace of the domestic gourd (*Lagenaria siceraria*) in the coprolites. It seems probable that the seeds of this latter species were discarded when the gourds were turned into containers.

It is noticeable that the amounts consumed of the plant materials already mentioned reach a maximum in the Flacco culture, except in the case of *Setaria*. In the Guerra culture, only *Setaria* and *Cucurbita* consumption has increased in the coprolites, and bone debris in the subsequent Mesa de Guaje. As maize was apparently introduced during the Flacco phase, in subsequent cultures its use must have been responsible for the reduction in consumption of other plant materials.

When the coprolites were received, some were riddled with circular, pit-like holes, containing larvae and pupae of blow flies or flesh flies, and the discarded larval skins of

* Golden ball epidermis and tissue have now been identified as *Capsicum*.

Fannia scalaris, the latrine fly. Plentiful remains of *Musca domestica*, the house fly, as well as several adult fungus gnats and other dipterous insects, were also present. All these have certainly entered the coprolites after they were deposited at the back of the cave. However, the presence of *Drosophila* larvae and pupae of at least three species indicates the consumption of ripe or even overripe fruit.

Other insect material identified includes parts of grasshoppers, bees, wasps, ants, spiders, beetles and even mites and termites. The spiders and the darkling (tenibrionid) beetles are complete and undamaged, which is not surprising, as the darkling beetles colonize faeces, and the spiders are of the small variety that would crawl into cavities and holes. The other insects and beetles are in fragments, and have almost certainly been eaten.

Bones of all sorts and sizes have been recovered. Some were obviously bird bones, and consisted of vertebrae, leg and foot bones, and pieces of sternum. Interesting is the fact that some of these bones are charred at one end, and not at the other. Even egg shell and immature feathers have been recovered. Several small lower jaws turned up, making specific identification possible. One has been tentatively identified as that of a pygmy mouse, and others as those of deer mice. A lizard mandible and other bones have been recognized, and there is mammalian hair of several types, including human. Deer hair and fragments of bone as large as 12 × 16 mm in the same coprolite suggest *Mazama*, bones of which were recovered from the cave.[1]

Although this work on the Sierra Madre coprolites is incomplete, much information can already be pieced together from it to show the value of this new technique. Apart from the actual plant and animal remains that can be identified, and which have not been found in the refuse, the relative amounts eaten and the types eaten together, as well as whether cooked or not, can all be determined from the coprolites. But it has to be borne in mind that these caves were only occupied at certain seasons of the year, and that the picture of the food habits that is being built up only represents that particular season of the year, and which may not be typical.

ACKNOWLEDGEMENTS

The writer is greatly indebted to Mr Junius Bird and Dr Richard (Scotty) MacNeish for placing their materials and knowledge at his disposal; to Dr C. E. Hubbard and Dr C. R. Metcalfe of the Royal Botanic Gardens, Kew, and many colleagues at McGill University, especially Prof. T. W. M. Cameron, a never-failing source of help and encouragement.

REFERENCES

1 MacNeish, R. S. 1958. *Trans. Am. Phil. Soc.* 48 (6), 1–210
2 Callen, E. O. and Cameron, T. W. M. 1960. *New Scientist* 8 (190), 35
3 Bird, J. B. 1948. *Natural History* 58 (7), 296, 334
4 Whitaker, T. W. and Bird, J. B. 1949. *Amer. Mus. Novitates*, no. 1426, 1
5 Willey, G. R. 1960. *Science* 131, 73
6 Whitaker, T. W., Cutler, H. and MacNeish, R. S. 1957. *Am. Antiq.* 22 (4), pt. 1
7 Kaplan, L. and MacNeish, R. S. 1960. *Bot. Mus. Leafl. Harv. Univ.* 19 (2), 33

20 Fauna

ERIC HIGGS

THE INVESTIGATION of Pleistocene fauna began as early as the eighteenth century. Recognition of the association of the bones of extinct animals with artifacts was one of the events which led to the realization of the true antiquity of man.

The faunal changes during the Pleistocene consisted of the extinction of some forms, the evolution of others, and migrations of animal populations from one area to another. These changes took place against a background of at least four major ice advances which in Europe covered, at their maxima, most of the British Isles and Scandinavia, parts of Germany, Central Russia and Poland and in North America more than half the continent.[1] Between the glaciations occurred interglacial or warmer periods during which times it has been postulated North America was completely deglaciated and in Europe there was less ice than there is now. These climatic changes were not immediate and complete. A number of warmer and colder oscillations have been demonstrated during the last glaciation of varying severity and no doubt similar minor fluctuations occurred in earlier glaciations. Climatic change, however, was not necessarily a slow process for in the Mankato advance 'the ice came so fast it overrode the living forest'.

In so far as faunal changes can be related to particular ice advances or recessions, they are of assistance in forming a relative chronology. The extinction of some species of animals occurred in Europe early in the Pleistocene and their bones suggest an early date for related deposits. Similarly the evolution of the elephant from *Elephas meridionalis* through *E. trogontherii* and the forest *E. antiquus* to the cold open-country mammoth, forms a relative chronology for associated artifacts.

During the glaciations the floral zones, tundra, coniferous and deciduous forest probably moved southwards in the Northern Hemisphere. With them went their appropriate fauna. In the warmer interglacials the floral zones probably moved northwards. A living site inhabited during these climatic changes may show in its layers alternating warm and cold faunas and indicate changes in the vegetation surrounding it. Tundra conditions are said to be indicated by such animals as the Arctic fox and the mammoth, coniferous forest by the brown bear, the lynx and the elk, temperate forest by *Elephas antiquus* and the hippopotamus.[2] The mere absence or presence of a particular animal, however, in an assemblage is of itself usually of uncertain import.

As with the ice advances the rain belts are thought to have moved southwards it is tempting to correlate the supposed pluvials of Africa with glaciations in the Northern Hemisphere. Certainly there were periods when the sea-water temperature of the

Mediterranean fell below present levels and the rainfall over the Sahara may have been greater than it is now. Cattle, for example, were able to penetrate to areas at present desert. The presence of Eurasiatic animals such as bear, wolf and deer in North Africa shows a time existed when the deserts were open to the passage of animals and therefore of man. On the other hand deserts expanded under drier conditions and animal communities isolated in refuge areas died out or sometimes evolved on different lines from those elsewhere. Similarly the rising of sea level, due to the melting ice, interrupted the free passage of animals and isolated other communities. The dwarf elephants of the Mediterranean islands are said to be due to such isolation[3] although others have suggested the migration of already existing small species to these areas, or a food deficiency, to account for this dwarfism.

Apart from these climatic and geographic inferences to be made from bones, it has been possible to make further deductions as to the customs, habits and way of life of prehistoric man. Hunting and fishing methods have been inferred and the mobility of peoples from the seasonal occupation of living sites.[4]

With the introduction of the domestication of animals man increased his control over his environment, a process which had begun in temperate Europe with the fall of the tree to the Mesolithic axe. The imbalance which took place by the protection and hence proliferation of Neolithic flocks and herds resulted in erosion and denudation, the creation of barren lands and deserts over many millennia, a process which has been underestimated and the extent and speed of which at the present day are little appreciated. The domestic animal, as Childe put it, is a walking wardrobe and a living larder. It necessitated a profound difference in the way of life of prehistoric peoples, as did cultivation. The preservation of the animal against predators and against the seasonal food shortage of winter cold or summer drought, becomes a new form of preoccupation. The animals themselves are a new source of exchangeable, transportable, inheritable and cumulative wealth which can be passed from one generation to another, a form of wealth essential to the economic developments which were to take place.

Evans-Pritchard[5] records the absorption of the Nuer in their cattle and how they necessitated a certain mode of distribution and transhumance. He describes the concepts of time and space which arose largely from ways of livelihood and disposition of settlements. The importance and effect of the pastoral way of life upon these peoples is of overwhelming significance. It is to the evidence from the bones of the domestic animals that we must look for many of the more important characteristics of prehistoric peoples and for an understanding of them.

REFERENCES

1 CHARLESWORTH, J. K. 1957. *The Quaternary Era*, London
2 ZEUNER, F. E. 1950. *Dating the Past*, London
3 VAUFREY, R. 1939. *Arch. Inst. Paléont. Hum. 20*
4 CLARK, J. G. D. 1952. *Prehistoric Europe*, London
5 EVANS-PRITCHARD, E. E. 1940. *The Nuer*, Oxford

K. A. JOYSEY

THE PIECE OF BONE described here is not important in itself, and the investigation based upon it has not led to any world-shaking conclusions. But it is a story with a moral, and it can be used to illustrate several points of general application.

In 1956 my geological colleague Dr C. L. Forbes of the Sedgwick Museum, Cambridge, came to visit me with a piece of bone (D.5762). It had been collected by Mr W. E. Doran, Chief Engineer of the Great Ouse River Board, from the new flood-relief channel, about half a mile north of Saddlebow village, near King's Lynn in Norfolk.

It was clearly a piece of bird bone, and consisted of three fused thoracic vertebrae, broken from the anterior end of the synsacrum. The bird from which it had been derived was of unusually large size, and so I compared it with the skeletons of the larger British birds. Swan, goose, heron, barn-owl, gannet, gull, cormorant and golden eagle—none of them matched the bone. A search among the birds of Europe proved more fruitful, and after some time the bone was found to be derived from a pelican.

The most recent check-list of the birds of Great Britain and Ireland[3] does not include any species of pelican. How then had a pelican come to leave its bones in Norfolk? Was it an escape from a zoo, or was it a stray migrant which had wandered beyond its normal range?

There are several reports of pelicans having been shot or sighted in England during relatively recent times. Sir Thomas Browne recorded that a pelican was shot at Horsey Fen, Norfolk, in 1663, but he suggested that it might have been one of the King's pelicans which had escaped from St James's Park at about the same time.[15] Nearly two hundred years later, Tristam[21] recorded that a dead pelican had been found on the coast of County Durham, but gave no indication of the species. Gurney[10] reported a pelican at Breydon, Norfolk, in 1906, which later spent several months near Whitstable, Kent, where it was identified by Saunders[20] as a White Pelican, *P. onocrotalus*. Another pelican was sighted at Breydon in 1915 but this time the species was not recorded.[19]

There are two species of European pelican, namely the White Pelican, *Pelecanus onocrotalus* Linné, and the Dalmatian Pelican, *Pelecanus crispus* Bruch. According to Dresser[4] the ranges of *P. onocrotalus* and *P. crispus* overlap to a large extent. Both species live in South and South-eastern Europe and range into North Africa and eastwards into Asia. *P. onocrotalus* occurs rarely in Central and Northern Europe although it has been recorded in North Germany, Poland, Denmark, Sweden, and Finland. In contrast, *P. crispus* has not been observed either in Scandinavia or France. Hence, on the basis of the present distribution supported by the evidence of the only specimen which has been identified, it seems likely that the stray pelicans which have been recorded in Britain during the last few hundred years would have been *P. onocrotalus* rather than *P. crispus*.

At this point in the investigation it appeared that by some remote chance the mechanical excavator working in Norfolk had brought to light the bones of a stray *P. onocrotalus*, but the species could not be determined with any certainty because the anterior region of the synsacrum does not provide any characters on which it is possible to distinguish between the two European species.

While searching through the collection of pelican skeletons in the University Museum of Zoology, Cambridge, we found in the same cupboard a box containing two sub-fossil pelican bones, from the peat of East Anglia. Further inquiry revealed that there were two more in the Sedgwick Museum.

It appears that Milne-Edwards[13] and Newton[14] recorded the first pelican bone from Britain in 1868. This bone (Sedgwick Museum no. D.5760) was among an old collection of bones from the lower peat of Cambridgeshire. It is a left humerus, which was judged to have been derived from a young bird, presumably bred in this country, rather than from an adult migrant. Newton stated that it was larger than the corresponding bone of the White Pelican, *Pelecanus onocrotalus*, and on the same basis Milne-Edwards suggested that it might belong to a new species.

In 1871, Newton[16] described another pelican humerus from Feltwell Fen, Norfolk. This bone was presented by J. H. Gurney to the University Museum of Zoology, Cambridge (no. 260a). Newton noted that it was from an adult bird, and suggested that both this and the previous humerus were comparable in size to that of the Dalmatian Pelican, *Pelecanus crispus*.

Harmer[12] recorded the discovery of the fractured, but associated, humerus, radius, and ulna of a pelican from Burnt Fen, near Littleport, Cambridgeshire, in 1897. These bones, which are also in the University Museum of Zoology, Cambridge (no. 258D), were identified by him as belonging to *Pelecanus crispus*.

In 1901, Newton[17] recognized a right tarso-metatarsus of a pelican among the same collection of bird bones in which he made his first discovery and he suggested that they might have been collected from the same deposit. He also identified this bone (Sedgwick Museum no. D.5761) as *Pelecanus crispus*.

We decided to make an attempt to recover the rest of the skeleton of our bird. Here was an opportunity to find out which of the two species of pelican had lived in East Anglia, and it was essential to determine the exact horizon in the peat from which it had come. For this latter purpose, Dr Forbes and myself were accompanied by our botanical colleague, Dr R. G. West. On arrival at the site we measured up the section, collected samples of the deposits, and searched for more bones—in vain.

The section of Fenland postglacial deposits exposed where the pelican bone was found is as follows: (4) Grey silt, weathering brown above, penetrated from the surface by *Phragmites* rhizomes. 0 to 3 ft. (3) Chocolate-brown fen peat with wood and *Phragmites* rhizomes. 3 ft to 5 ft 6 in. (2) Transition to next. Brown clay penetrated by *Phragmites* rhizomes. 5 ft 6 in. to 5 ft 11 in. (1) Grey-blue fen clay, with *Cardium edule* abundant in the top 6 in.; seen to water level. 5 ft 11 in. to 17 ft 11 in.

The sequence—fen clay, peat, silt—is repeated in the section described by H. and

M. E. Godwin[8] at Wiggenhall St Germans, about a mile and a quarter south of the pelican site. Our peat bed no. 3 corresponds to the 2 ft peat bed 'E' at Wiggenhall St Germans.

The pelican bone was stained brown and contained peat in its crevices and hollows, so there is no doubt that it came from the peat bed, although it was found lying on the peat in a slumped part of the section. In order to find the horizon within the peat from which the bone had come, Dr West made a pollen analysis of peat scrapings taken from within foramina in the bone. He then compared the results of this analysis (given in Table A), with analyses made from successive levels of the peat bed itself.

TABLE A

Pollen analysis of peat scrapings from the pelican bone, given as percentages of total (150) tree pollen.

Trees	%	Trees	%
Betula (Birch)	20	Tilia (Lime)	1
Pinus (Pine)	1	Alnus (Alder)	27
Ulmus (Elm)	6	Carpinus (Hornbeam)	1
Quercus (Oak)	36	Fraxinus (Ash)	8

Non-Trees	%	Non-Trees	%
Corylus (Hazel)	62	Ranunculus (Buttercup)	1
Salix (Willow)	3	Umbelliferae (Umbellifers)	1
Gramineae (Grasses)	29	Myriophyllum verticillatum	
Cyperaceae (Sedges)	12	(Whorled water-milfoil)	4
Artemisia (Mugwort)	3	Nymphaea (Water-lily)	3
Calluna (Ling)	1	Sparganium (Bur-reed)	20
Chenopodiaceae (Goosefoot		Typha latifolia (Great reed-	
family)	3	mace)	1
Rubiaceae (Bedstraw family)	1	Filicales (Ferns)	55
Plantago lanceolata (Ribwort)	3	Pteridium (Bracken)	1

Samples were taken at 6 in. intervals through the peat bed a few yards from the pelican site. The samples from the top 2 ft of the bed contained sparse tree pollen, but abundant fern spores, values of which reached from 600 to 6,000% of the total tree pollen.

The results indicated that the bone had come from the lowest 6 in. of the peat bed, where values for the fern spores were found to be considerably lower and tree pollen much more abundant. A similar horizon for the provenance of the bone is suggested by comparison with the pollen diagram of the synchronous 2 ft peat bed at Wiggenhall St Germans,[8] where the analysis from the pelican bone is best matched in the section of the diagram taken from the lower part of the peat bed.

Godwin and Willis[9] have recently obtained radiocarbon dates for the peat bed at Saddlebow, immediately adjacent to the pelican site. Two samples from the top few centimetres of peat (Q.549; Q.550) give the dates AD 85 and 110 BC, respectively (both ± 110 years). Two other samples, Q.489 from the Transition Bed between the top of the Fen Clay and the base of the peat, and Q.490 from the base of the peat itself, both indicate a date of approximately 2000 BC. Hence, in archaeological terms this peat bed is now known to cover a range including both Bronze Age and Iron Age times. Previously, the peat bed was believed to be of Iron Age date,[6] and so when this pelican bone was first described it was attributed to this period.[5] The pollen analysis showed that the pelican bone was derived from the basal part of the peat, and so it must now be attributed to the Bronze Age.

As described by Godwin,[6] the fen clay was formed under brackish-water conditions, the freshwater 2 ft peat bed was deposited after a regression of the sea, and the change to the upper silt was caused by a later marine transgression. H. and M. E. Godwin[8] have described the vegetational conditions obtaining during the growth of the peat in this area, as indicated by their pollen diagram from Wiggenhall St Germans. The basal part of the peat contains indicators of salt-marsh conditions (e.g. the 3% of Chenopodiaceae pollen seen in the analysis from the pelican bone). Such conditions would appear on the regression of the sea at the change from the fen clay to the fen peat. The lower middle part of the peat was formed during alder carr conditions, when brackish water gave way to freshwater conditions. In the analysis from the bone the presence of shallow open freshwater is suggested by the presence of pollen of *Myriophyllum verticillatum* and *Nymphaea*, and of reed swamp by *Typha latifolia* and *Sparganium*. The remaining upper part of the peat was formed under fen wood conditions. This change from alder carr to fen wood is the normal vegetational succession to be expected. Thus, the pelican bone came from the vegetational stage during the replacement of the salt-marsh by freshwater fen, and prior to the growth of the fen wood, but there is no clear evidence from the site, of former climatic conditions or changes which might have affected the distribution of the pelican.

While Dr West was engaged on the foregoing pollen studies, I re-examined all of the pelican bones previously found in East Anglia, and compared them with skeletons of *P. crispus* and *P. onocrotalus* in the Cambridge and London museums. The seven skeletons of *P. onocrotalus* available for study in the British Museum fall into two size groups, five of the skeletons being distinctly smaller than the other two. The sex of only two of the specimens is definitely known and these are both female, and both belong to the smaller size group; this is consistent with the assumption that the differences in size may be due to sexual dimorphism.

Only a single complete skeleton of *P. crispus* was available for study, and its sex is unknown. The bones of the wing are comparable in size with the two larger (male?) skeletons of *P. onocrotalus*, but the leg bones are relatively small and comparable in size with those of the smaller (female) skeletons of *P. onocrotalus*.

All the wing bones of the pelicans found in the peat of East Anglia are comparable in size with the skeleton of *P. crispus* and the two male (?) skeletons of *P. onocrotalus*.

These fossil wing bones were originally referred to *P. crispus* on the basis of their large size, but it is evident that some specimens of *P. onocrotalus* attain an equivalent size, and one of them (British Museum no. 1903.3.6.2) is larger than any of the East Anglian fossils. It has not been possible to find any characters of the humerus, radius, or ulna which distinguish *P. crispus* from *P. onocrotalus*, and so all the East Anglian fossil wing bones should strictly be referred to as *Pelecanus* of uncertain species.

The remaining pelican bone previously found in the East Anglian peat is the tarso-metatarsus recorded by Newton.[17] The tarso-metatarsus of the single skeleton of *P. crispus* in the British Museum shows differences from those of *P. onocrotalus*. In *P. crispus* the hypotarsus projects relatively further and its posterior face is relatively smaller than in *P. onocrotalus* (Fig. 29). As there is only one skeleton of *P. crispus*, it seemed possible that these differences were due to individual variation. Fortunately, when a bird skin is prepared as a study specimen the leg bones are usually left in position. A single specimen (British Museum no. 1895.2.10.112) was chosen at random from the large collection of skins of *P. crispus*, and the tarso-metatarsus was carefully exposed. It was found that the shape of the hypotarsus matched that of the single skeleton of *P. crispus*, so confirming

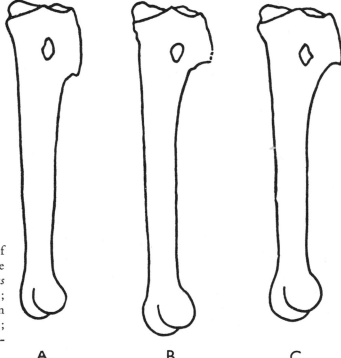

Fig. 29 Right tarso-metatarsi of pelicans, viewed from the left side (× 2/3): A: *Pelecanus onocrotalus* (British Museum, 1903, 3.6.1); B: fossil pelican from East Anglian peat (Sedgwick Museum, D.5761); C: *Pelecanus crispus* (British Museum, 1896. 2.7.1).

A   B   C

that this character could be used to distinguish between the two European species of pelican. As a further check, the tarso–metatarsus in the skin of an immature specimen (British Museum no. 1908.2.29.1) of *P. onocrotalus* was similarly exposed, and it was found to conform to the type expected in this species.

The tarso-metatarsus from the peat of East Anglia is of the type found in *P. crispus*, so confirming the conclusion reached by Newton.

Elsewhere in Britain, a single femur of a pelican has been found in the peat of Hull, Yorkshire,[18] and the remains of *P. crispus* have been recorded from the Lake Village at Glastonbury, Somerset, which was the site of an Iron Age settlement shortly before the Roman occupation. Andrews[1,2] described numerous bones, including nine tarso-meta-tarsi, so representing at least five individuals, some of which were young birds. It has been possible to re-examine eight of the Glastonbury tarso-metatarsi. Five of these bones have the hypotarsus preserved and all of them are of the *P. crispus* type.

There now appears to be no doubt that the Iron Age pelican of Somerset was the Dalmatian Pelican, *P. crispus*, and not the White Pelican, *P. onocrotalus*, the latter being the species which visits parts of north-west Europe at the present time. The Bronze Age pelican vertebrae from East Anglia and the several pelican wing bones from East Anglia could belong to either of these species, but the single tarso-metatarsus from East Anglia can be identified with certainty as *P. crispus*. This change in the distribution of the Dalmatian Pelican appears to be more than a local phenomenon, since Winge[22] has reported the occurrence of fossil *P. crispus* in Denmark, which is also outside the present range of the species.

In an extensive study of references to birds in early literature, Gurney[11] found no evidence that the pelican was native to Britain either during or subsequent to Roman times. This indication is supported by the absence of the pelican among bird bones which have been recovered from sites of Roman occupation in Britain.

Looking back on this project, the following general points have emerged:

1. Certain material is so rare that one cannot go out into the field and collect it at will. Such material only becomes available in our museums as the product of hundreds of man-hours of observation by interested amateurs. In order to receive and enjoy the fruits of such labour the museum specialist must also be prepared to spend many hours checking hundreds of bone fragments of recently deceased horse, sheep and cow.

2. When first collected this pelican bone was roughly cleaned, but by good fortune some of the matrix was preserved in the foramina. Subsequently, this matrix was used to determine the exact provenance of the specimen. The natural urge to clean a specimen may lead to loss of information. As a general principle some of the matrix should always be preserved.

3. In many museums there is a tendency to regard specimens lacking stratigraphical data as practically worthless. The advent of pollen analysis and of certain petrological techniques has now made it possible to match very small quantities of adherent matrix. Such techniques have given new value to old material which was originally collected without stratigraphical detail.

4. This investigation was not the outcome of an archaeological project at a former habitation site, but it has provided corroboration of the previous find at Glastonbury. It was the product of collaboration between engineer, geologist, zoologist and botanist, none of whom had enough specialized knowledge to complete the work alone. Such

team work is fruitful and will become essential as more specialized techniques are applied to archaeological problems.

5. Comparative osteology for its own sake is not at present a fashionable zoological pursuit, and the present trend of biological research is such that archaeologists will find it increasingly difficult to contact zoologists who are either able or willing to undertake bone identification. Under pressure for space some zoological institutions have already disposed of their supposedly outdated osteological collections. Large and comprehensive collections of skeletons are essential for the accurate identification of bone fragments. Such collections take many years to accumulate and many specimens are virtually irreplaceable. The time has now come when archaeologists must be trained to specialize in this field, and archaeological departments must be prepared to accommodate the necessary comparative collections.

ACKNOWLEDGEMENTS

The piece of bone which prompted this investigation has been kindly presented to the Sedgwick Museum by the Great Ouse River Board. I am indebted to Mr J. D. Macdonald and Mrs P. A. Cottam for their help in the British Museum (Natural History), to Dr M. Bird and Miss M. T. Prior for arranging the loan of specimens from the Glastonbury Lake Village Museum. Sections of this chapter, including Fig. 29, have been reprinted from the *Geological Magazine*, vol. 95 (1958), by kind permission of my co-authors, Drs C. L. Forbes and R. G. West, and the publishers, Stephen Austin and and Sons, Ltd.

REFERENCES

1 ANDREWS, C. W. 1899. *Ibis* (7) 5, 351
2 —— 1917. In BULLEID, A. and GRAY, H. ST. G., *The Glastonbury Lake Village*, II, 631
3 BRITISH ORNITHOLOGISTS' UNION. 1952. *Checklist of the birds of Great Britain and Ireland*, London
4 DRESSER, H. E. 1881. *A History of the Birds of Europe*, London, 6, 191
5 FORBES, C. L., JOYSEY, K. A. and WEST, R. G. 1958. *Geol. Mag.* 95, 153
6 GODWIN, H. 1940. *Phil. Trans. Roy. Soc. Lond.* B 230, 239
7 —— 1961. *Proc. Roy. Soc. Lond.* 153, 287
8 —— and GODWIN, M. E., 1933. *Geol. Mag.* 70, 168
9 —— and WILLIS, E. H., 1961. *Am. J. Sci. Radiocarbon Suppl.* 3, 60
10 GURNEY, J. H. 1907. *Zoologist* (4) 11, 131
11 —— 1921. *Early annals of ornithology*, London
12 HARMER, S. F. 1897. *Trans. Norf. and Norwich Nat. Soc.* 6, 363
13 MILNE-EDWARDS, A. 1868. *Ibis* (2) 4, 363
14 NEWTON, A. 1868a. *Proc. Zool. Soc. for 1868*, 2
15 —— 1868b. Editorial note to Milne-Edwards[13]
16 —— 1871. *Proc. Zool. Soc. for 1871*, 702
17 —— 1901. *Trans. Norf. and Norwich Nat. Soc.* 7, 158
18 NEWTON, E. T., 1928. *The Naturalist*, 167
19 PATTERSON, A. H., 1916. *Zoologist* (4) 20, 364
20 SAUNDERS, S., 1906. *Ibid.* (4) 10, 431
21 TRISTAM, H. B. 1856. *Ibid.* 14, 5321
22 WINGE, H. 1901. *Ibis* (8) 1, 516

22 Osteo-Archaeology

CHARLES A. REED

IN REMEMBERING my own experiences, and hearing those of others, of bones and archaeologists together, it seems to me that the archaeologists usually lack understanding of, and appreciation for, bones. For the archaeologist, a bone definitely lacks the emotional appeal of pottery, stone, statuettes, and architecture. He understands the artifacts, and can visualize the kinds of conclusions to be derived from them. He feels that they were human-made and tell him of human cultures. He does not usually understand bones, and considers them to be unpleasant biological matters, a second-class category of objects, to be treated with less care, to be chopped across in cleaning a vertical excavation face, to be saved perhaps if they are hard but to be destroyed if time is pressing or if they are soft, or perhaps to be tossed on the dump-heap willy-nilly whether salvageable or not.

Yes, lack of understanding leads to lack of appreciation.

Bone is a particular kind of dense connective tissue, produced to some extent by most living vertebrate animals except the cyclostomes, sharks and rays. Bone in the living animal is not solid, but is penetrated by multiple microscopic canals, in which lie capillaries, cells, and tissue fluid in an intricate but organized pattern. It is penetrated in all directions with circulating fluids, so that molecular exchanges occur at all times between the fluids and the inorganic portion of the bone, no part of which is more than a micron or so from a source of replenishable supplies. Molecular replacement in the crystalline bone is constant; in the living animal, bone is an active, dynamic tissue with a complex biochemical life.[6] Only after death do we see the 'dead' bone that too often is regarded as the real thing.

If we shift our emphasis from bone as a tissue to bones as skeletal parts, we find the palaeontologist and comparative anatomist sharing intellectual adventures. Bones occur in myriad shapes and sizes, but each bone is exquisitely designed in correlation with the particular animal, position, and function it serves. The ultimate design of the adult bone, both within and without, is the result of complex physiological processes, controlled primarily by genes but influenced greatly by such environmental factors as nutrition, sex hormones, use or disuse, and possibly distorting forces (e.g. head-binding).

The genes in turn are chromosomal molecules of desoxyribonucleic acids (DNA), which have been passed through generation after generation of populations (gene-pools); they have been modified by mutation and screened for survival by multiple selective factors, most of which cannot now be analysed.

A bone is an identification tag of the animal to which it belonged. Having solved the problem of identification, we can see the animal entire, not merely a single bone; we see an animal in its functioning whole, with the psyche, behaviour, nutritional demands, and environmental requirements of that species of animal. The animal lives in a particular kind of a world; seeing the bone and knowing the animal, we know something of flora, other animals, terrain, water supplies, temperature.

Who—except possibly archaeologists—would dig for artifacts when there are bones to be salvaged?

In the discussion that follows, my own personal experiences naturally obtrude in matters of technique and interpretation. In various places here, and in prior papers, I stress the importance of the zoologist knowing the country and its ecology where the digging occurs, and also I stress that he should be an active excavator and general participant in the expedition. There is nothing more deadly than having someone else go out, do the digging, and bring back the bones to be 'experted', although Heizer[21] recommends this latter practice to American archaeologists.

FIELD TECHNIQUES

The skulls and long bones in the prehistoric sites I have helped excavate were almost invariably broken. Most of this breaking is ancient—done in the original butchering, by the cook, or by the diner. Under such circumstances, the broken bones from many animals will ultimately get mixed together, and those from one animal, possibly distributed between several households, become scattered; there is little or no hope of reconstructing any one animal or even parts thereof.

Such mixed and broken bone, if it has not rotted over the millennia, can then be removed as found, stratum by stratum. On a large excavation, where many local workmen have been hired, the bone from each stratum and square is then assembled in piles to be sorted by a zoologist. One realizes that some possibilities of interpretation are necessarily lost in such large-scale operations. Particularly for a foreign expedition, the rigid limitations of a short field season and high operating costs make impossible the meticulous excavation which is possible to the local excavator elsewhere.

At the same time, the archaeologist must be looking for any unusual concentration of bone, for articulated pieces, and for pieces too large or too broken to be lifted casually. Such situations call for more time than the supervising archaeologist has, and demand the particular skills of the zoo-archaeologist.

Field sorting and packing of bone. At large excavations where, as happened at Jarmo and Sarab, quantities of broken bone rapidly accumulate, preliminary field sorting is necessary, since 90% of the bulk may be unidentifiable chips. One should then weigh all the excavated bone or measure its volume in boxes of predetermined sizes, after which the bulk of this 'trash' may be discarded. Some, perhaps 2–3 cubic feet, should be saved; this can be weighed in the home laboratory, and a rough constant worked out as to the relation between weight and volume, to be applied to the bone discarded in the field. Further, unidentifiable chips can serve as a source of collagen for C^{14} determinations[46] and to have as a reservoir for serological (or other) techniques as yet undeveloped.

One naturally saves all the pieces that experience determines may be identifiable; one does not merely save what is thought to be a satisfactory sample (I thus disagree with

Meighan[27] concerning sampling techniques). It is most disconcerting to visit an old site later and find the ground and dump-heap strewn with identifiable bone and to realize that the published conclusions, based upon a small sample, are most erroneous.

Hard, dry, broken bones do not usually need special packing. The bulk of them from one square and stratum can safely be placed together in one or more tough paper bags and recorded on the bag in ink.

Any treatment with shellac, alvar, glue, or other compound is generally unnecessary for good firm bone. If the bone is at all damp, shellac and some other compounds have definite disadvantages. The use of alvar I particularly dislike, for, as it dries after a year or so, it sometimes peels off in thin sheets, which take with them the adherent surfaces of the bone, and thus destroys the bone as an object of identification and comparison. Further, if the bone was not cleaned, the alvar or shellac must be removed before cleaning can be accomplished.

Using the technique of the plaster jacket,[8,56,21] there is *no* material, bone or otherwise, which cannot be lifted intact from the ground and transported safely to the laboratory. The major drawback of the plaster technique is that the jackets are bulky and heavy. An enclosing jacket of papier-mâché, light-weight and non-bulky, is as satisfactory as is that of plaster for all except the largest and heaviest pieces of archaeological bone. As with plaster, papier-mâché has the advantage that it can be applied to wet bone; indeed, wetting the bone is part of the process.

The one basic fact to be remembered is that no substance non-miscible with water should be applied to the bone, which, as it lies in the ground, is often wet or at least damp. Thus shellac, alvar, and all other compounds which do not dissolve in, or mix with, water are at once excluded. On wet or damp bones shellac and kindred substances will not penetrate, but form only a film. If the damp bone and the enclosing film are then packed for shipment, slowly the bone dries, and slowly it may fall to powder. Alvar, as mentioned above, often peels as it dries. I thus disagree definitely with any and all field-manuals[51] which ignore the value of water-soluble glues.

One must achieve *penetration* with any substance to be applied to soft or crumbling bone, and it is exactly this penetration that the shellacs, alvars, and plastics fail to accomplish. Glues, including gum arabic, are the water-miscible substances of choice. My own experience in the Near East is that the glue used by the local carpenters (this glue is purchasable as small, dry, brown pellets) is satisfactory, cheap, and easily available. One simply takes a bucket of water at air-temperature and drops in and mixes the pellets until the water feels quite sticky between the fingers.

Drip glue into the specimen successively, letting it dry somewhat between applications. During rains, such preparations must be covered. When the crumbling or cracked bone is firmly adherent to itself and the surrounding earth, dig a trench around the glued bone (or other object being so prepared), and gently undercut the trench, so that the object sits upon a pedestal. Wet the surface of the object once again with the thin glue, and apply cleansing tissue to it, the paper to be patted down firmly with a paint brush wetted in the glue, until no air bubbles remain beneath the paper. Successive pieces of tissue are then applied in the same way, to a depth of several layers, covering the whole of the object and being tightly wrapped around, and down under, the edge of the pedestal. Following the tissue, torn pieces of newspaper are then *soaked* in the glue, to be applied in a similar way over the layers of tissue. Apply newspaper until it, too, is several layers thick. One now waits for the structure to dry; in an area where the papier-mâché technique is necessary, the place soon sprouts a number of thick-stemmed, paper-capped 'mushrooms'. When one of these is dry, the 'stalk' is carefully broken (stiff wires poked through it will aid this process), the structure is turned over, and the former lower side is cleaned of dirt, and the same process is repeated on the newly exposed surface.

Pieces of bone which are firm and do not need the papier-mâché treatment can be soaked in warm glue until they cease to bubble air.

Glues, being of biologic origin, are subject to invasion by moulds if the objects containing them are stored in damp places. One can either plan to store the glued bones dry and warm (as museum storage should be), or mix carbolic acid with the glue in the field.

My own experience would indicate that objects of the size and relative fragility of a cracked human skull or the horn-core of an aurochs (*Bos primigenius*) are more safely preserved in plaster.

The use of either the plaster or the papier-mâché jackets is very simple, and both should be among the basic techniques possessed by every archaeologist, zoological or otherwise.

For the preservation of very small bones, and other small, delicate objects, one should always have a plentiful supply of the largest gelatin capsules in pharmaceutical use. A surprising number of small bones can be tucked into one capsule. Other handy and non-shatterable containers are plastic vials.

At Star Carr[10] the removal of bones from a bog was achieved by the complex technique of infiltration of plastic into the bone under vacuum. I wonder, however, if the bones could not have been lifted directly, with the use of glue and papier-mâché; I have successfully used this technique under circumstances so wet that a small drainage ditch had to be dug away from the trench around each pedestal; as the water drained out below the glue soaked in above, and eventually the bone was lifted without distortion due to drying.

Other zoo-archaeological field activities. For the zoologist who co-operates with archaeologists close to home, the local animals are well known, or at least accessible for study. Additionally there may be a good museum collection and considerable publishep literature on the behaviour, ecology, microclimatic necessities, food preferences, etc., of the animals expected to be found.

To the man going abroad, perhaps to an area new to him and one poorly known zoologically, the problems are multiplied: (1) Some of the commonest animals of the area may not have been reported in the scientific literature. (2) Skeletons of any animals from the area will be a great rarity in any museum, and to acquire a comparative collection is one of the first—and most difficult—tasks of the zoologist.[38,39,40] (3) Between collecting, skinning, skeletonizing, excavating, sorting, and packing, there is little time for the detailed ecological observations which one needs to *understand* fully the meaning of each bone dug from the excavation; thus we cannot yet give the degree of ecological interpretation for excavations in Iran or Iraq that Neill[29] was able to do for those for Florida, for instance. (4) There is little time to consider whether changes in faunal composition with time are due to climatic changes, to human cultural differences, or to man-produced environmental changes (deforestation, soil-erosion, etc.), although one makes preliminary efforts in this direction.[42]

It is assumed that the zoologist will know, or learn, the necessary techniques for capturing, measuring, and preparing animals under field conditions.[2,23] Most of the smaller forms he must trap, but larger specimens are better purchased.[3]

Small skeletons can merely be dried and packed thus for shipment home. While drying, they (and all other 'fresh' bones) must be hung safe from local birds and carnivores, and must be protected from flies by cheesecloth or netting. Larger animals already decomposing must have the flesh stripped off and buried; here the zoologist works alone, although often with an audience—both his fellow scientists and the local inhabitants—held in horrid fascination in an encircling ring.

Two absolute necessities for cleaning large carcasses are a place to hang the body while stripping the skin, and enough enveloping netting to keep out flies. Without the netting, particularly in warm weather, one would be driven to immediate madness. Another necessity for the zoo-archaeologist is a boiling-vat, made from the half of a large steel drum. The bones are cleaned in soapy water at a gentle boil for about four hours; however, care should be taken not to overcook immature specimens, in which the teeth will loosen and the epiphyses will separate from the shafts.

Since, as mentioned, the area may be one for which little zoological knowledge is available, the zoologist on an archaeological expedition abroad should collect other specimens as he can, to contribute to general scientific knowledge, even though such collections (as in entomology, herpetology, or parasitology) have little direct archaeological application.

LABORATORY TECHNIQUES

Bone from archaeological sites does not usually require the elaborate laboratory preparation so typical of many palaeontological specimens. Usually washing and some gluing of small bones or teeth are all that need be done. Larger broken pieces should be repaired with plaster and dextrin, as done by palaeontologists.

Plaster or papier-mâché jackets must be removed; if unfamiliar with the removal of plaster, follow the directions in Camp and Hanna.[8] Papier-mâché jackets are much simpler; one merely wets small portions of the glued paper, and removes the paper thus softened. The internal bone, as exposed, may be strengthened with more water-soluble glue as necessary.

Bone (and/or artifacts) in breccia, or with adherent masses of calcareous soil, must be treated with weak acid, which dissolves the calcium carbonate.[43] We have used 4% hydrochloric acid quite successfully, and, at this concentration, found no need to protect exposed bone surfaces with polystyrene, other plastics, or thin Duco, as recommended

Wild pig, Kermanshah, west-central Iran; January 1960. Skin and skeleton were salvaged as museum specimens.

(b) A compact mass of sub-Recent bones at the bottom of Tepe Asiab, near Kermanshah; May 1960. The bone was fragile and each piece had to be removed in a separate papier-mâché jacket.

(see page 204) PLATE XI

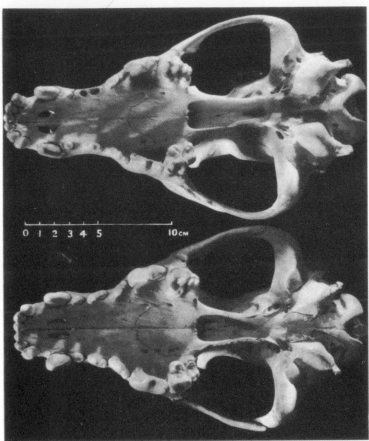

(a) Palatal views of the skulls of *Canis lupus lupus*, from the collection of the British Museum (Natural History). In the bottom skull the teeth are very large and they are abnormally compacted. There is no diastema between the first premolar and the canine, and the second premolar overlaps the third premolar (no. 1680; locality, Europe). In the top skull the teeth are evenly spaced and there is no overlap or displacement of the teeth. This skull represents the normal condition of wolves (no. 28.5.4.1; locality, north Sweden).

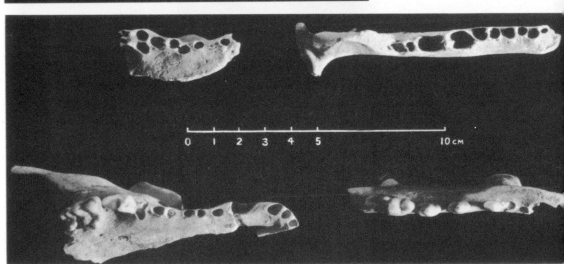

(b) Dog jaws from the Bronze Age site of Chios in Greece, to show the variability in tooth formation. Top left: fragment of maxilla with tooth sockets that are compacted and which held large teeth, crowded together; top right: mandibular ramus with the same type of tooth sockets as the maxilla at left. Bottom left: maxilla with the carnassial tooth and the two molars in position. These teeth are smaller and are not compacted in the jaw. Bottom right: fragment of mandibular ramus with the second, third and fourth premolars in position; small, widely-spaced teeth as in the previous specimen.

PLATE XII (see page 269)

by palaeontologists, since archaeological materials are usually in quite soft calcareous deposits and the dissolving of the calcium carbonate proceeds so rapidly that the bone is not affected. Several washings in water are necessary to remove all acid.

Rare specimens can be duplicated by rubber moulds.[35-37,53]

In general, techniques of handling archaeological bone in both field and laboratory are essentially simple; zoo–archaeology has not found need for the complexities more typical of pollen–studies, or of the physical techniques used in archaeology.[1] It is very probable that we are, thereby, missing some of the possibilities of identification and interpretation that future development of physico–chemical techniques will open. One thinks of the possibility of serological testing of archaeological bone for species identification, or if possibly there is different molecular orientation in the bone or teeth of one species or genus, as contrasted with another (handy for sorting the sheep from the goats?). Still other techniques, as yet unconsidered or undeveloped, will certainly be standard laboratory procedures in the future; for instance, such an observation as that by Peabody[32] that annual and seasonal differences in weather are reflected in bone structure of some cold-blood vertebrates may prove to be useful to some zoo-archaeologist. We must be alert to use such possibilities.

It is my firm opinion, agreed with by every zoo–archaeologist known to me personally, that identification of animal bones should be done by vertebrate zoologists with extensive experience. Thus I must disagree with such efforts as those of Cornwall[11] and Olsen[30] to the degree that they imply that the average archaeologist can be adequately trained to identify bone, and interpret its meaning.

This general situation works in reverse, also. The biologist should not consider himself competent to identify and study all the artifacts (flint, pottery, etc.) that are the particular field of the archaeologist, but at the same time the biologist should be aware of the problems of cultural evolution, and how his particular data fit into, and possibly contribute, to a solution of these problems.

INTERPRETATION

With interpretation, one leaves technique behind, and zoo–archaeology becomes a fascinating maze of intermixed science and art. Considerable of what I might have said here has already been discussed by Meighan[27] and Heizer.[21]

Eventually, in the home laboratory, the bones are sorted, identified, counted and measured. At this point the zoologist who does not know the biology of the area of the excavation will write a short report—often only a faunal list—and desist (at least, he is wise if he desists, for if he does not know the ecology of the area he must rely only on written reports and hearsay). But it is at this point that the participants in the excavations, especially if in a foreign area poorly known biologically, will begin the interpretative analysis, in co-operation with the archaeologist. Whatever valuable conclusions may emerge as by-products, the important emphasis is always on the cultural history, and this ultimate emphasis should never be forgotten.

It would seem hardly necessary to mention that correct interpretations depend upon accurate identifications. One source of erroneous interpretations has been a general lack of comparative skeletal materials for many parts of the world. Thus Perkins,[33] in attempting to determine the constant skeletal differences between goats and sheep, was forced to discard many previously published criteria which had been used to separate these closely related genera. Obviously, interpretations based on invalid identifications (stemming, in turn, from lack of adequate series of comparative skeletons) cannot in turn be valid, but such conclusions have often been published.

Statistics. The use of statistics has been uncommon in zoo-archaeological work, or at best has typically been of a simple sort. Numbers of specimens, and measurements on each, are often published as raw data, possibly with comparative measurements of modern populations of related wild or domestic animals. Conclusions are almost on an intuitive basis, derived from working with the specimens and examination of the tabulated data.

Vertebrate palaeontologists and physical anthropologists, who also work with the concepts of the theoretical populations of which the bones are representative, are usually much more sophisticated in their use of mathematics than have been most zoo-archaeologists. For instance, Kurtén's reworking[26] of Degerbøl's data, with subsequent refinement of conclusions, is an excellent example of what is possible with the use of more modern mathematical concepts, still generally unknown to most zoo-archaeologists.

Available statistical tools should be learned, and new ones sought, for particular use in such instances where there are available large samples of several populations for hundreds or thousands of years, where a change in general environment is occurring (with possible increase in evolutionary rates), or where changes to domestication are occurring.[40] For each of these situations, involving evolutionary changes in the sampled fauna over short periods of time ('short', evolutionarily speaking), statistical technique involving the analyses of correlated changes in many characters should be used, as is being done by palaeontologists[31] and physical anthropologists.[20]

Too often we are not even informed of the normal limits of variation of either the bones of the archaeological sample or the modern population with which the bones are being compared, nor are we given any indication of the shape of the population curve within those limits. In general, until we learn to interpret our data, we will not be deriving from it the potential information it actually contains. (For those not statistically orientated, a good pathway into this maze is that of Simpson.[45])

Environment. Prehistorians in general have long been interested in problems of the environment: What was the environment at the time of a particular culture, what changes in environment occurred with time, how did man change the environment, what influence did a changing environment have on human culture? The study of zoological remains in conjunction with associated botanical, geological, and cultural evidences, can often answer these questions in major part, and valuable studies of this kind are available, particularly for the late Quaternary.

However, the use of faunal evidence, as based on archaeological bones, has certain pitfalls, not always realized. The basic fact to be remembered is that one is dealing with a 'cultural filter'; the bones are in a site because people dropped them there. For whatever purpose the animals were used (food, hides, pets, or for religious purposes perhaps) there may have been others in the area not used, or only rarely so, due to taboo, habit, or lack of certain hunting skills. With time, the faunal composition of the site might change, without a concomitant change in the general fauna of the area, due to changing hunting techniques, etc.[9]

Each excavation may present its own unique possibilities for environmental interpretation. Thus, the late Pleistocene fauna from the cave of Hazar Merd in north-eastern Iraq[10] indicated definitely that the environment at that time was very similar to that of today,[42] and was not frigid, as sometimes claimed. The fauna was typical of that of the area today, and none of it was specifically northern or cold-loving. The presence of certain birds, also to be found in the area today, particularly indicated little difference between the present environment and that of the time, perhaps 40,000 years ago, when the cave was occupied; the key point is that the area of overlap of the distribution of these particular avian species is very narrow, but this narrow area includes today the region of the cave, as presumably was also true 40,000 years ago. In this case, a study of the ranges, and specifically the area of overlap of the ranges, of the birds is the key factor; at another site another set of circumstances will probably furnish the important environmental evidence.

It is often true that the bones of the small, microclimatic animal indicators are the ones either never represented at a site or destroyed before excavation. However, such small mammals and birds are often the best environmental and habitat indicators, and should be given the attention they deserve. On the other hand, badgers, many rodents, and some other animals too, burrow into the deeper strata of earlier deposits, often with the most misleading results!

Many hunting societies seemingly did not bother with the small animals or, if they did catch them, perhaps did not bother to bring them home. Thus, at the site, we would find only bones of medium-sized and larger animals (as at Shanidar Cave, for instance, where most of the bones are of wild goat, with some wild sheep, pig, deer and little else). However, where the small vertebrates were gathered, and we have remains of what would appear to be every last bird and tortoise, then zoologists who really know the behaviour and ecological peculiarities of each bird, mouse, and tortoise can do an amazing piece of work, not only on the palaeo-environment but on the reconstruction of the necessary behaviour of the human hunters and gatherers.[29]

Census problems. Where the yield of bones from a site has been large, detailed study may yield evidence not only on the kinds of animals present but also on the relative numbers of each, and the ages represented. Thus a more complete reconstruction of the human culture can be made, and eventually questions answered, such as: In what proportions were different animals being hunted? Was there selective hunting for certain age groups, or was the distribution the random one to be expected in a wild population? For each kind of domestic animal, what proportions were killed at what ages? (That is, what was the population structure of the herd?) Was the age at death the same for both sexes or was one sex preserved preferentially?

Obviously, we must have adequate samples if we are to reproduce a population structure for each species involved. Also we must have considerable morphological knowledge, for each species, of both the sequence and the time of occurrence in the individual life-cycle of several ageing phenomena which can be detected osteologically. Some such information as to age is available; for instance, a standard veterinary anatomy lists the time of eruption of deciduous and permanent teeth for the domestic horse, cow, sheep, pig, and dog.[47] Even for domestic animals, research in this field continues (see Brown et al.[7] for studies on cattle).

Another source of age information is the time of fusion of the epiphyses to the shafts of long bones and vertebrae. The general sequence of fusion is similar in most mammals, but the time of fusion of each epiphysis is not known for most species of mammals. As with the more extensive studies of this kind on man, proper application of X-ray techniques leads to solution of the problem.[48,49]

Unfortunately, we have no way of knowing yet to what degree information derived from a study of the time of epiphyseal fusion in one breed of modern domestic sheep, to take but one example, can be applied to other domestic breeds, to primitive domestic sheep, or to wild sheep. Furthermore, when such studies on the same species disagree remarkably in part[52] on the time of epiphyseal fusion in sheep, which is to be followed?[48]

Considerable information can be deduced by the degree of wear on the teeth, *if* one has a standard for comparison, as exists for some of the North American deer.[34,44] However, lacking such careful studies, and ignorant of the environmental (dietary) factors under which early domestic animals, at least, were kept, one can distinguish in this way only general age ('mature', 'very old', etc.). I have occasionally seen long bones of wild animals with the walls of the shafts eroded internally to become very thin; this condition, senile osteoporosis, is indicative of extreme age. Size of antler-shafts or horn-cores, or degree of fusion of skull sutures, gives some indication of age, but these subjects have been little studied and each investigator has to depend upon his own judgement and the comparative evidence available in his own collection.

Domestication. Particularly in Near Eastern areas, but not unknown elsewhere, the discrimination between bones of wild but potentially domesticable animals of an earlier archaeological horizon and those undergoing preliminary domestication in a later horizon is a fundamental and difficult problem. The associated artifacts from the same excavations offer no clue to 'incipient domestication'; one must deal with the problem biologically. Sometimes there is a definite change in shape of one of the bones, as seemingly is true of early domestic male goats, which have a flattening of the medial side of the horn-core,[58,40] but usually one has to rely upon the general observation that domestication typically resulted in a decrease in size of the animals involved. Unfortunately, one often recovers only meagre samples of any similar parts of the same species from different time and/or cultural horizons. One first has to establish, for the modern wild and domestic populations being used as norms, the limits of variation and then the *kind* of variation (i.e. the type of distributional curve) within those limits. These are standard statistical techniques for handling this type of biological data,[45] and they should be used. Once the standard has been established for a wild population, the degree and direction of change of the population suspected of undergoing domestication can be determined, and conclusions drawn with some assurance of validity.

Adequate skeletal series of the wild populations are the primary and fundamental necessity for studies of this kind, but for many species in many parts of the world such series do not exist.

However, where occurring, as for instance for wild pigs from south-western Asia,[41, 16] conclusions as to prehistoric domestication can be reached, but without such series—a situation existing in the case of wolves from south-western Asia—we are at a loss in our attempt to establish the facts of early domestication.[41]

The lack of adequate series of skeletons, plus the lack of realization of the need for them, has been a major factor in leading many zoo-archaeologists of an older generation astray in their published criteria.[33]

Animals in a period of incipient domestication may show little or no morphological differences when contrasted with their wild kin, but study of their bones taken in correlation with other data may still indicate domestication. Such is the case at Zawi Chemi Shanidar, a settlement in northern Iraq of some 10,500 years ago, where grinding-stones and other artifactual evidences indicate the possibility of some agriculture and some permanence of settlement.[50] The unpublished studies of Dexter Perkins on the bones from Zawi Chemi and from the nearby Shanidar Cave indicate that for much of the later Pleistocene wild goats were the predominant animal hunted, with wild sheep in a definite minority. However, quite suddenly (within a period of two or three thousand years, or even less), coincident with the shift from cave-living to an open site, remains of sheep outnumber those of goats by 16 to 1, and the percentage of animals one year old or less increases from approximately one-fourth to three-fifths. The conclusion is unmistakable that the people of Zawi Chemi Shanidar were able to control the sheep directly and no longer relied upon the hunting of goats (that is, the sheep are presumed to have been domesticated).

Detailed study of bone from successive archaeological horizons will, of course, indicate changing of human food habits, from the eating of wild animals to domestic ones, or from one group of wild or domestic to some other group (correlated, perhaps, with a taboo against one animal), or perhaps to the eating of a single major food animal. These and some other aspects of the archaeological evidence for domestication have been mentioned by Meighan *et al.*[27]

Hunting, butchering, food. It is of course quite possible for animals from varied habitats (stream-side, meadow, plains, mountain, forest) to be hunted by men going out in different directions from a single village, and thus bones of animals (gazelles and wild goats, for instance) whose natural niches do not overlap may become jumbled in the same prehistoric midden. However, given this situation, and knowing the animals of each such habitat, it would be possible to judge which were the favourite hunting areas. It might, indeed, be possible to show that the people of several villages, each itself in a slightly different habitat area, were hunting different animals with slightly different weapons, all in a relatively circumscribed region; a pattern of this type would appear to be emerging in the study of the sequence of late Quaternary pre-agricultural and agricultural settlements in the Zagros Mountains of south-western Asia.[17] Obviously, only a zoologist who has worked at the excavations in a particular area is capable of such difficult interpretations; 'identifier', working solely with a museum collection, cannot in fairness be expected to do anything more than identify.

White,[54] in a notable series of papers, opened new possibilities concerning interpretation, in cultural terms, of osteological observations. He showed that discriminating study by a zoologist with anthropological knowledge could lead to understanding of butchering techniques (including knowledge of which parts of a carcass were left in the field, which brought into camp), of distribution of parts of a carcass within a settlement, and of the weight of meat which could be calculated to be represented by the bone excavated.

Clark,[10] at Star Carr, made the logical transfer from excavated bone to calories in relation to population size, duration of settlement, and energy expenditures of the people. These data were investigated further by Braidwood and Reed[5] in an attempt at a more detailed ecological study.

From age and seasonal data, too, we may be able to deduce the season of occupancy of a site; for this, knowledge of migratory birds, seasonal fishes, and the like, is most useful. Star Carr, from the evidence of the deer antlers (shed annually, but at different times by different species), is known to have been a winter-spring site,[18] while Sarab, in western Iran,[5] is known to have been occupied at least during late winter and/or early spring, because of the presence of snail shells (snails are collectable there only during the winter–spring rainy season) and because the bones of newborn lambs or kids were found, indicating occupancy during February or March.

Archaeologists have been increasingly interested in the food resources available to, and used by, ancient cultures. One method of translating from excavated bone into weight of meat has been to determine the minimum number of animals of each kind represented, to multiply this number by an average weight for each such animal, and then to multiply by a further factor which supposedly represents actual meat available for eating; White[55] used 50% for most larger animals hunted, but 70% for relatively short-legged ones. This technique involves identifying all of the bones to species, and, for each species, determining the minimum number of individuals possibly present. This latter count is made by determining the number of animals which must have been involved. The degree of approximation of the final figure, however, to the real truth cannot ever be known; it will vary with the condition of the bone (the more broken, the less identifiable it is, to bone or to species), and will vary with the ability of the investigator. The result, in any case, is that the fewer the pieces identified the lower will be the amount of meat calculated.

Kubasiewicz[25] considered these and correlated problems in some detail, from experience gained on the identification and study of tens of thousands of bones from medieval settlements in Poland. Kubasiewicz still identifies each bone (as possible) to species, but has tested various assumptions and practices as to the percentage of meat originally derived from each species represented in the total osteological sample excavated. The proportion of meat assumed to have been derived from each species varied remarkably whether one considered methods of calculation based on the number of bones for each species, the number of individuals for each species, or the total weight of bone for each. Kubasiewicz concluded that the latter method is by far the more valid, and advocates thus the weighing of archaeological bone after preliminary identification.

Kubasiewicz stated that for each of the domestic food animals, and presumably for wild food animals of corresponding size, the bones are approximately 7·0–7·7% of the total weight (for average-fed individuals: pigs, 7%, cattle, 7·3%, sheep, 7·7%).

It occurs to me that, if we are interested primarily in the weight of consumable meat, we can for most sites: (1) excavate all bone, (2) sort out that presumably from non-food animals, (3) weigh the remainder, (4) calculate the total weight of food animals involved, if the bone represents c. 7·5% of the weight of each animal, (5) multiply this weight by one-half (somewhat more if many pigs or other short-legged animals are involved), a conservative figure of utilizable meat.[55] The proportion of such meat derived from each species could then be calculated, after identification of the individual bones. Naturally, as with any technique, precautions will have to be taken where the bone is mineralized (heavier than normal), where leached (lighter than normal), or where skull portions (which constitute a higher bone-to-meat ratio than does the remainder of the skeleton) are either abnormally numerous or rare. In other words, there is no single magical formula, but judgement must still enter the calculations. Further, the weights of dry skeletons relative to the total weights should be checked for individuals of a number of species, both wild and domestic.

Lastly, I would like to mention the work of Dart and his colleagues[12–15] as an outstanding example of meticulous extraction, identification, sorting, analysis, and interpretation of bone fragments. At times Dart's interpretations seem to me to outrun his evidence, but in general his careful and meticulous work will continue to stand as a monumental achievement in osteological archaeology.[24]

REFERENCES

1 AITKEN, M. J. 1961. *Physics and Archaeology*, London and New York
2 ANDERSON, R. M. 1948. *Bull. Nat. Mus. Canada 69, passim*
3 BARNETT, L. 1960. *The Wonders of Life on Earth*, New York
4 BOURNE, G. H. (ed.) 1956. *The Biochemistry and Physiology of Bone*, New York
5 BRAIDWOOD, R. J., HOWE, B. and REED, C. A. 1961. *Science 133*, 2008–10
6 —— and REED, C. A. 1957. *Cold Spr. Harb. Symp. Quant. Biol. 22*, 19–31
7 BROWN, W. A., CHRISTOFFERSON, P. V., MASSLER, M. and WEISS, M. B. *Am. J. Vet. Res. 21*, 7–34
8 CAMP, C. L. and HANNA, G. D. 1937. *Methods in Paleontology*, Berkeley, Calif.
9 CLARK, J. G. D. 1952. *Prehistoric Europe*, London
10 —— 1954. *Excavations at Star Carr*, Cambridge
11 CORNWALL, I. W. 1956. *Bones for the Archaeologist*, London and New York
12 DART, R. A. 1957. *Mem. Transvaal Mus. 10*
13 —— 1959. *J. Dent. Assoc. S. Afr. 14*, 164–78
14 —— 1960. *S. Afr. J. Sci. 56*, 71–74
15 —— and KITCHING, J. W. 1958. *S. Afr. Arch. Bull. 13*, 94–116
16 FLANNERY, KENT V. 1961a. *Skeletal and radiocarbon evidence for the beginning and spread of pig domestication*, M.A. thesis, Faculty of the Division of Social Sciences, Univ. of Chicago.
17 —— 1961b. Early village farming in south-western Asia, *Proc. 1961 Ann. Spring Meet. Am. Ethnol. Soc.* 7–17
18 FRASER, F. C. and KING, J. E. 1954. In CLARK[10], 70–95
19 GARROD, D. A. E. 1930. *Am. Sch. Prehist. Res. Bull. 6*, 8–43
20 GILES, E. and BLEIBTREU, H. K. 1961. *Am. Anth. 63*, 48–61

21 HEIZER, R. F. (ed.) 1958. *A Guide to Archaeological Field Methods*, Palo Alto, Calif., 3rd ed.

22 —— 1960. Physical analysis of habitation residues, *Viking Fund Publ. Anthr. 28*, 93–157

23 HERSHKOVITZ, P. 1960. *Collecting and Preserving Mammals for Study*, Chicago

24 HOWELL, F. CLARK. 1959. *Science 230*, 831

25 KUBASIEWICZ, M. 1956. *Materialy Zachodnio—Pomorskie 2*, 235–44

26 KURTÉN, B. 1959. *Cold Spr. Harb. Symp. Quant. Biol. 24*, 205–15

27 MEIGHAN, C. W. 1961. *The Archaeologist's Note Book*, San Francisco

28 —— PENDERGAST, D. M., SWARTZ, B. K., Jr. and WISSLER, M. D. 1958. *Am. Antiq. 24*, 131–50

29 NEILL, W. T., GUT, H. J. and BRODKORB, P. 1956. *Am. Antiq. 21*, 383–95

30 OLSEN, S. J. 1960. *Pap. Peabody Mus. Arch. & Ethn.*, Harvard Univ. *35*, pt. 4, i–vii, 1–15.

31 OLSON, E. C. and MILLER, R. L. 1958. *Morphological Integration*, Chicago

32 PEABODY, F. E. 1961. *J. Morph. 108*, 11–62

33 PERKINS, D. 1959. *The post-cranial skeleton of the Caprinae: Comparative anatomy and changes under domestication*, Ph.D. thesis presented to the Biology Department of Harvard University

34 QUIMBY, D. C., and GAAB, J. E. 1957. *J. Wildl. Manag. 21*, 433–51

35 QUINN, J. H. 1940. *Field Mus. Nat. Hist. Tech. Ser. 6*, 1–21

36 —— 1952. *News Bull. Soc. Vert. Paleo. 36*, 28

37 —— 1957. *Ibid. 49*, 31

38 REED, C. A. 1955. In BRAIDWOOD, R. J. *et al. Sumer 30*, 134–6

39 —— 1957. *Zoology. Publ. Nat. Acad. Sci.—Nat. Res. Council 565*, 43–44

40 —— 1959. *Science 130*, 1629–39

41 —— 1961. *Z. Tierzüchtung u. Züchtungsbiologie 76*, 34–38

42 —— and BRAIDWOOD, R. J. 1960. *Stud. Anc. Orient. Civiliz. 31*, 163–73

43 RIXON, A. E. 1950. *Mus. 49*, 116–117

44 ROBINETTE, W. L., JONES, D. A., ROGERS, G., and GASHWILER, J. S. 1958. *J. Wildl. Manag. 21*, 134–53

45 SIMPSON, G. G., ROE, A., and LEWONTIN, R. C. 1960. *Quantitative Zoology*, New York, 2nd ed.

46 SINEX, F. M. and FARIS, B. 1959. *Science 129*, 969

47 SISSON, S. and GROSSMAN, J. D. 1953. *The Anatomy of the Domestic Animals*, Philadelphia, 4th ed.

48 SMITH, R. N. *Vet. Rec. 68*, 257–8

49 —— 1960. *Ibid. 72*, 75–79

50 SOLECKI, R. S. 1959. *Trans. New York Acad. Sci.* ser. 2, *21*, 712–17

51 SPAULDING, A. C. 1959. *Am. Antiq. 24*, 434

52 TODD, T. W. and TODD, A. W. 1938. *Am. J. Anat. 63*, 1–36

53 TUGBY, D. J. 1953. *Am. J. Phys. Anth. 11*, 437–440

54 WHITE, T. E. 1952–55. *Am. Antiq. 17*, 337 f.; *19*, 160–4, 254–64; *21*, 170–8

55 —— 1953. *Ibid. 18*, 396–8

56 —— 1955. *Ibid. 21*, 85–87

57 —— 1956. *Ibid.* 401–4

58 ZEUNER, F. E. 1955. *Palest. Expl. Quart. 1955*, 70–86

23 The Rate of Evolution

BJÖRN KURTÉN

EVOLUTION is a process of secular change. Surely one of the most obvious questions is, 'At what rate does it occur?' Yet the first really systematic attempts to measure the tempo of evolution, as it is reflected in the fossil record, date from Simpson[7] and Zeuner.[9]

How can we measure the rate of evolution? One of the simplest methods would seem to be to study the change of a linear dimension in an evolutionary series. This is an example of what Simpson calls the morphological rates of evolution. A measure has been proposed by Haldane;[1] this is the *darwin*, defined as a change of $1/1,000$ in a millennium (equivalent to a change by the factor e in one million years). For instance, a number of dimensions in the teeth of Tertiary horses, studied by Simpson, evolved at rates about 0·01 to 0·08 darwins.

Most generalizations regarding rates of evolution have not been based on morphological rates, however, but on taxonomic rates. Zeuner, for instance, found that the average longevity of mammalian species is about half a million years. This is a way of measuring the rate of evolution: the time an evolving lineage needs to pass through one of a series of successive species-stages in its evolution. The reciprocal (two species per million years) is a direct rate measurement.

Simpson used the next higher category, the genus. He found that the rate of evolution was variable, but within a given group of organisms the rates tended to cluster about a mean value, with relatively few lineages evolving at rates considerably faster or slower than the mean. Thus, a frequency histogram showing the rates of evolution within a group of organisms will have a unified pattern with a 'peak', representing the rates at which the majority of lineages have evolved, and two 'tails', representing the fewer lineages that have evolved at markedly faster or slower rates. Fig. 30, showing the distribution of evolutionary rates for genera of land carnivores in the Tertiary, illustrates a taxonomic rate distribution. The mean rate in this case (the reciprocal of the mean longevity) is $\frac{1}{8}$ genus per million years.

It may be objected that the reciprocal of the longevity is an adequate measure of the rate of evolution only in the case of genera actually forming temporal segments of continuously evolving lineages: genera that have vanished by extinction without issue should be left out. Perhaps this may account for some characteristics of the pattern in Fig. 30, such as the peculiar skewing of the distribution, but it is doubtful whether the mean value has been much affected. Simpson[8] found almost exactly the same average rate (0·13 genera per million years) in truly ancestral-descendant sequences of genera in horses and chalicotheres.

A more serious objection is that results on the genus level are less reliable because a genus is a less 'objective' taxonomic category than a species. A species in neozoology is

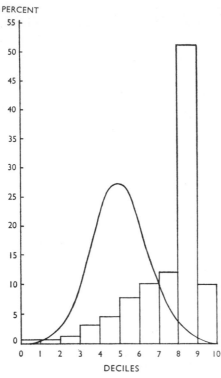

PERCENT

Fig. 30 Distribution of rates of evolution in genera of land carnivores, based on survivorship of extinct genera. A normal curve equal in area to the histogram has been drawn for comparison. The distribution is skewed, with a mode in the right part of the range (indicating that relatively fast rates are more common than relatively slow ones). After Simpson.

defined by Dobzhansky as 'the most inclusive Mendelian population' and is in most cases quite an objective unit. For various reasons the palaeontological species will be less objective, but in practice it is delimited in much the same way as present-day species. Unfortunately, the great majority of fossil faunas have not been revised according to modern taxonomic principles, and so material for a study on this level simply was not available to Simpson.

Another objection may be illustrated by the use of a hypothetical example. Genus A contains several species, one of which evolves rapidly and in a short time gives rise to genus B. Here the pattern is repeated, and one species gives rise to genus C. At the same time, other species of genera A and B carry on with little change, and both genera may be very long-lived. In this case the fact that there has been a rapidly evolving component in both will not be reflected in the computation of rates of evolution. In short, the use of a high taxonomic category leads to blur. But this objection is valid on the species level too.

Of course the measurement of morphological rates of evolution may also be affected by blurring. Suppose, for instance, that an animal species tended to increase in size, at the rate of 1 darwin, from 20,000 BP to 10,000 BP then to remain stable to the present day. If we were to have no material except a sample 20,000 years old, and the living form, we would conclude that the lineage evolved at a rate of about 0·5 darwins. Measurement of rates during the Tertiary, where successive populations are usually many millions of years apart, is particularly liable to bias of this kind.

The Quaternary land mammals of Europe are exceptionally valuable for the study of rates of evolution. The sequence is fairly well dated, and chronologically closely spaced successive populations are known; furthermore, some modern taxonomic revisions have been carried out. Of course, much remains to be done in all these respects.

The information on evolution in Postglacial and Late Glacial times is particularly detailed. Fig. 31 shows the evolution in size of a number of mammal species (this example is analysed and discussed in more detail elsewhere[3]). The size of the animals is expressed as a percentage of the Recent mean size, and thus all the trend lines converge towards 100% at the present day.

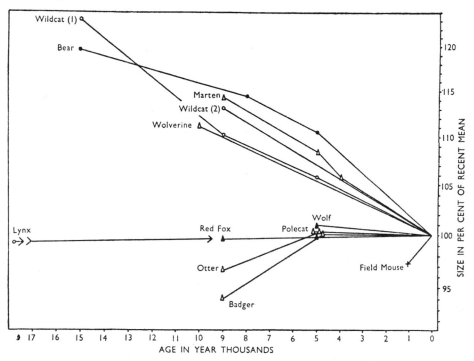

Fig. 31 Evolution in size of some European mammals in Late Glacial and Postglacial times. The size of the fossil forms is expressed as a percentage of the Recent mean size. From Kurtén.[3]

A number of these animals are now considerably smaller, on an average, than their ancestors at the end of the Pleistocene. Successive samples indicate that the dwarfing has proceeded continuously during the last 10,000 years or more. In this group belong the bear (*Ursus arctos*), the pine marten (*Martes martes*), the glutton (*Gulo gulo*), and the wildcat (*Felis sylvestris* with two distinct lineages leading to the British and the Continental populations of the present day). Some other forms have increased in size, but these trends have apparently been of shorter duration: both the badger (*Meles meles*) and the otter (*Lutra lutra*) became larger in early Postglacial times, and the field mouse (*Apodemus sylvaticus*) has become much larger locally after its introduction in Iceland about a thousand years ago.

The rates at which these changes have occurred are easily computed, and were found to vary between 7 and 35 darwins. If the rate units are scaled logarithmically, the rates are found to form a single unified distribution, marked A in Fig. 32. Calculation shows that the (logarithmic) mean rate in this distribution is 12·6 darwins, and the standard range (or expected variation in a sample of 1,000 rates) extends from 3·7 to 43 darwins.

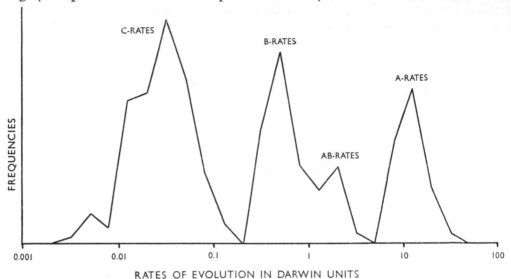

Fig. 32 Distribution of rates of evolution in size of mammals, expressed in darwins (1 darwin = a change of 1/1,000 in 1,000 years), showing the separation into three distinct distributions. After Kurtén.[3]

That these A-rates are tremendously fast rates of evolution is easily appreciated when it is noted that evolutionary growth at this rate (12·6 darwins) for one million years would result in a 150,000-fold increase in size! Obviously evolution at this rate can go on for a very limited span of time only. This means that we can hope to find sequences of this type only in the youngest part of the Quaternary, where the dating is accurate enough to give reliable chronological intervals down to 10,000 years.

The next main distribution in Fig. 32 is that of the B-rates, which have a mean of 0·51 darwins, and range from 0·12 to 2·3. This distribution represents some of the animals in Fig. 31: the wolf (*Canis lupus*), the red fox (*Vulpes vulpes*), the lynx (*Felis lynx*), and, finally, the badger and otter during the last 5,000 years or so. All of these have changed very little in proportions. Furthermore, a number of lineages have been followed throughout the Pleistocene (see Kurtén;[3] also unpublished data), and they were also found to have evolved at B-rates.

Some measurements appear to form a separate peak, intermediate between the A and B distributions. It may perhaps be suggested that they are due to blurring in the manner suggested above: a short-term change at A-rates diluted in a long–term B-rate history. The available data suggest that the B distribution represents the normal or basic rates during the Pleistocene, and that the A-rate changes occur as episodes, adding up to perhaps not more than 5% of the total time of the evolutionary sequence.

The third group, the C-rates, is the distribution found in mammalian lineages during the Tertiary (especially the Miocene and Pliocene)—for instance, in the horses. The mean rate in this group is 0·023 darwins, and the range 0·003 to 0·2. The difference between the distributions for the Tertiary and the Pleistocene mammals may well mean that the basic tempo of evolution was slower in the Late Tertiary, reflecting the greater stability of the environment.

The flexibility of the evolutionary mechanisms is impressive. The means for the rate groups are related almost as 1/25/625, and the fastest recorded rates are 10,000 times as fast as the slowest.

The existence of three groups of rates was theoretically predicted by Simpson in 1944.[7] The A-, B- and C-rates do not exactly correspond with the separation into tachytelic, horotelic and bradytelic rates of Simpson (there is here no bradytelic group as he defined it, and the B- and C-rates represent different horotelic groups). However, the A-rates seem to be exactly what Simpson visualized, but was unable to exemplify, as tachytelic rates. These very fast rates evidently result from adaptation, under strong selective pressure, to notable environmental changes—for instance in climate, as in Europe in Postglacial times.

An entirely different method for the computation of evolutionary rates was proposed by the author.[2,3] It is based on the differentiation index described else wherein this book (pp. 224–34). The index gives the percentage of allometric growth patterns found to be significantly different in two populations. In closely related species, most of the growth patterns, usually 80% or more, are dissimilar. In subspecies of the same species, the figure is usually lower, about 50% on an average. In local demes of a single subspecies it tends to be still lower, down to zero. Of course, if an ancestral and a descendant population are compared in this respect, a rate of evolution (e.g. in per cent per millennium) may be computed.

A number of lineages of Quaternary mammals studied in this way appeared again to show a distribution of the rates into two distinct groups. In the majority of forms, the 'index rates' formed a unified distribution with the mean 0·20% per 1,000 years, and a standard range extending from 0·044 to 0·90. On the other hand, a number of observations indicated the existence of very much higher rates, extending from 3 (glutton) through 11 (badger) and 14 (pine marten) to a freakish 60 (field mouse). Though these determinations have a large standard error, it seems evident that there must be a distribution of very fast, or tachytelic, rates in addition to the normal or horotelic rate group. The mean of the tachytelic group is 6·9% per 1,000 years, which is about 35 times the value of the horotelic mean (0·20), so the difference is of the same order of magnitude as that between the A- and B-rates. Furthermore, the two seem to be correlated in such a way that animals evolving rapidly with regard to size (A-rate) tend also to change rapidly as regards the allometry patterns, and vice versa.

This correlation indicates that about 10,000 years of evolution at a tachytelic rate may produce a new subspecies, and about 30,000 years a new species, on an average; whereas the corresponding figures for evolution at a horotelic (B-) rate would produce the same categories in about 300,000 years and about 1,000,000 years, respectively. If the two tempos of evolution were mixed in the proportions suggested previously (5% A-rate years, 95% B-rate years), the average duration of a species may be set at about half a million years: the figure actually suggested by Zeuner[9] on the basis of fossil lineages.

The study of actual species longevity is, however, very difficult. Most observations with any accuracy pertain to species which are still in existence, and they should be left out, as their life-span has not yet been terminated (though, unfortunately, there is every reason to fear that the remaining span of life for most larger forms is very limited indeed). This would mean cutting away the best-dated part of our material.

I have tried to devise a different approach to the problem. The method suggested is to determine the rates of change (extinction and origination) of the species-composition of a fauna. This can be expressed as a half-life, that is, the time in which 50% of the species have vanished (by extinction or transformation) and have been replaced by new species. It can be shown, furthermore, that the half-life has a constant relation to the mean species longevity. (These concepts and methods are discussed in detail by the author elsewhere.[4,5,6])

A preliminary census of the Pleistocene faunas indicates that, for a number of mammalian orders, the average species longevity would be about 600,000 years. It appears, however, that the rates of evolution, and hence the average length of life of the species, were somewhat different in the Middle and Late Pleistocene. The rates were apparently somewhat higher in the Middle Pleistocene, especially the Cromer-Mindel stages, and this may perhaps be interpreted as a reflection of the impact of the first great glaciations on the faunas.

The average longevity of the species appears to differ in different orders of mammals. In the carnivores, about 750,000 years was the average, but the rodents had a mean of 450,000 years and thus evolved somewhat more rapidly. An even lower mean was suggested for the insectivores, whereas the bats had an average species longevity of more than a million years. These differences may possibly be correlated with the length of generations, which permit particularly rapid evolutionary change in the short-lived and prolific rodents and insectivores, in contrast with the long-lived and slow-breeding bats.

Though these figures are, of course, only very rough approximations, it is quite clear that they differ strongly from analogous values for Tertiary mammals. The average species longevity in the mammalian faunas of the Miocene and Pliocene seems to have been about five million years, or almost ten times higher than in the Pleistocene. Some species have actually survived for upwards of twenty million years: the two mastodons *Turicius turicensis* and *Trilophodon angustidens* apparently were in existence from the Lower Miocene to the Middle Pliocene! In contrast, the oldest living mammalian species date back no further than the late Villafranchian, or perhaps 600,000 years.

This difference between the species longevities in the Late Tertiary and the Quaternary seems, like that between the B- and C-rates, to indicate a difference in the basic tempo of evolution. It is of interest to note that the tempo seems to have been higher, again, in the earliest Tertiary: a tentative estimate indicates a mean longevity of only about 1,500,000 years. This is closer to the value for the Pleistocene than to that for the Mio-Pliocene.

It should be remembered that the Early Tertiary was the time in which the mammals rose to terrestrial dominance, clearly a situation in which rapid evolutionary advance may be expected.

The high evolutionary rate in the Quaternary is also evident in the history of man. The age of *Homo sapiens*, even if this species is taken to include the Steinheim-Swanscombe type, probably does not exceed 300,000 years; and similar, or even lower, figures seem probable for the extinct species of man, *Pithecanthropus*, *Australopithecus*, and *Paranthropus*. Human brain volume evolved at B-rates, probably with episodes at A-rate (especially on the *Pithecanthropus* stage). Clearly the Ice Age was a blessing in disguise. It seems probable, however, that the repeated oscillation of the climatic belts, and the consequent profound stirring and mixing of the faunal components, making for almost continuous environmental change, was the important thing, not just the cold.

REFERENCES

1 HALDANE, J. B. S. 1949. *Evolution* 3, 51–56
2 KURTÉN, B. 1958. *Ibid.* 12, 146–157
3 —— 1959a. *Cold Spr. Harb. Symp.* 24, 205–15
4 —— 1959b. *Soc. Sci. Fennica, Comment. Biol.* 21 (4), 1–14
5 —— 1960a. *Ibid.* 21 (5), 1–62
6 —— 1960b. *Ibid.* 22 (5), 1–14
7 SIMPSON, G. G. 1944. *Tempo and Mode in Evolution*, New York
8 —— 1953. *The Major Features of Evolution*, New York
9 ZEUNER, F. E. 1946. *Dating the Past*, London

24 The Cave Hyena, an Essay in Statistical Analysis

BJORN KURTÉN

THE LOWER CARNASSIAL of the cave hyena is a particularly characteristic and easily identified tooth (see Fig. 33). Its main part is a shearing blade, consisting of two cusps, the anterior one being termed the paraconid and the posterior one the protoconid. In addition there is a small basal element behind the protoconid. This is the talonid or heel, which may carry one or a few very small cusplets. The talonid is quite large in vegetivorous members of the order Carnivora, as bears and badgers. In the hyenas there is a strong tendency towards a reduction of this element, and the cave hyena is one of the most advanced forms in this respect.

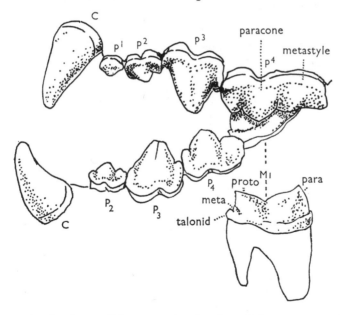

Fig. 33 Left upper and lower cheek teeth of spotted hyena (*Crocuta crocuta*) in partial occlusion, external view. C: canines; P: premolars, with serial numbers (P⁴: upper carnassial); M_1: lower carnassial, also shown separately in internal view (reversed, front end to the right) to exhibit dental elements: paroconid, protoconid, vestigial metaconid, and vestigial talonid.

At the base of the posterior border of the protoconid there may also, in some specimens, be seen another element, the metaconid. It is a small cusp, usually situated just to the inner side of the protoconid; but in some individuals it has migrated backward on to the talonid. This is the vestige of a cusp that is present as a prominent and distinct denta element in less advanced Hyaenidae, for instance in the striped hyena.

In the living African population of the spotted hyena, the carnassial is built on exactly the same plan as that of the cave hyena. In fact the two animals are now generally regarded as members of one and the same species, *Crocuta crocuta* (Erxleben). The typical cave hyena is distinguished from the living form mainly by its somewhat larger size and different limb proportions, and may be regarded as a distinct subspecies, *Crocuta crocuta spelaea* (Goldfuss). This implies the belief that the European and African populations, during the Pleistocene, were contiguous, and that there was a gradual transition from one geographic type to the other. In fact, this contention is strongly supported by fossil finds from southern Russia and Lebanon.[2]

About 10% of the present-day African spotted hyenas carry the vestigial metaconid in their lower carnassial. In the cave hyena some interesting differences in the frequency of this trait may be noted. Soergel[4] pointed out that the metaconid was present in all of the 13 specimens collected from the Lindental Cave at Gera in Germany, whereas out of 21 specimens from other localities only nine, or 43%, carried the cusp. Soergel concluded that the universal presence of this archaic character in the Lindental sample was due to its greater antiquity, and represented a primitive condition. It may be mentioned that the probable ancestor of the species, the earliest Pleistocene *Crocuta sivalensis* (Falconer and Cautley), in most cases has a small metaconid in M_1, though it may be absent occasionally.

Accordingly, we might expect to find that the frequency of the metaconid would be steadily reduced during the later part of the Ice Age—for instance, during the time span from the last interglacial to the last glaciation. The facts, however, do not agree at all with this contention (Table A).

TABLE A

Incidence of the metaconid in M_1 (the lower carnassial).

Age and locality	Number of specimens		%
	Total	Metaconid present	
Eemian Interglacial			
Tornewton Cave (Hyena Stratum)	103	10	10
Kirkdale Cave	16	2	12
Joint Mitnor Cave	33	6	18
Barrington Gravels	8	—	0
Würm Glaciation			
Kent's Cavern	199	85	43
Brixham Caves	4	3	(75)
Uphill Cave	10	3	(30)
King Arthur's Cave	6	2	(33)
Coygan Cave	2	—	(0)
Ffynnon Beuno	5	3	(60)
Long Hole	2	2	(100)
Creswell	2	2	(100)
Total, Eemian	160	18	11
Total, Würm	230	100	44

The faunas of the Barrington Gravels, Joint Mitnor Cave, Kirkdale Cave and the Hyena Stratum of the Tornewton Cave are characteristically interglacial, with hippopotamus and other warmth-loving forms present (see Sutcliffe[5]). In all of these the incidence of the metaconid in the cave hyena is very low, varying from zero in the Barrington sample to 18% in that from Joint Mitnor Cave. The average for the three smaller samples is 14%, which is of the same order of magnitude as the 10% recorded for Tornewton Cave.

The incidence is much higher in the material from Kent's Cavern, and it can be shown that the difference between this sample and that from Tornewton Cave is of the highest order of statistical significance. We must conclude that the two samples represent two quite distinct hyena populations. Of course, the distance between the two caves, both of which are in the Torbay area, is so small that a geographic differentiation is ruled out as the explanation. The difference must represent a difference in time, and it may be concluded that the Kent's Cavern hyena does not date from the Eemian interglacial. In actual fact good reasons may be brought forth for a Würm date.

The samples from the seven caves of Würm age except Kent's Cavern are mostly too small to give reliable statistics. If the data are combined, however, we may note that 15 out of the total of 31 specimens, or 48%, carry a metaconid. Obviously, this frequency is similar to that in the sample from Kent's Cavern. It may be concluded that the vestigial metaconid was retained to a much greater extent in the British cave hyena population of the last glaciation than in its forerunners during the last interglacial.

This is contrary to some of the palaeontological 'laws' or 'principles' of evolution, and indicates that these principles may have only limited validity. The facts show that a vestigial character, present only in a small fraction of the population, may secondarily increase in frequency. The explanation of this retrogressive trend in the cave hyena is unknown. Most probably it has something to do with a selective advantage, perhaps not so much in the visible character itself as in some genetic factor linked with it. We may even speculate whether these unknown genetic conditions had something to do with, for instance, climate tolerance. Such speculation is relatively pointless, though, unless analogous correlations between climate and metaconid incidence might be demonstrated in other cases. Such possibilities are provided by earlier glacial-interglacial cycles.

However this may be, it is evident that, as far as Britain is concerned, the presence or absence of the metaconid in the lower carnassial is a useful character for the differentiation between last-glacial and last-interglacial cave hyena populations. A relatively high frequency is suggestive of a Würm date, a low frequency of an Eemian age. To be reliable, however, such conclusions usually necessitate the collecting of a statistically respectable sample.

Fortunately, this is not the sole character distinguishing the two hyena populations. Several others are available, and in practice almost any reasonably complete sample of the cave hyena may be dated.

One of the simplest characters is the size of the dental elements. The lower carnassial, or M_1, may be used once more, this time considering the breadth of the tooth. The greatest breadth of M_1 is measured over the anterior part of the tooth, in the region of the paraconid. In some very old individuals this measurement cannot be taken, as the wear facet may extend down to the base of the crown in this region.

The width of M_1 was measured with calipers calibrated to 0·1 mm. For the calculation of statistical parameters, to be discussed later, the measurements were secondarily grouped in 0·2 mm groups, but for the construction of frequency distribution graphs 0·5 mm groups were used. In the present case the initial group is 11·3–11·7 mm with the midpoint 11·5; the second 11·8–12·2 with the midpoint 12·0; and so on (Fig. 34).

The peaks or modes of the two main distributions (from Kent's Cavern and Tornewton Cave) in Fig. 34 are decidedly distinct. The difference is slightly exaggerated by some (probably accidental) asymmetry in the Tornewton Cave sample. The two smaller samples (from four Würm caves and three Eemian localities) exhibit a similar difference in the modes.

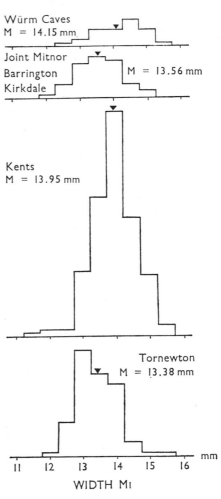

The mean values (Table B) fall into two groups. In one of them, comprising the samples of Eemian interglacial date, the means range from 13·38 to 13·57; in the other, from the Würm, from 13·86 to 14·30. The difference between the two groups can easily be shown to be highly significant by means of statistical tests. In contrast, however, none of the differentiation within the groups (e.g. between the Kent's Cavern mean of 13·95 and the Ffynnon Beuno mean of 14·30) is statistically significant. It may be concluded, then, that the lower carnassial of the Würm-age cave hyenas in Britain tends to be broader, on an average, than that of the Eemian ones.

Naturally, as Fig. 34 shows, there is a broad overlap between the Würm and Eem populations, and in practice a single specimen from unknown horizon cannot be dated on this character. What is needed is, of course, a sample which should be large enough to give a reliable mean. It does not necessarily mean a very large sample. Even the five specimens from Coygan Cave are adequate to give a quite distinctive mean.

Fig. 34 Width of lower carnassial in samples of the cave hyena.

The carnassial teeth dating from the Würm tend to be longer, as well as broader, than those of the Eemian; and the size difference may suggest that the Glacial cave hyena was actually a somewhat larger animal, on an average, than its Interglacial predecessor. There is some corroboration of this, for instance in the size of the jawbone. It is somewhat difficult to get adequate samples, for the young individuals, which form an appreciable proportion of most cave fossils, have to be left out. It can be shown, however,

TABLE B
Greatest width of the lower carnassial.

Age and locality	No. of specimens	Mean width	Standard Deviation	Coefficient of Variation
		mm	mm	
Eemian Interglacial				
1 Tornewton Cave	93	13·38±0·06	0·60	4·5
2 Kirkdale Cave	15	13·55±0·18	0·68	5·1
3 Joint Mitnor Cave	27	13·55±0·13	0·70	5·1
4 Barrington Gravels	7	13·57±0·27	0·72	5·3
5 2–4 combined	49	13·55±0·10	0·69	5·1
Würm Glaciation				
6 Kent's Cavern	177	13·95±0·05	0·65	4·7
7 Uphill Cave	10	13·86±0·18	0·56	4·0
8 King Arthur's Cave	7	14·21±0·30	0·79	5·6
9 Coygan Cave	5	14·15±0·32	0·72	5·1
10 Ffynnon Beuno	5	14·30±0·22	0·50	3·5
11 7–10 combined	27	14·15±0·14	0·72	5·1

that the mandibles from Kent's Cavern tend to be significantly more robust than those from the Hyena stratum of the Tornewton Cave, or from the Barrington Gravels (Table C); and a composite sample from a number of Würm Caves shows the same thickening of the jawbone.

TABLE C
Width of the jawbone under the third premolar.

Age and locality	No. of specimens	Mean width	Standard Deviation	Coefficient of Variation
		mm	mm	
Eemian Interglacial				
1 Tornewton Cave	15	21·47±0·35	1·34	6·3
2 Barrington Gravels	12	21·25±0·29	1·01	4·8
Würm Glaciation				
3 Kent's Cavern	69	23·09±0·40	1·92	8·2
4 Four Würm Caves★	6	23·67±0·56	1·37	5·8

★ The four Würm Caves are: Creswell, Uphill, Ffynnon Beuno, and Coygan.

This change must not be thought of as a harmonious enlargement of all skeletal parts in the same proportion. In fact, some dimensions have not been enlarged at all. A particularly surprising change is found in the anterior lower premolars, P_2 and P_3 (P_1 was lost long ago in the hyenas). In common with most other dimensions, the length of P_3 increased from the Eemian to the Würm; but that of P_2 actually decreased

(Table D). It follows that the relative sizes of these two teeth are useful in distinguishing between Eemian and Würmian hyenas, and the distinction is particularly well brought out if a scatter diagram of the two dimensions is constructed (Figs. 35–6). In both

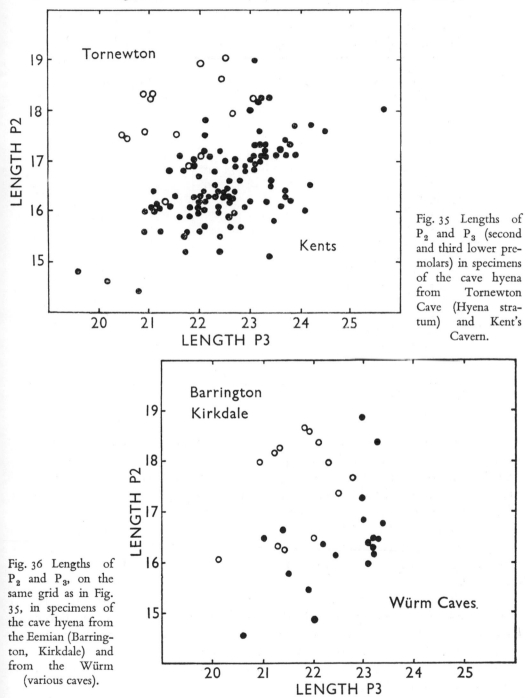

Fig. 35 Lengths of P$_2$ and P$_3$ (second and third lower pre-molars) in specimens of the cave hyena from Tornewton Cave (Hyena stratum) and Kent's Cavern.

Fig. 36 Lengths of P$_2$ and P$_3$, on the same grid as in Fig. 35, in specimens of the cave hyena from the Eemian (Barrington, Kirkdale) and from the Würm (various caves).

diagrams the dots represent the Würm populations, and the open circles the Eemian ones. There is partial overlap in the areas covered, but the displacement is characteristic, and will usually permit the classification of even a moderately large sample.

TABLE D
Lengths of second and third premolars.

Age and locality	No. of specimens	Mean length	Standard Deviation	Coefficient of Variation
		mm	mm	
P_3, Eemian Interglacial				
1 Tornewton Cave	52	21·52±0·10	0·74	3·4
2 Barrington Gravels	16	21·75±0·22	0·88	4·0
3 Joint Mitnor Cave	26	21·67±0·08	0·42	2·0
P_3, Würm Glaciation				
4 Kent's Cavern	210	22·56±0·07	0·96	4·3
5 Coygan Cave	8	22·94±0·26	0·73	3·2
6 Five Würm Caves*	21	22·43±0·20	0·93	4·1
P_2, Eemian Interglacial				
1 Tornewton Cave	27	17·44±0·17	0·87	5·0
2 Barrington Gravels	11	17·50±0·33	1·09	6·2
3 Joint Mitnor Cave	10	17·22±0·25	0·79	4·6
P_2, Würm Glaciation				
4 Kent's Cavern	156	16·53±0·06	0·80	4·8
5 Coygan Cave	5	16·42±0·10	0·22	(1·3)
6 Five Würm Caves*	22	16·72±0·20	0·95	5·7

* The five Würm caves are: Creswell, Uphill, Brixham, Ffynnon Beuno and King Arthur's Cave.

At present no definite explanation can be given of these evolutionary changes. The size increase may be related to the cooling of the climate, in accordance with Bergmann's rule. Such a correlation between size and temperature is found in the present-day spotted hyenas.[2] On the other hand, the size increase might be related to the size of the prey, or of the carcasses available as food. Finally, the increase of P_3 at the cost of P_2 may be related to the jaw mechanics; P_3 is closer to the jaw joint and hence has a greater strength of bite. There are other possible explanations, but the main point is that we recognize these changes as adaptive in nature, not just as characters shuffled to give convenient time-markers.

The teeth may change in shape as well as size. The third upper premolar (Fig. 33) is an example. A scatter diagram of the length and width of this tooth shows a displacement of Würmian and Eemian specimens analogous to that in the previous instance (Fig. 37). Actually the width of the tooth remained constant, on an average, whereas the length increased (Table E). As a result, the shape of the P³ tended to be more elongate in the Würmian than in the Eemian.

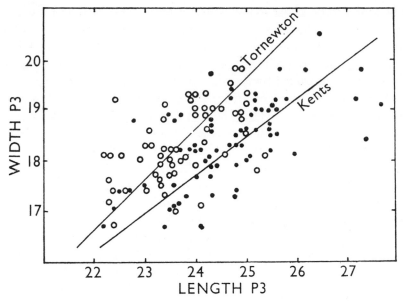

Fig. 37 Width and length of third upper premolar in specimens of the
cave hyena from Tornewton Cave (Hyena stratum) and Kent's Cavern,
with trend lines for the two samples.

TABLE E

Dimensions of third upper premolar.

Locality	No. of specimens	Mean	Standard Deviation	Coefficient of Variation
		mm	mm	
Width of P³				
Tornewton Cave	59	18·32±0·11	0·82	4·5
Kent's Cavern	54	18·33±0·11	0·82	4·5
Length of P³				
Tornewton Cave	61	23·70±0·10	0·82	3·5
Kent's Cavern	68	24·72±0·13	1·09	4·4

There is a significant correlation between length and width in both samples, and we may construct trend lines for each sample in the graph. The lines pass through the points determined by the mean widths and lengths for the two samples, their slopes being obtained as the quotients of the standard deviations for width and length respectively. The slope is 1·00 for the Tornewton Cave sample, and 0·75 for that from Kent's Cavern.

A method alternative to the construction of scatter diagrams, and to the study of trend axes, would be to calculate the quotient between width and length, which may be called the width index, and study the variation of the index. The mean value of the index will be found to be lower in the Würm sample. This method is used very commonly, but while it has the advantage of being simple and easily understood, it may occasionally be seriously misleading. Consider, for instance, the trend line for the Tornewton P³ sample in Fig. 37. It has the slope 1 00. Thus an increase in the length will, on an average, be accompanied by an equal increase in width. A change in the mean length from 23·70 mm to 24·70, or 4·2%, would correspond to a width change from 18·32 to 19·32 mm, which is 5·5%. The increase in width is relatively greater than that in length, and a general size increase will result in a gradual change in the width index (from 0·77 to 0·78 in this case) and in the shape of the tooth. This is the well-known phenomenon of allometric growth.[1] In the present case its influence is slight, but if the allometry is stronger, or the range of size greater, it may render the index method invalid as a means of establishing evolutionary affinity.

There are several other differences between the Eemian and Würmian hyena populations in Britain. It would carry us too far afield to consider each of them in similar detail, but as far as the dentitions are concerned, the following may be mentioned:

The canine teeth, both uppers and lowers, tend to be larger in the Würm population.

The second upper premolar is somewhat larger in the Würm hyena.

The upper carnassial is of the same length in both populations, but the width is greater in the Würm hyena. This heavier build is a character which is quite easy to see. Furthermore, the posterior lobe or metastyle (see Fig. 33) of the carnassial blade is longer in the Würm hyena, whereas the middle lobe or paracone is shorter.

The fourth lower premolar is no longer, but markedly broader, in the Würm hyena.

With the help of these average tendencies and trends it will usually be possible to classify a local sample as Glacial or Interglacial in age. However, there must have been some kind of continuity between the populations of the Eemian and those of the Würm. They assuredly did not change overnight in all the characters enumerated here. On the contrary, as well-dated populations are studied, and temporal gaps are filled, we may expect to find gradual transitions: perhaps populations combining traits characteristic of the Würm with others characteristic of Eem, as well as being perfectly intermediate in other respects.

There is at least one sample suggestive of such a condition. This is the collection from the initial excavations at Joint Mitnor Cave.[5] The material dates from the Eemian, and in most respects it conforms exactly to the pattern found at Tornewton Cave, Kirkdale Cave, and Barrington. In one character, however, this sample differs quite definitely from the other Eemian ones, and is similar to the Würm hyenas. This is the width of the upper carnassial. It is significantly broader than in the typical Eemian samples, and there is excellent agreement with the Würm form (Table F).

A possible explanation of this condition may be that the material from Joint Mitnor Cave may represent a relatively late stage in the Interglacial, in which the hyena population had already acquired some of the characters that we associate with the Würm. The excavations so far have touched only a small part of the very great talus cone in the cave, and perhaps only the outermost and hence youngest part. However this may be, the Joint Mitnor Cave hyena demonstrates that the transition from the Eemian type of

TABLE F

Blade width of the upper carnassial.

Age and locality	No. of specimens	Mean width	Standard Deviation	Coefficient of Variation
		mm	mm	
Eemian Interglacial				
Tornewton Cave	58	11·89±0·07	0·56	4·7
Kirkdale & Barrington	5	11·58±0·33	0·73	6·3
Joint Mitnor Cave	21	12·40±0·14	0·62	5·0
Würm Glaciation				
Kent's Cavern	86	12·19±0·08	0·72	5·9
Three Würm Caves*	17	12·29±0·15	0·63	5·1

* The three Würm caves are: Uphill, Ffynnon Beuno and Coygan.

cave hyena to that characteristic of the Würm must have been a gradual one. Once the history of this transition is mapped, a fairly sensitive chronological tool will be available.

A gradual transition; yet, it seems, at a relatively fast rate. The difference between the Eemian and Würmian populations is surprisingly great, considering that the chronological distance between (say) the Tornewton and Kent's Cavern populations may be rather less than 50,000 years, or in any case a small fraction of the entire Ice Age.

To measure the amount of evolution separating the two populations, we may perhaps proceed as follows. Consider the trend lines indicated in Fig. 37; the difference in growth patterns apparently reflects a difference in the genetic constitution of the two populations. In other cases, however, for instance the length-to-width relation of P^2, the Eemian and Würmian populations show identical growth patterns. When a number of character pairs are studied in this way, it turns out that about 60% of the growth patterns are significantly different in the two populations, whereas the remaining 40% cannot be shown, on available data, to differ. These percentages may be used as a measurement, or index, of the differentiation between the two populations (see Kurtén[3]).

If the Late Pleistocene cave hyena is compared, by this method, with the ancestral form, the Villafranchian *Crocuta sivalensis*, the differentiation index is found to be about 80%. At a constant rate of evolution, the index will approach 100% asymptotically in such a way that an index of 80 will represent precisely twice the amount of time corresponding to an index of 60. Yet the time span separating *Crocuta sivalensis* from the late Pleistocene cave hyenas must be well over 600,000 years, or more than ten times the distance in time separating the Eemian and Würmian populations. In this way it can be shown that the evolution of the hyenas in the late Pleistocene was particularly rapid.

For the study of micro-evolutionary events of this type, which are of great interest from the point of view of the theory of evolution, in addition to their stratigraphic usefulness, it is of course important that excavations are made with the utmost care, and that bones are collected with the same precision and attention to level as artifacts.

This pertains not only to the teeth, but to other skeletal parts also; for instance, the Eemian and Würmian cave hyenas differ in the relative proportions of their limb bones.

Much work remains to be done on the pre-Eemian evolution of the species, and the material at hand is far from satisfactory. The Tornewton Cave, however, has yielded some specimens of Penultimate (Riss) Glaciation date, and they indicate that analogous differences will be found. The lower carnassial, for instance, is significantly shorter, on an average, than in the Eemian, the mean length of four specimens being only $29 \cdot 78 \pm 0 \cdot 25$ mm, whereas the corresponding mean for 100 Eemian specimens from the same cave is $31 \cdot 91 \pm 0 \cdot 12$ mm.

Finally, it should be pointed out that many other mammals may be profitably studied by quantitative methods. The bear, the fox, the badger, and many other species, show remarkable evolutionary changes during the course of the Pleistocene. The careful excavator will render the student of evolution great service by putting stratigraphically dated material at his disposal. In return he may expect new possibilities of dating 'difficult' finds.

REFERENCES

1 HUXLEY, J. S. 1932. *Problems of Relative Growth*, London
2 KURTÉN, B. 1957. *Quaternaria 4*, 69–81
3 —— 1958. *Evolution 12*, 146–57
4 SOERGEL, W. 1935. *Beitr. Geol. Thüringen, Jena 4*, pt. 5, 171–89
5 SUTCLIFFE, A. 1960. *Trans. Torquay Nat. Hist. Soc. 13*, pt. 1, 1–28

25 *The Science and History of Domestic Animals*

WOLF HERRE

THE WILD ORIGINS of domestic animals are of fundamental importance. The archaeological record reveals that at first man was only a food-gatherer who hunted wild animals for their meat, so that, in the settlements of the Palaeolithic and Mesolithic, remains of animals of the chase alone are found. It is only in Neolithic sites that the number of bones of the many species of game animals decreases: now only a few species occur frequently. Man had formed a new relationship with these animals—he had domesticated them. This event was of the highest significance for the development of human culture: man was freed of the vicissitudes of hunting by the adoption of an economy based on food production. When considering this general subject the discipline of zoology must be applied properly if sound conclusions regarding the history of civilization are to be reached.

Wild animals are adapted to different habitats and their geographical distribution differs according to their species, while their various qualities enable them to take part in the natural struggle for existence. Wild animals lack many characteristics which, today, constitute the value of their domestic counterparts. Thus the wild sheep and guanaco have a hairy coat like most mammals, but their wool is not of the type produced by the domestic sheep and alpaca, which can be spun. The aurochs and wild goat have only enough milk to rear their young; they cannot produce those quantities of milk which in their descendants, the domestic cow and domestic goat, are so important to man. Wild boars and wolves do not have the amount of fat or the growth of meat that make the domestic pig and domestic dog sources of food for many peoples. Similarly, the wild hen does not lay the large number of eggs that its domestic counterpart does. These are characteristics of domestication just as are peculiarities of colouring, morphological changes or modifications of behaviour, surveys of which have been compiled by Klatt,[22] Nachtsheim [27] and Herre.[10,11]

It can be seen, therefore, that wild animals have undergone considerable changes during the course of domestication; man has developed different specialities in them which often render them unfit for the struggle for existence in the wild and which characterize them as domesticated. One is thus led to consider the zoological causes of these peculiarities, and the cultural problems concerning the general causes of the adoption of domestication and the development of domestic animals in different cultures in particular.

THE CONCEPT OF SPECIES

Many discussions on the domestication of animals are based on the fact that domestic animals occur in more varied forms than wild species. It often seems incredible that such a variety should have evolved from so few wild species. For this reason some people were of the opinion that domestic forms had sprung from a crossing of different wild species. Let us therefore elucidate the term 'species'.

In order that zoology might progress it was necessary to arrange animal forms in some sort of order. At first current scientific thought used the term 'species' in a static sense so that the important characteristics were those which made a simple diagnosis possible. Hence an individual would be described as a type-specimen of the species; its characteristics served as a guide for classifying other individuals as belonging to that species. Linnaeus, the founder of zoological systematics, realized however that it was the group that determined the characteristics and not the characteristics that determined the group. He knew that characteristics varied, but later the fact that variation existed led to the conclusion that only the individual constituted a real unit and that supra-individual units were merely man-made abstractions, and hence 'artificial' rather than 'natural'.[25] In the last decades the opinion that the individual belongs to a supra-individual unit, especially and clearly in the case of the higher animals, has once more gained ground. This supra-individual unit is the breeding community, and populations which, given free choice in selecting a mate, represent breeding communities, are defined as 'species'. Thus the species is a biological reality.[15,16]

This thesis of modern zoological systematics, for the perfection of which the work of Kleinschmidt,[23] Rensch,[35] Huxley[19] and Mayr[24] has been especially valuable, has important consequences affecting research into domestic animals. The populations of domestic horses, asses, cattle, sheep, pigs, dogs, etc., form, among themselves and with only that wild species from which they originate, a natural breeding community, given free choice of mate. Each of these communities therefore constitutes a species. It has not been possible, as yet, to break down the barrier between *natural* breeding communities in domestication. Man has, for instance, crossed domestic horses and donkeys for at least 4,000 years to produce mules.[17] He has not, however, succeeded in producing a new natural breeding community, a species.[15,16] Research into domestic animals is, therefore, faced with the task of showing clearly the origin of the various domestic animals from their wild species, and it is wrong to speak of phylogeny as applying to domestic animals. The changes that have come about during domestication must be regarded as morphological development within the species (a significant fact in the formation of biological theories).

THE NATURE OF DOMESTICATION

In order to study the causes of the special changes of wild animals under domestication it is necessary to examine the nature of domestication in the biological sense. Very different opinions have been expressed on this subject; Röhrs[41] has produced the most recent critical summary of this question.

Domestication is a relationship between man and some species of animals, but while domestic animals are of use to him, the fact that man makes use of these animals does not constitute parasitism, since with domestication man took on responsibilities as well. The unrestrained life of the hunter was replaced by an existence which gave freedom for the development of his mental faculties. At first domesticated animals received little tending; the primitive domestic animal found its own food and was not kept in stalls. But man formed a sexual barrier against the wild individuals of the species, made a selection of the more tractable animals and, instead of the small groups formed by animals in the wild state, he made his animals live in large flocks and herds from which he was able to take animals for slaughter, when needed. Man was king over his herd, but there are limits to any form of husbandry that merely exploits its resources; in intensive husbandry, a higher quality animal is eventually achieved. The more man aims at this higher quality in his domestic animals, the greater the attention they must receive, so that man becomes the servant of his animals. A remarkable psychological readjustment was necessary to bring this about, entailing a readjustment of social structure.

There are indications that animals seem to appreciate the advantages offered by man—they seek association with him of their own accord. A relationship between two animal species for their mutual benefit is called, in zoological parlance, symbiosis. Thus domestication has been described as symbiosis between man and the domestic animals. Other species of animals are thought to have a relationship comparable to domestication: ants, for example, are supposed to keep domestic animals.[20,46]

The decisive factor in domestication by man is, however, the sexual isolation of parts of the wild species and the keeping of large herds under his control and for his own use. This new social structure requires suitable forms of behaviour, and steps are therefore taken to eliminate animals that hinder the formation of large herds.[10] Thus, even in the early stages of domestication, man begins using a method of selection which is different from natural selection. The formation of large herds offering greater protection for the individual than the smaller natural group[39] also brings about a change in the working of selection. Consequently other and fewer individuals fall victim to selection than would do so in the natural struggle for survival. The conditions of domestication widen and alter the *Lebensraum* of the wild species so that more variations within the species survive. In addition to this, man isolates only small sections of the wild species. The result of this, as Sewall Wright[45] has shown, is that, in isolation, combinations of genes become different from those resulting from free mating; thus characteristics become frequent which are uncommon in the wild species. This is another reason why the breadth of variation of characteristics must become greater in domestication. Man is able to derive benefit from such circumstances and he starts selecting characteristics which are of particular value to him. If he sets up new sexual barriers among the domestic animals, the formation of selected breeds is brought about, a step which must be regarded as a new cultural achievement demonstrating an ability to direct consciously processes which are conditioned by domestication.

Such brief observations alone show that domestication is more than mere symbiosis in the zoological sense. Domestication is an expression of the constructive abilities which man owes to the evolution of his brain. Röhrs[41] is therefore right when he says that only man possesses genuinely domesticated animals. The domestication of animals represents an achievement peculiar to man; he actively influences the relationship between himself and the animals.

If this interpretation is valid, it leads one to the conclusion that the greater variety of domestic animals compared with their original species is not a result of particular physiological conditions in the domesticated state, for example being kept in stables, the kind of food, etc., but that it comes about through special selection. In order to examine this statement further, one must look for domestic animals which have always been kept in relatively free and primitive conditions which, on the whole, differ from those of the original species only in the conditions of selection and not in their immediate environment. Such animals are the domesticated reindeer of northern Europe and Asia, and the llama and alpaca of South America.[7,9,10,12,13]

The domesticated reindeer enables groups of human beings to settle in desolate areas because it is capable of finding its food even under a thick cover of snow. To do this it ranges over great distances. Man follows the herds as a nomad and has thus adapted his way of life to that of the domestic animal. Domestic reindeer are never kept in stables and no fodder for them is provided by man; but he creates large herds to satisfy his demand for food. This has only become possible through the elimination of rutting-fights by the castration of all fully grown stags, leaving the business of reproduction to the younger males. This intervention may seem unimportant but its result is that the reindeer has all the characteristics of domestication which are known from other domesticated animals.

The llama and alpaca are the domesticated forms of the guanaco, the llama serving as beast of burden, the alpaca as a supplier of wool. These herds of domestic animals live in parts of the Andes that can only be described as unsuitable for habitation by man. They are never kept in stalls either, and they find their own food; but they live in large herds. And they, too, show the general characters of domestic animals. The variability in the herds of domestic reindeer as well as of llama and alpaca is very much greater than in the original species. This variability offers material for many directions of selection. Both through the forces of environment and the mental abilities of man certain directions of selection are brought into effect.

WHAT CHARACTERIZES A DOMESTIC ANIMAL?

The archaeologist who wants to find out the origin of domestication will want to know whether there are characteristics which distinguish the remains of wild animals from those of domestic ones. The numerical ratio of the species of animals found on pre-historic sites gives the first clues to any domestication. In the case of hunters the number of species present is usually larger and the distribution of age and sex is generally more even than in the case of a herding community. In domestication some species of animals predominate and the distribution of, for instance, age groups indicates habits of utilization.

More important still is the analysis of changes within the breed after the transition to domestication. An accurate knowledge of the variability of the wild species is neces-sary and any examination of the history of domestic animals must be based on systematic zoological studies. Wild species are not static units, but change in space and time. Thus some original species have died out after the beginning of domestication, e.g. the aurochs; others have changed their areas of distribution, e.g. wild sheep and wild horses, while others have a different geographical distribution of their sub-species today from that of the time of domestication. Such factors make the study of the history of domestic animals more difficult.

Today, the value of domestic animals is determined above all by their physical qualities; the study of material from prehistoric settlements tells us nothing about these. Skeletal remains play a special part in research into the history of domestication. If the bones of the wild species of the old domestic animals, for example, sheep, cattle, pigs, horses and dogs, are compared with those of the domestic animals, at first an extension of the range of variations and eventually a selection in favour of smaller size and variation of form become apparent.

It has frequently been concluded from the decrease in physical size in the earliest stages of domestication, that the animals degenerated compared with the wild species. This overlooks important biological facts. In the initial stages of domestication man did not yet make adequate provision for the animals' fodder and he prevented the animals from roaming around freely. Thus when food was scarce domestic animals suffered more than wild ones and small individuals with smaller food requirements had a better chance of survival than large, so that the proportion of small animals increased. In addition to this, it is probable that primitive man preferred small animals as he could control them better. Reduction in size is not however a necessary result of domestication; fundamentally, the state of domestication produces variation extending in all directions: in domestication there also appear individuals which are larger than in the wild species. If man knows how to preserve these variations he is also able to increase the physical size of an animal beyond the range realized in the wild species. The domestic horse, the rabbit and the domestic fowl are examples of this.

A change in size generally brings about changes in morphology and individual characteristics. Peculiarities can be more striking between large and small domestic animals, or between domestic animals and their original species, than differences between wild species. If, therefore, only peculiarities of morphology are taken into account and the differences of proportion, which are correlated to size, are not explained, the wrong conclusions may be reached on the origins of domestication, as Klatt[21] showed in 1913; more recently Röhrs[40] has applied the allometric formula to these problems, a decisive contribution to research on this subject.

Studies into the influence of physical size on the form of the body and its parts show that there are governing factors that change single characteristics. Such factors are, among others, sex, growth pattern, age and nutrition. Female animals are generally smaller than males, but there may be considerable sexual dimorphism in other characteristics also. This fact used to be overlooked and differences that were due to sex were regarded as a peculiarity of the domestic animal or as a characteristic of a breed. In the case of cattle, it was especially Siewing[44] who pointed out the significance of such influences; in the case of sheep, Reitsma[34] showed that discussions concerning special centres of domestication lose their basis if the sexual dimorphism of sheep is taken into consideration. In general, sexual differences decrease in domestication.

Klatt has drawn attention to another important phenomenon. In every population there are lightly and heavily built individuals. In domestication, the range of even these characteristics widens. Klatt, therefore, distinguished growth patterns because skull, skeleton and organs often differ in the same sense. Growth patterns occur in all sizes; and because of variations in size and growth pattern many peculiarities of morphology can be understood. Meunier[26] has done particularly valuable work on their theoretical elucidation and recording. Hammond[5] has studied the influence of feeding on physical proportions.

From research into the origin of domestic animals, we have shown that in the gradual transition from wild animals to domestic animals the range of variation of all characteristics reached in the wild species is extended and eventually moved outside this range. However, the greater variation between domestic animals calls for a very careful consideration of correlative ties and modifying changes if conclusions on the origin of domestication are to be sound. One has to examine again and again the way in which the characteristics of domestic animals are to be classified within the ranges of variation; there are no characteristics which are absolutely valid for distinguishing a state of domestication.

The living conditions of wild species bring about severe selection which keeps the range of variation narrow. As a result of this, inferences can, with a high degree of probability, be drawn from single characteristics to apply to the whole body. This is no longer the case with domestic animals. Here single characteristics do not always vary correspondingly with each other,[8,4,29] and must thus be first considered within the range of variation in order to exclude merely coincidental individual variations before significant conclusions are drawn from them.

WHAT IS A BREED?

This question leads one to the problem of making subdivisions among the domestic animals. The increase in the breadth of variation under domestication often leads to extreme individuals of very different physiques; these are often subdivided into breeds, but individuals whose characteristics result from special gene combinations or hereditary changes do not yet constitute a breed so long as they are merely extremes of a uniform variation. They are only potential preliminary stages towards breeds. One may only speak of breeds when groups of individual domestic animals (populations) show certain accumulations of characteristics which can be statistically recorded within the overall range of variation. The environments of domestic animals and man bring about the selection of such combinations of characteristics.

A population with accumulations of characteristics brought about by its environment is called a geographical breed;[15-16] it will exhibit broad variability. Of greater relevance to the history of civilization are the selected breeds, created by man through the selection of animals according to definite breeding objectives and through sexual isolation, which show a narrow range of variation. Such selected breeds are a sign of a highly developed culture; nor are they static units immune to change. Often, it is true, the name remains the same but qualities change and with them morphology. Selected breeds are 'improved' towards higher performance when man's abilities increase, or they disappear when sexual isolation discontinues. If breeds of domestic animals which, isolated in space as geographical breeds or isolated sexually as selected breeds, have been developing in their own way for some length of time are then intermingled, new and remarkable variations will occur which will often range beyond that of the two original breeds. Thus the way is opened for new selection. Modern animal breeding and its selective breeding are characterized by such processes.

THE PROCESS OF DOMESTICATION

The number of animal species hunted by man is large, but the number of species that became important to him as domestic animals is small. He must have made a choice.

It can be seen that nearly all domestic animals originated from social wild species, i.e. in the individuals of the wild species there was already an inclination towards sociability which facilitated an association with man. But a choice was made even from social species. Species with dangerous offensive equipment and with fierce rutting–fights (such as fallow, roe and red deer) became domesticated animals only when, through some special biological factor, they made habitable by man areas which otherwise would have been uninhabitable. This happened, for instance, in the case of the reindeer.[10,11]

Domestic animals did not all originate in the same part of the world; this can be seen from the fact that the original species live in different geographical areas. Any given wild species can, however, only have become domesticated in its natural area of distribution. Reed[33] has recently emphasized this point. At the time of its domestication the wild horse had its home exclusively north of the Caucasus, the wild ass in north-eastern Africa; consequently they could not have been domesticated in the same area. The wild form of the domestic llama and alpaca, the guanaco, which lives only in South America, may be cited as a further example. It may be assumed on this basis that the domestication of wild animals is carried out when a certain level of civilization is reached, as Zeuner[46] and Reed[33] also suggest. There is also the conception of the pre-historian Schwantes to be considered, that ideas travel faster than goods; with this in mind one might think that only the idea of domestication was passed on and put into practice with different species at different places.

Cattle are of interest in this connection. Of them several wild species with differing ecological peculiarities have been domesticated. *Bos primigenius*, the aurochs, was an animal of the open deciduous forests and of parkland; from it came the domestic cow. The sub-tropical areas are the home of the buffalo, *Bubalus arnée*, used in hot and moist areas instead of the descendants of the aurochs. The Gayal, which goes back to the Gaur as wild cattle, is also adapted to tropical swampy areas. The domestic yaks, on the other hand, are the cattle of the cold high mountains of Tibet. Similar observations apply to geese. In Europe and North Africa *Anser anser*, the grey goose, was domesticated, in East Asia *Anser cygnoides*. It can therefore be assumed that there are cases of the new domestication of animal species after the pattern of older ones.

However, a comparison of the areas in which domesticated animals originated shows that a certain level in the cultural development of the peoples was a prerequisite for domestication. The numbers of domestic animals whose homes are in Europe and Asia are large, while in Africa, where wild species abound, only the domestic ass and the domestic guinea-fowl came into being. In Australia and North America no domestication took place, disregarding the turkey, which probably originated in Mexico. In South America, it was only in parts of the Andes where a high standard of civilization developed that guanaco and guinea-pig were domesticated.

If one seeks reasons for such domestication, the following is of importance. All wild cattle have found a similar use in the economy of man; the donkey takes the place of the horse as transport; the camel and llama fulfil a similar task, and the equivalent of the sheep is found in the alpaca. It is possible, therefore, that similar universal requirements have led to the domestication of animals, that experience of the possibilities of the uses that they could be put to spread more rapidly than the animals themselves, so that the same demands were met by different animals.

It is beyond doubt however that domestic animals were brought to areas in which the original species were unknown. This is certainly true of the horse which came to occupy an important position among the domestic animals south of the Caucasus; that is, in areas which were the home of other wild equids. Goats and sheep also became important domestic animals quite early in areas where the wild species had long since died out or had never existed.

From such examples of the influence of man on their distribution domestic animals have come to be considered as originating in essentially the same area and from there starting a march of conquest. Zoological data do not support this view even if one species alone is considered. Pigs may be used as an example. The subspecies of the wild boar show peculiarities between western Europe and eastern Asia. Such differences also occur between the domesticated pigs of these areas, evidence of different instances of domestication of the same wild species.

Archaeological finds support this; in several places gradual transitions from wild populations to domestic animals can be demonstrated; Pira[30] was the first to draw attention to this fact with his study of pigs in the Baltic area. In more recent times Reed[33] has recorded the same phenomenon in pigs from prehistoric settlements in Iraq.

Such findings apply also to cattle; Röhrs and Herre[42] have described a population in transition from the aurochs to the domestic cattle on the southern shore of the Bosphorus, and Nobis[29] one in Schleswig-Holstein. Another aspect of this question may be mentioned to support the assumption that the same species was domesticated several times. It is now certain that the first settlements in the Near East, in which the first domestic animals occurred, are earlier than those of northern Central Europe. Had the domestic animals been imported one would expect those in the earlier settlements of the north to show a clear difference from the wild species. However some direction transitions from the wild populations of Central Europe have been found, suggesting an indigenous domestication.

THE BEGINNING OF DOMESTICATION

After these predominantly zoological considerations it is necessary to consult the evidence relating to the history of civilization in order to discover the point of time at which the domestication of the various species occurred. In the older literature quite a number of erroneous views are expressed because archaeological research did not progress at an equal rate in all fields. Apart from this, errors occurred because the fauna from areas where domestication had happened was rarely so well known that the gradual changes during domestication could be recorded with accuracy; also the shifting of the ranges of variation in local populations was ascertained in such a way as to make statements on the actual beginning of domestication hardly possible. So far, the best preparatory work for such an analysis has been done on the Cimbric peninsula.[3,38]

For a long time it was generally thought that the chronological order in which domestic animals followed one another was the same in all parts of the world, and, for a long time, the Near East was considered to be the original home of domestic animals— *ex oriente lux!* The dog was considered to be man's oldest domestic animal; but results from recent excavations must lead one to a different conclusion.

Reed[33] made a critical examination of the new data according to which sheep are shown to be the oldest domestic animals. In Zawi Chemi, Shanidar (Iraq), groups of humans kept sheep as domestic animals as early as 9000 BC. A little later the goat was domesticated; even in the oldest levels of Jarmo and Jericho the goat is recognizable as a domesticated animal, therefore the practice of domestication must have been carried on for some time before the deposition of the strata. The domestic pig has also a long history. It is true that in the pre-pottery levels of Jarmo only remains of large wild boar were found, but with the occurrence of pottery the presence of domestic pigs is also clear. The distinct differences that can immediately be recognized here between wild boar and domesticated pigs force the conclusion that the pig was not domesticated in Jarmo but earlier, in another place. It may be assumed that this happened around 6500 BC.

According to the archaeological evidence available so far, domestic cattle are of a more recent origin. Their first identifiable occurrence as such is at the Halafian site of Banahilk, which places the date for domestication in the period 5000–4000 BC. For this reason the reports of Röhrs and Herre on the animal remains from the oldest Neolithic permanent settlement of Fikirtepe on the southern shore of the Bosphorus are of interest. Bittel dates the settlement in the early fourth millennium BC. Röhrs and Herre found undoubted remains of domestic sheep, domestic goats and domestic pigs; the cattle, however, formed a population of transition from aurochs to domestic cattle. Independently of Reed's conclusions, the same picture emerges from this evidence of the order in which the domestication of these species took place in the Near East.

In the same way, the new ideas on the appearance of the domestic dog in the Near East gain in importance because of the independent nature of their evidence. It was previously thought that the dog was the oldest domestic animal in the Near East because Bate[1] had reported a domestic dog from the Natufian, that is, 8000 BC. Röhrs and Herre were puzzled that no evidence of domestic dogs could be found in the varied material from Fikirtepe; they only found the humerus of a wolf. Bate's statements were then checked and found to be without foundation. Other early prehistoric settlements in the Near East yielded no evidence of dogs either, and Röhrs and Herre called for an accurate

analysis of wild canids from that area before conclusions were made on the domestication of the dog. Such a study has meanwhile been presented by Clutton-Brock.[2] It
showed that the remains of a canid which Bate had regarded as a domestic dog were of a
small subspecies of wolf. Reed examined the remains of canids from Jarmo; he too was
forced to allocate these few bones to wolves. Thus it was not possible to find any evidence
to establish the domestic dog among the first domestic animals. Whether Zeuner's
view[47] concerning a domestic dog from Jericho can be maintained remains to be seen.
The domestic dog is certainly not the oldest domestic animal in the Near East.

In Central Europe, especially to the north, on the other hand, the dog is certainly
the oldest domestic animal.[4] It is probable that dogs originated from the wolves of
Central Europe and were domesticated at a stage of cultural development as early as the
Mesolithic. This is, therefore, a case of autochthonous domestication and not one of the
importation of a domestic animal. There is evidence also of the domestication of aurochs
and wild boar in Central Europe,[30,29] which seems to be more recent than that in the
Near East (this must, however, be clarified by further dating), while the order in which
species were domesticated is different. This is more evidence to indicate that the idea of
domesticating wild animals spread faster than the domestic animals themselves. This is of
great significance especially in evaluating the sequence of domestication from a zoological point of view.

The mounting archaeological evidence, taken as a whole, shows that the beginning
of domestication is not to be regarded as a uniform process but as a varied one. Present
ideas may be extended and modified by further new archaeological findings. In this
connection, fresh information provided by Ducos, as well as by Samson and Radulesco,[31]
is important as it indicates that the domestication of sheep may also have occurred at
several different places, such as Asia Minor, south and south-east Europe.

THE REASONS FOR DOMESTICATION

Both the zoological facts and recent archaeological finds again pose the question of why
men domesticated animals, thereby not only creating advantages for themselves but
also taking on the responsibility of looking after the animals. As an answer the psychological explanation was advanced that among primitive peoples the social instinct of
man had extended to young wild animals and that thus a more intimate relationship
developed between individuals and social animal species in particular, which resulted
in domestication. However, Reed has said, quite rightly, that the rearing and fondling of
young animals is practised a good deal to this day without any further consequences.
The above explanation overlooks the fundamental fact that it is the sexual isolation of
parts of wild populations which constitutes the decisive step towards domestication.

The view that hunting peoples invented domestication became more important, and
the idea of the dog as the first domestic animal fits into this line of thought. This
theory has been varied in many ways, especially in Europe. It was thought that wolves
realized the advantages of hunting together with man, joined him voluntarily and thus
brought the domestic dog into being. Sauer[43] has already said sharply that such ideas
arose from romantic minds and were without foundation. Modern hunting peoples do

not know the use of the dog as a helper in hunting and it is certain that the dog only became a hunting companion in fairly recent times. Furthermore, Degerbøl[4] discovered that wherever the dog appeared as the oldest domestic animal it had been used as food. Even today the dog is eaten in wide areas of the world, in Asia and among the aborigines of South America. It must also be remembered that as a beast of prey the wolf has its special food requirements and that it is unlikely that the food refuse of small groups of prehistoric men was sufficient to make the domestication of this animal possible. Nor does archaeological evidence now support the thesis of the dog as the oldest domestic animal.

Another major theoretical standpoint recently demolished is that religious factors were of primary significance in the origins of domestication, particularly of the ox. The latest archaeological evidence shows that the ox was not present at the first stage, although it became one of the most important and versatile domestic animals at a very early date. One must therefore examine whether the religious ideas of prehistoric men were already so deep-rooted as to provide the impetus for such a culturally significant act as domestication. What has been discovered so far hardly supports such a thesis.

So far it has become certain that the first domestic animals were easily fed herbivorous animals whose main importance lay in their meat-producing qualities, as the wild animals did not form wool or produce large quantities of milk. The first domestic dogs, too, served as producers of meat. The provision of meat seems, therefore, to have been an important reason for domestication, a view supported by the fact that the same animal species, or other wild species that were similar to the domesticated form, were domesticated at different times, but at presumably similar cultural stages. As Reed, too, points out, it is becoming increasingly clear that domestication begins when a growing human population changes over to a more settled and culturally higher form of life. So the view suggests itself that the keeping of domestic animals arises from the necessity of ensuring a regular food supply for larger groups of people. Therefore domestication is probably dependent on a certain cultural stage and at the same time a prerequisite for the further development of culture. However, this is another matter about which archaeology will have to provide further information.

THE MAIN HISTORICAL FEATURES OF THE DOMESTICATION OF HORSES AND CATTLE

It is not intended to give here a general survey of the historical development of all domestic animals. Some data on the horse and ox may serve as examples of the most important domestic animals.

The home of wild horses lies to the north of the big mountain chains which run through Europe and Asia from east to west. Once their numbers were large; the wild horse was an important animal of the chase for Palaeolithic men. In the course of the early Holocene the area of distribution and the numbers of animals decreased greatly, and today it is only in east Asia that there are small populations of the wild horse. If the up-to-date palaeontological evidence and the results of modern zoological systematics are considered, *Equus przewalskii* is the only species from which the domestic horse can have originated.[15,16] It is difficult to give a complete and accurate picture of the beginnings and the place of the domestication. Hančar[6] mentions the early Tripolje culture in the South-East European wooded steppe and the Afanasje culture of the Siberian wooded steppe, and the end of the third millennium BC as places and times at which wild horses were domesticated. Huppertz[18] adds the view that horses were domesticated in central Asia and came, domesticated, from there to China as early as 4000–3000 BC.

According to what is known today, the horse had little importance at first as a domestic animal because it was only a supplier of meat, but after it had crossed the Caucasus probably in the middle of the third millennium BC., following the example of the use of the ox, it was harnessed to the cart. In the ancient East, in the mountain country of Syria, Asia Minor, the Caucasus, the cart developed into the horse-drawn chariot which helped to overthrow and form empires. The use of the horse in war gained it a special position as an important element of political power. The riding of the horse is more recent than the chariot, at least in the orient. According to Hančar, the development of the horse into a riding animal took place in the Altai-Sajan area around 1500 BC, with the mounted warrior replacing the chariot from 1000 BC. Huppertz thinks that the development of the horse into a riding animal began in central Asia, and it is certain that it was from Asia that mounted warriors and their horses came into world history. The horse, however, gained importance also as a helper to the animal breeder, at first probably in Caucasian and South Siberian areas. In Central Europe, its chief use for a long time was as a beast of burden, a draught animal before the plough and a source of meat. Thus the 'social position' differs very much from one area to another. In Europe it is predominantly a working animal, in the region of Asia Minor and in parts of Asia it is the companion of the socially privileged classes. It needs further ethnological study to determine how far this statement is true.

When it comes to the question of the biological change undergone by the horse in domestication, modern research permits quite accurate statements, particularly for Europe. On average the Przewalski horses stand 140 cm high at the withers. At the beginning of domestication, this height is known to have been decreased without the formation of a breed becoming immediately evident. Horses of the La Tène period grew to a height of 130 cm. Horses of the pre-Roman Iron Age in Britain are said to have reached a height of only 120–125 cm at the shoulder. It is certain that in the ancient Mediterranean civilizations thoroughbreds were already being developed, though evidence from osteological remains is not yet conclusive. In Central Europe, differences between geographical breeds of horses become distinguishable only as late as 300 BC: in the region immediately to the north of the Alps, horses were of lighter build than on the North Sea coast. According to studies made by Nobis[28] a rapid development took place in the Migration period: the original heavy cart-horse was developed from smaller geographical breeds of horses of broad build, and big horses became frequent. This process continued into the Middle Ages when, through selection, bigger and bigger domesticated horses were developed, reaching a height of up to 160 cm at the withers. These were the knights' chargers and side by side with them survived the small country horses of the farmers. The first horses to reach Iceland during the time of the Vikings were of heavy build but developed into ponies in the course of adaptation to the un-favourable environment.

All this shows that wild animals extended their range of variation when domesticated. From this wide variation selections were made which led to widely different forms in domestic horses. In modern times crossing and subsequent selection became important as a method of breeding.

Domestic horses became so important to mankind because they did not remain mere meat animals, but lightened human toil and were eventually decisive in warfare. The ox, on the other hand, has remained in a more modest position as a domestic animal, though more important in the development of early mankind than the horse.

It is true to say that all domestic cattle descend from the aurochs, *Bos primigenius*. Adametz named a further species of origin, *Bos brachyceros*; this turned out to be a mis-interpretation, a domestic ox having been incorrectly dated. The same applies to Reed's assumption[32] that, side by side with the aurochs, another smaller species of wild cattle had lived in the Near East.[33]

India is generally believed to be the area where the aurochs originated, spreading thence to much of Eurasia and Africa. From Africa it was not, however, able to populate south Europe, as from the Pleistocene there was no longer a land bridge with Europe. The Pleistocene aurochs was of massive build, and was divided up into subspecies; *Bos primigenius trochoceros* lived in Europe, *Bos primigenius hahni* in Egypt, and *Bos primigenius namadicus* in India. The aurochs of the Holocene was smaller; it is called *Bos primigenius primigenius*. This subspecies was widely distributed, became rarer in the Middle Ages and died out in the seventeenth century. There are, however, many records available concerning the appearance of the aurochs.[36,37]

In the several different regions where the aurochs was domesticated a notable and uniform variation appeared at a very early stage. Domestic oxen became generally smaller than the wild species. In the larger animals, the skull still showed a predominance of the characteristics of the wild animal; hence the term 'primigenius cattle'. In the smaller animals, changes dependent on size led to stronger morphological differences;[21] such animals are called 'brachyceros cattle'. As the development towards the domestic ox progresses, brachyceros cattle become predominant; it is however not justifiable to regard these individuals as a separate breed, as the variability in their stock is very large. Only when the breadth of variation narrows down and special characteristics become frequent that are not connected with sexual differences or with castration can breeds be designated, as indicating the breeders' intention and ability. Such phenomena can be identified in highly developed cultures, such as those of Egypt and Rome. In Central Europe, influence through breeding remained slight for a long time. The number of small animals, which could survive times of food scarcity, increased up to the Middle Ages. Neolithic cattle stood from 115 to 138 cm high at the withers, that is, they resembled modern medium-sized breeds. From the Middle Ages, a minimum size of 95 cm is known.

Concerning the history of breeding, it is noteworthy that large cattle, different from the smaller country cattle, lived in the area of the Roman castella north of the Alps.

These large animals have been called 'pseudoprimigenius cattle'; they did not, however, attain any great importance in breeding. By the ninth and tenth centuries, no effects of such animals can be traced in the area of the Rhine. Crossing as a method of breeding does not seem to have been practised in the Middle Ages, it has assumed importance only in modern times. Selection from the geographical breeds offered sufficient possibilities for the realization of breeding aims.

What had first been a meat animal was soon used to draw the plough; the cart was invented for it and it also became important as a milking animal. Cattle have to be considered as the most important domestic animals of peaceful men. Sheep, goats and pigs are also distributed widely as domestic animals. According to the evidence so far known concerning the history of sheep and goat, it seems probable that they were widely distributed as domestic animals even in early times, while the pig was domesticated in Europe as well as in Asia Minor and East Africa.

Altogether the domestic animals illustrate that a high degree of adaptability is inherent in wild animals. Man therefore found it possible to change radically the shape and qualities of an animal according to his needs, and it cannot be predicted how far such endeavours will lead. Man has the ability to change domestic animals today as much as ever.

REFERENCES

1 BATE, D. M. A. 1937. In GARROD, D. *The Stone Age of Mount Carmel*, Oxford, vol. 1
2 CLUTTON-BROCK, J. 1962. *Z. Tierzüchtung u. Züchtungsbiologie 76*, 326–33
3 DEGERBØL, M. 1933. *Danmarks Pattedyr i Fortiden*, Copenhagen, vol. 1
4 —— 1962. *Z. Tierzüchtung u. Züchtungsbiologie 76*, 334–41
5 HAMMOND, J. 1960. *Farm Animals*, London, 3rd ed.
6 HANČAR, F. 1956. *Das Pferd in prähistorischer und früher historischer Zeit*, Vienna and Munich
7 HERRE, W. 1943. *Zool. Anz. 141*, 196–214
8 —— 1951. *Anat. Anz. 98*, 49–65
9 —— 1952. *Zool. Garten N-F. 19*, 70–98
10 —— 1955a. *Das Ren als Haustier*, Leipzig
11 —— 1955b. Domestikation und Stammesgeschichte, in HEBERER. *Die Evolution der Organismen*, Stuttgart, 2nd ed., 801–56
12 —— 1958a. Abstammung und Domestikation der Haustiere, *Handbuch der Tierzüchtung*, Hamburg, Bd. I
13 —— 1958b. *Z. Tierzüchtung u. Züchtungsbiologie 71*, 252–72
14 —— 1959. *Naturwissenschaftl. Rundschau* 87–94
15 —— 1961a. Der Art- und Rassebegriff, *Handbuch der Tierzüchtung*, Hamburg, Bd. III, 1, 1–24
16 —— 1961b. *Z. Tierzüchtung u. Züchtungsbiologie 75*, 57–78
17 —— RÖHRS, M. 1958. 71. *Win. Veröffentl' d. deutschen Orient-Gesellschaft*, 60–79
18 HUPPERTZ, J. 1962. *Z. Tierzüchtung u. Züchtungsbiologie 76*, 190–208
19 HUXLEY, J. 1948. *The New Systematics*, London
20 KELLER, G. 1905. *Naturgeschichte der Haustiere*, Berlin
21 KLATT, B. 1913. *Arch. Entw. Mech. 36*, 387–471
22 —— 1927. Entstehung der Haustiere, *Handb. d. Vererbungswissenschaft*, Berlin, Bd. III, 1–107
23 KLEINSCHMIDT, O. 1902. Der Formenkreis Falco-Hierofalco, *Aquila 9*, 1–49
24 MAYR, E. 1957. *The Species problem*, Washington
25 —— LINSLEY, E. G. and USINGER, R. L. 1953. *Methods and principles of systematic zoology*, New York
26 MEUNIER, K. 1959. *Z. wissenschaftl. Zoologie 162*, 328–55
27 NACHTSHEIM, H. 1949. *Vom Wildtier zum Haustier*, Berlin, 2nd ed.

28 NOBIS, G. 1955. *Z. Tierzüchtung u Züchtungsbiologie 64*, 201–46

29 —— 1962. *Ibid. 77*, 16–31

30 PIRA. 1909. *Zoolog. Jahrb.*, Suppl. Bd. X, H.2

31 RADULESCO, C. and P. SAMSON. 1961. *Z. Tierzüchtung u. Züchtungsbiologie 75*, 282–321

32 REED, C. A. 1960. A review of the archaeological evidence on animal domestication in the prehistoric Near East, in BRAIDWOOD, R. J. and HOWE, B. *Prehistoric investigations in Iraqi Kurdistan*, Chicago

33 —— 1961. *Z. Tierzüchtung u. Züchtungsbiolgie 76*, 34

34 REITSMA, G. C. 1932. *Het Schapp*, Wageningen

35 RENSCH, B. 1929. *Das Prinzip geographischer Rassenkreise und das Problem der Artbildung*, Berlin

36 REQUATE, H. 1957. *Bonner Zoologische Beiträge 8*, 207–29

37 —— 1957. *Z. Tierzüchtung u. Züchtungsbiologie 71*, 297–328

38 —— 1962. *Ibid. 77*

39 RÖHRS, M. 1958. Ökologische Beobachtungen an wildlebenden Tylopoden Südamerikas, *Verhandl. Dtsch. Zoologen 1957 in Graz*, 538–54

40 —— 1959. *Z. wissenschaftl. Zoologie 162*, 1–95

41 —— 1961. *Z. Tierzüchtung u. Züchtungsbiologie 76*, 7–22

42 —— and HERRE, W. 1961. *Ibid. 75*, 110–27

43 SAUER, O. 1952. *Agricultural Origins and Dispersals*, New York

44 SIEWING, G. 1960. Das Hausrind, in HERRE, W. *Die Haustiere von Haithabu*, Neumünster, 19–71

45 WRIGHT, S. 1940. The statistical consequences of Mendelian Heredity in relation to speciation, in HUXLEY, J., 161–83

46 ZEUNER, F. E. 1954. Domestication of animals, in SINGER, C., HOLMYARD, E. J. and HALL, H. R. *A History of Technology*, Oxford

47 —— 1958. *Palestine Exploration Quarterly 19*, 52–55

26 The Ageing of Domestic Animals

I. A. SILVER

THE METHODS for determining the age at death of domestic animals by examination of their hard parts differ little from those used in ageing any other animals. However, owing to the close association of domestic animals with man much more detailed information is available in relation to age changes in the skeleton and dentition than in the case for any animals other than man himself. The science of ageing an animal by the appearance of its teeth in life (or death) is probably as old as animal husbandry.

Really accurate estimates of the age of an animal can be made only when the following conditions are fulfilled—(a) that it belongs to a species or breed of which the age characteristics are well documented, (b) that its plane of nutrition is known, (c) that most of the teeth and a representative selection of bones are available and (d) that it is not yet fully adult. Archaeological material cannot satisfy all these criteria, since, first, age characteristics are well known only for modern domestic animals, most of which are considerably selected and inbred. Tooth eruption dates and epiphysial fusion dates differ very significantly between individual breeds within a single species. It is a reasonable assumption that bony remains from sites dated before intensive selective breeding began will show age characteristics similar to the more primitive of modern domestic animals rather than to those more highly specialized, provided that the archaeological material is definitely the same species as its modern counterpart. Second, the plane of nutrition of the animal can only be guessed at, usually from the bones whose age is to be determined, which leads to a danger of circular argument. Third, it is only under rather favourable circumstances that several bones can be identified positively as belonging to one animal. Fourth, it is fortunate that where food animals are concerned many are slaughtered before reaching adulthood and this slightly simplifies the task of ageing many bones.

METHODS—BONES

Assessment of age. This relies on a number of factors which are linked with the embryological, foetal and post-natal method of bone development and growth. With the exception of the clavicle and some parts of the skull, bones are first preformed in cartilage which then ossifies and becomes rearranged structurally. The process of ossification is constant for each bone. Long bones usually show a primary centre of ossification in the middle of the shaft and at least one epiphysial centre at each end (Fig. 38a). Complex bones such as vertebrae have more centres (Table A). Cartilaginous zones, the epiphysial plates, persist between the primary and secondary centres, allowing growth, until a relatively constant age for each particular epiphysis when the cartilage becomes ossified and the primary and secondary centres fuse. There are, however, some regions of cartilage which do not ossify, even in old age, although calcium salts may be deposited within cartilage, giving it a superficial appearance of bone. The costal cartilages and the proximal parts of the suprascapular cartilages of large animals may be affected in this way.

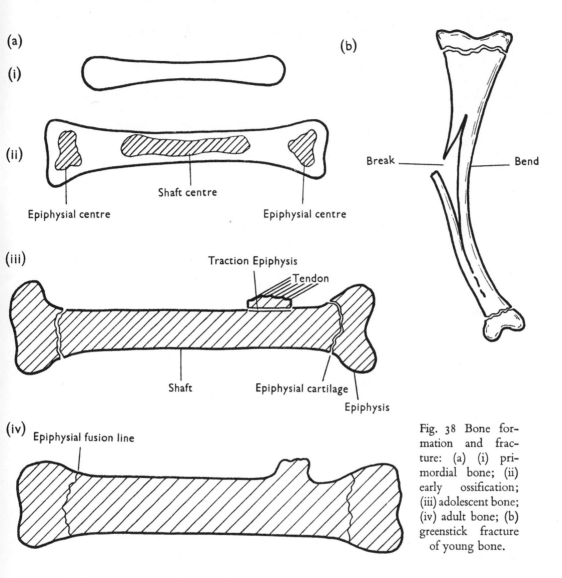

(a)

(i)

(ii)

Epiphysial centre   Shaft centre   Epiphysial centre

(iii)   Traction Epiphysis

Tendon

Shaft   Epiphysial cartilage

Epiphysis

(iv) Epiphysial fusion line

(b)

Break   Bend

Fig. 38 Bone for-
mation and frac-
ture: (a) (i) pri-
mordial bone; (ii)
early ossification;
(iii) adolescent bone;
(iv) adult bone; (b)
greenstick fracture
of young bone.

Once a skeleton has started to ossify, the age of an animal may be determined fairly accurately by noting the regions where epiphysial fusion has occurred. From the point of view of the skeleton, full adulthood is reached when all epiphyses are fused and from this time onwards the indications of advancing age are very much less precise. The following changes in bones take place during the adult period, and serve as a rough guide (if evidence of tooth wear is lacking) as to whether the animal is a young, middle-aged or elderly adult. At first the shafts of the limb bones are relatively long and slender and the extremities are large. There are few surface marks on the bone and prominences for tendon and muscle attachments are small. In the mid-adult phase the bones become more rugged in appearance and the extremities are relatively narrower.

TABLE A

Ossification centres and ages of fusion in post-cranial skeleton of domestic animals.

Bone	Ossification Centres	Fusion
Vertebrae	Body 1 Arch 2 + Spine 1 Epiphyses 2	Horse, ox—body and arch fuse at or just after birth; bodies fuse with epiphyses at 5 years. Pig, sheep, dog—body and arch fuse at 3–6 months.
Atlas Axis*	4 7	Horse and ox—wings not fused till 6 months. Epiphysis between body and odontoid in horse open till 3–4 years.
Sacrum†		Body epiphyses may never fuse. Unite with each other before uniting with body.
Costal cartilages‡		
Sternum	Manubrium 1 Sternebrae, 2 each	Sternebral centres fuse early except in last sternebra of ruminants which remain in 2 parts till old age.

* Anterior notch of axis becomes a foramen in old horses.
† Bases of spines fuse in old horses. Spines fuse in young adult cattle and sheep.
‡ Ossify or calcify commonly in old age.

Bone	Ossification Centres	Fusion					
		Horse	Ass	Ox	Sheep	Pig	Dog
Scapula	Bicipital tuberosity	1 yr 8 mo.		7–10 mo.	6–8 mo.	1 yr.	6–7 mo.
	Tuber spinae	3 yrs					
Humerus	Proximal epiphysis	3–3½ yrs.		3½–4 yrs	3–3½ yrs.	3½ yrs	15 mo.
	Distal epiphysis	15–18 mo.		12–18 mo.	10 mo.	1 yr.	8–9 mo.
Radius	Proximal epiphysis	15–18 mo.		12–18 mo.	10 mo.	1 yr.	11–12 mo.
	Distal epiphysis	3½ yrs		3½–4 yrs	3 yrs	3½ yrs	11–12 mo.
Ulna	Olecranon*†	3½ yrs		All at 3½–4 yrs	3 yrs	3–3½ yrs	9–10 mo.
	Distal end	Before birth	2 mo.				11–12 mo.
Metacarpus	Proximal epiphysis‡§	Before birth		Before birth	Before birth	Before birth	Before birth
	Distal epiphysis	15–18 mo.		2–2½ yrs	18–24 mo.	2 yrs	8 mo.
1st Phalanx	Proximal epiphysis	13–15 mo.		Before birth	Before birth	2 yrs	7 mo.
	Distal epiphysis	Before birth		1½ yrs	13–16 mo.	Before birth	Before birth

TABLE A continued:

Bone	Ossification Centres	Fusion					
		Horse Ass	Ox	Sheep	Pig	Dog
2nd Phalanx	Proximal epiphysis	9–12 mo.	Before birth	Before birth	1 yr	7 mo.
	Distal epiphysis	Before birth	1½ yrs	13–16 mo.	Before birth	Before birth
3rd Phalanx	No true epiphysis¶	Partly ossified at birth				
Pelvis (os innominata = os coxae)	Fusion of main bones Ilium—Tubercoxae Ischium—sciatic tuberosity Pubis–Acetabular bone	1½–2 yrs All fused at 4½–5 yrs	7–10 mo. All fused by 4½ yrs	6–10 mo. All fused by 3½ yrs	1 yr. All fused by 6–7 yrs	6 mo. Sciatic tuberosity at 2 yrs
Femur	Proximal end (2 epiphyses)‖	3–3½ yrs	3½ yrs	2½–3 yrs	3½ yrs	1½ yrs
	Distal end (1 epiphysis)	3–3½ yrs	3½–4 yrs	3–3½ yrs	3½ yrs	1½ yrs
Tibia	Proximal epiphysis	3–3½ yrs	3½–4 yrs	3–3½ yrs	3½ yrs	1½ yrs
	Distal epiphysis**	20–24 mo.	2–2½ yrs	1½–2 yrs	2 yrs	13–16 mo.
Fibula	Proximal epiphysis	Doubtful 2–3 yrs	Fused with tibia 2–3 yrs		3½ yrs	15–18 mo.
	Distal epiphysis	Fuses with tibia 1–3 mo.	Separate bone	Separate bone	2½ yrs	15 mo.
Fibular Tarsal (Calcaneum)	Tuber calcis	3 yrs	3–3½ yrs	2½–3 yrs	2–2½ yrs	13–16 mo.
Metatarsal	Proximal epiphysis	Before birth	Before birth	Before birth	Before birth	Before birth
	Distal epiphysis	16–20 mo.	2¼–3 yrs	20–28 mo.	2¼ yrs.	10 mo.

* Interosseus radio–olecranon ligament ossifies in horse at 3–4 yrs.
† Radio–ulnar ligament ossifies in dog at 2 yrs.
‡ Metacarpals 3 and 4 of ruminants are joined by cartilage at birth.
§ Ossification occurs at 3–8 mo. (old figures give 12–15 mo.).
¶ In old horses the lateral cartilages may ossify to form 'side bones'.
‖ A traction epiphysis at 3rd Trochanter in horse ossifies variously from 2 to 4 yrs.
** Lateral malleolus separate at birth to 3 mo. in foal.

Marks caused by blood vessels become obvious and tendon attachments may ossify to give 'traction epiphyses'. Smaller prominences associated with muscle attachment appear, and depressions at muscle origins are deep. The cortex of the bone is thick and the bone is heavy. In senility, calcium resorbtion takes place resulting in a bone with a thin cortex and large medullary cavity. Rarefaction is common. Similar changes may occur in pregnancy.

Certain pathological features may be present which can also be a guide to the probable age. For instance, so-called 'greenstick' fractures occur only in young bones (Fig. 35b); malignant bone tumours usually appear in the adolescent or young adult but arthritic changes and signs of healed inflammatory changes, especially on the legs of large animals, are commonest in middle to late life. Changes in the alveoli of the jaws where teeth have been lost in life may be useful as guides to age. The alveolar cavity is slowly filled with bone after loss of a tooth, and if no cavity at all is present, particularly at the site of a deep-rooted tooth, it is an indication that the jaw is probably not from a young adult. The size of the maxillary sinuses in horse, ox, sheep and goat gives a fairly close correlation with age even when teeth or other parts of skull are missing. The lower the floor of this sinus, the older the animal. In extreme old age, high-crowned teeth may grow right out of the jaw leaving the floor of the maxillary sinus below the level of the palate. In the foal, the maxillary sinus is almost full of developing teeth, at $5\frac{1}{2}$ years it is full of embedded parts of permanent teeth and in old age it is largely filled with air.

In the horned domestic animals the cavity of the frontal sinus extends into the bony horn-core. A horn-core from a young animal normally has a rather narrow cortex and a large sinus cavity. With advancing age the cavity is reduced and the cortex thickens. Horn-cores showing signs of repaired damage are more likely to come from mature animals. If the horn itself survives it will be found to show annual growth rings, the first of which appears at two years of age in cattle.

Detailed assessment of age. The tables above indicate the ages at which the epiphyses of the major bones fuse with the shaft in the common domestic mammals. There is unfortunately no complete agreement on exact fusion ages and the figures given in the tables are means and as far as possible these data refer to 'scrub' crossbred animals. High planes of nutrition and sheltered conditions tend to accelerate epiphysial fusion.

Certain features may be amplified as these are not obvious in tables. The proportions of the skull change strikingly with age. In young mammals the brain case is large relative to the face, but during the growing period the face usually increases in size faster than the cranium. Taking the horse as an example (Table B), in a young foal the bones of the forehead are convex, but as growth occurs the frontals and nasals flatten and may become concave in old age. The maxillary region of the face is also primarily convex but it becomes concave as the cheek teeth grow out of the skull. The relationship of the rostral end of the facial crest to the cheek tooth immediately below it, is as follows: in the new-born, the posterior part of the third premolar, in the three-year-old the posterior part of the fourth premolar, and in the mature adult the first molar. The premaxilla in young horses has a downward curve which is gradually lost with age. The caudal border of the vertical ramus of the mandible becomes narrow and sharp in very old horses. The long axis of the bony orbit in the young adult is on a line passing through the necks of the incisor teeth and the external auditory opening but in old age it is lower and on a line joining the occipital tubercle and the rostral end of the zygomatic crest.

The cranium behind the post-orbital bars is wider in a young than in an adult animal: the various prominences, especially the lachrymal tubercle and nuchal and sagittal crests, increase with age, and the infra-orbital foramen, which in early life is present as a slit, becomes large and almost round in old age.

METHODS—TEETH

General. The teeth are the most durable and in many ways the most informative hard

TABLE B

The skull of the horse—centres of ossification and fusion ages.

Bone	Centres of ossification	Fusion ages	Notes
Occipital	Supraoccipital 2 × exoccipital Basioccipital	Supra with exocc. at 18 mo. Basi with exocc. at 3–4 mo.	4 bones at birth but only 1 bone in adult
Sphenoid	One in each of 4 wings One in body = 5	With occip. at 5 yrs	
Ethmoid	2 in each lateral mass 1 in perpendicular plate = 5		At birth perpendicular and cribriform plates are cartilaginous Often paired in young animals
Interparietal	2 main centres	With parietals at 3–4 yrs With supraoccipital at about 5 yrs	Fusion v. variable Central part more convex in foal than adult
Parietal	Each has one centre	Parietals fuse across midline about 4 yrs Parieto-occipital fusion 5 yrs Parieto-squamous fusion 12–15 yrs	No external parietal crest in foal
Frontal	Each has one centre	With each other or parietals only in old age	
Squamosal (Squamous temporal)	Each has a single centre	With parietal at 12–15 yrs	
Periotic (Petrosal or Petrous temporal)	At least 2	At or soon after birth	Rarely fuses with adjoining bones
Pterygoid Maxilla Lachrymal Palatine Zygomatic	1 each (Some may have small secondary centres)		Normally remain separate. May unite with adjoining bones in old age
Premaxilla	1	The two bones fuse across mid line at about 4 yrs	
Nasal	1	Mid line suture is unfused even in old age	
Mandible	2 in each branch	The 2 centres fuse before birth. The 2 halves fuse at 2–4 mo.	

structures of the body. It may be possible to infer, from a single tooth, not only the species or feeding habits of an animal, but also its age and approximate size. However, for accurate determination of age from teeth it is necessary to have at least a selection of them from an animal, preferably still embedded in the jaw. The teeth which give the best indication of age in the adult are those of the 'high-crowned' or hypsodont type which grow out of the jaw at an approximately constant rate as they are worn away, and whose character changes not only in regard to length but also in respect of the crown pattern of the interfolded layers of cement, enamel and primary and secondary dentine. It is unfortunate that maximum accuracy in ageing of teeth can be accomplished only in the infantile and adolescent animal, the same periods in which bones give their most reliable indication of age. There are, however, as in the case of bone, certain signs to be found in the teeth of adults which will indicate whether they are from young, middle-aged or senile animals. Although changes in horse teeth are dealt with in detail in the tables it is worth noting that the first molar is rather commonly attacked by caries in the young to middle-aged adult, whereas caries in other cheek teeth is much less common and is usually an indication of advanced age. In cattle, the incisor teeth are always movable in the jaw in life, so that there is a relatively large amount of soft tissue in the incisor alveoli. Thus it is common to find in normal cattle that the roots of the incisors are much smaller than the alveolar cavity. On the other hand, especially in carnivores, if the teeth show roots which are markedly smaller than the alveoli, and the alveolar walls are rough, then it is probable that the specimen suffered from paradontal disease and was old. A common sequel to this condition is readily detectable in archaeological material due to the resorbtion and destruction of bone at the original abscess site. The tooth most often affected by abscesses of the root is the carnassial tooth of the upper jaw (premolar 4) in old dogs. Frequently the maxillary bone over the roots of this tooth is eroded so that a sinus develops between alveolus and the surface.

Very heavily worn teeth, or jaws showing alveoli from which teeth have been lost in life, naturally indicate an old animal, but considerable caution must be exercised in coming to such a conclusion unless there is confirmatory evidence from other (skeletal) sources. Young dogs which eat large quantities of bones or play with and chew hard materials such as wood or stones, may present a pattern of tooth wear suggestive of extreme senility, whereas old animals which have eaten mainly meat and have not had to scavenge may have almost unworn teeth. In this latter case, however, there is nearly always some wear on the canines and carnassials and the tips of the incisors. Among herbivores the type of soil and herbage plays a major part in tooth wear. Animals on sandy soil and short grass show the highest rate of wear, whereas animals feeding largely on foliage or on lush grass from soft soils with a low silica content show only slow tooth abrasion. Certain areas are well known at the present time to produce rapid tooth wear. For instance, ponies living on Dartmoor often seem, on the evidence of their teeth, to be as much as two years older than they are in fact.

Details of ageing by teeth in individual species. (1) *Horse.* Table C gives tooth eruption dates in live horses, that is the age at which the tooth cuts the gum and not the age at which it first appears out of the bone. In archaeological material teeth which are unworn and project only slightly above the jaw line are best regarded as being at a stage represented by the earliest dates given here. If a tooth shows the slightest evidence of wear then it must have been erupted, and in all probability will have been erupted for at least 2–3 months. Teeth usually take about six months from eruption to come into full wear.

TABLE C
Tooth eruption ages in the horse.

Tooth	Deciduous teeth	Permanent teeth
Incisors*		
Central 1/1	Present at birth	$2\frac{1}{2}$–3 yrs
Lateral 1/1	3–4 wks	$3\frac{1}{2}$–4 yrs
Corner 1/1	5–9 mo.	$4\frac{1}{2}$–5 yrs
Canine 1/1	Rarely emerges from jaw	4–5 yrs
Premolars		
1 1/1 Wolf tooth	Inconstant, 6 mo.	Inconstant, $2\frac{1}{2}$ yrs
2 1/1	⎫	$2\frac{1}{2}$ yrs
3 1/1	⎬ Present at birth	$2\frac{1}{2}$ yrs
4 1/1	⎭	$3\frac{1}{2}$ yrs
Molars		
1 1/1	⎫	Wide variation. 7–14 mo. Usually present by 1 yr
2 1/1	⎬ Absent	2–$2\frac{1}{2}$ yrs
3 1/1	⎭	$3\frac{1}{2}$–$4\frac{1}{2}$ yrs

* It is usual for the upper milk incisor teeth to be replaced by permanent teeth slightly earlier than those of the lower jaw.

It is of great importance to distinguish permanent from deciduous incisor teeth and the following characteristics may be used. The milk teeth have a definite 'neck'; they are grooved on the lingual and smooth on the labial surfaces; they are small and the enamel is white; they often show signs of resorbtion of the root due to the presence of following teeth; when present in the jaw they are arranged in a semi-circle. The permanent incisors appear as follows (Fig. 39a): they are long and curved and diminish gradually from crown to root without a neck, the curve being restricted to the crown region, the root being straight; they are grooved on the labial aspect; the enamel is a dirty white and the infundibulum is much deeper than in milk teeth; there is a

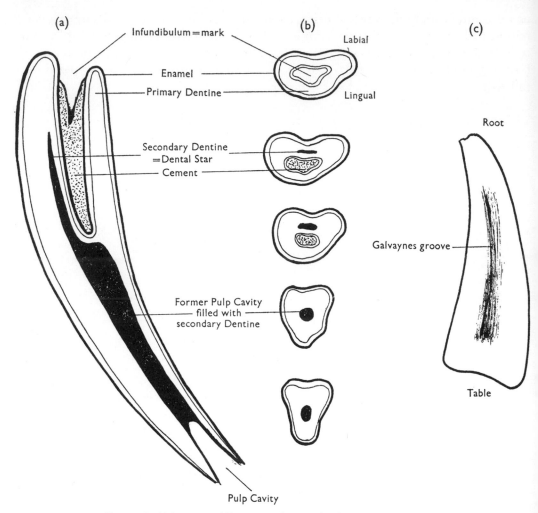

Fig. 39 Incisors of horse: (a, b) lower middle incisor: longitudinal section and cross-sections viewed from above (note the outer layer of cement has been omitted to avoid confusion); (c) upper lateral incisor, showing Galvayne's groove.

considerable change in cross-section from the crown to root, the crown being twice as wide laterally as it is antero-posteriorly whereas in the root region the antero-posterior diameter is twice the lateral (Fig. 39b).

When all the teeth have erupted and are in wear, it is necessary to resort to other characters for determining age. The incisor teeth of horses show valuable clues to age provided that tooth wear has remained within normal limits. The first is the infundibulum or mark, and the second is the star, which is formed by the filling of the pulp cavity with secondary dentine of a colour different from that of the primary dentine. (Fig. 39a, b). The third is that the shape of the table (the biting surface) varies with age in a constant manner. Lastly, the labial groove (of Galvayne) of the upper corner incisor is confined to the middle third of the tooth so that it remains within the jaw

until approximately the tenth year (Fig. 39c), it is half-way down the erupted front of
the tooth at 15, the full length at 21 and only the distal half shows a groove at 30 years.
The following list shows the expected appearance of teeth at differing ages.

Birth	Milk central incisors and premolars
1–5 months	Milk central plus lateral incisors and premolars
6–12 months	Milk central plus lateral plus corner incisors and premolars plus first molar
1 year	Infundibulum worn out of central incisors. Corner incisors in wear but thin walled. Incisor teeth close together
18 months	Infundibulum lost from lateral incisors. First molar in wear
2 years	Incisor teeth wide apart. Infundibulum lost from corner incisor. Second molar appears
2½ years	Permanent central incisor and first and second permanent premolar cut. Second molar in wear
3 years	Permanent central incisor and first and second permanent premolar in wear
3½ years	Permanent lateral incisor and third permanent premolar cut plus lower canines
4 years	Permanent lateral incisor in wear. Upper canine may appear (males). Third molar appears
4½ years	Permanent corner incisor appears. Upper canine usually present as a sharp knife edge—but only in males. Third molar in wear
5 years	Permanent corner incisor in wear, but inner wall still level with jaw and the upper tooth is much longer laterally than antero-posteriorly. Canine in wear. Star on central incisor
6 years	Upper corner incisors, diameters almost equal laterally and a.p. and inner walls in wear. Infundibulum very shallow on central. Star on lateral incisor
7 years	Upper corner square, often with a posterior 'hook'. Lower corner in wear on inner as well as outer walls, all of which are thick. Infundibulum lost from central incisor. Canines blunt
8 years	Infundibulum lost from lateral incisors and very shallow on lower corners
9 years	All infundibular marks absent on incisors. No labial groove on upper corner beyond alveolar cavity. Central incisor table is triangular
10 years	Appearance of Galvayne's groove on labial aspect of upper corner incisor. Lateral incisor table triangular
11 years	Corner incisor table becoming triangular
12 years	All incisor table markedly triangular
13 years	Often a posterior hook on corner incisor
15 years	Galvayne's groove ½ down erupted part of upper corner incisor
18 years	Central incisor table width = thickness a.p.

21 years   Galvayne's groove reaches full length of erupted part of tooth.
                  Narrowing of lower jaw and separation of roots of incisors marked
26 years   Width of central incisors = $\frac{1}{2}$ a.p. diameter
30 years   Galvayne's groove half-way off upper corner incisor

The rate of wear of horse teeth is not constant, e.g. between 5 years and 7 years the incisors are worn away at about $\frac{1}{4}$ inch per year while later in life the rate is much reduced so that over 20 years of age the incisors are ground off at about $\frac{1}{4}$ inch per 5 years. The lower cheek teeth tend to wear faster than the upper as they have a smaller surface area; also the central cheek teeth wear faster than those at each end of the row. In old horses this often leads to an undulation of the surface of cheek teeth. Very smooth molars and premolars are also characteristic of old age.

Lastly, the arrangement of the incisor teeth in the jaw is referable to the age of the animal. In youth the upper and lower teeth meet to form a vertical line with their labial surfaces (Fig. 40). As the animal ages the angle at which the teeth meet becomes progressively less than 180° until in old age, the incisors, especially of the lower jaw, protrude almost horizontally from the jaws (Fig. 40).

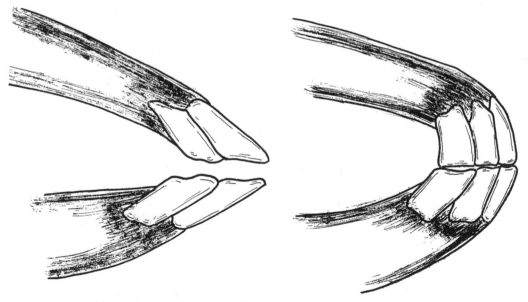

Fig. 40 Change of the angle of profile of teeth; this is due to the curvature of the crown and straight roots.

No doubt horse dealing is almost as old as domestication of horses and dealers are distinguished by the ingenuity they show in attempting to improve on the natural appearance of horses' teeth, to the confusion of their clients. The common forms of deception consist of the production of an 'artificial infundibulum' in old incisor teeth by burning a hole and the filing away of the front of the incisors to reduce the acuteness of the angle at which they meet. Both of these practices help to produce a 'young' old horse. Both are easily detected if the normal arrangement of dentine and enamel is

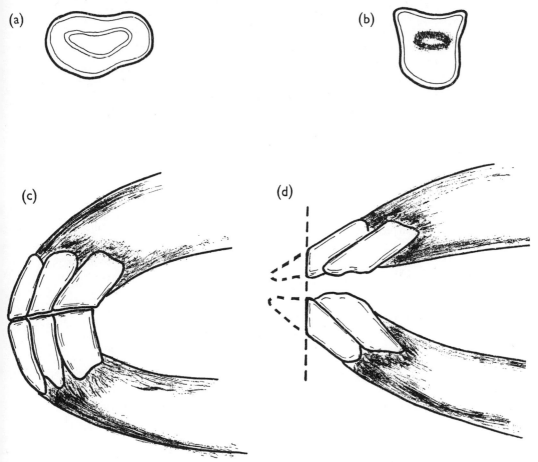

Fig. 41 'Bishoping'; (a) natural mark; enamel surround is present; tooth is wider than long; (b) false mark; no enamel surround; tooth is longer than wide; (c) young teeth, meeting at 180°; (d) old teeth, filed to give 180° front surface.

understood (Fig. 41). In the first case no enamel surrounds the false 'mark' and in the second the enamel will be missing from the front of the filed incisors (Fig. 41). This type of 'faking' used to be very common and is known as 'Bishoping', which suggests a rather disreputable connection with the church. Another trick which has a long history is that of removing the milk incisors in order to 'force' the permanents and give a very young horse a more mature appearance. This is easily detected by reference to the molars and premolars.

(2) *Ox.* The teeth of cattle show great variation in eruption dates depending on breed, management and nutrition. The better the housing and feeding and the more highly bred, the earlier the eruption of teeth. It is noticeable in the early works on domestic animals that the ages given for tooth eruption may be as much as twice that given by modern authors for improved breeds—see Table D. It seems reasonable to take the older figures as more applicable to archaeological material unless there is independent

TABLE D
Tooth eruption ages in the ox.

Tooth		Deciduous teeth	Permanent teeth	Chauveau 19th century	Commercial Crossbred stock 1950. MR*	Ranch cattle MR*
Incisors						
1 central o/1	⎫	Present at birth		14–25 mo.	18 mo.	20–24 mo.	22–24 mo.
2 middle o/1	⎬	Present at birth		17–36 mo.	30 mo.	30 mo.	30–36 mo.
3 lateral o/1	⎭	Present at birth or in first 2 wks		22–40 mo.	42 mo.	36 mo.	42 mo.
Canine o/1 (= incisiform corner)		At birth or in first 2 wks		32–48 mo.	54 mo.	42–48 mo.	54–60 mo.
Premolars						
1		Occasional	Occasional, always lost before 3 yrs			
2	1/1	Birth to 3 wks	24–30 mo.	18 mo.	30 mo.	
3	1/1	Birth to 3 wks	18–30 mo.	30 mo.	30 mo.	
4	1/1	Birth to 3 wks	28–36 mo.	42 mo.	36 mo.	
Molars						
1	1/1		5–6 mo.	6–9 mo.	6 mo.	
2	1/1	Absent	15–18 mo.	30 mo.	15–18 mo.	
3	1/1		24–30 mo.	4–5 yr	24 mo.	

* MR: Miller and Robertson.[18]

evidence that the system under which the animals were kept afforded good protection against weather and periodic starvation. Some features not obvious from the table are given below:

Birth to 3 months	Incisor crowns overlap
6 months	Incisors are side by side
1 year	Spaces between incisors, heavily worn
2 years	Central permanent incisors show some wear
2½–3 years	2 pairs permanent incisors in wear
3–4 years	3 pairs permanent incisors in wear
4–5 years	4 pairs permanent incisors in wear with some overlapping of teeth

5–10 years	Progressive wearing of incisors and reduction of overlap with eventual almost complete loss of crown leaving root stumps with 'tips' of enamel only
12–14 years	Widely separated stumps of incisors
14–16 years	Gradual closing up of stumps of incisors

Separate incisor teeth can be placed as young if the labial surfaces bear longitudinal wavy lines, or aged if these are absent. The incisors are at first convex in outline and are levelled by wear. This wear removes the enamel to expose a line of yellow dentine. Within this a darker streak appears later (the secondary dentition) which changes in shape with age; from being long (transversely) it shortens, then widens into a square and finally becomes round in the root.

It is worth noting that the last milk premolar of the lower jaw is very large in ruminants and has 3 cusps. It may be easily mistaken for a permanent tooth.

TABLE E

Tooth eruption ages in the sheep.

Tooth		Deciduous teeth	Permanent teeth	
			Modern figures (improved breeds)	Semi-wild, hill sheep, old figures (1790)
Incisors				
Central	0/1	Birth to 1 wk	12–18 mo.	18 mo.
Middle	0/1	Birth to 1 wk	18–24 mo.	30 mo.
Lateral	0/1	Birth to 2 wks	27–36 mo.	42 mo.
Canine (corner incisor)	0/1	Birth to 3 wks	33–48 mo.	50 mo.
Premolars				
1		Usually absent	Usually absent	
2	1/1	Birth to 6 wks	21–24 mo.	30 mo.
3	1/1	Birth to 6 wks	21–24 mo.	30 mo.
4	1/1	Birth to 6 wks	21–24 mo.	40 mo.
Molars				
1	1/1		5 mo. (upper) 3 mo. (lower)	6 mo.
2	1/1	Absent	9–12 mo.	18 mo.
3	1/1		18–24 mo.	3–4 yrs

(3) *Sheep*. Sheep vary widely in the age at which they reach maturity, the so-called improved breeds maturing much earlier than hill breeds. Figures published by authors in the late eighteenth and early nineteenth centuries suggest that at that time sheep were regarded as having similar tooth eruption dates to cattle, but modern authorities, referring to modern breeds of sheep, give eruption dates which are considerably younger. The incisors of sheep are long and narrow so do not show the same changes as those of the ox. They are normally held rigidly in the jaw. Sheep teeth come into wear 3–5 months after they are erupted.

(4) *Goat* (Table F: improved breeds early dates, rough goats late dates).

(5) *Pig*. Like sheep, pigs have been selected into a great many breeds whose maturation varies considerably. Only very general reliance can be placed on eruption dates as indication of age. The pig is peculiar in that the first premolar is not deciduous and is

TABLE F
Tooth eruption ages in the goat.

Tooth		Deciduous teeth	Permanent teeth*
Incisors†			
Central	o/1	Birth	15 mo.
Middle	o/1	Birth	21 mo.—27 mo.
Lateral	o/1	Birth	27 mo.—36 mo.
Canine (corner incisor)	o/1	1–3 weeks	36 mo.—40 mo.
Premolars			
1		Usually absent	Usually absent
2	1/1	3 mo.	17–20 mo.—30 mo.
3	1/1	3 mo.	17–20 mo.—30 mo.
4	1/1	3 mo.	17–20 mo.—30 mo.
Molars			
1	1/1		5–6 mo.
2	1/1	Absent	8–10 mo.—12 mo.
3	1/1		18–24 mo.—30 mo.

* Early dates: improved breeds; later dates: rough goats.
† Incisors are frequently broken in old goats due to eating twigs.

TABLE G
Tooth eruption ages in the pig

Tooth		Deciduous teeth
Incisors		
Central	1/1	1–3 wks 4–14 days
Lateral	1/1	10–14 wks 6–12 wks
Corner	1/1	Birth
Canine		Birth
Premolars		
1	1/1	
2	1/1	7–10 wks
3	1/1	1–3 wks 1–5 wks
4	1/1	1–4 wks 2–7 wks
Molars		
1	1/1	
2	1/1	
3	1/1	

* As usual, data from late 18th-cen

variable in appearance, also alone of the domestic animals it possesses a tooth, the canine, which grows throughout life. Very long lower canines (more than 8 inches) indicate an old animal.

The lower incisors become heavily worn from digging and in old pigs the molar and premolar crowns may be worn flat or even concave.

(6) *Dog and Cat.* The domestic carnivores are relatively long-lived yet their teeth provide little evidence of age after the first eight months of life.

At one year all dog incisors are in wear but still have the *fleur-de-lys* shape which is completely lost by two years. Cats frequently lose the incisor teeth in middle age.

(7) *Camel.* Although the ageing of camels by their teeth has been practised in Arabia since before the tenth century, information on the subject is still rather vague.

TABLE H
Tooth eruption ages in the dog.

rmanent teeth	Old Data* Permanent	Tooth		Deciduous teeth	Permanent teeth
		Incisors			
2–17 mo.	2½–3 yrs	Central	I/I	⎫	
		Lateral	I/I	⎬ 4–6 wks	3–5 mo.
7–20 mo.	2½–3 yrs	Corner	I/I	⎭	
–12 mo.	6–12 mo.	Canine	I/I	3–5 wks	5–7 mo.
–12 mo.	12 mo.	Premolars			
		1	I/I	Absent	4–5 mo.
½–6½ mo. nconstant		2	I/I	⎫	
2–16 mo.	2 yrs	3	I/I	⎬ 5–8 wks	5–6 mo.
2–16 mo.	2 yrs	4	I/I	⎭	
2–16 mo.	2 yrs	Molars			
		1	I/I		4–5 mo.
–6 mo.	1 yr	2	I/I		5–6 mo.
7–13 mo.	1½–2 yrs	3	I/I		6–7 mo.
7–22 mo.	3 yrs				
rs give late eruption dates.		Similar ages are given by 18th-century authors.			

TABLE I

Tooth eruption ages in the cat.

Tooth		Deciduous teeth	Permanent teeth
Incisors			
Central	1/1	} 3–4 wks	3½–5½ mo.
Lateral	1/1		
Corner	1/1		
Canine	1/1	3–4 wks	5½–6½ mo.
Premolars			
1		Absent	Absent
2	1/0	} 5–6 wks	4–5 mo.
3	1/1		
4	1/1		
Molars			
1	1/1	Absent	5–6 mo.

Domestic Fowl. Owing to the very short period during which growth takes place it is not practicable to age skeletal remains except into 'young' and 'old'. Long bones in birds do not have epiphysial centres of ossification, the whole epiphysis being cartilaginous in youth. The epiphyses of long bones all ossify early (under six months). The 'keel' of the sternum is largely cartilaginous in young birds, and gradually ossifies. This process is completed between 5 and 8 months according to breed. Spurs develop on the metatarsals of males and their length is some indication of age. Old females may also develop spurs.

CONCLUSIONS

The ageing of animals from skeletal remains of any antiquity cannot be an exact science, and calls for the exercise of considerable judgement. Despite selective breeding the horse and dog seem to have retained a more constant skeletal development with age than have other domestic species. In particular, sheep and pigs are very difficult to age on the evidence of teeth alone owing to their responsiveness to feeding and management changes. It is unfortunate that the translations from Arabic of works of the thirteenth century are not always clear in respect of nomenclature of teeth and that earlier writers such as Aristotle and Varron are far from objective in their methods of ageing. Nevertheless medieval authors from Asia and Europe provide useful information on unimproved

TABLE J
Tooth eruption ages in the camel.

Tooth		Deciduous teeth	Permanent teeth
Incisors			
Central	o or 1/1	4–6 wks	0/1 4 yrs
Middle	1/1	3–4 mo.	0/1 5 yrs
Lateral	1/1	8–9 mo.	1/1 6 yrs
Corner (Canine)	1/1	10–12 mo.	1/1 6½ yrs
Premolars			
1 (canine type)	0/0		1/1
2	1/0		0/0 ⎫ 4–5 yrs
3	1/1	⎬ 4–6 mo.	1/(1) ⎱ Lower P.M.3 if erupted is usually shed by 6–7 yrs
4	1/1		1/1 ⎭
Molars			
1	1/1		1 year
2	1/1		3 yrs
3	1/1		5 yrs

For further details *see* Cornevin and Lesbre,[7] Monod,[19] and Lesbre.[16]

animals in many instances. Where it can be established that one breed of animal only is present in an excavation site, and if a reasonably complete set of bones and teeth for one or two individuals can be assembled, then relationship of tooth wear to epiphysial fusion dates may be determined and applied to the rest of the more fragmentary material from the same site.

There is little difficulty in classifying animals as young, aged or senile, but to decide ages to the nearest six months or year clearly requires very close study and considerable luck in obtaining appropriate bones or teeth.

REFERENCES
1 ARISTOTLE. *Natural History of Animals*, bks 2 and 4; first detailed record of observations but with many errors
2 ABU-BEKR. c. 1400. *Le Naceri*, bk 2, p. 54; transl. PERRON, M., Paris, 1859; difficult translation but earliest good details on horse, camel, sheep and goat; also, first details of tooth forgery in Arabia
3 BROWN, G. T. 1860. *Dentition as indicative of the age of the animals of the farm*, London

4 CHAUVEAU, A. 1888. *Traité d'anatomie comparée des animaux domestiques*, Paris, 4th ed.
5 —— 1891. *Comparative anatomy of the domesticated animals*, transl. FLEMING, G., London; useful for summary of nineteenth-century views on ageing by bones and teeth
6 COLUMELLE. *De Re Rustica*, bk 4; early observations on horse teeth
7 CORNEVIN, C. and LESBRE, X. 1894. *Traité de l'âge des animaux domestiques*; the most comprehensive book available on ageing of sheep, goats, camels, horses, dogs, cats, rabbits and guinea-pigs by examination of teeth; well illustrated
8 CRESCENZI, P. DE. *c.* 1260. *Opus ruralium commodorum*, bk 12; ageing in medieval Europe
9 DAUBENTON. *Instruction pour les Bergers*, Pamphlet *c.* 1800; ageing sheep up to 5 years
10 DUPONT, M. M. 1893. *L'âge du cheval et des principaux animaux domestiques*, Paris
11 FRANCINI, HORACE DE. 1607. *Hippiatrique*, bk 1, ch. 7
12 GIRARD FILS. 1824. Receuil de médecine veterinaire, *Mémoire sur les moyens de reconnaître l'âge du cheval*; good practical account of horse teeth
13 GIRARD, J. 1834. *Traité de l'âge du cheval augmenté de l'âge du bœuf, du mouton, du chien et du cochon*
14 HAYES, M. H. 1915. *Veterinary notes for horse owners*, London, 8th ed.; excellent photographs of horse teeth at various ages
15 HUIDEKOPER, R. S. 1891. *Age of the domestic animals*, Philadelphia
16 LESBRE, F. X. 1893. *Bulletin de la société centrale vétérinaire*, p. 147 ; dentition des camélides
17 MAYHEW, E. 1849. *The horse's mouth, showing the age by the teeth*, London; illustrations
18 MILLER, W. C. and ROBERTSON, E. D. S. 1947. *Practical animal husbandry*, Edinburgh, 5th ed.; good diagrams on horse and cow. Useful for modern horse, cattle, sheep, pig and dog
19 MONOD, O. O. 1892. Receuil de mémoires et observations sur l'hygiène et la médecine vétérinaire militaire, *De l'âge du Chameau*, Paris
20 NEHRING, 1888. *Landwirtschaftliche Jahrbücher*; comparison of teeth in wild and domestic pigs
21 NICKEL, R., SCHUMMER, A. and SEIFERLE, E. 1960. *Lehrbuch der Anatomie der Haustiere*, Berlin; the most recent information on bones and teeth
22 PESSINA. 1830. *Sul modo di conoscere dai denti l'età dei cavalli*; extremely detailed ageing of horse teeth
23 PLINY. *Natural History*, bk VIII; repetition of Aristotle
24 RUINI, CARLO. 1626. *Anatomia de Cavallo, infermità e suoi remedii*, Venice, bk 1, ch. 41; the most detailed information on horse up to that time
25 SAUNIER, GASPARD DE. 1734. *La parfaite connaissance des chevaux*, La Haye
26 SIMONDS, J. B. 1854. The age of ox, sheep and pig, *Roy. Agricultural Soc.*, London; good detail; distinguishes well-bred and common stock
27 SISSON, S. 1953. *Anatomy of the domestic animals*, ed. CROSSMAN, J. S., Philadelphia, 4th ed.; the best information in English on epiphysial fusion dates except for sheep and goat
28 SOLLEYSEL, DE. 1664. *Le parfait maréchal*, Paris; details of horse teeth up to 8 years and of faking practices in Europe
29 TAQUET, J. 1607. *Phillipica ou haras de chevaux*, Paris, Anvers ed.
30 VARRON. *De Re Rustica*, bk 2
31 VEGETIUS, PUBLIUS. *c.* 450. *Artis veterinariae sive mulo medicinae*, bk 4
32 VIBORG. 1823. *Mémoires sur l'éducation, les maladies, l'engrais et l'emploi du porc*, Paris; the first useful information on pig teeth
33 XENOPHON. *On Equitation*, bk 1, ch. III; first reference to ageing by teeth

JULIET CLUTTON-BROCK

IN 1787 John Hunter submitted a paper to the Royal Society on 'Evidence to show that the dog, wolf, and jackal are all of the same species'. He postulated that because the dog will interbreed with both wolf and jackal to produce fertile progeny, the three groups should be considered as a single species. This discussion was one of the first essays written on a subject that has become increasingly popular with anatomists and archaeologists. That is, whether the dog is descended from the wolf, from the jackal or from a wild dog that is now extinct.

There are two main problems that confront the osteologist working in this field, firstly, the detection of very early domestic dogs and the features that distinguish their remains from those of wild canid species, and secondly from what wild ancestors the dog has actually evolved.

Because the skulls and particularly the teeth are the most commonly found remains of canids on archaeological sites, osteologists have concentrated on their distinctive features rather than on those of the appendicular skeleton. The skulls of modern breeds of dog can be distinguished from those of wild wolves and jackals and it is usually possible to identify dog skulls from archaeological sites in Europe and Asia when these sites are Neolithic or later. It is, however, extremely difficult to distinguish dog remains from Mesolithic sites. It is probable that Mesolithic man kept dogs but they were very similar in skull structure to their wild progenitors so that distinguishing their fragmentary remains is a difficult task. Dog remains have been identified from the Natufian levels of Mount Carmel in Palestine by Bate,[8] and from Maglemosian sites in Denmark,[6] and recently from the Mesolithic site of Star Carr in Yorkshire, by Degerbøl.[7] Canid remains were excavated from a microlithic site in north India, but it has not been possible to distinguish these from the wild Indian wolf.[1] A reinvestigation of the so-called dog remains from Mount Carmel shows that they also cannot be certainly distinguished from the local Arabian wolf although the palate is somewhat wider and this is a characteristic feature of the domestic dog. The Star Carr animal has been identified as dog on the crowding and displacement of the teeth which is also a characteristic feature of the dog, but it is not known how frequently this abnormality is found in wild European wolves (p. 271; Plate XIIa). It can be stated, however, that these Mesolithic canid remains bear no resemblance to the skull of the jackal and that they are closely similar to that of the local wolf.

A vast amount of literature has been written on the distinctions between the skulls of dogs, wolves and jackals. Goudry and Boule[9] listed the characters, as known to them in 1892, that were believed to be specific and amongst these they stated that in the wolf the length of the upper carnassial tooth is greater than that of the two molars, measured together, whereas in the dog and jackal the length of the carnassial is less than, or at the most equal to, the length of the two molars. The authors stated that the Indian wolf, *Canis lupus pallipes* Sykes, 1831, was an exception to this rule and that it had short carnassial teeth like the dog. This exception has been lost sight of and the character has been frequently used as a supposedly distinctive feature to identify canid remains from archaeological sites. It is a potentially useful diagnostic feature because the part of the maxillary bone that holds these teeth is a most commonly found fragment. It was thought necessary therefore to reassess the results of Goudry and Boule. The appropriate measurements were made on all the skulls of European and Indian wolves, jackals and dogs that are in the collection of the British Museum (Natural History).[2] These measurements are presented in the form of a graph (Fig. 42) where the central axis represents a carnassial index of unity. Those skulls in which the carnassial length exceeds the combined lengths of the two molars fall to the left of the central axis, whilst those in which the carnassial length is shorter than the length of the two molars fall to its right.

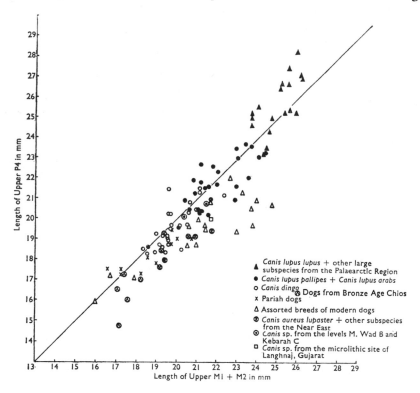

Fig. 42 Graph to show the relationship of the length of the upper carnassial tooth to the combined lengths of the upper first and second molars in dogs, wolves and jackals and in the canid specimens from Natufian levels in Palestine. The diagonal line represents a carnassial index of unity.

It can be seen from the graph that as far as modern dogs are concerned, the results of Goudry and Boule are strikingly confirmed, for only a single specimen had a carnassial index greater than unity. The European wolves, however, although significantly different from dogs, do in a number of individuals show a carnassial index less than unity. The Indian and Arabian wolves as stated by Goudry and Boule overlap the dogs in carnassial index. The Natufian canid remains fall well within the range of the Arabian wolf. So they cannot be identified as dog on the basis of this measurement, nor can it be stated that they were derived from the Egyptian jackal, *Canis aureus lupaster* Hemprich and Ehrenberg, 1833, as Bate[8] contended.

Reduction in size of the carnassial teeth is typical of highly domesticated dogs and it becomes exaggerated in those of very large body size. This is well illustrated in the graph, where the carnassial teeth of the largest specimens of domestic dog, these being Great Danes and Bloodhounds, are, for the size of dog, very short and considerably shorter than the length of the two molars. The upper carnassials of these specimens are very much smaller than those of the large European wolves, although the dogs have the greater body size. The tooth measurements of this group of dogs are shown on the extreme right of the range for dogs on the graph.

The changes that occur in the size and shape of canid skulls as the result of domestication or even of taming alone, are well authenticated. Not only are these changes shown by the remains of primitive domestic dogs from archaeological sites but they are also to be seen in captive wolves.[6,7] The first alteration to the animal as a result of taming or domestication is an overall reduction in size. In the skull this reduction in size is seen as a shortening of the jaw bones without a corresponding reduction in the width so that the characteristic wide muzzle of the dog is produced. This feature is present in the canid remains from the Natufian levels of Mount Carmel that were identified as dog by Bate[8] and were believed to be the earliest remains of dog known. The wide muzzle is in fact the only feature that distinguishes these fragments from the skull of the small Arabian wolf, *Canis lupus arabs* Pocock, 1934.

As a result of this shortening of the muzzle, the teeth become compacted in the jaw and they may be much displaced. It is especially common for the third upper premolar and the fourth lower premolar to overlap the carnassial teeth that lie behind them. It is not known, however, how frequently the teeth of wild European wolves are displaced in this way and the condition may be more common than is generally supposed, so that this feature alone should not be taken as proof of taming or domestication. Plate XIIa shows the palatal views of two skulls of *Canis lupus lupus* L. Both of these were, as far as is known, wild animals and yet one of the skulls (bottom) has teeth that are considerably displaced.

The next stage of alteration in the domestic dog is reduction in the size of the teeth, especially the canines and carnassials. With the development of long-faced breeds of dogs the muzzle may be secondarily lengthened so that the teeth are widely and irregularly spaced and lose the feature of crowding, as in the Greyhound. The jaws can be distinguished, however, from those of the wild wolf or jackal by the relatively small size of the teeth.

In highly domesticated dogs the cusp pattern of the teeth is often reduced in complexity, especially that of the premolars, where the posterior accessory cusps may be much reduced in size if not entirely absent.

Paradontal disease occurs in the teeth of a very high percentage of present-day dogs and if evidence of this bone disease is found in canid fragments from archaeological sites it is more than likely that they belong to a dog or at least to a tamed canid. For paradontal disease is caused by an unnatural soft diet consisting mainly of slops, such as is often fed to dogs by man. The disease can be recognized by a spongy growth of the jaw bone, by evidence of abscesses or by the bone and teeth having 'rotted' away in life.[3] The mandible of a dog with the first stages of paradontal disease was found on the Bronze Age site of Snail Down in Wiltshire (Clutton-Brock and Jewell, in prep.).

Amongst a collection of dog remains from an archaeological site there is commonly found to be a marked variability in the size of the teeth relative to the length of the jaw, although the dog population as a whole may be of approximately the same sized animals. An example of this was found on the Bronze Age site of Chios in Greece.[1] On this site the dogs were rather small animals that were slightly larger than an English Fox Terrier. There were 22 mandibles and 11 maxillae found throughout all levels of the Bronze Age trenches. Some of these had large teeth that were compacted in the jaw and others had small widely spaced teeth. Presumably breeding was at random amongst such a dog population and the size and degree of crowding of the teeth must be a natural variation that is probably augmented by the effects of domestication. Measurements of two extreme variants from Chios are given in Table A.

TABLE A

Measurements of two extreme variants of Bronze Age dogs from Chios in Greece.

	Type I	Type II
	mm	mm
Length of tooth row from the anterior edge of premolar 2 to the posterior edge of molar 3	58·5	62·0
Depth of mandible below premolar 4	c. 18·0	c. 19·7
Length of premolar 2	7·8	6·6
Length of premolar 3	10·0	8·2
Length of premolar 4	10·5	9·8
Length of molar 1	21·0	18·6
Length of molar 2	8·4	7·7
Length of molar 3	3·0	4·0

If the added lengths of the teeth, premolar 2 to molar 3, are expressed as a percentage of the directly measured length of the tooth row from the anterior edge of the second premolar to the posterior edge of the third molar, then this index can be used to show the degree of crowding of the teeth. In the mandible of type I (Plate XIIb, top right) whose tooth measurements are given in the table, where the tooth row is short and the teeth large the index is 102·8%, whereas in the second type (bottom right), where the tooth row is absolutely longer and the teeth smaller, the index is 72·6%.

In the material from Chios the second type of jaw, that is with small widely spaced teeth, is more common than the first type, only two mandibles from a total of nine having large compacted teeth. (The remaining thirteen mandibles were too fragmentary to allow any assessment to be made of their tooth development.) This material may be compared with a collection of dog remains from the Bronze Age barrow site of Snail Down in Wiltshire. In these specimens the teeth are very large and are compacted in four out of five of the mandibles. The dogs from Snail Down were considerably larger animals than those from Chios and they represent a different type of dog, with large heavy jaws and powerful teeth, showing the influence of the great wolf of northern Europe.

The question remains of what was the ancestry of the domestic dog. Trouessart[11] believed that all domestic dogs of Europe and Asia and the dingo were derived from the Indian wolf, *Canis lupus pallipes*, with the exception of the Ancient Egyptian dogs which he believed were derived from the Egyptian jackal, *Canis aureus lupaster*. Since his time there has been a general neglect of the Indian wolf as the supposed ancestor of the dog, despite its very close resemblance to primitive domestic dogs. The Indian wolf is extraordinarily similar in size and skull shape to the dingo and also to the Indian pariah dog with which it freely interbreeds. There can be no doubt, at least, that these two forms of the dog have evolved from the Indian wolf. It seems probable also that the dog remains from prehistoric sites in the Near East, such as Jericho[12] and Chios, were descended from this subspecies of wolf. On the other hand the much larger dogs from the Maglemosian sites in Denmark and from the Mesolithic site of Star Carr in Yorkshire must have evolved from tamed European wolves, because the occupants of these northern sites had no contact with Asia. It has recently been demonstrated by Crisler[4] how easy it is to tame the large wolves of northern Canada and how dog-like their behaviour becomes. The northern wolf is not the fierce untamable beast that legend has reputed him to be.

There is no osteological evidence to suggest that the jackal is the ancestor of any breed of dog but it is possible that interbreeding has at some time occurred. For it is interesting that the dog will interbreed with both the wolf and the jackal to produce fertile offspring whilst there is no case known to the author of a wolf-jackal cross. The interbreeding of dogs with wolves is well authenticated and indeed Pliny wrote of how the Gauls tied their female dogs up in the woods so that they might mate with wolves and strengthen the breed. Similarly interbreeding must have occurred between the dogs derived from European wolves and those from Indian wolves so that their identity is now lost. The dingo is probably the only breed of dog that can be considered as derived purely from the Indian wolf. This hypothesis of the poly-specific origin of the dog was believed in and expounded by Darwin[5] and it is in fact surprising how little knowledge has been gained on the much discussed subject of the ancestry of the dog since he wrote his book, *The Variation of Animals and Plants under Domestication*, first published in 1868.

ACKNOWLEDGEMENTS

I am greatly indebted to Dr F. C. Fraser, Keeper of Zoology at the British Museum

(Natural History), and to Miss J. E. King of the Osteology Department for the facilities they have offered to me during the course of this work.

Miss Ann Grosvenor Ellis took the photographs of the canid skulls. I wish to acknowledge permission granted to me by the trustees of the British Museum (Natural History) to reproduce photographs of the two wolf skulls.

REFERENCES

1 CLUTTON-BROCK, J. 1962a. Ph.D. thesis, University of London
2 ——1962b. Z. Tierzüchtung u. Züchtungsbiologie 76, 326–33
3 COLYER, F. 1936. Variations and Diseases of the Teeth of Animals, London
4 CRISLER, L. 1959. Arctic Wild, London
5 DARWIN, C. 1868. The Variation of Animals and Plants under Domestication, London
6 DEGERBØL, M. 1943. Saertryk of Dyr Natur Og Mus. København 1942–43, 11–36
7 —— 1961. On a find of a preboreal domestic dog (Canis familiaris L.) from Star Carr, Yorkshire, with remarks on other domestic dogs. Proc. Prehist. Soc. 27, 35–55
8 GARROD, D. A. E. and BATE, D. M. A. 1937. The Stone Age of Mount Carmel, Oxford, vol. I, 157–253
9 GOUDRY, A. and BOULE, M. 1892. Matériaux pour l'Histoire des Temps Quaternaires, Paris, vol. IV 123–9
10 HUNTER, J. 1787. Observations tending to show that the wolf, jackal and dog are all of the same species. Phil. Trans. Roy. Soc. Lond., 1787
11 TROUESSART, E.-L. 1911. C.R. Acad. Sci. Paris 152, 909–13
12 ZEUNER, F. E. 1958. Palestine Exploration Quarterly 19, 52–55

28 The Palaeopathology of Pleistocene and more Recent Mammals

DON BROTHWELL

DISEASE is the result of biological variability, trauma, or malfunction, and as such one expects to find traces of it throughout time, both in invertebrate and vertebrate remains. The study of anomalous fossil remains can supply valuable information regarding the exact extent to which animal groups were prone to a particular disorder. As evolution is likely to have taken place in pathogenic organisms no less than other animal varieties, it is also evident that such remains are likely to provide evidence of the antiquity of a particular variety of disease. Owing to the nature of the remains, only abnormalities affecting bone can usually be identified.

Pathological studies on ancient animal remains are as yet few, but with the increasing interest and study in the field of such osteological material, it seems only a matter of time before far more data are assembled. The information to be revealed is threefold:

(1) It helps to establish the range and antiquity of various diseases found in animals other than man.

(2) In some instances it may directly reflect upon the environment of the animal and of man.

(3) In the case of certain infectious diseases, it might eventually be possible to identify the precursor, that is the carrier, of a specific type of disease before man emerged or contracted it.

The present essay is meant to be a very brief review of what has been discovered about one particular group of animals, the mammals, during the period of man's existence, and what may still be revealed by further work.

One of the earliest references to the pathology of fossil animal bones was made by E. J. C. Esper (1742–1810),[3] on the femur of a cave bear (*Ursus spelaeus*). Admittedly, his diagnosis would appear to be quite wrong, for he suggested an osteosarcoma, whereas the deformity seems likely to have been the result of a fracture and callus formation, with some necrosis.[5] Later, in 1820, Cuvier[2] described the skull of a hyena from Gaylenreuth displaying a severe injury to its occipital crest, which had healed before death. Interest in the pathology of animal bones was also developing in England about that time and William Clift,[1] in a paper on cave fauna, notes inflammatory changes in the metacarpal and metatarsal bones of bovines present. A wolf mandible also displayed chronic abscessing and periodontal disease of the alveolar bone.

Other papers noting pathological upsets in Pleistocene animals followed, and in particular the cave bear has been well described (for further references see Moodie;[6] Pales[7]).

VARIETIES OF DISORDER

In Table A, a synopsis of the palaeopathology of Pleistocene and more recent mammals is given. In particular, fractures, periostitis, osteomyelitis, and arthritic disorders are well

TABLE A

A synopsis of the pathological conditions recognized in Pleistocene and more recent mammals.★

Order *Carnivora*
    Family *Canidae*
        Canis familiaris: fracture, 'osteophytic growth', periostitis
        Canis lupus: tumour (? myositis), abscesses, periodontal disease
        Aenocyon dirus (giant wolf): fracture, osteo-arthritis, osteomyelitis
    Family *Hyaenidae*
        Hyena: fracturing, osteo-arthritis
    Family *Ursidae*
        Ursus spelaeus: osteomyelitis, fractures, osteo-arthritis, 'necrosis', 'amputa-tion,' kyphosis, vertebral collapse, caries, chronic abscesses, periodontal disease
    Family *Felidae*
        Panthera pardus: fracture
        Smilodon californicus (sabre-tooth cat): spondylitis, periostitis, exostosis, fractures
Order *Perissodactyla*
    Family *Equidae*
        Equus sp. Pleistocene: hyperostoses (? the result of an osteogenic sarcoma)
Order *Primates*
    Family *Cercopithecidae*
        Papio hamadryas (baboon): Paget's disease (?), rickets, spondylitis (?)
Order *Edentata*
    Superfamily *Megalonychoidea*
        Mylodon robustus (ground sloth): fracture, 'necrosis'
Order *Proboscidae*
    Family *Mammutidae*
        Mammut americanus: fracture, necrosis, caries, abscess
Order *Artiodactyla*
    Infra-order *Palaeodonta*
        Platygonus (peccary): periostitis
    Sub-order *Tylopoda*
        Camel, Texas Pleistocene: pathological phalanx
    Family *Cervidae*
        Rangifer tarandus: ankylosed phalanges, fracture, osteitis
    Family *Bovidae*
        Symbos cavifrons (musk ox): fracturing, chronic suppurating sinusitis
        Bos primigenius: osteo-arthritis, chronic abscess, periodontal disease, dental tumour (?)
        Ovis: osteo-arthritis
        Bos longifrons: osteo-arthritis

★ The list is not meant to be an exhaustive compilation.

represented. As accidental injury and blood-stream infection produced fracturing and inflammatory changes in the Dinosaurs, millions of years before the mammalian radiation, it is not surprising to see such anomalies in fauna of the last million or so years. An added factor is however the appearance of man, and a number of cases of animal injury may have resulted from his quest for food or as a result of defending himself. Pales,[7] for example, describes an inflammatory reaction to be seen on the lower jaw of a cave bear from Ariège which he considers may have resulted from a wound by a human artifact. Another type of deduction is sometimes possible, as demonstrated by Saint-Périer.[8] He describes a fractured, osteomyelitic, and partly healed reindeer metacarpal. He concludes that as the beast lived many months in this incapacitated condition without being killed by man, there was probably a surplus of game in that area at that time.

Arthritic disorders are also clearly in evidence in giant Jurassic/Cretaceous reptiles, and are therefore not surprising in the mammals. Much evidence is at present rather obscured by lack of agreement as regards terminology, and as Zorab[10] has recently pointed out, various earlier authors would appear to have used the term 'ankylosing spondylitis' (an arthritic disorder which may result in ossifications at the vertebrae uniting them into a single block) rather than 'osteo-arthritis', which seems a much more common condition—producing 'lipping' and deformity at some articular surfaces. Union of some lumbar vertebrae by extensive bony bridging in *Smilodon californicus* may be an example of the former, whereas the latter disorder seems to be fairly common in the European cave bear. In man, osteo-arthritic deformity may be broadly correlated with age, and it would be interesting to know whether similar information could be obtained from its occurrence in other mammals.

Disorders of the mouth do not appear to be so common, relatively speaking, although this difference may result as much from a lack of interest—and thus of recording—as of actual infrequency. *Ursus spelaeus* has provided examples of caries cavities, chronic abscessing and alveolar bone destruction through periodontal infection. A recently discovered skull of *Bos primigenius* from Cambridgeshire[9] is of interest in that restricted alveolar destruction and possibly chronic abscessing are associated in this case with lack of dental alignment on the left side, presumably resulting initially in food impaction and gum irritation.

There seems little doubt that the considerable variety of tumours affecting modern men were not all present even a few thousand years ago. Their infrequency in earlier mammals is even more marked. A pelvic fragment of *Canis lupus* (Pleistocene) displays a bony projection of a spongy appearance, which might be the result of a tumour. The molar of a Pleistocene bovid from Charente has an extremely swollen root which Pales thinks could be a tumour, but could on the other hand be hypercementosis. Another very debatable case is to be seen on a posterior cannon bone of a Pleistocene horse from Gironde, France. Pales[7] describes a 'diaphysial hyperostosis' which could perhaps be the result of an osteogenic sarcoma.

Few other anomalies have so far been noted, and some of these are questionable.

DISCUSSION

As I have already said, the palaeopathology of earlier animal forms, as of man, is a multi-purpose study. It is to be hoped that with the increasing detailed examination of excavated animal remains, some attempt at establishing the more common diseases, such as arthritis, will be made. Radiographic examination, at least of the more complete bones, might be revealing, especially as regards 'lines of arrested growth'. As in the study of ancient human pathology, there is also a need for very precise description and careful diagnosis, especially in the case of the rarer anomaly, where a single example may be of extreme importance. So far it has not been possible to link up the origin of some human diseases with the pathology of earlier or contemporary mammals. It seems reasonable to suppose, however, that some human parasites were originally carried by other mammalian forms. The transmission of the plague bacillus from rats to men immediately comes to mind as an example of the adaptability of a parasitic organism to another host, but there is in fact a variety of parasitic groups affecting both man and other animals (either the same species or similar ones). As Hare[4] points out, the *Salmonella* which produce typhoid and paratyphoid fever have cousin-species in oxen and pigs, which closely resemble the human varieties. *Corynebacterium diphtheriae*, causing diphtheria, resembles to some extent *C. ovis* of horses, *C. pyogenes* of cattle, pigs and sheep, and *C. murium* a pathogen of mice. Some human viruses also have relatives producing disease in animals. For example, the main habitat of the yellow-fever virus is certain species of monkeys, and it is transmitted from these to man by *Haemagogus* mosquitoes.

By Neolithic times, contact between some forms of animal and man had become closer than ever before, and it is possible that this period in particular is a critical one from the point of view of the transmission of certain forms of disease to man. The continued study of animal palaeopathology may help to substantiate this.

Finally, it must be remembered that disease may be as much a killer in other vertebrate populations as in man, and in the case of food animals, epidemics have obvious repercussions for the particular human society concerned.

REFERENCES

  1 CLIFT, W. 1823. *Phil. Trans. Roy. Soc. Lond. 113*, 81 (quoted by Moodie)
  2 CUVIER, G. 1812. *Recherches sur les Ossemens fossiles*, Paris (quoted by Moodie)
  3 ESPER, E. J. C. 1774. *Ausführliche Nachrichten Von neuentdeckten Zoolithen unbekannter vierfüssiger Thiere*, Nuremberg
  4 HARE, R. 1954. *Pomp and Pestilence. Infectious Disease, Its Origins and Conquest*, London
  5 MAYER, DR. 1854. *Nova Acta Leopoldina*, 673–89
  6 MOODIE, R. L. 1923. *Paleopathology. An introduction to the study of ancient evidences of disease*, Chicago
  7 PALES, L. 1930. *Paléopathologie et Pathologie comparative*, Paris
  8 SAINT-PÉRIER, R. DE 1936. *Arch. Inst. Paléont. hum. 17*
  9 SHAWCROSS, F. W. and HIGGS, E. S. 1961. *Proc. Camb. Antiq. Soc. 54*, 3–16
 10 ZORAB, P. A. 1961. *Proc. Roy. Soc. Med. 54*, 415–20

29 Bird Remains in Archaeology

ELLIOT W. DAWSON

REMARKABLY little appreciation has been shown of the value of bird remains in archaeo-logical sites in Europe despite the stimulus provided by Clark's [37,38] major reviews of the fowling activities of prehistoric man, and the knowledge of domestic associations of many kinds of birds in historic times.[86]

The reasons for this lack of study are, firstly, that large mammal bones, often the predominant faunal remains from such sites, have provided what seemed to be an adequate picture of the food supply and hunting of the ancient peoples, and the extra information from the relatively few bones of birds was not considered worth their detailed examination. Secondly, it has often been supposed that identification of small bird bones is difficult. This is quite true, the difficulties being comparable with those for many of the smaller mammals, which have been equally neglected. Had a book such as Cornwall's[47] guide been available for even the larger or commoner birds much more could have been attempted by the informed archaeologist who had only Lam-brecht's[109] treatment for reference. The lack of comparative skeletons in museums has meant that the identification of bird remains has become essentially specialist work limited to those few zoologists who have managed, largely through their own enthusi-asm, to build up adequate collections of bones of living birds, so that the third reason for the neglect of bird remains in archaeology is the lack of adequate collections and interested specialists.

In other parts of the world the situation has varied from this extreme, through North America where bird remains have been studied from a considerable number of sites and where correlations and discoveries of some interest have emerged, to the other in New Zealand where a whole phase of Maori culture, the *Moa*-hunter (or 'Archaic') Period, was largely based on the hunting of these giant ratite birds, the Dinornithiformes. The relative abundance and importance of various animals in the supply of food or clothing materials for prehistoric peoples has determined the proportions of bird, fish, shell-fish, and mammal remains found in their occupation sites. In Europe, large mam-mals were a chief source of these materials; in North America both birds and mammals were used for particular purposes, while in New Zealand, with its lack of native land mammals, *Moas*, small birds, seals and whales, fish, and shell-fish were used in varying proportions from the *Moa*-hunter Period to European times, and the tracing of these variations, as the *Moa* became rarer, has been beautifully demonstrated by Lockerbie.[117] Hence, in New Zealand, the study of bird remains has become of very great importance both in view of the current intensive archaeological research, and in relation to the many natural deposits, in caves, swamps, and sand-dunes, of extinct birds, some of which were known to the earliest Maoris.[48,49,51,52,56,59,60]

Lately, increased interest has been shown in bird remains in Europe and the work of Bramwell and some others in Great Britain is providing results of some significance.

It was in Europe that the pioneer work was done on birds in archaeological sites, and this makes it surprising that their significance has been overlooked to a great extent. The work of Japetus Steenstrup in 1848 on the Danish shellmounds of Jutland showed that from the identification of the bones of birds and mammals found in these places one could derive quite an amount of information about the climatic conditions and the vegetation at the time when the middens were being formed in addition to purely cultural information about the hunting range of the former inhabitants. Winge[193] carried on such studies and the tradition has been maintained by Troels-Smith[173] and others in assessing the value of bird remains found at early Neolithic sites in west Zealand.

What can one derive from a study of bird remains? What has already been achieved in this way from various sites throughout the world? How can these bird remains be identified, and what are the problems involved? Some answers to these questions, with examples and references for further reading, follow and may provide suitable encouragement for archaeologists likely to encounter such material.

THE USE OF BIRD REMAINS IN ARCHAEOLOGY

The 'remains' of birds found in archaeological sites include bones, feathers, mummies, eggshell, guano, and, perhaps, the painting and carving of replicas of the contemporary avifauna on caves, trees, stones or artifacts. Each of these kinds of relic has its value in interpreting the everyday life and background of the dwellers in these sites. From identification of the bones a list of species can be compiled and comparisons can be made with the present-day avifauna of the region. From what is known of the present habits of movement or migration of these birds, evidence may be found of seasonal occupation of the sites or of a particular hunting or trading range of the peoples formerly inhabiting them.

Although there have been several later studies (e.g. an analysis of animal remains in preceramic sites of 5,000 to 3,500 years old in Florida by Neill, Gut, and Brodkorb[138]) the classic example is Howard's[93] interpretation of the bird remains from the Emeryville shellmound, a large prehistoric Indian site on the shore of San Francisco Bay, California. The bones found there were predominantly of water birds, indicating a hunting range restricted to the vicinity of the shore. Most of the birds were ducks, mainly winter visitors, and geese, at present entirely winter visitors from October 1st to the end of April. Bones of the Merganser were correlated with the present-day occurrence from January 1st to April 11th. Howard concluded: 'On this evidence, then, we can say with certainty that the shellmound was occupied during the winter months.' From the abundant bones of cormorants (Phalacrocoracidae), of which nearly half were of young nestling birds, it was concluded, based on the knowledge of the habits and nesting times of the present-day species in the area, that the 'optimum time' of taking young cormorants of the age found in the mound is from the middle of June to the end of July; and, therefore, the Emeryville mound must have been inhabited by the Indians during the summer months also. The avifauna of the mound indicated a continued occupation by the Indians throughout the year even though there are no bones of birds limited to the intervening spring and autumn months.

While such correlations are justifiable, some caution must be observed when account-
ing for the presence or absence of bones of certain birds in occupation sites (cf. Gilmore[79]). A comparison has been made between birds from Indian middens in Oregon
and those in Puget Sound, Washington, by Professor Loye Miller.[134] At the latter site
many groups of birds, well represented in Oregon, were rare or completely absent,
notably condors and eagles. Some correlation seemed likely between their absence and
the ritual usage of condors, eagles, and ravens by Indians of various tribes.[133] Owls
and crows were also, according to him, 'shielded by Indian psychology' in North
America (cf. Friedmann[74]), and, in Roman Britain, ravens had peculiar semi-domestic
associations which accounted for their abundant remains near dwelling sites.[86] Trade
with distant tribes may account for the presence of some otherwise inexplicable
bones,[55] and intermingling with earlier deposits may provide a complex situation.[48,49,55]

Broken bones or artifacts made from bird bones are of very great interest also. In
most New Zealand sites bone awls, needles, or bird spear-points occur. Discussing those
from the *Moa*-hunter camp at the Wairau Bar, Duff[60] provided an example: 'The chief
value of these awls to archaeology is that they were selected from the stoutest and
soundest portions of the skeleton . . . and being preserved in large numbers provide a
ready indication of the presence of extinct creatures, whose bones have not otherwise
survived. Thus at Wairau the only indication of the extinct eagle (*Harpagornis*) is, apart
from a practically indestructible claw, three awls worked from the distal tibia and ulna.'

Eggs and eggshell may provide useful information, as in New Zealand, where *Moa*
eggs were found with *Moa*-hunter burials at Wairau presumably used as water-bottles,
replacing the *Lagenaria* gourds of the tropical homeland, and suggesting, because of
their increasing rarity, 'some superiority of rank of the deceased'.[60] Engraved or painted
eggs also occur in some sites (cf. Breuil and Clergau[26]). Ceremonial bird burials, a feature
of some Indian cultures, have been discussed[175, 90] (cf. also Blanc and Blanc [16]), and the
use of captive macaws and other parrots in providing feathers for 'religious para-
phernalia' accounts for isolated skeletons in certain Pueblo sites.[103] A later report on
the Pueblo del Arroyo provides an amusing archaeological sidelight interpreted by
bird bones: 'Another interesting find . . . the incomplete skeleton of a macaw, one of
those gorgeous red-blue-and-yellow parrots (*Ara macaw*) from tropical Mexico and
south. The skeleton is especially interesting to me because the sternal apparatus had
been fractured by a blow and subsequently healed. Presumably the bird had bitten a
careless finger somewhere on the trail to Chaco Canyon, or after arrival there, and had
been felled by a stick in angry hands.' This find 'provided evidence of an apparent clash
of tempers. We may imagine a sudden painful bite from an irritated beak and a sharp,
angry blow in retaliation. Landing full on the bird's breast, the blow resulted in a
permanent injury', which was described in full anatomical detail.[104] Mummies of birds,
as made in ancient Egypt, are also of interest.[127,161]

Some indication of the former presence of various birds, which may confirm the
identification of bones found in the sites or may indicate a wider knowledge of the
natural world by the peoples concerned, can be derived from pictographs,[86,25] petro-
glyphs,[134] dendroglyphs,[100] and artifacts (e.g. Webb and Baby[176]). Again on the New

Zealand scene some of the large birds of rock paintings of South Canterbury are possibly contemporary work of the *Moa*-hunters.[60] Guano, also, has its role in aiding the archaeologist, and an example is Kubler's[107] attempt at a chronology based on guano deposition.

EXAMINATION AND IDENTIFICATION OF BIRD BONES

With a little experience bird bones can be easily separated from those of the smaller mammals, such as the rabbit, and, provided a few bones of birds now common in the area can be studied, most archaeologists, aided by a good memory, should be able to attain a working knowledge of at least the major families of birds encountered. This is about as far as the non-zoologist can go with safety, and for many archaeological purposes this is sufficient. The archaeologist rarely wants detailed identification but rather help in interpreting what material information he has.

For the ornithologist concerned with the more detailed identification of the bones, there are a number of problems and pitfalls, some of which may be mentioned here. There is the problem of the palaeontologist, the fitting of what is essentially a fossil, a 'thing dug up', devoid of feathers and the other external characters used by the present-day ornithologist, into the framework of the zoologist dealing with living animals, a problem comparable with that of the palaeobotanist who must name fossil pollens which are identical with those of Recent plants but may have had different leaves. Many zoologists are sceptical of how far such correlation can be carried, and as a concession to those who insist that an identical *part* (bone, or pollen) may not be correlated with an identical *whole* (bird with feathers, or plant with leaves) one has to make the identification, *Corvus* aff. *corax*, for example, meaning a species closely comparable with *corax*, the present-day Raven, if not identical. This naming problem arises with all fossils, even those characterized by morphological features common to both fossil and living specimens, but, since palaeontology, and indeed any science, can only advance by making or assuming provisional correlations, one may be justified in making specific identifications. This is just how Owen[149] deduced the former existence in New Zealand of 'a struthious bird nearly, if not quite, equal in size to the ostrich, belonging to a heavier and more sluggish species', from an unprepossessing fragmentary limb bone. Lydekker[120] and Miller[128] have also demonstrated that, within reason, such a correlation is the most practical procedure; but it is important that those concerned should be familiar with this problem. However, a number of workers insist on identifying down to subspecies on a basis of the present-day distribution, particularly where geographical subspecies, not necessarily separable osteologically, inhabit different regions or different islands (cf. Wetmore[187]). For example, a New Zealand crow bone found in a North Island deposit would be *Callaeas cinerea wilsoni*, the Blue-wattled Crow (or North Island *Kokako*), despite the absence amongst the bones of the coloured wattles distinguishing it from the Orange-wattled (South Island) Crow, *C. cinerea cinerea*. Provided that this assumption is stated no great harm may be done but to the archaeologist, not 'in the know', a confusing picture of events may result. An undifferentiated *Kokako* population may have been widespread in New Zealand at the time of the deposits since it is evident that many profound changes in the New Zealand avifauna have occurred within Recent times and not all of these are solely attributable to the advent of Polynesian Man.[50] One must not assume that the present range or habitat of a bird is identical with its distribution in former times when the archaeological deposit was forming. In New Zealand a large rail, the *Takahe* (*Notornis*), now restricted to small colonies in the mountainous, snow-grass country of the south-west of the South Island, was formerly widespread[87,192] and the virtually extinct flightless ground parrot or *Kakapo* (*Strigops habroptilus*) occurred within living memory in many parts of the country.[191] The specialized habitat of *Notornis* might imply differences in tolerance of the bird towards its environment in earlier times or the wider distribution of its present habitat and climate.

Similarly, Blanc[15] used the presence of the remains of the Great Auk (*Alca impennis*) in the Grotta Romanelli in southern Italy as an indicator of a cold climate,[28] but Bate[8] has said of the Great Auk remains from Gibraltar: 'The occurrence of the Great Auk in Mediterranean region in Palaeolithic times does not necessarily imply a very different climate to that obtaining at the present day. That this bird was commonly known only from more northerly latitudes within historic times may be responsible for its being usually considered an entirely northern, though not an arctic species.'

A fine example of the danger of assumption of present-day distributions is provided by the pelican remains in the Iron Age peat of East Anglia (cf. K. A. Joysey, elsewhere in present volume). Records of living stray pelicans in Britain during the last few hundred years have been of *Pelecanus onocrotalus*, the White Pelican. It was reasonable to assume, therefore, that the peat bones (Pollen Zone VII–VIII, 500 BC) would be those of the same species. K. A. Joysey's thorough critical examination of the peat birds has established them as *Pelecanus crispus*, the Dalmatian Pelican, also recorded as presumably breeding birds at the Iron Age settlement of Glastonbury[1,2] up to the Roman occupation.[68]

In some areas, notably sand-dunes where the wind may scour out deposits intermingling the remains from different strata, another problem arises, one that the field archaeologist can do much to eliminate. In New Zealand, bones of *Moas* which had died probably in pre-human times became mixed with overlying midden debris, which might or might not have contained *Moa* bones once used for food.[48] This situation resulted in earlier workers identifying the site as a *Moa*-hunter camp or, if indeed there were *Moa* bones in the later midden, in providing a longer species list of *Moas* used for food than warranted and, hence, of projecting the existence of certain genera into human times. Only careful field work in collecting and the distinguishing of such primary and secondary associations can save the zoologist this embarrassment.

Similarly care must be used in analysing and interpreting the size ranges of the essentially selected animals found in midden debris; their robustness, perhaps, is not necessarily indicative of the normal size range in the region.[32] Again, it is not often realized, even by ornithologists, how much variation in size there is in living birds and this must be considered when making comparisons with earlier faunas.[132] Gilmore's[80] guide to the organization and significance of the identification of mammal remains can be read with profit by every archaeologist desirous of the services of the specialist zoologist, and by every such zoologist invited to undertake such identifications. A number of references should also be consulted by those seeking ecological information from midden debris.[198,79,81,116,189,190,43,44,45,201,170,124,125,126] Correlations between climatic conditions and the presence of various bird remains are feasible by ornithologists conversant with the living bird, and reference should be made to A. H. Miller's[130,131] work in California and to Gentilli's[77] treatment of the Australian scene. The preparation of illustrated guides or keys to the bones likely to be encountered may be useful, modelled on those produced for mammals.[20,47]

GEOGRAPHICAL SUMMARY

A selected listing of the main work involving collections, identifications, and inter-pretations of bird bones from archaeological sites includes the following references, although many published reports on late Pleistocene and Recent bird faunas not directly associated with human activities are also relevant.

Europe

Scandinavia: Investigations of the Danish 'kitchen middens' of Jutland provided the first evidence of the archaeological significance of bird bones.[167] Winge published a number of lists of identifications from later excavations,[193–197] and birds have been reported from other sites[75] including rock shelters in Norway[29] and in other Danish sites,[171,146,136] although little interpretation of their significance has been made. An imaginative picture has been provided by Troels-Smith[173] from an early Neolithic site in Denmark, e.g.: 'A large number of birds lived at the lake—swans, mallards, pintails, and shovellers had their nests in the swamp, and in the twilight the teal passed over the peat islet with whirring wings.' Here the bird remains were interpreted in relation to the possible seasonal occupation of the site: 'Bones from barely fledged birds indicate a habitation in June and July, and finds of bittern and other migratory birds point to the summer half year. Characteristic winter visitors among the migratory birds have not been found.' And it was concluded—'Hence we can be sure that the dwelling place was inhabited in the months, June, July, August, and September, while there is nothing to indicate that it was inhabited during the rest of the year.'

Brønsted,[30] recounting the excavation of the Gokstad Viking ship (AD 870), related the 'exotic and unexpected discovery' of bones and feathers of a peacock lying beside the steering oar. In Sweden, within recent years, interesting work has been carried out in medieval and prehistoric sites by Lepiksaar,[113,115] notably at the Iron Age Vallhagar in Gotland (AD 200–550) and in Lund (AD 1020–1040).[13] Investigations have also been made on the sea birds of early middens including an unknown species of petrel.[112,114] In another Swedish publication, Rausing[153] has discussed the application of natural sciences to archaeology, and the work of Sirelius[165] should be noted for Finland.

Germany: A number of Neolithic sites, especially Magdalenian and Azilian caves in southern Germany,[160] have produced notable bird faunas (see also Soergel[166]). Particu-lar interest is attached to the Late-Glacial site of the 'Reindeer Hunters of Meiendorf' near Hamburg[157] where the birds found were largely species found in tundra environment, confirming the findings from the age of the reindeer calves that it was only a summer camp (cf. also Rust[158]).

Switzerland: The lake dwellings have provided bird bones and some discussion has been made.[156,105,139,154] Neolithic sites near Berne have been investigated more recently.[101]

France: Excavation reports, mentioning identifications or offering interpretations of the bird fauna in France, are relatively numerous, and the classic work is Milne Edwards's contribution[135] in Lartert and Christie's *Reliquiae*, dealing with the fauna of caves and sites in the south-west of France. Other Magdalenian and Azilian sites in the Dordogne and in the Pyrenees have been discussed by Astre,[5, 6] and there are notes of interest on other caves and shelters.[121, 110, 10]

The Monaco grottoes have been investigated by Boule[18] and the figures of the bones may be helpful as a guide.[19]

Great Britain: During the earlier part of this century, E. T. Newton, already noted for his researches into the extinct bird fauna of the Mascarene Islands, published numerous lists of birds identified from Pleistocene and later occupation caves; however little ecological interpretation was attempted.[141–145] Alfred Newton, also, was interested in bird remains, especially those of the Great Auk, from middens,[140] and Auk bones are still an interesting feature of some sites elsewhere.[85,119,172,37,28] Gurney[86] presented an historical review of prehistoric birds in general terms with some interesting information on the ancient domestication of geese, fowls and pigeons, particularly in Romano-British times; cf. also the prehistoric origin of the fowl[169] and the domestic goose.[155] Gurney's records of the keeping of birds in medieval England, taken from various 'Household Books', are of particular interest in urban archaeology following reconstruction in Britain. Lowe[118] has discussed the introduction of the pheasant and fowl based on distinguishing osteological features. Fowl bones have also been reported on from beneath a Romano-British floor (AD 130) at Cirencester [41] and a reviewer noted: 'Well-attested remains of *Gallus* from early Roman sites in this country are not yet sufficiently common to pass unnoticed.' (*Ibis 92*, 335). Bird remains were common at Glastonbury and have been reported on by Andrews;[1, 2] they include evidence of the breeding of pelicans in England shortly before Roman times (cf. also Forbes *et al.*[68]).

Many of the British (and Middle East) bird remains were identified by Miss D. M. A. Bate, formerly of the British Museum (Natural History), e.g. Hawkes and Hull.[9] The death of Miss Bate in 1951 prevented many important findings being published, and much material still awaits identification. Arkell's[4] tribute to her still challenges future workers to follow her lead. For this reason the current work of Bramwell in caves in Somerset and Derbyshire is very welcome.[21–23] Bell[11,12] had earlier given a detailed summary of sites containing bird remains, with lists of the species found, but no ecological correlations were discussed. Bramwell's[24] excellent treatment of Late-Glacial and Postglacial distribution of British birds, with a useful map showing locations of sites, must be commended. Lydekker's[120] earlier account of the difficulties of identifying bird remains in Britain should also be considered.

At other occupation sites, bird bones may appear of less importance, as at Star Carr;[39],[40] here, 'Fowling played' what Clark called 'a definite, though very subordinate part in the quest for food. . . . The good representation of water birds . . . is only what might be expected from the location of the site, but the rarity of land birds . . . can only mean that no serious attempt was made to secure the avifauna of the forested hinterland.'[39]

Ireland: Many caves throughout the Irish Republic and Northern Ireland have produced bird remains in sufficient quantity to make them of considerable interest.[168] Coleman[42] has produced an important paper which lists caves, the birds found, and gives many references to the original sources.

Gibraltar: A rich bird fauna was found in the Devil's Tower rock-shelter and 33 species, including the Great Auk, were identified by Miss Bate,[8] indicative of a mild climate with cool summers. This conclusion was verified by the finding of both the Alpine Chough (*Pyrrhocorax pyrrhocorax*) and the Red-billed Chough (*P. graculus*), the former being now restricted to high mountains. Both species have been found also in the Monaco caves.[19]

Italy: A. C. and G. A. Blanc[14],[15],[16] have published various lists of bird remains from late and post-Monastirian deposits in southern Italy, many species of which are now restricted to more northerly regions (but cf. Bate[8]). They have recently given an intriguing account of the identification of bones of a black or a griffon vulture sacrificed in the sixth or seventh century BC in the area of the Comitium in the Roman Forum. An interesting correlation was suggested between this find of a bird 'sacred to Mars and preferred to any other bird for taking omens' and the story of the founding of Rome when Romulus saw his flight of twelve vultures.

General: Clark has presented several accounts of early man's activities in Europe associated with the bird fauna. Correlations were made of the birds and climatic conditions and, from the literature, he has summarized lists of the fauna of Mesolithic sites throughout Europe covering the range 8300 to 500 BC. References to the original sources can be found in his bibliography.[35],[36] Later, he correlated the movements of the Magdalenians of the Dordogne with the movements of the reindeer to their summer grazing grounds and he provided a brief summary of the European scene.[38]

Clark's [37] review of fowling activities, read in conjunction with accounts of more modern fowling,[123] is especially valuable, and, with Moreau's[137] account of 'vicissitudes of the European avifauna since the Pliocene', is the basic reference for Europe.

North Africa, the Middle East and India

Bird remains feature in some of the North African cultures investigated by McBurney, but little has yet been published except from the earlier sites on which McBurney and Hey[122] have remarked: '. . . in contrast with later North African cultures no use seems to have been made of marine shell-fish, snails, or birds.' From the Sahara, Breuil and Clergeau[26] have reported on a Palaeolithic decorated ostrich egg.

Hilzheimer[92] calculated that 2·5% of his animal bones in his Mesopotamian site were birds but he could not identify them for lack of comparative material. Reports on other

Middle East sites have been given by Vaufrey[174] and by Josien.[102] Bird bones were collected in quantity from the Mount Carmel excavations[76] but, owing to Miss Bate's death, the identifications have not been completed and much material still awaits examination. Coon[46] gave a more detailed account of the fauna of Belt Cave, Iran, and, although the species of birds had not been identified, he was able to analyse the material quantitatively and correlate the percentages of birds found with the hunting and gathering activities of the inhabitants of the various caves, providing an illustration of what the archaeologist can do even if no zoologist can be induced to identify his material.

In India and Pakistan, a few reports have been made, notably Rang Mahal,[115] Mohenjo-Daro,[163] and in West Pakistan.[61] Basham[7] has given some account of the capture and domestication of birds in pre-Muslim India.

North America

Several lists of identifications of bird remains from archaeological sites in this region have appeared and those of Howard,[93] Brodkorb (in Neill et al.[138]) and Miller[133] may be cited as containing ecological or archaeological interpretations of interest. A further selection of reports on bird remains from Indian occupation sites follows:

Alaska: Friedmann[69-74] on Eskimo sites ranging from 50 to 1,500 years old.

British Columbia.[64]

Washington State.[134,33]

California.[93,98,57,58] Attention is also drawn to Howard's[96] survey of trends in avian evolution in Pleistocene to Recent times and her treatment of direct ancestral forms of birds in a continuously forming site in relation to 'temporal' subspecies,[97] and, hence, to subspecific identification of bird bones.

Nevada: Heizer and Kreiger[91] recorded 19 species of birds from the Humboldt Cave.

Oregon.[182,133]

Utah and Arizona.[129,89,27,134]

Ohio.[82-84,184]

Illinois.[150-152]

Florida: Close co-operation between zoologists and archaeologists has produced some reports of note, especially relating to earlier cold phases in the climate of Florida.[28,138,177,178,88,34,162,164]

New Mexico:[94,95,183,184] The use and distribution of turkeys, particularly among the Pueblo people, has also been of interest here, in other parts of America,[27,111,108,104,161] and in Europe.[17]

Central and Southern America and the West Indies

The Yucatan caves have been reported on by H. I. Fisher,[65] and pre-Columbian mounds in the Argentine by Kraglievich and Rusconi[106]. Middens and caves in the West Indies have been extensively investigated by Wetmore;[179-181,185,186,188] see also Chabanaud[34] and R. R. Howard.[99]

Australia

Although subfossil birds have been recorded in considerable number, little mention has been made of birds in midden debris. Gill[78] has recorded birds from one aboriginal midden, and Gentilli's[77] geographical summary provides the necessary background information for future studies.

New Zealand

With the earlier phase of Maori culture based on the hunting of *Moas*, these birds, together with their contemporary small birds, form an important feature of midden debris in early archaeological sites and persist into later sites in the form of worked bone artifacts often made from subfossil remains. Extensive accounts of the *Moa* have been given by Archey[3] and by Oliver,[147] while Duff[60] has dealt, in great detail, with the cultural aspect of *Moa* remains. Oliver[148] and Falla[63] have provided the background information on the New Zealand avifauna as a whole. Falla[62] has reported also on the small birds of the *Moa*-hunter middens at Wairau. Since Duff's work, the use of radiocarbon dating has enabled Lockerbie[117] to demonstrate a gradual change in the diet of the early inhabitants of southern New Zealand from *Moa*-hunter (or 'Archaic') to 'Classic' Maori culture up to European times, based on his own skilful excavations. At Pounawea, Lockerbie found a *Moa*-hunter layer (AD 1145) with plentiful *Moa*, whale and seal bones with a few shellfish. Above this was an occupation layer (AD 1455) where the *Moa* was less abundant and fish had become common. In the uppermost part of the site (AD 1665), *Moa* bones were very scarce and shellfish must have provided most of the menu. Later sites closer to European times (False Island, 1636, 1762; Murdering Beach, 1817) contain nothing typical of the *Moa*-hunter Period.

Many New Zealand sites are in shifting sand-dunes where secondary or false associations may be formed by the mingling of midden debris with earlier deposits,[48] giving a longer list of birds from a site than should be the case (cf. Dawson[49]). Despite Lockerbie's[117] demonstration that many species of *Moa* can occur in the one site, great care in collecting and identifying *Moa* remains still has to be observed in all localities. Stratification in most New Zealand sites is undeniable and excavations in the earlier natural deposits can reveal much of the history of the site (Dawson and Yaldwyn[56] and unpubl.). Study of the many species of small birds which disappeared in a geologically short space of time on the arrival of Polynesian Man, as well as others already on the way to extinction due to climatic effects, is a necessary adjunct to the examination of archaeological bird remains and many points of interest are becoming evident.[50-54,66,67] *Moa* remains from known occupation sites are being examined more critically and lists of purely archaeological *Moa* bones are appearing.[159,199,200]

The zoologist is as busy with his own researches as the archaeologist is with his and to many zoologists making such identifications would be the 'drudgery' that Gilmore[80] mentioned. The archaeologist would do well to enlist the sympathy and enthusiasm of his consulting zoologist in explaining the particular interest attached to the remains submitted for identification and he should avoid unnecessary duplication of material.

Cultural inferences must be left to the archaeologist but the zoologist should provide all the biological evidence that can be deduced from the material and he should ensure that publication of results of biological significance is made in purely biological journals as opposed to the zoologist's report added as an appendix in an archaeological journal far removed from the eye of fellow zoologists.

REFERENCES

1 ANDREWS, C. W. 1899. *Ibis* (7) 5 (19), 351–8.
2 —— 1917. In BULLEID, A. and GRAY, H. ST G., *The Glastonbury Lake Village*, II, 631.
3 ARCHEY, G. 1941. *Auckland Inst. and Mus. Bull.* no. 1.
4 ARKELL, A. J. 1951. *Arch. News Letter 3* (11), 169–70.
5 ASTRE, G. 1949. *Bull. Soc. Hist. nat. Toulouse 84*, 233–6.
6 —— 1951. *Ibid. 85*, 151–71.
7 BASHAM, A. L. 1954. *The Wonder that was India*, London.
8 BATE, D. M. A. 1928. *J. Roy. Anth. Inst. 58*, 92–113.
9 —— 1947. In HAWKES, C. F. C. and HULL, M. R. *Rep. Res. Comm. Soc. Antiq. London 14*, 354–5.
10 BAYOL, J. and PAULUS, M. 1947. *Bull. Soc. Etud. Sci. nat. Nimes 48*, 79–99.
11 BELL, A. 1915. *Zoologist* (4) 19 (893), 401–12
12 —— 1922. *Ibid.* 251–3
13 BERGQUIST, H. and LEPIKSAAR, J. 1957. Medieval animal bones found in Lund, in *Archaeology of Lund. Studies in the Lund Excavation Material*, I, 11–84
14 BLANC, G. A. 1921. *Arch. Antrop. Etnol.* (Firenze) *50*, 1–39, 7 pls.
15 —— 1928. *Ibid. 58*, 3–24
16 —— and BLANC, A. C. 1958. *Nature 181* (4627), 66
17 BÖKÖNYI, S. and JÁNOSSY, D. 1959. *Aquila 65*, 265–9
18 BOULE, M. *et al.* 1919. *Les Grottes de Grimaldi (Baouse–Rousse)*, Monaco
19 —— and VILLENEUVE, L. DE. 1927. *Arch. Inst. Paléont. hum. 1*
20 BRAINERD, G. W. 1939. *Ohio Sta. Archaeol. & Hist. Qtly. 48*, 324–8
21 BRAMWELL, D. 1957. *Proc. Univ. Bristol Speleol. Soc. 8* (1), 39
22 —— 1960a. Some research into bird distribution in Britain during the late glacial and postglacial periods, *Bird Report, 1959–60, of the Merseyside Naturalists' Assoc.*, pp. 51–8
23 —— 1960b. *Proc. Somerset Archaeol. and Nat. Hist. Soc. 104*, 87–90.
24 —— 1960c. The Excavation of Dowel Cave, Earl Sterndale, *Peakland Archaeol. Soc.* (Newsletters 14–17, 1957–60, reprinted, and *J. Derbyshire Archaeol. and nat. Hist. Soc.* 1959, 79)
25 BREUIL, H. 1938. *C.R. 13th Congr. préhist. France*, 478–88, 559–64, 673–84
26 —— and CLERGEAU, A. 1931. *Anthropologie 41*, 53–64
27 BREW, J. O. 1946. Archeology of Alkali Ridge, Southeast Utah, *Papers of the Peabody Museum, Harvard 21*, 121
28 BRODKORB, P. 1960. *Auk 77* (3), 342–3
29 BRØGGER, A. W. 1908. *Vistefundet. En aldre stenalders Kjøkkenmødding fra Jaederen*, Stavanger, 332–47
30 BRØNSTED, J. 1940. *Danmarks Oldtid*, Copenhagen
31 BULLEN, R. P. and SLEIGHT, F. W. 1959. Archaeological investigations of the Castle Windy midden, Florida, *William L. Bryant Found. Amer. Studies, Report* no. 1
32 BYERS, D. S. 1951. *Am. Antiq. 16* (3), 262–3
33 CARLSON, R. L. 1960. *Ibid. 25* (4), 562–86
34 CHABANAUD, P. 1946. *Mém. Mus. Hist. nat. Paris 22*, 121
35 CLARK, J. G. D. 1936. *The Mesolithic Settlement of Northern Europe*, Cambridge
36 —— 1944. Man and nature in Prehistory with special reference to Neolithic settlement in Northern Europe, *Occ. Pap. Univ. London Inst. Archaeol.*, no. 6
37 —— 1948. *Antiquity 22*, 113–30
38 —— 1952. *Prehistoric Europe*, London
39 —— 1954. *Excavations at Star Carr*, Cambridge

40 CLARK, J. G. D. 1956. Star Carr, a Mesolithic site in Yorkshire, in BRUCE-MITFORD, R. L. S. (ed.), *Recent Archaeological Excavations in Britain*, London, 1–20

41 CLIFFORD, E. H. 1948. *Trans. Brist. & Glos. Archaeol. Soc. 67*, 381–95

42 COLEMAN, J. C. 1947. *J. Roy. Soc. Antiq. Ireland 77* (1), 63–80

43 COOK, S. F. and HEIZER, R. F. 1947. *Am. J. Phys. Anth. N.S. 5*, 201–20

44 ——— and TREGANZA, A. E. 1947. *Am. Antiq. 23* (2), 135–41

45 ——— ——— 1950. *Univ. Calif. Publ. Amer. Archaeol. Ethnol. 40* (5), 223–62

46 COON, C. S. 1951. *Mus. Monogr. Univ. Mus. Pennsylvania 1*, 156–7

47 CORNWALL, I. W. 1956. *Bones for the Archaeologist*, London and New York

48 DAWSON, E. W. 1949a. *N.Z. Bird Notes 3* (5), 132–3

49 ——— 1949b. *J. Polynes. Soc. 58* (2), 58–63

50 ——— 1952. *Emu 52* (4), 259–72

51 ——— 1958. *Ibis 100* (2), 232–7

52 ——— 1959a. *Proc. XVth Int. Congr. Zool. 1958*, 450–2

53 ——— 1959b. *Notornis 8* (4), 106, 111–5

54 ——— 1961. *Ibid. 9* (5), 171–2

55 ——— 1962. A possible association of Maori and Kakapo (*Strigops habroptilus*; Aves, Psittacidae) in the Wellington district, N.Z. *Rec. Dominion Mus. 3* (6)

56 ———and YALDWYN, J. C. 1952. *J. Polynes. Soc. 61* (3–4), 283–91

57 DeMAY, I. S. 1941. *Condor 43* (6), 295–6

58 ——— 1942. *Ibid. 44* (5), 228–30

59 DUFF, ROGER. 1949. *Pyramid Valley. The Story of New Zealand's Greatest Moa Swamp*, Christchurch

60 ——— 1956. *The Moa-hunter Period of Maori Culture*. Canterbury Mus. Bull. 1, Wellington

61 FAIRSERVIS, W. A. 1956. *Anth. Pap. Amer. Mus. nat. Hist. 45* (2), 169–402

62 FALLA, R. A. 1942. Bird remains from Moa-hunter camps, *Rec. Canterbury (N.Z.) Mus. 5* (7), 43–9

63 ——— 1955. New Zealand bird life past and present, *Cawthron Lecture Series* no. 29 (Cawthr. Inst. Sci. Res., N.Z.)

64 FISHER, E. M. 1943. *Bull. Bur. Am. Ethnol. 133*, 133–42

65 FISHER, H. I. 1953. In HATT, R. T., FISHER, H. I., and LANGEBARTEL, D. A., Faunal and archaeological researches in Yucatan caves, *Cranbrook Inst. Sci. Bull. 33*

66 FLEMING, C. A. 1952. *Rep. 7th Sci. Congr. Roy. Soc. N.Z., 1951*, 114–23

67 ——— 1957. *J. Polynes. Soc. 66* (3), 271–90

68 FORBES, C. L., JOYSEY, K. A. and WEST, R. G. 1958. *Geol. Mag. 95* (2), 153–60

69 FRIEDMANN, H. 1933. *Condor 35* (1), 30–1

70 ——— 1934a. *J. Wash. Acad. Sci. 24* (5), 83–96

71 ——— 1934b. *Ibid. 24* (5), 230–7

72 ——— 1935. *Ibid. 25* (1), 44–51

73 ——— 1937. *Ibid. 27* (10), 431–8

74 ——— 1941. *Ibid. 31* (9), 404–9

75 FRÖDIN, O. 1906. En svensk kjökkenmödding. *Ymer 1906*, 17–35

76 GARROD, D. A. E. and BATE, D. M. A. 1937. *The Stone Age of Mount Carmel*, Oxford, vol. I

77 GENTILLI, J. 1949. *Emu 49* (2), 85–129

78 GILL, E. D. 1954. *Mankind 4* (6), 249–54

79 GILMORE, R. M. 1946. *Am. Antiq. 12* (1), 49–50

80 ——— 1949. *J. Mammal. 30* (2), 163–9

81 GOGGIN, J. M. 1948. *J. Wash. Acad. Sci. 38* (7), 225–33

82 GOSLIN, R. M. 1945. *Wils. Bull. 57* (2), 131

83 ——— 1955. *Ohio J. Sci. 55* (6), 358–62

84 ——— 1957. Food of the Adena people, WEBB and BABY, *The Adena People* (q.v.)

85 GRIEVE, S. 1885. *The Great Auk, or Garefowl (Alca impennis, Linn.)—its History, Archaeology, and Remains*, London

86 GURNEY, J. H. 1921. *Early Annals of Ornithology*, London

87 GURR, L. 1952. *Trans. Roy. Soc. N.Z. 80* (1), 19–21

88 HAMON, J. H. 1959. *Auk 76* (4), 533–4

89 HARGRAVE, L. L. 1939. *Condor 41* (5), 206–10

90 HEIZER, R. F. and HEWES, G. W. 1940. *Am. Antiq. 42* (4), 587–603

91 HEIZER, R. F. and KREIGER, A. D. 1956. *Univ. Calif. Publ. Amer. Arch. & Eth.* 47 (1), 1–190
92 HILZHEIMER, M. 1941. *Stud. Ancient Orient Civiliz.* no. 20
93 HOWARD, H. 1929. *Univ. Calif. Publ. Zool.* 32 (2), 301–94
94 —— 1931a. *Condor 33* (5), 206–9
95 —— 1931b. *Ibid.* 216
96 —— 1947a. *Auk 64* (2), 287–91
97 —— 1947b. *Condor 49* (1), 10–13
98 —— and MILLER, A. H. 1939. *Publ. Carnegie Inst. Wash.* 514, 39–48
99 HOWARD, R. R. 1956. *Am. Antiq.* 22 (1), 47–59
100 JEFFERSON, C. 1955. *J. Polynes. Soc. 64* (4), 367–441
101 JOSIEN, T. 1952. *Arch. Suisses d'Anth. gén. 21* (1), 28–62
102 —— 1955. *Israel Explor. J. 5* (4), 246–55
103 JUDD, N. M. 1954. *Smithson Misc. Coll.* 124
104 —— 1959. *Ibid. 138* (1), 1–222
105 KELLER, F. 1866. *The Lake Dwellings of Switzerland and Other Parts of Europe*, London
106 KRAGLIEVICH, L. and RUSCONI, C. 1931. *Physis 10*, 229–41
107 KUBLER, G. 1948. Towards absolute Time: Guano Archaeology, in A Reappraisal of Peruvian Archaeology, *Soc. Amer. Archaeol. Mem.* 4, 29–50
108 LANGE, C. H. 1950. *El Palacio 57* (7), 204–9
109 LAMBRECHT, K. 1933. *Handbuch der Palaeornithologie*, Berlin
110 LANTIER, R. 1945. *Proc. Prehist. Soc. 11*, 49
111 LEOPOLD, A. S. 1948. The wild turkeys of Mexico, *Trans. 13th N. Amer. Wildlife Conf. 1948*, 393–400
112 LEPIKSAAR, J. 1950. *Göteb. Mus. Årstr. 1949–50*, 143–6
113 —— 1955. The bird remains from Vallhagar, in STENBERGER, M. (ed.), *Vallhagar, a Migration Period Settlement on Gotland Sweden*, Copenhagen, vol. II, 814–31
114 —— 1958a. *Zoologisk Revy 4*, 77–85
115 —— 1958b. Bone fragments from Rang Mahal, in HANNA RYDH (ed.), 'Rang Mahal. The Swedish Archaeological Expedition to India 1952–1954', *Acta Arch. Lund 3*, 196–200
116 LEROI-GOURHAN, A. 1952. Étude des vestiges zoologiques, in LAMING, A. (ed.), *La Découverte du Passé*, Paris
117 LOCKERBIE, L. 1959. From *Moa*-hunter to Classic Maori in Southern New Zealand, in FREEMAN, J. D. and GEDDES, W. R. (eds.), *Anthropology in the South Seas. Essays presented to H. D. Skinner*, New Plymouth
118 LOWE, P. R. 1933. *Ibis* (13) 3 (2), 332–43
119 LUCAS, F. A. 1890. *Rep. U.S. Nat. Mus. 1887–88*, 493–529
120 LYDEKKER, R. 1891. *Ibis* (6) 3 (11), 381–410
121 MAYET, L. and PISSOT, J. 1915. *Lyon Ann. Univ. 39*, 74–7
122 McBURNEY, C. B. M. and HEY, R. W. 1955. *Prehistory and Pleistocene Geology in Cyrenaican Libya*, Cambridge
123 MACPHERSON, H. A. 1897. *A History of Fowling*, Edinburgh
124 MEIGHAN, C. W. 1958a. *Am. Antiq. 24* (1), 1–23
125 —— 1958b. *Ibid.* 131–50
126 —— 1958c. *Ibid.* 383–405
127 MEINERTZHAGEN, R. 1930. In NICOLL, *Birds of Egypt*, London
128 MILLER, A. H. 1929. *Univ. Calif. Publ. Bull. Dept. Geol. Sci. 19* (1), 1–22
129 —— 1932. *Condor 34* (3), 138–9
130 —— 1937. *Ibid. 39*, 248–52
131 —— 1939. *Proc. Sixth Pacific Sci. Congr.*, pp. 807–10
132 MILLER, L. 1944. Ornithology of the looking glass, in *Science in the University*, Berkeley, Calif., 267–78
133 —— 1957. *Condor 59* (1), 59–63
134 —— 1960. *Wils. Bull. 72* (4), 392–7
135 MILNE EDWARDS, A. 1876. Observations on the birds whose bones have been found in the caves of the South-West of France, in LARTER, E. and CRISTY, H., *Reliquiae Aquitanicae*, London, 226–47

136 Møhl, U. 1957. Contribution on animal bones, in Klindt-Jensen, O., *Bornholm i Folkevandringstiden*. Nationalmus. Skr., Større Beretninger II, 1–323

137 Moreau, R. E. 1954. *Ibis 96* (3), 411–31

138 Neill, W. T., Gut, H. J. and Brodkorb, P. 1956. *Am. Antiq. 21* (4), 383–95

139 Neuwiler, E. 1924. *Mitt. Antiq. Ges. Zürich 29* (4), 109–20

140 Newton, A. 1870. *Ibis* (2) 6 (22), 256–61

141 Newton, E. 1922. *Proc. Univ. Bristol Speleol. Soc. 1* (2), 64, 73

142 —— 1923a. *Naturalist* Aug. 1923, 264–5

143 —— 1923b. *Proc. Univ. Bristol Speleol. Soc. 1* (3), 119–21

144 —— 1924. *Ibid.* 2 (2), 121

145 —— 1925. *Ibid.* 2 (2), 159–61

146 Nordmann, V. 1936. *Danm. Geol. Unders.* (3) 27, 128

147 Oliver, W. R. B. 1949. *Dominion Mus. Bull.* no. 15

148 —— 1956. *New Zealand Birds*, Wellington

149 Owen, R. 1840. *Proc. Zool. Soc. London* 7, 169–71

150 Parmalee, P. W. 1956. Faunal analysis, in Fowler, M. L. and Winters, H., Modoc Rock Shelter, preliminary report, *Illinois Sta. Mus. Rep. Investig.*, 4 (and see *Am. Antiq. 24*, 257–70)

151 —— 1957. *Trans. Ill. Sta. Acad. Sci. 50*, 235–42

152 —— 1958. *Auk 75*, 169–76

153 Rausing, G. 1958. *Lund Hist. Mus., Från Forn. och Medell.* no. 3

154 Reinerth, H. 1926. *Die jüngere Steinzeit der Schweiz*, Augsburg

155 Riddell, W. H. 1943. *Antiquity 17*, 148–55

156 Rütimeyer, L. 1862. *Neue denks. allg. Schweiz Ges. Naturwiss. 19*, 113–15

157 Rust, A. 1937. *Das altsteinzeitliche Rentierjägerlager Meiendorf*, Neumünster

158 —— 1943. *Die alt und mittelsteinzeitlichen Funde von Stellmoor*, Neumünster

159 Scarlett, R. J. 1952. *Rep. 7th Sci. Congr. Roy. Soc. N.Z.* 1951, 198–9

160 Schmidt, R. R. 1912. *Die diluviale Vorzeit deutschlands*, Stuttgart

161 Schorger, A. W. 1961. *Auk 78* (2), 138–44

162 Sellards, E. H. 1916. *Eighth Ann. Rep. Florida Sta. Geol. Surv.*, 121–60

163 Sewell, R. B. S. and Guha, B. S. 1931. Zoological remains, in Marshall, J. (ed.), *Mohenjo-Daro and the Indus Civilization*, London, vol. II, 649–73

164 Shufeldt, R. W. 1917. *Ninth Ann. Rep. Florida Sta. Geol. Surv.*, 35–42

165 Sirelius, U. T. 1934. *Die Volkskultur Finnlands. I. Jagd und Fischerei*, Berlin and Leipzig

166 Soergel, E. 1955. *Jh. ver. vaterl. Natur. Würtemb. 110*, 121–4

167 Steenstrup, J. 1857. Et bidrag til Gerrfuglens, *Alca impennis* Lin., naturhistorie, og saerligt til kundskaben om dens tidligere Udbredningskreds, *Vid. Medd. nat. For. Kjøbenhavn. 1855* (3–7), 33–116

168 Stellfox, A. W. 1938. *Irish Nat. Journal 7* (2), 37–43

169 Stubbs, F. J. and Rowe, A. J. 1912. *Zoologist* (4) 16 (347), 1–14

170 Taylor, W. W. (ed.). 1957. The identification of non-artifactual archaeological materials, *Nat. Acad. Sci. Publ. 565*, Nat. Res. Council, Washington

171 Thomsen, T. and Jessen, A. 1907. *Mém. Soc. Roy. Antiq. Nord*, 1902–7, 161–232

172 Ticehurst, N. F. 1908. *Brit. Birds 1* (10), 309–11

173 Troels-Smith, J. 1960. *Ann. Rep. Smithson. Inst.* 1959, 577–601 (transl. from *Natur Verd.*, July 1957)

174 Vaufrey, R. 1931. *Anthropologie 41*, 262

175 Wallace, W. J. and Lathrap, D. W. 1959. *Am. Antiq. 25* (2), 262–4

176 Webb, W. S. and Baby, R. S. 1957. *The Adena People No. 2*, Ohio State Univ. Press

177 Weigel, P. H. 1958. *Auk 75* (2), 215–16

178 Weigel, R. D. 1959. *Florida Anth. 12* (3), 73–4

179 Wetmore, A. 1918. *Proc. U.S. Nat. Mus. 54*, 513–22

180 —— 1922a. *Bull. Amer. Mus. Nat. Hist. 46*, 297–333

181 —— 1922b. *Smithson. Misc. Coll. 74* (4), 1–4

182 —— 1928. *Condor 30* (3), 191

183 —— 1931. *Ibid. 33* (2), 76–7

184 —— 1932. *Ibid. 34* (3), 141–2

185 —— 1937. *J. Agric. Univ. Puerto Rico 21* (1), 5–16

186 WETMORE, A. 1938. *Auk 55* (1), 51–5
187 —— 1956. *Smithson. Misc. Coll. 131* (5), 1–105
188 —— 1959. *Ibid. 138* (4), 1–24
189 WHITE, T. E. 1953. *Am. Antiq. 18* (4), 396–8
190 —— 1956. *Ibid. 21* (4), 401–4
191 WILLIAMS, G. R. 1956. *Notornis 7* (2), 29–56
192 —— 1960. *Trans. Roy. Soc. N.Z. 88* (2), 235–58
193 WINGE, H. 1900. Report on bird remains, in MADSEN, A. P. *et al.*, *Affaldsdynger fra Stenalderen Danmark*, Copenhagen and Paris, 179–82
194 —— 1903a. *Vid. Medd. fra naturhist. For. Kjøbenhavn., 1903*, 61–110
195 —— 1903b. Knoglerne (pp. 194–5), in SARAUW, G. F. L., En Stenalders Boplads i Maglemose ved Mullerup, Sammenholdt med Beslaegtede Fund. Bidrag til Belysning af Nystenalderns Begyndelse i Norden, *Aarbog. Nord. Oldkynd. Hist.* (2) 18, 194–5
196 —— 1920. *Mém. Soc. Roy. Antiq. Nord. 1918–19*, 241–359
197 —— 1931. *Ibid. 1926–27*, 1–128
198 WINTEMBERG, W. J. 1919. *Canad. Field Nat. 33*, 63–72
199 YALDWYN, J. C. 1959a. *N.Z. Arch. Assoc. Newsletter 2* (4), 20–5
200 —— 1959b. *Ibid. 25*
201 ZEUNER, F. E. 1959. *The Pleistocene Period*, London

30 *Remains of Fishes and other Aquatic Animals*

M. L. RYDER

THIS ACCOUNT concentrates on vertebrate fishes, but all aquatic animals of archaeological interest are mentioned because there is little distinction archaeologically between the group of animals known zoologically as fishes, and the other aquatic animals that are gathered, caught, or hunted in water. Table A classifies the aquatic animals that are likely to be found on an archaeological site; most of these have been mentioned in this account, and there are no doubt others that have been omitted.

TABLE A
Aquatic animals of archaeological importance.

Invertebrates (skeleton, if any, mainly external)	Phylum *Coelenterata*	corals
	Phylum *Arthropoda*	crayfish, crabs, lobsters, barnacles (*Crustacea*)
	Phylum *Mollusca*	shell-fish, cuttlefish, octopus
	Phylum *Echinodermata*	sea urchin
Vertebrates (internal skeleton)	Phylum *Chordata*	fishes Amphibia—frogs, newts Reptiles—turtles Mammals—Rodents: beaver Carnivores: otters, seals, sea-lions, walruses *Cetacea:* whales, dolphins *Sirenia:* dugong (sea-cows)

FISHES

Fishes breathe by gills. They have a body that is divided into a trunk and a muscular tail. There is a tail fin with dorsal and ventral lobes, and there are paired pectoral and pelvic fins representing limbs. On the back and belly are median unpaired dorsal and ventral fins. In the lowest fishes (including the sharks and rays, Fig. 43a) the skeleton is cartilaginous; in the more advanced fishes, the teleosts (Fig. 43b), the skeleton is bony, and the gill slits are covered by a bony flap, the operculum. Most fishes have an external skeleton of small scales which are formed in the skin.

There seems to be no agreed way of classifying fishes; different sources often give a different name and status to even the major groups. The classification of Goodrich[1]

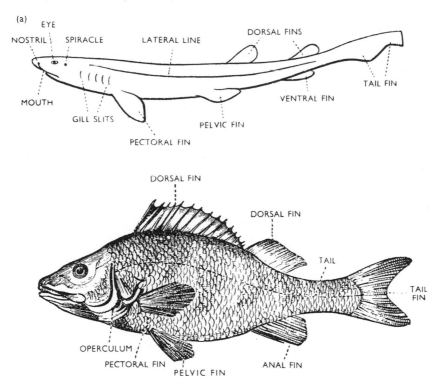

Fig. 43 External features (a) of the dogfish, a cartilaginous fish, and (b) of the perch, a bony fish.

is authoritative and detailed, and another is given by Norman[2] for British fishes, which Wells[3] apparently follows. The classification given in Table B is simplified from Romer[4] with additions from Young.[5]

Evolution of the fish skeleton and survey of fish types. A brief consideration of its evolution will give a better understanding of the fish skeleton. The eel-like lampreys, lacking jaws and fins, are the most primitive living vertebrates, and they live parasitically on other fishes. Their skeleton is cartilaginous and includes a simple cranium, gill-bars, and a poorly developed backbone. The evolutionary advance to bony fishes is accompanied by the development of jaws with teeth, and paired fins. Jaws are thought to have arisen from the first pair of skeletal bars that lay between the gill openings in the ancestors of the lampreys. The possible way in which this took place is illustrated by Zeuner.[6] Teeth have their origin in the shark group. The skin of sharks contains pointed scales (denticles) that give it a rough texture (shagreen). The teeth of sharks are similar to denticles, and it seems likely that teeth arose from the denticles along the edge of the mouth, becoming enlarged in the process. The first function of teeth was to prevent prey escaping from the mouth, and for this reason the teeth of fish usually point backwards into the mouth.

Sharks (the *elasmobranchs*) range in size from the small dogfish, common around Britain, to the large whale sharks of the tropics, but form only a small proportion of

TABLE B
Brief classification of main fish groups.

Class *Agnatha* (jawless vertebrates)
    Three fossil orders
    Order *Cyclostomata* (*Petromyzan*—lampreys)
Class *Placodermi* (archaic jawed fishes)
    Two fossil orders
Class *Chondrichthyes* (cartilaginous fishes)
    Order *Cladoselachii* (primitive fossil sharks)
    Order *Elasmobranchii* (sharks, skates and rays)
    Order *Holocephali* (chimaeras)
Class *Osteichthyes* (bony fishes)
    Sub-class *Crossopterygii* (lobe-finned fishes)
        Order *Osteolepidoti*
        Order *Coelocanthini*
        Order *Dipnoi* (lung-fishes)
    Sub-class *Actinopterygii* (ray-finned fishes)
        Order *Palaeoniscoidei* (*Polypterus*—bichir)
        Order *Chondrostei* (*Acipenser*—sturgeon)
        Order *Holostei* (*Amia*-bowfin, *Lepidosteus*—gar-pike)
        Order *Teleostei*
            Sub-order *Isospondyli*: *Clupea* (herring), *Salmo* (trout)
            Sub-order *Ostariophysi*: *Cyprinus* (carp), *Tinca* (tench), *Silurus* (catfish), *Leuciscus* (roach)
            Sub-order *Apodes*: *Anguilla* (eel), *Conger* (conger eel)
            Sub-order *Mesichthyes*: *Esox* (pike), *Belone* (gar-fish), *Exocoetus* (flying-fish), *Hippocampus* (sea-horse), *Gasterosteus* (stickleback), *Syngnathus* (pipe-fish)
            Sub-order *Acanthopterygii*: *Zeus* (john dory), *Perca* (perch), *Labrus* (wrasse), *Uranoscopus* (star gazer), *Blennius* (blenny), *Gadus* (whiting), *Pleuronectes* (plaice), *Solea* (sole), *Lophius* (angler-fish)

---

living fishes. The rays and skates eat shell-fish, and their teeth have been modified into flattened crushing plates. In addition, their body has become flattened for living on the sea-bed; their pectoral fins have become enlarged, and their tail has been reduced. Some of the denticles in the tail have enlarged to form spines.

A much more important group are the *Osteichthyes*. In these the cartilaginous skeleton has become replaced by bone, and additional bones, known as dermal or membrane bones, have arisen. These have no cartilaginous precursor in the embryo. At the beginning of their evolution the *Osteichthyes* divided into two groups: the *Crossopterygii* (lobe-finned fishes) and the *Actinopterygii* (ray-finned fishes). The *Crossopterygii* were not successful as fishes, but were important in giving rise to the land vertebrates. The first order (Table B) is extinct and the second order (*Coelocanthini*) was thought to be extinct until the first of several specimens was caught off South Africa in 1939. The third order (*Dipnoi*, or lung-fishes) has only three types, one in each of Australia, South America and Africa. These have short jaws and fan-shaped crushing teeth. The skeleton of the paired fins consists of pre- and post-axial jointed radials articulating with a median jointed axis, a structure that gave rise to the limb of land vertebrates.

In the *Actinopterygii*, except in rare instances, the paired fins are composed only of a web of skin supported by slender rays. The oldest ray-fins (*Palaeoniscoids*), a living representative of which is the Nile bichir, have thick, shiny, rhomboid scales. The bichir has a dorsal fin that is divided into a series of parts, and the pectoral fins have a fleshy lobe. The sturgeon (*Chondrostei*), like the bichir, is a survivor of an ancient group. The tail fin is shark-like, the jaws lack teeth, the skeleton is almost entirely cartilaginous, and the scales comprise many small denticles, and five rows of large bony scutes. The *Holostei* are represented today by the fresh-water gar-pike (Central and North America) and bowfin (North America).

The *Teleostei* include all fishes familiar to us, except those already mentioned, and number about 20,000 species. The scales have become thin and flexible, and overlap, and the hind ends of the jaw bones are not fixed to the skull, allowing a wide gape. Most of the group live in the sea, and are more abundant in shallow coastal waters where food is plentiful. The smaller numbers that inhabit the high seas are unlikely to be encountered by archaeologists. Many teleosts live in fresh water and there are 34 species of fresh-water fishes in Great Britain,[7] to which have recently been added 10 aliens, e.g. rainbow trout, bass and carp; Fitter[7] thinks that the carp might have been introduced in the Middle Ages. Wells[3] describes 164 British sea fishes (of all types). The majority of teleosts lay numerous eggs that float near the surface, but some lay eggs that develop on the bottom. The salmon lives in salt water, but ascends fresh-water streams to breed; that is, it is anadromous. The eel on the other hand is catadromous, it lives in streams, and migrates to the ocean, crossing the Atlantic, to spawn; the young elvers spend three years on the return journey.

There are great variations in size and body shape among the teleosts from the 'standard' streamlined bodies (Fig. 43b) of fast-swimming fishes such as the trout, to the elongated eel shape, as well as many bizarre shapes, e.g. the sea-horse. The teleosts are on the whole flattened laterally, so that the flat-fishes (plaice and sole) have become adapted to bottom living by turning over on to their side, the dorso-ventral flattening found in the rays being impossible in fish that were already thin laterally. The head appears incongruous, having two eyes on one side, because the eye of the underside migrates around to the upper surface in the young flat-fish. Despite these different shapes, the teleosts are a difficult group to classify, and it is a disadvantage to those students interested in the skeleton that the classification is often based on external features.

The classification into sub-orders followed here (Table B) is that of Young.[5] The *Isospondyli* (salmon, trout and herring) show primitive features in the large maxillae (upper jaw bones), and the posterior position of the pelvic fins. In the *Ostariophysi* (carp, roach and catfish) the anterior vertebrae are modified to form a separate chain of bones, the Weberian ossicles, joining the swim-bladder to the ear. The *Apodes* (eels) have many primitive features. The *Mesichthyes* (pike, flying-fish, sea-horse) link the more primitive types with the more highly developed *Acanthopterygians* (perches, flat-fishes and Gadids—cod, haddock, ling). These have stiff spines at the front of their dorsal and anal fins, the body is short, as is the maxilla bone, and the pelvic fins lie far forward (Fig. 43b).

The skeleton of fishes in detail. What are fish bones like when encountered in archaeological excavations? The only parts that are likely to be preserved from cartilaginous fishes are teeth and denticles—particularly any that have become enlarged to form spines (Fig. 44a). The bones of bony fish are irregular in shape, and have a rough texture.[8] They often have sharp points, and are often brown in colour as opposed to the yellow-white bones of higher vertebrates. Some fish bones appear very like horn. One has done well if one can state that fish bones have been found, because to go further and identify species is very difficult even when comparative material is available. Skull bones on the whole have specific differences, but in my experience the most common fish bones are vertebrae, and although these can be reported as say 'of cod size', the difficulty is that large vertebrae from a small species might be similar in size to the small ones of another, but larger, species. As with the identification of any animal material, the only way is to build up a reference collection of known skeletons from the area in question. However, it is advisable to measure the diameter of each vertebra found, and to report the frequency with which each diameter occurs. Then, later, someone with a greater knowledge of fish bones may be able to use these statistics to identify the species to which they belong.

The cartilaginous elasmobranchs are described by Daniel.[9] The denticles (placoid scales), like teeth, are made of a core of dentine (ivory), the base of which is surrounded by cement (bone), and the point of which is covered with a cap of enamel. The point of spines is bent acutely upon the base, which is bean-shaped, and much larger than the spine itself (Fig. 44a). The cartilaginous skeleton is impregnated with calcium salts and may well be preserved

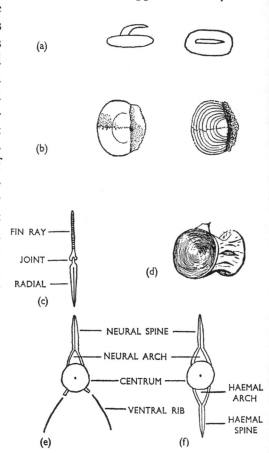

Fig. 44 (a) Spine of a ray (enlarged placoid scale), side view (left), top view (right); only the spine projects above the skin surface: the oval baseplate lies within the skin; (b) cycloid scales of herring: one annual growth ring (left), eight growth rings (right); (c) dorsal fin of bony fish showing supporting radial; (d) archaeological specimen of vertebra from bony fish—note broken arch; (e) trunk vertebra and (f) tail vertebra from bony fish. (b) After Kyle,[11] (d) from Ryder.[8]

in certain conditions. The brain-case or cranium has a nasal capsule at the front, a large orbit at each side, and an auditory capsule at the back. Attached to the back of the skull is the vertebral column. The upper jaw is not fused to the cranium, but is suspended by a cartilage and some ligaments. Both upper and lower jaws bear teeth. Behind the jaws are the skeletal arches of the gill slits. The cartilaginous vertebrae consist of a basal centrum or body, with concave ends, on top of which lies the neural arch. In the tail there is also a ventral haemal arch. In some elasmobranchs (e.g. the rays) the vertebrae of the trunk region are fused into a continuous rod. The median and paired fins are supported by jointed cartilaginous rods known as radials. The edge of the fin is strengthened by horny dermal fin rays known as ceratotrichia. The radials of the paired fins form a series starting with larger rods at the base. These basal rods articulate with the girdles lying transversely across the body. The pectoral (shoulder) girdle is an incomplete hoop, whereas the pelvic girdle is merely a transverse rod.

The typical bony teleostean fishes have a relatively shorter body than the elasmo-branchs, and in some of them the pelvic fins are in front of the pectoral fins. The thin bony scales may be circular or oval in shape; some have smooth edges (cycloid scales), others have serrated edges (ctenoid scales), and are rough to the touch.[10] This distinction can sometimes help to distinguish species, e.g. the dab has ctenoid scales, whereas the plaice has cycloid scales.[11] The eels do not have visible scales, and the Silurids never have them. The scales show rings of growth which indicate the age of the fish. In spring and summer when growth is rapid many rings are laid down, but as the growth slows and almost ceases in winter the rings become fewer in number, and closer together. These winter rings form a band which marks off a year's growth, though some may be due to unequal growth in summer[11] (Fig. 44b).

Age can also be determined from similar rings on the otoliths or ear-stones. These are elongated and often angular, porcelain-like aggregations of calcium carbonate found free in each ear cavity. They have a flattened appearance, and show growth rings on their broad face (Plate XIII). As otoliths are sure to be as old as the fish, they probably give a more accurate indication of age than scales, which can begin to grow during life. Otoliths are also useful in indicating fish when all other remains have decayed. Gregory[12] states that certain species have characteristic otoliths that allow identification, and Mr J. M. Moreland of the Dominion Museum, Wellington, New Zealand, has found oto-liths useful in the identification of archaeological material.[13] Certain bones, too, exhibit growth rings; Kyle[11] illustrates them in an opercula bone, and Wells[3] states that the fin rays (of cod), when sectioned transversely, show microscopic growth rings. Such a microscopic approach, similar to that described in other chapters by Sandison and my-self, is likely to be used increasingly in the future.[14, 15] The horny plugs in the ears of whales show six-monthly growth rings that indicate age.

The skull can be divided into brain case, additional dermal bones (bones lacking a cartilaginous precursor in the embryo) and splanchno-cranium (jaws and gill arches). It is a complicated structure of often flattish irregular-shaped bones (Fig. 45). Gregory[12] illustrates the skulls of many teleosts, but the bones readily separate from one another, as can be seen if the head of a fish is boiled, so the skull is unlikely to be found intact.

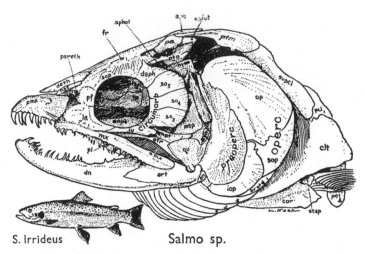

Fig. 45 Skull of bony fish (*Salmo irrideus*—a Pacific Salmon). Key from Gregory[12] (some bones not mentioned in the present text are omitted): dn—dentary, art—articular, qu—quadrate, pmx—premaxilla, pl—palatine, mx—maxilla, pareth—parethmoid, fr—frontal, sphot—sphenotic, soc—supra-occipital, epiot—epiotic, ptm—post-temporal, supcl—supra-cleithrum, clt—cleithrum, pcl—post-cleithrum, cor—coracoid, scap—scapula, brste—branchiostegal rays. From Gregory.[12]

Apart from the jaws, other bones in the roof of the mouth bear teeth. The gill cover or operculum is supported by four flat bones, and the branchiostegal membrane below the operculum is supported by branchiostegal rays. These are often found as archaeological remains, and consist of stoutish, curved bones, not unlike the ribs of a mammal, ending in a blunt point. There are five gill arches; the inner surface of these often bears teeth, and the posterior border often has small spine-like processes known as gill rakers. The teeth of teleosts are like those of the cartilaginous fishes. The vertebral column is composed of distinct bony vertebrae. The body of each vertebra has concave ends, and is constricted in the middle into the shape of an hourglass (Fig. 44d). Dorsally there are a pair of processes that unite to form the neural arch. In the trunk region each vertebra bears a pair of ventro-lateral processes to which ventral ribs are attached (Fig. 44e). In the tail region these processes are bent downwards and united to form the haemal arch. The haemal arches are extended to form the haemal spines (Fig. 44f). In the region of the ventral fins (Fig. 46) there are radials below the haemal spines, and the radials articulate with the fin rays. In some fishes the radials of the tail fin are flattened to form plates lying in the median plane of the body.

The neural arches are prolonged to form neural spines. These are surmounted by radials (Fig. 44c) in the regions of the dorsal fins, and the radials articulate with the dermal rays that support the fins. The fin rays of bony fishes (lepidotrichia) are bony, jointed, and often branched, unlike the horny unjointed ceratotrichia of cartilaginous fishes. In the more highly evolved bony fishes the joint between the fin rays and the radials enables the fin to be raised and lowered.

The bones of the pectoral (shoulder) girdle (Figs. 45 and 46) corresponding to those of the cartilaginous fishes comprise the dorsal scapula, the ventral coracoid, and the meso-

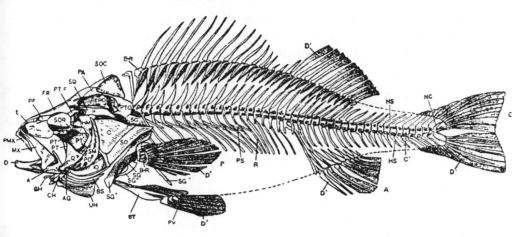

Fig. 46 Skeleton of perch. Key from Young[5] (some bones omitted): A—anal fin, B+R radials, BS—branchiostegal rays, BT—basipterygium, C—caudal (tail) fin, C'—centrum, D'—dermal fin rays, HS—haemal spine, NS—neural spine, O—operculum, P—pectoral fin, PS—rib processes, PV—pelvic fin, R—ribs, SG—shoulder girdle. After Dean.

coracoid. There are also some dermal bones, the cleithrum, post-cleithrum and supra-cleithrum. The supra-cleithrum articulates with the post-temporal of the skull, attaching the pectoral girdle to the back of the skull. The pectoral fin articulates with the girdle by means of several short radials, and the web of the fin is supported by rays that articulate with the radials. The first (anterior) ray is larger than the rest, and often articulates directly with the scapula. In some fishes, e.g. the Silurids (catfish), this articulates independently from the rest of the fin and is armed with spikes on each side. These rays are very characteristic, and some were found in the recent Seelands dig in Australia (see below). The pelvic skeleton consists of only a single, flat triangular bone, the basipterygium, on each side, and the radials of the pelvic fin are much reduced.

ARCHAEOLOGICAL SURVEY

1. *Fish remains in Europe and the Near East.* Perhaps the earliest aquatic animals used for food were shell-fish. The Neanderthal men of Devil's Tower, Gibraltar, derived much of their food from limpets and mussels, and shell-fish appear to have contributed to European subsistence ever since.[17] However, a diet in which shell-fish are the mainstay is normally associated with a low level of attainment and shell-fish occupied only a subsidiary place in communities which hunted and fished with vigour. On the other hand, a hominid older than *Zinjanthropus* found recently in Tanganyika[18] had apparently eaten catfish.

(a) Upper Palaeolithic hunter-fishers. Although remains of fishing gear are rare, abundant fish bones, and representations in Magdalenian cave art, show that fishing was already carried out in Upper Palaeolithic times.[16,17] The Magdalenians of the Dordogne caves (France) caught pike, trout, dace, chub, bream and white bream, as well as salmon. It is likely that the salmon were caught at some distance away when they came upstream in summer. The lack of salmon skull bones in the caves, whereas skull bones of the frailer Cyprinids (dace, chub and bream) were preserved, shows that the head was removed elsewhere. This suggests a seasonal migration to catch the salmon, which were dried, as done recently by North American Indians to be eaten in the caves in winter.

Representations in cave art in northern Spain and southern France include pike, trout and salmon, and also, near the coast, flat-fish and tunny. But the latter do not prove sea-fishing. Well-preserved fish bones are rare on coastal sites, and these are mainly from species like wrasses that could be taken close inshore. The inhabitants of the Grimaldi caves on the Mediterranean shore ate many shell-fish. Perhaps these people were unable to fish at sea because of the lack of boats.

(b) Mesolithic hunter-fishers. The boat first appeared in Mesolithic times together with the hook, net and funnel-shaped trap.[16,17] Apparently the most common fish caught was the pike, but the Maglemosian people of the north European plain also caught bream, perch, tench and eels in Boreal times.[16] Remains of pike were found impaled on spear-points in lake deposits at Kunda, Esthonia, and in southern Sweden. On one lake site in north Zealand 80 upper and 64 left lower jaw bones of pike were found. The preponderance of skull bones at Svaerdborg may indicate that the pike were dried to be eaten elsewhere. The suggestion quoted by Clark[16] that the head bones were more likely to survive is not borne out by my experience, which is that the most common fish bones to survive are vertebrae. Surprisingly, no osteological evidence of fishing was found at Star Carr,[19] the early Mesolithic lake-side site at Seamer near Scarborough, Yorkshire.

Towards the end of Mesolithic times there is evidence for the beginning of sea-fishing from boats.[16,17] The Tardenoisian middens of Téviec and Hoëdic on the south coast of Brittany yielded bones of sea-fish. Although fishing was more important than hunting, shell-fish still predominated and wrasse and other Labrid remains indicated inshore fishing only.

Cod bones were found in an Early Atlantic level at Cushendun in Northern Ireland, and early sites on Oronsay have yielded remains of black sea-bream, probably caught from the rocks, as well as conger, haddock, common sea-bream, ballan wrasse, thornback ray, skate, a number of sharks, and claws of crabs, which suggest fishing from boats.

Several Mesolithic III sites on the Littorina shores of Denmark had middens containing marine shell-fish, yet the vertebrate fish were mainly fresh-water types.[16] At Ertebölle most of the fish remains were from eel, roach and pike, yet bones from cod, flounder and gar-fish indicate sea-fishing. The occurrence of remains of large haddock and coalfish, which live at depths of from 40 to 100 metres, shows that the Ertebölle people of Denmark must have caught fish by line from boats at a good distance from the shore. Clark[17] considers that this off-shore fishing was more effective after the advent of farming: there were numerous haddock and cod bones in the Sölanger midden, most of which is Neolithic.

(c) The Neolithic period to the Iron Age. The advent of farming, and its continued development, increased the population, and this increased the demand for fish. Improved tackle (barbed hooks, metal fish-spears, net sinkers, and the development of weirs) increased the efficiency of fishing. But the full possibilities were not realized until historical times, the development of herring fishing, for example, being associated with the rise of an urban economy.

From Neolithic times then the fisherman was usually a farmer, fishing being a seasonal occupation that led to seasonal settlements. At Jarmo in Iraq, a few fish and fresh-water crabs added to protein variety.[20] The 'lake dwellings' of Europe have yielded many fish scales and fish bones. The most common species from the Swiss sites were pike, and Clark[16] considers that many of the roach, dace, chub and perch caught may have been used as live-bait for pike. Other fish caught by the inhabitants were carp, burbot, and a salmon.

Although most lakes and rivers were fished to satisfy day-to-day needs, certain fisheries were developed around the anadromous salmon and sturgeon, and the catadromous eel. Clark[16] gives evidence of salmon fishing at certain points on Irish rivers (cf. the North American Indians); the lack of fish remains at such sites supports the suggestion that the fish were cured and taken away. It is likely that the sturgeon was fished seasonally in the Danube, remains having been found on two sites.[16] Although eel remains have been recovered from Stone Age sites in Jutland and Gotland, there is little evidence that eels were fished extensively. Young may have been taken in the run upstream, but remains of these are unlikely to survive.

There is evidence for a line fishery off the northern and western shores of Britain based on cod, but including coalfish, dogfish, skate, other rays, conger, gurnet, grey mullet, wrasse, haddock, tope, angel-fish, bream, rudd and accompanied by crab catching.[16] Petrie in 1866 found 'apparently sillock or coalfish' bones in the midden at Skara Brae on Orkney, as well as cod bones and a building mortar to which ground fish bones had been added.

Off-shore fisheries were carried on in the Skagerrak by people occupying the northern parts of the west coast of Sweden at the close of the Stone Age.[16,17] The contents of three middens yielded mainly cod, ling and haddock with smaller numbers of ballan wrasse, whiting and pollack, all of which are bottom feeders. One of the eight haddock from Rotekärrslid, and two of the ninety-seven from Rörvik were larger than the maximum size caught there today, and many of the ling were large. This apparent reduction in size might appear to be associated with recent over-fishing, but it must be noted that only two of the forty-eight cod from Rörvik were as much as 0·97 m. long as compared with the present maximum of 1·5 m. and there is evidence that fishing, by reducing competition among the fish, stimulates growth.[5]

A midden at Anneröd yielded cod and numerous haddock, as well as whiting, pollack, tunny and flounder. That this fishery was by line is suggested by a Bronze Age rock-engraving in south Sweden showing men fishing from a boat with a hook and line.[17] A Neolithic settlement at Hemmor, Gotland, yielded 5,343 cod bones, and numerous fish-hooks, indicating line-fishing. Sea-fishing in Denmark continued to be concentrated on the southern shores of the Kattegat. The Sölanger midden has already been mentioned; cod was also found at the Bronze Age site of Fyen, and at the Iron Age site of Borrebjerg on Sejerö.

Clark[17] considers that the biggest sea fisheries in prehistoric Europe were those of Norway; the deep fjords bring bottom-feeding fish close in to shore. The earliest traces were found at Viste, near Stavanger, which was occupied by hunter-fishers probably before farming spread to Norway. Here cod was the most common fish; other remains came from haddock, ling, pollack, torsk, conger, ballan wrasse and striped wrasse.[16] Later, fishing accompanied farming and became seasonal in character, which must have resulted in the drying of fish (see medieval period below). Two engravings of skin-covered boats show halibut caught on a line.

Herring remains are almost absent from prehistoric sites in Europe, although herring fishing was well established by Domesday. Clark[17] considers that herring fishing was not developed because the needs of small communities of farmer-fishers did not justify the labour involved in making the nets.

(d) The ancient Mediterranean civilizations. The classical archaeologists of Mesopotamia, Egypt, Greece and Rome tended to concentrate on art treasures, and it is not often that animal remains appear in publications about these periods. Hilzheimer,[21] in what he states is the first study of bones from a *Mesopotamian* site, lists fish among the remains from Tell Asmar, the period of which is given as from Early Dynastic III to Gutian. These formed 3·4% of the total remains from both domestic and wild animals; no species are given. Bird bones formed only 2·5% of the remains. Braidwood and Reed[20] state that the irrigation canals of Sumer were a source of fish.

Engravings and other representations of fish become more common in this period. One species that is abundantly represented in ancient art is the Nile fish *Tilapia nilotica*. Thompson[22] illustrates an engraving of one of these from a Vth Dynasty tomb. He also shows an engraving of two men carrying a giant Nile perch (*Perca nilotica*) from Medum (*c.* 2780 BC). According to Childe[23] the ancient *Egyptians* imported dried fish from the Arabian Sea, and Thompson[22] states that salted fish are well preserved on Egyptian sites. Along with many other animals fishes were mummified.[24] With the advent of these civilizations literary sources are added to representations and remains, and with the ancient *Greeks* the first interest in biology arose; Aristotle knew a great deal a boutfishes. Thompson[22] lists ancient Greek names for fishes, and gives many illustrations, e.g. his frontispiece illustrates a well-known vase of the fourth century BC showing a tunny-merchant cutting up fish. The ancient Macedonians are said to have been the first to fish with artificial flies.

The *Romans* held fishing contests, cultivated oysters, and had fish-ponds in their markets to ensure that fish would be fresh, although they imported sea-fish from Germany.[25] In Rome there was a sacrificial custom in which small fishes were caught in the Tiber and burnt alive in honour of the god Vulcan.[26] One oyster shell comprised the only remains from fish that I found among some animal bones from the Roman cemetery in Trentholme Drive, York, excavated by Mr L. P. Wenham in 1957–58. There had been other shells in previous years among these bones which came from food buried with the dead for their journey into the next world.

(e) The medieval period. The only fish bone reported from an Early Christian Crannog in Northern Ireland was a branchiostegal ray that was probably from cod.[27]

The inhabitants of a tenth-century settlement at Mawgan Porth, Cornwall, ate mussels, but the only evidence of fishing came from a few perforated stones that may have been used as net or line sinkers.[28]

The animal remains of thirteenth-century date found at Clough Castle, Co. Down,[29] included the following marine mollusca: edible cockle (*Cardium edule*), great scallop (*Pecten maximus*), common periwinkle (*Littorina littorea*), edible mussel (*Mytilus edulis*) and oyster (*Ostrea edulis*). In addition there were remains from cod (including vertebrae) and probably wrasse, haddock and perch (scales). Some of the cod bones showed a diseased condition known as hyperostosis (extra growth of bone). The cause of this is unknown; it is found today and may be associated with age.

The excavations carried out during the last ten years at Kirkstall Abbey (1152–1540) yielded numerous oyster and mussel shells, as well as a few cockles and whelks (*Buccinum undatum*).[30] These are thought to have been eaten more before the monks were allowed to eat meat, because fewer were found in a midden associated with the meat kitchen built about 1450. These shell-fish must have come from the coast and some fifteenth-century records of Fountains Abbey[31] refer to oysters being bought at York, Hull and Scarborough (respectively 25, 50 and 70 miles from Leeds). I know of no records of the way in which these were transported; they may have been carried in barrels of salt water, but it is now known that if oysters are kept cool and moist they become dormant and remain alive for months.* It is of interest that the same records mention 'seal fish' which were apparently regarded as being fish rather than 'flesh'. The oyster shells at Kirkstall were only about half the size of modern adult oysters, and had only one or two (annual) growth rings, indicating that they were young.[32]

The midden yielded only a small proportion of fish bones among the thousands of animal bones found.[33] There were about as many fish bones as bird bones, and most were apparently too large to have come from fresh-water fish. In 1956 eight large vertebrae, probably from cod, were found, and there were branchiostegal rays of cod size. In 1957 forty fish bones were found; one vertebra had a diameter of 7 mm being comparable in size to a modern salmon vertebra. There were eleven other vertebrae, and the frequencies of the diameters (in mm) of those found in 1956 and 1957 are: 12 mm (1), 13 (1), 16 (4), 17 (3), 18 (2), 19 (3), 20 (1), 22 (2), 23 (2). There were also branchiostegal rays, fin rays, ribs, and skull bones that could not be identified. One skull bone was from a fish larger than cod. In addition, there was a dermal spine from a large ray (Fig. 45). In 1958 the fish bones were of cod size; there were two skull bones, two branchiostegal rays, and three vertebrae with diameters of 13, 16 and 17 mm. Some of the unidentified bones may have been from haddock, ling or the fresh-water pike. Fitter[7] says that this was transported to likely ponds in the Middle Ages, and Kirkstall along with other monasteries had its own fish-ponds. The records of Fountains[31] mention salmon, cured sprats (*Clupea sprattus*), and that 'stock-fish' (dried or salted fish, probably cod and ling) were bought at the above three ports. Speed (1631) said that dried fish were imported from Norway and Iceland.

* The Inca runners could carry fish and shell-fish from the Pacific 170 miles over the mountains and deliver it fresh to Cuzco.

Excavations carried out at Pontefract Priory (1090–1540) from 1957 to 1959 yielded about 300 animal bones of which thirteen were from fishes, and only six of these were stratified.[34] One bone was definitely from cod, and most of the others were of cod size; three vertebrae had diameters of 12, 13 and 23 mm. There was one mussel shell, and thirty-five oysters, which were larger than those from Kirkstall.

About 400 animal bones, of which five were from fishes, were found in excavations in Petergate, York, in 1957 and 1958, through levels dating from the fourteenth century back to the eleventh century.[35] These comprise two parts of the pectoral girdle, of which one had a knife cut, and was identified as cod, a skull bone, and two vertebrae 14 and 16 mm in diameter. The second of these was from the extreme anterior end (disk-shaped) and was therefore the largest in the body. There were 147 oyster shells, 49 cockles, one scallop and one whelk. It is known that the Archbishop of York had 'salmon garths' on the river Ouse, and a record of 1465 mentions the large number of pike that were eaten at one of his feasts.

Of about 3,000 bones found during the first ten years' excavation at the village of Wharram Percy, deserted about 1500, perhaps 50 were from fishes.[36] Cod bones were identified amongst these, and many were of cod size, but there were a few smaller ones, possibly from fresh-water fish. The diameters (in mm) and dates of the vertebrae (frequency in brackets) were as follows: thirteenth century, 14, 22; fourteenth century, 5 (2), 6, 8, 9, 11, 16, 17, 18, 20 (first of column), 20 (2), 24; fifteenth century, 5, 12, 13. There was one oyster shell, and a fragment that was possibly from a whelk shell. It is most interesting that sea-fish, including shell-fish, reached this isolated village on the Yorkshire Wolds.

2. *Whales and Seals in Europe*. Whales[37] and seals[38] were hunted off European shores as early as the Stone Age, but space forbids a consideration of the details, which are discussed by Clark.[17]

3. *Findings outside Europe*.

(a) *Africa*. Goodwin[39] describes prehistoric coastal fishing methods in *South Africa*. He describes tidal fish-traps (*vywers*) made of 'dry' stone walls. These occur for at least 1,000 miles roughly from Cape Town to Zululand. Many are still in use, often with ground-bait; they are covered at high tide, and as the tide ebbs, water is lost through the stones leaving any fish stranded. At Oakhurst shelter near George, some distance from and 300 feet above the sea, there is a series of local Later Stone Age strata. In the pre-Wilton levels few fish bones or otoliths occur, whereas above that level they increase in number and variety and include scales. As otoliths would not have disappeared, the appearance of fish remains is comparatively recent, and is associated with the discovery of a means of catching fish in quantity. The lack of other implements indicates these traps which are accordingly Wilton and post-Wilton in date.

Species identified include bishop (*Pagrus*), elft (*Pomatomus*) and eagle ray (*Myliobatus*). At Klip Kop cave, Hermanus, fishes of the genera *Pagrus*, *Dentex*, *Sparus*, and *Diplodus*, all in the modern fauna, were identified. This local Wilton culture is characterized by the replacement of microliths with shell implements. The shells used were *Mytilus* (common mussel) and *Donax*. The same sequence occurs in many middens along the coast: the earliest levels have neither fish nor pottery; the next have fish but no pottery, and the most recent levels contain fish and pottery. Some middens associated with some *ywers*, possibly used a century ago, comprised conical heaps of shells 3–4 ft high, and 9–10 ft in diameter, and each heap contains only one type of shell, possibly reflecting the way in which available supplies were used.

(b) *Asia*. Mongait[40] does not mention sea-fishing in his general survey, *Archaeology in the USSR*. But in the third or Serov phase (third millennium BC) of the Siberian Neolithic he says that fresh-water fishing played as great a role as hunting. Fish were caught with nets, harpoons, and arrows, the fish-hook being invented later in the same phase. Stone images of fish are common, and even though schematic, they are good representations of salmon, whitefish, ling, sturgeon and others. Two of these are illustrated;[40] one 28 cm long is an exact representation with mouth, eyes, fins and scales, wheresa the other has only the shape of a fish, with a mouth. It was thought that these images were used in a ritual to ensure fishing success. Now it is considered that they were used as decoys, and each has several holes from which the stone could have been suspended. A pile settlement in the Charozero District of the second millennium BC had heaps of fish scales and bones between the dwellings, as well as remains of woven fish-traps and bone harpoons. In the early *Chinese* Neolithic between 3500 and 2000 BC there were at least two riverine cultures in which farming activities were supplemented by well-developed fishing and mollusc-collecting activities. The later Neolithic in south China had a maritime orientation.[41]

(c) *Oceania*. Gifford[42] excavated a coastal site in Fiji and another not far inland. These have since been dated as belonging to the first century BC. The artifacts resemble those of Melanesia to the west, rather than Polynesia to the east. He found two main cultural levels: lower layers without shell, upper layers with shell, and either the earlier people did not eat shell-fish, or they dumped the shells elsewhere. Bones of vertebrate fish, domestic pig, and evidence of cannibalism were found in each level. The weight of the fish bones found was 3,113 g. compared with 4,950 g. of bones from other animals. Although most of the fish bones could not be identified, e.g. vertebrae, some identifications were made from jaws, and evidence of 20 species as well as several genera was obtained. Five of the species had not been reported from Fiji before. The weight of bones found at the different levels, and the depths at which the different species were found, are indicated in tables. The only other aquatic vertebrate found was the green turtle (*Chelonia mydas*). This is the shore turtle of tropical seas that is commonly eaten by man.

There was so much shell material that only sufficient shells were collected to indicate species; the many species identified (shown in tables) are all found in Fijian waters today, and some are still eaten. The large white cowry (*Ovulum ovum*) which is used today as an external house decoration was not found in the excavations; on the other hand, a smaller cowry (*Cypraea eburnea*), used as a personal ornament, was found. When spider shells (*Pterocera lambis*) are collected today, the sharp projections are immediately broken off. The animal is often obtained by shattering the shell, and the fragmentary specimens indicate that this was done in the past. Shell had been used to make knives, fish-hooks and ornaments. A few small crustacean fragments were found, and these were mainly concentrated in the shell layer. Four species of crab were identified, and only one of these was among the two species eaten today. Two echinoderms—a sand dollar and a heart urchin—were identified, as well as specimens of coral.

Gifford and Shutler[43] excavated eleven sites in New Caledonia, a large island about 1,000 miles off the coast of Queensland, which has cultural relationships with other parts of Melanesia. There were fewer fish bones than in Fiji, although nine of the eleven sites were on the coast; whereas in Fiji 1·08 g. of fish bone per cubic foot was found, here the weight was only 0·75 g. Whether this represents a true difference in the use of fish, or whether the smaller yield in New Caledonia is due to the reported practice of burning fish bones is not clear. Nevertheless, a total of 5,652 g. of bones from fishes was found, compared with 4,316 g. from other animals, including mammals introduced by Europeans. But the uneven distribution of fish bones, the absence of bones from domestic animals, and the scanty evidence of cannibalism, suggested that molluscs, and possibly also decapods (crustaceans), had been the principal sources of protein. Many of the fish bones could not be identified, but of the fourteen species recorded, nine had not been reported from New Caledonia before. Bones of the green turtle and also the loggerhead turtle (*Caretta caretta*) were found.

Mollusc shells were the most abundant animal remains; these were more plentiful in the coastal sites, and whereas in Fiji it was clear that the shells had been carried to the sites by man, here this is certain only in the inland sites. The 255 species identified were mostly marine types and comprised both bivalves and univalves, with which *Nautilus* was included, but two, *Arca scapha* and *Gafrarium tumidum*, were found in large quantities indicating frequent use for food. The author, however, admits that in some instances he has taken the liberty of omitting the doubt in the identification expressed by the malacologist, and instead listed the species as a definite identification. As there is no indication of where this has been done, the value of all the identifications is in my opinion reduced. The heaviest concentration of shells at one site was in the 24- and 30-in. levels, which later radiocarbon dating has shown to be of the sixth century BC. One level of another site was dated as first century AD. The change of species at different levels in one site suggested an environmental change; an increase in *Arca scapha* and decrease of *Potamides semitrisulcatus* suggested more sand and less mud in earlier times. Shell artifacts were next in abundance to potsherds; these comprised net sinkers, fish-hooks, money and personal ornaments. Octopus lures were also found.

Decapod shell fragments, chiefly from crab, with occasional lobster, were abundant at one site. Of the total of 6,550 g. of decapod shell from various sites, 6,369 g. came from this site. The abundance here may be explained by its proximity to shallow water, and the scarcity of shell on other sites suggested that crabs did not form a prominent part in the diet. Sea-urchin shell fragments, mostly spines, came from three sites and there were stone-like coral remains; these may merely represent beach debris, but a possible use of coral additional to the hair bleach suggested at Fiji is as a file in the manufacture of shell artifacts.

Gifford[44] excavated five sites at Yap, 'the island of stone money' which lies at the western edge of Micronesia. It is in the longitude of Tokyo, about 750 miles east of the Philippines, and is culturally associated with the Marianas Islands to the north. Radio-carbon dates show the sites to range from the second to the nineteenth century AD. Fish bones (4,053 g.) were the most abundant vertebrate remains, and the density of 2 g. per cubic foot shows that fish were used more than in Fiji and New Caledonia. In general the upper levels yielded more than the lower levels and the distribution is indicated in tables. Six species were determined, but eight genera and three families had representatives that could not be specifically determined. The frequency of each identification was indicated, and these are of interest because few fishes have ever been recorded from Yap. Again the only other aquatic vertebrate found was the turtle.

Except for coral, molluscs were the most abundant organic remains; 167 species were identified of which 52 were bivalves and 115 univalves (including *Nautilus*). The distribution by site and depth is shown in tables. The stratigraphic distribution of species indicated a constancy of food habits.

Fleming[45] discussed the use of the stratigraphical succession in a marine fauna to establish a chronology in New Zealand. He said that differences in species of mollusca in successive midden groups that had suggested changes in the distribution of the tohemanga = toheroa (*Amphidesma ventricosum*) could have been due to different food habits of the successive peoples, but the status of the toheroa is still changing on modern beaches. Decrease in the size of molluscs in more recent middens suggested the silting of estuaries, but no indication had been found of local changes in molluscan faunae comparable with those of the Yoldia and Littorina seas of the Baltic. Seal remains, however, suggested a more extensive prehistoric distribution than at present.

The first period of New Zealand prehistory is known as the Archaic Phase of New Zealand Eastern Polynesian culture.[46] This period was originally known as the *Moa*-hunter culture; *Moa*-hunter sites have been shown by radiocarbon dating to range from the eleventh to the fifteenth century. These sites commonly have shell middens and artifacts include bait-hooks, stone and bone lure-hooks and barracouta harpoon points. Ornaments found include shells and teeth from the sperm whale, porpoise and shark (*Carcharadon*). An excavation of a *Moa*-hunter site at Sarah's Gully on the Coromandel Peninsula in the North Island of New Zealand yielded abundant seal remains.[47] At the coastal site of Pounawea, which according to radiocarbon dating was first occupied before AD 1140, the diet at first consisted principally of *Moa*, with some other birds, and fish, seal and whale, but few shell-fish.[48] By AD 1450 the *Moa* had become less plentiful, and more fish and shell-fish were being eaten. Finally by AD 1660 the *Moa* had become very scarce (as a result of continued killing by the Maoris) and the diet consisted principally of shell-fish, fish, seal and small birds. The scarcity of the *Moa* caused many sites to be abandoned, new settlements being established near the new source of food on the coast. Some coastal sites, e.g. on False Island, were almost wholly connected with fishing. A large midden dated AD 1480±50 contained great quantities of fish bones, as well as mussel, paua and large cockle shells.

When European contact was established in the eighteenth century the Classic Maori phase of New Zealand Eastern Polynesian culture was dominant.[48] Sites of this period have yielded whalebone weapons, metal fish-hooks with and without barbs, more highly developed barracouta points, and lures with hooks, often in the shape of small fish. Again there were whale and shark-tooth ornaments; and there were trumpets made from a *Charonia* shell. Fortified *pa* sites are common in this period but it is not certain whether or not these extend back into the archaic period. Green[49] in a survey of *Moa*-hunter sites on the Coromandel coast said that they had mussel, limpet, periwinkle and paua shells in that order, along with bones of seal, whale and a variety of birds in addition to the *Moa*. The middens of *pa* sites on the other hand contain primarily pipi and cockle shells.

Australia, to prehistorians, is the least-known continent. At most, this vast area has been covered by five excavations of chronological or cultural significance.[50] In the excavation of a rock shelter at Fromm's Landing on the Lower Murray river, South Australia, eleven distinct levels were encountered.[51] The tenth of these has been dated by the C^{14} method as being 4850 ± 100 years old. Fish bones were found in most levels, but in only two instances was it possible to distinguish species. These were *Oligorus macquariensis* (Murray cod) which was found in several levels, and the broken spine of *Bathytoshea* (Sting ray). Four bone muduks, thought to have been used as fish gorges, were found in levels five to seven. Mollusc shells were found at all levels, and there was no significant change of species with depth. The following aquatic molluscs were identified: univalves, *Notopala hanleyi*, *Lenameria tenuistriata* (*waterhousei* and *confluens*), and *Plotiopsis tetrica*; bivalves, *Corbiculina angasi*, *Velusinio ambiguus* and *Alathyria jacksoni*, the last two of these being fresh-water mussels common in the Murray today.

Finally, in 1960, the excavation of a rock shelter was commenced at Seelands on the banks of the Clarence river in northern New South Wales. Five levels down to a depth of four feet six inches were encountered and a radiocarbon date[52] of level II gave the result AD 1040 ± 80. The fish bones, vertebrae (diameter relatively small, e.g. about 3–8 mm and often compressed laterally or dorso-ventrally), ribs, branchiostegal rays, and a few jaws were submitted by the present author to Mr G. P. Whitley of the Australian Museum in Sydney. He reported that owing to their fragmentary nature and the lack of a representative collection it was on the whole impossible to identify species. There was, however, a movable fin-ray from a catfish, and three other bones were probably from catfish. There are two species of catfish in NSW today. The shells were submitted to Dr D. F. McMichael at the same museum. He reported that there were five species of aquatic molluscs, all bivalves. There were two fresh-water mussels (*Cucumerunio novaehollandiae* and *Velesunio ambiguus*) both found in the Clarence today. The others were marine types, although the sea is at least thirty miles away, including the common pipi (*Plebidonax deltoides*), well known to have been eaten by the aborigines; a ship worm probably belonging to the genus *Nausitora*; and finally a member of the family *Gariidae*.

CONCLUSIONS

1. There has been a tendency for all animal remains to be neglected, and 'fish' remains

have probably received the least attention. This is probably mainly due to the difficulty of identifying species: even experienced people require a full collection of comparative specimens which takes a long time to acquire, especially in a new area such as Australia, in which there are many species.

2. Diet helps to indicate the cultural attainment of a people. Fishes, and other aquatic animals, have apparently been important as food from earliest times. In some collecting communities with a riverine or maritime orientation fish formed the main source of food. Shell-fish were probably the first aquatic animals to be collected, and remains of shell-fish on their own probably indicate a primitive people with a low level of attainment.

3. Shells provide a useful raw material, and the artifacts of some cultures are based almost entirely on shell.

4. The identity of fish species can indicate: (a) the extent to which different fishing methods were developed; (b) zoological distribution; and (c) changes in climatic as well as geological environment.

5. The identity of different bones of the body can indicate practices such as fish-drying, in which the head is removed.

6. The study of fish remains in future is likely to depend more and more on specialized knowledge possibly involving microscopical and chemical techniques.*

* A method has recently been evolved in South Africa to obtain a relative dating of shell middens.[54] Shells of *Mytilus perna* from stratified coastal middens were dissolved in dilute acetic acid, and the ratio of conchyolin (horn-like substance) to calcium carbonate in the shell was estimated. This ratio was found to decrease with the increasing age of the shells, and could therefore be used to indicate the relative age of the middens. The method was applied to Later Stone and Iron Age deposits on the Natal coast, and the results obtained were consistent with the relative dating deduced from stratification. The method is apparently capable of distinguishing between middens of different age providing the soil environments are identical. This is important because clearly an acid soil will remove calcium carbonate, and the conchyolin may decay more rapidly in some conditions than others.

ACKNOWLEDGEMENT

I wish to thank my colleagues in the History and Zoology departments of the University of New Zealand for their helpful advice during the preparation of this article.

REFERENCES

1 GOODRICH, E. S. 1909. *Cyclostomes and Fishes*, Part IX of LANKESTER, SIR RAY (ed.), Treatise on Zoology, London
2 NORMAN, J. R. 1953. *Fishes* in List of British Vertebrates, British Museum (Natural History)
3 WELLS, A. L. 1958. *The Observers Book of Sea Fishes*, London
4 ROMER, A. S. 1941. *Man and the Vertebrates*, 3rd ed., Chicago
5 YOUNG, J. Z. 1954. *The Life of Vertebrates*, Oxford
6 ZEUNER, F. E. 1958. *Dating the Past*, 4th ed., London
7 FITTER, R. S. R. 1959. *The Ark in our Midst*, London
8 RYDER, M. L. 1960. *Animal Bones in Archaeology*, Wakefield and London (on microfilm: Micro Methods Ltd.; originals in the possession of the Thoresby Society, Leeds)
9 DANIEL, J. F. 1934. *The Elasmobranch Fishes*, Berkeley, Calif.
10 GOODRICH, E. S. 1908. *Proc. Zool. Soc.*, 751
11 KYLE, H. M. 1926. *The Biology of Fishes*, London

12 GREGORY, W. K. 1959. *Fish Skulls*, Laurel, Florida (originally published 1933 in *Trans. Am. Phil. Soc. 33*)

13 Personal communication

14 ANDERSON, H. and JORGENSEN, J. B. 1960. *Stain. Technol. 35*, 91–95

15 MOSS, M. L. and POSNER, A. S. 1960. *Nature, 188*, 1037

16 CLARK, J. G. D. 1948. *Ant. J. 28*, 45–81

17 ⸺ 1952. *Prehistoric Europe: The Economic Basis*, London

18 LEAKEY, L. S. B. 1961. *Nature 189*, 649f.

19 CLARK, J. G. D. 1954. *Star Carr*, Cambridge

20 BRAIDWOOD, R. J. and REED, C. A. 1957. The achievement and early consequence of food production, *Cold Spr. Harb. Symp. Quant. Biol. 22*, 19–31

21 HILZHEIMER, M. 1941. Animal remains from Tell Asmar, *Studies in Ancient Oriental Civilization*, no. 20

22 THOMPSON, D'ARCY W. 1947. *A Glossary of Greek Fishes*, Oxford

23 CHILDE, V. G. 1936. *Man Makes Himself*, London

24 LORTET, L. C. and GAILLARD, C. 1907. *Arch. Mus. Lyon 9*, Mém. 2

25 BROGAN, O. 1936. *J. Rom. Stud. 26*, 195–222

26 ROSE, H. J. 1933. *Ibid. 23*, 46–63

27 JOPE, M. 1955. *Ulster J. Arch.* 3rd ser., *18*, 77–81

28 BRUCE-MITFORD, R. L. S. (ed.) 1956. *Recent Archaeological Excavations in Britain*, London

29 JOPE, M. 1954. *Ulster J. Arch.* 3rd ser., *17*, 103–63

30 RYDER, M. L. 1959. *Agric. Hist. Rev. 7*, 1–5

31 FOWLER, J. T. (ed.). 1918. Memorials of Fountains, III, *Surtees Soc.* 130

32 YOUNG, C. M. 1960. *Oysters*, London

33 RYDER, M. L. 1961. In OWEN, D. E., Kirkstall Abbey Excavations, 1955–59. *Pub. Thoresby Society*, Leeds

34 ⸺ 1962a. In BELLAMY, C. V., Excavations at Pontefract Priory, *Yorks Arch. J.*

35 ⸺ 1962b. In WENHAM, L. P., Excavations in Petergate, York, *Ibid.*

36 ⸺ 1962c. In HURST, J. G., Excavations at Wharram Percy, *Medieval Arch.*

37 CLARK, J. G. D. 1947. *Antiquity, 21*, 84–104

38 ⸺ 1946. *Proc. Prehist. Soc. 12*, 12–48

39 GOODWIN, A. J. H. 1946. *Antiquity 20*, 134–41

40 MONGAIT, A. 1959. *Archaeology in the USSR*, Moscow; 1961. Harmondsworth

41 FAIRSERVIS, W. A. 1959. *The Origins of Oriental Civilization*, New York

42 GIFFORD, E. W. 1951. Archaeological Excavations in Fiji, *Anth. Recs. 13*, 3, Berkeley, Calif.

43 ⸺ and SHUTLER, D., JR. 1956. Archaeological Excavations in New Caledonia, *Anth. Recs. 18*, 1

44 GIFFORD, W. S. and GIFFORD, D. S. 1959. Archaeological Excavations at Yap, *Ibid.* 2

45 FLEMING, C. A. 1953. Materials for a Recent Geochronology of New Zealand, *Report of 7th Sci. Congress, Roy. Soc. N.Z.*

46 GOLSON, J. 1959. Culture Change in Prehistoric New Zealand, in FREEMAN, J. D. and GEDDES, W. R. (eds.), *Anthropology of the South Seas*, New Plymouth

47 ⸺ 1959. Excavations on the Coromandel Peninsula New Zealand, *N.Z. Arch. Assoc. News Letter* 2, (2), 13–18

48 LOCKERBIE, L. 1959. From Moa-Hunter to Classic Maori in Southern New Zealand, in FREEMAN, J. D. and GEDDES, W. R. (eds.), *op. cit.* [46]

49 GREEN, R. 1959. A Survey of Sites on the Coromandel Coast, *N.Z. Arch. Assoc. News Letter* 2 (2), 23

50 MULVANEY, D. J. 1959. *Nature 184*, 918

51 ⸺ 1960. *Proc. Roy. Soc. Victoria 72* (2), 53–85

52 McBRIDE, I. 1961. *Antiquity 35*, 312–313

53 McMICHAEL, D. F. 1961. *J. Malac. Soc. Austral.* no. 5, 51

54 SCHOUTE-VANNECK, C. A. 1960. *S. Afr. J. Sci. 56*, 67–70

NOTE

The address of Dr Ryder is now: Animal Breeding Research Organization Field Laboratory, Dryden Mains, Roslin, Midlothianshire.

31 Non-Marine Mollusca and Archaeology

B. W. SPARKS

THE STUDY OF THE PAST DISTRIBUTIONS, occurrences and associations of non-marine Mollusca in the Quaternary period has two main aims: first, to find out as much as possible about such Mollusca for their own sake, and second, to use the Mollusca to determine the age of the beds in which they were found and the natural conditions prevailing during their deposition. The very fact that the first aim exists indicates that knowledge is incomplete and that, therefore, the second aim cannot be fully realized. In addition, the incompleteness of knowledge about modern Mollusca limits the inferences that may be drawn from the accumulations of dead Mollusca found in deposits. Further work on modern Mollusca, in the identification of species in the juvenile state and on their ecology in particular, might be expected to illuminate the past, while studies on past Mollusca are necessary to understand some aspects of present distributions. The position is exactly similar when one considers studies of non-marine Mollusca made in conjunction with other studies, for example, Quaternary botany, archaeology, or geomorphology, because it is not only a question of interpreting, for example, the archaeology in the light of the Mollusca, but of gleaning information from the archaeology concerning the distribution and occurrence of Mollusca at different periods.

Mollusca are useful because of their wide distribution, their preservation in a variety of deposits, their large numbers and their comparative freedom from human influences, at least when compared with such vulnerable larger animals as the vertebrates. They prefer habitats with a sufficiency of lime for building their shells and, although different species have different degrees of tolerance of non-calcareous habitats, only one species, *Zonitoides excavatus*, is at present a calcifuge, though it does not seem to have been one always in the past.[5] Thus, the richer the base-status of the locality, whether it be land or freshwater, the richer the fauna generally is. In non-calcareous localities not only is the number of species restricted, but the shells produced are thinner and hence less adapted to preservation. Furthermore, the shells are more readily weathered and destroyed by the acid deposits formed in such localities. Provided, then, that the district is not one of acid rocks, soil and vegetation, Mollusca may be expected in a wide variety of river, lake, marsh, woodland and open-land deposits.

Preservation varies enormously. Although the shells will be preserved in well-aerated oxidized deposits, they are affected by leaching. Most of them are very thin and hence even though the shell itself may not be destroyed, the fine detail of ornamentation, often a diagnostic feature, may suffer severely. Percolating water may precipitate calcium carbonate and, even though this may not cement the shells into the deposit, it may encrust and obscure features of the shell. The differences between the degrees of

preservation are so great that Quaternary faunas as old as that from the organic parts of
the Cromer Forest Bed are sometimes far better preserved than Postglacial specimens
from superficial deposits on Chalk downland.

If the shell survives at all, its shape is likely to be preserved accurately simply because
of the rigid form of the shell. In certain sediments crushing does occur, especially of
bivalve shells and particularly the large ones such as the species of *Unio* and *Anodonta*.
Small closely coiled gastropods, such as *Vertigo* and *Vallonia* spp. (Fig. 47), are probably
the least susceptible to crushing. But even though crushing may remove a whorl or two
it often leaves the first two or three whorls intact and the species may very often be
identified from that part of the shell. Again the large numbers of Mollusca preserved
usually means that not all the specimens will be broken and, even though broken and
juvenile specimens are unidentifiable, there will be a residue of unbroken identifiable
specimens.

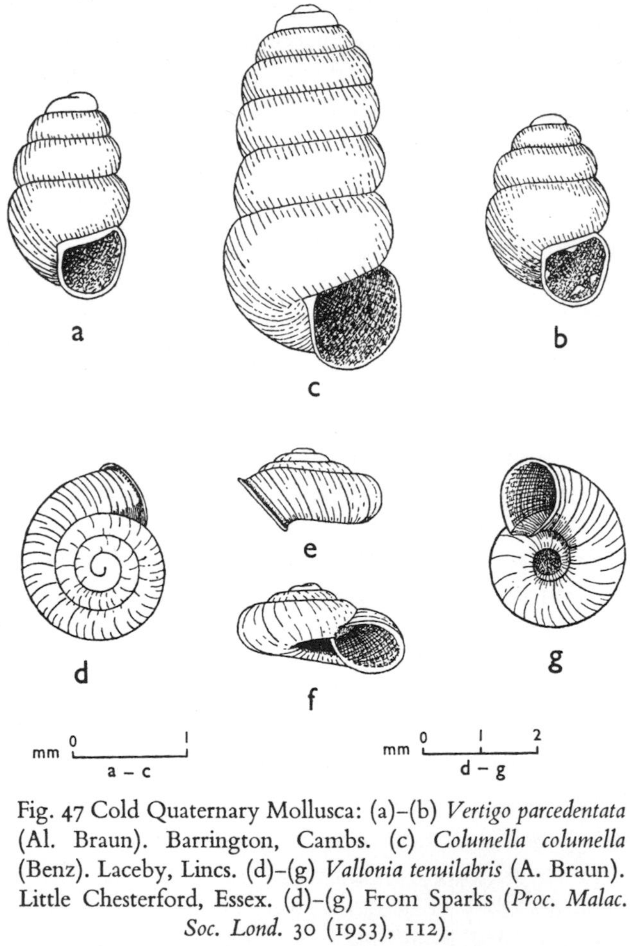

Fig. 47 Cold Quaternary Mollusca: (a)–(b) *Vertigo parcedentata*
(Al. Braun). Barrington, Cambs. (c) *Columella columella*
(Benz). Laceby, Lincs. (d)–(g) *Vallonia tenuilabris* (A. Braun).
Little Chesterford, Essex. (d)–(g) From Sparks (*Proc. Malac.
Soc. Lond.* 30 (1953), 112).

It is not completely true to say that Mollusca, being small and lowly creatures, are not
subject to human interference, because the Postglacial spread of widespread alteration
and cultivation of the earth's surface by man seems to have wrought greater changes in

Mollusca faunas than occur from one interglacial to another, largely because the micro-climate near the surface has generally become drier. Yet it is probably safe to assume that, on the one hand, Mollusca have occupied most of their climatic and ecological range and, on the other, that these ranges have not been so reduced by human persecution as to be unrepresentative and, therefore, useless in reconstructing conditions from past distributions of Mollusca.

With these introductory remarks made, it seems possible to discuss the use of non-marine Mollusca in archaeology under the three headings of their value as indicators of age, climate and local conditions.

MOLLUSCA AS INDICATORS OF THE AGE OF A DEPOSIT

The idea that certain species of Mollusca might be usable to date deposits of Quaternary age was probably inherited from the use of zone fossils in geology. The ideal zone fossil is one either with a very wide distribution, such as a floating marine creature, or one widely dispersed after death, often by flotation, such as an ammonite. Rapidly evolving species are also required so that the length of time it is possible for an animal to represent is limited. None of these three conditions is met by Quaternary non-marine Mollusca. They are far from widely dispersed, being, on the contrary, controlled in their distribution by local conditions. Further, it seems practically impossible to detect evolutionary changes in non-marine Mollusca in the Quaternary period—at least that is my own experience mainly with British species.

Certain species are or appear to be limited to one particular horizon. For example, *Viviparus diluvianus* seems to be confined in England to the Hoxne Interglacial, *Viviparus glacialis* to the Cromer Interglacial and earlier beds, and *Nematurella runtoniana* (Fig. 48e, f) to the Cromer Interglacial. But each species is known from very few localities, two of them from only two localities, so that whether they are really as confined in their distribution as they seem to be awaits further discoveries of older Quaternary deposits. Such deposits need to be dated independently for obvious reasons. Some idea of the possibilities may be gathered from the fact that in the Netherlands *Viviparus diluvianus* also occurs in the much earlier Tiglian horizon, so that, in view of the proximity of the two countries, it may well turn up at this level in England when more deposits are known.

An extension of the idea of zone fossils is to be found in the linking of particular types of fauna with certain phases of the Pleistocene. The clearest example of this is in the attribution of the 'loess' fauna to the cold period associated with the Last Glaciation. The main features of this type of fauna are a very high frequency of *Pupilla muscorum* associated with *Columella columella* (Fig. 47c) and *Vertigo parcedentata* (Fig. 47a ,b). These occur with marsh species, such as *Succinea arenaria* or *oblonga*, species characteristic of small bodies of water, for example *Planorbis leucostoma* and sometimes with *Pisidium obtusale lapponicum* and *Pisidium vincentianum*. On the Continent *Vallonia tenuilabris* (Fig. 47d–g) is also commonly found. Of course, all the species may not occur in a single deposit, as the fauna will vary somewhat with the local conditions. Probably the first five or six examples of this fauna to be found in Britain proved to be Last Glaciation in age, but

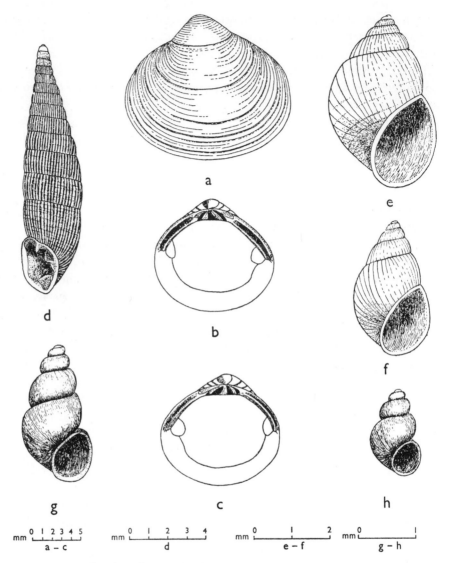

Fig. 48 Interglacial Mollusca: (a)–(c) *Corbicula fluminalis* (Müller). Swanscombe, Kent. (d) *Clausilia pumila*, C. Pfeiffer. Barnwell, Cambs. (e) *Nematurella runtoniana*, Sandberger. Little Oakley, Essex. (f) *Ditto*, ditto. West Runton, Norfolk. (g)–(h) *Belgrandia marginata* (Michaud). Bobbitshole, Ipswich, Suffolk.

examples were later found at Little Chesterford in Essex and Thriplow in Cambridgeshire, which are unlikely to be as recent and more likely to represent a period of cold climate associated with the previous Gipping glaciation. The same has proved true on the Continent: faunas of this type, but earlier in date than the Last Glaciation, have been found in the Netherlands, Germany and Czechoslovakia. It is clear that the fauna is an indication of distinctive local conditions, which were repeated in the Pleistocene, the apparent relation with the Last Glaciation being due to the fact that so many more deposits of this age are preserved. It is still true, however, that when such a fauna is found the odds are that the deposit is Last Glaciation in age, but the inference can no longer be fully relied on.

It is generally unsafe to attempt to correlate deposits by the nature of their assemblages of Mollusca, except perhaps within short distances within one river basin. For example, four or five fossiliferous sites are known in the highest terrace at Cambridge within a distance of about four miles. Certain features of the faunas recur from site to site and within the same area it ought to be possible to link in any future discoveries of the same type of Last Interglacial fauna. But to correlate on the basis of Mollusca faunas from one river basin to another is an extremely uncertain operation. An extremely interesting and important application of the numerical study of Mollusca to the interpretation of the subaerial deposits of the North Downs in Kent, especially the Late Glacial deposits, is at present being made by Dr M. P. Kerney, of Imperial College, London, who has shown that it is possible to recognize definite periods of the Postglacial in that area by the Mollusca contained in the beds.

Another possibility, the use of percentage of extinct species present as a guide to the age of a deposit, fails because of the comparatively small differences in such percentages and because the variations between deposits of a single age are so great. Of the species of Mollusca known from the Cromer Interglacial approximately 21% are now extinct: for the Hoxne Interglacial the figure is about 17%, for the Ipswich Interglacial it is about 15% and for the early part of the Postglacial it is about 5%. These figures are obtained by lumping faunas. When individual faunas are compared it is found, for example, that the Hoxne deposit itself has no extinct species, while some rich Postglacial deposits may contain 4 or 5% of extinct species.

Perhaps the clearest examples of snails being introduced at certain definite periods are to be found in the Postglacial period. It has long been known[3] that many of our most common snails are late in their introduction into the British fauna and their presence or absence may point to a Postglacial age and sometimes to a particular part of the Post-glacial period. *Pomatias elegans*, a species characteristic of dry, friable calcareous soils, occurs in large numbers in many Postglacial deposits, but is only known by isolated fragments from two or three interglacial deposits. In abundance, then, it is fairly safe to conclude that it indicates a warm part of Postglacial time. The two largest British land snails, *Helix pomatia* and *Helix aspersa*, are nearly everywhere indicative of a date no earlier than Roman except that the latter is reputed to occur earlier in the south-western peninsula. *Helicella virgata*, *Helicella caperata* and *Helicella gigaxii* are all late. The first is reputed to occur early in the Postglacial in the south-west but elsewhere to be absent from Roman deposits: it is known from a few interglacial deposits but such could probably be differentiated by other features of the mollusc faunas. The second, *Helicella caperata*, only occurs late in Postglacial time as a rule, though it has been found in deposits which are probably Bronze Age or earlier in dry valleys near Hitchin, while it is known fossil in south-west England. The third, *Helicella gigaxii*, is known fossil in south-west England but is only common in post-Roman times. *Monacha cantiana*, which is very common on cultivated land at the present time, is probably even later and Kennard[3] suggested a Norman age for its introduction. Many of these species, which are largely or entirely confined to the Postglacial, are xerophilous and have been found mainly in subaerial deposits at the foot of chalk slopes, in dry valleys and on the Chalk itself, often in association with archaeological remains. Deposits of this type of interglacial age are virtually unknown, largely because either glacial or preglacial denudation has removed them or because they have had any Mollusca weathered out of them. This may explain the very rare occurrence of some species in interglacials and their Postglacial abundance, but it does not explain a complete absence in interglacials because other xerophiles have become incorporated in river deposits in small numbers, e.g. *Pupilia muscorum* and *Helicella itala*. There are other species in the Postglacial period which do not everywhere survive the early part of that period and, where they persist later, do so in greatly reduced numbers. In eastern England *Lauria anglica, Acanthinula lamellata, Acicula fusca, Vertigo substriata, Vertigo parcedentata* (or *genesii*), *Vertigo angustior, Vertigo moulinsiana, Vertigo alpestris* and *Ena montana* all fall into this class and indicate an early Postglacial date.

Non-marine Mollusca, then, may sometimes be used for giving approximate ideas of dating, though rarely is the indication precise and often it is non-existent. The more that these creatures are studied carefully, especially in conjunction with the archaeology of the Postglacial period, the greater will become our knowledge of the spread across England or disappearance locally of certain species and hence the more exact the indication of dates to be gleaned from the snails in other deposits.

MOLLUSCA AS INDICATORS OF CLIMATE

Most non-marine Mollusca have a wide distribution. For example *Vallonia pulchella* is known from the Ahaggar region of the central Sahara, from most of Europe up to and within the Arctic Circle in Scandinavia, from much of northern Asia and also from North America. Such a distribution is probably an extreme one, but commonly one reads that the species occurs from Sicily to the North Cape and over most of Europe and western Asia. On the face of it animals of this sort offer little hope of drawing useful climatic deductions, but the position is not as hopeless as it seems to be. The problem can be approached in two ways: either by considering the presence or absence of certain key species or by considering the overall composition of the fauna.

Certain species occur only in cold deposits. These have mainly been mentioned in considering the loess type of fauna earlier in this chapter. They are *Columella columella, Vertigo parcedentata* (Fig. 47), *Pisidium vincentianum* and *Pisidium obtusale lapponicum*. On the other hand there are species which are confined to the interglacials and to the warmer parts of the Postglacial. Most famous of these is the bivalve *Corbicula fluminalis* (Fig. 48 a–c), which at present occurs in the Nile and thence eastwards to Kashmir, but there are other useful species as well. *Pisidium clessini* (= *astartoides*, Fig. 49j), *Theodoxus serratiliniformis* (= *cantianus*, Fig. 49a, b) and *Helicella crayfordensis* (Fig. 49c–e) are not known living but may be presumed southern from their occurrence only in association with true interglacial faunas. *Belgrandia marginata* (Fig. 48g, h) now known only from a few localities in the south of France; *Helicella striata* and *Clausilia pumila* (Fig. 48d), south-east

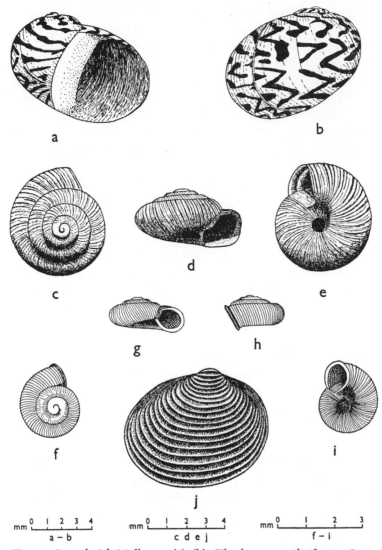

Fig. 49 Interglacial Mollusca: (a)–(b) *Theodoxus serratiliniformis*, Geyer.
Swanscombe, Kent. (c)–(e) *Helicella crayfordensis*, Jackson. Grantchester,
Cambs. (f)–(i) *Vallonia enniensis*, Gredler. West Runton, Norfolk. (j)
Pisidium clessini, Neumayr. Swanscombe, Kent. (f)–(i) From Sparks (*op. cit.*).

European species, which spread north-westwards in interglacial periods; *Vallonia
enniensis* (Fig. 49f–i), another species known from interglacials and now found mainly
in the southern half of Europe; all these are more southern species now extinct in
Britain. In addition many of the British species reach their northern limits in Britain
and in Denmark or the very south of Scandinavia on the continent. Among these are
Acicula fuscza, *Azeca goodalli* (not found in Scandinavia), *Helicodonta obvoluta* (northern
limit in Holstein), *Ena montana* (reaches southern Sweden), *Vertigo moulinsiana* (northern
limit in Denmark) and *Truncatellina cylindrica* (extends as far as Oslo). The presence of

these species indicates climatic conditions no cooler than those now prevailing in Britain.

Depending on the presence or absence of species such as these listed above, the climate can be classed as truly interglacial or cold and steppe-like. But even here there are certain difficulties. In the case of the cold species of Mollusca very little is known about their survival into periods of warmer climate. By analogy with plants one might expect them to linger in certain places from which they would eventually be ousted by the spread of more thermophilous species in interglacial or Postglacial time. *Vertigo parcedentata* seems to have done this, for it is known (at least under the name of *Vertigo genesii*) from a warm Postglacial deposit near Takeley in Essex. The fauna should, then, be judged as a whole and not by the presence or absence of small numbers of key species. Again, all such reconstructions of past climates and local conditions from biological evidence rely on the assumption that species do not change their ecological requirements. There is little evidence from Mollusca of such changes, but an exception must be made of *Discus ruderatus*, a Boreo-Alpine form which is known in interglacial and warm Postglacial deposits, but not in the cold deposits in which it might be expected. The opposite is true of *Pisidium vincentianum*, found in cold deposits, but now living in south-east Europe and Asia.

The presence of the southern species is an indication of reasonably warm climatic conditions, but again care needs to be exercised. In the first half of an interglacial period or in the Postglacial period, Mollusca presumably will not immigrate until the climate suits them, so that there will be a lag reflecting the rate of immigration. Southern species may, however, be found in the deposits from the second half of an interglacial for a number of reasons. They may survive in less favourable climates for a while before they die out in the area concerned. They may survive in favourable habitats, where the micro-climate allows, even though the regional climate has deteriorated. Limestone slopes facing the south come to mind as most likely to provide highly favourable micro-climates. Mollusc faunas, after all, really reflect small-scale variations of environment, although one tends to interpret them in more regional terms. Finally it is very difficult to distinguish in deposits between contemporary and derived shells. The shells are too fragile to stand much battering, but such limited derivation as the washing out of a bed of river alluvium after a few millennia with the redeposition of the included Mollusca is sufficient to confuse the climatic interpretation. This is known to have happened with pollen and the possibility of it happening with Mollusca cannot be eliminated.

More may be learned about the nature of the climate from a careful study of the Mollusca. For this purpose the frequency of different species must be known and this requires the extraction of Mollusca from a bulk sample of the material concerned rather than their selection by eye from the material in the field. Owing to variations in size and colour-contrast between the shells and the matrix containing them, selection by eye gives a very distorted picture of the fauna. Hence washing followed by sorting of the sample under a low-power microscope is required both for the deduction of the climate and the local conditions indicated by the fauna.[7]

As a rule it is not possible to consider the variations of a single species through a deposit as an indication of climate, because the local conditions prevailing during de-position rarely remained sufficiently stable for the species of Mollusca to reflect solely climatic change. As a result, it is necessary to form the Mollusca into distributional groups to offset local ecological changes.[6-9] About four such groupings suffice and they are based upon present distributions in Scandinavia:

(a) Species reaching to or almost to the Arctic Circle
(b) Species reaching approximately 63°N
(c) Species reaching 60°–61°N, i.e. approximately the limit of the oak
(d) Species only reaching the very south of Scandinavia or being confined to the Continental mainland

A model distribution of these groups through an interglacial period would show their successive appearance and disappearance in reverse order, the peaks of the warmer groups probably occurring a little after the middle of the interglacial. The distribution of the Mollusca is somewhat asymmetrical with respect to the climatic optimum, partly because appearance depends on the rate of immigration, while disappearance depends on ability to withstand deteriorating conditions. It is clear, however, that the periods of colder climate at the beginning and end of interglacials are characterized by highly tolerant faunas, while the middles have still a majority of species of such type, although less tolerant species are present in varying, usually small, amounts.

In practice, acquaintance with such distributions, allied with a consideration of such factors as the number of species, and the dominance or otherwise of the fauna by one or two species, and the relative proportions of land and freshwater species, would enable an experienced fossil malacologist to make a shrewd estimate of the climate. The position is, however, too complex to allow a hard and fast rule whereby simple proportions of the fauna can be used to infer the climate directly.

MOLLUSCA AS INDICATORS OF LOCAL CONDITIONS

Just as the distribution of Mollusca is exceedingly broad, so often is the range of habitat in which a given Mollusc is found. It is true that certain of them are restricted, for example *Ancylus fluviatilis* is only characteristic of streams with a stony bottom and an absence of mud, while *Pomatias elegans* is more or less confined to friable soils in calcareous districts, but many have a wide range of either land or freshwater habitats. This leads to a considerable degree of uncertainty at times in inferring the local conditions represented by a fauna. If Mollusca with very restricted distributions are present they probably define the local conditions fairly precisely, but with fossil assemblages the possibility of mixed faunas is always present. That this happens is easy to see for example in the case of river deposits containing a small proportion of dry-land Mollusca. It is easy to infer the washing in and transporting of the latter by the stream. When one finds, on the other hand, a predominantly marsh fauna, together with *Pomatias elegans*, *Vallonia costata*, and *Carychium tridentatum*, the inference of local conditions becomes more difficult. Unless the ecology of species has changed—and if one makes that assumption too easily the basis of fossil work disappears—such mixtures must imply two environments in close juxtaposition. But is it to be assumed that the juxtaposition is spatial or that it is temporal? Mollusca vary so much with small differences of vegetation and elevation that a mixed marsh and dry-land fauna of the type suggested above might be interpreted as meaning dry calcareous hummocks projecting through a marsh. A consideration of the minor relief might suggest whether such an idea is plausible or not. Alternatively, there may have been a marsh, in which calcareous muds were deposited and which dried out sufficiently for its invasion by dry-loving species. There would then be a mixture of faunas more or less at one level. It might be possible to tell whether this happened by taking samples above and below the mixed horizon—assuming, of course, a fair thickness of deposits, which is by no means always present.

A good example of the mixed type of faunas representing spatial variations in the detail of environment is provided once more by many of the cold loess faunas. These usually contain a very high percentage of the xerophilous species, *Pupilla muscorum*, in association with smaller numbers of species characteristic of marshes and poor bodies of water, such as *Succinea* spp., and *Planorbis leucostoma*. Such a mixture is probably best interpreted as representing a set of hummocks of, at least partly, wind-blown silt separated by marshy slacks.

But there are many deposits the faunas of which are less readily interpretable because of the range of possible conditions. However, although many species have a range of habitat,[1,2] it commonly appears that if one were searching for living specimens one particular sort of habitat would be more likely to yield specimens than others. If it is assumed that this habitat is indicated by the species concerned, it becomes possible to start to interpret local conditions by forming ecological groups of species, comparable with the distributional groups outlined above, and studying their percentage variations.[7-9] As with the latter groups, if some such assumptions are not made, it is hardly possible to start serious work on the interpretation of fossil groupings of Mollusca. One hopes that a predominance of Mollusca of a particular group, made up of different species, is cumulative evidence of a particular form of environment. It may not be, but the chances are that it is.

The groups of freshwater Mollusca used have been:

(a) Slum species, i.e. those which will stand exceedingly poor water conditions, such as poor aeration, periodic drying, large temperature changes consequent upon the small size of the body of water. Only certain species can stand such conditions, although such species may be found elsewhere.

(b) Catholic species, i.e. those which are found in practically every type of freshwater environments except the worst 'slums'.

(c) Ditch species: a term designed to cover those species which prefer plant-rich slow streams.

(d) Moving water species, i.e. those more commonly found in larger bodies of water, streams, or ponds, where movement is assumed either by currents or by winds. The bodies of water are 'larger' and 'moving' by mollusc standards.

With land Mollusca it may be possible to separate such groups as marsh and associated species, xerophiles, open-habitat species and 'woodland' species, the last being a vague term designed to cover rather retiring Mollusca and those commonly found in damp scrubland.

Such groupings have been used and checked in several ways:

(a) By the consistency of the results. For example, high percentages of 'slum' fresh-water Mollusca are usually associated with a predominance of marsh and associated species among the land Mollusca. Also, one begins to see recurring groupings of the species of large genera, for example with the small bivalve *Pisidium*, the combination of *casertanum* with *personatum* seems to point to slums, the combination of *subtruncatum*, *milium* and *nitidum* is a typical catholic one, while *amnicum* (possibly with *clessini*) and *henslowanum* and *moitessierianum* is more characteristic of moving water.

(b) By inferring local conditions from the form of the deposit and checking that the Mollusca agree. This is most easy to do in Postglacial deposits, for example alluvial valley fills, where marginal samples differ from central samples in the land/freshwater ratios and in the percentages of the subdivisions of each group.

(c) Most important, by comparison with the conclusions drawn from the study of macroscopic plant remains taken from the same samples. Very close agreement has been reached mainly from the study of Pleistocene freshwater and marsh deposits for it is in these that plant remains are well preserved. Many archaeologically important deposits are not of this type but were formed on dry land. Nevertheless, the fact that the conclusions drawn from Mollusca have been cross-checked by several methods gives more confidence in the interpretation of the Mollusca of those deposits where no such checks are available.

CONCLUSION

Mollusca may therefore be used in deriving conclusions about climatic and local conditions and less certainly about the age of deposits. Their abundance and comparative freedom from human interference make them very useful for percentage variation studies. The interpretations are probably most accurate when a deposit is thick enough to show variation through time, but even single samples yield something of value. It must be remembered, however, that human beings usually take a wider view of environment than snails, so that the conclusions drawn from the latter are valid only for small sections of the human environment.

REFERENCES

1 BOYCOTT, A. E. 1934. *J. Ecol.* 22, 1–38
2 —— 1936. *J. Anim. Ecol.* 5, 116–86
3 KENNARD, A. S. 1923. *Proc. Malac. Soc., Lond.* 15, 241–59
4 ELLIS, A. E. 1926. *British Snails*, Oxford
5 KERNEY, M. P. 1959. *Proc. Geol. Assoc.* 70, 322–37
6 SPARKS, B. W. 1957. *Phil. Trans. Roy. Soc. Lond.*, B, 241, 33–44
7 —— 1961. *Proc. Linn. Soc. Lond.* 172, 71–80
8 —— and LAMBERT, C. A. 1961. *Proc. Malac. Soc. Lond.* 34, 302–15
9 —— and WEST, R. G. 1959. *Eiszeitalter und Gegenwart* 10, 123–43

SECTION III MAN

32 *The Biology of Earlier Human Populations*

DON BROTHWELL

PERHAPS THE OLDEST of all specialist fields associated with archaeology is that concerned with the analysis of the remains of man himself. Oddly enough, however, it is a field which seems to cause more unhappiness to the excavator than interest, especially to those who are unfortunate enough (they think) to come across the remains of many bodies. In the Mediterranean area, Egyptologists have shown themselves to be the most calm and collected in the face of large numbers of burials, and as early as 1910 large and detailed monographs were appearing on East African material.[6] Excavators in Britain have certainly not behaved so commendably, and for example, as I have pointed out in a recent study of Yorkshire Bronze Age skeletons,[3] many skeletons have been lost, badly stored or partly thrown away.

The various articles concerned with the remains of man included in this book show clearly that the biology of earlier populations is by no means purely a matter of measuring skulls and computing indices. Even in death, there is a considerable range of data which can be obtained from the close study of parts of the human body, including the determination of the morphological affinities of a group by means of measurement, relative frequencies of age groupings, sex ratios, variations in height and robustness, the general health of the people, and even the variability of soft tissue traits.

In the case of skeletons, the traditional procedure was to take various measurements of the skull, and estimate the lengths—and less often the shaft diameters—of the long bones. The elaboration of head measurements has come under criticism in recent times, and there is no doubt that a number are highly correlated, and are probably not always the best from the point of view of determining growth variations in bones. Nevertheless, considerable mean differences of numerous measurements have been detected in various populations and, excluding cultural deformation and the minor effects of environment, must represent genetic differences in these groups—probably involving many genes. Because of the complex nature of the genetics of bone form, and the lack of knowledge in this field, extreme care has to be taken in considering the affinities of groups by means of skull measurement.

The fact that the British Bronze Age people had a far greater proportion of short-headedness[3] is very probably indicative of a new intrusive element, but on the other hand, the fact that the Etruscans were craniologically similar to the modern inhabitants of northern Italy is negative evidence which need not mean that one is in any way ancestral to the other.[1] In other words measurement is principally of value to demonstrate variability rather than close affinity. Long bone measurements—by their relative proportions and the stature estimates which can be calculated from them—may also provide evidence of group differences, although it seems likely that overall body length may be modified by climatic and, especially, nutritional factors. Certain diameters of these post-cranial bones are, incidentally, also of considerable value in sexing skeletons.

More recently, investigations on the frequencies of certain discontinuous traits of the skull (Fig. 50) offer to provide very useful additional information about earlier groups. These non-metrical features include the presence of extra sutures (such as the metopic

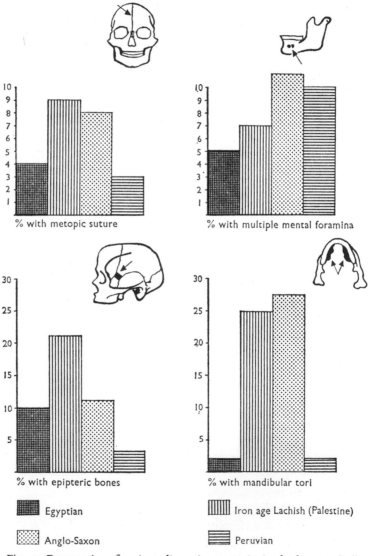

Fig. 50 Frequencies of various discontinuous traits in the human skull.

suture of the frontal bone), additional small bones along various sutures, differences in the articulation of bones, the presence of extra foramina, and the development of compact bony protuberances or tori in the mouth and ears. A number of these traits are already being studied from a genetic point of view, the findings so far suggesting that at least some are likely to be controlled by a simple genetic background.[10,13-15] Data of this kind have already been employed in the differentiation of both modern and ancient populations.[2,9] Various dental characteristics, for example the number of cusps, the presence of 'shovel-shaped' incisors, and the congenital absence of teeth also show considerable frequency differences in human groups (Table A), and offer further profitable lines of research.

TABLE A

Percentage frequencies for a number of populations to show the degree of variability present in man for shovel-shaped (median) incisors, missing third molars, and cusp numbers and patterns.

		Chinese	Eskimo	Negro	European
Shovel-shaped median incisors		89·6	95·3	11·6	8·4**
Total of marked and semi-shovelling		(1094)	(116)	(1000)	(2000)
Congenitally missing third molars		31·2	11·0	11·0*	19·7
Per cent of jaws lacking one or more M_3		(64)	(319)	(119)	(461)
	Y5	100	95·7	77·9	87·0
Cusp numbers and patterns on	+5		2·8	10·6	2·0
lower first molars	Y4		0·0	4·1	7·0
	+4		1·4	0·8	4·0
Number of individuals		(26)	(143)	(133)†	(98)

Data from Dahlberg[5] and Chagula[4]
The number of individuals is shown in parentheses; if the frequency for more than one sample has been published for a group, the largest is given here.
* American Negro
** Average of male and female samples, each of 1000
† Sample from East Africa. Frequencies for Y6 and +6, amounting to 6·6%, are not given in the table.

Bones need not, however, be complete to yield information about an individual. Fragments may indicate with some certainty the number of individuals represented and even their possible sex, although great caution is needed, and sex determinations are especially questionable in remains antedating Upper Palaeolithic man. Cremated remains present even greater problems than unburnt pieces for there is often considerable fissuring and distortion which may obscure some features, and evidence of attrition—of use in age estimations—is usually destroyed by the splintering off of the dental enamel under heat. Much information may however be gleaned from such uninspiring material. Yet again, pieces of bone (unburnt) may give an idea of the original histology of the bone, or be suitable for blood-typing research.

Because of the chemical nature of bones and teeth, there is obviously far more likelihood of these remaining than any of the soft tissues. Nevertheless, other parts of the body may remain, and it is my belief that even in English soils hair may be preserved long after most other parts have decayed. It is to the archaeologist of the future to be particularly careful when excavating skeletons in case other tissues do in fact remain! For example the Negro hair from Nkudzi Bay, near Lake Nyasa, described below (p. 429), was upon excavation found to be adhering to the skull in typical spirals—evidence which could have been completely overlooked and destroyed by a person overzealous at trowelling out bones! Recently, also, shrunken pieces of brain were discovered inside the skull of a Romano-Briton from Droitwich, Worcestershire,[11] and this also could easily have been broken up and missed during the cleaning of the bones.

Ancient soft tissues have come from a variety of other sites, and especially Egypt, Peru, and the bogs of Denmark and Schleswig-Holstein. Many of these bodies have been submitted to extensive examination, and of the recently discovered ones, those found in peat at Grauballe in Denmark[8] and Windeby in Schleswig-Holstein[12] have resulted in exhaustive analysis. Even the fingerprints, features which show considerable variability in modern peoples, were studied for possible deviations from modern norms.

An important and revealing aspect of the study of early peoples is that of mortality. As is evident from modern populations, age at death is highly correlated with living standards in a community, economic status, and pressure of disease.

Unfortunately, investigations of this nature are somewhat hampered by the difficulties in ageing adult remains accurately, especially when the important evidence of the pubic symphysis is absent. However, the data so far are most revealing and yet controversial. It is commonly thought, for example, that the mortality of earlier groups would be as high in the childhood and early adult age-groups as in, say, India of the present day, but there is in fact evidence from various groups of various periods that the number of people surviving into adulthood was far more like that found in modern Europe (Fig. 51). It is also

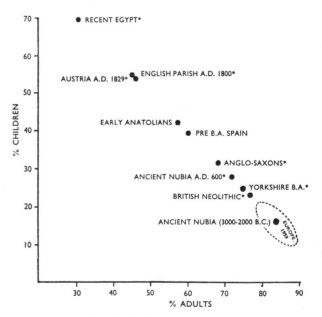

Fig. 51 Adult and child mortality in recent and early groups.

evident that the average life-span for males need not necessarily be lower than the females as in modern Europeans, and in a study of Texas Indian material (AD 850–1700) Goldstein[7] found the females to have a greater mortality.

If these mortality figures are not the result of selective burial, there is then increasing evidence that the hardships of early less civilized groups were not as great as previously imagined. An important point which is often forgotten is that the earlier human groups were probably not exposed to so many varieties of disease as known in modern groups. Such diseases as tuberculosis, leprosy, yaws, smallpox and syphilis seem unlikely to have taken on their present wide distribution before the first millennium AD at the earliest. Many earlier populations, especially those enjoying some degree of isolation from other groups, may thus have enjoyed good health comparable with the famous inhabitants of Tristan da Cunha at the turn of this century.

The biological study of earlier human remains is thus a multi-faceted discipline which can tell us far more than that population A had shorter heads or longer faces than population B. Indeed it is vital to the complete understanding of man's cultural and social development.

REFERENCES

1 BARNICOT, N. A. and BROTHWELL, D. R. 1959. In CIBA Symposium, *Medical Biology and Etruscan Origins*, London, 131–49
2 BROTHWELL, D. R. 1959. In *Bericht über die 6 Tagung der Deutschen Gesellschaft für Anthropologie in Kiel*, Gottingen, 103–9
3 —— 1960. *Advancement of Science 17*, 311–22
4 CHAGULA, W. K. 1960. *Am. J. Phys. Anth. 18*, 83–90
5 DAHLBERG, A. A. 1951. In *Physical Anthropology of the American Indian*, New York, 138–76
6 ELLIOT SMITH, G. and WOOD JONES, F. 1910. Report on the human remains. *Archaeological survey of Nubia. Report of 1907–08*, Cairo
7 GOLDSTEIN, M. S. 1953. *Hum. Biol. 25*, 3–12
8 VARIOUS PAPERS on Grauballe Man in *Kuml 1956*
9 LAUGHLIN, W. S. and JØRGENSEN, J. B. 1956. *Acta Genet. 6*, 3–12
10 MOORREES, C. F. A., OSBORNE, R. H., and WILDE, E. 1952. *Am. J. Phys. Anth. 10*, 319–30
11 OAKLEY, K. P. and POWERS, R. 1960. *Man 60*, 122, 123
12 VARIOUS PAPERS on human remains from Windeby in *Praehist. Z. 1958, 36*
13 SUZUKI, M. and SUKAI, T. 1960. *Am. J. Phys. Anth. 18*, 263–72
14 TORGERSEN, J. 1951. *Ibid. 9*, 193–210
15 —— 1954. In JANSEN, J. and BRODAL, A. *Aspects of Cerebellar Anatomy*, Oslo, 396–418

33 Microscopy and Prehistoric Bone

ANTONIO ASCENZI

THE MICROSCOPE has been profitably used in the study of prehistoric bone for more than a hundred years. Many problems had to be dealt with, but they can be arranged, as Jaekel pointed out some 70 years ago, under three main headings. Under the first heading comes the vast number of studies directed towards the microscopic investigation of the process of fossilization and the chronological data which can be obtained therefrom. The second heading covers the comparative histology of prehistoric vertebrate skeletons yielding information essential to palaeontological research. Under the third heading are grouped all those studies which concern the microscopic investigation of skeletal pathology. These three groups will be dealt with separately; however only the first group will receive extensive treatment, as the other two have been amply discussed in other chapters.

MICROSCOPIC CHARACTERISTICS AND THE STATE OF PRESERVATION

Prehistoric bone and *fossilized bone* are certainly not synonymous terms. There are famous instances where animal remains have become embedded in frozen mud and preserved almost unaltered throughout many thousands of years, not only in their bone but also in their soft parts. As regards the bones, such material is particularly valuable, because it furnishes a large amount of organic substance (ossein) which can be microscopically compared with fresh bone as has recently been done by Ezra and Cook.[34] Similarly Randall and his colleagues[78] were able to obtain a quantity of collagen sufficient for electron microscopic study from a tusk of *Elephas primigenius*, aged between 10,000 and 15,000 years, found in the frozen mud of Siberia. They were able to show that the periodic structure of the fibrils had remained unchanged. Moreover, complementary studies with wide-angle X-ray diffraction showed that even the minutest periodic structures had been preserved. These results confirmed the previous observations of Bear[19] who examined the collagen of a tusk of *Elephas primigenius* by low-angle X-ray diffraction and found that the overperiod of the fibrils averaged 640 Å.

The fortunate circumstance of finding animal and human remains preserved in frozen terrain is unhappily not the rule. Usually bones buried in the earth are subject to far-reaching changes which finally lead to fossilization.

The first students who applied microscopy to fossil bones[77] were forcibly struck by the fact that in general their specimens showed no substantial changes of structure, making it possible to compare them histologically with the bones of present-day animals. This led to the investigation by microscopic, chemical and physical methods of the process of fossilization in the hope of finding laws which could be used to make chronological deductions. The fruitfulness of this microscopic research which was already considerable in the past has recently become greatly enhanced by technical refinement and the introduction of new apparatus.

In order to appreciate the results hitherto achieved, it may be as well to recapitulate briefly some fundamental concepts on the structure of bone tissue. Bone contains cells, the osteocytes, furnished with fine branching processes. Between these cells lies a meta-plasmic ground-substance, consisting of an organic component (ossein) and an inorganic component. Ossein consists of collagen fibres running in bundles which are cemented together by osteomucoid. Depending on the orientation of collagen fibres, coarse fibred bone and parallel finely fibred bone can be distinguished. The inorganic component has a micro-crystalline structure corresponding to an apatite, the nature of which is still uncertain.[26] The crystallites are orientated in the direction of the collagen fibres.[35,57,12,37] Finally the bone contains vascular cavities, known as Haversian canals, and marrow cavities.

In the process of fossilization the bone's components are modified as follows: (a) gradual disappearance of all organic structures, i.e. the osteocytes and the ossein; (b) their replacement by material carried in the water of the ground; (c) substitution of the chemical elements constituting the crystalline lattice of the apatite. These various trans-formations can be followed microscopically.

The disappearance of the marrow cells and of the osteocytes is the first phenomenon to occur after death and is due to autolysis following the activation and the setting free of intracellular enzymes. This is the main reason why it is impossible to establish the blood group in fossil bones, group specific elements being present only in the marrow. Though the osteocytes are no longer directly visible, their external profile can still be seen, because the surrounding calcified metaplasm faithfully follows the original out-lines. Moreover, the cavity which was previously occupied by the osteocyte and its processes often stands out clearly, owing to the deposits of brown or blackish foreign material which it contains. This also applies to teeth in which this material collects in the canaliculi of the dentine, replacing the fine processes of the odontoblasts that filled them in the living tissue. This was already noted by those authors who were the first to apply the microscope to the study of fossilized bones [77] and to fossilized teeth.[2,71] In fact, Quekett was of the opinion that the essential factor in the process of fossilization was exactly the substitution of the osteocytes and the contents of the major cavities of the bone by material coming from the earth. This view was opposed by Aeby[1] who systematically investigated bones of various geological ages and found that the filling of the cavities previously occupied by the osteocytes is not a constant phenomenon syn-chronized with the process of fossilization. Actually it can happen that in highly fossilized bone these cavities are completely empty. Aeby, therefore, concluded that fossilization is not due simply to foreign material being deposited in cavities previously occupied by cells, but rather to a chemical metamorphosis of the inorganic components of the meta-plasm or apatite. In this he saw the explanation for the excellent state of the histological structure.

That was definitely the end of Quekett's belief in the possibility of dating fossil bone by the filling of the osteocyte cavities.

What has been said about the filling of the osteocyte cavities applies equally to the filling of the larger vascular and marrow cavities. The material in these larger cavities being more abundant, it can be studied by means of the polarizing microscope along mineralogical lines as was done by Rogers [80] on a wide scale.

A further step in our understanding of the process of fossilization by means of the microscope is to the credit of Schaffer.[87] It was known that the metaplasm of fresh bone is optically anisotropic. This applies both to the apatite and the collagen fibres of the ossein. Before Schaffer this had been established by Valentin[96] and by von Ebner.[31,32] The latter author had also noted that whenever bone is artificially deprived of ossein, it retains its birefringence, but that this is susceptible to variations of intensity and sign, depending on the refractive index of the fluids in which the sections are embedded. Thus the birefringence which is monoaxially positive with reference to the orientation of the collagen fibres in fresh bone, might in the presence of fluids with a suitable refractive index become negative (Fig. 52). Taking these discoveries as his starting point, Schaffer examined vertebrate bones of various geological ages ranging from the Lias to the 'Diluvium' under the polarizing microscope. He found that only the bones from 'Diluvial' beds behaved as regards optical anisotropy in the same manner as fresh bones, while animal bones of greater age showed a behaviour of the birefringence which with increasing age of the specimen became more and more similar to that of tissue artificially deprived of ossein. The author concluded that in the course of fossilization bone slowly but progressively loses its collagen fibres.

Schaffer[88] subsequently extended his investigations to fossil teeth and obtained exactly analogous results.

The physical bases of von Ebner's experimental findings which led to Schaffer's discoveries were established much later by Wiener[98] who worked out the theory of optical anisotropy of composite bodies. The merit of having recognized how this theory could also be applied to bone belongs to Schmidt.[90] Today quantitative studies on the optical anisotropy of bone tissue based on Wiener's theory are a fruitful field of research on the question of solving some of the basic problems of ultrastructure.[8,10,13]

The correctness of Schaffer's conclusions was recently confirmed by Baud and Morgenthaler[16], Ascenzi[11] and Oakley.[70] By using the optical as well as the electron microscope, these authors demonstrated the persistence of ossein in skeletal fragments which were thousands and even tens of thousands of years old. Baud and Morgenthaler's material was obtained from 7 human skeletons ranging in age from a minimum of 450 years (the beginning of the sixteenth century) to a maximum of 10,000–12,000 years (Magdalenian epoch). After decalcification, the yield of ossein from these fragments decreased in proportion to the duration of their preservation. Whether they were examined by optical, polarizing or electron microscope, the results were in full agreement. The normally birefringent ossein was markedly stainable with fuchsin by van Gieson's method, owing to its high content of collagen. The electron microscope showed the fibrils to be well preserved and their overperiod measured on the average 640 Å.

Even more significant were the studies of Ascenzi,[11] because they were conducted on bone of an even earlier geological age. He used a small fragment of the Neanderthal mandible Circeo IIa and some fragments of the fauna accompanying the Neantherthal mandible Circeo IIIb. Considering that it was possible to establish the exact age of the

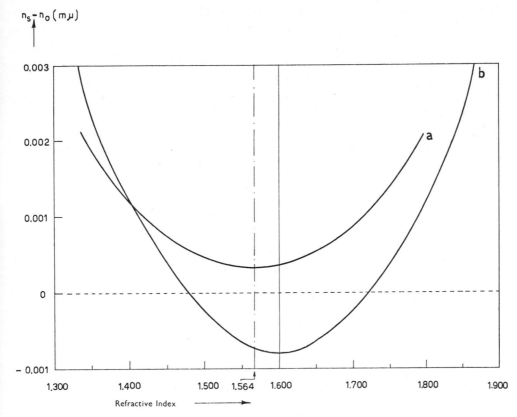

$n_s - n_o$ (mμ)

Refractive Index

Fig. 52 Curves of form birefringence pertaining to highly calcified normal bone (a) and to bone deprived of ossein (b), according to Ascenzi and Bonucci. For embedding fluids with range of refractive index between 1·420 and 1·640, the birefringence of the bone deprived of ossein is negative. → Ivory ~ fresh

deposits in which these bones were found, the importance of these studies is evident. The mandible Circeo IIa was discovered in 1939 by A. C. Blanc together with the Neanderthal cranium Circeo I in the Grotta Guattari, Monte Circeo. The mandible Circeo IIIb was found in 1950 by Ascenzi and Lacchei[92] in the ossiferous wall outside the entrance of the above-mentioned cave. According to Blanc these remains belong to the Epiwürm II. From the fragment of the Circeo IIa mandible as also from those of other bones a relatively large amount of organic material was obtained. As the mandibular fragment was small, it was only examined under the optical microscope, while the rest of the material was also investigated by the electron microscope.

The ossein of the Circeo IIa mandible appeared surprisingly well preserved. Its structure was that of a lamellar bone which in some areas showed some osteonic units (Plate XIVa). Between the lamellae the small elongated lacunes formerly occupied by the osteocytes were clearly visible. The tissue showed a feeble affinity for haematoxylin, a transitory metachromasia with toluidin-blue, a fair staining with methyl-blue by

★ Cf. *Man 51*, January 1951, Art. 7.

Mallory's method and no affinity for Schiff's reagent (Plate XIVc). On the other hand the ossein obtained from the fragments of animal bones showed staining qualities more akin to those of fresh bone, i.e. a marked affinity for haematoxylin, persistent metachromasia, intensive staining both with Mallory's methyl-blue and van Gieson's fuchsin and little affinity for Schiff's reagent. The electron microscope showed the collagen fibres to have preserved their periodic structure and the average size of the overperiod was 640 Å (Plate XIVb).

The significance of this work lies in the fact that it shows it to be possible to estimate the state of preservation of ossein obtained from bones in the process of fossilization by means of histological staining.

These findings are in accord with those of Oakley[70] who isolated collagen fibrils from the remains of a rhinoceros of the Upper Pleistocene found in the Piltdown deposits. Under the electron microscope the fibres were in a poor state of preservation and had no visible periodic structure.

The finding of collagen in fossilized or presumedly fossilized bones proved useful in determining whether skeletal remains of dubious origin do or do not belong to the same individual. This was so in the case of the Piltdown cranium. The electron microscopic examination of fragments from the mandible and of the cranial vault showed collagen to be present in the mandible while it was completely absent in the cranium. It was thus possible, in conjunction with other methods, to show that the mandible was of a much more recent date than the cranium and could not therefore have belonged to the same individual.[69]

The histological demonstration of the persistence of ossein in bone undergoing fossilization is borne out by chemical and physical methods of dating with nitrogen [50] and with C^{14}.[93] In fact both elements used in these techniques are derived from the collagen.

When in advanced fossilization the ossein has disappeared, the fine canaliculi which are left when the bundles of collagen fibres have gone are filled with extraneous material which, usually being dark in colour, gives to the tissue a finely striated appearance.[87,21]

Various methods have been employed in the microscopic study of the transformations undergone by the bone's apatite in the course of fossilization. In the past, measurement of the refractive index by means of Becke's line was used. Actually the refractive index of fossil bone cannot be regarded as an exponent of only the chemical changes in the apatite's crystalline lattice, but rather as an exponent of the whole complex process of substitution of the organic structures by penetrating mineral material. Normally the refractive index of ossein alone is 1·530,[14] while that of apatite alone is 1·600.[7,8,10,14] Obviously the whole bone has an intermediate refractive index which in adult animals in whom the depositing of calcium salts has been completed is 1·564.[14] As regards fossilized bone, the systematic measurements conducted by Rogers[80] on a large series of animals of various geological ages, ranging from the Ordovician to the Pleistocene, established two important facts: first, that there is no constant relationship between geological age and the refractive index; second, that the refractive index often greatly exceeds that of the apatite alone, suggesting that in the bone as a whole and in the

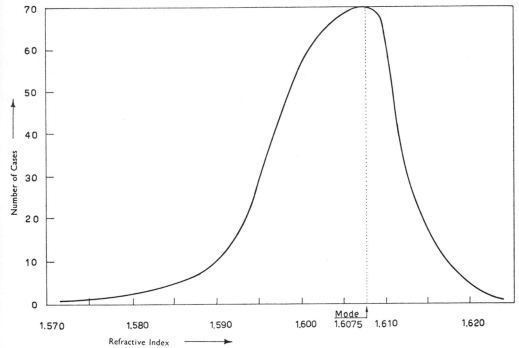

Fig. 53 Frequency diagram of the refractive index of a series of fossil bones, according to Rogers. The mode of the measured refractive indices (n=1·6075) is higher than the refractive index of fresh bone deprived of ossein (n=1·6)

apatite in particular dip changes have taken place through the influx of extraneous material (Fig. 53).

Autoradiography is a highly selective microscopic technique for the study of the changes taking place in the apatite's lattice during fossilization.[60],[23] However, this can only be used when radioactive elements are present. Strutt[95] was the first to report the presence of radioactive elements of the uranium series in fossilized bones, but it was only in the last ten years that specific research was undertaken.[52],[54],[28],[25],[3] It could be shown that though the radioactivity varied considerably from one specimen to another, it was always greater than that of the surrounding earth. Smith and Bradley[94] reported that in the dinosaur bones which they examined the uranium content varied from 0·04 to 0·135%, while the adjoining rock contained only 0·001 to 0·005%. Oakley [69],[70] was able to establish that as a general rule the uranium concentration in cenozoic human and animal bones increases proportionately with the passage of time. Moreover, a strict correlation between uranium and fluorine was noted.[3]

These findings led to the conclusion that the uranium is localized in the apatite where, as elsewhere in phosphates, it finds suitable chemical and structural conditions. The demonstration of the elective depositing and the mechanism by which it takes place was largely the result of studying autoradiograms microscopically. These investigations were made (a) on fossilized bones containing uranium, (b) on fossilized bone which did not contain uranium, but was exposed to the action of a dilute solution of uranium,

(c) on fresh bones from which the ossein had been artificially removed and which were then exposed to the same solution of uranium.

Bowie and Atkin[24] conducted research of the first type. They used remains of the dermato-skeleton of a specimen of *Homosteus* which on preliminary examination appeared to have a radioactivity equivalent to $0 \cdot 5\%$ U_3O_8. Closer investigation supplemented by chemical analysis, however, showed that the radioactivity of the remains was due to the simultaneous presence of uranium and thorium and that the respective percentage of the two elements was $0 \cdot 32\%$ U_3O_8 and $0 \cdot 51\%$ ThO_2. The autoradiographic examination of sections together with measurements of the *alpha* tracks showed that only uranium was present in the bone tissue, while the thorium was contained in the material that filled the cavities.

Recently Baud and Morgenthaler[18] studied autoradiographically the mode of distribution of uranium in sections of non-radioactive fossilized bone which was immersed in a $1‰$ solution of uranium nitrate buffered with a solution of $0 \cdot 025N$ $NaHCO_3$, as suggested by Neuman and colleagues.[65] Baud and Morgenthaler found (a) that the radioactivity was greater along the margins of the outer and inner surfaces of the sections which had come into direct contact with the solution, as also in osteones with a low degree of calcification and along the zones through which ran the abnormal canaliculi due to the action of micro-organisms (see below); (b) that there was no radioactivity in Haversian canals obstructed by calcite; (c) that the distribution of radioactivity wherever present was diffuse. The authors, therefore, concluded that the amount of uranium present in a fossil bone depends, apart from extrinsic, also on intrinsic factors. These are the porosity and the permeability of the tissue which in turn depend on its submicroscopic structure as also on the physical and chemical composition of the inorganic component. It is the inorganic component which conditions the processes of adsorption and exchange. This is generally in accordance with the results obtained by Amprino[4] who conducted similar investigations, using fresh, instead of fossil bone, which he artificially deprived of ossein.

The way in which uranium attaches itself to phosphates in general and bone apatite in particular is still controversial. If in the case of the bone it can be excluded that this constitutes a separate phase[18] in the form of UO_2 or UF_4 or $Ca(UO_2)_2(PO_4)_2.8H_2O$ (autunite), there remain the following possibilities to be considered: either the uranium is chemically adsorbed on the surfaces or internal discontinuities of the crystalline lattice in the form of U^{+4} ions or as isolated $(UO_2)^{+2}$ radicals;[51] or else the uranium (U^{+4}) substitutes the calcium present in the apatite lattice;[58,28,38] or the $(UO_2)^{+2}$ radical substitutes two Ca^{+2} ions.[66,67]

The fact that fluorine and uranium behave analogously in fossil bone makes it possible to use measurements of the radioactivity of the latter element for relative chronological calculations and this has led to the establishment of important data.[70]

Only few electron microscopic studies of the apatite of fossilized bone have been made and it would be worth while to take them up again with more suitable methods. Ascenzi[9] found that fragments of *Elephas antiquus* from Saccopastore (Rome) contained no collagen and showed a mineral structure which was not unlike that of fresh bone artificially deprived of ossein. In the following year (1950) Barbour[15] reported similar findings. Moreover she pointed out variations in the size of the mesh of the mineral structure due to the process of fossilization. She did not express an opinion on the significance of this finding, but it is probable [9,16] that this is caused either by an increase in crystalline material or by a reduction of that which was originally present. The latter alternative, that is, a rarefaction of the mineral framework, might find a confirmation in the work of Baud and Morgenthaler,[18] who in fossil bone found microradiographically visible zones of far-reaching demineralization.

It remains to be mentioned that as far back as 1864 Wedl described, in both recently deposited and fossil bones, canaliculi which had no similarity with those present in normal tissue (Plate XIVd) and which contained fine brownish filaments. He was of the opinion that these findings were caused by a fungus. They were also observed by Roux[86] in fossil bones and fully confirmed by Schaffer,[87, 89] who designated them 'Bohrkanäle', that is, drilled canals. They have been recently studied by Morgenthaler and Baud.[64] The appearance of this type of canal leads to the progressive elimination of any structure.

In those cases in which greater or lesser parts of the bone tissue become destroyed they are replaced by material which is brought in from the ground.[21]

From what has been said it follows that the microscopic changes which take place in bone undergoing fossilization not only depend on the passage of time, but above all on the environmental conditions of the deposits in which they are found. Therefore, in the present state of our knowledge, they do not furnish criteria for absolute dating.

THE HISTOLOGICAL STRUCTURE OF THE SKELETON IN THE PREHISTORIC VERTEBRATES

The fact that fossil bone retains its microscopic structure makes comparative histological research possible. This has been done systematically in fishes and reptiles.

It was Owen,[71] Williamson[99] and Pander[73-76] who undertook the first histological studies of the skeletons of fishes. After the death of Pander, these studies lay dormant for over 40 years, except for a few isolated contributions[27] and Rohon's publications.[81-85] However the latter author's microscopic interpretations are often inexact (cf. Gross[46]). In 1907 Gebhardt's work was published, as also that of Goodrich. After the first World War there arose a renewed interest in the palaeontology of palaeozoic fishes and this led to a revival of histological studies in the field by Stensiö, Obrutschew, Heintz, Hoppe, Bryant, Stetson, Brotzen (cf. Gross[46,47]). But the most valuable body of research, both in scope and thoroughness, is that published by Gross between the years 1930 and 1959. Leaving aside the many problems which concern the structure of the exoskeleton, it can be briefly said of the histology of the endoskeleton that the bone is structurally primitive. It is primary or coarse fibred bone of variable feature containing primary osteones. This last are particularly abundant in the Arthrodires and the Crossopterygians. Secondary osteones on the other hand are rare. However, it is probable that if specimens of the same species, but of different size, were examined, they would show that the differentiation of bone in fossil fishes, as judged by the number of secondary osteones, is largely a function of the bodily mass and thus a mechanical and mineral metabolic exigency. That this does in fact apply to the vertebrae of *Thynnus thynnus* L. has recently been shown by Amprino and Godina.[5]

Valuable studies on the skeletons of fossil reptiles have been made by Kiprijanoff,[56] Seitz[91] and Gross.[45] Minor contributions limited to specific problems are those of Broili[22] and Moodie[63] on the ossified vertebral tendons of *Trachodon* and those of Nopcsa[68] concerning the development of the ribs also of *Trachodon*.

These various studies go to confirm that reptilian skeletal development follows the same laws in the geologically oldest and in surviving forms. Nevertheless the gigantic dimensions reached by the Dinosaurs of the Cretaceous induced a structural complexity similar to that of the largest surviving mammals. On that particularly touches the structure of the diaphyses of the limbs which has been the object of major attention; this does not differ, even in its most simple expression, from that of the amphibians. Thus the diaphysial shaft consists of primary periostal bone of homogeneous structure with a trace of stratification which can be more or less pronounced. It is traversed by vascular canals which have primary osteones. More rarely one comes across that particular type of periostal bone which Gross calls 'laminar Periostknochen' owing to its peculiar structure. In it laminae are orientated concentrically with reference to the axis of the bone and are separated from each other by an ample vascular network which is also arranged concentrically. This has been seen in *Thermomorpha* (*Kannemeyeri*), *Thecodontia* (*Erythrosuchus*), *Dinosauria* (*Plateosaurus*). Secondary osteones, though usually rare, reach their maximum development in *Brachiosaurus*, *Diplodocus*, *Bronthosaurus* and *Iguanodon*.

The ossified intervertebral tendons of *Trachodon* also have a complex structure and are rich in longitudinally orientated secondary osteones.[22] It may be assumed that this is due to their particular mechanical function of making the vertebral column rigid. Contrary to Dollo,[30] Broili expressed the opinion that the abundance of Haversian canals and hence of blood vessels could be the result of the direct ossification of muscles, a view which hardly seems acceptable.

The histological structure of skeletons of other classes of fossil vertebrates has received less attention (Moodie[62]). From what is known it may be concluded that generally speaking the bone structure of extinct forms is no different from that of surviving ones (cf. also Ezra and Cook[34]). This also applies to fossil man in whom microradiography has shown that the statistical distribution of the osteones in relation to the degree of calcification is identical with that of modern man.[17]

A problem of great palaeontological as well as of forensic interest is the possibility of determining microscopically the species to which a bone fragment belongs when this cannot be ascertained macroscopically. Demeter and Mátyás[29] claimed to be able to distinguish about 40 mammalian species by the histological characteristics of their bones. This was doubted by Eggeling[33] and recently by Amprino and Godina.[5] The latter showed that within the Order, the Genus and the Species the type of bone structure varies, depending upon which bone is examined, the size of the species, the age of the individual and differences in the speed of growth, as also in relation to other less easily recognizable factors. Undoubtedly the problem requires further study.

THE HISTOLOGICAL PATHOLOGY OF PREHISTORIC BONE

Bone is the only tissue which can bear evidence of the diseases which have afflicted the vertebrates in the most distant past. Histological contributions on the pathology of the skeleton are not numerous and are scattered in the vast literature pertaining to medicine, palaeontology and anthropology. Particularly valuable, therefore, was the work of Moodie who, as long ago as 1923, produced the first collection and treatment not only of the macroscopic, but also of the microscopic lesions found in prehistoric vertebrates. A similar collection of all known data was made by Pales.[72]

The earliest indications of skeletal pathology reach back to reptiles of the Permian and it may be said that in this as well as in subsequent periods traumatic lesions, i.e. fractures, dominated the scene. In these fractures the histological appearance of the callus showed no features that were essentially different from those of ordinary present-day pathology. Moodie's observation that in fossil reptiles the structural complexity of the callus is greater than that of the normal bone, it having a particularly large number of secondary osteones, certainly needs checking. In calluses which complicating osteomyelitis had rendered septic, histological examination showed only indirect signs of inflammation, such as more or less conspicuous structural irregularities consisting of communicating cavities with fistular pathways. But those formations which Renault[79] interpreted as fossilized microbes cannot be regarded as direct evidence of a causal agent, because they are often seen in perfectly healthy bone and are probably due to post-mortem putrefaction. The same can be said for inflammations not resulting from fractures, for instance maxillary alveolitis and osteomyelitis of dental origin.

Chronic arthritis which was already present among the large Tertiary dinosaurs and became increasingly common in later epochs, as in *Machairodus* and above all in *Ursus spelaeus*, showed nothing of histological significance as compared with the findings of modern pathology.

The microscope has furnished certain indications for the recognition of some tumours of the bone which produce rather characteristic features, as do the angiomas.

In a comprehensive study of pachyostosis Kaiser[55] has recently confirmed that, subject to the structural differences among species, skeletal pathology is remarkably uniform.

Finally, Michaëlis[59] pointed out in fossilized human bones microscopic signs which would prove the pre-Columbian origin of syphilis.

Before concluding this brief section, it might be as well to mention that, taken singly, the various contributions on the pathological histology of fossil bones often reveal, specially in the older papers, a lack of terminological precision which creates some uncertainty in the value of their findings. It is to be hoped that in future research there will be a stricter adherence to generally accepted pathological concepts.

PROSPECTS FOR FURTHER STUDY

What has been said regarding the contribution to the study of prehistoric bone which microscopy has made, should give some idea of the length of the road that has been travelled, but it should also provide an orientation for future research.

As for our knowledge of the way in which the process of fossilization takes place, there can be no doubt that the greatest use will be made of systematic studies on the progressive disappearance of the ossein and the ultrastructural modifications which take place in the apatite of the bone. As far as the ossein is concerned, this will have to be further investigated by histochemical methods, by the use of the electron microscope and by employing the polarizing microscope for quantitative estimations. The electron and polarizing microscope will also be of the greatest use in the analysis of ultrastructural modifications of the apatite. Wherever possible it will be necessary to associate these studies with (a) the chemical analysis of ossein; (b) chemical and X-ray spectrographic analysis of the apatite; (c) absolute chronological measurements by the C^{14} technique, using specimens of ossein; (d) studies on the manner in which liquids from the ground circulate in skeletal parts; (e) geological and geochemical investigations to clarify the conditions in the environment in which fossilization takes place. In this way it would become possible to arrive at precise conclusions concerning the microscopic aspects of the process of fossilization in bone making reference to the nature of the deposits and to absolute time.

Autoradiographic studies, on the way in which various radioactive elements are exchanged for elements making up the bone's apatite, would increase our knowledge of the transformations which the inorganic fraction of bone tissue undergoes.

As regards palaeontology, histological studies on the skeletal structure of those groups of vertebrates which have hitherto received little attention would be welcome. It might also be worth while to study systematically the characteristics of bone collagen of extinct species wherever this has been preserved. It might also be profitable to go further into the question of histologically ascertaining the species to which a bone belongs.

It seems superfluous to stress the already considerable interest in the histological investigation of palaeopathological problems.

REFERENCES

1 AEBY, CHR. 1878. *Arch. f. mikrosk. Anat. 15*, 371–82
2 AGASSIZ, L. 1833–43. *Recherches sur les poissons fossiles*, Neuchâtel
3 ALTSCHULER, Z. S., CLARKE, R. S. and YOUNG, E. J. 1958. *Geological Survey, Professional Paper* 314-D, pp. 45–90
4 AMPRINO, R. 1953. *Experientia 9*, 291–3
5 —— and GODINA, G. 1947. *Commentationes Acad. Pontificia Scientiarum 11*, 329–464
6 —— 1956. *Pubbl. Staz. Zool. Napoli 28*, 62–71
7 ASCENZI, A. 1948. *Rend. Accad. Naz. Lincei* (Cl. Sc. Fis. Mat. e Nat.) (VIII) *4*, 777–83
8 —— 1949a. *Nature 163*, 604
9 —— 1949b. *Riv. di Antrop. 37*, 143–8
10 —— 1950. *Science 112*, 84–86
11 —— 1955. *Am. J. Phys. Anth. 13*, 557–66
12 —— and BENEDETTI, E. L. 1959. *Acta anat. 37*, 370–85
13 —— and BONUCCI, E. 1961. *Ibid. 44*, 236–62
14 —— and FABRY, C. 1959. *J. Biophys and Biochem. Cytol. 6*, 139–42
15 BARBOUR, E. P. 1950. *Am. J. Phys. Anth. 8*, 315–30
16 BAUD, C.-A. and MORGENTHALER, P. W. 1952. *Arch. Suisses d'Anth. Gén. 17*, 52–65
17 —— 1956. *Ibid. 21*, 79–86
18 —— 1959. *Ibid. 24*, 45–52
19 BEAR, R. S. 1944. *J. Am. Chem. Soc. 66*, 1297–305

20 BLANC, A. C. 1939. *Rend. Accad. Naz. Lincei* (Cl. Sc. Fis. Mat. e Nat.) (VI) *29*, 205–10
21 BLEICHER 1893. *Bibliographie anatomique 1*, 93–96, 123–8
22 BROILI, F. 1922. *Anat. Anz. 55*, 464–75
23 BOWIE, S. H. U. 1951. *Bull. Geol. Survey G.B. 3*, 58–71
24 —— and ATKIN, D. 1956. *Nature 177*, 487–8
25 —— and DAVIDSON, C. F. 1955. *Brit. Mus. Nat. History Bull. Geology 2*, 276–82
26 CARLSTRÖM, D. and ENGSTRÖM, A. 1956. Ultrastructure and distribution of mineral salts in bone tissue in BOURNE, G. H., *The Bio-chemistry and physiology of Bone*, New York
27 CLAYPOLE, E. W. 1894. *Proc. Amer. Micros. Soc. 15*, 189–91
28 DAVIDSON, C. F. and ATKIN, D. 1953. *C. R. XIX Congr. géol. internat. Alger* Sec. 11, 13–31
29 DEMETER, G. and MÁTYÁS, J. 1928. *Z. Anat. u. Entwg. 87*, 45–99
30 DOLLO, L. 1887. *Arch. de Biol. 7*, 249–64
31 EBNER, V. v. 1874. *Sitzgsber. Akad. Wiss. Wien., Math.-naturwiss. Kl.* (III) *70*, 105–43
32 —— 1875. *Ibid. 72*, 49–138
33 EGGELING, H. v. 1938. Allgemeines über den Aufbau knoecherner Skeletteil, in BOLK L. v., GÖPPERT, E., KALLIUS, E. and LUBOSCH, W. *Handb. d. vergl. Anat. d. Wirbelt. 5*, 275–304
34 EZRA, H. C. and COOK, S. F. 1959. *Science 129*, 465–6
35 FERNANDEZ-MORÁN, H. and ENGSTRÖM, A. 1957. *Biochim. et biophys. acta 23*, 260–4
36 GEBHARDT, F. A. M. W. 1907. *Verhandl. anat. Ges., 21 Vers. Würzburg*, 72–90
37 GLIMCHER, M. J. 1959. *Revs. modern Phys. 31*, 359–93
38 GOLDSCHMIDT, V. M. 1954. *Geochemistry*, Oxford
39 GOODRICH, E. S. 1907. *Proc. Zool. Soc. London*, 751–74
40 GROSS, W. 1930. *Geol. Paläont. abh. 18*, 121–56
41 —— 1931. *Paläontographica 75* (A) 1–62
42 —— 1933a. *Abh. Preuss. Geol. Landesanst. H. 145*, 41–77
43 —— 1933b. *Paläontographica 79* (A) 1–74
44 —— 1933. *Abh. Preuss. Geol. Landesanst. H. 154*, 4–83
45 —— 1934. *Z. Anat. u. Entwg. 103*, 731–64
46 —— 1936. *Paläontographica 83* (A) 1–60
47 —— 1947. *Ibid. 96* (A) 91–158
48 —— 1957. *Ibid. 109* (A) 1–40
49 —— 1959. *Ibid. 113* (A) 1–35
50 HEIZER, R. F. and COOK, S. F. 1952. *Am. J. Phys. Anth. 10*, 289–303
51 HENDRICKS, S. B. and HILL, W. L. 1950. *Proc. Nat. Acad. Sci. Washington 36*, 731–7
52 HILL, W. S. 1950. *Ciencia e Investigación 6*, 43–44
53 JAEKEL, O. 1891. *Neues Jahrbuch f. Mineral., Geol. u. Paläon.*, I, 178–98
54 JAFFE, E. B. and SHERWOOD, A. M. 1951. *U.S. Geol. Survey, Trace Elements Memorandum*, Rep. no. 149, 1–19
55 KAISER, H. E. 1960. *Paläontographica 114* (A) 113–96
56 KIPRIJANOFF, V. 1881–3. *Mem. Acad. Sci. St. Petersburg 28*, 1–103; *30*, 1–55; *31*, 1–57
57 KNESE, K.-H. and KNOOP, A.-M. 1958. *Z. Zellforsch. 48*, 455–78
58 McKELVEY, V. E. and NELSON, J. M. 1950. *Econ. Geology 45*, 35–53
59 MICHAËLIS, L. 1930. *Veröffentl. Kriegs- und Konstitutionspathol. 6*, 1–92
60 MILLER, B. L. and HOECKER, F. E. 1950. *Nucleonics 8*, 44–52
61 MOODIE, R. L. 1923. *Paleopathology*, Urbana, Illinois
62 —— 1926. *Biologia generalis 2*, 63–95
63 —— 1928. *Am. Museum Novitates*, No. 311, New York
64 MORGENTHALER, P. W. and BAUD, A.-C. 1956–7. *Bull. Soc. Suisse Anthrop. et Ethnol. 33*, 9–10, 1956–7
65 NEUMAN, W. F., NEUMAN, M. W., MAIN, E. R. and MULRYAN, B. J. 1949a. *J. Biol. Chem. 179*, 325–33
66 —— 1949b. *Ibid. 179*, 335–40
67 —— 1949c. *Ibid. 179*, 341–8
68 NOPCSA, F. B. 1933. *Proc. Zool. Soc. London*, 221–6
69 OAKLEY, K. P. 1955a. Analytical methods of dating bones, *Advancement of Science 11*, 3–8
70 —— 1955b. *British Mus. Nat. History Bull. Geology 2*, 254–65
71 OWEN, R. 1840–5. *Odontography*, London

72 PALES, L. 1930. *Paleopathologie et pathologie comparative*, Paris
73 PANDER, CH. H. 1856. Monographie der fossilen Fische des silurischen Systems der russisch-baltischen Gouvernements, *Buchdruck. d. keis. Akad. d. Wiss.*, St. Petersburg
74 —— 1857. Ueber die Placodermen des devonischen Systems, *ibid.*
75 —— 1858. Ueber die Ctenodipterinen des devonischen Systems, *ibid.*
76 —— 1860. Ueber die Saurodipterinen, Dendrodonten, etc des devonischen Systems, *ibid.*
77 QUEKETT, J. 1849. *Trans. Micros. Soc.*, London 2, 40–42
78 RANDALL, J. T., FRASER, R. D. B., JACKSON, S., MARTIN, A. V. W. and NORTH, A. C. T. 1952. *Nature* 169, 1029–33
79 RENAULT, B. 1896. *Ann. des Sci. nat. bot.* (VIII) 2, 275–349
80 ROGERS, A. F. 1924. *Bull. Geol. Soc. Am.* 35, 535–56
81 ROHON, J. V. 1889. *Mém. Acad. Imp. Sci. St. Petersburg* (VII) 36, no. 14
82 —— 1892. *Ibid.* (VII) 38, no. 13,
83 —— 1893. *Ibid.* (VII) 41, no. 5,
84 —— 1899. *Sitzgsber. Böhm. Ges. Wiss., Math.-naturwiss. Kl.*, no. 8, 1–77
85 —— 1901. *Ibid.*, no. 16, 1–31
86 ROUX, W. 1887. *Ztschr. f. wissen. Zool.* 45, 227–54
87 SCHAFFER, J. 1889. *Sitzgsber. Akad. Wiss. Wien., Math.-naturwiss. Kl.* (III) 98, 319–82
88 —— 1890. *Ibid.* (III) 99, 146–52
89 —— 1894. *Anat. Anz.* 10, 459
90 SCHMIDT, W. J. 1933. *Ber. Oberhess. Ges. Natur- u. Heilk., Naturw. Abt.*, Giessen 15, 219–47
91 SEITZ, A. L. L. 1907. *Nova Acta Abh. keiserl. Leop.-Carol. deutsch. Akad. Naturf.* 87, 231–370
92 SERGI, S. and ASCENZI, A. 1955. *Riv. di Antrop.* 42, 337–403
93 SINEX, F. M. and FARIS, B. 1959. *Science* 129, 969
94 SMITH, K. G. and BRADLEY, D. A. 1951. *Papers Michigan Acad. Science, Arts and Letters* 37, 257–63
95 STRUTT, R. J. 1908. *Proc. Roy. Soc. London* (A) 81, 272–7
96 VALENTIN, G. 1861. *Die Untersuchung der Pflanzen- und Tiergewebe in polarisiertem Lichte* ENGELMANN, W., Leipzig
97 WEDL, C. 1864. *Sitzgsber. Akad. Wiss. Wien. Math.-naturwiss. Kl.* (I) 50, 171–93
98 WIENER, O. 1912. *Abh. sächs. Ges. Wiss., math. phys. Kl.* 32, 509–604
99 WILLIAMSON, W. 1849. *Phil. Trans. Roy. Soc. London* 140, 435–75

34 Sex Determination in Earlier Man

SANTIAGO GENOVÉS

OFTEN A MAJOR STUDY of skeletal remains is made with practically no more than a cursory investigation of sexual differences, and much laborious and useful work is undertaken, particularly on small samples or on 'unique' specimens, which would lose almost all its usefulness if the sex assignment proved to be incorrect. Consequently, it seems a good idea to lay stress on certain points before giving a general account of the methods followed in order to reach a reasonably accurate sex diagnosis.

In his celebrated memoir *L'Homme fossile de La-Chapelle-aux-Saints* Marcellin Boule[1] wrote (p. 5): 'la méthode des mensurations, employée comme méthode directrice a le très grave inconvénient de donner l'illusion d'une précision mathématique dont la Nature, essentiellement mobile et changeant, ne saurait s'accomoder'. Quite often the measuring of bones instead of being a tool has become practically the master of the physical anthropologist; and, as Leakey[2] pointed out, the fact that two things, whether skulls or teeth or pieces of bone, have the same length, breadth, and height does not necessarily mean that they have the same shape or that both are, morphologically speaking, identical. I agree with Leakey that it is important to stress at all times that no single measurable character of any bone will serve by itself to distinguish two different individuals racially or sexually as the case may be, but that only after critical examination of the combination of all the characters can we arrive at results which will be of value. Furthermore, characters which by their own nature might have escaped measurement or expression in an equivalent way may have to be called in to help supply the correct answer.

In spite of the great advance in genetics and the views of authorities like W. C. Boyd[3] who have strongly criticized the traditional methods of physical anthropology, advocating that practically the only approach to the subject is the genetical one, the fact remains that in practice the anthropologist is often confronted with the problem of assigning sex to a bone, and the only practical way in which this can be accomplished is by combining measurements and morphological observations in a fashion as logically valid as possible. It must be admitted that from a strictly genetical point of view the worker may be observing or measuring 'characters' which are of different orders and fall under the influence of different factors. On the other hand, if the measurements and observations are generally in keeping with the normal patterns of growth, morphology, and function of the bone, they may prove to be of value in sex discrimination in spite of the fact that a phenotype is being considered which perhaps in the future might be subdivided into smaller factors. This may be so no matter how obscure or inexplicable the different genetic or other forces concerned in the adult appearance of the complete character may be. We are still far from understanding to what extent genetic, environmental, hormonal, or other factors are responsible for the final shape a bone assumes.

To return to the anthropological problem, it may at first sight appear that metrical and morphological methods are too crude to determine sex differences in bones which have been affected by these various factors. However, the fact is that if the analysis does not rely on the infallibility of just one character, it may be possible to discriminate unless, as it sometimes happens, a picture of what can be called intersexuality appears. Thus it is not advisable to trust to a single metrical or morphological character, no matter how seemingly infallible, when undertaking sex-determinations.

THE SEX-RATIO

In earlier populations as in modern ones we have examples of varying sex-ratios. Among the Pecos Indians, Hooton[4] reported an excess of males (of more than 10 years of age) in all the periods extending into the last phase of occupation, the sex-ratio being 176·5 males to 100 females.

Angel[5] finds in ancient Greece that in most cemeteries the males preserved for study outnumber the females two to one. On the other hand, Neel[6] shows with data from a recent census that in the United States 50% of the women give birth to 88% of the boys born in each generation, and Ferembach[7,8] shows that in prehistoric groups the sex-ratio, as also the differential fertility and mortality, can greatly modify the outward appearance of a population.

We have considered the above explanation pertinent in order to show:

(1) That contrary to what is usually believed in earlier populations it is not uncommon to find unequal proportions between the sexes.

(2) That factors are constantly changing the sex-ratio, so that this changes from one age to another amongst the individuals of a population and from one generation to the next.

Therefore, what is found in one archaeological stratum *need not* serve as a pattern for postulations about remains found in adjacent strata, whether above or below.

SEXUAL DIMORPHISM IN PREHISTORIC REMAINS

The question of whether the sexual dimorphism in prehistoric populations is greater or less than in recent ones is a fruitless one unless we specify the prehistoric remains to which we are referring. The various modern human groups do not have the same degree of sexual dimorphism. For example, it is known that the sexual dimorphism in Bantu pelves is much less marked than those of Bushmen and Europeans[10] and that some characters (e.g. the pre-auricular sulcus) are of practically no value in a Bantu population.

If we depend on indirect data from other primates, there are several facts which suggest that a pronounced sexual difference *in size* is a primitive condition. Prehistoric races of orang-utan[11] as well as of the Celebes macaque[12] possess a more marked sexual difference in canine size than the corresponding living forms.[13]

In what ways do ancient human remains display sexual dimorphism? Morant[14] and von Bonin[15] find that Upper Palaeolithic European populations are, in many respects, similar to their more recent descendants, whence Brothwell[16] infers a similar type and degree of sexual dimorphism. Keith[17] believed that sexual dimorphism was less pronounced in Neanderthal 'races' than is the rule among modern ones[18] and Hooton[4] contends that sex differences are less pronounced in primitive peoples than among Europeans.

In the remains of Tabun I, there were found in the superior ramus of the pubis (McCown and Keith[19]) characteristics which, whilst separating them from the rest of the known Neanderthals—including the specimens from Skhul—could not be duplicated in modern man. It was thought that they might possibly be attributed to the sex factors. Later, however, Stewart[20] showed that in Shanidar I and III (both Neanderthals and apparently male) the same situation is produced in the superior pubic ramus as found in Tabun I, which proves that *these pelvic features are not sex-induced changes.*

What is reasonable in the question of sexual dimorphism of prehistoric remains is that we can make more or less legitimate suggestions from these remains, from comparisons with other primates, or with more recent populations. However, such suggestions will frequently be erroneous, attributing to sexual dimorphism what might be in fact a simple intra or extra group variation, or a stage in evolutionary development.

Elsewhere,[21] the present author reached the following conclusions with reference to prehistoric skeletal remains:

'Since the relation between skulls and post-cranial bones from different sites of more or less contemporary deposits is still very far from being elucidated, sexing one specimen on the evidence afforded by corresponding bones of another should be attempted only with great caution.

'Sexing palaeanthropic material on the basis of bones that do not correspond is very inadvisable, even with specimens from contemporary deposits.'

That extreme caution in this respect should be observed when dealing with prehistoric bones of great age is exemplified by the great numbers of them which have opposed diagnoses from specialists (Table A).

One could, of course, make a larger table with other remains for in the above table are figured only those which have Neanderthal affinities. One can also quote cases from America. Thus Minnesota *Man* seems in fact to be a *Girl*[22-24] and Tepexpan Man is very probably Tepexpan Woman.[25,26] It is clear that in these and in other cases, the original error was due largely to natural ignorance of the progress which has been made in sex diagnosis in recent years.

Apart from a series of standards and techniques to which we shall briefly refer later, it must be stressed that one cannot judge prehistoric remains by the same criterion as modern ones. Frequently the diagnosis was based on traces of muscular insertions, forgetting that in early remains, and in the majority of our so-called 'primitive contemporaries', the cultural environment and different division of work, amongst other factors, can put a good part of the female population to fulfilling tasks which require considerable muscular exertion. This would certainly affect bone size and form.

TABLE A

Sexes assigned to Neanderthal remains by different anthropologists.

Anthropologists	Spy I	Spy II	Skhul IX	Galilee	Gibraltar I	La Quina H₅	Ehringsdorf III
Fraipont & Lohest (1886)	♀	♂	—	—	—	—	—
Virchow (1887)	♂	♂	—	—	—	—	—
Schaaffhausen (1887)	♂	♂	—	—	—	—	—
Sollas (1907)	♂	♂	—	—	♂	—	—
Keith (1911)	♂	♂	—	—	♂	—	—
Henri Martin (1913)	—	—	—	—	—	♀	—
—— (1923)	—	—	—	—	—	♂?	—
Keith (*ante* 1925)	—	—	—	♂	—	—	—
—— (1925)	—	—	—	—	Probably ♀	Probably ♀	—
—— (1927)	—	—	—	♀	—	♀	—
Morant (1927)	♂?	♀?	—	♀?	♀?	♀?	—
Weidenreich (1927)	—	—	—	—	—	—	♀
Hrdlička (1930)	'Weak' ♂, or ♀	♂	—	♂	♀	♂	♂
Keith (1931)	—	—	—	o?	♀	♀	♂
Vallois (1937)	♂	♂	—	o?	—	Probably ♀	♀
McCowan & Keith (1939)	—	—	♂	♂	♀	♂	—
Howells (1946)	—	—	—	—	—	—	'Seemingly' ♀
Trevor (*post* 1949)	♂	♂	—	—	—	—	—
Clark Howell (1951)	♂	♀	♂	♂	♀	♀	♂
Boule & Vallois (1952)	—	—	—	—	—	♀	—

Thus Wood Jones,[27] working on Egyptians, found foetuses in pelves with characteristics which were to him distinctly masculine, and Faulhaber[28] says, referring to the prehispanic remains of Tlatilco (Mexico): 'As for the sexual characteristics, the number of cases in which the female skeletons have an extremely robust appearance, similar in this character to the males, is surprising, although according to the pelvic characters they are unquestionably women.'

METHODS OF SEX DETERMINATION

In agreement with Keen,[29] Stewart[30] and others, and contrary to the opinion of Hanna and Washburn,[31] I believe it impossible to base sex determination on one character alone—either metric or morphological. Masculine characteristics in one bone may be accompanied by feminine traits in another, or in another segment of the same one. This is equally true of both modern and prehistoric remains.

Up to now, I have outlined the various difficulties which exist. I believe, however, that with care and by using diverse methods, one can, both in populations and even in individuals, arrive at a wholly satisfactory sex diagnosis. Obviously, the further away we are in time from the present, the more difficult it will be, especially if we are dealing with specimens whose phylogenetic affinities are still somewhat incomprehensible. In anatomy books, in anthropometric works, or in works on identification from skeletal remains,[32-40] there is a résumé of the traits, mostly anatomical, to observe and evaluate for sex diagnosis. Although they are not all in agreement with each other (and neither is the author with the evaluation of some of the criteria given), I believe nevertheless that it is easy and within the reach of all archaeologists to familiarize themselves with these, and also to undertake sex diagnosis. As various authors have reviewed the traits of value in sexing, I will not enter into great detail here.

Practically all the bones in the human body have at some time been an object of study with a view to determining the degree of sexual dimorphism. To a certain degree, all make a contribution towards arriving at a diagnosis. However, we can say that there are three areas to be considered in the first instance, and these afford the best results. They are the pelvis, as a whole and for its particular traits; the skull and face, as a whole and for their particular traits; and the articular surfaces of the bones, chiefly long bones.

PELVIS

The prepuberal pelvis. According to some authors, several of the pelvic characters enabling a determination, or a good assessment, of sex are established early in development, in some instances even before birth.[41-43] However, others[44-48] maintain that features of the pelvis strongly indicative of sex only become apparent at puberty when the bones of the female pelvis, and in particular the pubic bones, respond by active growth changes to the hormonal stimuli produced by the sex hormones. Nevertheless, Boucher[49] finds significant statistical differences in the greater sciatic notch, using British foetal material, and also in the sub-pubic angle[50] in prenatal remains of American Whites and Negroes. With her method $\frac{\text{Breadth} \times 100}{\text{Depth}}$ of the greater sciatic notch, she managed to distinguish without error the 34 foetal pelvic specimens which she had at her disposal. Although her results are very promising, they need confirmation.

The adult pelvis as a unit. For obvious reasons, the number of works on the female pelvis far surpasses those on the male pelvis; the former has been studied above all in relation to childbirth, and to the various stages of pregnancy, giving rise to the frequent confusion between the characteristically female pelvis and that of the childbearing woman. That is to say, in normal circumstances, female pelves are not so wide, brachypellic or platypellic, as the case may be, as it has been supposed and described.

Innominate bone. Whilst it is rare to be able to reckon upon a complete pelvis, one very frequently has at one's disposal nothing more than some fragments. Generally speaking, certain parts of the innominate bone can be of more value to us than fragments of other bones in the matter of sexing.

Genovés[51,52] after the analysis of forty-four absolute measurements, nine indices and thirteen morphoscopic characteristics on this bone concludes that one index, three absolute measurements, and four morphoscopic characteristics are valuable for sex diagnosis.

It has been made evident[53,54] that the main sexual difference in the *sciatic notch* is not its width or depth or the index between both measurements, but the fact that the perpendicular from the maximum-width line to the deepest point of the notch divides the width into roughly two equal chords in females, whereas in males the upper chord is the smaller. Thus the features of the innominate bone to be considered in sexing are as follows:

1. The sciatic notch index: composed of the distance in projection between the perpendicular at the point of greatest depth, starting from the line determining the width of the greater sciatic notch, and the highest point of this width, times 100, divided by the width of the greater sciatic notch.

2. Middle width of pubis. This is the distance from the mid-point of the anterior border of the pubic symphysis to the nearest point on the inner border of the obturator foramen.

3. Minimum lower width of the ilium, which is the shortest distance between the supra-acetabular point and the anterior border of the greater sciatic notch.

4. Maximum vertical diameter of the acetabulum, following the direction of the general axis of the body of the ischium.

5. Pre-auricular sulcus. In the postero-inferior border of the ilium.

6. Composite arch of the anterior border of the auricular facet and the anterior border of the greater sciatic notch.

7. Shape of the greater sciatic notch.

8. Relative massiveness of the upper area of the medial portion of the pubis or pubic crest.

By using either a series of metrical characters, standardized morphoscopic characters or a combination of both composed in the manner described above, an accuracy of 95% can be expected.

Although it was in favour for some years, and has a certain amount of utility, I shall not deal with the ischio-pubic index of Hanna and Washburn[31] for it presents many technical deficiencies.[30,51,55]

SKULL AND FACE AS A WHOLE

The skull has traditionally been the anatomical unit most used in sex diagnosis. In general terms the male skull has a higher cranial capacity than the female. Moreover, a female skull capacity rarely reaches 1,500 cc. To Hrdlička a capacity of above 1,450 cc suggests a male whereas a capacity of 1,300 cc or less suggests a female.

The male skull, besides being generally bigger than the female skull, looks more solid, and usually has a more receding frontal.[56] The malars and the mandible are stronger and more solid, and the facial skeleton in general is relatively bigger and longer.

The supra-orbital ridges are more prominent in male remains. They have more marked mastoid processes and also external occipital protuberances. Keen[29] arrives at an 85% accuracy in sex determination by using (a) the supra-orbital ridges, (b) the occipital crest and nuchal lines and (c) the ridge at the upper rim of the auditory meatus (posterior root of the zygomatic process of the temporal). In the experience of

Keen,[29] of Machado de Sousa[57] and of the author, this last characteristic is of considerable value, for it is well marked in the majority of male skulls and generally weak in females.

In the mandible, the gonial angle is more open in females, whilst the ascending ramus, the condyle and the symphysis are higher amongst men.[58] The ascending ramus is also wider in males, and the chin more square, quite frequently showing lateral protuberances.[59] After a metrical and morphoscopical examination, Morant says, 'It will be safe to conclude that sexual differences are more marked for the mandible than for the cranium.' Anatomically, following Morant's methods,[58] Cleaver[60] managed to sex accurately 85% of his samples.

ARTICULAR SURFACES OF THE BONES—ESPECIALLY THE LONG-BONES

Just as the vertical diameter of the acetabulum is found amongst the four characteristics of greatest value in the innominate bone for sex discrimination, the femur and humerus heads, as also their distal articular surfaces and those of the other long-bones, are very valuable for sex determination. Generally, in male and female long-bones of the same general size, the articular surface of the second will be appreciably less than that of the first. Obviously, this is better appreciated in femur and humerus heads, although others (e.g. the sigmoid notch of the ulna or the upper articular surface of the astragalus) can be very useful.[26]

Although long-bone criteria are not commonly used, there is an extensive literature dealing directly with sex differences in these bones.[61-64] Dwight,[65] in a fairly ample series, found that the diameter of the femur head has a mean of 49·7 mm and 43·8 mm for men and women respectively, with only one male specimen having a value lower than the female one, and only two females above the male mean. Thieme and Schull[66] in a study of North American Negroes calculated means of 57·17 mm and 41·52 mm for the diameter of the femoral head in men and women respectively. They conclude that it is 'the best single measurement for discriminating the sexes in this series' of the eight characters studied. By using for preference the femur head, the epicondylar width of the humerus and other characteristics of the long-bones and pelvis they were able to reach an accuracy of 98·5% in known material and one of 97% when the material was unknown.

SOME OTHER CHARACTERISTICS

Apart from what has been said about the scapula by Bainbridge and Genovés[67] and apart from the various data provided by Vallois,[68] Olivier and Pineau[69] give the following data: (1) A scapula is female if the breadth of the glenoid fossa is less than 2·61 mm; (2) the height of the bone less than 144·4 mm; (3) the length of the spine less than 127·9 mm; and (4) the weight less than 38·58 g; the bone is male if these dimensions are more than 26·8 mm, 15·75 mm, 141·4 mm, and 61·78 g respectively.

From the articles by Olivier et al.[70] on the clavicle the useful data in Table B have been taken.

Although it has traditionally been desirable to use the sacrum for sex determination, Piganiol and Olivier[71] reach the conclusion that the only element of any value in this respect is the weight. This is of little use in fragmentary material.

TABLE B

Dimensions of clavicle used in determination of sex.

	Female if less than	Male if more than
Maximum length	138 mm	150 mm
Maximum breadth	20·5 mm	25·5 mm
Perimeter at the middle of the diaphysis	32 mm	36 mm
Weight	8 g	20 g

Various authors have attempted to use the sternum in sex discrimination, but I believe that its use is too open to error, and in any case, it is very rare to find a complete sternum of prehistoric date (*see* Serra[72] and especially Ashley[73] in this respect).

Some authors[74,75] have revived in recent years the method of using the weight of the bones as characteristics of sex discrimination, but its value seems to be very low and almost never applicable to early remains.

Gejvall[76] has suggested standards for verifying sex (and age) of cremated remains. This method seems promising, but certainly needs further elaboration.

CONCLUSIONS

Although some important aspects of sex determination have been neglected in the past, new statistical procedures are gaining greater attention, not only for their application to articular surface measurements, but also in that these methods are being applied to other parts of the skeleton such as the skull, sternum, pelvis and scapula.

Pons[77] achieves 95%, 94% and 89% correct estimates using four femoral, six pelvic, and five sternal measurements respectively. Bainbridge and Genovés[67] applied their method to various metrical characteristics of the scapula from a population of known identity, comprising twenty-six males and twenty females, with the following results:

At the 99–87% limits 21 individuals were 'sexed'.
At the 87–80% limits 2 more individuals were 'sexed'.
At the 84–20% limits 10 more individuals were 'sexed'.

Giles[78] achieves 86% and 85% correct determinations in skulls of Whites and of Negroes respectively, using various measurements.

Other authors, such as McKern and Munro,[79] Brothwell[80] and later Giles and Elliot[81] have applied discriminant functions or the concept of 'size and shape' introduced by Penrose[82] for racial diagnosis. Perhaps, by following these methods, we shall in the future possess true limits of accuracy for the sex determination of various parts of the skeleton, and for a range of human populations both prehistoric and recent. This is a desirable goal which is not so far distant.

REFERENCES AND NOTES

1 BOULE, M. 1911–13. *Ann. Paléont.* 6, 106–72; 7, 21–192; 8, 1–70

2 LEAKEY, L. S. B. 1953. *Adam's Ancestors*, London, 4th ed.

3 BOYD, W. C. 1950. *Genetics and the Races of Man*, Boston

4 HOOTON, E. A. 1930. *The Indians of Pecos Pueblo; a Study of their Skeletal Remains*, New Haven

5 ANGEL, J. L. 1954. Human Biology, Health and History in Greece from First Settlement until Now. *Yearbook Am. Phil. Soc.*, 168–74.

6 NEEL, J. V. 1958. *Hum. Biol. 30*, 43–72

7 FEREMBACH, D. 1960. *Boletim da Soc. Portug. de Ciencias Naturais* sér. 2a, *8*, 1–6

8 —— 1960. *Trabalhos de Anthropologia e Etnologia 18*, 5–23

9 ORFORD, M. 1934. *S. Afr. J. Sci. 31*, 586–610

10 HEYNS, O. S. 1945. *A Critical Analysis of the Bantu Pelvis with Special Reference to the Female*; D.Sc. thesis, Univ. of the Witwatersrand, Johannesburg

11 HOOIJER, D. A. 1948. *Zoo. Med. Museum Leiden 29*, 175–301

12 —— 1950. *Verh. Ken. Ned. Akad. v. Wetenschappen Amsterdam, Afd. Natuurk II, 46*, 1–164

13 —— 1952. *Proc. Ken. Ned. Akad. v. Wetenschappen Amsterdam*, ser. C, *55*, 375–81

14 MORANT, G. M. 1930. *Ann. Eugen. Lond. 4*, 214

15 BONIN, G. VON. 1935. *Hum. Biol. 7*, 196–221

16 BROTHWELL, D. R. 1961. *Man. 61*, 113–16

17 KEITH, SIR ARTHUR. 1931. *New Discoveries Relating to the Antiquity of Man*, London

18 Though he expressed this opinion cautiously and stated that it was subject to modification in the light of further discoveries

19 MCCOWN, T. D. and KEITH, SIR ARTHUR. 1939. *The Stone Age of Mount Carmel*, Oxford, vol. II

20 STEWART, T. D. 1960. *Science 131*, 1437–8

21 GENOVÉS, S. T. 1954. *J. Roy. Anth. Inst. 84*, 131–44

22 JENKS, A. E. 1936. *Pleistocene Man in Minnesota: a fossil Homo Sapiens*, Minneapolis

23 HRDLIČKA, A. 1937. *Am. J. Phys. Anth. 22*, 175–99

24 JENKS, A. E. 1938. *Am. Anth. 40*, 328–36

25 DE TERRA, H. J. ROMERO and STEWART, T. D. 1949. Tepexpan Man. *Viking Fund Publications in Anthropology*, no. 11

26 GENOVÉS, S. T. 1960. *Am. J. Phys. Anth. 18*, 205–18

27 WOOD JONES, F. 1907–8. *The Archaeological Survey of Nubia, II: Report on the Human Remains*, Cairo

28 FAULHABER, H. (unpublished). La Población de Tlatilco Caracterizada por sus Entierros

29 KEEN, J. A. 1950. *Am. J. Phys. Anth. 8*, 65–78

30 STEWART, T. D. 1954. *Ibid. 12*, 385–92

31 HANNA, R. E. and WASHBURN, S. L. 1953. *Hum. Biol. 2*, 21–27

32 TESTUT, L. 1928. *Traité d'Anatomie humaine* (ed. LATARJET, L., Paris)

33 KROGMAN, W. 1939. *FBI Law Enforcement Bull. 8*, no. 8

34 STEWART, T. D. 1948. *Am. J. Phys. Anth. 6*, 315–28

35 BRASH, J. C. (ed.) 1951. *Cunningham's Text Book of Anatomy*, London, 9th ed.

36 HRDLIČKA, A. 1952. *Practical Anthropometry* (ed. STEWART, T. D.), Philadelphia, 4th ed.

37 BOYD, J. D. and TREVOR, J. C. 1953. Problems in Reconstruction; I: Race, Sex, Age and Stature from Skeletal Material, in SIMPSON, C. K. (ed.) *Modern Trends in Forensic Medicine*, London, 133–52

38 CORNWALL, I. W. 1956. *Bones for the Archaeologist*, London

39 OLIVIER, G. 1960. *Pratique anthropologique*, Paris

40 MONTAGU, M. F. A. 1960. *A Handbook of Anthropometry*, New York

41 FEHLING, H. 1876. *Arch. Gynaek. 10*, 1–80

42 THOMSON, A. 1899. *J. Anat. Lond. 33*, 359–80

43 VILLEMIN, F. 1957. *Strasbourg Méd. J. 3*

44 KONIKOW, M. 1894. *Arch. Gynaek. 45*, 19–42

45 LE DAMANY, 1904. *J. Anat. Paris, 40*, 387–413

46 KAPPERS, J. ARIENS. 1938. *Biemetrische Bijdrage tet de Kennis van de ontogenestische entwikkeling van het menschelijk Pekken*, Assen

47 YAMAMURA, H. 1939. *Jap. J. Obstet. Gynaec. 22*, 268–341

48 HEYNS, O. S. 1947. *S. Afr. J. Med. Sci. 12*, 17–20

49 BOUCHER, B. J. 1955. *J. Forensic Med. 1*, 51–54

50. —— 1957. *Am. J. Phys. Anth. 15*, 587–600

51 GENOVÉS, S. T. 1959a. *Diferencias sexuales en el hueso coxal*, México

52 GENOVÉS, S. T. 1959b. *Bull. et Mém. de la Soc. d'Anth. de Paris* 10ème sér., *10*, 3–95
53 LAZORTHES, G. and LHEZ, A. 1939. *Arch. Anat. Strasbourg 27*, 143–70
54 LETTERMAN, G. S. 1941. *Am. J. Phys. Anth. 28*, 99–116
55 GAILLARD, JEAN. 1961. *Bull. et Mém. de la Soc. d'Anth. de Paris* 11ème sér., *2*, 92–108
56 WOO, J. K. 1949. *Am. J. Phys. Anth. 7*, 215–26
57 MACHADO DE SOUSA, O. 1954. *Revista de Antrop. 2*, 11–18
58 MORANT, G. M. 1936. *Biometrika 28*, 84–122
59 ALBUQUERQUE, R. M. 1952. *Contribuições para o Estudo da Antrop. Portug. 5*, 65–196
60 CLEAVER, F. H. 1937–8. *Biometrika 29*, 80–112
61 DWIGHT, T. 1894. *Boston Med. and Surg. J. 22*, 1–12
62 —— 1904. *Am. J. Anat. 4*, 18–31
63 PARSONS, F. G. 1914. *J. Anat. Lond. 48*, 238–67
64 PEARSON, K. 1915. *Biometrika 10*, 479–87
65 DWIGHT, T. 1900. *J. Anat. Lond. 24*, 61–68
66 THIEME, F. P. and SCHULL, W. J. 1957. *Hum. Biol. 29*, 242–73
67 BAINBRIDGE, D. and GENOVÉS, S. T. 1956. *J. Roy. Anth. Inst. 86*, 109–29
68 VALLOIS, H. V. 1928–46. *Bull. et Mém. de la Soc. d'Anth. de Paris* 7ème. sér., *9* (1928), 129–68; 7ème sér., *1* (1929), 110–91; 8ème sér., *2* (1932), 3–153; 9ème sér., *7* (1946), 16–110
69 OLIVIER, G. and PINEAU, H. 1957. *Arch. d'Anat. 5*, 67–88
70 —— 1951–6. *Bull. et Mém. de la Soc. d'Anth. de Paris* 10ème sér., *2* (1951), 67–99 and 121–57; 10ème sér., *3* (1952), 269–79; 10ème sér., *4* (1953), 553–61; 10ème sér., *5* (1954), 35–56 (with CHALBEUF, M. and LALUQUE, P.) and 144–53; 10ème sér., *6* (1955), 282–302; 10ème sér., *7* (1956), 225–61 (with CAPLIEZ, S.) and 404–47
71 PIGANIOL, G. and OLIVIER, G. 1958. *C.R. de l'Assn. des Anatomistes (54e. réunion)* no. *100*, 589–94
72 SERRA, J. A. 1941. *Contribuições para o Estudo da Antrop. Portug. 4*, 33–159
73 ASHLEY, G. T. 1956. *J. Forensic Med. 3*, 27–43
74 VALLOIS, H. V. 1957. *L'Anth. 61*, 45–69
75 OLIVIER, G. and PINEAU, H. 1958. *Bull. et Mém. de la Soc. d'Anth. de Paris* 10ème sér., *9*, 328–39
76 GEJVALL, N.-G. 1959. Vanligaste Ben: Nagot om Bearbetning Av Branda Ben Och Deras Vetenskapliga Värde. *Särtryck ur Fvnd*, Göteborg
77 PONS, J. 1955. *Trabajos del Instituto Bernardino de Sahagún. 14*, 137–59
78 GILES, E. 1960. *Race and sex in crania by discriminant analysis*; paper presented to the Fifth International Congress of Anthropological and Ethnological Sciences, Paris
79 McKERN, T. W. and MUNRO, E. H. 1959. *Am. Antiq. 24*, 375–82
80 BROTHWELL, D. R. 1959. *Deutschen Ges. f. Anth. 6*, 103–9
81 GILES, E. and ELLIOT, O. 1961 (Abstract). *Am. J. Phys. Anth. 19*, 99
82 PENROSE, L. S. 1954. *Ann. Eugen. London. 18*, 337–43

35 *Estimation of Age and Mortality*

SANTIAGO GENOVÉS

THERE ARE TWO SIDES to the problem of determining the age of prehistoric remains: first, what we can ascertain about the age distribution and life expectation of earlier populations, either by analysing their skeletal remains, or by examining the vital statistics of present-day human groups whose state of cultural development is comparable with the peoples being studied by the prehistorian; second, starting with the data provided by well-identified remains, and by legitimate morphological methods of deduction obtaining formulae for the estimation of age in skeletal remains. During the last few years the criteria for the second point have changed considerably. Nevertheless, the data regarding this aspect are far more abundant than for the first.

Precision in the diagnosis of age in a skeleton has been a subject for study chiefly owing to the interest displayed in it by physical anthropologists, and to its application in the field of forensic medicine. Only recently have we taken account of the value it holds in the study of earlier populations. It must, however, be said at the outset that recent studies have shown once more that, although we can arrive at a fair degree of exactness in age estimates, the variability *within* and *between* the races is considerable. Indeed, there remains much to be discovered in this field of study, which means that the estimation of age in either individuals or populations is still subject to a variable margin of error.

Before continuing, a few explanations are necessary. In the first place we cannot depend on having skeletal series representing prehistoric populations which are statistically large enough in number and which are perfectly identified as regards the characteristics of age. We base our deductions chiefly on data taken from more recent and better known groups, and from those which we have reason to believe possess—because of their racial affinities, geographic location, and cultural similarities—characteristics homologous to the peoples we are trying to analyse. Moreover, we shall be concerned here solely with prehistoric man belonging to the species *Homo sapiens*, for if we venture into previous morphological stages, the problem becomes greater and more complex.[1]

Apart from the cultural elements often associated with skeletal remains—which can indirectly shed some light on the subject of age estimation and the numbers and demographic characteristics of a population—we rely in the first instance on the number and state of development of the bones, and on certain characteristics in them which have been successfully related to definite ages.

It may be noted here that although we are at present considering age, it has in fact quite a close relationship with sex. It is well known that in general the developmental stage of bone growth in relation to chronological age is more advanced in females than in males. Thus it is estimated, for example,[2] that in girls the ischio-pubic ramus is joined at approximately $4\frac{1}{2}$ years whilst in boys this occurs at about 7 years; also that fusion of the three primary elements of the pelvis takes place at about 10 years and 14 years respectively.

DEMOGRAPHY AND MORTALITY

Until very recently the essential criteria for age estimation in adults consisted of observing the degree of obliteration of the cranial sutures. It is because of this that excessive age estimates were misguidedly made in the past on prehistoric man.

Expectation of life in prehistoric groups. At the very beginning of this century[3] investigations began to be made into the life expectation of earlier man, finding that chances of long life were very small. Lately, a fair number of authors have concerned themselves with this problem.[4-12] Vallois,[5] for example, has considered in detail life expectation in Upper Palaeolithic and Mesolithic man (Table A). It will be seen that an age of over 50 years was very seldom attained, and although he considered suture criteria in this work, the evidence of the post-cranial remains does not fundamentally contradict these findings. Further data on age variability in earlier groups is given in Tables B and C. From other considerations there is no doubt that there exists a close relationship between the cultural level and the expectation of life in earlier times.

TABLE A

Expectation of life of Upper Palaeolithic and Mesolithic man.

	No.	Age				
		12–20	21–30	31–40	41–50	51–60
Upper Palaeolithic and Ibero-Maurusian men	86	15 (17·4 %)	31 (36 %)	27 (31·4 %)	11 (12·8 %)	2 (2·3 %)
Mesolithic men	50	6 (12 %)	35 (70 %)	6 (12 %)	1 (2 %)	2 (4 %)

From Vallois.[5]

Mortality of sub-adults. Until recently, little attention has been given to this subject. The small quantity of sub-adult remains, their lack of inclusion in normal population statistics, and their frequent state of severe fragmentation, have contributed to their being overlooked for quite a long time. A further complicating factor is the possible practice of burying stillbirths or young infants in places away from the main cemeteries, and which thus are usually missed. Nevertheless, after considering such problems, Howells[8] deduces that the percentage of mortality among sub-adults was between 55 and 60%.

Sex differences in mortality. Many authors are in agreement that in prehistoric times and early historic periods mortality among females was considerably more frequent before the age of 40 years than for males.[4-7,9,11,13-15] This greater female mortality during the earlier age periods (contrary to what happens today) is usually attributed to causes related to pregnancy, although other reasons have also been suggested.

TABLE B
Mortality by age in populations of different epochs.

Origin	Period	n	0–12 %	13–20 %	21–40 %	41–60 %	61–x %	Authors
Several	Lower Palaeolithic (*H. neanderthalensis*)	20	40·0	15·0	40·0	5·0	0·0	Vallois (1937)**
—	Upper Palaeolithic	102	24·5	9·8	53·9	11·8	0·0	**
—	Mesolithic	65	30·8	6·2	58·5	3·0	1·5	**
Spanish Levant	Neo-eneolithic	101	24·7	14·8	41·6	17·8	1·0	Fusté (1952)
Anatolia	Chalcolithic and Copper Age	104	31·7	12·5	34·6	17·3	3·8	Several (Senyürek, 1951)
—	Chalcolithic to 13th cent. BC	122	20·4	13·1	40·9	19·6	5·7	Senyürek (1947)†
Aulnay-aux-Planches	Neolithic	28	0·0	7·1	64·3	25·0	3·6	Riquet (1943) and Fusté (1952)*
Austria	Bronze	273	6·9	17·2	39·9	28·6	7·3	Franz and Winkler (1936)**
Ancient Greeks	—	2,022	18·7	23·4	33·8	13·6	10·1	Several (Richardson, 1933)†
Egyptians	—	141	19·8	14·1	39·7	16·3	9·9	Pearson (1901–1902)†
Ancient Romans	Roman era	8,065	38·1	19·9	30·0	7·1	4·6	MacDonell (1913)†
Spain and Lusitania	Roman era	1,996	9·4	16·4	38·8	19·9	15·2	—
Africa	Roman era	10,697	9·9	9·4	28·4	19·6	32·4	—
Lower Austria	1829	—	50·7	3·3	12·2	12·8	21·0	Franz and Winkler (1936)**
—	1900	—	44·3	2·0	12·1	15·7	25·9	—
—	1927	—	15·4	2·7	11·9	22·6	47·4	—
France	1896–1905	—	25·3	2·6	11·5	17·3	43·3	Vallois (1937)**

Origin	Period	n	0–14 %	15–19 %	20–39 %	40–59 %	61–x %	Authors
Spain	1948	299,178	21·8	2·3	11·8	16·3	47·7	Statistical Year Book, 1950
—	1949	315,512	20·7	2·0	10·8	16·2	50·3	1951
—	1950	300,112	19·7	1·9	10·1	15·9	52·4	1952
—	1951	321,083	17·6	1·5	8·7	15·7	56·6	1953

From Fusté,[6] p. 328.
* Compilation of the Aulnay-aux-Planches series (Riquet 1943) and of the Dolmen des Bretons (Fusté 1952), of the same locality.
** The limit between the first two categories of ages is at 14 years.
† According to Senyürek, 1951.

TABLE C
Percentage of male and female deaths in relation to age at death.

Age Group	Bronze Age of Lower Austria		Egyptians of Roman times	
	%M.	%F.	%M.	%F.
Adolescents (14–20 yrs)	10	25·9	6·5	18·1
Adults (21–40 yrs)	37·5	52·8	44·2	65·9
Mature Adults (41–60 yrs)	45	13	29·5	11·3
Senile (> 60 yrs)	7·5	8·3	19·6	4·5

From Vallois,[4] p. 530.

METHODS OF DETERMINING SKELETAL AGE[16]

Up to the age of about 30 years, the estimation of age for fairly complete specimens can be made with reasonable accuracy by considering methodically three groups of processes. These are dental eruption, synostosis of the bones, and epiphysial union of the bones—especially the long-bones. For later age periods, transformations on the articular surface of the pubic symphysis and certain structural changes within the bones themselves are employed.

DENTAL ERUPTION AND OTHER CHANGES

Milk dentition. Although sex differences in dental maturation are slight, there is good evidence that eruption can be influenced by outside factors.[17] In Table D data for Korean, North American and Japanese boys are compared to show the degree of variability.

TABLE D
Eruption of primary teeth (in months): comparison of Korean, American and Japanese infants.

	Maxillary			Mandibular		
	Korean	American	Japanese	Korean	American	Japanese
Central incisors	9–11	6–9	7–9	7–9	5–7	7–9
Lateral incisors	11–14	7–11	8–11	11–14	6–8	8–11
Canines	15–19	16–20	17–20	15–19	14–18	16–19
First milk molars	13–19	10–18	15–20	13–19	8–16	15–20
Second milk molars	19–29	20–28	23–36	19–29	16–24	22–26

From Duk Jin Yun. 1957. *Am. J. Phys. Anth.* 15, 261–8.

Permanent dentition. Hurme,[18] in what is probably the largest sample of actual populations, provides the data presented in Table E. In regard to this he writes: 'A glance at the table shows that the minima and maxima at the 95% level are quite apart, ranging from a little over 3 years to more than $6\frac{1}{2}$ years, not counting the third molars. Thus

TABLE E

Normal variability in emergence of human permanent teeth.

Sequence	Tooth		95 % range (yrs)		Sex diff. (yr)
	Max.	Mand.	Males	Females	
1	—	M_1	4·64 – 7·78	4·37 – 7·51	·27
2	M^1	—	4·83 – 7·97	4·65 – 7·79	·18
3	—	I_1	5·01 – 8·07	4·73 – 7·79	·28
4	I^1	—	5·88 – 9·06	5·61 – 8·79	·27
5	—	I_2	5·98 – 9·42	5·62 – 9·06	·36
6	I^2	—	6·75 – 10·59	6·28 – 10·12	·47
7M 8F+	P^1	—	7·52 – 13·28	7·15 – 12·91	·37
8M 7F+	—	C	8·30 – 13·28	7·37 – 12·35	·93
9	—	P_2	7·94 – 13·70	7·30 – 13·06	·64
10	P^2	—	8·10 – 14·26	7·80 – 13·96	·30
11	—	P_2	8·18 – 14·76	7·60 – 14·18	·58
12	C	—	9·00 – 14·38	8·29 – 13·67	·71
13	—	M_2	9·45 – 14·79	8·99 – 14·33	·46
14	M^2	—	9·99 – 15·37	9·58 – 14·96	·41
15	—	M_3	16·5(?) – 27·0(?)	16·5(?) – 27·0(?)	small
16	M^3	—	16·5(?) – 27·0(?)	16·5(?) – 27·0(?)	small

From Hurme,[18] p. 379.

the chances of error are considerable in using teeth for purposes of estimation of age, and the desirability of supplementing this estimate with evidence of some other kind becomes easy to understand.'

With this in mind, and only then, should we apply tooth emergence data (Table F) to earlier material. As regards the third molars, we can say that for Europeans (and those of European origin) the main eruptional period is 17–22 years, although sometimes they are much later. Account should of course be taken of the fact that congenital absence of one or more thirds is not uncommon, the frequency of absence for modern populations ranging from a few per cent to over 30%.

Dental attrition. The degree of wear on the teeth can be used in populations where we *already know* the cultural circumstances, in order not to fall into considerable error, and in the total absence of other data. To rely on attrition in populations of whom we know little can lead to serious errors.

Other dental procedures. Approaching the problem from another angle, Zander and Hurzeler[19] have clearly shown that cementum thickness is directly related to age for single-rooted teeth with healthy supporting tissues. Likewise, Nalbandian and Sognnaes[20] have initiated studies in which they correlate chronological age with criteria such as secondary dentine, periodontal attachment, cementum apposition and root sclerosis. Employing the multifactorial approach introduced by Gustafson[21] to various modifications amongst which are figured those mentioned above, it is possible that valid results will be obtained in the future.

Mandibular Teeth

Group	Source	Method	Range of Size of n	$_1I_1$	$_2I_2$	$_1C_1$	$_1P_1$	$_2P_2$	$_1M_1$	$_2Mt_2$
Male										
American Negro	Steggerda & Hill	L, m	From 9 to 50	6·95 / ·59	7·94 / ·76	10·99 / ·94	10·86 / ·87	11·48 / ·90	6·97 / ·70	12·33 / 1·02
Zulu	Suk	C, med.	492	5·47 / ·73	5·96 / 1·04	9·63 / 1·31	10·11 / 1·38	10·75 / 1·28	5·23 / ·71	11·04 / 1·17
Maya	Steggerda & Hill	L, m	25 to 67	7·41 / ·67	8·40 / ·53	11·16 / ·90	11·14 / 1·00	11·99 / 1·08	6·76 / ·62	11·86 / 1·07
Pima	Dahlberg	C, med.	470	6·26 / ·89	7·65 / 1·21	10·78 / 1·28	10·43 / 1·29	11·39 / 1·45	5·89 / ·67	11·29 / 1·25
American	Cattell	C, med.	3,863	6·25 / ·68	7·58 / ·79	10·66 / 1·02	10·58 / 1·36	11·33 / 1·54	6·16 / ·79	11·66 / ·86
English	Ainsworth	C, med.	2,000	6·49 / ·69	7·72 / ·71	10·80 / 1·09	10·86 / 1·33	11·80 / 1·50	6·24 / ·69	11·86 / 1·09
New Zealand	Leslie	C, med.	1,427	6·38 / ·59	7·42 / ·83	10·78 / ·93	11·34 / 1·42	12·18 / 1·44	6·46 / ·76	11·89 / 1·13
Female										
American Negro	Steggerda & Hill	L, m	8 to 50	6·28 / ·79	7·19 / ·70	9·73 / ·92	10·23 / ·87	10·77 / ·90	6·33 / ·62	11·43 / ·99
Zulu	Suk	C, med.	516	5·85 / ·73	6·23 / 1·03	9·12 / 1·07	9·76 / 1·12	10·24 / 1·32	5·49 / ·75	10·61 / 1·49
Maya	Steggerda & Hill	L, m	13 to 55	7·15 / ·78	8·09 / ·81	10·32 / ·81	10·24 / 1·16	11·16 / 1·16	6·68 / ·75	11·49 / 1·10
Pima	Dahlberg	C, med.	487	6·15 / ·78	7·32 / 1·02	9·66 / 1·25	9·87 / ·87	10·73 / ·90	5·43 / ·76	10·80 / 1·10
American	Cattell	C, med.	3,826	6·08 / ·75	7·25 / ·68	9·66 / ·91	10·08 / 1·30	11·08 / 1·46	6·00 / ·99	11·42 / 1·05
English	Ainsworth	C, med.	2,000	6·19 / ·65	7·50 / ·72	9·90 / ·95	10·36 / 1·22	11·21 / 1·46	5·95 / ·68	11·52 / 1·03
New Zealand	Leslie	C, med.	1,335	6·09 / ·60	7·16 / ·62	9·74 / ·94	10·54 / 1·18	11·73 / 1·35	6·30 / ·59	11·36 / 1·47

From Dahlberg A. and Menegaz-Bock, R. 1958. *J. Dent. Res. 37*, 1123–40, Table VIII.

TABLE F *Estimates of age of tooth emergence, medians or means (in years), + one standard deviation, in Negro, American Indian, Caucasoid American and English populations.*

Group	Source	Method	Range of Size of n	Maxillary Teeth						
				$1I^1$	$2I^2$	$1C^1$	$1P^1$	$2P^2$	$1M^1$	$2M^2$
Male										
American Negro	Steggerda & Hill	L, m	From 9 to 50	7·77	8·45	11·74	10·82	11·92	6·79	12·64
				·66	·81	·97	1·09	1·03	·79	·92
Zulu	Suk	C, med.	492	5·98	6·98	10·17	10·11	10·66	5·26	11·36
				1·07	1·40	·17	·11	·69	·69	1·21
Maya	Steggerda & Hill	L, m	25 to 67	8·35	9·30	11·79	10·29	11·63	6·88	12·49
				·67	·88	1·55	1·35	1·19	·55	·99
Pima	Dahlberg	C, med.	470	7·83	8·74	11·66	10·08	11·33	5·98	11·67
				·71	·75	1·13	1·01	1·03	·77	1·21
American	Cattell	C, med.	3,863	7·33	8·42	11·50	10·33	11·08	6·33	12·16
				·74	·79	1·41	1·28	1·36	·79	1·13
English	Ainsworth	C, med.	2,000	7·42	8·81	11·73	9·96	10·89	6·34	12·33
				·69	·94	1·20	1·59	1·31	·68	1·06
New Zealand	Leslie	C, med.	1,427	7·26	8·32	11·40	10·01	11·74	6·47	12·47
				·80	·90	1·12	1·42	1·50	·78	1·33
Female										
American Negro	Steggerda & Hill	L, m	8 to 50	7·13	8·31	10·39	10·07	10·97	6·90	11·85
				·60	·88	·85	·79	·81	·45	·75
Zulu	Suk	C, med.	516	6·18	7·14	9·72	9·76	10·06	5·77	10·92
				·93	1·25	1·44	1·27	1·23	·57	1·38
Maya	Steggerda & Hill	L, m	13 to 55	8·27	8·63	10·89	9·96	10·92	6·69	12·09
				·85	·76	1·00	·94	·94	·70	1·01
Pima	Dahlberg	C, med.	487	7·47	8·34	10·94	9·63	10·73	5·80	11·38
				·69	·98	1·59	1·23	1·34	·79	1·29
American	Cattell	C, med.	3,826	7·08	8·00	11·08	9·92	10·92	6·16	12·08
				·68	·79	1·07	1·31	1·42	·57	1·13
English	Ainsworth	C, med.	2,000	7·20	8·37	11·20	9·77	10·72	6·12	12·07
				·63	·94	1·12	1·13	1·33	·68	1·03
New Zealand	Leslie	C, med.	1,335	6·83	7·86	10·82	10·52	11·24	6·38	12·20
				·69	·61	1·02	·99	1·20	·78	1·28

SYNOSTOSIS OF BONES

The pelvis. Although a certain degree of variability exists, the union of the ischium and pubis in the ischio-pubic ramus and the union of the three elements composing the acetabulum, are of use in the case of pre-adolescents (Table G).

TABLE G

The pelvis: union of the conjoined rami and of the acetabulum.

Year of Union of Conjoined Rami	Author	Year of Union Acetabulum
—	Stevenson (1924)[22]	at 15–16
7th year	Wood Jones in *Buchanan's Anatomy* (1949)[23]	14–16
4–4½ in females	Francis (1952)[24]	females at 10
7 in males		males at 14
8 in females	Smout (1943)[25]	—
later in males		
9th year	Grant (1952)[26]	—
—	McKern and Stewart (1957)[27]	at 17 (final age)

The sacrum. Allowing for bone variations, union of the bodies of the sacral vertebrae begins at about 16 years and proceeds from the lower segments upwards. At about 23 years, ossification is complete, although in a number of cases the union between the upper segments S_1 and S_2 is not completed until about 30 years.

The skull. Contrary to the criteria traditionally accepted until recent times, the process of suture obliteration in *Homo sapiens* does not follow a well-defined pattern.[27,28] Various authors have thrown grave doubts on the idea that the sutures are directly related to the growth of the skull, and as a result, to the age of the individual.[29–37] Thus the only union of bones in the skull which we are now able to employ is at the basi-sphenoid synchondrosis. This gap between the basi-sphenoid and basi-occipital is obliterated about adulthood, as various authors have found (Table H).

TABLE H

Closure of the basi-sphenoidal synchondrosis.

Author	Begins–Ends
	yrs
Cunningham (1951)[34]	18–25
Prinsloo (1953)[35]	23
Hrdlička (1952)[36]	18–19
McKern and Stewart (1957)[27]	18–21
Genovés and Messmacher (1959)[37]	18–20
Vallois (1960)[5]	17–23
Singer—Comments to Vallois, 1960	17–25

EPIPHYSIAL UNION OF THE BONES, ESPECIALLY THE LONG-BONES

The distal epiphysis of the humerus and proximal epiphyses of the ulna and radius. These show the first signs of union, which is generally complete by 18 years.

The epiphyses of the femur, tibia and fibula. According to the majority of authors, the process of epiphysial fusion of these bones has already been completed by the age of 19 years, making it possible to estimate 17–18 years for a specimen with partial ossification and less than 17 years if the process has not yet begun.

The ischial tuberosity. The epiphysial portion of the ischial tuberosity unites with the rest of the ascending ramus of the ischium at about 19 years, and towards 20 years completes its process of ossification.

Iliac crest and vertebral epiphysial plates. If the plates and crest are separate the person is under 19 years. If there is partial obliteration, the age is probably between 19 and 20 years. Over the age of 20 years union is usually complete.

Proximal epiphysis of the humerus and distal epiphyses of the ulna and radius. The ossification process of the epiphyses is relatively slower, for it begins at about 18 years and does not end until about 21–22 years of age. Although these three epiphyses have been grouped together, there is evidence that the humerus head undergoes a slight retardation in its ossification relative to the other two.

Medial extremity of the clavicle. This presents certain difficulties on account of the polymorphism of the articular surfaces. Nevertheless we can say that although the process of fusion generally begins at about 18 years, it is quite often retarded and may begin as late as 25 years. Normally the fusion ends between 27 and 30 years, with the last site of union being located in the form of a fissure along the inferior border.

CHANGES AT THE ARTICULAR SURFACE OF THE PUBIC SYMPHYSIS

Todd[38] described ten phases through which the symphysial surface of the pubis passes in its metamorphosis from adolescence up to 50 years or more. With slight variations other authors have since corroborated the usefulness of this method.

Whilst the non-specialist can, with sound criteria and within certain limits, use the guides which have so far been indicated for the estimation of age, it is far more difficult for him to succeed in using the criteria of the pubic symphysis in the same form. Nevertheless it seems worth giving here, at least very concisely, the ten phases of Todd, with slight corrections proposed by Brooks[28] (McKern and Stewart[27] have reproduced these basic changes in plastic casts which can be obtained):

(1) 17·5–19·5 years: surface crossed by horizontal crests separated by a distinct groove; margins not defined. (2) 19·5–21·5 years: the grooves begin to fill up, starting from the posterior margin which begins to be noticeable. (3) 21·5–24·0 years: the grooves become progressively obliterated and the posterior margin shows up more clearly; the anterior margin is slightly bevelled. (4) 24·0–26·0 years: posterior margin clearly delimited by the 'dorsal plateau'. The bevelled anterior margin acquires a considerable extension, with the lower border beginning to appear. (5) 26·0–27·0 years: sporadic beginnings of the formation of a 'ventral rampart'; the posterior and inferior borders become more and more defined and the upper border begins to appear.

(6) 27·0–33·5 years: upper and lower borders are better defined; ventral rampart reaching its final stage of evolution. (7) 33·5–38·0 years: the granular surface of the symphysial area grows smaller and exotoses appear on it. (8) 38·0–42·0 years: the surface becomes smooth, having for the first time a complete border on the articular area. (9) 42·0–50·5 years: the posterior border becomes more visible and more prominent than the rest. (10) 50·5 or more years: the surface acquires an eroded appearance and a look of dis-ordered ossification; the border begins to disintegrate.

These, then, are certainly the best criteria for age estimates after 18 years. Indeed, because of the very favourable results, too much attention is being paid to them, forgetting other criteria which are still of value as supporting evidence.

MORPHOSCOPIC ALTERATIONS IN BONES

From birth until death the bones experience a series of primary changes. To these we have just referred. There are others, however, which we can call secondary, being of a morphoscopic or sometimes metrical nature. These are more subtle and less well defined but, when used with discretion, can be of some little value. For example, from 35 years onwards, the sciatic portion of the major sacro-sciatic ligament begins to ossify, thus forming a characteristic bony lip. Because we have no other guide than the pubic symphysis between the ages 30 and 50 years, the ossification of this ligament can be

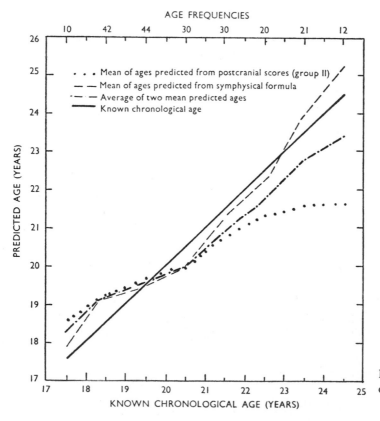

Fig. 54 Relationship between certain known and predicted skeletal ages.

very useful. Another feature of interest is that of vertebral 'lipping' (osteo-arthritis), which develops fairly regularly and especially after the age of about 40 years.[40] Hence the feature can be used to separate the older age groups.

It must be noted that McKern[40] establishes, first, that in complete remains, instead of the usual practice of emphasizing complete skeletal coverage, dependable age estimations can be obtained from the combined maturational activity of a small number of critical areas. Second, that the use of other criteria than the pubic symphysis is only justified when this region is missing or damaged. Although this seems correct from the statistical point of view, it does not agree with the criteria of Brooks[28] nor with my own. In the first place it is a very rare thing to have for examination complete skeletons, and in the second, it is preferable to base one's opinion on different processes, especially when, as in the case of the pubic symphysis, the margin of error can be great for the non-specialist. Nevertheless, it seems

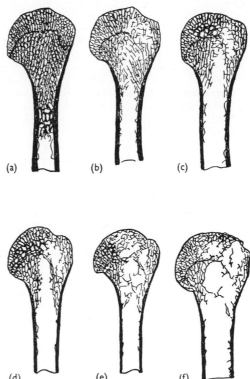

Fig. 55 Morphological changes in the upper epiphysis of the humerus from younger (a) to older (b–f) ages. From Nemeskéri et al.[45]

worth reproducing here the graph from McKern,[40] demonstrating the relationship between certain known and predicted skeletal ages (Fig. 54).

OTHER METHODS

Continuing along the lines of Wachholz[41] in the past century, Schranz,[42] Berndt,[43] and Hansen[44] distinguish a number of phases in the spongy structure of the femoral and humeral heads. Although the margins of error are very great, and thus it cannot be used by itself, there is no doubt that great benefit can be gained from it. Nemeskéri and others[45] have tried with similar results to subdivide the types of structural change. Considering this evidence, six phases of structural modification can be identified as shown in Fig. 55.

REFERENCES AND NOTES

1 Weidenreich, for example, estimated the ages of the 'Sinanthropus' individuals and those from Ngandong—but they are likely to be far from the truth:
WEIDENREICH, F. 1943. *Palaeontologica Sinica 10*
—— 1951. *Am. Mus. Nat. Hist., Anth. Papers* no. 43, 205–90
2 FRANCIS, C. C. 1952. *The Human Pelvis*, London
3 PEARSON, K. 1901–2. *Biometrika 1*, 261–4
4 VALLOIS, H. V. 1937. *Anthropologie 47*, 499–532
5 —— 1960. Vital Statistics in Prehistoric Populations as Determined from Archaeological Data, in

HEIZER, R. F. and COOK, S. F. (eds.) 'The Application of Quantitative Methods in Archaeology', *Viking Fund Publications in Anthropology* no. 28, 181–222

6 FUSTÉ, M. 1955. La duración de la vida en las poblaciones humanas del levante español durante el período neo-eneolítico. *Homenaje Póstumo al Dr D. Francisco Pardillo Vaquer*, Barcelona, 325–33

7 —— 1954. *Trabajos del Inst. 'Bernardino de Sahagún' Antrop. Etnol. 14*, 81–104

8 HOWELLS, W. W. 1960. Estimating population numbers through archaeological and skeletal remains, in HEIZER, R. F. and COOK, S. F. (eds.) *op. cit.*[5]

9 GOLDSTEIN, M. S. 1953. *Hum. Biol. 25*, 3–12

10 NEMESKÉRI, J. 1956. *V. Int. Congr. Anth. Eth. Sci.* (From Howells[8])

11 MACDONELL, W. R. 1913. *Biometrika 9*, 366–80

12 WILLCOX, W. F. 1938. *Congr. int. de la Population, Paris*, no. 2, 14–22

13 FRANZ, L. and WINKLER, W. 1936. *Z. f. Rass. 4*, 157–63

14 SENYÜREK, M. S. 1947. *Am. J. Phys. Anth. 5*, 55–66

15 —— 1951. *Belleten 15*, 447–68

16 Without doubt the most complete work on the subject of ageing is that of McKern and Stewart (a). Together with those of Vandervael (b) and Cabot Briggs (c) it has been used widely here, for these improve on and add to earlier works such as Stevenson (d), Todd and Lyon (e and f) and Augier (g).

    (a) MCKERN, T. W. and STEWART, T. D. 1957. *Skeletal Age Changes in Young American Males, Analyzed from the Standpoint of Age Identification.* Quartermaster Research and Development Center, Massachusetts.

    (b) VANDERVAEL, F. 1952. *S.A.S.* no. 25–26

    (c) CABOT BRIGGS, L. 1958. *Initiation à l'Anthropologie du Squelette*, Algiers

    (d) STEVENSON, P. H. 1924. *Am. J. Phys. Anth. 7*, 53–93

    (e) TODD, T. W. and LYON, D. W. JR. 1924. *Ibid.*, 7, 325–84

    (f) —— —— 1925. *Ibid. 8*, 23–71

    (g) AUGIER, M. 1932. *Anthropologie 42*, 315–22

17 HURME, V. O. 1954. *Child Development 19*, 213

18 —— 1957. *J. Forensic Sci. 2*, 377–88

19 ZANDER, H. A. and HURZELER, B. 1958. *J. Dental Res. 37*, 1035

20 NALBANDIAN, J. and SOGNNAES, R. F. 1960. *Am. Ass. Adv. Sci.*, Pub. no. 65, 367–82

21 GUSTAFSON, G. 1950. *J. Am. Dental Ass. 41*, 45–54

22 STEVENSON, P. H. 1924. *Op. cit.*[16(d)]

23 WOOD JONES, F. (ed.) 1949. *Buchanan's Manual of Anatomy*, London, 8th ed.

24 FRANCIS, C. C. 1952. *Op. cit.*[2]

25 SMOUT, C. F. V. and JACOBY, F. 1943. *Gynaecological and Obstetrical Anatomy of the Female Pelvis*, London; 2nd ed., 1948; 3rd ed., 1953

26 GRANT, J. C. B. 1952. *A Method of Anatomy*, Baltimore, 5th ed.

27 MCKERN, T. W. and STEWART, T. D. 1957. *Op. cit.*[16(a)]

28 BROOKS, S. T. 1955. *Am. J. Phys. Anth. 13*, 567–97

29 MOSS, M. L. 1954a. *Ibid. 12*, 373–84

30 —— 1954b. *Am. J. Anat. 94*, 333–61

31 MEDNICK, L. W. and WASHBURN, S. L. 1956. *Am. J. Phys. Anth. 14*, 175–91

32 LACHMAN, E. 1958. *Am. J. Roentgenol. 79*, 721–5

33 CHRISTENSEN, J. B., LACHMAN, E. and BRUES, A. M. 1960. *Ibid. 83*, 615–27

34 BRASH, J. C. (ed.) 1951. *Cunningham's Text Book of Anatomy*, London, 9th ed.

35 PRINSLOO, I. 1953. *J. Forensic Med. 1*, 11–17

36 HRDLIČKA, A. 1952. *Practical Anthropometry* (ed. STEWART, T. D.), Philadelphia, 4th ed.

37 GENOVÉS, S. T. and MESSMACHER, M. 1959. *Cuadernos del Inst. de Historia (Mexico)*, Ser. Antrop. no. 7

38 TODD, T. W. 1920. *Am. J. Phys. Anth. 3*, 285–334

39 STEWART, T. D. 1958. *The Leech 28*, 144–51

40 MCKERN, T. W. 1957. *Am. J. Phys. Anth. 15*, 399–408

41 WACHHOLZ, L. 1894. *Friedrichs Beitr. ger. Med. 45*, 210–19

42 SCHRANZ, D. 1933. *Dt. Z. ges ger. Med. 22*, 332–61

43 BERNDT, H. 1947. *Z. ges. Inn. Med. 2*, 122–48

44 HANSEN, G. 1953–4. *Wiss. Z. Humboldt-Univ. Berlin 3*, 1–73

45 NEMESKÉRI, J. I., HARSÁNYI, L. and ASCÁDI, G. 1960. *Anth. Anz. 24*, 70–95

36 Stature in Earlier Races of Mankind

L. H. WELLS

STATURE IS ONE OF THE CHARACTERISTICS on which we chiefly rely in identifying individual human beings and also, in some measure, human population types or 'races'. Accordingly, in building up a living mental image of men of earlier periods, stature is among the characteristics which we most wish to be able to assess.

As late as the eighteenth century opinions on the stature of early man belonged to the realm of folk-lore rather than science. With the expansion of the horizons of human prehistory in the nineteenth century, inquiry into the stature of early man acquired a new significance; Broca's discussion of the stature of the Cro-Magnon fossil skeletons may be taken as marking the beginning of serious study of this problem.

THE VARIATION OF STATURE IN LIVING MAN

Anthropologists have attempted to attach absolute values to the otherwise elastic concepts of 'tall' and 'short' stature. From accumulated evidence, the mean stature of the male half of the world's living population appears to be approximately 165·0 cm (5 ft 5 in); Morant[16] gives the actual mean value from nearly four hundred samples recorded up to 1926 and representing populations from all parts of the world as 164·6 cm. Taking this mean value as a starting point, it has been found consistent with experience to label statures below 160·0 cm as 'short', and those of 170·0 cm and upwards as 'tall'. By a further extension, statures below 150·0 cm may be termed 'very short', and those of 180·0 cm and upwards 'very tall'. Both individual statures and the mean statures of population groups can be placed in these categories. The terms 'dwarf' and 'giant' are applied respectively to individuals below 130·0 cm and above 199·9 cm, limits which appear effectively outside the range of normal human variation. The term 'pygmy' is applied not to individuals but to populations whose mean stature is less than 150·0 cm, so that at least half of their members are likely to belong to the 'very short' category. There is no corresponding term for 'very tall' populations, which in fact hardly exist; Morant[16] observes that a mean stature of 180·4 cm appears to be the largest on record, whereas at the other extreme a mean as low as 143·0 cm is to be found.

The mean stature of females is approximately 10·0 cm less than that of males, the difference being about 6% of the male stature; this proportion holds with increasing and decreasing stature, and the limits of the stature categories for the female are adjusted accordingly.

Morant[16] points out that it is only in very extreme cases that the variations in stature of human populations do not overlap considerably. For some purposes it is useful to know the actual range of a series of measurements, that is the highest and lowest individual measurements encountered. Statistically, however, the variation around a mean is measured by the average amount by which individual measurements exceed or fall short of the mean; this figure is known as the standard deviation. By expressing the difference between an individual measurement and the mean of a series as a proportion of the standard deviation of the mean, the probability that the individual could have belonged to this particular series can be evaluated. In the case of stature the standard deviation varies for different population samples between 5·0 and 8·0 cm. A statistical argument against including an individual in a certain group on the ground of stature requires a difference between the individual stature and the group mean at least 2·5 times the standard deviation of the mean, e.g. the chances that an individual with a stature of 138·2 cm could have belonged to a population whose mean stature is 162·4 cm with a standard deviation of 6·5 cm are only about 1 in 10,000, the difference being 3·7 times the standard deviation.

Normal stature is known to be controlled genetically by the interaction of a large number of inherited factors. At the same time environmental influences, in particular nutrition, operating during the growth period may affect stature very considerably, preventing the genetic potentialities of the individual from being realized. Thus an appreciable fluctuation of stature from generation to generation could be caused by external circumstances in a genetically stable population.

STATURE AND THE SKELETON

Stature is divisible into two moieties, axial (head + trunk) length and lower limb length. Within a single population the proportion between these moieties varies appreciably from individual to individual, some being long-trunked and short-legged, others short-trunked and long-legged. The mean ratio between these moieties may differ from one population to another; thus leg length forms a greater proportion of stature in American Negroes than in White Americans.[26] Leg length in turn has two main components, femoral length and crural (tibio-fibular) length; the relation of femoral to crural length varies from individual to individual, and the mean femoro-crural ratio may differ from one population to another.

Upper limb length, though not a direct component of stature, in the normal individual is broadly proportionate to leg length and so indirectly to stature. However, in addition to individual and group variations in the proportion of arm length to stature and of upper-arm to forearm length, the length of the upper limb bones is affected by differential use of the two arms (handedness). Unfortunately it cannot be simply assumed that the preferred limb has been overdeveloped, nor alternatively that the neglected limb is underdeveloped; under different conditions both effects may be found in varying degrees.

In the most advantageous circumstances it would be difficult, and usually completely impossible, to assemble the trunk skeleton accurately enough for an estimate of axial length, although a method for estimating stature from the length of the vertebral column was developed by Dwight (Telkkä[24]). Stature estimates from the skeleton are therefore practically always founded on the lengths of the long bones of the limbs. From what has been said, it would be inferred that the stature could best be assessed from the combined femoro-crural length, less accurately from either the femoral or the crural length, and still less accurately from the lengths of the upper limb bones. This has in fact proved to be the case (e.g. Trotter and Gleser[26]). At the same time it follows that all these estimates, even the femoro-crural, are subject to a measure of inescapable uncertainty. Even in one population group, individuals of identical stature may have appreciably different limb-bone lengths, and conversely bones of identical length may have belonged to individuals differing appreciably in stature; these variations will be even more accentuated if individuals belonging to distinct population groups of differing limb proportions are compared.

DEVELOPMENT OF TECHNIQUES FOR STATURE ESTIMATION

The credit for the first scientific contribution to this subject may perhaps be claimed for the English surgeon-anatomist William Cheselden (1668–1752), who in 1712 communicated a paper to the Royal Society on 'The dimensions of some bones of extraordinary size which were dug up near St Albans.'[6] Of these bones (possibly Romano-British), Cheselden concluded that 'if all the parts bore a due proportion this man must have been eight foot high'. From the measurements given by Cheselden, it appears probable that his specimen was a pituitary giant, so that his estimate may well have been of the correct order; it is however his qualifying clause, 'if all the parts bore a due proportion', which deserves notice.

The history of successive attempts to devise formulae for estimating stature from limb-bone lengths has been reviewed by Telkkä[24] and by Trotter and Gleser.[25] The widely followed methods of Manouvrier and of Pearson are founded upon Rollet's study on the limb-bone lengths of 50 male and 50 female southern French individuals, published in 1888; Telkkä rightly comments on the small size of the foundation on which a great edifice has been erected.

Manouvrier's and Pearson's methods held the field for several decades, the former, as Telkkä notes, being more frequently used by continental European, and the latter by British and American workers. Some workers have questioned the validity of these methods even as applied to all European populations; in particular, Pearson's method has been considered to underestimate the stature of tall individuals. To remedy the supposed defects of the Manouvrier and Pearson techniques, Breitinger[3] attempted to develop a method using limb-bone lengths measured by indirect methods in living European subjects of known stature. This procedure allowed data from a much greater number of subjects to be used, but in the opinion of some other workers it merely substituted one set of uncertainties for another.

Both Manouvrier and Pearson regarded their methods as applicable to human material of all physical types, regarding differences in average proportions between types as less considerable than individual variability in proportion within a single type. Pearson[18] deals with the inescapable error due to individual variability in a surprisingly off-handed way, so that his reference to the matter may easily pass unnoticed, and his estimates are presented with a spurious impression of precision.

Alternative formulae have been presented by Stevenson[22] for Chinese material, by Telkkä[24] for Finns, and by Dupertuis and Hadden[8] for American Whites and Negroes. The work of the last-named authors is however superseded by that of Trotter and

Gleser,[25],[26] which is revolutionary in being based on directly measured limb-bone lengths of individuals whose stature was recorded during life. Their first study was based on comparatively small American White and American Negro series, their second on much larger series of both these groups and on a smaller Mongoloid series. These series are of males only; in their earlier study Trotter and Gleser correlated their living-stature series with cadaver-length series for both male groups, and on the basis of this comparison developed estimation formulae from cadaver-length series of American White and American Negro females to replace those of Dupertuis and Hadden.

In both their studies Trotter and Gleser lay great stress on the inescapable range of error in estimation. They maintain that the limits of 95% certainty in estimation are between 7·0 and 8·0 cm on either side of the estimate for the lower limb bones, and 8·0 to 9·0 cm for the upper limb bones. However distressing these wide limits may be, Trotter and Gleser insist that they cannot be reduced by statistical juggling, as some authors have suggested. These errors of estimate apply strictly only to populations substantially identical with those upon which the formulae were founded; for other populations they may well be considerably too small.

Most earlier investigators have taken as the best estimate of stature the average of the estimates obtained from all available bones and combinations of bones. Trotter and Gleser regard this procedure as statistically fallacious, and argue forcibly that the best single estimate available, i.e. that with the lowest error of estimate, should be adopted. They also reject the pooling of results obtained from different populations to derive 'general' or inter-racial formulae, such as that constructed by Dupertuis and Hadden,[8] who combined Pearson's data with their own data for American Whites and American Negroes.

Telkkä[24] has compared some estimates obtained by his own method and those of Manouvrier, Pearson, and Breitinger; estimates by Manouvrier's methods tend to be lower than those by Pearson's method for short statures, and higher for tall statures, while estimates by Breitinger's and Telkkä's methods are consistently somewhat higher than those by Pearson's method. Almost all the discrepancies are very much less than the error of estimate by any of the formulae. The author[31] has similarly compared estimates by Pearson's formulae, the 'general' formulae of Dupertuis and Hadden, and the original and revised Trotter-Gleser formulae for American Whites and Negroes. Dupertuis and Hadden's general formulae and the revised Trotter-Gleser White American formulae give closely similar results; those obtained by Pearson's method are lower, the difference being usually small at the lower end of the range but rising considerably with increasing bone length. The revised Trotter-Gleser American Negro formulae give estimates surprisingly close to those obtained by Pearson's formulae, so that the latter would appear, contrary to expectation, to predict the stature of present-day American Negroes better than that of White Americans.

Applied to modern Sicilian measurements published by Graziosi,[11] Pearson's formulae for the lower limb bones give estimates agreeing much better with records of living Sicilian stature than do those obtained by the American formulae. It is also to be noted that Trotter and Gleser's American White formula for tibial length overestimates the mean stature of Allbrook's[1] present-day British series by about 2·5 cm (1 in), although the mean statures of the British and American White groups differ very little, whereas Pearson's formula founded on a French series of shorter stature comes very close to the true value. It is by no means certain, therefore, that the American White formulae are to be preferred for estimating the stature of earlier European populations.

Allbrook,[1] in estimating East African Negro statures by a modification of Breitinger's technique, has found that different estimation formulae are needed for 'Nilo-Hamite' and 'Bantu' groups; the Trotter-Gleser Negro formulae give reasonable estimates for the former of these groups, but are very unsatisfactory for the latter.

'NEAR-GIANT' AND 'NEAR-DWARF' STATURES

Pearson found that his formulae failed conspicuously to predict the stature of true giants (above 200 cm) and true dwarfs (below 130 cm). He concluded that the formulae gave an approximation to the middle part of a complex curve representing the varying relationship between limb-bone lengths and stature, and that they broke down for statures below 150·0 cm and above 179·9 cm, that is for 'very short' and 'very tall' individuals: 'In the region of what may be termed sub-giants and super-dwarfs, namely, from about 180–200 cm and 150–130 cm, a very small change in the long bone length makes a remarkable change in stature.' He therefore suggested that outside of the limits of 150 cm and 180 cm his formulae should not be used, but that stature should be estimated from curves plotted for the different long bones. Further he suggested that the points of inflection of the curves might have 'a biological as well as a mathematical significance', that is presumably that at these levels the genetic mechanism controlling stature changed significantly. Pearson seems to have regarded these critical levels as absolutely fixed; it would seem more natural to suppose that they are fluctuating, and that there is a zone of overlap between 'normal' tall or short individuals and true sub-giants or super-dwarfs.

More recent investigators have largely passed over this question of limits. Telkkä has tabulated his results for the range 155–185 cm, and does not discuss the validity of his formulae outside this range. Trotter and Gleser[25] did not extrapolate below 152·0 cm (5 ft), which was the lower limit of stature for acceptance into the US forces; they regard their formula as valid up to 198·0 cm stature, i.e. over the whole of Pearson's 'sub-giant' range. The question of limits is in fact very pertinent since it affects the estimation of stature in individuals belonging to very tall and very short or pygmoid races of living men, especially in Africa, and also of some of the most notable examples of early man.

STATURE ESTIMATES IN EARLIER HISTORIC AND PREHISTORIC PERIODS

Broca[5] prefaced his discussion of the stature of the Cro-Magnon skeletons with the comment: 'It is impossible to determine correctly the stature of any imperfect and disarticulated skeleton; it is not even safe to apply to this determination the relationship between the length of the femur and the height of the body that medical jurisprudence has adopted; for these relations have been determined for men of our own race, and we know that the proportions of the body notably vary among existing races; and there is more reason why they may have varied in races which have died out in the course of ages.'

Trotter and Gleser[25] have expressed even stronger reservations: 'It is perhaps impossible to determine which equations are best for application to skeletal remains of older races for which there are no records of actual stature. In fact, Kurth has suggested on the basis of his recent experience in estimating stature of middle Europeans of the 8th to 10th century that measurement, when possible, of the overall length of the skeletal remains *in situ* is preferable to stature estimated from the long bones according to equations based on more recent populations.' This defeatist conclusion would limit the possibility of stature estimation to undisturbed burials in the extended position. Against this it may be urged that available formulae, provided we do not press the result too hard, can in fact give a reasonable indication of the probable stature of earlier groups. In dealing with individual specimens, the full range of inescapable variation attending any estimate has to be borne in mind, but estimates based on the means of population samples of reasonable size are more likely to be near the truth.

There are now available as alternatives, for material of European origin, the formulae of Manouvrier, Pearson, Breitinger, Telkkä, Trotter and Gleser, and Allbrook; for Mongoloid material, those of Stevenson and of Trotter and Gleser; and for Negroid material, the American formulae of Trotter and Gleser and at least two sets of formulae devised by Allbrook, one founded on 'Nilo-Hamite' and the other on East African 'Bantu' data. For remains which can be assigned with confidence to one of these groups, the choice can be reduced to a few alternative methods. The problem of choice is much more difficult when dealing with remains which cannot confidently be assigned to one of these groups, and which may not even belong to the species *Homo sapiens*.

No attempt at a complete review of all the data available concerning stature in past times will be made in this paper; consideration will be given only to certain classes of evidence: (1) the mean stature of a number of populations, mainly west European, belonging to historic and later prehistoric periods; (2) estimates of individual stature of some pre-Neolithic European specimens, (3) estimates of individual stature of some prehistoric African specimens, and (4) estimates related to individuals possibly or probably not of the species *Homo sapiens*. To further simplify the problem consideration will be limited almost wholly to male specimens.

Historic and late prehistoric European populations. The data considered have been divided into two groups, one consisting of mean femoral lengths of British population samples ranging from medieval to Neolithic, and the other of femoro-tibial lengths mostly of west European populations over the same range. Where other evidence was not available, series quoted by Pearson[18] have been included; these have previously been reconsidered by Dupertuis and Hadden.[8] When both femoral and femoro-tibial length estimates for British series are available, the difference between the two estimates is well below the error of estimate by either formula.

The fluctuation of British mean femoral stature estimates from the Neolithic to the medieval period (Table A) covers a range of about 7 cm (3 in) by the Pearson formula and 9 cm ($3\frac{1}{2}$ in) by Trotter and Gleser's American White formula. If the Pearson estimates were considered better for shorter, and the American for taller statures, this range might be increased to as much as 12 cm (5 in). The lowest value is found for the

TABLE A

Mean femoral stature estimates for some British male series.

	No.	Femur Length	Pearson	Trotter-Gleser (1958)
		cm	cm	cm
Medieval (Rothwell) (Parsons[11])	76	45·6	167·0	171·3
Anglo-Saxon (Munter[17])	161	46·4	168·5	173·2
Iron Age (Maiden Castle) (Goodman and Morant[10])	26	44·1	164·2	167·8
Round Barrow (Beddoe, in Pearson[18])	27	47·8	171·2	176·4
Neolithic (Beddoe, in Pearson[18])	25	45·8	167·4	171·8

Iron Age population of Maiden Castle, the highest for Beddoe's Round-Barrow series, who appreciably exceed Munter's Anglo-Saxons (this larger series gives a lower femoral length than Beddoe's for the same period). Over this whole period it may be said that British mean stature has fluctuated between medium and tall.

It is valuable to have some idea of the variation around these means. In this instance a consideration of the greatest and least femoral lengths (Table B) may serve as a measure of this variation. The least femoral lengths of the medieval, Anglo-Saxon, and Iron Age series differ but little, corresponding to stature estimates in the upper part of the 'short' range on both Pearson's and the American formulae. The greatest lengths differ more widely; the medieval series has one exceptionally high measurement, the next being much lower. Disregarding this, the fluctuation of the upper end of the range appears to follow that of the mean. Preferring the American formula to that of Pearson may raise the estimates for the tallest statures by as much as three inches. On the other hand, recourse to Pearson's curves would increase the estimates for the tallest statures in both the medieval and the Anglo-Saxon series very considerably; the stature of the

TABLE B

Extreme femoral stature estimates for some British male series.

		Femur Length	Pearson	Trotter-Gleser (1958)
		cm	cm	cm
Medieval (Rothwell):	least	40·9	158·2	160·4
	greatest	49·0	173·4	179·2
		(54·3)	(183·4)	(191·5)
Anglo-Saxon:	least	40·4	157·3	159·3
	greatest	52·7	180·4	187·8
Iron Age:	least	40·0	156·5	158·3
	greatest	47·7	171·0	176·2

exceptionally tall medieval specimen would be raised into the 'giant' category. A single exceptional specimen of this type may well be that of an abnormal individual, but in the Anglo-Saxon series the number of long femora is so considerable that it seems highly doubtful whether they can be claimed as abnormal 'sub-giants' in Pearson's sense.

The tibio-femoral stature estimates for west European series (Table C) show a similar range in mean values, between 164 cm and 171 cm by Pearson's formula, and between 167 cm and 175 cm by the American formula; thus Pearson's formula makes most of these populations to be of medium average stature, whereas the American formula makes most of them tall. The Reihengraber, Anglo-Saxon and Frankish series, compared with the Gallo-Roman and British Iron Age series, suggest that the Teutonic migrations produced a shift towards taller stature in western Europe. The Franco-Belgian 'Neolithic' series should probably be taken, in more modern usage, to cover also the Chalcolithic and Early Bronze Age periods. For comparison it may be noted that an Early Bronze Age series from Austria[9] gives a mean stature estimate of 164·7 cm by Pearson's formulae, and 168·2 cm by those of Breitinger. The predynastic Egyptian population of Nagada[29] had a mean stature just below or just above 170 cm, depending on whether the Pearson or the American formulae are used.

TABLE C
Mean femoro-tibial stature estimates for some European series.

	Femoro-tibial Length	Pearson	Trotter-Gleser (1958)
	cm	cm	cm
French (10th–11th century)	82·6	167·0	171·2
Franks (500–800 AD)	82·0	166·3	170·4
Anglo-Saxon	83·5	168·1	172·3
S. German Reihengraber	85·5	170·4	174·8
Gallo-Roman	81·4	165·6	169·7
British Iron Age (Maiden Castle)	80·5	164·6	168·5
French and Belgian 'Neolithic'	79·9	163·9	167·8
Predynastic Egyptian (Nagada)	83·9	168·5	172·8
Mesolithic (Teviec, Brittany)	76·5	159·9	163·5

At the end of last century considerable play was made with the idea that during the Neolithic period, at least in central Europe, a 'pygmy' type existed alongside of the normal medium-statured population. The original evidence for this view, according to Pearson,[18] consisted of three adult skeletons only, one probably male and two female. The lower limb-bone lengths of these three are at the extreme lower end of the range of variation of British Neolithic, Iron Age, and Dark Age series. In themselves, these specimens afford no more evidence of a distinct pygmy population than individuals of similar proportions in a Dark Age Scottish series[32] do of the 'dwarf Picts' of tradition.

Pre-Neolithic Europeans. Since prior to the Neolithic period stature has to be deduced from individual skeletons rather than from the means of series, the estimates must be presumed liable to an even greater margin of uncertainty. A comparison of Upper Palaeolithic and Mesolithic male stature estimates by the methods of Manouvrier, Pearson, and Breitinger has been made by Pittard and Sauter;[19] in the present survey this has been supplemented by a comparison of femoral, and where possible also of tibio-femoral, stature estimates by Pearson's method and that of Trotter and Gleser. Some observations on Upper Palaeolithic female stature estimates have been assembled by von Bonin.[27]

Short male series of the Mesolithic period have been recorded from Teviec, Brittany (Table C) and from Mugem, Portugal.[12,19] Both groups give mean stature estimates around the boundary between 'low' and 'medium' stature, with a range from 'low' or even 'very low' to the boundary of 'tall' stature. The single skeleton of this period from Cuzoul de Gramat (Table D) has limb bones considerably longer than the average for both these groups though within the upper limit of both; stature estimates for this skeleton place it within the upper half of the 'medium' stature range. The evidence that the Mesolithic population of western Europe was appreciably shorter in stature than its successors from the Neolithic period onwards is thus by no means conclusive. There are however some grounds for considering that the varieties of the European physical type became differentiated during the Mesolithic period; this may have included differentiation in mean stature.

Of male skeletons belonging to the latter part of the Upper Palaeolithic (Magdalenian and contemporary phases), that from Chancelade is notable for its low femoral length, slightly below the mean of the Teviec Mesolithic group and approximating to the least measurements in historic British series. The estimated stature of this man is on or slightly below the boundary between 'short' and 'medium'; this has been advanced along with other arguments for dissociating the Chancelade specimen from other Late Palaeolithic remains and looking for its affinities among short-statured types of man. Other Late Palaeolithic male skeletons from western Europe, such as those of Veyrier, Haute-Savoie, Obercassel near Bonn, and Gough's Cave, Cheddar, Somerset, are unquestionably of modern European type. These all have considerably longer femora than the Chancelade man, their estimated statures approximating to the means of Neolithic and later west European populations. It is perfectly possible, and indeed probable, that the Chancelade individual belongs to the same group as the others, and that the average stature of the inhabitants of western Europe at that period was very much the same as in later periods.

In point of stature, two skeletons from San Teodoro Cave, Sicily,[11] might well be grouped with these, but some craniological arguments as well as their geographical separation may make it preferable to keep them apart.

Broca,[5] in spite of his reservations already quoted, considered that the taller of the two males from Cro-Magnon (the 'old man') must have exceeded 180·0 cm in stature. It must be pointed out that the limb-bone lengths for this skeleton cited by Pearson and later workers are estimations; the only intact lower limb bone is the tibia of the second

TABLE D
Pre-Neolithic European male statures.

	Length	Pearson	Trotter-Gleser (1958)
	cm	cm	cm
Cuzoul de Gramat			
Femoral	44·7	165·3	169·2
Femoro-tibial	81·5	165·7	169·8
Chancelade			
Femoral	40·8	158·0	160·2
Obercassel			
Femoral	44·7	165·3	169·2
Veyrier			
Femoral	46·1	168·0	172·5
Gough's Cave			
Femoral	44·0	164·0	167·6
San Teodoro 1			
Femoral	44·2	164·2	168·1
Femoro-tibial	81·6	165·8	169·9
San Teodoro 4			
Femoral	42·5	161·2	164·1
Gr. des Enfants			
Femoral	52·2	179·4	186·6
Femoro-tibial	97·2	183·9	189·6
Barma Grande I			
Femoral	53·2	181·3	189·0
Femoro-tibial	96·8	183·5	189·1
Barma Grande II			
Femoral	49·1	173·6	179·4
Femoro-tibial	89·3	174·8	179·6
Gr. de Cavillon			
Femoral	47·0	169·7	174·6
Femoro-tibial	87·4	172·6	177·2
Paviland			
Femoral	47·6	170·8	176·0
Combe-Capelle			
Femoral	42·5	161·2	164·1

male, which measures 37·5 cm, corresponding to statures of 167·8 cm by Pearson's formula, 172·7 cm by the Trotter-Gleser formula for White Americans, and 170·0 cm by Allbrook's modern British formula.

Four skeletons from the Grimaldi (Mentone) group of caves provide more satisfactory evidence. A skeleton from the Grotte des Enfants and the taller of two from Barma Grande (B.G. I) appear to have had longer limb bones than the taller Cro-Magnon individual, who was more closely matched by the shorter Barma Grande skeleton (B.G. II). The skeleton from the Grotte de Cavillon agrees with the second Cro-Magnon skeleton; that from Paviland Cave, Glamorgan, comes close to these two (Sollas[21]). From Table D it will be seen that stature estimates for these skeletons by the Pearson and Trotter-Gleser formulae differ by more than 5 cm and sometimes as much as 8 cm (2 to 3 inches), but by both methods the two tallest individuals (Grotte des Enfants and B.G. I) both fall into the 'very tall' class and the other three into the 'tall' class. It must be noted that if Pearson's curve of stature variation is used instead of his formula, the stature estimates for the two tallest skeletons would be increased almost to the lower limit of 'giant' stature. Verneau, using Manouvrier's methods, ascribed to this group of skeletons a mean stature of 187 cm; Sollas, using Pearson's method, reduced this to 179 cm. The estimates assembled by Pittard and Sauter give averages of 175 cm for Pearson's method, and 180 cm for both Manouvrier's and Breitinger's.

While the Grimaldi group of skeletons could be regarded as those of a local isolated group of special genetic character, the Cro-Magnon, and still more the Paviland examples suggest that tall stature was a widely dispersed character in western Europe at this period. The evidence of the Predmost III skeleton[19] shows that it occurred also in eastern Europe. However, the Combe-Capelle skeleton, which is regarded as probably the earliest Upper Palaeolithic specimen from western Europe, has a much shorter femoral length, placing its estimated stature in the lower half of the 'medium' range. These divergent pieces of evidence can be regarded as indicating either two population groups of quite different stature, and so presumably having a distinct history, existing simultaneously in the earlier Upper Palaeolithic, or a very thinly scattered population derived from a single origin, within which local foci of distinctive character, possibly of a purely transitory nature, might appear as a consequence of temporary isolation and in-breeding. How far the strikingly tall men of the earlier Upper Palaeolithic were ancestral to their shorter successors at the end of this period is not, even now, completely clear.

TABLE E
Prehistoric African femoral lengths (male).

	Length	Pearson	Trotter-Gleser Negro (1958)	Trotter-Gleser White (1958)
	cm	cm	cm	cm
Asselar	45·0	165·9	166·7	169·9
Nakuru IX	50·2	175·7	177·6	182·0
Makalia I	48·4	172·3	173·9	177·8
Willey's Kopje I	49·2	173·8	175·5	179·7
II	51·6	178·3	180·6	185·2
III	52·2	179·4	181·8	186·6
Elmenteita I	51·5	178·1	180·4	185·0
3	45·5	166·9	167·8	171·1
Naivasha	41·5	159·3	159·4	161·8
Gamble's Cave 4	51·0	177·2	179·3	183·9
5	52·0	179·1	181·4	186·2
Fish Hoek	43·5	163·1	163·6	166·5
Tuinplaats (Springbok Flats)	50·0	175·3	177·2	180·5

In this connection it must be remembered that the duration of the Upper Palaeolithic may well have been comparable with the whole span of post-Palaeolithic time.

Prehistoric Africans. Table E presents femoral stature estimates for a number of noteworthy prehistoric specimens from Africa south of the Sahara.

The rather insecurely dated Asselar skeleton from the southern fringe of the Sahara[2] is important as probably the earliest specimen to show a predominance of Negroid characters. On this ground the stature estimate by Trotter and Gleser's Negro formula might claim preference; however, it differs hardly at all from that obtained by Pearson's formula. All the estimates indicate a medium stature comparable with the means for living central and southern African Negro groups.

The long series of East African specimens recorded by Leakey[13,14] are divisible into three chronological groups, Neolithic (Nakuru, Makalia, Willey's Kopje), Mesolithic (Elmenteita), and Upper Palaeolithic (Naivasha, Gamble's Cave). All appear to be predominantly 'Europoid' rather than Negroid, and may perhaps be included under the term 'Palaeo-Mediterranean' proposed by Briggs.[4] A noteworthy feature of the whole series is the great femoral length and inferentially tall stature of most of its members. The Elmenteita specimens however show a considerable range of variation, and equal variability might be expected also in the earlier and later groups. Nevertheless the short femoral length of the Naivasha specimen[14] contrasts so strongly with the others as to bring the correctness of its sexing under consideration; if it is truly male, it raises the possibility of a second, much shorter statured element in this population.

The two South African specimens considered both have substantial claims to more than merely relative antiquity.[33] The Fish Hoek skeleton, despite its strongly paedomorphic cranial characters, is clearly not pygmoid in stature; the femoral stature estimates place it closer to the mean stature of modern Hottentots than of modern Bushmen. It is to be noted that no pygmoid remains of unquestionable geological antiquity have yet come to light in Southern Africa. The great length of the Tuinplaats femur sets it far apart from all later South African human types, and suggests some affinity with the East African series, but in its craniology this individual displays Bushmanoid traits not observed in any of the East African specimens; it is not completely impossible that this anomalous combination of characters might find a counterpart in the Naivasha skeleton.

Earlier humans. The myth of the 'gorilloid' build and stance of the 'classic' Neanderthal type must now be considered completely exploded;[23] nevertheless the massive lower limb bones of this type present almost as distinctive a character as does its skull. It is to be noted that in these respects the Neanderthal type specimen is not as extreme as are the Spy skeletons which have done most to foster our conception of the type. These bones, it must be urged, are not especially short. The results in Table F, for what they are worth, indicate that the Neanderthal and Spy individuals could both have fallen into the medium range of modern human statures. Two arguments can be adduced for discarding this inference, one that the stature was reduced by a slouching stance, the other that the lower limb was disproportionately short so that the stature is underestimated; these arguments appear to cancel each other out.

McCown and Keith[15] demonstrated that the limb bones from the Skhūl Cave at

TABLE F
Femoral and femoro–tibial stature estimates for earlier human types.

	Length	Pearson	Trotter–Gleser (1958) White	Trotter–Gleser (1958) Negro	Trotter–Gleser (1958) Mongoloid
	cm	cm	cm	cm	cm
Neanderthal					
Femoral	44·1	164·2	167·8	164·8	167·4
Spy					
Femoral	42·8	161·8	164·8	162·1	164·6
Femoro-tibial	75·9	159·2	162·7	159·0	163·0
Skhūl IV					
Femoral	49·0	173·4	179·2	175·1	177·9
Femoro-tibial	92·4	178·4	183·5	178·0	183·0
Trinil					
Femoral	45·5	166·9	171·2	167·8	170·4

Mount Carmel were entirely different from those of the classic Neanderthal type both in length and morphology, being much more closely paralleled by those of the tall group of European Upper Palaeolithic skeletons. This is clearly demonstrated by the lower limb bones of Skhūl IV (Table F); the limb bones of other specimens in the Skhūl group are even longer but are not so well preserved. The interpretation of these findings has been much debated; recent evidence however tends very forcibly to dissociate the Skhūl group from other Near Eastern 'Neanderthaloids', and there are good arguments for regarding this group as 'proto-*sapiens*' and genetically ancestral to the tall Upper Palaeolithic stock of Europe.

Among the skeletal fragments plausibly associated with the Broken Hill skull from Northern Rhodesia is a complete tibia, the length of which is 409 mm;[20] the entirely normal character of this bone has sometimes but quite baselessly been considered an obstacle to associating it with the 'Neanderthaloid' skull. A very wide range of stature estimates can be obtained from this bone: Pearson 175·8 cm, Trotter–Gleser 'White' 180·9 cm, Trotter–Gleser 'Negro' 174·9 cm, Allbrook 'British' 177·9 cm, Allbrook 'Nilo-Hamite' 173·0 cm, Allbrook 'Bantu' 167·3 cm. All except the last point to a tall stature comparable with those of the Skhūl remains; this resemblance can be interpreted in more than one way.[30]

Finally, the only measurable limb bone which may possibly be attributable to the Java-Pekin group of fossil men is the femur belonging to the original Trinil group of finds. The essentially 'modern' character of this bone[7] was again at first an obstacle to its acceptance; latterly it has been seen as consistent with the probable sequence of man's structural evolution as interpreted e.g. by Washburn.[28] Whatever estimation formulae are applied to this bone, the inferred stature comes out to be close to, though somewhat above, the average of modern humanity. Other limb-bone fragments from the Java and Pekin deposits are consistent with the conclusion that early hominines tended to a stature round about, and perhaps slightly above, the average of *Homo sapiens*. Whatever may be the case as regards pre-hominine types, there is no positive evidence to suggest that the earliest true hominines were either giants or pygmies; both these extreme variations in stature appear to be confined to *Homo sapiens*, in whom they may have been developed only in comparatively recent times.

REFERENCES

1 ALLBROOK, D. 1961. *J. Forensic Med.* 8, 15–28
2 BOULE, M. and VALLOIS, H. V. 1932. *Arch. Inst. Paléont. Hum.* 9
3 BREITINGER, E. 1937. *Anth. Anz.* 14, 249–74
4 BRIGGS, L. C. 1955. The Stone Age races of Northwest Africa. *American School of Prehistoric Research, Peabody Museum, Harvard University.* Bulletin no. 18
5 BROCA, P. 1865–75. On the human skulls and bones found in the cave of Cro-Magnon, near Les Eyzies. In LARTET, E. and CHRISTIE, H. *Reliquiae Aquitanicae*, London, 97–122
6 CHESELDEN, W. 1712. *Phil. Trans. Roy. Soc. London* (abridged) 5 (1703–12), 671–2
7 DRENNAN, M. R. 1936. *Am. J. Phys. Anth.* 21, 205–216
8 DUPERTUIS, C. W. and HADDEN, J. A. 1951. *Am. J. Phys. Anth.* N.S. 9, 15–53
9 EHGARTNER, W. 1959. *Mitt. Anth. Ges. Wien* 88–89, 8–90
10 GOODMAN, C. N. and MORANT, G. M. 1939. *Biometrika* 31, 295–312
11 GRAZIOSI, P. 1947. *Riv. Sci. Prehist.* 2, 123–223
12 LACAM, R., NIEDERLANDER, A. and VALLOIS, H. V. 1944. *Arch. Inst. Paléont. Hum.* 21
13 LEAKEY, L. S. B. 1935. *The Stone Age Races of Kenya*, London
14 —— 1942. *J. E. Afr. Nat. Hist. Soc.* 16, 169–77
15 McCOWN, T. D. and KEITH, A. 1939. *The Stone Age of Mount Carmel. Vol. II. The fossil human remains from the Levalloiso-Mousterian*, Oxford
16 MORANT, G. M. 1939. *Biometrika* 31, 72–98
17 MUNTER, H. 1936. *Ibid.* 28, 258–94
18 PEARSON, K. 1899. *Phil. Trans. Roy. Soc. London* (A) 192, 169–244
19 PITTARD, E. and SAUTER, M. R. 1946. *Archives Suisses d'Anthrop. Generale* 11, 149–200
20 PYCRAFT, W. P. 1929. Description of the skull and other human remains from Broken Hill. *Rhodesian Man and Associated Remains*, London, 1–51
21 SOLLAS, W. J. 1913. *J. Roy. Anth. Inst.* 44, 325–74
22 STEVENSON, P. H. 1929. *Biometrika* 21, 303–21
23 STRAUS, W. L. and CAVE, A. J. E. 1957. *Quart. Rev. Biol.* 32, 348–63
24 TELKKÄ, A. 1950. *Acta. Anat.* 9, 103–17
25 TROTTER, M. and GLESER, G. C. 1952. *Am. J. Phys. Anth.*, N.S. 10, 463–514
26 —— 1958. *Ibid.* 16, 79–123
27 VON BONIN, G. 1935. The Magdalenian skeleton from Cap-Blanc in the Field Museum of Natural History. *Univ. Illinois Bull.* 32, no. 24
28 WASHBURN, S. L. 1951. *Trans. N.Y. Acad. Sci.*, Series II. 13, 298–304
29 WARREN, E. 1897. *Phil. Trans. Roy. Soc. London* (B) 189, 135–227
30 WELLS, L. H. 1957. The place of the Broken Hill skull among human types. *Proc. 3rd Pan-African. Congr. Prehist. Livingstone, N. Rhodesia, 1955*, London, 172–4
31 —— 1959a. *J. Forensic Med.* 6, 171–7
32 —— 1959b. *Proc. Soc. ant. Scot.* 90, 180–91
33 —— 1959c. *Man* 59, 158–60
34 PARSONS, F. G. 1914. *J. Anat.* 48, 238–67

NILS-GUSTAF GEJVALL

THE INTEREST IN PREHISTORIC cremated bones displayed by archaeologists has increased to a very remarkable extent during the last ten years. From being considered either valueless or at any rate not worth the trouble, either of recovery in the field or of the great care demanded for their proper storage, samples of cremated bone have suddenly become most important, and a large number of excavation reports, in Sweden at least, are nowadays accompanied by an analytical study of cremated remains. It is only the shortage of qualified bone specialists that seriously restricts the progressive expansion of such studies.

Just over thirty years ago the celebrated Swedish anthropologist and anatomist, Professor C. M. Fürst, made the following declaration in reply to an inquiry from the then Chief Inspector of Antiquities in Stockholm: 'I would straight away place on record my considered opinion, based on experience, that cremated remains of human bones in burial urns are almost always devoid of any anthropological interest, especially in cases of such in a mass cemetery. From an anthropological point of view, therefore, these bones are of no scientific value, and I consider that nothing is lost if they are neither submitted to nor preserved in the Museum.'[1] Archaeologists, however, continued to recover such material, and in the discussions that followed the above-mentioned declaration on the principles to be adopted at the National Museum of Antiquities in Stockholm, it was resolved nevertheless that all cremated bones should be collected, in the expectation that methods would be devised in the future which would make it possible to use them for scientific purposes.

Opinions on such osteological remains have, however, varied very considerably; some scholars have sought to find indications of anthropological characteristics in them,[2] and this in itself is neither an impossibility nor an exaggeration for those who have in fact come to recognize how much can, under favourable conditions, survive in the way of identifiable fragments, even after cremation. Others, doubtless on the *a priori* assumption that it is too fantastic even to venture on making a morphological examination of shattered and distorted skeletal fragments, and insufficiently acquainted with material from prehistoric cremation burials, have adopted a pessimistic attitude towards all attempts to make a categorical estimate of the age or sex of a dead person on the basis of surviving cremated remains.[3]

In England, too, there has been a markedly increased interest in prehistoric cremations in latter years. A series of meticulous studies have been published by F. P. Lizowski,[4-6] and Calvin Wells' recent paper on the cremated bones from a fifth- to seventh-century urn-field at Illington, Norfolk,[7] is a further indication that this subject is becoming much more widely recognized.

On the Continent, a series of investigations were carried out during the Second World War on the bone material recovered from a number of urn cemeteries, but these papers (like so many anthropological studies and not least those of the author) have appeared in a large number of local periodicals that are difficult to come by or as appendices attached to archaeological excavation reports, so that it would not be easy to give an exhaustive catalogue of them all. Two authors may be mentioned here, Ursula Thieme in Germany[8] and Aemilian Kloiber in Austria.[9] Unfortunately, neither of these gives any information about the procedures·employed, and this was one of the reasons why the author, in a short and fully illustrated summary,[10] has tried to draw the attention of archaeologists to the fact that it really is profitable to make such investigations as a matter of course.

A later paper, dealing with the cremated bones from 200 graves of the late Celtic period in a cemetery in south-west Sweden,[11] includes a description of the methods that have been consistently followed since then at our Osteological Laboratory in Stockholm. At the time of writing, the contents of no less than over 5,000 cremation burials have already been examined, using the same procedure throughout.

Before proceeding to a closer study of the material, we will add a reminder that the first stages in the investigation of cremations are the same as in all studies of skeletal material, namely to establish the *number of interred individuals*, their approximate *age at death* and their *sex*.

PHYSICAL CHARACTERISTICS OF THE MATERIAL

These must, of course, depend directly on the firing temperature, any treatment that may have taken place before deposition (e.g. crushing to reduce the fragments to a standard size), also the nature of the encasement of the bones, under which we must include the various kinds of container (urn with or without lid or covering stone, comparatively perishable tree-bark boxes caulked with resin, etc.), and finally the amount of pyre debris, charcoal and ash, and the soil type and precipitation conditions in the burial area.

As a result of a series of comparisons with present-day cremations from the Northern and Southern Crematoria in Stockholm, the former an old and the latter a modern establishment, and of a number of experiments with the re-burning of pulverized bone samples from prehistoric (including late Celtic) cremations, the author has become convinced that cremating techniques in prehistoric times must have attained a very high level of efficiency. This in turn presupposes a tradition extending far back in time. Thus it very frequently happens, even after modern cremation, that a proportion of blue or blue-grey areas of bone are found, especially in the cross-section of compact bony parts, e.g. in the diaphyses of long bones, showing that organic matter still survives there. When such samples are re-heated under blast, after they have been pulverized, the blue colouration disappears, and it can be demonstrated that a slight diminution in weight has occurred.

In prehistoric times, of course, burning took place in the open, on a pyre that was exposed to wind and weather. There was no restriction on the duration of a cremation other than (perhaps) nightfall; there was no great risk of deficient oxygenation, while the remains were accessible throughout the whole process and could be pushed back into the flames with sticks or other implements to ensure effective combustion. Only heavy rain or snow would be needed to minimize or delay the completion of cremation.

Nowadays, because cremation is carried out in an enclosed chamber, oxygen has to be forced by various means through air vents into the incinerator (the cremation oven), and indeed the effectiveness of the combustion cannot be assessed until the whole process has been completed and the 'ashes' collected in a receptacle. The time taken for a modern cremation is normally in the order of $1\frac{1}{2}$ to 2 hours, and the oxygen deficiency usually occurs while the 'ashes' are cooling in the receptacle, in which they lie in a fairly compact mass.

Size. In prehistoric samples this varies from microscopically small parts and fragmentary bones up to pieces a couple of decimetres in length. The latter are rare, however, and in fact occur only in large, intact urns. Otherwise, the fragments in any given sample can usually be characterized without further ado as being of a certain average size (e.g. 1·5–2·5 cm), and this, together with the general appearance of the individual pieces of bone, is a fairly reliable indication that some mechanical breaking-up must have taken place. The bone remains were perhaps simply crushed with a stone after they had cooled, in order either to get them into the burial container or to make them easier to handle. Precisely the same is done with the remains after the cremation process at the present day; special apparatus is used, consisting of a powerful fan to blow away the ash (the true ash), a magnet to extract all the coffin nails and the large numbers of various metal fittings which the undertaker insists on using to make the coffins more expensive, and finally a crusher to reduce the bone remains (nowadays mistakenly called the 'ashes') to suitable dimensions, normally 1–2 cm.

In the Second World War, as in the First, it became expedient to make urns from paper pulp. Several of these have subsequently been disinterred and their contents transferred to metal containers. On inspection of such re-interments one can immediately see that, even during the short time that the cremated bones have lain in the earth, they have completely assimilated the soil colouring from it, and it is impossible to distinguish them from prehistoric samples—this is worth remembering for the field archaeologist. It is also worth noting that even in urns from the Bronze Age the characteristic smell of burning can still hang over the cremated bones.

As regards changes suffered by the sample after interment, it is obviously to be expected that in areas with a high water content in regions where winters are cold, further fragmentation will take place as a result of repeated frosts, that soils with a high acidity can erode the bone, and again that depositions lying at shallow depth may sometimes have served as a substratum for the roots of plants and thus have suffered secondary erosion. Uncalcined or incompletely combusted parts may in some instances be affected by processes of decay, but as a general rule the bones from cremation burials have undergone little alteration. Only the remains of aborted foetuses and new-born babies, and poorly combusted cremated bones may, on occasion, crumble into a morphologically unrecognizable state.

Colour. Cremated bones can vary from chalk-white, through grey, grey-brown and brown, or grey-blue and blue, to coal-black. Blue-green and bright verdigris green shades also occur, but these are usually a result of lying close to metal objects among the grave goods. The general rule is that large bone amounts of lightish colour shades, comprising a high proportion of big fragments (high mean size) and with unaltered, sharp fracture edges, derive in the main from well-protected interments (urns with lids or covering stones in dry soils), whereas strongly humus-stained or charcoal-mixed fragments bespeak simpler cremation pits. Cremated burials of the pre-Roman Iron Age embrace the remains of individuals of all age groups, from foetuses to the elderly, both males and females, from well-preserved urns with covering stones and containing the whole of the bones recovered from the pyre, to simple cremation pits with a very few scraps of charcoal and a mere token deposition of a tiny fraction of the burnt bones. All this, like the factors mentioned above, must to a considerable extent determine the chances of developing a method by which the material can be made scientifically productive, and the fundamental principle must be to recover every single scrap of information that the fragments can be made to yield. The results achieved by an investigation are thus a measure of the length of time that can be spent on repeated re-examinations of the material. The important factors are primarily the following: quantity and weight of the bones and the ratio between the two; size of the fragments; identifiable fragments and morphological observations on them (Plate XV); and certain metrical series of wall thicknesses and the statistical use of these (discussed in DETERMINATION OF SEX, below).

IDENTIFICATION OF THE FRAGMENTS

During the process of cremation of the human (or animal) cadaver on the funeral pyre, the soft parts are the first to disappear, followed by the distortion and shattering of the bones that makes it so difficult to identify individual fragments among the burnt remains. An intensively trained and experienced eye, research at a crematorium and comparative studies between modern cremated bones before crushing and prehistoric bone samples, are the essential prerequisites for learning to recognize more and more fragments (Plate XVa shows a typical sample of cremated bones). One important difference that may be pointed out is between the ways in which compact bone tissue, e.g. the shaft bones, and spongy bone, e.g. the epiphyses, are altered during cremation. The compact bone normally cracks and breaks into pieces, as do the crowns of all teeth that had erupted at the time of burning, whereas teeth that were not yet ready but lie in various stages of growth in the jaw, and the roots of the erupted teeth can normally be recovered whole or reassembled. The spongy bone tissue, which of course has this texture specifically in order to withstand pressures from different directions, shrinks slightly during burning but in general retains its shape. The articular heads of thigh bones and upper arm bones, complete vertebrae and various bones of the middle hand and middle foot are among the normal finds.

The way in which the compact bone shatters is not completely haphazard. Some degree of regularity can be observed, and one factor that is often overlooked is the common tendency for the lines of the cracks to follow trajectories of the bone, i.e. features indicating 'the interdependence of structure and function' . . . 'one of the fundamental laws of biology.'[12] By studying this fracture formation on the different bones of the body caused by cremation (Plate XVb, c, e, and f show examples from the thigh bone and radius) and at the same time memorizing the shape of the different cross-sections of these bones at different points along their lengths, it is possible to train oneself to pick out a given part of a given bone of each individual from a sample of bones from cremation burials. The various morphological details can be learnt either from a text-book or on an uncremated skeleton.[13]

ENUMERATION OF INDIVIDUALS

One may expect, especially when examining all the interments from a large cemetery, to come across graves that contain remains of more than one individual. It is also important for the archaeologist to know the total of individuals, since it may otherwise be impossible to reach a correct interpretation of particular associations of finds. There is, moreover, the accidental chance that at some time in the history of a given population there befell some misfortune, some passage of arms, an epidemic or some other event that resulted in the simultaneous deaths of a number of individuals, who were thereupon buried together. Religious beliefs and customs may also on occasion lie behind multiple interments.

The prerequisites necessary for a reliable estimate of the total of individuals in a grave are: that a sufficient quantity of the remains from the pyre were deposited to provide a reasonable chance of success; that some *singly-occurring* or *paired* bones of every individual are present; and, of course, that they have not been broken up beyond recognition. In practice, the author normally looks for such skeletal parts as the odontoid process of the second cervical vertebra (a *dens axis* is shown in Plate XVd), the petrous part of the inner ear (*petrosum .. mastoid*) (Plate XVj, k, l), the supraorbital region (Plate XVg, i), the glabella (the protuberance above the nasal root) (Plate XVh, i), jaw parts and their articulating processes (*processus articulares mandibulae*), the articulating heads of the upper arm and thigh bone (*capita humeri et femoris*), the pilaster region of the thigh bone and all teeth and tooth fragments (cf. Plate XVo), including root parts, etc. The above are then used throughout the whole investigation and should be placed separately in a box or bag for control on any future occasion. In addition, certain other pieces from the middle regions of the shaft bones are extracted for sex determination, of which more will be said below (DETERMINATION OF SEX). By grouping together those skeletal parts that occur singly or in pairs in each individual, it is possible to calculate the number of persons represented (or at least the minimum number), but of course the smaller the volume of bones deposited, the less certain will be the results. If there are only few fragments, it will be impossible to estimate the total of individuals at all. Nevertheless, there are individual similarities in form between paired bones, e.g. that part of the petrous region that faces the brain cavity and contains the outlet for the auditory nerve (*meatus auditorius externus*), that make it possible, if one left and one right section of this region are both represented, to distinguish between different individuals (cf. Plate XVk, l). Similarly, if there is a wide divergence in age between two individuals in the same grave, this can be demonstrated from a large variety of different skeletal parts (DETERMINATION OF AGE, below). If different individuals were cremated on separate occasions, or interments deposited at different times, this too will be detectable, in which cases this fact is usually reflected in different shades of colouration and peculiarities in the stratigraphy, which it is the duty of the archaeologist to observe and record meticulously.

As an example of a burial rite where the cremated bones of one individual after another (probably of the same family) were scattered horizontally, ultimately forming what almost amounted to a small burial mound, we may cite the Middle Grave Field of late Celtic date at Vallhagar on Gotland. This type of grave, before the osteological analysis showed it to represent a concentration of several individuals, had surprised archaeologists by the occurrence of several specimens of the same class of iron objects, e.g. shield-bosses and swords, in each structure.[14]

DETERMINATION OF AGE

The determination of the individual ages at death is based mainly on the same principles as for uncremated skeletal material, but the same limitations apply as in the calculation of the total number of individuals. As far as adults over the age of thirty are concerned, any anthropological age determination must necessarily be both relative and subjective, not least because we have no means of knowing how those characteristics on which such estimations are based were manifested when the individual was alive; still less do we know of the genetical background of the population from which the individual came. All these points were underlined by the author in his dissertation on 364 medieval skeletons from North Sweden.[15]

Cremated remains of foetuses, new-born babies, children of various ages, adolescents and young adults up to the age of 25–30 years can be aged no less precisely than un-cremated skeletons, with the aid of the surviving teeth and tooth fragments and the degree of synostosis of the various articulating processes (epiphyses and certain other bones in the body become firmly fused with their respective diaphyses according to a known time-scale to be found in text-books on anatomy).[13] The various sutures of the skull also change with increasing age, and it is always worthwhile extracting from the sample all the vault fragments (cf. Plate XVn) and examining their cross-section by eye. A combination of the shape of the tooth roots, the width of the root canals, the root apices, the cross-section of the vault, the degree of sutural obliteration and the ratio of the weight of the sample to its volume, will give a good indication of the relative gradation of the age groupings above twenty years into *adult*, *mature* and *senile*. Further than this it is dangerous to venture, even in cases where the complete inventory of bones is available.

A number of comprehensive series of age determinations carried out by these methods formed the basis of the mortality curves published by the author in various papers and collated in his doctorate theses.[16]

DETERMINATION OF SEX

Anyone who has been engaged in skeletal studies knows how difficult it can sometimes be to sex uncremated bones. Surely, then, it must be quite impossible to grapple with the problems of cremated ones? The answer is No; and in the following paragraphs the author will proceed to try to explain the way in which he has attempted to deal with the question.

The difference between the sexes is most often sought on skeletal material in the so-called secondary sexual characters; in males a more robust cranium with more powerful and coarser supraorbital parts, a more prominent region above the nasal root (or glabella) (cf. Plate XVg, h), larger *processus mastoides*, more powerful and larger *capita humeri et femoris* and, in general, more pronounced muscle relief. All these characters are *normally* less strongly manifested in the females (cf. Plate XVi). Every population, however, exhibits a certain number of intersexes or intermediates between the definitely male and the definitely female individuals from an osteological point of view. We may expect at least 20% of the adult individuals in a collection of cremated material to be morphologically indeterminable, partly comprising these intermediate types, partly pathological cases and partly because sex-determinative fragments will probably have failed to survive in some of the samples under investigation.

There will always still remain, therefore, after the sexing of the individuals with

TABLE A
Statistical treatment of the comparative material.

	Maximal measured wall thickness in measurement area Ia.	Wall thickness at 1b.	Wall thickness of femur in measurement area 2.	Vertical diameter of caput humeri	Transversal diameter of caput humeri	Wall thickness of caput humeri in measurement area 3c.	Wall thickness of radius in measurement area 4
Males							
Mean value ($\bar{x}$)	6·5	13·0	6·7	44·4	38·9	4·1	2·7
Standard deviation (σ)	1·3	3·3	1·6	2·3	2·7	0·8	0·5
Mean error ($\Sigma\bar{x}$)	±0·2	±0·8	±0·2	±0·3	±0·4	±0·1	±0·1
Total (n)	46	17	47	56	44	30	32
Coefficient of variation	20·0	25·4	23·9	5·2	6·9	19·5	18·5
Range	10·0–4·5	23·0–8·5	11·5–4·0	52·5–40·0	47·5–37·0	6·6–2·6	3·6–1·8
Females							
Mean value ($\bar{x}$)	5·9	11·5	5·3	41·8	35·5	2·7	2·0
Standard deviation (σ)	1·3	2·3	1·1	2·4	2·4	0·8	0·4
Mean error ($\Sigma\bar{x}$)	±0·2	±0·5	±0·2	±0·3	±0·4	±0·1	±0·1
Total (n)	45	22	41	47	39	32	26
Coefficient of variation	22·0	20·0	20·8	5·7	6·8	29·6	20·0
Range	9·2–4·0	17·0–8·0	8·5–2·2	45·0–34·5	40·5–32·0	5·0–1·7	2·9–1·2
t for the difference	2·14	1·59	4·95	6·12	6·01	9·90	4·95
Probability value (P)	0·02	0·1	<0·001	<0·001	<0·001	<0·001	<0·001

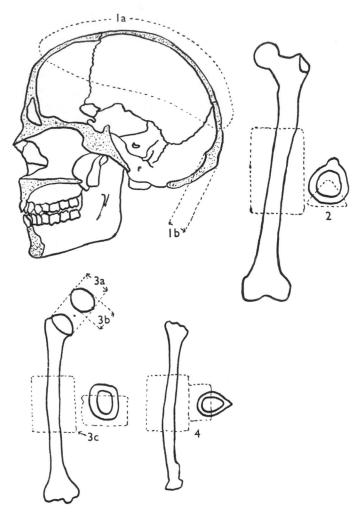

Fig. 56 Schematic diagram of measurements, showing the approximate areas for the metrical series and the position of the measurements within each area. The figures correspond to the headings of the relevant columns in Tables A–D as follows: 1a: maximal measured wall thickness of the vault in measurement area 1a; 1b: wall thickness of the cranium between *protuberantia occipitalis externa* and *eminentia cruciata* (these are easily recognizable fragments); 2: wall thickness of the thigh bone within an area near the middle of the diaphysis and directly opposite the pilaster; 3a, 3b, and 3c: vertical and transversal diameters of the articular head of the upper arm, and wall thickness at the middle of the diaphysis; 4: wall thickness of the radius within an area near the middle of the diaphysis. From Weinmann and Sicher.[12]

typically male or female supraorbital regions, *capita humeri et femoris*, etc., a number of individuals that cannot be sexed by direct means.

   For such cases the author has attempted to evolve a procedure based on the established fact that, out of any two individuals of equal size, the walls of the bones of the female will on average be $\frac{1}{3}$–$\frac{1}{4}$ thinner than those of the male. In 1948 the author was able to demonstrate statistical proof of this hypothesis when an opportunity arose of taking

TABLE B

Sex determination of cremations by various methods.

Females	mm	Males
	69 2·5	
	95 2·6	
	209 2·7	
	107 2·8	
	2·9	
	114 3·0	
51 49	53 3·1	
	204 3·2	
166 73	207 3·3	
164 97	175 3·4	
133 199 160 68 67 31 174 59 222 196	71 3·5	
224 198 96 92 80	47 3·6	
61 13	173 3·7	
159 44 128	55 3·8	116
110	39 3·9	12 77 130 33 90
158 11	211 4·0	137 153 84 144 219 120 134
180 170	100 4·1	105 146
125 119 124	214 4·2	138 139 30 45 184 205
	4·3	21 27 87 88 115 118 197
	216 4·4	14 149 188 127 65
	63 4·5	117 121 123 155 189 17 104 206
	4·6	58 113
	4·7	101 194
	4·8	167 215 182
210	4·9	190 62 162
	5·0	29 143 157 102
41	5·1	171 176
	5·2	74 140
	5·3	91 60
	5·4	20 32 25
	5·5	
	5·6	148
	5·7	
	5·8	
	5·9	141
	6·0	23

In the framed column in the middle, the mean thickness of the vault wall in mm; on the left side the female burials, on the right the males. On either side of the central frame, enclosed with solid lines, the determinations based on morphological features (supraorbital regions, shoulder joint heads, etc.); between the solid and the dotted lines, the determinations on biometric grounds, arranged in descending order of certainty from the middle outwards. From Gejvall.[11]

TABLE C

Example of a points system for interpolation of a prehistoric cremated individual into the metrical series for modern cremations.

Grave 59, containing 1½ litres of bones, i.e. low in the range of bone volumes.

	Column							
	VI.	1a	1b	2	3a	3b	3c	4
Grave 59	3·5	5·0	6·6+	5·0	—	—	2·6	1·6
Mean value for ♀ in the modern sample (*cf.* Tab. A)	—	5·9	11·5	5·3	41·8	35·5	2·7	2·0
Points	—	♀	♀	♀	—	—	♀	♀

The result is 5 ♀ points in 5 columns (considering the similarity of the measurements), implying that the individual should be placed on the female side of Table B. This position is further supported by the value of 3·5 for the mean thickness of the vault wall shown in col. VI.

This procedure makes it possible to build onto Table B; outside the solid line delimiting the morphologically sexed individuals are interpolated the determinations arrived at by statistical means, arranged in descending order of certainty from the middle outwards.

From Gejvall.[11]

measurements, following the same procedure throughout, on 50 male and 49 female modern cremations selected at random and placed at his disposal in Stockholm. There was no question here of any difficulty in finding the skeletal parts required for measuring. The relevant metrical series are shown in Table A and Fig. 56, and the statistical treatment of the values derived from these measurements shows that a proven sexual difference exists in the majority of the experimental metrical series.

At the same time, all the morphological sexual characters listed above in connection with prehistoric cremations were recorded for this material, and age determinations were also carried out, which the author was able to check directly against the records of the crematorium offices several days later. The age determinations proved to a great extent to fall within the correct limits, and only two of the sex determinations were wrong. A multitude of information of forensic and criminological value was recovered from these studies, but they lie outside the scope of the present discussion.

When applying the results thus achieved to the prehistoric material, it is most convenient to start with morphologically sexed individuals (i.e. on the basis of supraorbital regions, etc.) and then, for the remainder, to employ statistically the average wall-thicknesses given by the male and female individuals thus determined. In practice this can be done either by straight comparisons or by using a simple points system such as that described by the author in his 1948 paper on cremations (an example of which is given in Tables B and C).

It would be wrong to leave the subject of prehistoric cremations without some mention of the animal bones that occur in them together with the human bones. First, a curiosity. A prehistoric cremation can sometimes be assigned even to a specific season of the year, as in the case of a number of early Roman Iron Age graves, if jaw fragments of

TABLE D

The mean values of the biometric series and the division of the comparative material into different age groups.

Age Group	Ia ♂	Ia ♀	Ib ♂	Ib ♀	2 ♂	2 ♀	3a ♂	3a ♀	3b ♂	3b ♀	3c ♂	3c ♀	4 ♂	4 ♀
I. Over 70 yrs	7·1	6·2	12·1	11·9	6·8	5·1	44·1	39·5	41·1	35·6	3·9	2·5	2·9	1·7
n	14	26	9	13	16	23	15	22	15	21	9	16	10	11
II. 50–70 yrs	6·3	5·5	13·9	11·4	6·7	5·3	44·8	37·5	42·4	34·6	4·1	2·8	2·6	1·9
n	24	12	6	8	22	10	26	12	21	11	14	9	15	9
III. under 50 yrs	6·0	5·7	14·8	9·7	6·7	5·7	44·2	39·5	41·8	36·4	4·3	3·0	2 6	2·4
n	8	8	2	2	9	9	15	10	12	8	7	8	7	7

From Gejvall.[11]

lamb (the remains of a burial feast?) are included. Lambs are born in March–April, and their age can be determined from the associated tooth fragments. The occurrence of various animal species in prehistoric cremation graves (bear, in the form of the first claw phalange, from the skin in which the corpse was wrapped (cf. Plate XVm), dog, horse, ox, sheep and/or goat, pig, elk, deer, various kinds of bird, fish, etc.) and the distribution of these species over the various periods and regions, open up a completely new field of research which the author has discussed in a recently published paper,[17] and which sheds fresh light on burial rites, economy and hunting activities, and on the incidence of want and plenty at different periods in earlier times.

REFERENCES AND NOTES

1 Letter dated 22nd August 1930 in the Stockholm Archaeological and Topographical Archives, D. no. 1394 1930

2 KRUMBEIN, C. N. 1934–5. *Anthropologische Untersuchungen an urgeschichtlichen Leichenbränden, Forschungen und Fortschritte 10–11*, 411

3 HUIZINGA, J. 1952. In Dubiis Abstine. In *Proc. State Service for Archaeological Investigations in the Netherlands*

4 LIZOWSKI, F. P. 1955–6. *Proc. Soc. Antiq. Scot. 89*, 83

5 —— 1956. The Cremations from Barclodiad y Gawres, in POWELL, T. G. E. and DANIEL, G. E., *Barclodiad y Gawres*, Liverpool

6 —— 1959. *J. Roy. Soc. Antiq. Ireland 89*, 26

7 WELLS, C. 1960. *Antiquity 34*, 29

8 THIEME, U. 1940. Untersuchungsergebnis des Leichenbrandes aus 7 Gräbern von Bornitz, Kr. Zetz. Nachrichtenblatt für deutsche Vorzeit, Leipzig, 16 Jahrg. Heft 10–11

9 KLOIBER, AE. 1943. *Mitt. Anth. Ges. Wien. 72*

10 GEJVALL, N.-G. 1947. *Bestämning av brända ben från forntida gravar, Fornvännen*, Stockholm, H 1 (English summary)

11 —— and SAHLSTRÖM, K. E. 1948. Gravfältet på Kyrkbacken i Horns socken, Västergötland in *Kungl. Vitterhets Historie och Antikvitets Akademiens Handlingar*, Stockholm, Del. 60:2 (German summary)

12 WEINMANN, J. and SICHER, H. 1955. *Bone and Bones. Fundamentals of Bone Biology*, St Louis, 127

13 BRASH, J. C. 1937. *Cunningham's Text-book of Anatomy*, Oxford, 7th ed. or: u.p. RAUBER-KOPSCH, *Lehrbuch und Atlas der Anatomie der Menschen* I, Leipzig, 1947, 17 Aufl.; in the present edition (19th) the valuable tabular summaries of obliteration and epiphysis-fusion have unfortunately been omitted—interest in osteology is apparently not in the ascendant in medical schools!

14 GEJVALL, N.-G. 1955. The Cremations at Vallhagar, in STENBERGER, M. (ed.), *Vallhagar, A Migration Period Settlement on Gotland Sweden*, Stockholm, II, 705

15 —— 1960. *Westerhus, Medieval Population and Church in the Light of Skeletal Remains*, Kungl. Vitterhets Historie och Antikvitets Akademien, Stockholm, 42 (Monograph Series)

16 —— *Ibid.*, plate 5

17 —— 1961. *Acta Archaeologica Lundensia*, ser. in 4°, 5, 157–173

38 The Palaeopathology of Human Skeletal Remains

MARCUS S. GOLDSTEIN*

PALAEOPATHOLOGY, a term apparently first used by Sir Marc Armand Ruffer,[39] is concerned with the diseases which can be demonstrated in earlier human and animal remains. Thus the materials of study in human palaeopathology have been the skeletal and soft tissue remains of 'ancient' peoples, occasionally also the art objects left by these people which depict the human figure in ways suggestive of morbid conditions.

Obviously the physical anthropologist and physician who usually undertake the studies in human palaeopathology are dependent on the archaeologist for their material. In turn, the role of pathology in prehistory, so far as it can be ascertained, should be of relevant interest to archaeology. For disease, disability, and death are integral aspects of the biology of a population and its culture. Angel,[3] for example, has pointed to the close relationship between health and the course of civilization in ancient Greece. Studies in palaeopathology in recent years, as noted by Sigerist,[43] Ackerknecht,[4] Brothwell,[9] and no doubt others, have tended to include, in addition to a description of diseased conditions of bones, an 'epidemiology' of the skeletal population recovered by the archaeologist. That is, there has been a consideration of health status of the group in terms of prevalence of disease, age and sex distributions, estimates of age at death and average life span of the group, and relationships with culture changes observed in different strata or periods of time. An early example of such a 'reconstruction of the growth and decline' of an early population is the classic work on the Pecos Indian Pueblo by Hooton[23] in 1930. Such studies, regrettably enough, tend to be limited in number and scope because a large 'population' of skeletal material is not often uncovered, especially of early man. Even when a large burial site is found, the remains may be too fragmentary or in too poor a state of preservation for study.

SCOPE OF THE PRESENT CHAPTER

This essay is meant only as a brief general survey, and will thus note only the major literature on the subject, especially since about 1945, and indicate briefly what palaeopathology has revealed.

Several previous publications have reviewed in detail the field of palaeopathology. Moodie[28] in 1923 published a comprehensive work on animal and human palaeopathology which includes an extensive bibliography. A volume by Pales[35] in 1930, *Paléopathologie et Pathologie comparative*, gives the most complete bibliography (660 titles) and exhaustive treatment of the subject to that time. Sigerist[43] in his illuminating

* The views here expressed are the author's and do not necessarily represent those of the Public Health Service or of the Department of Health, Education and Welfare of Washington, D.C.

book *Primitive and Archaic Medicine* published in 1951, reviews the field and lists the literature published between about 1930 and 1944. A recently published study by Brothwell[9] provides an extensive review and a provocative discussion of the palaeo-pathology of early British man. Shorter but nevertheless excellent general reviews of the subject have also been published in recent years by Vallois,[52,53] Krogman,[26] Angel,[3] and Ackerknecht.[4]

THE FINDINGS OF HUMAN PALAEOPATHOLOGY

Disturbances in development. The older literature[35,43] cites congenital club-foot in ancient Egypt and deformity attributed to hydrocephalus in an Egyptian of the Roman period, and instances of open sacrum and possible Paget's disease from Neolithic France. More recently Angel[1] reported a case of congenital hip dislocation in a series of 132 skeletons (31 well preserved) of Greeks dating from Neolithic to Byzantine times. The skeletal remains of 9 prehistoric Huron Indians from Ontario, Canada,[25] showed a 'strong, active male, at least 50 years of age' with two congenital anomalies: an asymmetrical distortion of the skull involving all the bones of the face which, according to the author, probably caused 'a severe tilting of the head on the neck' (torticollis?); and a lesion of the lumbar region of the vertebral column that probably caused low-back pain and sciatica. Brothwell[9] reports on a Neolithic skeleton from Britain in which the long bones of the left arm are much shorter than those of the right, and of scoliosis of an apparently congenital origin found in five early British skeletons, one dating back to the Bronze Age. Instances of hip dislocation have been found in skeletons from Neolithic France[35] (Fig. 57e), Bronze Age Britain,[9] Early Iron Age Greece,[1] and pre-Columbian America.[21,25]

Mention may also be made of a possible case of mongolism in an Anglo-Saxon population. According to Brothwell,[8] the skull of a child of about nine years of age manifested symptoms generally associated with mongolism, such as marked micro-cephaly, hyperbrachycephaly, small sphenoid body and high angle of basi-occipital, thinness of cranial bones, small maxilla but fairly normal mandible size, and minor anomalies of the dentition.

Inflammation of bone. Sigerist[43] has remarked that inflammation in the skeleton is a normal defence reaction to a pathological agent or injury, occurring in the periosteum (periostitis) or in the marrow (osteomyelitis), and that the great majority of all pathological changes found in early human bones are the results of inflammatory processes. Chronic inflammatory diseases that affect the joints (arthritis deformans), or spondylitis deformans when it is in the spinal column, are included under this category.

According to Straus and Cave,[51] the 'old man' of La Chapelle-aux-Saints, a member of the Neanderthal groups, was afflicted with spinal osteoarthritis that caused him 'to stand and walk with something of a pathological kyphosis'; these authors also point to a flattening and deformation of the right mandibular condyle in the La Chapelle man, 'attributable to an osteoarthritis of the temporo-mandibular joint', and note a like but more severe condition in two other Neanderthal mandibles, those of La Quina and La Ferrassie.

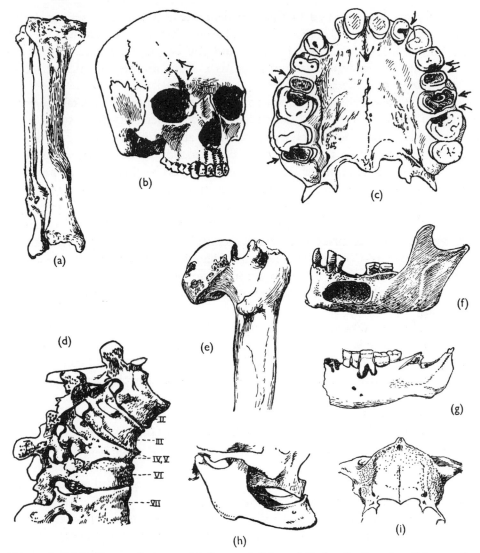

Fig. 57 (a, b) Evidence of trauma: (a) fractured tibia and fibula of a Peruvian; (b) an early Egyptian skull. (c) The palate of Rhodesian Man; arrows point to the caries cavities. (d) Part of the vertebral column of a Neolithic skeleton from Germany, with vertebral collapse and fusion strongly suggestive of tuberculosis. After Moodie.[28] (e) Deformed femur head of the French Neolithic period; the anomaly probably indicates a congenital dislocation of the hip. After Pales.[35] (f–i) Examples of early Egyptian oral pathology: (f) a large cystic cavity; (g) chronic abscessing at the root of a lower first molar; (h, i) lateral and palatal views of edentulous skulls. After Ruffer.[39a]

Stewart[49] has reported osteoarthritis in Shanidar I from Iraq: this Neanderthaloid skeleton, judged to be about 45,000 years old, shows osteophytes or 'lipping' in his cervical and lumbar vertebrae, as well as a pathological flattening of the mandibular condyle similar to that of La Chapelle man noted above.

Several reports have pointed to the prevalence of inflammatory lesions (arthritis, periostitis, and osteomyelitis) in the skeletons of prehistoric American Indians,[10,21,25,38,46] Neolithic France,[29] Greece,[1] and Britain,[9] and the late Copper Age in Hungary.[18] Such inflammatory conditions are not indicative of specific diseases, since they could have been caused by different agents.[43]

Tuberculosis of bone. Perhaps the first definite evidence of human skeletal tuberculosis, according to Morse,[30] is from a Neolithic cemetery in Germany (Fig. 57d). Sigerist[43] notes that Elliot Smith and Ruffer, in 1910, found an Egyptian mummy of the XXIst Dynasty (*c.* 1000 BC) with inflammation and destruction of bone indicative of Pott's disease. Possible manifestations of Pott's disease have also been reported in pre-Columbian American Indian remains.[36,38,46] American Indian clay figurines and effigy water-bottles of pre-Columbian times are cited by Ritchie[36] as '. . . faithful representations of persons afflicted with Pott's disease . . .' although this view has been questioned sharply by Morse.[30] The latter, after detailed consideration of the evidence for skeletal tuberculosis in the pre-Columbian American Indian, found it all negative and concludes that tuberculosis did not exist in the prehistoric American Indian.

Brothwell[9] describes two possible cases of tuberculosis in British remains from Saxon times.

Syphilis and Yaws. Whether syphilis originated in the New World or Old has been an uncertain and moot issue for many years.[45] Possible syphilitic lesions have been noted recently in pre-Columbian remains in Oklahoma,[10] Texas,[21] and California,[38] although in each instance the diagnosis was far from being definitive and the number of cases was very small.

Of interest in this connection is the citation quoted by Brothwell[9] of '. . . an edict of Edward III to the Mayor and Sheriffs of London in 1346, which describes a disease of a syphilitic nature communicated by "carnal intercourse with women in stews and other secret places".'

It seems fair to say that the evidence as to where syphilis originated is still too meagre and uncertain to warrant any firm conclusions.

Yaws, a treponemal disease largely limited to tropical regions and at times mistakenly diagnosed as syphilis, has been discovered by Stewart and Spoehr[50] in the skeleton of an individual from a prehistoric site (*c.* AD 854 ± 145) in the Mariana Island group in the Western Pacific (Fig. 58c). They note that the specimen '. . . gives evidence not only of the presence, but of the character of yaws in the Western Pacific before the introduction of syphilis.'

A provocative suggestion has recently been made by one authority,[15] that the various species of treponemal infections have been 'mere variants of one basic organism', and that 'Interspecific competition may partially determine whether a population contracts yaws or syphilis.'

Leprosy. According to Møller-Christensen,[27] the earliest case of leprosy found in the skeleton is that of a Copt (mummy) from the sixth century. Brothwell[9] notes that only one questionable case of leprosy has previously been reported in the literature on excavated British material, but describes a fairly definite case of seventh-century date AD.

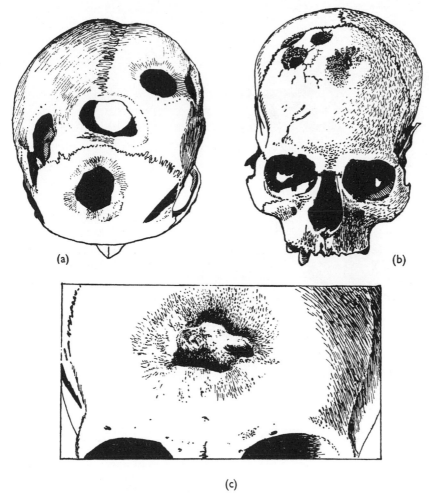

Fig. 58 (a) Upper aspect of a pre-Columbian skull from Cusco, Peru, with seven trephine openings. After Oakley *et al.*[33] (b) Facial aspect of a Bronze Age skull from Jericho. After Oakley *et al.*[33] (c) Part of the frontal region of a skull from the Western Pacific, dated to the ninth century AD; a crater-like lesion is suggestive of yaws. After Stewart and Spoehr.[50]

Møller-Christensen, it may be mentioned, on examining the skeletons representing about 200 persons who had been inmates of a Danish medieval leper hospital, discovered a diagnostic characteristic of the disease in the skeleton, namely, '. . . changes in the distal part of the *aperture piriformes* . . . roentgenologically characterized by atrophy of the anterior nasal spine and the maxillary alveolar process', or *facies leprosa*. Some 76 per cent of the examined crania manifested this diagnostic criterion. Typical bone changes in leprosy are shown in Fig. 59.

Traumatic injury. Cranial injuries (e.g. Fig. 57b) as a possible cause of death, or traumatic lesions in the form of fractures healed by the formation of calluses (e.g. Fig. 57a), have occurred at all times before and since the advent of man, as evinced in skeletal remains from all parts of the world.[1,9,10,17,21,29,38,43]

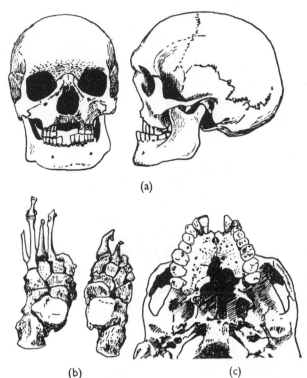

(a)

(b)   (c)

Fig. 59 Bone changes in leprosy, after Møller Christiensen.[27] (a) Facial and lateral aspects of Case 2, showing bone changes in the upper alveolar region. (b) Both feet of Case 1, displaying considerable deformity and loss of bone. (c) Palatal aspect of Case 4, showing a large perforation.

Tumours. Except for benign osteomata, tumours in prehistoric man are apparently rare.[43] According to Brothwell,[9] only about 12 cases in earlier peoples have appeared in the literature. Nemeskéri and Harsányi[31] cite a case of 'Tumor multiplex (Myeloma)' in a skeleton from a medieval site in Hungary (ninth to twelfth centuries AD; 1 case in 1055 skeletons). The oldest example of a tumour in man appears to be a sarcomatous overgrowth (Fig. 60b) on the chin of the Kanam mandible from Kenya, East Africa, which has been dated as possibly Middle Pleistocene.[34] A honeycomb type of hyperostosis over the vertex of a skull from the Egyptian XXth Dynasty (c. 1200 BC), according to Rogers,[37] 'suggests the reaction to an angioblastic or sarcomatous meningioma'. Other examples of tumours are shown in Fig. 60.

Trephination. Trepanning should perhaps be mentioned in a review of palaeopathology since it is evidence of possible surgical therapy for the alleviation of pathological conditions. Thus Brothwell[9] remarks on a Beaker period skeleton in Britain with signs of congenital scoliosis associated with a trephined hole in the head, and suggests the latter may have been an attempt to cope with the scoliosis. Evidence indicative of at least a possibility that early peoples performed trephination to alleviate mastoid inflammation has been noted,[33] as well as to relieve pressure on the brain due to injury.[26] Trepanning was practised in Europe during Neolithic times,[29,40] in Africa in the Bronze Age,[33] and in ancient Peru.[47] Stewart[48] has recently reviewed the skull surgery performed by Stone Age man in different parts of the world. Examples of trepanning from the New World and Old World are shown in Fig. 58.

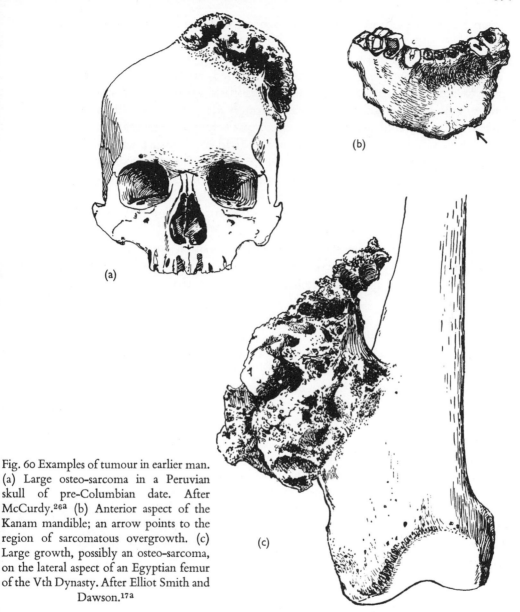

Fig. 60 Examples of tumour in earlier man. (a) Large osteo-sarcoma in a Peruvian skull of pre-Columbian date. After McCurdy.[26a] (b) Anterior aspect of the Kanam mandible; an arrow points to the region of sarcomatous overgrowth. (c) Large growth, possibly an osteo-sarcoma, on the lateral aspect of an Egyptian femur of the Vth Dynasty. After Elliot Smith and Dawson.[17a]

Dental pathology. A large literature is extant on dental palaeopathology. Only some representative examples of recent papers on the subject are here mentioned.

Caries have been observed in the teeth of the Australopithecine apes of South Africa and in *Pithecanthropus*.[6,13,14] Neanderthal man evidently suffered from periodontal disease and abscessed roots,[43,52] as well as from tooth fracture and faulty dental micro-structure.[24,44] The relationship of nutrition to dental pathology in early human populations has been discussed by Brothwell,[6] who also reports on caries and periodontal disease in British remains extending from the Neolithic to the seventeenth century.[9]

Others have reported on dental disease among the ancient Minoans in Crete (*c.* 1750–1550 BC),[11] and pre-Columbian American Indians.[19,38] A few cases of early oral pathology are given in Fig. 57.

Longevity of early peoples. As already mentioned, an effort has been made in recent years to consider rates of mortality in prehistoric groups, based on age at death as determined on their skeletal remains. A rough idea of average life span can thus be ascertained and related with the incidence of pathology and general biology and culture of the group. Since about 1945, data in this field have been published on the ancient Greeks,[2] the ancient inhabitants of Anatolia,[42] Bronze Age British,[7] groups in Hungary during the late Copper Age and ninth to twelfth centuries,[18,31] and several pre-Columbian Indian groups,[10,12,16,20,38] virtually all indicating that relatively few individuals lived beyond middle life, and that mortality among females in the earlier years of life tended to be greater than in males.

Since estimates of age on skeletal material have often been based on cranial suture closure, mention may be made of a recent critique of this method,[5] as well as a report on the rate of development of vertebral osteoarthritis as a means of identifying skeletal age.[49]

COMMENTS AND CONCLUSIONS

Plainly, human palaeopathology reveals that our prehistoric ancestors were also subject to disease and disabilities even as we; that mortality in infancy and the early years of life was very high, with individual survival generally limited to very young adulthood.* No doubt acute infectious diseases eliminated whole families and even larger groups in prehistoric times, as they have done throughout history until very recently even in west European countries.[22]

Archaeology, both as an essential contributor of the source material to, and a potential beneficiary of the findings from, the field of palaeopathology, has a legitimate and considerable interest in the progress of the latter. It may be appropriate therefore to mention several ways in which, in the author's opinion, the skeletal material provided by the archaeologist might be better utilized in studies of palaeopathology.

First, there are still large lacunae in the diagnoses of lesions on the dry bone. Hooton[23] long ago suggested that the clinical pathologist and anatomist co-operate in the preservation of skeletal material of known clinical history for the purpose of acquiring satisfactory criteria in the study of palaeopathology. In any event, there is surely a need for closer collaboration between the physical anthropologist and the pathologist in the detection and diagnosis of diseases in the skeleton, thereby making the results of palaeopathology more meaningful for the archaeologist as well as for others. Second, there is a definite need for compiling the bits of information on palaeopathology that are often 'buried' in archaeological reports and the like. In many instances the skeletal remains uncovered in an archaeological excavation are few in number, and hence a report on

---

* According to the basic studies of Schultz,[41] diseases and developmental defects are common even in monkeys and apes in their natural environment, although many so affected nevertheless survive and successfully compete in their natural habitat.

them, including observations on pathology, appears as a brief addendum to the archaeological monograph. Such fragmentary data on skeletal remains and palaeopathology may or may not be significant in any single instance; when multiplied a hundredfold they might well reveal much of interest to a large circle of workers. It is suggested therefore that 'clearing-houses' be established at places willing to assume the responsibility, to which could be sent all publications containing data on palaeopathology. And third, deriving from the second suggestion, it is proposed that broad surveys of the palaeopathology of a whole country or region be developed, especially with knowledgeable respect to archaeological relationships, as was recently done by Brothwell[9] for Britain. Such surveys, appearing at periodic intervals, should be of pertinent interest to the medical historian and physical anthropologist as well as to the archaeologist.

ACKNOWLEDGEMENT

I wish to thank Miss Rosemary Powers of the British Museum (Natural History) for the excellent illustrations.

REFERENCES

1 ANGEL, J. L. 1946. Am. J. Phys. Anth. 4, 69–97
2 ——1947. J. Gerontol. 2, 18–24
3 —— The Interne (Jan.–Feb. 1948), 15–17, 45–48
4 ACKERKNECHT, E. H. 1953. Paleopathology, in KROEBER, A. L. (ed.) Anthropology Today, New York, 120–126
5 BROOKS, S. T. 1955. Am. J. Phys. Anth. 13, 567–597
6 BROTHWELL, D. R. 1959. Proc. Nutrit. Soc. (Great Brit.) 18, 59–65
7 —— 1960. Advancement of Science 64, 311–322
8 —— 1960. Ann. Human Genetics (London) 24, 141–150
9 —— 1961. The paleopathology of early British Man: An essay on the problems of diagnosis and analysis. J. Roy. Anth. Inst. 91, 318–344
10 BRUES, A. M. 1959. Bull. Oklahoma Anth. Soc. 7, 63–70
11 CARR, H. G. 1960. Man 157, 1–4
12 CHURCHER, C. S. and KENYON, W. A. 1960. Hum. Biol. 32, 249–273
13 CLEMENT, A. J. 1956. Brit. Dental J. 101, 4–7
14 —— 1958. Ibid. 104, 115–123
15 COCKBURN, T. A. 1961. Science 133, 1050–1058
16 COOK, S. F. 1947. Hum. Biol. 19, 83–89
17 COURVILLE, CYRIL B. 1950. Bull. Los Angeles Neurol. Soc. 15, 1–21
17a ELLIOT SMITH, G. and DAWSON, W. R. 1924. Egyptian Mummies, London
18 GÁSPARDY, G. and NEMESKÉRI, J. 1960. Acta Morphologica (Budapest) 9, 203–218
19 GOLDSTEIN, M. S. 1948. Am. J. Phys. Anth. 6, 63–84
20 —— 1953. Hum. Biol. 25, 1–12
21 —— 1957. Am. J. Phys. Anth. 15, 299–312
22 HARE, R. 1954. Pomp and Pestilence. Infectious Disease, Its Origins and Conquest, London
23 HOOTON, E. A. 1930. The Indians of Pecos Pueblo. A Study of Their Skeletal Remains, New Haven
24 KALLAY, JURAY. 1951. Am. J. Phys. Anth. 9, 369–371
25 KIDD, E. 1954. Am. J. Phys. Anth. 12, 610–615
26 KROGMAN, W. M. 1949. Scientific American 180, 52–56
26a McCURDY, G. G. 1923. Am. J. Phys. Anth.
27 MØLLER-CHRISTENSEN, V. Ten Lepers from Naestved in Denmark. A Study of Skeletons from a Medieval Danish Leper Hospital, Copenhagen
28 MOODIE, R. L. 1923. Paleopathology. An Introduction to the Study of Ancient Evidences of Disease, Urbana, Illinois

29 MOREL, C., JR. 1957. *La Médecine et la Chirurgie Osseues aux Temps Préhistoriques dan la région des Grands Causses*, Paris

30 MORSE, D. 1961. *Am. Rev. Respir. Dis. 83*, 489–504

31 NEMESKÉRI, J. and HARSÁNYI, L. 1959. *Homo 10*, 203–226

32 NETTLESHIP, A. 1954 *Bull. Hist. Med. 28*, 259–269

33 OAKLEY, K. P., BROOKE, W. M. A., AKESTER, A. R. and BROTHWELL, D. R. 1959. *Man 59*, 1–4

34 —— and TOBIAS, P. V. 1960. *Nature 185*, 945–947

35 PALES, L. 1930 *Paléopathologie et Pathologie comparative*, Paris

36 RITCHIE, W. A. 1952. *Am. J. Phys. Anth. 10*, 305–317

37 ROGERS, L. 1949. *Brit. J. Surg. 36*, 423–424

38 RONEY, J. G., JR. 1959. *Bull. Hist. Med. 33*, 97–109

39 RUFFER, M. A. 1921. *Studies in the Paleopathology of Egypt*, Chicago

39a —— 1920. *Am. J. Phys. Anth. 3*, 335–382

40 SCHRODER, G. 1957. *Fortschr. auf dem Gebiete der Roentgenstrahlen und der Nuklearmedizin 87*, 538–543

41 SCHULTZ, A. H. 1956. The Occurence and Frequency of Pathological and Teratological Conditions and of Twinning Among Non-Human Primates, in HOFER, H., SCHULTZ, A. H. and STARCK, D. *Handbook of the Primates*, New York, I, 965–1014

42 SENYUREK, M. S. 1947. *Am. J. Phys. Anth. 5*, 55–66

43 SIGERIST, H. E. 1951. *A History of Medicine*; vol. 1, Primitive and Archaic Medicine, New York

44 SOGNNAES, R. F. 1956. *Am. J. Path. 32*, 547–577

45 STEWART, T. D. 1940. Some historical implications of physical anthropology in North America. In Essays in Historical Anthropology of North America, *Smithson. Miscell. Coll. 100*, Washington, D.C.

46 —— 1950. Pathological changes in South American Indian skeletal remains, in STEWARD, J. H. (ed.), *Handbook of South American Indians 6, Bur. Am. Ethnol. 143*, 49–52

47 —— 1956. *Bull. Hist. Med. 30*, 293–320

48 —— 1958. Stone Age skull surgery: A general review with emphasis on the New World, *Smithson. Report for 1957*, publ. 4333, 469–91, Washington

49 —— 1958. *The Leech 28*, 144–51

50 STEWART, T. D. and SPOEHR, H. 1952. *Bull. Hist. Med. 29*, 538–553

51 STRAUS, W. L. Jr. and CAVE, A. J. E. 1957. *Quart. Rev. Biol. 32*, 348–363

52 VALLOIS, H. V. 1948. *La Clinique 43*, 7–13

53 —— 1949. Paléopathologie et paléontologie humaine. In *Homenaje a Don Luis de Hoyos Sainz*, Madrid, 333–341

39 The Radiological Examination of Human Remains

CALVIN WELLS

ROENTGEN ANNOUNCED HIS DISCOVERY of what later came to be called 'X-rays' in November 1895.[1] Almost at once they were applied to the study of man's pathology,[2] anatomy[3] and dentistry.[4] Within a few years they were being used to investigate ancient remains: mummy packs were examined by Pellegrin[5] in 1900 and by Lortet and Gaillard[6] in 1903. Yet it is remarkable that despite this early enthusiasm the scope of radiological investigation is today largely neglected by archaeologists.

These brief notes of a few of the uses of X-rays seek to lure the archaeologist to employ them more often in the future. Works listed in the brief bibliography are almost all chosen for their radiographic illustration of points mentioned in the text: some early examples have been selected for their historic interest.

EARLY SKELETAL REMAINS

Radiological investigation of early remains can yield information of great value about the normal structure of the body which is otherwise difficult to obtain.

For example, the size and shape of the frontal, maxillary and ethmoid sinuses can be seen in great detail on a radiograph. As the dimension of these cavities, especially the frontal sinus, is a secondary sexual character they should always be examined when important material presents any doubt as to its sexing. It is certain, too, that racial or group differences exist in sinus patterns, although little reliable work has been done on this subject. If the sinuses are obscured by foreign matter within, as in skulls which have lain in fine sand, clay or alluvial silt, it is usually a simple affair, before X-raying them, to pass a catheter and wash them out through their natural opening or to puncture a small hole in the wall with only negligible damage to the cavity. Long-rooted teeth sometimes encroach on the maxillary antrum and this should be looked for in skiagrams. The sella turcica is another intra-cranial feature that is not always easy to see in the intact skull. It lodges the pituitary gland and may become pathologically enlarged, as in acromegaly, or developmentally, as in scaphocephaly.[7] It is of individual and phylo-genetic interest and although located almost centrally in the skull it is well placed for radiographic investigation. It is in close relationship with the sphenoidal sinus, with which it may be confused.[8,9]

Carefully angled exposures will give much information about the less accessible cranial architecture, the relative thickness of compact bone and diploë, the internal structure of the mastoid apophysis and the petrous temporal. None of this evidence should be ignored when dealing with Palaeolithic or similarly important material. It is not only intra-cranial features that are suitable for radiological investigation. Projection of contours for 'shape' studies can conveniently be done by this means.[10]

Much can also be learned from radiological study of the rest of the skeleton. Indications of sex may be obtained from the internal structure of some of the bones and age changes may similarly be recognized long before they are detectable on external examination. The proximal end of the humerus is a particularly sensitive indicator[11] and the femoral head has also been used.[12] Variations in the volume of the medullary cavities, and the density or porosity of individual bones as life progresses throw further light on the subject, although inter-racial differences of this kind remain largely unexplored. Certain other characteristics of X-ray examination can be useful. One is the fact that the passage of the rays through a bone onto the film enables both sides to be seen simultaneously and superimposed on each other. This may be helpful when studying special aspects of cranial or vertebral structure, although allowance must be made for some degree of projection distortion in these cases.

MUMMIES

A peculiarity of mummies is the fact that they often occur swathed in a 'pack' which may be so fragile that its unwrapping can cause both the body and its draperies to crumble completely. Even with the best conservation techniques many museum curators are reluctant to unravel an elegantly assembled mummy on the off chance of finding some trait of anthropological interest. Radiology can help here. It not only gives information about the skeletal structure of the body but also reveals something of the soft tissues and, incidentally, it may detect a variety of objects placed within the pack which can even justify a change of policy about the desirability of undoing it.

If the angle of the radiograph is chosen with skill[13] it is often possible to assess not only the general skeletal development but also such special characters as dolichocrany or brachycrany, prognathism, the orbital margins, the pattern of jaws and teeth (especially the mandible), pelvic features, platymeria, platycnemia and much else. Anatomical variants of all kinds should be looked for, especially those such as the bony bridge of the atlas,[14,15] or atlanto-occipital synostosis[16] which are almost certainly familial and may point to close blood relationships in the group under study. Almost all the pathological conditions affecting bone can be detected, such as the tuberculosis in three Peruvian mummies described by García Frias,[17] but soft tissue abnormalities should also be sought. These include hypertrophic organs such as the enlarged spleen of malaria,[18] or the liver of hydatid disease; the large heart and liver of myocardial failure, and the pregnant or fibromyomatous uterus. Displacements, especially perhaps of the heart, are recognizable and a variety of calcifications of soft tissue are readily seen—the hard, tortuous blood-vessels of arteriosclerosis,[19] late changes in uterine fibroids, plaques of myositis ossificans, ossification of ligaments and the late results of cirrhosis of the liver. Calculi in the bladder and kidneys are visible though not easy to interpret in the presence of other foreign bodies in the pack, and gallstones may also be found. Erosion of bone may reveal primary soft tissue disease, as for example aneurysm or malignant growths.

Estimation of the individual age of the mummy can be obtained radiographically. In children this may be done by recognizing the state of dental eruption,[20] the calcification of tooth roots,[21] the progress of ossification in different areas,[22,23] and the extent of epiphysial union;[24] in adults more tentatively by balancing the evidences of such criteria as the extent of sutural fusion,[25] the dental state, the presence of arterio-sclerosis and the numerous other changes of advancing years. Sex determination, when in doubt, can be similarly estimated from the established criteria.

The interpretation of mummy radiographs is often extremely difficult. If the mummy is in a pack foreign material, such as sand, is almost always present to mask the film. In Egypt the ritual demanded removal of many of the organs and the body was often repacked with various radio-opaque objects and impregnated with bituminous resins.[26] The whole process of Egyptian mummification introduces an ambiguity into the radiographs which is largely lacking in natural sun-dried specimens or in the simpler Peruvian packs. On the other hand the separate bundles of the four canopic jars can occasionally provide additional information not obtainable elsewhere. A special watch should be kept for the 'faking' of mummies by the embalmers who were often careless or unscrupulous in their attempt to re-create the living appearance of their subject: human bones may be placed in the wrappings upside down or reversed as to side and animal bones of many sorts are commonly used as a makeshift.[27]

Methodical X-raying of mummies offers abundant scope for important discoveries. An excellent example is the recent identification (for the first time in palaeopathology) of what appears to be alkaptonuria—a rare congenital metabolic disease in which the urine turns black shortly after it has been passed, owing to the presence of homogentisic acid, and which is associated with specific changes in the vertebral column.[28]

BOG FINDS

Radiology offers precisely the same scope here as it does with mummies. The differences are merely those which depend on the necessary technical readjustments in filming or screening, which in turn depend on the difference in the two modes of preservation of the bodies. The rarity of human bog remains, other than skeletal elements, imposes limits on the dissectional destruction of these cadavers and makes X-ray examination all the more important.

PATHOLOGY

Apart from its specific use with mummies or bog finds the radiological investigation of a skeleton will almost always be used as supplementary to the inspection of the bones. It is difficult to think of any pathological condition which is not made more intelligible when the accompanying internal bony changes are revealed.[29,30] Indeed, it cannot be too strongly emphasized that the diagnosis of many diseases can only be made at all with the help of a radiograph.

A short review of some of the different types of skeletal abnormality is all that can be attempted here.

Trauma. Sometimes only a radiograph shows whether or not a fracture has occurred and it may also distinguish between a complete break and a greenstick. Foreign bodies are usually obvious: occasionally bone reaction leads to their becoming embedded and

X-rays are needed to reveal them. At times something can even be learned about the material of which a foreign body is composed.[31]

Infections. If the bone is intact, non-specific infections such as periostitis and osteomyelitis may only be distinguishable radiologically. Innumerable bones have been diagnosed as syphilitic both in the Old World and the New,[32,33] and the diagnosis has been as often refuted. Yet syphilis does produce changes in the internal structure of the skeleton and radiography can remove doubt in some of these instances. Tuberculosis,[34,35,36,37] leprosy,[38,39] actinomycosis,[40] hydatid disease,[41] mastoiditis,[42] and many other infections produce radiographic changes which help to identify them.

Neoplasms. Malignant growths such as sarcoma[43] or carcinoma are histologically complicated and X-ray investigation will sometimes distinguish between different types of tumour. Secondary deposits in bone from primary soft tissue cancers or diseases which, like multiple myeloma,[44] occur within the bone may be visible only on a film, if the cortex of the bone is intact. It is quite possible that far more cancer would be recognized in early populations if routine radiography of the skeleton was adopted. Such sites as the skull, vertebrae, humerus and femur are commonly invaded by secondary deposits of growth from cancers of the breast, prostate or thyroid. No doubt these cases pass unnoticed when death ensues from soft tissue spread before the deep bone secondaries have shown themselves by breaking through the compact cortex. New growths can also be distinguished from other conditions such as organized haematomata[45] or osteitis deformans (Paget's disease).[46]

Miscellaneous. Scores of diseases are known which attack bone either primarily or secondarily. These include rickets, frost-bite,[47] various types of gangrene, cystic disease, osteoporosis and other rarefactions,[48] petrosis or increased density, plumbism or fluorosis due to the ingestion of lead or fluorine from water or other sources, metabolic disorders of the renal rickets type, neurological sequelae from syringomyelia or hemiplegia,[49] and many other conditions. All these are interesting; many have a very precise significance in terms of the individual or the group.

Developmental. Abnormalities which are genetically determined should always be sought and carefully recorded. Many of these are rare, some are not, but if they are found with an unusually high frequency in a cemetery it suggests that we are dealing with members of a single family or closely related group. Not all these are unambiguous and X-rays help diagnosis as, for example, in distinguishing a congenital from a pathological synostosis.[50]

The pathology of any population is never a matter of random chance. It invariably expresses the total environmental circumstances of the group, both internal and external. It reflects their geographical background, their occupations, feeding habits, social customs and much else besides. The closest attention, therefore, should be given to every abnormality in a community and it must again be stressed that radiography almost always adds to our understanding of skeletal pathology. It ought to be a fixed rule that every pathological specimen, even common fractures and osteoarthritic lesions, should be X-rayed. Unfortunately few archaeologists give this subject the attention it deserves.

TEETH

Anthropologists have long been in general agreement on the importance of teeth in taxonomic, evolutionary, racial and individual studies.[51] But something like a third of the dental tissue may be hidden in the alveolus and is not readily available for inspection. With radiology this essential source of information can be revealed.

It is now realized that the particular enlargement of the pulp cavity known as taurodontism is neither a universal character of early or primitive man[52] nor is it confined exclusively to such types.[53] But although its phyletic significance has probably been exaggerated[54] it remains a feature of interest, about the distribution and variation of which we need to know more. It was recognized in dental radiographs at an early date;[55-57] it is easily seen and should be regularly looked for. The size and shape of tooth roots are important, especially when dealing with Palaeolithic remains. Bifid canines and premolars, three-rooted lower molars,[58] root fusion and other variants can be seen in detail in the jaw.[59] So, too, can internal characters such as pulp stones and canal patterns which vary from group to group.[60,61] The Piltdown mandible clearly shows the simian pattern of long-rooted teeth and it was only the technical inadequacy of the early radiographs taken soon after its 'discovery' that prevented this fact from being recognized.[62] Only very exceptional peculiarities of fossilization would mask such details today.

A trend towards the reduction in the size and number of teeth is commonly considered a progressive feature of dental morphology. A manifestation of this is the failure to erupt, or even to develop, of one or more third molars.[63] Often only radiography can distinguish between an unerupted tooth and its congenital absence, as in the case of the young female skeleton of Upper Palaeolithic date from Cap Blanc, Dordogne.[64] Supernumerary teeth are a common and interesting anomaly. Although they are frequently seen at some point in the tooth series their interpretation may depend on radiography and in many cases their presence would be quite unsuspected without an X-ray photograph. Apart from supernumerary teeth the orthodontic investigation of most of the malpositions needs radiological study.

In man slight sexual dimorphism is found in teeth[65,66] but because of its normal feebleness in tooth roots their radiography is of limited use for sexing human remains. By contrast, it is of considerable value in age determination. In young subjects the degree of calcification of the roots is a valuable guide;[67] somewhat later the size of the root canal gives useful information, but in assessing this other factors such as heavy attrition, leading to secondary dentine formation, must always be borne in mind. An increased translucency of the root tip has been described as a character of increasing age and may give additional information.[68]

An important aspect of dental dynamics is the replacement of the deciduous dentition. Some inter-group variation in the process seems probable[69] and more work needs to be done on the subject using X-ray techniques. Finally, a number of pathological conditions can be helpfully diagnosed radiographically. Fracture is one of these.[70] Contact caries may escape visual inspection, especially between tightly packed molars.[71,72] Apical rarefaction and cavitation when invisible in the tooth in situ may be obvious on a film. Root resorption, hypercementosis[73] and reactionary alveolar petrosis are likewise recognizable, and small paradontal abscesses can sometimes only be found radiologically.[74]

GROWTH STUDIES

A major limitation in studying an early population is that the individuals composing it can be observed at only a single moment of time—the moment of death. It is true that from pathological conditions present at that time much can be inferred about the processes leading up to the final appearance. But we are not permitted any glimpse, as it were, of the successive interim states. A new application of radiology has recently enabled us to see something of the development of the individual as a dynamic process through several years of the growing period.[75]

Growth in a long bone takes place at the epiphysial junction at each end of it.[76] In the presence of disease or starvation this growth is temporarily stopped. When it is resumed a transverse scar line is left in the bone and can be seen on a radiograph.[77] This arrest of growth may be repeated several times and the resulting scars are permanent (save in certain exceptional conditions) and remain as a record of the illnesses from which the growing child suffered.[78] H. A. Harris,[79-81] first paid special attention to the X-ray appearance of these lines though Wegner[82] had noted them macroscopically, in rabbits and chickens fed on phosphorus, even before the days of Roentgen. Different average frequencies of these 'Harris's lines' between various populations thus serve as an indicator of differences of morbidity rates among their younger members. Moreover, the distance of each line from the end of the bone can be measured and from this an estimate can be made of the length of the bone when the line formed and hence the approximate age of the child at that time.

It seems possible to recognize not only differences in disease rates between early groups but also, in cases of similar frequency, to differentiate between groups in which the incidence of disease falls principally at different periods of life. This gives a diachronic view of the progress and interruption of normal growth throughout most of childhood which can hardly be obtained in any other way. It must be noted, however, that it tells us nothing about the specific nature of the disease which has produced the bone scar.

The technique is simple, though its interpretation is far from easy, but in view of its potential promise we may hope that archaeologists will use and elaborate it until its full range and usefulness are defined. Harris's lines appear, as we might expect, to be correlated with stature variation and also with body proportions as well as with absolute size. Their association with dental hypoplasia, another condition caused by constitutional disorders, needs to be more precisely established.

Other forms of growth study in skeletal material have been conducted using laminographic X-rays on various aspects of cranial development.[83,84]

NON–HUMAN REMAINS

The radiological study of non–human remains is basically the same as that of man. It is, however, complicated by three principal differences:

(a) The much greater frequency of extreme mineralization. This makes the technical details of exposure time, etc. more variable and less predictable. Almost always the best exposure will only be found after repeated trial and error.

(b) Anatomical problems may make it difficult to select the best angle for X-raying.

(c) The massiveness of many specimens, for example giant saurian or mammoth bones, creates problems that can only be solved empirically.

DETECTION OF FORGERIES

We have already briefly mentioned the ancient Egyptian 'faking' of mummies. This falls into a category on its own and has its own legitimate points of interest for the specialist.

It is a happy circumstance of skeletal studies that (in sharp contrast to the world of archaeology and above all to the finance-ridden realms of art) deliberate forgery is exceedingly rare. It seldom happens, therefore, that radiology is needed to expose such deceptions. Modern faked mummy packs do exist, however, and dried shrivelled monkey heads are offered to unenlightened tourists as a substitute for the true tsantras or Jivaro shrunken human heads. In neither of these instances would an expert be deceived and it seems hardly worth using radiographs to disillusion gullible collectors who prefer to remain illuded. Deceptions of a sort are occasionally met in such objects as the alleged remains of saints and martyrs preserved in church reliquaries or even offered for sale to pilgrims, but the former, at least, are more likely to be examples of unreliable attribution rather than deliberate fabrication. In a few instances where there is a genuine doubt about holy relics, combined with an equally genuine desire to elucidate the mystery, radiology can play its part along with other methods of examining the remains. But as a rule church authority is conservative to dispel accepted tradition in these matters and the radiologist will seldom be called upon to investigate such problems.

The one outstanding forgery which we must mention is, of course, the Piltdown assemblage. The whole story is so well known thanks to J. S. Weiner's excellent and popular book on the subject[85] that we have no need to dwell on it extensively. The ambiguity of the early radiographs has been noted above. The modern films not only eliminated the original source of error about the root lengths but also revealed an unnatural fuzziness in the outline of the canine, due to its applied coat of Vandyke brown.[86] That the imposture was not suspected earlier is understandable enough. What, in retrospect, seems more curious is the fact that forty years of rapid advance in radiological techniques passed by without the specimen having been X-rayed again to take advantage of these developments.[87] (And this was by far the most controversial jaw ever known.) The Piltdown episode surely points a moral in more directions than one!

TECHNIQUE

This is not the place to give a detailed description of radiographic techniques but a few brief notes may be helpful to archaeologists and anthropologists alike, who ought at least to be aware of some of the basic methods of investigation.[88-90]

Firstly it should be remembered that portable X-ray apparatus of relatively modest cost and size is available and that models exist which, being powered from the engine of a truck, are independent of mains electricity. Some firms will hire out these machines and they can be useful in the field if for any reason it is undesirable or impossible to remove all the skeletal material which is discovered. The radiographic techniques needed for producing simple but serviceable films under field conditions can easily be learned.

The basic and most generally useful radiograph is the simple positive transparency obtained by transmitting the X-rays from a focal point through the subject on to the film. But increasing use is being made of gamma-ray sources from radioactive isotopes which can now be produced cheaply, are easily portable and are especially useful when high energy radiation is needed for the penetration of the largest animal fossils or to take advantage of the peculiar properties of teleradiography. Most excavated human bones are not mineralized and need only low exposures. For long bones, vertebrae, pelvis and cranium a suitable figure is 70 Kilovolts, 20 milliampères, an exposure time of two seconds and a distance of 42 inches. For the small adult bones and children's long bones the time can be cut to $1\frac{1}{2}$ seconds. If the specimen is fully fossilized a much higher value is required. For example, a tibia may need an exposure of the order of Kv. 80, m-a. 50, 2 secs. 30 in. The primary rays which are taking the picture are accompanied by a secondary scatter of radiation which produces some fogging. This can be eliminated by using a different type of film placed in a cassette between two intensifying screens. For our first example the equivalent exposure would then be about Kv. 50, m-a. 25, 0·3 sec., 36 in, or a little less for light bones. It is a great advantage to be able to reduce the time factor so much and the effect of this method is to give much more contrast of radio-densities on the negative, but at the expense of producing some 'grain' on the film. However, it should be remembered that a dried bone normally has a more sharply contrasted structure than a living one and the unintensified technique is probably best for routine archaeological work. With the increase of Kv. (which may go to MeV. 0·5 for large fossils) scatter is correspondingly increased. Here it is often useful to interpose a single lead screen 0·0015 in or 0·004 in thick between the source of the rays and the subject to absorb the scatter.

Films should be carefully selected. Some of the best for anthropological purposes are made by Ilford Ltd. For unintensified work 'Ilfex' should be used; for cassettes 'Standard' is excellent or 'Red Seal' which is approximately twice as fast. All these films resist tropical conditions of heat and humidity if properly handled. Positive prints can be made from transparencies by the usual photographic processes and have certain advantages both for inspection and storage but do not entirely replace the transilluminated film. Positive prints are also sometimes useful for obtaining further transparencies.

Stereoradiography is well developed and can give beautiful results. Normally, if a bone can be filmed from several angles there is no need to use this. It is, however, extremely useful if the subject cannot easily be moved, as, for example, when X-raying a fragile mummy. Superimposed radiographs and normal photos can be combined into a single print, a fact which is useful when preparing illustrations or slides as well as for studying the internal structure of a bone as related to its surface anatomy. Localization

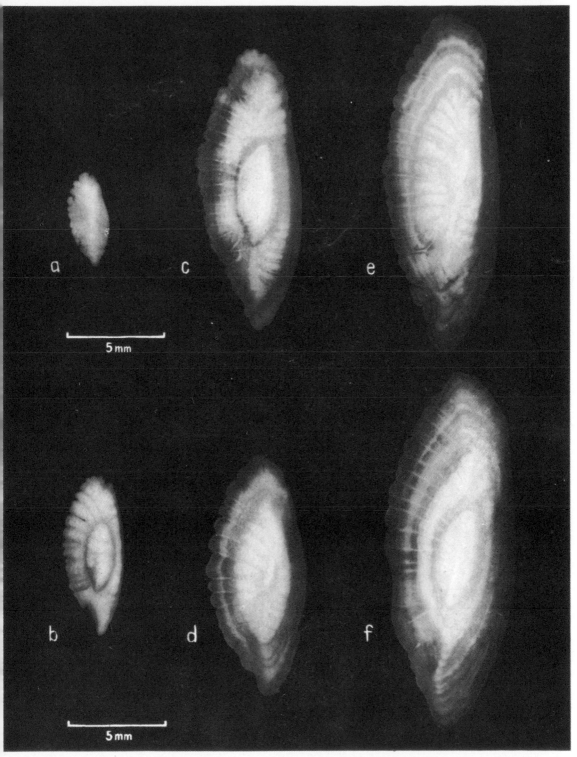

Otoliths (ear-stones) showing annual growth rings, from the tiger flathead (*Neoplatycephalus richardsoni*), an Australian sea fish; (a) no growth rings; (b) one ring; (c) two rings; (d) three rings; (e) four rings (first indistinct); (f) four rings (fifth forming). Photo courtesy Dr D. E. Kurth, C.S.I.R.O. Marine Laboratory, Sydney.

(see page 294) PLATE XIII

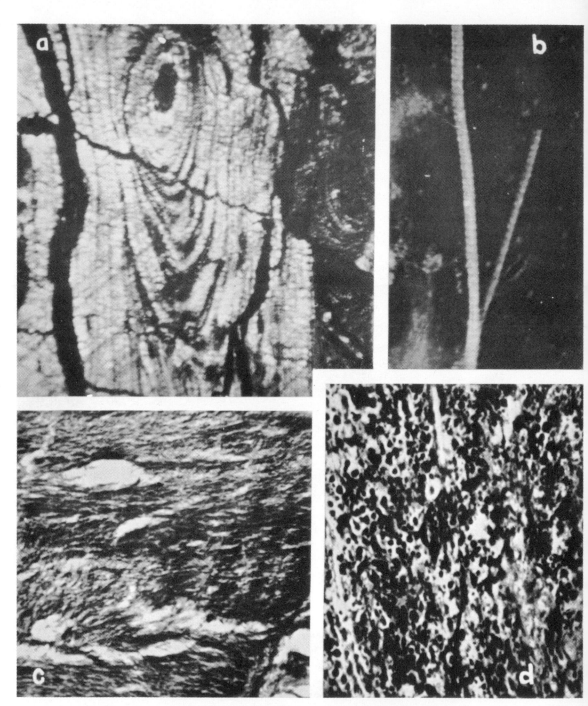

(a) Sample of mandible Circeo IIa: section of decalcified bone seen through a polarizing microscope; signs of tissue's deterioration are present. (b) Unidentified bone fragment found in close proximity to mandible Circeo IIIb. Electron micrograph of decalcified bone. Two collagen fibrils with the 640 Å overperiod. (c) Sample of mandible Circeo IIa. Section of decalcified bone, stained according to the Mallory method. A space previously occupied by an osteocyte is evident. (d) Unidentified bone fragment found in close proximity to mandible Circeo IIIb. Microradiogram of a section of decalcified bone. The tissue appears to be drilled by several 'Bornkanäle'.

PLATE XIV (see page 330)

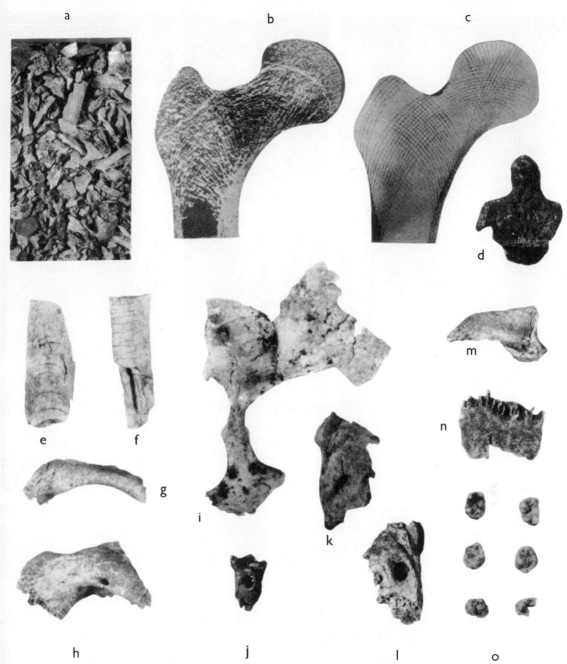

(a) A typical sample of cremated bones. (b) Proximal part of a thigh bone in action. (c) Trajectories in the proximal part of a thigh bone. (d) Fragment comprising the *dens* and part of the *corpus axis*. (e) Cracks caused by cremation in middle part of a femur. (f) Cracks caused by cremation in middle part of a radius. (g) Fragment of a male supra-orbital region. (h) Fragment of a male glabella. (i) Fragment (restored) of female orbit (right). (j) Fragment of petrous bone of new-born baby (NB: the sole find in the grave). (k, l) Fragments of petrous bones of different adults: (k) right, (l) left. (m) Claw phalange of bear (showing that the corpse had been cremated in a bearskin). (n) Fragment of the vault of an adult (part of the suture visible at top). (o) Crowns (partially restored) of milk teeth from the upper and lower jaws of a *c*. nine-month-old baby. All except (b) and (c) from prehistoric cremations; (b) and (c) after Koch, J. C. 1917. *Am. J. Anat.* 21, 177.

(see page 379) PLATE XV

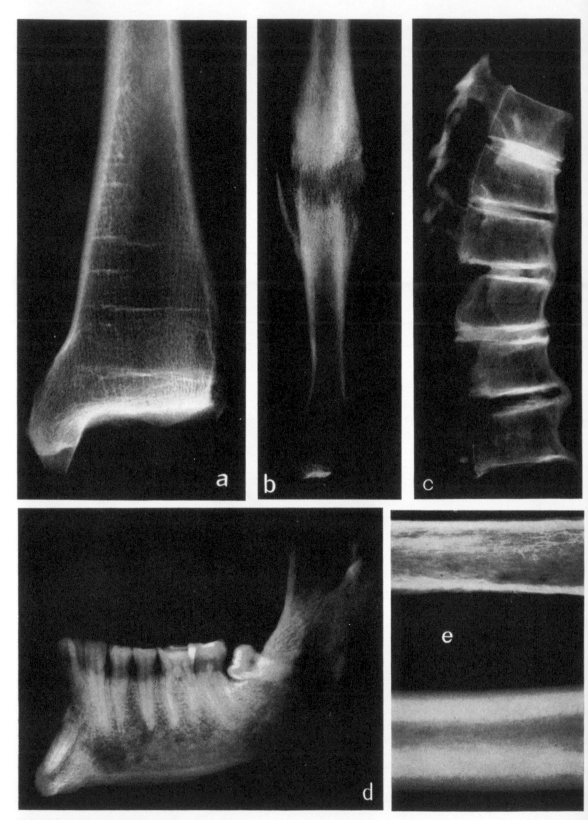

PLATE XVI (see page 401)

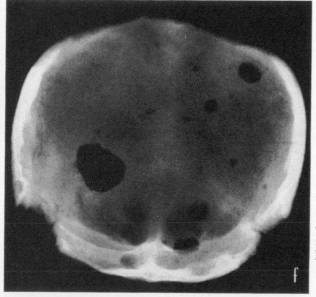

(a) Late Saxon: distal end of a left tibia which has fifteen Harris's lines across each end of the shaft. (b) Medieval: a fusiform swelling on an ulna. Radiography shows that this is callus round a fracture. (c) Early Saxon: ankylosing osteophytosis in six thoracic vertebrae ('bamboo spine'). (d) Early Saxon: jaw showing an impacted third molar with three divergent roots, also a deep unerupted canine. The 'abscess' cavity in the ramus is in fact wholly an effect of soil erosion. The 'pulp-stone' in the first and second molars are also post-mortem artifacts. This jaw is a good example of the rewards and pitfalls of radiography. (e) Bronze Age: mid-shaft sections of two femora to show variations in the medulla-cortex ratio: the Internal Index of Robusticity. (f) Medieval: a calva showing multiple myelomatosis. The bone is perforated by three holes; the radiograph reveals intra-diploic foci of disease which cannot otherwise be seen.

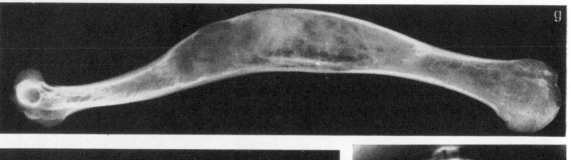

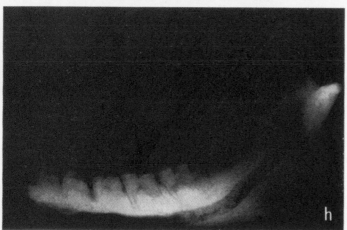

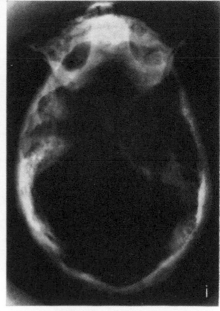

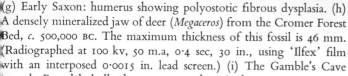

(g) Early Saxon: humerus showing polyostotic fibrous dysplasia. (h) A densely mineralized jaw of deer (*Megaceros*) from the Cromer Forest Bed, c. 500,000 BC. The maximum thickness of this fossil is 46 mm. (Radiographed at 100 kv, 50 m.a, 0·4 sec, 30 in., using 'Ilfex' film with an interposed 0·0015 in. lead screen.) (i) The Gamble's Cave 'pseudo-Paget's' skull: the appearance here is due to post-mortem changes. Radiographs: (a, f) B. M. Maxwell, (b–e, g, h) Ilford Ltd. (i) British Museum (Natural History). (a–e, g, h) Courtesy R. R. Clarke, Curator Norwich Museums.

(see page 401) PLATE XVII

(a) Striated muscle from a mummy stained by photo-tungstic haemotoxylin.

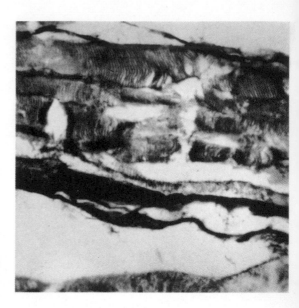

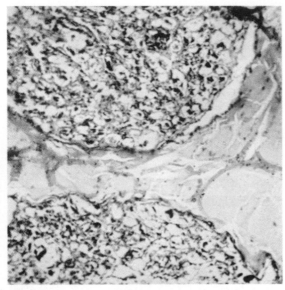

(b) Nerves of mummy leg stained by Heidenhain's iron haemotoxylin.

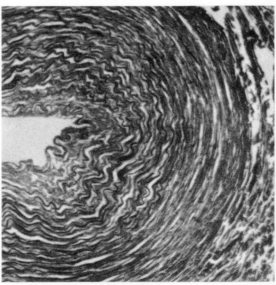

(c) Carotid artery from a mummy stained to show elastic tissue.

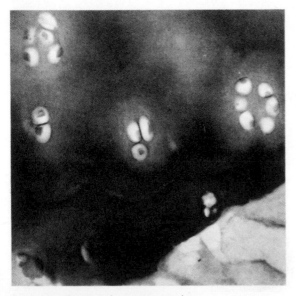

(d) Articular cartilage from a mummy stained brightly with Periodic-acid Schiff stain.

PLATE XVIII (see page 413)

(a) Skin from mummy wrist to show preservation of epidermis with surface keratin.

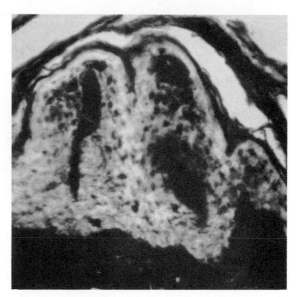

(b) Persistence of melanin in coats of a mummy eye.

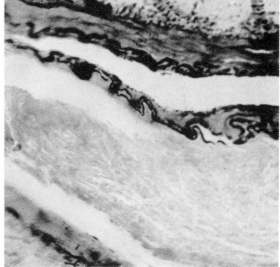

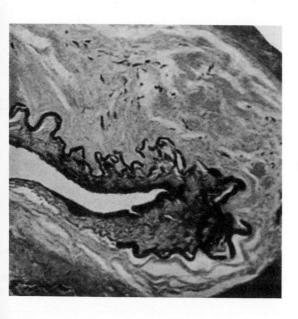

(c) Artheroma of artery of leg of a mummy; the light staining material is sub-intimal lipid.

(d) A mummy artery showing elastica reduplication and sectoral intimal thickening.

(see page 413) PLATE XIX

(a) Transverse section of an Egyptian mummy hair, showing dense melanin granules (× 800).

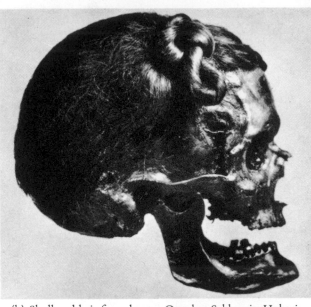

(b) Skull and hair from bog at Osterby, Schleswig-Holstein (first century AD).

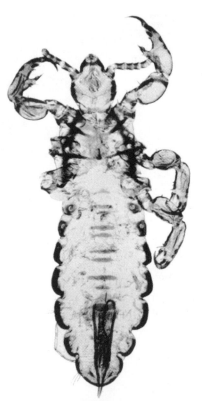

(c) Head louse (*Pediculus humanus*) found on a pre-Columbian mummy from Ancon, Peru.

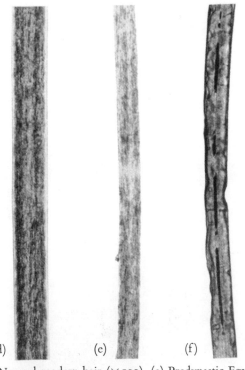

(d)   (e)   (f)

(d) Normal modern hair (× 100). (e) Predynastic Egyptian hair, showing some cuticular damage (× 100). (f) Hair from Hythe, Kent, probably of medieval date. There is considerable cuticular erosion. Air in the medulla shows up as a dark strand.

PLATE XX (see page 427)

of the depth of any feature, either a bone or an intrusive artifact, in a mummy pack can be accurately achieved by special techniques and its usefulness is enhanced by taking laminographic films. This process, known as tomography, is a means of obtaining on the positive a photo of structures at a desired depth inside the subject and at that depth only. Thus, a lateral tomograph of a skull could be taken to yield a section 1 cm or even as little as 2 mm thick along the nasion-sphenoidale-basion plane. Although the rays are penetrating the whole skull from side to side the remaining structures are excluded from appearing in the film by blurring them out and only the midsagittal cut remains.

The cone of rays which produces the image inevitably magnifies the subject to some extent so we cannot find the exact size of a bone by the simple process of measuring it directly on a film. To do so we need to make a factorial correction which may not be easy to compute accurately if we are dealing with a mummy. Scanography is a technique in which the image is produced by a narrow perpendicular beam moving along the subject. It eliminates linear distortion and enables measurements to be taken straight from the film with great accuracy. A multiple exposure method using the technique of orthodiagraphy can also be used.[91]

Miniature radiography is well known. It has the advantage of compactness and low cost if the apparatus is available. Ilford fluorographic films for this purpose are supplied in 35 mm and 70 mm sizes and large numbers of exposures can be obtained from a single spool. Microradiography is another useful process. This is not a technique of enlargement from a normal size negative: the subject is actually enlarged on the radiograph, usually by a factor not exceeding × 3, owing to loss of definition at higher magnifications. One of the most difficult regions to X-ray is the upper jaw, on account of the density and crowding of surrounding structures. Microradiography can be most helpful in elucidating doubtful tooth problems in this area and it deserves to be used much more extensively than it has been.

In autoradiography [92] the intrinsic radioactivity of a specimen is detected and photographed on a specially fast emulsion. It gives information unobtainable in any other way and was used on the Piltdown hippopotamus jaw.[93] It is almost impossible to give general guidance about this technique. The sensitivity of the film used needs to be carefully chosen to suit the peculiarities of the material. Archaeologists should not expect these emulsions to be available at short notice; plenty of time for their preparation must be allowed, the autoradiography itself may take days to complete, and subsequent processing is often complicated. Moreover, cosmic rays and local radioactivity lead to rapid deterioration of the unused plates or pellicles, in addition to which the emulsion gel needs refrigeration storage.

X-ray crystallography[94] and fluorescent analysis[95] are yet other techniques which are available for the study of human remains but these processes are somewhat marginal to those discussed here and will not be described. Direct visual X-ray screening without taking a radiograph has a limited but definite place in examining mummy and bog material.

To get the maximum information from radiographs it is important to take enough of them. For complicated regions like the face three or four shots from different angles may be needed, sometimes combining different techniques. Unless involved methods are used the cost of X-raying a complete, average size male body on five 17 in × 14 in films need not be more than £1 for basic materials, and this can permit two views of the skull and jaw. Excluding ribs, scapulae and pelvis it can be taken on no more than three films. As far as possible adherent or intrusive dirt should be removed before X-raying and if a long series of films is being taken it is essential to develop a few of the early plates immediately to check that a suitable exposure has been selected and that there is no defect in the apparatus. Finally a clear system must be devised for indicating left and right no matter whether an axial or a paired bone is being radiographed: without this there is no way of distinguishing one side from the other by simple inspection of the film.

GENERAL REMARKS

Brief though this chapter is, it is enough to indicate the scope of radiology in the examination of human remains. It is probably not too much to say that all important items should be X-rayed as completely as possible. This would certainly include every Palaeolithic specimen and most Mesolithic specimens too, all bog finds and all well-preserved mummies. We have already urged the desirability of including all pathological material. In addition, substantial samples of early populations or burial grounds should be tested for variation in internal structure, anatomical anomalies, growth peculiarities and bone-scar evidence of disease.

It cannot be too strongly emphasized that the interpretation of the films must invariably be the work of a professionally trained radiologist. After adequate instruction a few specially designed investigations of a simple sort, for example certain metrical studies, might be within the capacity of an archaeologist, and a medically trained anthropologist will undoubtedly be able to make an occasional study of limited range. But only a full radiological training and years of whole-time experience can ensure a correct evaluation of the infinite subtleties to be found in every radiograph. Even to the experienced radiologist a *caveat* must be given: the films of excavated bones are often very different from anything seen in clinical practice. Impregnation with calcium or mineral salts; surface abrasions; intrusive sand or silt; post-mortem changes due to bacterial, fungal or insect activity, all these agencies and many more can produce most deceptive appearances and lead the unwary to remarkable errors of diagnosis. For example, many bones from Bronze Age barrows on the chalk downs of Dorset give an appearance closely resembling that seen clinically in fluorosis or heavy metal poisoning. It is a golden rule that when reporting on the films of any bone the radiologist should have the specimen itself beside him for direct comparison and that he should also get from the archaeologist any additional information that is relevant about the nature of the soil and water in the burial area, grave goods or inhumation techniques, and, of course, post-excavation treatment of specimens. Effectively used, radiology is a tool of great value in archaeological research.

REFERENCES

1 ROENTGEN, W. C. 1895. Ueber eine neue Art von Strahlen. *S.B. phys-med. Ges.* Würzburg, 132–141
2 COX, J. and KIRKPATRICK, R. C. 1896. *Montreal Med. J. 24,* 661–665
3 BRYCE, T. H. 1896. *J. Anat. 31,* 59
4 CLARK, C. A. 1901. *J. Brit. Dent. Assoc. 22,* 610–617. There is a brief note in *Trans. Odont. Soc.* 1896, *28,* 170
5 PELLEGRIN, J. 1900. *Bull. Mus. d'Hist. Nat. Paris, 6,* 175–176
6 LORTET, L. C. and GAILLARD, C. 1903–1909. *Arch. Mus. Hist. Nat. Lyon 9,* Figs. 103 and 216
7 CAREY, E. J. 1927. Human anomalies, practical roentgenographic studies. Study I, abnormal crania— hydrocephalic, achondroplasic, oxycephalic and acromegalic, *Wisconsin Med. J.* 1–12
8 WEIDENREICH, F. 1951. *Am. Mus. Nat. Hist. Anth. Pap. 43* (3), 205–290
9 WASHBURN, S. L. and HOWELL, F. C. 1952. *Am. J. Phys. Anth. 10,* 13–21
10 YOUNG, R. W. 1956. *Ibid. 14* (1), 59–71
11 SCHRANZ, D. 1959. *Ibid. 17* (4), 273–277
12 JACQUELINE, F. and VERAGUTH, P. 1954. *Rev. de Rheumatism 21,* 237
13 CLARK, K. C. 1956. *Positioning in radiography,* London, 7th ed.
14 HADLEY, L. A. 1944. *Am. J. Roentgenol 52,* 173–195
15 SELBY, S., GARN, S. M. and KANAREFF, V. 1955. *Am. J. Phys. Anth. 13,* 129–141
16 McRAE, D. L. and BARNUM, A. S. 1953. *Am. J. Roentgenol 70,* 23–46
17 GARCÍA FRIAS, E. 1940. La tuberculosis en los antiguos Peruanos. *Actualidad Médica Peruana 5,* 274–291
18 MOODIE, R. L. 1931. *Field Mus. Nat. Hist., Anth. Mem. 3,* Chicago, Pl. 8
19 —— 1931. *Ibid.* Pl. 3.
20 SYMINGTON, J. and RANKIN, J. C. 1908. *An atlas of skiagrams illustrating the development of the teeth,* London
21 HESS, A. F., LEWIS, J. M. and ROMAN, B. 1932. *Dental Cosmos 74,* 1053–1061
22 FLECKER, H. 1942. *Am. J. Roentgenol. 47,* 97–159
23 GREULICH, W. W. and PYLE, S. I. 1959. *Radiographic atlas of the skeletal development of the hand and wrist,* 2nd ed.
24 STEVENSON, P. H. 1924. *Am. J. Phys. Anth. 7,* 53–93
25 TORGERSEN, J. 1951. *Acta Radiologica 36,* 374–382
26 ELLIOT SMITH, G. and DAWSON, W. R. 1924. *Egyptian mummies,* London
27 —— and WOOD JONES, F. 1910. *The archaeological Survey of Nubia, Report for 1907–1908,* Cairo, vol. 2, report on the human remains
28 SIMON, G. and ZORAB, P. 1961. *Brit. J. Radiol 34,* no. 402, 384–6
29 BRAILSFORD, J. F. 1953. *The radiology of bones and joints,* London, 5th ed.
30 SIMON, G. 1960. *Principles of bone X-ray diagnosis*
31 BAUDOUIN, M. 1918. *Bull. Soc. Prehist. Fr. 15,* 187
32 EATON, G. F. 1916. The collection of osteological material from Machu Picchu. *Mem. Connect. Acad. Arts and Sc.* New Haven, 5, 1–96
33 MOODIE, R. L. 1923. Palaeopathology. *An introduction to the study of ancient evidences of disease,* Urbana, Ill. Pl. 94, 95, 100
34 BARTELS, P. 1907. *Arch. f. Anth.* N.F. *6,* 243–255
35 SNURE, H. 1924. *Am. J. Roentgenol. 11,* 351–354
36 MEANS, H. J. 1925. *Ibid. 13,* 359–367
37 RITCHIE, W. A. 1952. *Am. J. Phys. Anth. 10,* 305–317
38 BARNETSON, J. 1949. *Acta Radiologica 34,* 47–56
39 MØLLER-CHRISTENSEN, V. and FABER, B. 1952. *Ibid. 37,* 308–317
40 MOODIE, R. L. 1922. *J. Parasitology* (Urbana, Ill.) *9,* No. 1, 28
41 LATHAM, W. J. 1953. *J. Fac. Radiologists 5,* 83–95
42 MOODIE, R. L. 1931. *Roentgenologic studies of Egyptian and Peruvian mummies,* Pl. 3, 38
43 MacCURDY, G. G. 1923. *Am. J. Phys. Anth. 6,* 217–329
44 RITCHIE, W. A. and WARREN, S. L. 1932. *Am. J. Roentgenol. 28,* 622–628
45 PALES, L. 1930. *Paléopathologie et Pathologie comparative,* Pl. 48
46 —— *Ibid.* Pl. 5
47 VINSON, H. A. and SCHATZKI, R. 1954. *Radiology 63,* 685–695

48 PALES, L. *Op. cit.*[45] Pl. 24
49 WELLS, C. 1961. *Norfolk Archaeology 32*, Pt. 4, 312–315
50 KIDD, K. E. 1924. *Am. J. Phys. Anth. 12*, No. 4, 610–615
51 CLARK, W. LE G. 1959. *The Antecedents of Man*, Edinburgh, p. 75
52 WEIDENREICH, F. 1937. The dentition of Sinanthropus pekinensis. A comparative odontography of the hominids. *Palaeontologia Sinica*, N.S.D. No. 1, Peiping
53 TODD, T. W. 1915. *Cleveland Med. J. 14*, 253–264
54 ROBINSON, J. T. 1956. *The dentition of the Australopithecinae*, Pretoria, 22, Fig. 5
55 GORJANOVIC-KRAMBERGER, K. 1906. *Der diluviale Mensch von Krapina in Kroatien*, Berlin
56 —— 1907. *Anat. Anz. 31*, 97–134
57 ADLOFF, P. 1910. *Deutsch. Mschr. f. Zahnhlk. 28*, 13–159
58 TRATMAN, E. K. 1938. *Brit. Dent. J. 64*, 264–274
59 PEDERSEN, P. O. 1949. *The East Greenland Eskimo dentition*, Copenhagen, Figs. 72, 138, 139
60 —— *Ibid.*, Figs. 42, 88
61 VALLOIS, H. V. 1957. *Bull. Mus. d'Anth. Préhist. de Monaco 4*, 111–117
62 LYNE, W. C. 1916. *Proc. Roy. Soc. Med. 9*, Pt. 3, 33–62
63 HENRY, C. B. and MORANT, G. M. 1936. *Biometrika 28*, 375–427
64 DAHLBERG, A. A. and CARBONELL, V. M. 1961. *Man 61*, 48
65 MIJSBERG, W. A. 1931. *Koninkl. Akad. v. Wetensch. te Amsterdam, Proc. Sec. Sciences 34*, 1111–1115
66 JANZER, O. 1927. *Vierteljhrsschr. f. Zahnhlk. 43*, 289–319
67 KRONFELD, R. 1935. *The Bur 35*, 18–25. Reprinted 1954 in *Basic readings on the identification of Human skeletons: Estimation of age*, New York
68 GUSTAFSON, G. 1950. *J. Am. Dent. Assoc. 41*, 45–54
69 STEGGERDA, M. and HILL, T. J. 1942. *Am. J. Orthodontics Oral Surg. 28*, 361–370
70 KALLAY, J. 1951. *Am. J. Phys. Anth. 9*, 369–371
71 BLAYNEY, J. R. and GRECO, J. F. 1952. *J. Dent. Res. 31*, 341–353
72 ARNETT, H. H. and ENNIS, L. M. 1933. *Dental Cosmos 75*, 561–569
73 PEDERSEN, P. O. *Op. cit.*[59] Fig. 185
74 MARSHALL DAY, C. D. and SHOURIE, K. L. 1949. *J. Am. Dent. Assoc. 39*, 572–588
75 WELLS, C. 1961. *Discovery 22*, 526–531
76 STEIN, I., STEIN, R. O. and BELLER, M. L. 1955. *Living bone in health and disease*, London
77 FOLLIS, R. H. and PARK, E. A. 1952. *Am. J. Roentgenol. 48*, 709–724
78 ACHESON, R. M. and STEWART, A. M. 1955. *Quart. J. Med. 24*, 415–416
79 HARRIS, H. A. 1924. Proc. Anat. Soc. Gt. Brit. and Ireland; in *J. Anat. 59*, 94
80 —— 1926. *Arch. Int. Med. 38*, 785–806
81 —— 1933. *Bone growth in health and disease*, London
82 WEGNER, G. 1874. *Arch. f. path. Anat. 61*, 44–76
83 GROSSMAN, J. W. and ZUCKERMAN, S. 1955. *Am. J. Phys. Anth. 13*, 515–519
84 ZUCKERMAN, S. 1955. *Ibid.* 521–539
85 WEINER, J. S. 1955. *The Piltdown forgery*, London
86 —— *Ibid.*, 48
87 OAKLEY, K. P. 1961. Personal communication
88 JACOBI, C. A. and HAGEN, D. E. 1960. *X-ray technology*, Kimpton, 2nd ed.
89 KEMP, L. A. W. and OLIVER, R. 1959. *Basic physics in radiology*, Oxford
90 SCHALL, W. E. 1961. *X-rays. Their origin, dosage and practical application*, Bristol, 8th ed.
91 GREEN, W. T., WYATT, G. M. and ANDERSON, M. 1946. *J. Bone and Joint Surg. 28*, 60–65
92 BOYD, G. A. 1955. *Autoradiography in Biology and Medicine*, New York
93 *Bull. Brit. Mus. (Nat. Hist.) Geol.* 1955. 2, no. 6
94 JAMES, R. W. 1953. *X-ray crystallography*, London, 5th ed.
95 HALL, E. T. 1959. *Endeavour 18*, 70

40 *The Study of Mummified and Dried Human Tissues*

A. T. SANDISON

TECHNIQUES FOR PRESERVATION of the human body in Ancient Egypt attained an elaboration perhaps only approached by contemporary mortuary practice in the United States of America. The methods used are, however, entirely different; modern embalming techniques utilize formaldehyde for tissue *fixation* while mummification implies virtual *desiccation* of tissues. Strictly speaking the term 'mummy' should be restricted to the product of Ancient Egyptian embalming; nevertheless preservation of the human body has been obtained by chance circumstance or deliberate intent in cultures widely separated in space and time. Such preservation, usually the result of simple dehydration, has been reported by anthropologists from the five continents. Places of interest to the anthropologist in this respect include the Canary Islands,[1,2] Peru, the Torres Straits Islands, Australia, Oceania, Central and West Africa and North America.[2,3] Anthropologists in the past[3,4] saw these phenomena as evidence of cultural diffusions but this view is no longer tenable. Other dried bodies have been reported, e.g. from the crypt of the Capucin convent in Palermo and St Michan's Church, Dublin.[1] True Egyptian mummies, sun-dried bodies, naturally desiccated bodies from the above locations as well as Moorleichen (bodies preserved in the peat-bogs of Schleswig-Holstein, Holland and Denmark),[45,57,63] all provide or could provide material of palaeohistological interest.

Mummification in Egypt had a sophisticated Osirian religious background but in the beginning was probably introduced as a substitute for the wonderful preservation of the body noted to result from simple desiccation in predynastic sand-burials.[5] As funerary practice became elaborate, entombment removed the body from close proximity to hot dry sand and some mode of preservation became imperative. Mummification, at first the prerogative of the pharaoh, then of royalty and nobility, became almost universal by the close of the New Kingdom. Despite this democratization it is certain that the techniques varied in complexity and cost.[6]

During the Old Kingdom the results of embalming were poor; the majority of Middle Kingdom specimens are friable and ill-preserved although notable exceptions are recorded. The New Kingdom has yielded many well-embalmed bodies especially from the XXIst Dynasty but continued deterioration set in after the XXVIth so that by Roman times preservation was usually mediocre and largely achieved by covering the body with hot resinous substances often described as bitumen. Excellent salted specimens have come from the Coptic period. Ironically perhaps the best preserved bodies are predynastic, preserved by simple desiccation by the hot sand.

The Ancient Egyptians were themselves the first Egyptologists and in later periods were keenly interested in their own history and archaic practices.[7] Nevertheless there is an unfortunate lack of information concerning embalming techniques in the ancient records; details are given only of liturgy and ritual. The most valuable account is given by Herodotus (*c.* 450 BC)[8] but this, although it is probably a reasonable account of later practice, may not have great relevance to the techniques of say the XXIst Dynasty. Diodorus Siculus (*c.* 60 BC)[9] also writes on embalming but adds little of scientific value. Briefly we learn that in the most expensive embalming the brain was removed via the nostrils by an iron hook, that the trunk viscera (except heart and kidneys) were removed and that the body was treated with natron. Debate continues as to whether natron was used in solution or solid form;[10] some experiments (to be published) made by the writer tend to support the argument that dry natron was used. Occasional comments on mummification by early Christian writers and medieval Arab scholars add little to our knowledge. In medieval Europe interest in mummies was largely confined to their therapeutic use. Bellonius[11] and Paré[12] in the sixteenth century and Greenhill,[13] Rouelle,[14] Hadley[15] and John Hunter in the eighteenth century made some observations. Napoleon's expedition to Egypt led in the nineteenth century to more important studies, e.g. those of Denon,[16] Baron Larrey [17] and in Britain those of Granville,[18] Osburn[19] and Thomas Pettigrew[1] whose fine book, published in 1834, was long the standard work. In the present century, the studies of Ruffer,[20-35], Lucas,[10] Elliot Smith,[6,36,37] Wood-Jones,[37] Derry,[37] and Warren R. Dawson[2,6,38] have consolidated our knowledge of the techniques and results of ancient embalming methods.

HISTOLOGICAL STUDIES

It did not occur to Pettigrew[1] to submit tissues from his mummies to microscopic examination although already mummy bandages had been thus studied. Mummy tissue is at first sight unpromising material so that it is in some ways surprising that as early as 1852 Johan Czermack[39] the distinguished Viennese laryngologist made accurate drawings of tissues from two mummies, which he had teased out in caustic soda. He depicted hair, tendon, cartilage, nerve, muscle and adipose tissue and used the micrometer to measure the structures. In 1904 Wilder[40] described the restoration of dried human tissues using 1–3% caustic potash for rehydration, checking the process at the desired stage with 3% formalin. Wilder studied Peruvian mummies and sun-dried bodies of Cliff-dweller and Basket-maker Indians of south Utah and demonstrated blood vessels, sarcolemma, neurilemma, adipose tissue, Meibomian glands of eyelid, medullary kidney tubules and portal tracts of liver. In 1909 Shattock[41] made frozen sections of the aorta of Pharaoh Merneptah and demonstrated calcification. Ruffer[21,26] at this time embarked on his important studies in Cairo and in a fine series of papers described naked-eye and histological appearances in normal and pathological mummy tissues. He used fluids containing alcohol and sodium carbonate to soften the brittle tissues, passed them through graded alcohol and chloroform to paraffin wax for section. He described many tissues, e.g. skin, muscle, nerve, blood vessels, heart, lung, liver, kidney, stomach, intestines, testis and breast. His death by drowning at sea in 1917 was a grievous loss to palaeopathology.

American palaeohistology was firmly consolidated in 1927 when Wilson[42] described tissues from Basket-Maker and Cliff-Dweller Indians using a softening fluid similar to

Ruffer's; he studied skin, muscle, lung, etc. In the same year Williams[43] reported studies of two Peruvian mummies, following his discovery that soft tissues could be dissected after soaking for a few hours in weak formalin. Histological preparations were made after submersion of tissues in 1% formalin then passing them through alcohols to paraffin or collodion. Later Williams[44] reported further work on bone sections from preserved bodies from Utah, Arizona and New Mexico including an Arizona Basket-Maker baby.

Turning now to Eurasia, Aichel[45] reviewed the histological appearances of German Moorleichen or peat-bog bodies; studies had been made of connective tissues, bone, nerves, alimentary tract, breast, etc.

Simandl[46] described the appearances of skin and muscle from a XIXth or XXth Dynasty female mummy after treatment in 30% alcohol followed by progressive alcohol dehydration to paraffin wax. He utilized many staining methods and also made frozen sections but failed to show convincing sudanophilia of adipose tissue. In 1938 Shaw[47] applied modern staining methods to canopic jar material from an XVIIIth Dynasty tomb; these tissues were soft and cut readily without special treatment; the results were of considerable interest.

Busse-Grawitz[48] reported a study of Egyptian mummy and American tissues; he found no cells nor nuclei but on culture observed cellular structures. On the basis of these findings he suggested altering Virchow's famous dictum 'Omnis cellula e cellula' to 'Omnis cellula e substantia viva'—a conclusion which will not be generally acceptable; probably the structures seen by Busse-Grawitz were of fungal nature. Following his studies Gürtler and Langegger[49] studied Theban mummy tissue before and after various treatments and found no evidence to support Busse-Grawitz. They noted that connective tissues were well preserved but saw neither cells nor nuclei. At this time Jonckheere[50] attempted to make sections of tissues from the Royal Scribe Boutehamon of the XXIst Dynasty at Thebes but was not successful. Graf[51] described histological studies of Egyptian tissues and of ancient Swedish skeletons; he used 1·2% saline to soften the tissues followed by 4% formalin.

Later Sandison[52] reported an elaboration of Ruffer's technique for mummified tissues which has also been used by Rowling[53] on human mummy material from different periods and by Ryder[54] on mummified Theban cat skin and parchments. This method involves softening by rehydration followed by conventional dehydration then double-embedding in celloidin and paraffin for section with any microtome.

Routine staining methods are readily applicable. A further modification by Sandison[55] introduced the use of an automatic Histokinette processing machine to accelerate the progress of tissues and obviate hand transference. Large specimens, e.g. entire temporal bone with external ear of a mummy, were cut in vertical section with ease. The method proved useful for such large bone-sections after decalcification utilizing an ion-exchange resin. This method has since yielded excellent sections of Bronze Age and medieval bone, the latter a portion of the femur of King William the Lion of Scotland recovered when his tomb was cleared at Arbroath in 1816. Sandison[52] had previously found the neutral decalcifying fluid of White useful for small bone fragments. Graf[51] used 5%

nitric acid or 1–3% trichloracetic acid respectively for ancient Swedish and Egyptian bones. Andersen and Jørgensen[56] used 2% citric acid and 20% sodium citrate at pH6 for decalcification of archaeological bones prior to histochemical examination.

Schlabow et al.[57] describe in a most elegant paper the detailed examination of a fourteen-year-old female bog body from Windeby, including a comprehensive histo-logical, histochemical and chemical examination of the well-preserved brain. Sandison[58] reported successful demonstration of sudanophilic lipid by frozen section of rehydrated mummy tissue and the application of some simple histochemical tests and polarimetry.

Leeson[59] cut ultra-thin sections of skin from an American Indian burial of uncertain date after embedding in methacrylate, submitted these to electron microscopy and demonstrated cell membranes, nuclear membranes and chromatin, although organelles, not surprisingly, were absent. Further electron microscopic studies on palaeohistological material are promised from Leeson's laboratory.

With regard to more recent preserved human tissues Born[60] describes the histological investigation of a naturally desiccated eighteenth-century European body using oil of cloves and double-embedding in celloidin and paraffin. Hunt[61] reported histological studies of naturally mummifying bodies from the notorious Christie murder case. He noted that tissues from these bodies (stored in an airy cupboard for about 50, 70 and 100 days), which had been firm, became soft and offensive in 4% formalin. An attempt to cut frozen sections failed but the tissues could be hardened in alcohol for twenty-four hours and then processed. Other specimens fixed in Heidenhain's Susa did not require hardening.

It should be mentioned here that mummified and dried tissues from all periods develop a brown turbidity in alcoholic solutions.

RESULTS

The conventional variants of the haematoxylin and eosin stains of the routine histologist give a poor histological picture, as a rule, with diffuse imprecise tinctorial renderings. This should not discourage investigators since very considerable detail may emerge with carefully chosen stains. In general cell outlines and nuclei are lacking although in the epidermis, for example, investigators[26,44,52] have noted persistence of cell membranes and nuclei, and cell and nuclear membranes have been seen on electron microscopy.[59]

All workers in the various fields of palaeohistology are agreed that connective tissues survive mummification and desiccation better than epithelia. Organs largely composed of epithelium, i.e. glandular organs, may only be identifiable by virtue of their connective tissue and vascular framework; nevertheless they are usually readily recognizable even in the absence of their delineated epithelial cells. For this reason stains such as van Gieson, Mallory, Masson, phosphotungstic acid haematoxylin, Heidenhain's iron haematoxylin, orcein, Verhoeff's and Weigert's elastica stains are often valuable. Sandison[52] has utilized these stains to distinguish connective tissues and to demonstrate muscle striations in appropriate instances (Plate XVIIIa). Nerves are well outlined also by such methods (Plate XVIIIb); if elastica and connective tissue stains are combined the structure of blood vessels in normal and pathological states may be studied with relative ease (Plate XVIIIc).

Adipose tissues, tendon, cartilage and bone are also readily visualized in well-preserved tissues. It is of interest to note the striking contrast in the staining of adjacent articular cartilage and bone in mummy sections stained by the periodic-acid Schiff method[52] (Plate XVIIId). Andersen and Jørgensen[56] have studied metachromasia of cartilage and bone in archaeological material.

It is possible to obtain excellent staining of the skin by phosphotungstic acid haematoxylin if the epidermis remains. Hair follicles, sweat glands and sebaceous glands may often be noted in the cutis while well-delineated squamous cells with nuclei may remain in the epidermis (Plate XIXa). Sandison[62] has demonstrated stainable and bleachable melanin in the coats of the mummy eye (Plate XIXb). It is sometimes possible to obtain a positive Perl's reaction in mummy tissues but it is not certain if such a reaction is reliable. Exogenous pigment, e.g. carbon, has been demonstrated in the lungs of Basket-Maker Indians,[40] in Egyptian mummy lungs[21] and in XVIIIth Dynasty canopic lung.[47]

Simandl[46] and Shaw[47] attempted staining for lipid in frozen sections but were unsuccessful: Sandison[58] demonstrated that frozen sections may indeed reveal sudanophilic lipid capable of study by polarimetry and special staining methods.

It may be stated confidently that many sections of mummy and dried tissues show bacterial bodies which have been present in the tissues since the onset of putrefactive changes which are checked by embalming. Moulds may also be present; further, if mummy tissue is allowed to become damp modern moulds may be detected on the surface of tissues.[62] Some moulds may readily be mistaken for red blood cells; Wilder,[40] Williams[43] and Busse-Grawitz[48] claimed to have recognized red blood cells but were probably mistaken. Sandison[52] noted erythrocyte-like structures in mummy thyroid gland; these had the tinctorial properties of red blood cells when stained by van Gieson, Heidenhain's iron haematoxylin, Lieb's phosphotungstic acid haematoxylin, Mallory's trichrome and Lendrum's eosin-phloxine tartrazine methods. They measured $3 \cdot 25 \mu$ in diameter while red blood cells from fresh human tissue similarly processed measured $4 \cdot 0 \mu$. Born[60] has discussed the probable fungal origin of red blood cell-like structures. It seems probable that 'white blood cells' described by some workers are also fungal. Occasional intrusive larvae may be noted in sections, almost certainly derived from eggs laid between the time of death and wrapping of the body and which may continue to develop for some time after wrapping. Sandison[62] noted the larva of a Piophila species in a section of mummy eye.

There are few studies of brain; Rowling[53] had disappointing results except in one instance where the provenance of the material is uncertain and is probably modern. Schlabow et al.[57] demonstrated remains of nerve fibres but no neurones in the wonderfully preserved brain of a fourteen-year-old female Moorleiche dating from about the beginning of the Christian era.

Turning again to more recent material Born[60] showed that, in a naturally mummified body dating from the early eighteenth century, collagen and elastic tissues were demonstrable but that the epidermis was lost and no nuclei could be demonstrated. This is of interest when compared with Ruffer's[26] study of naturally desiccated predynastic Egyptian bodies in which preservation was so good that epidermal nuclei and muscle striations were easily seen and in which even the intestinal contents were shown to contain vegetable cells, partially digested muscle fibres and starch granules. This latter information is of interest from the dietary point of view; a few similar studies have been made, e.g. by Glob[63] on Moorleichen and Wilder[40] on American dried bodies.

Mant[64] described natural mummification of parietes and internal organs (which were still recognizable) of a well-nourished man exhumed after four years in a sandy grave. He further described the excellent preservation of the body of a woman buried for 26 months in a mass grave in a concentration camp; histological examination of the neck tissues showed collagen, fatty tissue and the ghosts of muscle cells. Hunt[61] has shown that while skin structure was relatively normal 20 days after death, in a second body naturally mummified for 50 days much of the epidermis was lost, nuclei were scanty but muscle striation preserved. A third body dead for 70 days in similar conditions showed very scanty nuclei but still evident muscle striation; the latter was still evident in a fourth body dead for 100 days. In all these bodies there was extensive surface growth of moulds but these, being aerobic, did not penetrate deeply. The same author in a study of a body exhumed after three years' burial in a coffin states that no skin nuclei were then apparent but that fibrous tissue and adipose cell outlines were still evident when stained with haematoxylin laked by a wetting agent. It is hoped that further forensic medical investigations of this sort will also be reported: they may both throw light on natural mummification and aid our understanding of embalming.

Finally attention may be drawn to other laboratory studies of mummified tissues. Blood group serology has now been widely applied to archaeological tissue including bone. Graf[65] demonstrated a spasminogenic substance, presumably histamine, in mummy tissues while Sehrt[66] claimed to show glycolytic activity in mummy tissues put up with pancreatic extract and dextrose. Schmidt,[67,68] Mair[69] and Lipworth and Royle[70] investigated the lipids of ancient Egyptian brains while Aberhalden and co-workers[71,72] reported investigations on amino-acids. Trotter[73] studied hairs of Peruvian dried bodies from Paracas.

Unfortunately many of the earlier palaeohistological studies such as those of Ruffer are illustrated not by photographs but by drawings which are difficult to evaluate. Opinions on histological matters are frequently subjective to some extent so that if any of the material examined by earlier palaeohistologists is available in paraffin block form it would be of great interest to have further sections cut, stained by modern methods and published as photomicrographs.

Suggested procedures. The histologist or pathologist confronted with a wrapped mummy for study should consider radiological examination before unrolling the specimen. Apart from visualization of such artefacts as jewellery or amulets [74] much information can be obtained on the presence of bone and joint disease and of possible calcification of arteries.[75-79] If there is evidence of much disorganization of the skeleton or of multiple fractures without evidence of reaction the mummy is likely to be in poor condition (this state of affairs in a XXVIth Dynasty mummy examined radiologically by the writer was confirmed on unrolling). If the body is attractively bandaged it may be better to conserve it as a specimen for exhibition.

Many mummies show considerable carbonization of bandages and much dust may be released during unwrapping. This may irritate the eyes, nose and throat; a mask to cover the nose and mouth may be helpful. One is reminded of Belzoni's words:[80] '. . . though, fortunately, I am destitute of the sense of smelling, I could taste that mummies were unpleasant to swallow . . .' There may be difficulty in removing the last layers of bandages because of resinous materials and instruments may be necessary. This should be avoided if possible since epidermis, when present, may be lost. On the skin surface, and about the head especially, attention should be directed towards the presence of larvae or pupae; these may be of interest to the entomologist.[1,81,27,62] After unwrapping, further radiographs of areas of interest may be taken and better definition may thus be obtained. If it is desired to dissect large portions of the body these may be photographed and then placed in rehydrating fluid.[52] Much brown turbidity will develop in the fluid which may be changed as required. The specimen imbibes fluid and at this stage any adherent bandage may be removed. This process must be watched carefully to prevent maceration of the specimen; the process may be checked by transferring the specimen to 10% formal-saline in which it can safely be left. It may be of interest to rephotograph the specimen at this stage. A head treated as above will approach more closely to its original contours, especially eyelids, nose, mouth and ears.[40,62] (It might be worthwhile trying this technique on some of the Royal Mummies in the Cairo Museum in order to obtain a more accurate idea of their appearance in life; it would however require great courage to commit such priceless specimens to the rehydrating bath.) After rehydration dissection may be undertaken, e.g. in a limb the neurovascular bundles can readily be traced and removed.

At this stage selected specimens may be processed by the double-embedding method[52] or, if an automatic processing machine is available, by that of Sandison.[55] In the hand-transfer method the specimens are carried over in perforated glass tubes from one fluid to the next. In the automatic method the portions, which may be quite large, are processed in stainless steel cassettes. If the portion contains bone preliminary decalcification is essential; the method of Sandison[55] using ion-exchange resin may be recommended and has proved successful with large specimens. Andersen and Jørgensen[56] recommend 2% citric acid and 20% sodium citrate for decalcification; this also seems satisfactory.

After paraffin embedding the blocks may be cut on any conventional microtome, e.g. the Cambridge Rocking Model. As explained above, routine haematoxylin and eosin stains rarely give good results and resort should be made to methods which differentiate between collagen and epithelia. The writer has found phosphotungstic acid haematoxylin of particular value for bringing up latent detail. Heidenhain's iron haematoxylin, orcein, Verhoeff's and Weigert's elastica stains have proved valuable in the study of blood vessels. The histologist should not be shy of attempting more special methods such as the periodic-acid Schiff technique, Fontana silver stain, and others where appropriate. Andersen and Jørgensen[56] have employed carbolfuchsin-picro ponceau, toluidine blue and azure-A in studies of archaeological bone. In studies of lipids using frozen sections the tissues must, of course, not be exposed to fat solvents. The use of the cryostat should not be forgotten in planning such investigations.

PALAEOPATHOLOGICAL AND PALAEOHISTOPATHOLOGICAL STUDIES

'Palaeopathology' was coined by Ruffer in 1913 to indicate 'the science of disease which can be demonstrated in human and animal remains of ancient times' and it seems reasonable to extend the term as indicated above to imply the recognition of disease in ancient tissues by histological studies. Of course it is not only by examination of actual remains that we derive information about human disease in ancient tissues. For the historical period information is available from the great Egyptian medical papyri, from Greek and Roman writers etc. although there are sometimes conflicts in interpretation; art forms may also give information of value, e.g. Egyptian statues and statuettes, tomb painting,[25] Greek votive offerings, etc. Unexpected light is thrown by Mochica Peruvian pottery (c. 300 BC–AD 500) on the probable existence of *Uta* (a form of cutaneous leishmaniasis) at this period as well as information about amputation, circumcision and many variant sexual practices of which we would otherwise be ignorant.[82,83]

There is no modern comprehensive work on palaeopathology but an excellent synopsis is given by Sigerist[84] in his monograph on primitive and archaic medicine. Valuable older books include Ruffer's collected papers[85] and those of Moodie[86] and Pales;[87] Williams' paper[44] is also useful. None of these is now in print.

Much palaeopathological study concerns bones, considered elsewhere in this book by Dr Marcus Goldstein. Nevertheless, soft tissues have also provided considerable evidence of disease.

Mitchell[93] interpreted the appearances of an Old Kingdom mummy from Deshasheh as evidence of poliomyelitis. Gout in an early Christian of Philae was described by Smith and Dawson[6] and the presence of uric acid in tophae was confirmed by W. A. Schmidt. Smith and Dawson[6] also illustrate a case of leprosy of the hands and feet in an early Christian period Nubian specimen. Both of these cases were re-examined by Rowling[53] who agrees with the diagnoses. There is no doubt that Pott's disease (tuberculous spinal osteitis) occurred in Egypt: Smith and Ruffer[23] described a classical case with large psoas abscess in the mummy of a priest of Ammon of the XXIst Dynasty but failed to demonstrate acid-fast bacilli. Other cases are described by Derry.[37]

With regard to tumours there is a marked paucity of evidence possibly because the expectation of life in earlier times was short. Moreover, most examples are to be found in the skeleton, with a few exceptions. Smith and Dawson,[6] for example, suggested carcinoma of the ethmoid and of the rectum as being causal in the production of erosion of the skull base and sacrum in two Byzantine bodies; this is slender evidence but may be correct. Møller and Møller-Christensen[96] diagnose secondary carcinomatosis of the cranium in a medieval Danish skull. Possibly the most convincing evidence of neoplasm of soft tissues came from Granville[18] who diagnosed (without histological confirmation) cystadenoma of ovary, possibly malignant, in a mummy now known to be Ptolemaic. The writer has noticed a small squamous papilloma of skin in a mummy.

Ruffer and Ferguson[22] described a variola-like eruption of the skin in an XVIIIth Dynasty middle-aged male mummy from Deir-el-Bahari; histological section was consistent with smallpox. Elliot Smith[36] described a similar eruption on the skin of Ramesses V and Ruffer[29] further discussed these two cases and other cutaneous lesions in the

Royal Mummies. Ruffer tentatively diagnosed malaria in some Coptic bodies with splenomegaly[31] and conclusively proved the existence of bilharziasis in Ancient Egypt by demonstrating calcified ova of *Bilharzia haematobia* in the straight kidney tubules of two XXth Dynasty mummies.[20,21]

Other kidney lesions noted by Ruffer[21] included unilateral hypoplasia of kidney; in another XVIII–XXth Dynasty mummy the kidney showed multiple abscesses with gram-negative bacilli resembling coliforms. Long[97] described arteriosclerosis in the kidneys of the Lady Teye of the XXIst Dynasty. Shattock[98] described and analysed renal calculi from a IInd Dynasty tomb; oxalates and conidia were noted. A vesical calculus found in the nostril of a XXIst Dynasty priest of Amen contained uric acid covered by phosphates.[6] Ruffer[21] described three mixed phosphate uric-acid calculi from a predynastic skeleton. A bladder stone in a Basket-Maker Indian body is reported by Williams.[99]

Smith and Dawson[6] also refer to the finding of multiple stones in the thin-walled gallbladder of a XXIst Dynasty priestess. Two faceted gallstones were discovered between ribs and iliac crest of an arthritic male skeleton in Grave Circle B at Mycenae of date about 1600 BC.[100] Shaw[47] noted in the canopic-preserved gallbladder of an XVIIIth Dynasty singer that spaces resembling Aschoff-Rokitansky sinuses were present: this suggests chronic cholecystitis. Ruffer[26] mentions fibrosis of the liver in a mummy and equates this with cirrhosis but insufficient evidence is given to evaluate this. Little has been written about alimentary disease in mummies. Smith and Dawson[6] report appendicular adhesions in a Byzantine period Nubian body: these are almost certainly the result of appendicitis. Ruffer[26] describes what may well be megacolon in a child of the Roman period and prolapse of rectum in Coptic bodies.[31] A section of mummy bowel prepared by J. Thompson Rowling shows structures like helminth ova; these will be further studied and published in due course. Elliot Smith[36] mentions two probable cases of scrotal hernia—Ramesses V shows a bulky scrotum now empty after evisceration, while the scrotum of Merneptah was excised after death by the embalmers, possibly because of the bulk of a hernia.

Some interesting studies of lung have been published. Anthracosis in Egyptian mummy lungs was described by Ruffer[21] and by Long.[97] Wilder noted similar changes in Basket People bodies of Utah.[40] Shaw[47] reported anthracosis in the lungs of Har-mosĕ of the XVIIIth Dynasty but he had also suffered from emphysema and lower lobe bronchopneumonia. Ruffer[21] reported pleural adhesions and diagnosed pneumonia in two mummies, one XXth Dynasty and the other Ptolemaic; the latter may have been pneumonic plague although the evidence is far from complete. Long[97] reported caseous-like areas in the lung of a XXIst Dynasty lady and Wilder recognized possible broncho-pneumonia in a Basket-Maker Indian baby. In the writer's opinion these diagnoses must be accepted with some reserve in view of the possible confusion of moulds as leucocytes. With regard to anthracosis this seems to enhance lung preservation; in the lungs of a much decomposed coalminer exhumed $2\frac{1}{2}$ years after burial in a wet cemetery the writer noted that dust disease was still easily diagnosed and bronchial cartilages and vessels were relatively well preserved.

Elliot Smith[36] described lactating breasts in the recently delivered Queen Makere and Wilder[40] noted parous breasts and os cervix in a Basket People Indian woman. Williams[44] reported an observation by Derry that Princess Hehenhit of the XIth Dynasty had a narrow pelvis and died not long after delivery with vesicovaginal fistula. Smith and Dawson[6] described violent death in an unembalmed sixteen-year-old pregnant Ancient Egyptian girl and postulated illegitimate conception. The Archaeological Survey of Nubia revealed a deformed Coptic negress who died in childbirth as a result of absent sacro-iliac joint contracting the pelvis.[37] Male Egyptian mummies show circumcision throughout the dynasties until abandoned in the Christian period. Cameron[90] described a eunuchoid Middle Kingdom mummy with a curious penile appearance reminiscent of incisional operation.

With regard to vascular disease, we are here on firm ground and have direct evidence. Blood vessels are often well preserved in Egyptian mummies and dried bodies. Czermack[39] described aortic calcification and Shattock[41] made sections of the calcified aorta of Pharaoh Merneptah. Elliot Smith[36] noted this change in his macroscopic description of the royal body and also described calcification of the temporal arteries in Ramesses II. Ruffer[21,24,26] described histological changes in Egyptian mummy vessels from the New Kingdom to the Coptic period. Long[97] examining the mummy of the Lady Teye of the XXIst Dynasty described degenerative disease of the aorta and coronary arteries with arteriosclerosis of the kidney and myocardial fibrosis. Moodie[76] described radiological evidence of calcification of superficial vessels of a predynastic body. Williams[44] reported arteriosclerosis with calcification and calcified thrombus in a Peruvian mummy of AD 700. Buchheim[101] gives a good review of arterial disease in Ancient Egypt. It is often difficult to assess the older descriptions which are unaccompanied by photographs; Sandison[102] examined and photographed mummy arteries using modern histological methods (Plate XIXc, d). Arteries were tape-like in mummy tissues but could readily be dissected. Arteriosclerosis, atheroma with lipid depositions, reduplications of the internal elastic lamina and medial calcification could readily be seen. (A word of warning may be given here that atheromatous lesions in mummy arteries tend to form sectoral clefts: this should not be interpreted as dissecting aneurysm.)

Miscellaneous conditions noted in mummies include pediculosis, baldness in men and women and comedones of face (Ruffer[29]). The writer has also noted and confirmed histologically comedones in an elderly male mummy head. Wilder[40] described infantile eczema in a Utah Indian baby and an infective dermatosis in a Peruvian mummy. Wood Jones[103] described judicial hanging and decapitation in Roman Egyptian skeletons and Elliot Smith[36] reconstructs the death by violence of Pharaoh Seknenre. Glob[63] illustrates sacrificial hanging and throat-cutting in Moorleichen. Examinations of more recent remains include those of Don Francisco Pizarro[104] where the autopsy, 350 years after his murder in Lima, confirmed the historical account of his death. Porter[105] gives an account of the autopsy on John Paul Jones 113 years after his death; the body had been preserved in alcohol. The findings of pulmonary scarring and of interstitial nephritis fit well with his known medical history.

In conclusion it may be said that future palaeohistopathological studies might give further information on vascular disease, the presence of lesions inducing fibrosis, both inflammatory and neoplastic, and the presence of parasites such as helminth ova and others. It is to be hoped that such studies as well as gross examinations of bones and joints will continue to be made since information of value to the archaeologist, anthropologist, and pathologist, as well as to the general and medical historian, might be forthcoming.

ACKNOWLEDGEMENTS

I am grateful to Messrs J. G. Scott, J. D. Boyd and Cyril Aldred for assistance in obtaining material for my studies; to Cyril Aldred for continued advice on Egyptological matters; and to Messrs W. Penny, N. L. Russell, D. McSeveney and W. Mason (all Fellows of the Institute of Medical Laboratory Technology) for technical assistance.

REFERENCES

1 PETTIGREW, T. J. 1834. A History of Egyptian Mummies, London
2 DAWSON, W. R. 1928. J. Roy. Anth. Inst. 58, 115
3 ELLIOT SMITH, G. 1929. The Migrations of Early Culture, Manchester
4 PERRY, W. J. 1937. The Growth of Civilization, Harmondsworth, 2nd ed.
5 BREASTED, J. H. 1912. Development of Religion and Thought in Ancient Egypt, London
6 ELLIOT SMITH, G. and DAWSON, W. R. 1924. Egyptian Mummies, London
7 ALDRED, C. 1960. The Egyptians, London
8 HERODOTUS 1921. Text and trans. by A. D. Godley, London, vol. I
9 DIODORUS SICULUS 1933. Text and trans. by C. M. Oldfather, London, vol. I
10 LUCAS, A. 1948. Ancient Egyptian Materials and Industries, London, 3rd ed.
11 BELLONIUS 1553. De Admirable Opera Antiquorum, Paris
12 PARÉ, A. 1575. Les Oeuvres, Paris
13 GREENHILL, T. 1705. NEKPOKHΔEIA or the Art of Embalming, London
14 ROUELLE, M. 1754. Mem. de l'Acad. Royale des Sciences, Paris
15 HADLEY, J. 1764. Phil. Trans. Roy. Soc. 54, 1
16 DENON, V. 1803. Travels in Upper and Lower Egypt, London, vol. 1
17 LARREY, D. J. 1812. Memoires de Chirurgie Militaire, Paris
18 GRANVILLE, A. B. 1825. Phil. Trans. Roy. Soc. 1, 269
19 OSBURN, W. 1828. An account of an Egyptian Mummy, Leeds
20 RUFFER, M. A. 1910. Br. Med. J. 1, 16
21 —— 1910. Cairo Sci. J. 4, 1
22 —— and FERGUSON, A. R. 1910. J. Path. Bact. 15, 1
23 ELLIOT SMITH, G. and RUFFER, M. A. 1910 Zur Historischen Biologie der Kranksheitserreger, 3 Heft
24 RUFFER, M. A. 1911a. J. Path. Bact. 15, 453
25 —— 1911b. Bull. Soc. arch. Alex. 13, 1
26 —— 1911c. Mém. Inst. Égypte, 6 (3)
27 —— and RIOTTI, A. 1912. J. Path. Bact. 16, 439
28 —— —— 1912. Bull. Soc. archéol. Alex. 14, 1
29 —— 1914. Mitt. Gesch. Med. Naturw. 13, 239
30 —— 1914. Ibid. 13, 453
31 —— 1913. J. Path. Bact. 18, 149
32 —— and WILLMORE, J. G. 1914. Ibid. 18, 480
33 —— 1917. Cairo sci. J. 9, 34
34 —— 1918. J. Path. Bact. 22, 152
35 —— 1920. Am. J. Phys. Anth. 3, 335
36 ELLIOT SMITH, G. 1912. The Royal Mummies, Cairo

37 ELLIOT SMITH, G.,— WOOD-JONES, F. and DERRY, D. E. 1908–10. *Archaeol. Survey of Nubia, Bulls. & Report on Human Remains*

38 DAWSON, W. R. 1929. *Mém. Inst. Égypte 13*

39 CZERMACK, J. N. 1852. *S. B. Akad. Wiss., Wien 9, 427*

40 WILDER, H. M. 1904. *Am. Anth. 6, 1*

41 SHATTOCK, S. G. 1909. *Proc. Roy. Soc. Med. 2, 122*

42 WILSON, G. E. 1927. *Am. Nat. 61, 555*

43 WILLIAMS, H. U. 1927. *Arch. Path.* (Chicago) *4, 26*

44 —— 1929. *Ibid. 7, 890*

45 AICHEL, O. 1927. *Anth. Anz. 4, 53*

46 SIMANDL, I. 1928. *Anthropologie* (Prague) *6, 56*

47 SHAW, A. B. 1938. *J. Path. Bact. 47, 115*

48 BUSSE-GRAWITZ. 1942. *Arch. exp. Zellforsch. 24, 320*

49 GÜRTLER, J. and LANGEGGER, P. A. 1942. *Anat. Anz. 93, 185*

50 JONCKHEERE, F. 1942. *Autour de l'autopsie d'une Momie*, Brussels

51 GRAF, W. 1949. *Acta. Anat.* (Basel), *8, 236*

52 SANDISON, A. T. 1955. *Stain Technol. 30, 277*

53 ROWLING, J. T. 1961. *Disease in Ancient Egypt: evidence from Pathological Lesions found in mummies.* M. D. Thesis. Univ. of Cambridge

54 RYDER, M. L. 1958. *Nature 182, 781*

55 SANDISON, A. T. 1957. *Nature 179, 1309*

56 ANDERSEN, H. and JØRGENSEN, J. B. 1960. *Stain Technol. 35, 91*

57 SCHLABOW, K., HAAGE, W., SPATZ, H., KLENK, E., DIEZEL, P. B., SCHÜTRUMPF, R., SCHÄFER, U. and JANKUHN, H. 1958. *Prähist. Z. 36, 118*

58 SANDISON, A. T. 1959. *Nature 183, 196*

59 LEESON, T. S. 1959. *Stain Technol. 34, 317*

60 BORN, E. 1959. *Zbl. allg. Path. path. Anat. 99, 490*

61 HUNT, A. C. 1953. In CAMPS, F. E., *Medical and Scientific Investigations in the Christie Case*, London, Appendix 6

62 SANDISON, A. T. 1957. *Medical History 1, 336*

63 GLOB, P. V. 1959. *Jernaldermanden fra Grauballe*, Aarhuus

64 MANT, K. 1953. Recent Work on Changes after Death, in Simpson, K. (ed.), *Modern Trends in Forensic Medicine*, London

65 GRAF, W. 1949. *Nature 164, 701*

66 SEHRT, E. 1904. *Berlin, klin. Woch. 41, 497*

67 SCHMIDT, W. A. 1907. *Z. allg. Physiol. 7, 369*

68 —— 1908. *Chemikerztg. 32, 769*

69 MAIR, W. 1913. *J. Path. Bact. 18, 127*

70 LIPWORTH, A. and ROYLE, F. A. 1915. *Ibid. 19, 474*

71 ABERHALDEN and BRAHM. 1909. *Z. physiol. Chem. 61, 419*

72 ABERHALDEN and WEIL. 1911. *Ibid. 72, 15*

73 TROTTER, M. 1943. *Am. J. Phys. Anth. 1, 69*

74 WINLOCK, H. E. 1936. *Bull. Met. Mus. Art 31, 274*

75 BERTOLOTTI, M. 1913. *Nouv. Icongr. Salpêt 26, 63*

76 MOODIE, R. L. 1931. Roentgenologic Studies of Egyptian and Peruvian Mummies. *Field Mus. Nat. Hist.* III

77 DANFORTH, M. S. 1939. *Bull. Mus. Art. Rhode Isl. Sch. of Des. 27, 36*

78 JONCKHEERE, F. 1942. *Autour de l'Autopsie d'une Momie*, Brussels

79 ZORAB, P. A. 1961. *Proc. Roy. Soc. Med. 54, 415*

80 DISHER, M. W. 1957. *Pharaoh's Fool*, London

81 MURRAY, M. A. 1910. *The Tomb of Two Brothers*, Manchester

82 MASON, J. A. 1957. *The Ancient Civilizations of Peru*, London

83 POSNANSKY, A. 1925. In *Festschrift. zur Feier des. 25-jährigen Bestehens der Frankfurter Gesellschaft für Anthropologie and Urgeschichte*

84 SIGERIST, H. E. 1951. *A History of Medicine*, New York, vol. 1

85 RUFFER, M. A. 1921. *Studies in the Palaeopathology of Egypt*, Chicago (This volume includes references 20–35 and some other papers of interest)
86 MOODIE, R. L. 1923. *Palaeopathology, an Introduction to the Study of Ancient Evidences of Disease*, Urbana
87 PALES, L. 1930. *Paléopathologie et Pathologie comparative*, Paris
88 HRDLIČKA, A. 1914. In *Smithsonian Miscellaneous Collections, 61*
89 SALIB, P. 1961. *J. Bone Jt. Surg. 43A*, 303
90 CAMERON, J. 1910. In Murray, M. A. *Tomb of Two Brothers*, Manchester
91 BUDGE, E. A. W. 1924. *A Guide to the 1st, 2nd and 3rd Egyptian Rooms*, British Museum, London
92 STEWART, T. D. 1943. *Am. J. Phys. Anth. 1*, 47
93 MITCHELL, J. K. 1900. *Trans. Ass. Am. Phys. 15*, 134
94 MacCURDY, G. G. 1914. *Am. J. Phys. Anth. 6*, 217
95 ROGERS, C. L. 1949. *Br. J. Surg. 36*, 423
96 MØLLER, P. and MØLLER-CHRISTENSEN, V. 1952. *Acta. path. microbiol. scand. 30*, 336
97 LONG, A. R. 1931. *Arch. Path* (Chicago) *12*, 92
98 SHATTOCK, S. G. 1905. *Trans. path. Soc. Lond. 56*, 275
99 WILLIAMS, G. D. 1926. *J. Amer. med. Ass. 87*, 941
100 MYLONAS, G. E. 1957. *Ancient Mycenae, The Capital City of Agamemnon*, London
101 BUCHHEIM, LISELOTTE. 1956. *Therap. Berichte 28*, 108
102 SANDISON, A. T. 1962. *Medical History 6*, 77
103 WOOD-JONES, F. 1908. *Brit. med. J. 1*, 736
104 McGEE, W. J. 1894 *Am. Anth. 7*, 1
105 PORTER, H. 1905. *Century Magazine 70*, 927

TABLE A
General report on samples of earlier human hair.

Site	Period	Keratin preservation	Pigmentation	No. of specimens
York	Romano-British	Damage*. Slight erosion of cuticle. Internal structure of hair intact. No fibre splitting. Brittle. Bluish fluorescence	Light brown	I
Irish peat bog	? Early Christian	Damage*. Erosion of cuticle. Internal intact. No fibre splitting. Brittle. Bluish fluorescence	Dark brown	I
St. Brides, London	17th/18th century AD	Generally badly damaged: ★ ★ ★ ★ Erosion of cuticle. Extensive fibre splitting and hair breakage. Very brittle. Red fluorescence	Reddish brown to brown	3
Hythe, Kent	12th/16th century AD	Damaged ★ ★ ★. Cuticular erosion. Cortex altered but no fibre splitting. Slight reddish fluorescence	Medium to light reddish brown	3
Rougham, Suffolk	Romano-British	Damaged ★ ★ ★. Cuticular erosion. Brittle. Red fluorescence	Orange brown	I
Egypt (various sites)	Predynastic	Damage generally ★ ★ ★ ★. Cuticular erosion. Red fluorescence	Dark brown to medium brown	7
Egypt	Vth–XVIIth Dynasties	Damage ★ ★. Cuticular erosion. Red fluorescence	Dark brown to blond	II
Aleutian Islands	Probably post AD 1500	Damage ★★ generally. Mainly some cuticular damage. Bluish green fluorescence	Dark brown to medium brown	10
Peru (various sites)	Pre-Columbian	Damage ★ ★. Mainly cuticular damage. Red fluorescence	Dark to reddish medium brown	6
Lake Nyasa (Negro)	18th century AD	Damage ★ ★ ★. Some cuticular damage. Brittle. Red fluorescence	Dark brown	I
Canary Islands	AD c. 700–1200	Damage about ★ ★ ★. Cuticular erosion. Brittle. Overall red fluorescence	Dark brown to blond	4
Denmark (various sites)	Bronze Age to Early Christian	Damage generally ★. Slight cuticular erosion. Ranges from bluish green to slight reddish fluorescence	Very dark to reddish lighter brown	12

41 The Hair of Earlier Peoples

DON BROTHWELL and RICHARD SPEARMAN

RESEARCH ON ANCIENT HAIR is by no means a new approach to the study of early human remains and in fact as early as 1860 Browne in the United States examined mummy hair from Lima, Pachacamac, Arica, Pisco, Mexico, Brazil, although it is questionable whether mummy material did in fact come from two of the sites. A few years later in 1877 Pruner-Bey reported on Egyptian and Peruvian specimens; his studies of Amarask mummies of Peru and those from ancient Egypt included work on both pigmentary and structural variations. Later in the century Virchow[20] produced a more extensive study of early Egyptian hair; again his work was confined to colour and structure. Yet later, Minakow[12] reported on similar material in a Moscow journal. Since then only early American hair has received any real attention and in particular Paracas Indian mummies from Peru,[19] and also Basket-Maker and Mesa Verde Indians from North America.[21] Recently a detailed study has been made of hair from a body preserved in a Schleswig-Holstein bog and dated to the Iron Age period.[9] Other authors have studied ancient hair; Shrubsall (1896) noted that quite a number of Guanche mummies have fair hair, and gave this as supporting evidence for his hypothesis that the Canary Islands had in the past a fair-haired population. Our own work through the co-operation of various museums in America, Europe and Africa, is on hair from over 50 individuals from about 25 different geographical sites (see opposite). However, not all the preserved material has been made available to us and in a number of instances we have not as yet traced the whereabouts of some specimens mentioned by previous workers. Fig. 61 shows the geographic and time range of all recorded early hair so far traced in the literature. In some cases where the sites were very close together only one symbol is given. It will be seen that hair has come from a great number of countries and different types of burial environment, and there is no doubt that with the increase in care at excavations many more specimens will come to light. The age of the hair samples varies considerably, that from Egypt dating back as far as predynastic times (c. 4,000 BC). In Europe, particularly from Danish and British sites, it appears to date back as far as Bronze Age times. Hair from Western Siberia, belonging to Scythians is also very early and may be as much as 2,500 years old. Hair from America and Africa (excluding Egypt) is generally very much more recent, many samples being little more than a thousand years old.

THE ANATOMY OF HAIR

A typical human hair has an outer layer of flattened imbricated scales. Inside this layer is the broad cortex and in the centre of the fibre there is usually a slender medulla of less compact cells, sometimes separated by distinct cavities. These three layers can be readily seen in transverse sections and whole mounts. The identification of human and

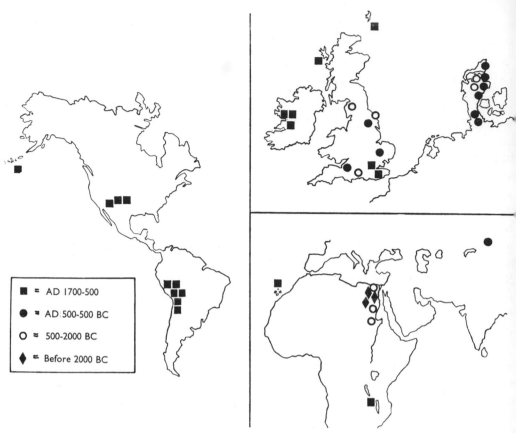

Fig. 61 Sites which have yielded early hair specimens.

animal hairs is dealt with by Appleyard and Wildman in their chapter later in this book (p. 545). Only human scalp hair has yet been studied in sufficient detail to be of value in anthropology or archaeology.

Hair is largely made up of the fibrous protein keratin. This substance is extremely resistant to decomposition and enzymatic digestion, mainly owing to the presence of disulphide cross linkages of the amino acid cystine. These join together the long poly-peptide chains of the molecule. If these cross linkages are broken by reduction or oxida-tion, altered keratin is readily attacked by proteolytic enzymes.[16] This resistance of keratin explains the durability of hair in ancient burials, a point already emphasized in a previous study of bog hair.[9] Some fungi probably attack buried hair, but the chief factors which alter keratin are probably atmospheric oxidation, soaking in water, and alkaline pH of the soil. These changes can occur on the living animal; thus atmospheric weathering of the fleece in sheep results in loss of cystine from the exposed tips of the fibres.[1] Permanent waving alters the keratin cross linkages, and these changes have been detected by using fluorescence microscopy (Jarrett, unpublished). It is probable that if the preparations employed during mummification contained reducing or oxidizing agents or alkaline substances the hair keratin would be damaged. Once the hair has been sufficiently altered by these environmental factors, it becomes more easily attacked by micro-organisms. It is therefore evident that the age of a specimen is no criterion as to its state of preservation.

ENVIRONMENTAL FACTORS OF THE BURIAL SITES

An interesting aspect of this study has been the determination of any possible relationship between hair preservation and the wide variation in burial environments represented. Bogged and waterlogged ground has yielded hair at a variety of sites. From Somerset a possible Iron Age case is known, the Shetlands have yielded a seventeenth-century example, and over twelve sites in Denmark ranging from Bronze Age to early Christian times have produced hair. Cases as early as Bronze Age are known from Schleswig-Holstein and Ireland. Warm dry conditions, as are found in parts of the Americas, Africa, Canary Islands, and the volcanic caves of the Aleutian Islands, are also particularly favourable to the preservation of hair. Most of these sites had a dry sandy environment and in the case of the Aleutian mummies (over seventy in number), the limestone caves were kept dry by natural hotsprings. Less usual types of hair preservation have been found in ancient bog butter from Skye, and on the famous tattooed Scythian bodies from the ice of western Siberia. Sometimes the hair appears to have been preserved under slightly unusual conditions. Thus Hooton[10] mentions the fact that hair from the early Indians of Pecos Pueblo stood more chance of being preserved if the head had been covered by a pot or bowl. The Negro hair from Nkudzi Bay, near Lake Nyasa, has an exceptional environment and in fact ironwork from this site was exceedingly well preserved, much of it with cloth, reed and wood impressions remaining. The oldest Egyptian samples from dry sand showed less change after more than 1,000 years than samples from St Brides Church buried in damp clay for only a few centuries. Hair from Danish bog and other similar deposits showed little damage. Occasionally, what appears at first sight to be hair, turns out to be of non-animal origin. For example, fine hair-like material from a short cist in East Lothian was shown on microscopic examination to be a mass of thin roots with very long and fine root hairs.[11]

EXPERIMENTAL METHODS AND TECHNIQUES OF ANALYSIS

Work on early hair involves more than just microscopic examination for structural alterations. During the early phase of our own work on prehistoric and early historic hair it became obvious that valuable information might be gained by undertaking experimental work with modern hair; and also by applying various staining and microscopic techniques used in other fields.

The type of soil in which the hair was buried is of great importance in determining its subsequent state of preservation. In order to test the relative preserving potentialities of different soils, hair from the living scalp was placed in jars of damp chalk, damp sand, and damp peat for a period of eighteen months. After this time samples were examined by fluorescence microscopy using acridine orange. Chalk samples were badly damaged, and had an overall reddish fluorescence, whereas hairs from the same original sample buried in sand and peat were hardly altered.

Probably the alkali pH of the chalk soil produced the damage as it is known that dilute alkali rapidly denatures hair keratin.[8]

Hair placed in distilled water for three months appeared no different from hair dried in an oven at 60°C for this time. However, more prolonged immersion in water may produce some change. Water helps maceration and fungal attack. Atmospheric oxidation as may occur in dry sand probably alters hair keratin. The best conditions for preservation appear to be acidic waterlogged soil. This type of soil is often deficient in oxygen when much organic material is present and the conditions are unfavourable for many micro-organisms.

PROBLEMS OF ANALYSIS

Ancient hair does present special problems in analysis. Usually the number of hairs in a sample is small, and pieces are often too short to ascertain any possible waving of the hair. Also, the hairs in a sample are often too few to allow statistical analysis. The most characteristic property of all the hairs examined was their brittleness compared with modern hairs. There was also damage to the cuticle in many samples. The structure of the hair, however, remained intact in many very old specimens when preserved under suitable conditions. Damage was easily produced by manipulating with forceps, and great care had to be taken in handling specimens. Crushing when obtaining specimens in the field may cause much unnecessary breakage and longitudinal splitting of the fibres. The extreme brittleness of ancient hair makes transverse sectioning difficult. We found that many specimens fragmented on cutting, but as previously mentioned suitable sections could be obtained when a very sharp knife and a hard embedding wax were used. In addition, although some information concerning hair pigmentation of earlier peoples is possible in such material, it is evident that alteration of the pigment can occur on account of post-mortem changes.

MICROSCOPIC EXAMINATION

The internal structure of intact hairs can only be seen in fully cleared microscopic preparations. We found the following technique was the best for routine examination of whole mounts. The hair was degreased in diethyl ether, washed in distilled water, for one minute, stained in 0·1% methyl violet for ten minutes, washed in distilled water, dehydrated in cellosolve, two changes, total time fifteen minutes, cleared in xylene for five minutes, and mounted in DePex. Cellosolve is obtainable from microscopy dealers and is a more rapid dehydrating agent than alcohol. If the hair is so heavily pigmented as to obscure its structure, it can first be bleached in hydrogen peroxide (10 Vols). The medulla of hair in whole mounts appears as a central darker strand of cells. The medulla can be seen in unstained preparations when the microscope condenser is lowered.

Transverse sections of hairs can be cut with a Cambridge rocker microtome provided the knife is very sharp. A high melting point wax enables one to obtain good results because of its hardness. Just before sectioning the block can be further hardened by cooling with ice. A small bunch of hairs was degreased and then moulded into a spindle with paraffin wax; the hairs were arranged in a parallel manner. Dehydration and clearing were unnecessary. The wax spindle was then embedded and orientated in slightly fluid wax prior to cooling. A few hairs cut much better than a large number in a bunch. Seven to ten was a suitable thickness for sectioning. After cutting, these were mounted in the usual way on albumin-treated slides. Safranin (0·1%) was used as a general stain. It was applied for five minutes, followed by washing, in water, dehydration in absolute alcohol, clearing in xylene and mounting in DePex. The hair medulla stained red, the cortex was pink, and the scales a darker pink. Melanin appeared as dark granules in the medulla and cortex of the hair. For anthropometric measurements the sections should be as nearly transverse as possible. In oblique sections the medulla appears elongated but it is roughly circular in truly transverse sections.

FLUORESCENCE MICROSCOPY

This special technique applied to skin and hair has been described by Jarrett and others.[6-8] The principle of fluorescence is that when ultra-violet light instead of visible light is focused through the microscope condenser onto a slide preparation, certain substances in it emit light in the visible spectrum. As a result, they may appear strongly luminous, but cease to do when the U.V. light is turned off. Fluorescing dyes, such as acridine orange, may be used in the same way as ordinary stains. We employed a Richert microscope and fluorescence bench. Degreased hairs were washed in distilled water then stained in 0·1% acridine orange for five minutes. They were then washed in distilled water, rapidly dehydrated in absolute alcohol, cleared in xylene and mounted in DePex. Cellosolve was not used in this technique as it upset the subsequent fluorescence.

Normal human hair had a bluish green fluorescence with acridine orange but permanently waved hair had a reddish fluorescence with associated fractures in the fibres. Hairs left in 3% peracetic acid for 12 hours at room temperature to oxidize the keratin[16] had a uniform reddish fluorescence with acridine orange. Hairs altered in this way were more brittle than normal. Hair bleached with hydrogen peroxide also showed this change due to oxidation of the keratin.[8]

Many of the ancient hair specimens showed a uniform red fluorescence with acridine orange similar to that after oxidation with peracetic acid. In only slightly altered buried hair the reddish fluorescence was confined to the cuticle, but in some samples such as predynastic Egyptian hair and samples from St Brides Church, London, the whole hair was altered in this way. Even so, the structure of the hair was retained. Alteration of the keratin in ancient hair was also shown by the presence of air in the medulla of many specimens. This is unusual in modern human hair and generally signifies a pathological condition when present in comparable amounts. Air in buried hair can be explained by the porous nature of the keratin.

Hairs from the living scalp which had not been artificially waved or bleached normally had a small patch of red fluorescence in the medulla but the cortex and cuticle were greenish blue (in transverse sections). In Egyptian hair and a sample of hair from St Brides Church, London, the red colour was also found in the cuticle and cortex—again using transverse sections.

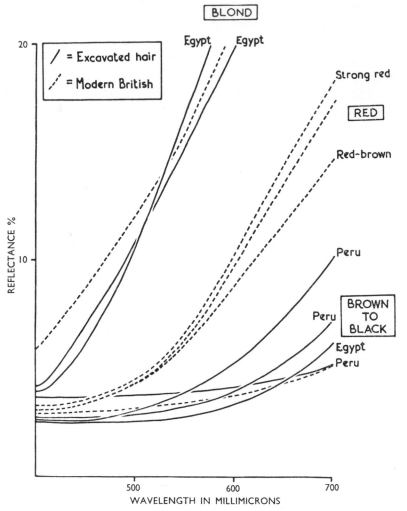

Fig. 62 Reflectance curves of ancient and modern hair.

PIGMENTATION

Hair colour showed considerable variability in these early cases. The samples varied from well-defined blond to near black, as shown by the reflectance curves in Fig. 62. These curves were obtained by submitting samples of hair to the automatic recording spectrophotometer at the National Physical Laboratory. Light of various wavelengths was shone on the hair sample and the proportion of light reflected was recorded by means of a photo cell. There was in the majority of specimens a tendency to increase values at the red end of the curve, that is in the 650–700 wavelength zone. In no case however did we note definite red hair, as claimed by earlier workers in Peruvian and Irish specimens. The blond hair is particularly interesting, especially as the cases noted in early material are from Egypt, Peru and the Canary Islands, areas now generally associated with dark hair. As far as we can tell this fair hair colour was not a result of

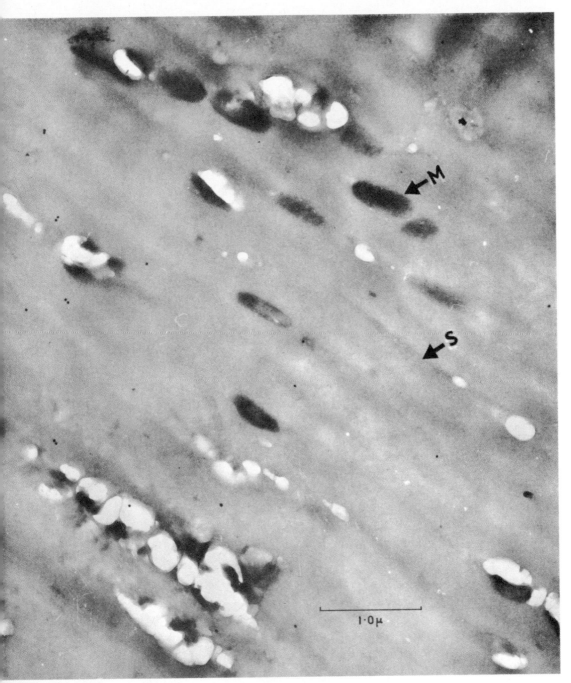

An electron micrograph of a section of one of the medieval Hythe hair specimens. The hair was a reddish-yellow colour. The longitudinal section shows part of the cortical zone containing melanin granules (M). The elongated form of the granules, their internal structure and size, suggest that the colour of the hair was originally dark. The granules in naturally red hair are smaller, rounder and have a different kind of internal structure. The direction of the keratin fibres diagonally from lower right is clear and at some points interstitial material (S) can be seen. The white areas around some of the melanin granules are holes in the section; they may be cutting artifacts or, more likely, are due to small pre-existing bubbles which were not penetrated by the embedding resin. The hair was embedded without previous treatment with fixatives.

(see page 427) PLATE XXI

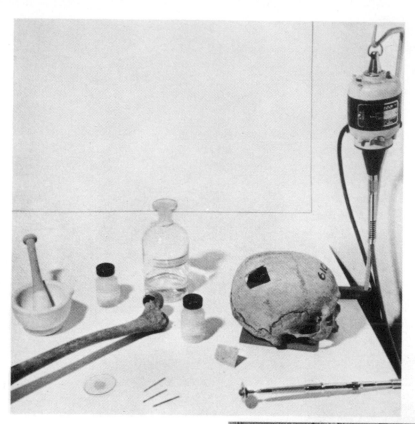

(a) The preparation of bone f[or] blood grouping. The skull m[ust] be sectioned with the aid of [a] fine saw attached to a den[tal] drill. After the removal of t[he] diploic bone the section [is] replaced. Where long bones a[re] available the necessary quanti[ty] of tissue is readily remov[ed] from the head of the fem[ur.] Both operations can be carri[ed] out without damaging the bo[ne] for anthropometric purpose[s.]

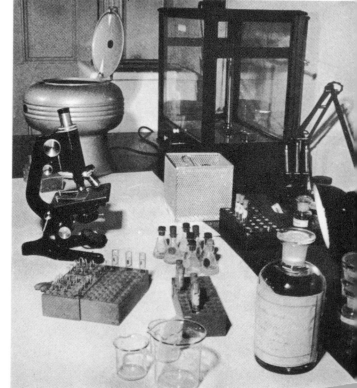

(b) Reading the results. Serum from the tissue under test has been removed from the sample after centrifugation, and titrated against fresh red cells. Results are read under the high power of the microscope.

PLATE XXII (see page 437)

intentional bleaching. The use of oxidizing substance as intentional bleach of the hair would probably be detected in specimens by changes in the fluorescence as we have found with hydrogen peroxide. Although burial can result in some degree of fading as evidenced by the changes in modern hair after burial for many months, it seems very unlikely indeed that such a light colour.could result from an originally dark specimen. A possible solution to this question might be in the examination of the actual melanin granules themselves under the electron microscope, Barnicot[3] and others having suggested a general relation between granule length and hair colour. Even if some of the blond samples are the result of staining by embalming fluid (as already suggested by Batrawi[4]) or ground solutions this might nevertheless help to indicate their true colour. Indeed, by means of the electron microscope, Barnicot has been able to show that the granule size in a reddish-haired medieval Hythe specimen suggests that the person had dark hair in life (personal communication; see Plate XXI). No direct correlation was noted between pigmentation and the general degree of hair damage, some very severely affected specimens being dark brown. Ancient hair keratin was often stained with yellowish brown patches from the deposits in all burial sites but causes no confusion with melanin as this appears as dark granules under the microscope. Dyed blond hair can usually be detected because it lacks many granules, and the dye is deposited and recognizable on the cuticle.

When black hair is partially oxidized in hydrogen peroxide the melanin is bleached from black to reddish brown colour. A similar unnatural colour was seen in only a very few ancient hairs, in particular in the St Brides specimens. Therefore, it is possible that oxidation of both melanin and keratin occurred in some buried samples, although melanin seems the most resistant of the two. Transverse sections of hair from an Egyptian mummy (Plate XXa) were interesting in that there was a strong uniform reddish fluorescence of the keratin with acridine orange, but the melanin granules in the medulla and cortex were black. In view of the covering of the body of the mummy with cloth it suggests that atmospheric oxidation was not responsible for this change, which may have been produced by the embalming preparation.

ANTHROPOMETRIC VARIABILITY

Although, as already mentioned, metrical work on hair sections has not been undertaken on our own specimens owing to the paucity of the available material, nevertheless comment deserves to be made as regards the metrical variability present in other excavated hair samples. Obviously, extreme care must be taken in measuring ancient hair and Topinard[18] in the last century, and more recently Trotter,[19] have suggested that hair size may be affected by the post-mortem environment, especially dehydration and erosion (Plate XX). The fact that human populations display considerable variability as regards the amount, size and shape of hair (Fig. 63) makes inquiries of an anthropological nature worthwhile, provided these drawbacks are realized. Only a few studies of statistical value have been made on excavated material, the earliest probably being that of Woodbury and Woodbury.[21] Their metric study involved hair from 156 individuals from twelve American Indian tribes, ten of these tribes being living peoples

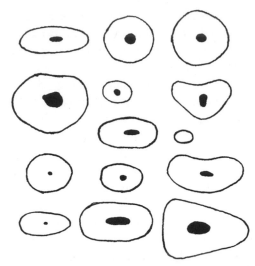

Fig. 63 Some of the drawings of hair sections made by Pruner-Bey in 1878, showing size and shape variability. In some cases, the central medulla is very noticeably spherical, showing that the sections were not always exactly transverse.

and two prehistoric. Ten hairs from each individual were measured for minimum and maximum diameters and the mean hair form was calculated from this data. From these individual means a total mean for the population sample was obtained. Hair form, that is the degree of roundness, was obtained by calculating the hair index (which is the minimum diameter times 100 over the maximum diameter); these results are given in Table B. The means for both early groups fall within the range for the living population of Indians, but it is nevertheless interesting to see that the two early groups can be differentiated by these readings, the Mesa Verde sample having an index noticeably smaller than that of the Basket-Maker Indians. Hair texture, expressed as the means of the maximum and minimum diameters of an individual hair and divided by two, was also found to be variable in these groups, and again the two early populations were differentiated by these methods (Table B).

A more recent study by Trotter[19] on the Paracas Indian mummies from Peru gives a form index between the Mesa Verde Indians and Basket-Maker Indians. Also the texture of the Paracas Indian sample differed from the North American Indian prehistoric groups. Trotter found that the Paracas hair was small in cross-sectional area when compared with hair of both modern and prehistoric Indian tribes and of French Canadians, but was larger than a Dutch sample given by Steggerda and Seibert.[17] Thus although the metrical aspect of ancient hair studies is still very much in its infancy they are of some value in demonstrating the variability of earlier populations. Obviously the number of individuals represented in the samples must be very large before the dissimilarities can be taken as reliable evidence of genetic differences between populations.

DISEASE, PARASITISM AND ANCIENT HAIR

No diseased or congenital anomalies of the hair have so far been detected in these early hair samples, but parasites have been found on both Egyptian and Peruvian specimens (Plate XXc). Indeed, conditions suitable for hair preservation seem to be favourable to

TABLE B

Hair form and texture of two prehistoric (*) and ten recent American Indian groups.

Tribe	$\dfrac{Min.\ D}{Max.\ D} \times 100$	$\dfrac{Max.\ D + Min.\ D}{2}$
Navajo	77·2	83·0
Shoshoni	77·8	89·5
Hopi	78·8	91·1
*MESA VERDE	79·7	86·6
Ute	80·0	85·0
Arapahoe	80·0	85·0
Chippewa	81·2	85·0
Gros Ventre	81·5	78·0
Paiute	81·5	89·0
*BASKET-MAKER	82·8	83·4
Sioux	83·0	74·0
Comanche	84·6	76·0

* Data from Woodbury and Woodbury.[21]

these large parasites and their eggs, particularly in mummified material. As early as 1926 the Peruvian form of louse was described under the name of *Pediculus humanis americanus*, but it is debatable whether this louse warrants the status of a new sub-species. Earlier taxonomists often failed to appreciate the degree of variability in a particular group, and thus in the case of the louse it is unlikely that these ancient specimens are distinct from the original sub-species of de Geer. Although the detection of hair parasites is ancillary to the study of early human hair, it is one of palaeopathological interest, and it would seem just as likely then as now that the louse was a carrier of disease.

ACKNOWLEDGEMENTS

We are indebted to Dr A. Jarrett for reading this paper and offering helpful suggestions. We also wish to thank Dr M. Garretts, Mr A. Bligh and Miss Rosemary Powers for their assistance. Professor N. A. Barnicot and Dr M. S. C. Birbeck kindly supplied the electron micrograph of an early hair specimen from Hythe; and similarly, Professor K. Kersten permitted us to use the photograph of the Osterby specimen. The Director of the Light Division, National Physical Laboratory, permitted one of us (D.R.B.) to use the Hardy Spectrophotometer.

Last, but not least, we wish to thank the following institutions for providing the hair specimens in this analysis: El Museo Canario, Las Palmas; Smithsonian Institution, Washington; Museum of Archaeology and Ethnology, Cambridge; National Museum of Ireland, Dublin; British Museum (Natural History), London; Rhodes-Livingstone Museum, Northern Rhodesia; National Museum, Copenhagen; York Museum, York.

One of the authors (R. S.) is a member of the Medical Research Council General Staff.

REFERENCES

1 ALEXANDER, P. and HUDSON, F. 1954. *Wool, Its Chemistry and Physics*, London
2 APPLEYARD, H. M. and WILDMAN, A. B. 1963. Fibres of archaeological interest, p. 545 *infra*
3 BARNICOT, N. A. 1957. *Man 57*, 114–120
4 BATRAWI, A. M. EL. 1935. Report on the Human Remains, *Mission Archéologique de Nubie 1929–1934*, Cairo
5 BROWNE, P. A. 1860. In SCHOOLCRAFT, H. R. *Archives of Aboriginal Knowledge*, Washington, vol. 3, 375–393
6 JARRETT, A. 1958. *Brit. J. Derm. 70*, 271–284
7 —— BLIGH, A. and HARDY, J. A. 1956. *Br. J. Derm. 68*, 111–119
8 —— and SPEARMAN, R. 1957. *J. Emb. Exp. Morph. 5*, 103–110
9 HIRSCH, VON F. and SCHLABOW, K. 1958. *Homo 9*, 65–74
10 HOOTON, E. A. 1930. *The Indians of Pecos Pueblo*, New Haven
11 LOW, A. 1943. *Proc. Soc. Antiq. Scot. 6*, 118–119
12 MINAKOW, P. A. 1899. Neue Ergebnisse bei Untersuchung von Haaren aus alten Grabstätten und von Mummien. Quoted by Woodbury and Woodbury.[21]
13 SUTTON, R. L. 1956. *Diseases of the Skin*, London
14 PRUNER-BEY, Dr. 1877. *J. Roy. Anth. Inst. 6*, 71–92
15 SHRUBSALL, F. C. 1896. *Proc. Camb. Phil. Soc. 9*, 154–178
16 SPEARMAN, R. and BARNICOT, N. A. 1960. *Am. J. Phys. Anth. 18*, 91–96
17 STEGGERDA, M. and SEIBERT, H. C. 1941. *J. Heredity 32*, 315–319
18 TOPINARD, P. 1885. *Eléments d'Anthropologie générale*, Paris
19 TROTTER, M. 1943. *Am. J. Phys. Anth. 1*, 69–75
20 VIRCHOW, R. 1898. *Über die Ethnologische Stellung der Prähistorischen und Protohistorischen Ägypter nebst Bemerkungen über Entfräbung und Verfärbung de Haarre*, Berlin
21 WOODBURY, G. and WOODBURY, E. T. 1932. *Differences between Certain of the North American Indian Tribes as shown by a Microscopical Study of their Head Hair*, Colorado

MADELEINE SMITH GLEMSER

THERE IS a growing interest in the biochemistry of the living body in its application to the study of population affinities. Research has included studies of the pigmentation of the skin, the hair and the eyes, basal metabolism and its inherited variation, allergies, haemophilia and sickle cell anaemia, the blood proteins and the blood groups. The biochemistry of the blood and tissue fluids has been intensively studied and provides good material for comparative purposes. The human blood group substances show variation between individuals; on this basis populations may also be distinguished, by statistical analysis.[1] These substances are highly complex mucopolysaccharides. The proteins of the blood and tissue fluids show species-specific differences; they have been used to show the degree of affinity between the primates, to identify breeds of cattle, and to show the systematic relationships of birds.

Both blood group mucopolysaccharides and species-specific proteins act as antigens; that is, their presence in the living body stimulates the production of antibodies, with which they will then react in an observable way, and by means of which they may be identified. Antibodies (bodies acting against introduced substances) are protective in their function; they form part of the body's defence against the introduction of alien substances, including the agencies of disease. They are found in the tissue fluids of the body, principally in serum, the liquid portion of the blood which remains after a blood clot has formed. Serum proteins can be placed in two classes: albumins and globulins. It is the globulins which amongst other functions act as antibodies.[2]

Before Landsteiner[3] discovered the human blood groups in 1900, it was already known that the bloods of varying species were not compatible. Attempts to transfuse animal blood into man were made in the seventeenth century, but failed on the observation of death by haemolysis. These reactions were explained at the end of the nineteenth century, by several workers who showed serological differences between animal species, and demonstrated agglutination (clumping) when human serum was mixed with animal blood. Landsteiner, by experimenting with the serum and red cells of a number of individuals, showed the same reactions in man, and from this information deduced the presence of the ABO groups.

While it is significant that the blood groups should first have been identified on red cells, it must be emphasized that they are to be found in most of the tissues of the body.[4] The ABO antigens are composed of four sugars: D-galactose, L-fucose, D-glucosamine and D-galactosamine; and a polypeptide portion with at least eleven amino-acids present. The antigen consists of an alcohol-soluble fraction and a water-soluble fraction. The relative distribution of these fractions in the body is not uniform, the alcohol-soluble fraction being more evenly distributed over the various organs than the water-soluble fraction. Water-soluble antigens are found in greatest concentration in the body fluids of secretors, i.e. those people with the capacity to produce relatively large quantities of A, B and H antigens in the secretions. These constitute about 75% of all studied populations. Non-secretors produce water-soluble antigens in their secretions but at much lower concentration. Alcohol-soluble antigens are found in most of the organs of the body. They are not found in the secretions, and their concentration is independent of secretor status. In consequence they are of much greater significance to the archaeologist than are the water-soluble antigens. There is relatively little variation in their concentration in individuals; they have been shown to be stable under moderate variations in pH and at normal environmental temperatures. Their presence in such tissues as muscle and bone makes possible the use of blood group studies in archaeology.

The human blood groups have become significant characters in the study of population variation because their mode of inheritance is known and comparatively simple, and their gene frequencies relatively high. In the ABO groups, the three allelic genes A(p) B(q) and O(r) produce six genotypes AA, AO, AB, BB, BO and OO. These are expressed as four groups, A, B, AB and O, according to their reaction with two sera, anti-A and anti-B. No serum has yet been found which will detect the O antigen in the heterozygous AO or BO individual. Naturally occurring human sera have been found which it is claimed will identify the O antigen in homozygous OO individuals. The exact nature of these sera is in doubt, and their use involves cautious interpretation.

The discovery that blood group frequencies varied between one population and another was made by the Hirszfelds in 1919.[5] This variation was shown to have anthropological significance. The many papers published on this subject since that date are summarized and discussed by Mourant,[1,6] and have been widely used in the study of racial origins and population affinities. Mourant[1] suggests a stability for ABO frequencies of 1,000 to 2,000 years, but he points out that the presence or absence of an expected gene may be of more value in the study of population affinities in the past than estimates of frequences. The influence of selection on the ABO groups is slight in comparison with its effect on other anthropological criteria such as stature, and their inheritance much simpler than that of others such as eye colour. Their use in discrimination between populations therefore presents many advantages. It was thought at first that environment had no selective effect on the distribution of these genes in the population. There is some evidence that this is not the case, and that individuals of certain blood groups are more susceptible to certain diseases.[7,8] The effects of selection are slow, however, and do not take away the value of the study of frequencies as a guide to the history of any given population. One of the more interesting examples is that of the Basques, who show the lowest B frequency in Europe, and a uniquely high frequency of the d (rhesus-negative) gene. These discoveries reinforce linguistic and skeletal evidence that the Basques are an old element in the population of Europe in which ancient blood group frequencies have survived because of isolation. Genes of other systems show peculiarities of distribution which are racially diagnostic. The Henshaw and Hunter genes, which are closely linked to the MNSs system, are almost exclusively confined to Africans. The Diego antigen appears to be found only in Mongoloids. Other genes, more widely distributed, show fluctuations in frequency which can be closely related to population movement and mixture.

Much of the initial work of identification of blood groups of the dead was inspired by criminal investigation. The need arose to identify the origin of blood stains; for this the precipitin reaction was developed and applied. This test distinguishes the blood proteins of one species from another. It is a highly sensitive test which has been applied to the taxonomy of the living animal and may have applications for the archaeologist. The first use of human precipitin reactions in forensic medicine was in 1916, when Lattes [9] presented evidence on the origin of blood stains before an Italian court. Species differentiation can have only a limited value in this field, in determining whether or not a stain is of human origin. As knowledge of the blood groups of the living became more extensive, medicolegal workers sought means of identifying these groups in the dead. It was found that the ABO groups could be identified in aged stains of many of the human secretions. Ducos[10] and his associates have shown the possibility of identifying other of the rarer blood groups in their recent work; the methods used are interesting, but the anthropological applications of such characters as the Kell antigen are more limited than the ABO antigens because of their rarer frequency.

First work on the blood groups of the dead in anthropology was carried out by the Boyds. They studied the methods of forensic medicine and applied them to the soft tissues of mummies.[11] Boyd and Boyd discuss the methods used, and give results of the grouping of Egyptian and American mummies, in a paper published in the same year.[12] The results quoted in this paper show that of a total of 327 individuals, 276 gave no reaction with anti-A or anti-B sera and were presumed to be group O while 37 gave reactions for either the A or B antigen or both. Fourteen gave no clear grouping. Similar results were used to speculate on the origins of the present blood groups in the American Indians. In a series of 226 individuals from the Aleutian Islands, Alaska, the SW United States and Peru, Wyman and Boyd[13] obtained positive results for the A and B antigens on 13 individuals. Of these, four were presumed to be group A, seven group B, and two group AB. Probably the most interesting point raised is the presence of B in the Peruvian material; unfortunately the evidence quoted for the presence of B in modern populations has since been discredited. Gene frequencies of from 0 to 3% are found in present-day peoples in this area. Boyd's frequency of 6% is considerably in excess of this. In their work on Egyptian mummies grouping was attempted on predynastic naturally preserved bodies and on dynastic artificially preserved material, and compared with grouping of bone taken at autopsy and preserved under varying conditions and for different periods.[14] This work illustrates many of the major problems in the field. The authors concluded that 'repeated tests on any one specimen are necessary and should be made with various sera, since the same specimen may effect no removal from some sera but show apparently specific removal from others.' Bacterial contamination is mentioned in discussing excessive agglutination in the XVIIIth Dynasty Priests of Amun, but the possibility discounted.

The Boyds concluded from this work that muscle gave clearer indications of blood group than bone.

The knowledge gained from a study of the results achieved by the Boyds would lead to the assumption that artificially preserved material is difficult to group accurately. Their work was of a high standard. Almost every problem in the field was uncovered by them, and pointed out. Matson, using similar techniques, attempted to blood group mummified American and Egyptian material.[15,16] He attempted extraction in both saline and alcohol, but was successful only with the former. He was the first to make use of bovine anti-O, now known to be anti-H, in order to obtain a positive result for group O. Candela showed that blood grouping could be carried out successfully on bone in the absence of clear results obtained from soft tissues of the same individual.[17] He found strong absorptive power in cancellous bone from long bones and from vertebrae. It is interesting to note his experience with autopsy material obtained from the Boyds, who had been unable to group it correctly.[18] Candela comments on the probable haemolyzing effects of decomposition products of the marrow. By meticulous attention to technique Candela was able to group all these specimens correctly.

The methods developed by these authors have been modified and used by a number of subsequent workers. Of particular interest are the comments of Salazar Mallen on the A-like reactions of the soil surrounding his Monte Alban remains;[19] and the work of Thieme and Otten on the effects of bacteria on the stability of blood groups.[20] Gray attempted alcohol extraction, but her results were not encouraging.[21]

In practice there are two techniques by which blood groups may be identified; that of alcohol extraction, and that of inhibition. As has been shown, both these methods have been used. The use of alcohol extraction presents problems which have not yet been overcome, however, and it is the inhibition test which is in present use.

The use of this technique makes necessary the careful preparation of the material under test. Spongy or cancellous bone contains detectable quantities of blood group substances; compact bone does not. In consequence, long bones are considered to present ideal material for grouping. Cancellous bone is removed with a curette or a dental drill, preferably from an area not previously exposed to the atmosphere. Unless soil particles or other extraneous matter are present, washing does not appear to be necessary. Provided that it is carried out in distilled water, it does not affect the possibilities of blood grouping adversely, and may be preferred. It is necessary to dry the material thoroughly to avoid uncontrolled dilution of sera during the test. This is done on filter paper in a drying oven at a temperature not exceeding 60°C. This process will not remove preservatives such as paraffin wax or lacquer, which will adversely affect the results obtained. It should be noted that their removal with the normal solvents may also affect the alcohol-soluble group specific substances it is desired to identify. It is preferable to use material which has not been treated with preservatives.

False positive results will be obtained in the presence of fats, including the normal body fats, or the products of decomposition. This was noted by Candela.[18] Material of any antiquity, which has been buried in soil or otherwise interred, will have lost most or all of its fat content and will not need further processing. Tissues obtained at autopsy, from the more recent dead, or from bodies preserved by adipocere formation or artificial mummification, will require fat extraction. It has been found that this material can be extracted in solvent ether in a soxhlet for periods up to 48 hours without detectable loss of specificity. Extraction must be complete, or slow hydrolysis of fats to fatty acids will continue in the specimen, and cause false blood group results. Following extraction, all material should be stored at − 20°C, to prevent any such degeneration.

The only further preparation required is to grind the sample in a mortar. This is usually done immediately prior to testing.

The inhibition test is a classic test in forensic medicine.[22] Its principle may be briefly stated, as follows: that if a given antigen is mixed with its appropriate antibody, the capacity of that antibody to agglutinate (clump) fresh red cells of the corresponding group will be diminished or totally removed. The degree of the effect will be related proportionally to the amount of antigen present and to the quantity and the strength of the antibody, and the value of the test is greatly enhanced when one of these factors is known. The test is carried out by direct mixing of the prepared tissue with a serum containing known antibodies. As the details of the test vary with most workers, it is proposed to describe the one in use at the British Museum (Natural History). The method must be subject to constant re-evaluation, especially in relation to the nature of the material under test.

A measured quantity of the prepared unknown tissue is put into a 75 mm × 12 mm glass tube. The amount used depends on what is available, and is usually 0·2 g. This quantity remains a constant for the specimen. To this is added 0·4 cc of antiserum, at a strength which will give a titration over three or four tubes against 2% suspension of fresh red cells of the appropriate group. This is thoroughly mixed with the tissue, and allowed to stand in the refrigerator at a temperature of approximately +4°C for 24 hours. Longer periods of inhibition have been recommended, but seem to increase the risk of non-specific reactions. At the end of this time the tube is centrifuged to throw down the tissue particles, and the supernatant removed with a Pasteur pipette. The use of a cotton-wool tip on the pipette helps to remove all the tissue particles. This is essential, as their presence causes both false positives and difficulty in reading results. The clear supernatant is then titrated against fresh red cells. Inhibition is considered to have taken place if the titre of the serum has been affected over three tubes. This result is always confirmed by repetition of the test and by the use of a 'panel' of sera. It has been found that results from the first test are often confused. Fresh serum is added to the same tissue sample for a second and third repetition of inhibition, and results taken from these two tests are compared. It is probable that on the first test some non-specific reactions are absorbed and removed. The second and third tests are almost always mutually consistent. Inhibition can be seen to occur to the seventh or eighth test on material containing a high proportion of organic matter. Candela reported inhibition to the eleventh test on recent specimens.[18]

The number of sera used in grouping any one specimen varies with the amount of tissue available. Ideally, it should never be less than three of each specificity. Pooled sera are not used; there is much value to be derived from the use of individual sera, whose reactions may be expected to vary with the genotype. This is illustrated very clearly by results obtained on a mother and child, both of group B, in inhibition testing with four individually occurring anti–B sera. Clear inhibition was obtained with three sera, but one serum failed to show inhibition with either specimen. This may be presumed to represent an individual and inherited variation in the nature of the *B* molecule.[23] The use of pooled sera in blood group reference laboratories is advocated in part to avoid this type of reaction, but in palaeoserology it is illustrative and highly desirable.

Anti-A and anti-B sera should be of human origin, naturally occurring and of comparable avidity and titre; that is, that they should show a comparable ability to agglutinate fresh red cells in the same time and at the same strength. The sera selected usually show the weakest agglutination at a dilution of about 1 in 64 or 1 in 128 where doubled dilutions are used to define this endpoint. Sera of other origins are also used. Rabbit immune sera, produced by injecting the human A and B antigens into rabbits, are useful in order to confirm the results obtained with naturally occurring sera. The use of anti-H and anti-O sera has presented many problems. If no sera specific for these two antigens are included in testing, the presence of group O can only be deduced from the absence of reactions for A or B. In the grouping of material of any antiquity this presents the hazard that the absence of reactions for A and B may also indicate the degeneration of blood group substances. Matson first made use of such sera in order to solve this very major problem.[16] The position of the H antigen in relation to the ABO groups is still uncertain; the intricacies of this relationship need not be understood by the palaeoserologist before he can make use of the H antigen, however. Reagents of both plant and animal origin have been shown to react specifically with the H antigen; the most useful seem to be eel and *Ulex europaeus*.[24-28] Human naturally occurring anti-O sera are described from time to time, and may be used provided that their reactions with controls of all groups are thoroughly understood. If the use of these sera shows the H antigen to be present where A and B are absent, this evidence may be used to presume the presence of the O antigen, and the possibility of degeneration dismissed.

Titre is determined by the use of fresh 1% suspensions of red cells in buffered saline. The use of A_2 cells with anti-A sera gives a more sensitive indication of inhibition of the anti-A molecule than A_1 cells. O cells must be carefully selected from non-secretor donors, to avoid confusion with the H antigen. Buffered saline containing 1% sodium azide as a preservative is used as a diluent throughout the test.

The presence of blood group substances in tissue can also be established by extraction techniques. Both the water-soluble and the alcohol-soluble fractions may be extracted, using appropriate techniques. Choice of the technique will be governed by the age of the material under test and the conditions in which it has been preserved. Water-soluble group-specific substances may be presumed to be present in recent dry blood stains; they will probably have been removed in tissues subject to leaching action in a moist environment. It is interesting to note that the blood group has been identified by direct inhibition in a stain on coarse fabric after thorough washing, although it is possible that this result was due to the presence of the alcohol-soluble fraction only. The H antigen has been identified on a stain five years old.[29] No ruling can be made as to a choice of extraction technique because no precise study has yet been made of the effects of environment on antigen stability. Where material is limited and of anthropological rather than forensic origins, it is probably safer to carry out alcohol extraction.

Extraction for water-soluble antigens is relatively simple. In standard forensic practice the stain is immersed for a period of from 12 to 24 hours, either in normal saline or in an aqueous solution of 2% sodium chloride and 0·5% mercuric chloride. Stains of any age may be immersed in 10% glycerine or in a saturated aqueous solution of borax. Encrusted stains may be scraped and the resulting powder dissolved in saline. The removal of stains from material of varying origin calls for specialist treatment; this is outlined in part by Polson.[30] It may be necessary to establish that the stain is blood, and that it is blood of human origin, before proceeding to the tests for blood group. The extracted stain is grouped by inhibition of appropriate sera, in much the same way as that outlined for pulverized bone or soft tissue.

Work on alcohol extraction has been done mainly with the aim of studying the biochemistry of the blood group substances, and has been concentrated on those tissues containing large quantities of these, such as ovarian cyst fluids. The techniques devised aim at a high degree of purification. This is not necessary for the purposes of blood grouping of tissue, and indeed could not be carried out. Most of the material available for assay is poor in blood group substances by comparison with meconium or ovarian cyst fluids, and limited quantities of it are available where it is of any antiquity. The simpler methods in use in the study of the distribution of blood group substances in the body can be applied to anthropological material.[4] These methods have the disadvantage that because no purification has taken place the danger of false or confusing results is not averted. In practice it has not been found to present any advantages over direct inhibition testing except where gross contamination with soil or similar agents is identifiable and cannot be eliminated by washing. It is also useful in cases of incomplete fossilization in aberrant circumstances (Kennedy; personal communication). Where quantity of material permits this some purification with phenol is practicable.[31]

The conditions in which bodies are preserved must determine the possibility of antigen stability, and should always be considered in the interpretation of results. Most of the work done on this subject has been for forensic purposes. In spite of the need for clarity on a vital issue, the effects of the environment on antigen stability are not sufficiently well known. It may be expected that in tissues exposed to the leaching action of water in the soil, water-soluble antigens would be removed, and that in consequence the diagnosis of blood group would depend on the alcohol-soluble fraction. The rate at which the water-soluble fraction is removed is not known; neither have studies been carried out on the effects of pH of soil on antigen stability. Some work has been done on the rate and type of decomposition of buried bodies under differing environmental conditions. These studies include exhumations from war graves and concentration camps,[32] and examinations of bodies of some antiquity from the bogs of NW Europe.[33] There is also the interesting case of the preservation of flesh on the bodies from Middle Bronze Age tombs in Jericho, although the causes of this preservation are obscure.[34] Mant was unable to show that soil type affected the rate of decomposition except where there was almost complete desiccation. It is known from predynastic Egyptian bodies and from Peruvian burials that bodies preserved under these conditions become mummified. Desiccation in both the heat and the cold can produce this result, as it has amongst the Aleut and the Eskimo. The lapse of time between death and burial is closely related to the degree of decomposition. In one case quoted by Mant the body of a woman was preserved for 26 months without gross change, following immediate burial at some depth. Physical type probably plays some part in the nature and rate of decomposition. In a damp environment a body with a fair distribution of fat probably converts to adipocere more rapidly than a thin one. In a dry environment there is reason to believe that the thin individual will become naturally mummified more readily than a fat one. The formation of adipocere would appear to be related to the feasibility of blood grouping. It is formed by the hydrogenation of fats, and in this process brings about mummification of the tissues by the removal of their water content. Putrefactive changes are thus retarded, as is bacterial activity. The understanding of these processes and of their role in post-mortem change in any given case, is of prime importance in assessing the value of blood grouping results.[35] The predominant organism found in tissue containing adipocere is *Clostridium welchii*. This organism is found in the bowel, from which it invades other areas at death. Schiff showed that strains isolated from this organism could decompose A and B blood group substances.[36] Stack and Morgan showed subsequently that *C. welchii* enzymes also act on O (H) substance.[37] Where the conditions following death may have been conducive to adipocere formation, great care must be taken in interpreting blood group results. Note should be taken of all the known conditions of death and burial, including the quantity of body fat, time between death and burial, the nature of any clothing, full details of the method of burial, time of year and the nature of the climate, and the type of soil. Where possible, age at death and the cause of death provide valuable information. It would appear that enzymes produced by other bacteria may also have this property; some micro-organisms have serological specificities very similar to certain of the blood group substances. No systematic investigation has ever been carried out in this field. Work done by Thieme showed that in tissue kept under varying conditions in the laboratory blood group specificity disappeared or had altered following the activity of certain anaerobic bacteria from soil.[20] He did not investigate adipocere formation, or post-mortem bacterial contamination. Much more knowledge is needed to estimate the nature and extent of bacterial activity in relation to blood group substances; the information already available should be applied to any discussion of the accuracy of blood grouping of the dead. Careful study is also needed of the effects of varying conditions of preservation. It is not known what effect there is on antigen stability under the conditions of crypt burial,[38] bog burial, or burial directly in the soil. The nature of the soil must play a big part in preservation. So also must the methods used in mummification. Naturally mummified Egyptian, Guanche, Aleut and Peruvian mummies have all been grouped, apparently with success. The reasons for their preservation vary; the preservation of soft tissues under cold wet conditions could be due to slow formation of adipocere where hot dry conditions result in preservation by rapid desiccation. Consideration of these factors must influence judgement of the results obtained in grouping, but again no systematic study of the variable effects of the environment has been carried out, and is badly needed.

Future research in palaeoserology must also consider the application of new techniques. In particular, the Coombs test[39],[40] and complement fixation may have applications in this field. The precipitin test will probably become an archaeological tool. This test for species-specific proteins is being widely developed as a technique in the systematics of the living animal. Its value in this field depends upon the fact that precipitating antisera are not absolutely specific for the species against which they are developed, but will give varying rates of reaction with related species. Comparison of the strength of the reaction illustrates systematic relationship, correspondence being highest amongst species of the same genus. The use of these techniques is discussed by Boyden.[41] The identification of animal remains from archaeological sites may well become practicable by this means, where it cannot proceed on morphological grounds; the essential element in its application is the survival of extractable protein. It must be borne in mind that environmental conditions may affect the stability of proteins in much the same way as they are thought to affect the mucopolysaccharides; specificity may be altered by bacterial activity, for instance. But the use of precipitation techniques offers rewarding results in archaeology, and should certainly be investigated.

These very new fields of research are complicated, time-consuming and full of hazards. Above all, they are not for use by the amateur. Their application must be carried out by those with a full understanding and appreciation of the serological, biochemical and bacteriological problems involved. Only then can their application to anthropology and archaeology give the reliable results for which we hope.

REFERENCES

1 MOURANT, A. E. 1954. *The Distribution of the Human Blood Groups*, Oxford
2 BOYD, W. C. 1956. *Fundamentals of Immunology*, London and New York
3 LANDSTEINER, K. 1901. *Wien Klin. Wschr.* 14, 1132
4 HARTMANN, G. 1941. *Group Antigens in Human Organs*, Copenhagen
5 HIRSZFELD, L. and HIRSZFELD, H. 1919. *Lancet* 97, 675
6 MOURANT, A. E., KOPEC, A. C., DOMANIEWSKA-SOBCZAK, K. 1958. *The ABO Blood Groups*, Oxford
7 SHEPPARD, P. M. 1959. *Brit. Med. Bull* 15, 2, 134
8 FRASER ROBERTS, J. A. 1959. *Ibid.* 129
9 LATTES, L. 1916. *Arch. antropol. criminale, psichiat. e med. legale* 37, 3
10 DUCOS, J. 1958. *Vox Sanguinis* 3, 385
11 BOYD, W. C. and BOYD, L. G. 1937a. *J. Immunol.* 33, 159
12 —— —— 1937b. *Ibid.* 32, 307
13 WYMAN, L. C. and BOYD, W. C. 1937. *Am. Anth.* 39, 583
14 BOYD, L. G. and BOYD, W. C. 1939. *Am. J. Phys. Anth.* 25, 421
15 MATSON, G. A. 1936a. *J. Immunol.* 30, 445
16 —— 1936b. *Ibid.* 459
17 CANDELA, P. B. 1939. *Am. J. Phys. Anth.* 25, 187
18 —— 1940. *Ibid.* 27, 365
19 SALAZAR MALLEN, M. 1951. *Gac. Méd. Méx.* 81, 122
20 THIEME, F. P. and OTTEN, C. M. 1957. *Am. J. Phys. Anth.* 15, 387
21 GRAY, M. 1952. Thesis, University of Oregon
22 BOORMAN, K. E. and DODD, B. E. 1957. *Blood Group Serology*, London
23 SMITH, M. Unpublished observations
24 GRUBB, R. 1949. *Acta Path. Microbiol. Scand., Suppl. 84*
25 RENKONEN, K. O. 1948. *Ann. Med. Exp. Biol. Fenniae* 26, 66
26 —— 1950. *Ibid. 28*

27 BOYD, W. C. and REGUERA, R. M. 1949. *J. Immunol. 62, 333*

28 BIRD, G. W. G. 1953. *Voc. Sang. 3*

29 DODD, B. E. Personal Communication

30 POLSON, C. J. 1955. *The Essentials of Forensic Medicine,* Edinburgh

31 MORGAN, W. T. J. and KING, H. K. 1943. *Biochem. J. 37, 640*

32 MANT, A. K. 1957. *J. Foren. Med. 4,* 18

33 SCHLABOW, K., HAAGE, W., SPATZ, H., KLENK, E., DIEZEL, P. B., SCHUTRUMPF, R., SCHAFER, U. and JANKUHN, H. 1958. *Praehist. Z. 36,* 118

34 ZEUNER, F. E. 1955. *Pal. Expl. Quar.,* 118

35 EVANS, E. G. In press. *Med. Sci. and the Law*

36 SCHIFF, F. 1935. *Klin. Wochschr. 14,* 750

37 STACK, M. V. and MORGAN, W. T. J. 1949. *Brit. J. Exptl. Pathol. 30,* 470

38 SMITH, M. 1959. *Nature 184,* 867

39 ALLISON, A. C. and MORTON, J. A. 1953. *J. Clin. Path. 6,* 314

40 RUFFIÉ, J. and DUCOS, J. 1956. *Ann. Med. legale et criminol. police sci. et toxicol. 36,* 1

41 BOYDEN, A. A. 1954. In *Serological approaches to the studies of protein structure and metabolism.* Rutgers U.P.

43 Blood Groups and Prehistory

J. P. GARLICK

IT IS OVER SIXTY YEARS since Landsteiner discovered the ABO blood groups. By the end of the First World War they had been shown to be inherited, and they seemed not to be affected in the individual by age or disease.

Anthropology came into the picture with the testing by Professor and Mrs. Hirszfeld of soldiers from many parts of the world brought by the fortunes of war to the Serbian Front. The frequency of Group B proved to be highest among Asians, especially Indians (more than thirty per cent), lowest among west Europeans (less than ten per cent) and intermediate among Africans. On the other hand Group A was commonest among Europeans. There was also considerable diversity of A, B and O rates within the continents.

To L. and H. Hirszfeld[12] it seemed 'étonnant que les résultats [obtenus par nos recherches] diffèrent des opinions anthropologiques courantes'. They offered two possible explanations: that classical theories were wrong; or that the biochemical and anatomical differentiation and mixture of races had taken place at different periods. Elsewhere[13] they avoided the conflict between the visible and blood group data and suggested two alternative origins for the world frequency differences. Firstly, 'when man appeared on the earth A and B were present in the same proportions in different races. In this case the differences which are now present in different races would depend on the assumption that for unknown reasons A is more suitable for increased resistance of the organism to disease in a temperate climate, while B is more suitable in a hot climate.' If this were so, it was argued, particular blood groups would no longer survive in regions where they were unfavourable. The existing distribution pattern, however, did not support this interpretation, and there were also peoples living in contrasted environments who showed similar frequencies (such as Siberian Russians and Madagascans), while peoples who had lived in the same region for several centuries could remain distinct (for example Monastir Jews and Slavs).

The alternative and favoured hypothesis was 'that there are two different biochemical races which arose in different places'. Present differences would then be explained by migration and mixture of the original 'Biochemical Race B', homeland India, and 'Biochemical Race A', homeland probably northern or central Europe. This approach gained increasing support, and several more complex schemes along the same lines were put forward as knowledge of blood group distributions increased.[5] At the same time the evidence of blood group frequencies was applied to specific ethnological and archaeological problems such as folk movements in Dark Age Europe and the origin of the Polynesians.

This essay attempts to assess the limitations, assumptions and difficulties of using present blood group distributions as evidence of past migration and hybridization, a procedure which is sound only if frequencies are stable. In the absence of fossil blood group evidence this in turn cannot be directly validated, and we must therefore use indirect means to reweigh the original Hirszfeld hypotheses and to give tentative answers to some basic questions. Do the forces which led to the original blood group divergences still operate; and if so are they powerful enough to interfere with historical reconstructions based on blood group frequencies? Or can blood groups be taken to have suffered for several thousand years from evolutionary apathy?

BLOOD GROUP ETHNOGRAPHY

With the discovery by Bernstein in 1924 of the three-allele mode of inheritance for the ABO system and the calculation of *gene* frequencies by simple mathematical methods,[22] populations could be compared more simply (one less variable) and more directly from the point of view of heredity (the genes being the actual units of inheritance). It has long been standard practice, therefore, to characterize and compare populations in terms of genes rather than phenotypes (blood groups), and this also aids the study of rates of frequency change and the effects of hybridization.

In 1927 Landsteiner and Levine discovered the MN blood group system, which places every individual in one of three categories (M, N and MN), independently of his ABO status. Many more inherited red cell antigens have since been discovered, most of them varying in frequency between populations. An individual's blood can now be tested for about a dozen genetically independent blood group systems, such as Rh (or Rhesus), Duffy and Diego, which in most cases have turned out to be much more complicated than they first appeared. In the ABO system, for example, there are two forms of the A gene (A_1 and A_2) and corresponding subdivisions of blood group A. In the Rh system at least ten antigens are now known, five of which may be carried by one person. There may well be further systems awaiting discovery, but many think (and hope) that the limit is in sight. Race and Sanger[25] give detailed descriptions of the serology and genetics of the systems known to date.

Distribution data have not expanded evenly for all systems, and in many cases only the bare outline of the world pattern is known. The ABO and the simple Rh-positive/negative status are routinely determined for transfusion purposes and have provided a mass of information in countries with developed hospital services, especially in Europe. The other systems are seldom important in transfusion and few data are produced as a by-product of clinical requirements. Most of the information has come from specially designed surveys, with increasing use of air transport from the more remote areas so that blood specimens can be tested in central laboratories within a few days of collection in the field.

Unfortunately most of the varieties of antisera needed for any but ABO tests are scarce and require delicate handling. Clear-cut reactions with them do not appear if the blood specimens have been left unrefrigerated for any length of time. In a cautious comment on L. and H. Hirszfeld's original report, a leading article in the same issue of

(a) Thin section of an axe-hammer from Pembridge, Herefordshire ($\times 25$).

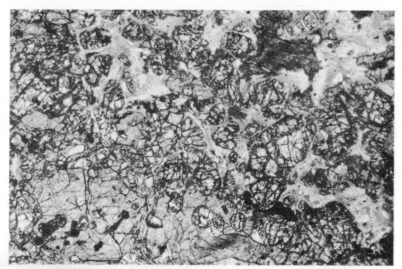

(b) Thin section of pictrite from an outcrop in Hyssington Parish, Montgomeryshire, for comparison with (a). In both these slides, the semi-rounded, greatly crushed grains are olivine; greyish material with cleavage, forming a large patch to the bottom and right, is augite; white is felspar, with the cloudy patches therein, apple-green chlorite and the black patches are iron ore.

(c) Thin section of the very distinctive metamorphosed laterite from Tievebulliagh, Co. Antrim ($\times 25$).

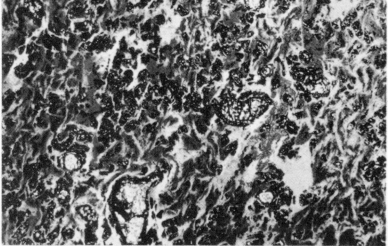

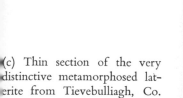

(see page 482) PLATE XXIII

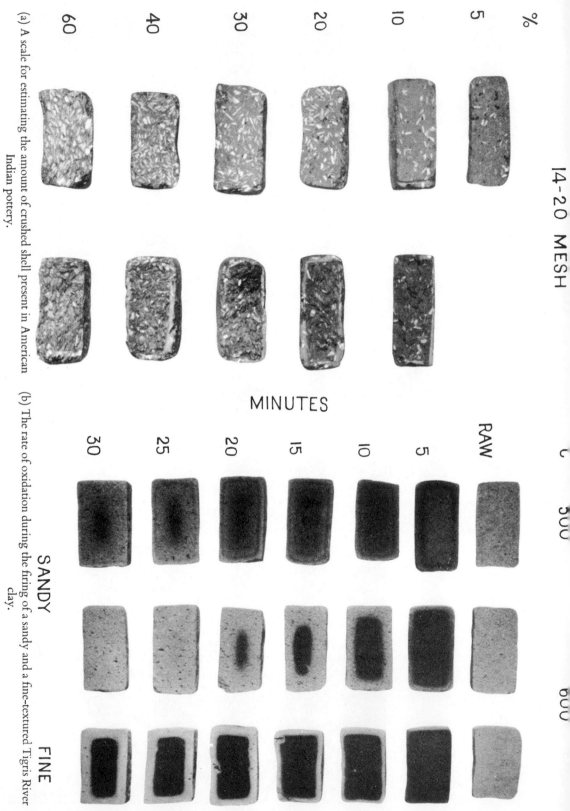

14-20 MESH

%

5

10

20

30

40

60

MINUTES

RAW

5

10

15

20

25

30

SANDY

FINE

(a) A scale for estimating the amount of crushed shell present in American Indian pottery.

(b) The rate of oxidation during the firing of a sandy and a fine-textured Tigris River clay.

PLATE XXIV (see page 489)

The Lancet emphasized the strict control of experimental technique necessary while 'serology is still in its perambulator'. Serology has come of age but the same careful controls are essential, now backed up by statistical methods; some published results, especially from hot climates, are open to doubt.

Apart from the laboratory hazards the selection of individuals to be tested presents difficulties. A statistically random sample (one which fairly represents all relevant sections of the population) must be carefully chosen. A series of blood donors may include an undue proportion of group O, Rh-negative persons, who are often wooed more assiduously than mere ordinary mortals by transfusion services. The blood group frequencies of hospital patients, often a ready source of data, may be biased in unpredictable directions (see blood groups and disease). Close kin should be excluded since they do not provide a random sample of a population's genes.

The definition of the population to be surveyed is often no easy matter. What is generally required is a sample of the mating population, which may or may not correspond to a linguistic, political or religious group. Considerable heterogeneity in blood group rates has been missed on occasion by sampling from too inclusive a grouping, for example 'Irish', whose A gene frequency varies from 15% in the extreme west of Eire to 20% in Dublin. Hardly any countries outside Europe have been adequately surveyed even for the ABO system, and within Europe many areas are still poorly explored. The United Kingdom is fast becoming one of the best known areas with the publication of carefully selected Transfusion Service data,[23] and over five hundred thousand results are at present being analysed at the Nuffield Blood Group Centre in London.

SUMMARY OF WORLD BLOOD GROUP DISTRIBUTIONS

Surveys of ABO frequencies soon extended to all major regions of the world. Pre-Columbian Americans (except Eskimos) seem to have lacked B altogether and many South American tribes both A and B (yet group A is frequent in North America, and some tribes, notably the Blackfoot and Blood, have very high rates). Among Australian Aboriginals the A rates again vary considerably and B is present only in northern Queensland. Throughout the rest of the world all three major genes—A, B and O—occur in variable proportions, but A_2 is seldom met with outside Europe, Africa and western Asia. The Lapps have far and away the highest A_2 frequency. Figs. 64 and 65, which are reproduced from the complete tabulation of world ABO tests published by Mourant *et al.*,[23] plot the world B and European O gene distributions.

The variations in the other systems, so far as they are known, often bear little or no relation to each other or to the ABO pattern (for instance MN and Rh in Europe); nor is there much agreement between the distributions of blood groups and visible racial characters such as pigmentation or hair form. The ABO frequencies of Australian Aboriginals, for example, can be matched only in Amerindians, yet these peoples are morphologically very different and for the MN groups occupy the two extremes of the world range. Exceptions include gene Di^a of the Diego system, probably restricted to Mongoloid peoples, although the gene is considerably more frequent in South America

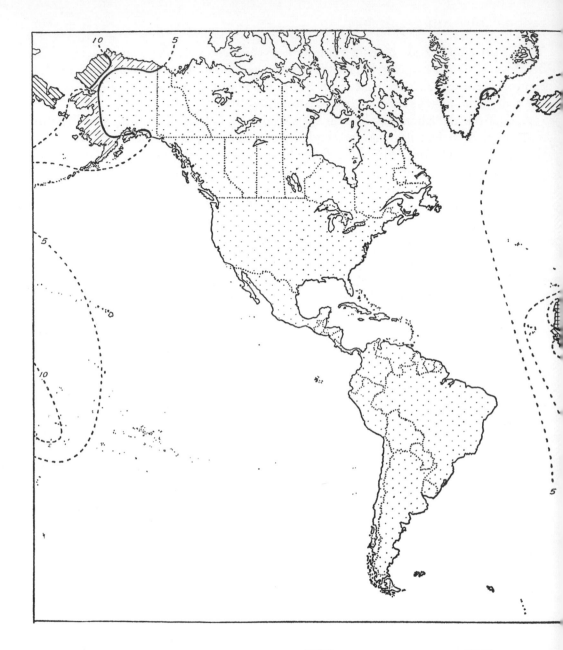

PERCENTAGE GENE B   ▨ 25 - 30   ▨ 20 - 25

Fig. 64 Distribution of blood group gene *B* in the aboriginal populations of the world. From Mourant.[23]

than elsewhere in the New World or in eastern Asia. In several systems there are genes which so far have been found to occur frequently only among Africans (and their New World descendants) and some neighbouring peoples.

Fig. 66, illustrating the tentative distribution of the *M* gene of the MN system, brings

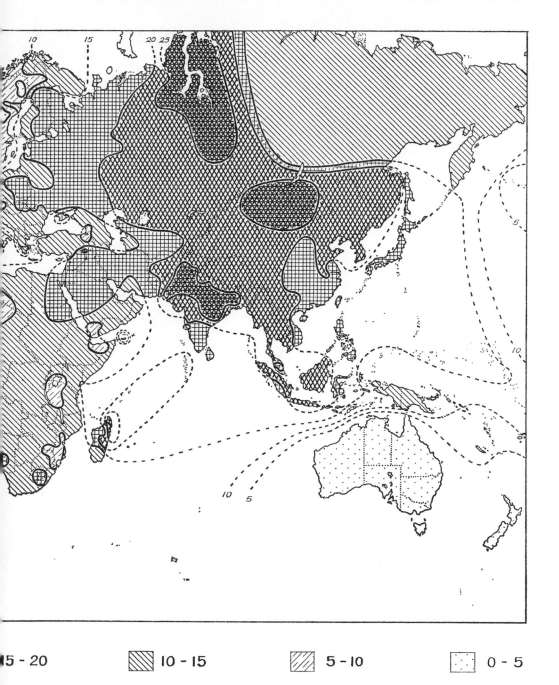

up to date the one in Dr A. E. Mourant's *Distribution of the Human Blood Groups*,[22] a study which deals fully with every anthropological aspect of blood groups, and from which many of the ideas expressed in this article have been consciously or unconsciously derived.

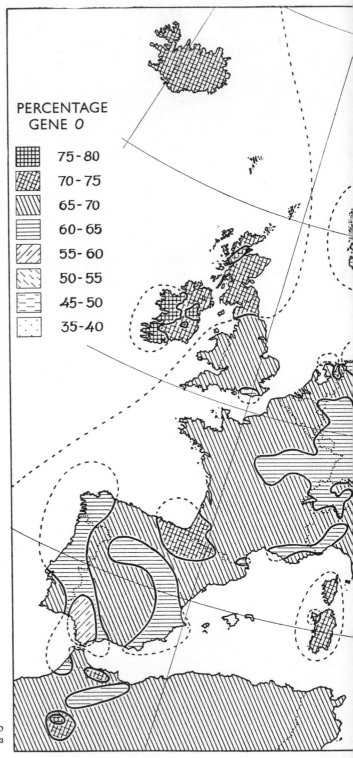

PERCENTAGE
GENE O

	75 - 80
	70 - 75
	65 - 70
	60 - 65
	55 - 60
	50 - 55
	45 - 50
	35 - 40

Fig. 65 Distribution of blood group gene O in Europe. From Mourant.[23]

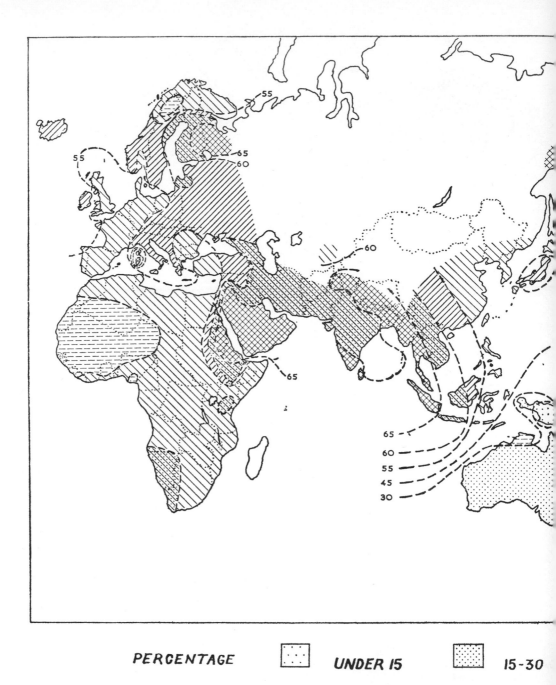

PERCENTAGE

GENE M

UNDER 15

15-30

60-65

65-75

Fig. 66 Tentative distribution of blood group gene *M* in the aboriginal population of the world.

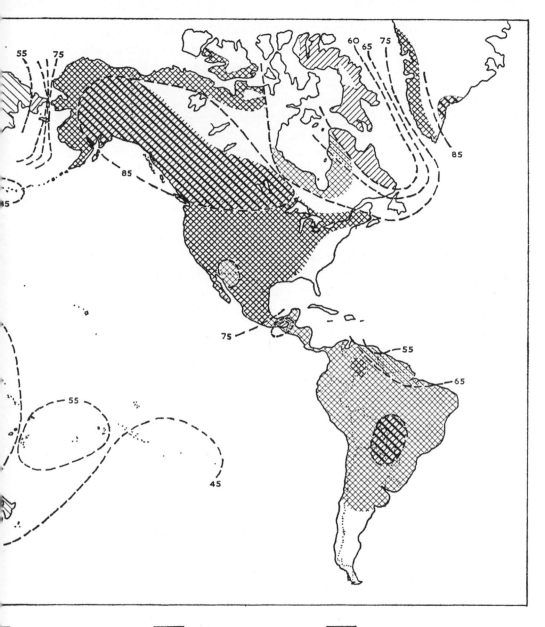

PRESENT DISTRIBUTIONS AS EVIDENCE OF FREQUENCY STABILITY

Similarity of blood group rates between migrant populations and their stay-at-home kin provides the available evidence for stable frequencies over the past few centuries, on the assumption that the descendants of emigrants have not paralleled the sedentes in evolutionary change. The greatest weight should be given to comparisons where the divided populations have come to live in contrasted environments, circumstances which should minimize parallel change through natural selection.

There is no lack of qualitative or roughly quantitative data. West Africans and North American Negroes, for example, share all known 'African' blood group genes at frequencies in accord with the generally accepted level of European admixture in US Negroes. Unfortunately the data do not allow useful quantitative comparisons even in the few cases where large samples have been tested, for the slave shipments from West and Central Africa were from a region with heterogeneous blood group frequencies, and their tribal origins are largely unknown.

The fullest and most reliable migrant data come from within Europe and from the peoples of European origin in Australia and the New World. In all systems studied these migrant populations lie within the European frequency range, but because of variation within Europe and the difficulty of weighting the series accordingly, the evidence is again not as critical as one would wish. Where the exact origin is known the samples have generally been too small to exclude any but rather gross changes. For phenotype rates around 10%, for example, European and emigrant series of about 2,000 each may be needed to exclude a true frequency difference of 2% between the populations.

Evidence of stability after more than a few centuries is not plentiful. The best known examples are the European Gypsy communities tested which have shown ABO frequencies closer to north Indian values than to those of their French and Balkan neighbours. Exceptions are small samples from Hungary[2] and Jugoslavia[27] with typical Balkan rates. The Hungarian Gypsies were admitted to be grossly diluted with European genes, and, despite the circularity of the argument, it is tempting to explain away the Jugoslav series (said to be unmixed, yet Rumanian-speaking with Serbian and Hungarian family names) as Balkan indigenes who had succumbed to the lure of the Gypsy life. Longer-range comparisons include several series of Madagascans with ABO frequencies rather closer to Indonesian than to East African values, and this up to two thousand years after their migration from Indonesia and subsequent mixture with Africans. Apart from a small series of Rh tests,[30] again with intermediate rates, there are no Madagascan data for other systems.

Inference from migrant data can be made quantitative only when there are records of the number of original settlers (to allow for random fluctuation in small populations—see below) and the degree of subsequent admixture. Studies are needed where these conditions are more nearly fulfilled and dealing with all the blood group systems. There may be scope for this in the Caribbean area, where the provenance of some ex-slave populations is roughly known, and where the fate of seventeenth- and eighteenth-century African genes for haemoglobin variants has already proved most interesting.[14]

BLOOD GROUPS IN ANIMALS

The story is taken even further back by the study of blood groups in animals. Most populations examined have blood group systems restricted to their own species or at least to low-level taxonomic categories. The ABO system is very widespread, on the other hand, and substances related to the human ABO antigens have been found in many animals including cattle, pigs, rabbits, frogs, guinea pigs and several micro-organisms and parasites of man. The search for other human blood groups in animals has concentrated on the Primates, and ABO-, MN- and Rh-like antigens have been found in both monkeys and apes. Probably in no case, however, are they identical with the human antigens. In general 'red-cell antigens reflect phylogenetic relationships within a group (e.g. primates) such that more closely related members, e.g. man and chimpanzee, have more antigenic factors in common than more distantly related members, e.g. man and monkey'.[15] It seems likely, then, that at least some of the human blood group systems were established before the advent of *Homo sapiens*, and that antigen diversification has continued within the Primates. On the other hand it is possible that equivalent systems have evolved independently in related species, perhaps in response to diseases common to the group, for the chances of genetic parallelism are surely much greater for simple traits than for the polygenic characters familiar in palaeontology.

BLOOD GROUPS AND EVOLUTION

Diversity of genetic types arises from change (mutation) or rearrangement of the hereditary material—the genes. Mutation is very rare and unaided may take tens of thousands of generations to replace one type of gene in a population by repeated production of allelic forms. Natural selection speeds up or slows down the spread of mutants if the genotypes differ even slightly in their fitness (the genetic equivalent of adaptive value, a measure of the mean relative viability and fertility of a genotype). A human gene mutating at an average rate and giving a 1% increase in fitness to homozygotes and heterozygotes, for example, would rise in frequency from 1% to 50% in about 15,000 years. On the other hand mutants which reduce the fitness of the homozygote or heterozygote, however little, cannot achieve more than a low frequency without the aid of random fluctuation.

We are concerned with the situation where two or more forms of a genetic character are fairly common in a population. This is known as polymorphism.[1,29] Polymorphism need not be fortuitous, the result of hybridization or long-past selection pressure. Nor need it be transient, as when one form of a gene is replacing its inferior allele. Nearly forty years ago Fisher and Haldane showed how balanced selective forces could indefinitely maintain polymorphism in a steady state.

Since animal studies, as we have seen, show that blood group variation is a zoological commonplace, and palaeoanthropology offers no evidence of increasing variability in human skeletal evolution, the weight of evidence points to an ancient origin for human blood group polymorphism. Yet it is now known to contain the seeds of its own downfall (see mother-foetus incompatibility), and we must therefore postulate some means of preserving the variability.

Random effects can hardly explain its persistence in time and space. Opposed muta-tion might play a part, for example from *M* to *N* and back from *N* to *M*, but such an equilibrium would be easily upset by other pressures. Much more effective stabilization is produced by opposed selective forces, in particular when the fitness of the heterozygote is greater than that of either homozygote. This situation has been widely found in plant and animal genetics and more recently for the sickle-cell gene in man.[1] Indeed it has been shown to occur in chicken blood group systems, where multiple heterozygotes are both more viable and more fertile than the average fowl.[29] Perhaps biochemical com-plexity is itself an adaptive character and antigen polymorphism a means to this end.[19,10] A specific contender among possible selective agents is disease, more especially infectious disease, which may have played a major part in human evolution since the rise in popu-lation density following the Neolithic Revolution.[11] Motulsky[21] has recently reviewed the role of infectious disease in human evolution.

BLOOD GROUPS AND DISEASE

Blood group studies were born into the world of immunology and it is not surprising that a link with disease was immediately sought. The search for a direct effect of disease on the blood groups of individuals soon drew a blank, but efforts to find indirect effects continued throughout the nineteen-twenties and intermittently thereafter. Interest has been particularly strong in the past ten years.

Two modes of selection have been postulated. Firstly, it may be disadvantageous to carry the same antigens as do invading micro-organisms, for generally speaking particular antibodies cannot be produced by an individual with the corresponding antigen. A second possibility stems from the discovery that micro-organisms when bound to the red cells are more readily removed by leucocytes.[24] Livingstone[18] pointed out that if certain disease-producing organisms were to stick more easily to cells carrying particular blood group antigens, individuals of that group would be favoured.

In fact no clear associations between blood groups and communicable disease have yet been found, although several possible associations await confirmation with large and carefully controlled series. Most of the disease associations which have been con-firmed[26] involve conditions such as peptic ulceration which, being rare, late in onset, or not severely disabling, can hardly be powerful selective agents. More important from the point of view of rapid evolution is selection during foetal life, of which the first discovered and best known occurrence is due to haemolytic disease of the new-born.[25]

If foetal red cells escape into the maternal circulation, the mother may produce anti-bodies to any foreign antigens they contain. This immune antibody diffuses across the placenta and destroys the foetal red cells. In practice mother-foetus blood group in-compatibility (where the foetal cells carry an antigen which the mother lacks) seldom leads to haemolytic disease. The most important case is when the mother is Rh-negative (homozygous for the *rh* gene) and the foetus is Rh-positive, that is whose cells carry the Rh antigen. Anti-Rh is produced by the mother in about one in twenty of such preg-nancies and about half the untreated cases die. Since affected offspring are always heterozygous (*Rh rh*) each fatal case of haemolytic disease removes two unlike alleles from the population. Simple calculation shows that this reduces and in time eliminates whichever is the rarer allele.

The Rh-negative gene is commonest in north-west Europe (about 40%) and becomes less frequent eastwards and southwards (25–30% in the eastern Mediterranean and Middle East, about 20% in Subsaharan Africa). Among the peoples of east and south-east Asia, the Pacific, Australia and the New World it is rare or absent. Within Europe the gene frequency rises above 50% only among the Basques and in one or two localities elsewhere. Notably low *rh* frequencies (20–25%) are found in northern Sardinia and among the Lapps. Selection by haemolytic disease must therefore be reducing the Rh-negative frequency among all European populations except the Basques, where, on the contrary, the rate should be slowly rising.

As soon as the selective consequences of haemolytic disease were appreciated the question arose how could the frequencies have reached their present levels? Both Haldane[9] and Wiener[33] suggested prehistoric hybridization between one population largely or entirely Rh-negative and another Rh-positive. The discovery a few years later of a population (the Basques) with an *rh* frequency above 50% and speaking a non-Indo-European language strengthened the hypothesis.

In a review of the case against the hybridization theory Sheppard[28] pointed out that the hypothetical Rh-negative race of early Europeans (represented today in its least mixed form by the Basques) must have accounted for a sizeable proportion of the ancestry not only of Europeans but also of Africans and Indians. This would put the time of mixture improbably far back in time, and in any case should have led to lower (or higher) *rh* frequencies in Europe today, unless the frequency change had been slowed up by reproductive compensation (the surviving children in families which can produce extra offspring to make up for their losses through haemolytic disease are usually Rh-negative).

There remains the possibility that either the homozygote or the heterozygote for *rh* is favoured in some other way. Where the gene frequency is about 40%, as in much of northern Europe, an increase of about 1% in the fitness of the heterozygote would balance the effect of haemolytic disease; if the gene frequency were 60% (rather more than among the Basques) a heterozygote advantage of about $1\frac{1}{2}$% would produce equilibrium. If the homozygote were favoured it would require an even lower selective advantage to achieve balance. Even these small differentials seemed unexpectedly large twenty years ago,[9] but today they arouse no misgivings. Unfortunately there is little chance of testing such a hypothesis, for, apart from the difficulty of identifying what could be an extinct selective agent, there is no available laboratory technique which infallibly distinguishes homozygous from heterozygous Rh-positive individuals.

The genetic results of haemolytic disease are complicated by interaction between the ABO and Rh groups. It seems that the initial immunization of the mother occurs only when the foetal red cells are also ABO-compatible with the maternal serum (if the foetal red cells are group A Rh-positive, for example, and the mother is group O Rh-negative, the naturally occuring maternal anti-A destroys the foetal cells before they are able to sensitize the mother to the Rh antigen they carry). This favours *A* and *B* genes at the expense of *O*, and we would expect populations with high Rh–negative rates to show lowered O rates too. The European data as a whole do not bear this out, and the Basques in particular have high frequencies of both Rh–negative and O genes. It is hardly reasonable to invoke this explanation in the few cases where the relation does hold, for example among the Sardinians, who enjoy the lowest Rh–negative rate in Europe (Lapps apart) and also a raised O frequency. Nor is it convincing to relate the similarity in the world trends of Rh–negative and A_2 rates to a similar process,[16] when the agreement within continents is so poor.

There is some evidence from family studies of pre-natal selection in the ABO and MN systems more powerful than that produced by haemolytic disease. The data are highly diverse and often contradictory. Some studies have suggested that a great number of ABO-incompatible foetuses are eliminated; others that heterozygous foetuses are favoured in ABO-compatible matings. Some series have also shown the latter effect for the MN system (too many MN offspring for MN × MN matings), but much of this surplus could be due to unreliable blood grouping technique. Two recent high-powered mathematical studies of all the available data, however, suggest that there is indeed considerable selection in both the ABO and MN systems, some of it favouring and some disfavouring the heterozygotes.[8,20]

There is clearly a pressing need to settle these problems one way or the other and to extend inquiry to other systems. In the unlikely event of the fitness differentials at present suspected being reversed in different conditions, the ethnological usefulness of these systems would be limited to a few centuries. If, as seems much more probable, the genetic effects of differential fertility were to vary slightly according to demographic patterns, especially the infant mortality and birth rate, the useful range might extend to millennia.

Infectious disease remains a possible selective agent of unpredictable power. Endemic diseases responsible for much infant mortality might be involved, for instance pneumonia or gastro–enteritis, or epidemic diseases such as plague or typhus. Vogel and others[32] have recently shown that the smallpox virus carries an A-like antigen, and the plague bacillus one resembling H (characteristic of group O, lacking in some group A_1 individuals). These diseases may therefore change ABO gene frequencies by striking particularly at persons of group A and AB (smallpox) and group O (plague). Some support is offered, as Vogel and his colleagues point out, by the world trends of the O gene and what is known of the history of bubonic plague (the smallpox/group A agreement is rather unimpressive). The hypothesis would gain weight not only from testing plague and smallpox cases, but also from demonstrating the expected blood group patterns on a smaller scale, for example in parts of Europe heavily and lightly attacked by the Black Death.

GENETIC DRIFT

Another means of producing genetic differences between populations is random frequency variation, or genetic drift. This is a consequence of random sampling errors in the genes passed on from one generation to the next. In large populations drift has little effect, for too many genes are passed on to allow the allele frequencies to be unrepresentative of the parental gene-pool, but in isolated communities numbering only a few hundred individuals drift is a force to be reckoned with and can overcome selective differentials of 1% or more. Such deviations can build up over the generations to large frequency changes and eventually to the elimination of some alleles. When the population increases in size the gene frequencies are fixed at the levels achieved by drift. This hazard of small samples is also present when a community is established by a small band of settlers or is periodically reduced to small numbers by famine or disease.

Genetic drift as an important force in human evolution is easy to postulate, unpredictable of effect in particular cases and impossible to prove. The most plausible case for drift effects is among the isolated Polar and Labrador Eskimos who show marked heterogeneity in the frequencies of both A and B and perhaps M.[17] The rather variable blood group frequencies in Polynesia can also reasonably be ascribed to the small numbers of original settlers.

When genetic drift is invoked to explain divergences far in the past (such as the origin of the hypothetical Early European Rh-negative race or the loss of A and B genes in the ancestors of South American Indians) conjecture is almost uncontrolled. Archaeological evidence may suggest the size of a local population but cannot supply data on the amount of hybridization between neighbouring communities. Present-day hunting peoples usually maintain contacts between tribes and a certain amount of gene-flow occurs between them. Estimates for Australian Aboriginals vary up to 10% per generation,[31] a sufficient rate to keep drift in check.

THE CHOICE OF EXPLANATIONS

Wherever it is reasonable to explain present distributions by genetic drift it is also reasonable to postulate natural selection as the agent of change. The fact that no appropriate selective agent has yet been discovered is not reason enough to doubt its existence. As Charles Kingsley remarked, aptly recalled by Cain:[6] 'To prove that no water-babies exist you must see no water-babies existing, which is not the same thing as not seeing water-babies.' Equally, as Birdsell[4] pointed out, 'water-baby-wise the non-existence of drift has not yet been proven'. Blood group-selective mortality can add to the confusion of causes, for a decimating epidemic may not only change the gene frequencies in its own right but also produce ideal conditions for genetic drift in the scanty survivors.

The impasse extends to alternative selection and migration hypotheses. It can hardly be haphazard coincidence that regions peculiar in their blood group frequencies are often also ecologically distinct (for example Highland Britain, the high rainfall area of the western Caucasus, or the gap in the West African rain-forest at the Ghana-Togo coast). A ready explanation in ethnological terms is usually available in such cases, but it is also possible that natural selection has been at work. Ecological zoning canalizes not only human migrants according to their technology but also disease-producing organisms. The epidemiological contrast induced by the habitat is enlarged by interaction between culture and environment through population density, hygiene, diet, contacts with other communities and so on. Again, a secondary demographic contrast may guide evolution through differential fertility (for example by haemolytic disease) at different rates or in different directions.

When blood group distributions and ecological patterns do not coincide selection may still be producing genetic divergence. This could apply, for example, to the gradient of decreasing B frequencies linking central Asia with western Europe (see Fig. 64). The obvious ethnological explanation, and one which has been generally accepted, derives the European B genes from central Asia, carried westwards by Dark Age invaders. On the other hand the pattern might be at least partly due to a selection gradient provided by, say, an epidemic disease periodically spreading from a focus in or near India. This could also explain the sharing of the highest B rates in the world by Caucasoid and Mongoloid peoples near the Himalayas. In fact, certain features of the European B distribution are not easily explained by an Asian hypothesis, whether ethnological or selective. To judge by present frequencies Asian influence would have lowered the O as it raised the B rate; consequently there should be a negative correlation between B and O frequencies in western Eurasia today. In central Europe this is generally true and it also holds among two particularly high O peoples—the Basques and the western Caucasians. But of the other two areas with especially high O rates Sardinia has a typical Mediterranean B frequency, while Celtic-speaking Britain boasts some of the highest B rates in north-west Europe.

Viewed on a world scale the contrasting patterns of the various systems are again open to alternative explanations. Each blood group system (or, for that matter, each visible racial character) tells a different story, and there is no way of knowing which, if any, is the best guide to closeness of descent. The greatest local fluctuation seems to be in ABO rates. This may reflect more intense natural selection for the ABO system (Mourant), but it could be argued that greater selective pressures in the other systems have smoothed out their local variation.

CONCLUSIONS

The blood groups of prehistory cannot be understood in isolation from the prehistory of blood groups. There is no doubt that mutation, genetic drift, natural selection, hybridization and migration have all played a part in the evolution of present-day blood group distributions. What *is* in doubt is the relative importance of these agents at different times and in different places. This multi-dimensional maze has no simple solution, and it would be rash to evade the difficulties and ambiguities which face the interpreter of present-day distribution patterns.

The best hope of progress (immunological advances apart) lies in the detailed study of selected regions, combining full blood group, other genetic and anthropometric surveys with historical, archaeological, demographic and epidemiological investigations. Sardinia, for example, distinctive in many genetic characters, provides an ideal field for such work.[7] In northern Europe a notable contribution is Beckman's[3] very detailed analysis of Swedish blood group distributions to show their partial agreement with anthropometric, historical and archaeological data. The full value of this work cannot be realized without similar studies in other parts of northern Europe. We may then know whether or not blood group evidence is a reliable guide to the movements and settlements of the Vikings, for example, and why Icelandic ABO frequencies are so different from those of Scandinavia but so similar to those of Ireland (for possible explanations see Mourant[22]).

Only when the rates of blood group frequency change are known will it be possible to offer a time-span for the ethnological usefulness of the various systems. In the meantime blood group anthropology remains underdeveloped territory in need of historical and archaeological aid.

REFERENCES

1 ALLISON, A. C. 1955. *Cold Spring Harbor Symp. Quantitative Biol. 20*, 239–255
2 BACKHAUSZ, R., NEMESKÉRI, J. and VAJDA, G. 1950. *Homo 1*, 193–202
3 BECKMAN, L. 1959. *Hereditas 45*, 1–189
4 BIRDSELL, J. B. 1950. *Cold Spring Harbor Symp. Quantitative Biol. 15*, 312
5 BOYD, W. C. 1950. *Genetics and the races of man*, Oxford
6 CAIN, A. J. 1950. *Cold Spring Harbor Symp. Quantitative Biol. 15*, 312
7 CEPPELLINI, R. 1959. Blood Groups and Haematological Data as a source of Ethnic Information; in WOLSTENHOLME, G. E. W. and O'CONNOR, C. M. (ed.) *Medical Biology and Etruscan Origins* (CIBA Foundation Symposium), London, 177–188
8 CHUNG, C. S. and MORTON, N. E. 1961. *Am. J. hum. Genet. 13*, 9–27
9 HALDANE, J. B. S. 1942. *Ann. Eugen. 11*, 333–340
10 —— 1953. Foreword to *Evolution*, Symposium no. 7 of the Society for Experimental Biology, Cambridge
11 —— 1957. *Acta genet. Stat. med. 6*, 321–332
12 HIRSZFELD, L. and HIRSZFELD, H. 1919a. *Anthropologie 29*, 505–537
13 —— —— 1919b. *Lancet ii*, 675–679
14 JONXIS, J. H. P. 1959. The Frequency of Haemoglobin S and Haemoglobin C Carriers in Curaçao and Surinam; in JONXIS, J. H. P. and DELAFRESNAYE, J. F. (ed.) *Abnormal Haemoglobins*, Oxford, 300–306
15 JOYSEY, V. C. 1959. *Brit. med. Bull. 15*, 158–164
16 KIRK, R. L. 1961. *Am. J. hum. Genet. 13*, 224–232
17 LAUGHLIN, W. S. 1950. *Cold Spring Harbor Symp. Quantitative Biol. 15*, 165–173
18 LIVINGSTONE, F. B. 1960. *Human Biol. 32*, 17–27*
19 MEDAWAR, P. B. 1953. Some immunological and endocrinological problems raised by the evolution of viviparity in Vertebrates; in *Evolution*, Symp. no. 7 of the Society for Experimental Biology, Cambridge, 320–338
20 MORTON, N. E. and CHUNG, C. S. 1959. *Am. J. hum. Genet. 11*, 237–251*
21 MOTULSKY, A. G. 1960. *Human Biol. 32*, 28–62*
22 MOURANT, A. E. 1954. *The distribution of the human blood groups*, Oxford
23 —— KOPEĆ, A. C. and DOMANIEWSKA-SOBCZAK, K. 1958. *The ABO blood groups: comprehensive tables and maps of world distribution*, Oxford
24 NELSON, R. A. 1953. *Science 118*, 733–737
25 RACE, R. R. and SANGER, R. 1962. *Blood groups in Man*, Oxford, 4th ed.
26 ROBERTS, J. A. FRASER. 1959. *Brit. med. Bull. 15*, 129–133
27 SCHMIDT, A. 1930. *Z. Rassenphysiol. 3*, 14–19
28 SHEPPARD, P. M. 1959a. *Brit. med. Bull. 15*, 134–139
29 —— 1959b. Natural Selection and some polymorphic characters in man; in ROBERTS, D. F. and HARRISON, G. A. (ed.) *Natural Selection in Human Populations*, Soc. for the Study of Human Biology, Symp. no. 2, London, 35–48

* Also published 1960 in LASKER, G. W. (ed.), *The processes of ongoing human evolution*, Detroit

30 SINGER, R., BUDTZ-OLSEN, O. E., BRAIN, P. and SAUGRAIN, J. 1957. *Am. J. Phys. Anth.* 15, 91–124
31 TINDALE, N. B. 1953. *Human Biol.* 25, 169–190
32 VOGEL, F., PETTENKOFER, H. J. and HELMBOLD, W. 1960. *Acta genet. Stat. med.* 10, 267–294
33 WIENER, A. S. 1942. *Science* 96, 407–408

SECTION IV ARTIFACTS

44 *Artifacts*

L. BIEK

STRICTLY, EVERY PIECE of evidence of early human activity should be categorized an artifact. In precise scientific terms this word denotes an accidental anomaly in a rigidly controlled experiment or observation, but in the present context the concept must be seen against a general background of human purpose impressed on inanimate material. While in this section of the book no special study deals with the modification of natural scenery, methods of construction or even craftsmanship, the implicit connection is clear enough and also extends into other sections of the book.

Thus prehistoric stone axes are linked with forest clearance,[1] certain baked clay objects with Roman reclamation works[2]—all are artifacts, whose effects have a direct bearing on pollen analysis and soil profile development. So have earthworks which in turn by their manner of construction determine the fate of smaller artifacts buried in them.[3] Perhaps the connection between the various aspects of a particular activity is shown most clearly in relation to something like the spectrographic analysis of bronzes. This cannot properly be considered in isolation from the nature of all the raw materials involved—ores, clay, wood or charcoal—or from the furnace characteristics, efficiency of crucibles and moulds, and forging skill.[4,5] In fact a piece of slag may in this sense be more significant than a dagger!

The recognition of a true artifact may be the most important task of all, especially for very early periods. Distinction between a natural and a man-made fire may be crucial,[6,7] and can be difficult; the same applies to problems of recognition in antiquity,[8] as for instance over the use of an iron ore as a building stone.[9] And the most obvious example is the establishment of true man himself as defined by his ability to make artifacts at all.[10]

Even when considered in this special sense, as small finds, the material must still be related first of all to its environment during burial. Any exposure of this kind produces in time an equilibrium between artifact and ambient medium which is disturbed on excavation,[18] and often constitutes evidence that may be easily and rapidly lost. The fragility of the principal object quite apart, if the object is simply considered for itself, certain details of structure which 'do not belong', or even altered features, may be overlooked and destroyed. Articles of wood and other organic material from water-logged deposits, as well as significant features contained in the attached soil, quickly suffer physical and chemical changes that alter their shape and nature unless protected from the atmosphere. As an overwhelming proportion of this material comes from

such deposits, at least in temperate climates, these considerations are of great importance, especially as they also involve clear evidence of the fate of the material during
and even before burial.[11,12]

Seen in isolation, artifacts present a variety of problems for scientific investigation.
Where the material remains essentially unaltered by working—as do stone, wood and
bone—its identification is best considered along with the natural environment and by
the same specialists. But usually some modification of the raw material occurs and the
preparation, in the widest sense, of the substance from which the artifact is made introduces further stages of appraisal. As the complexity of processes increases so specialties
are multiplied, yet equally we need all the more to consider the methods of preparing
and working the material in relation to one another.

Even in the simplest cases, such as the selection or crude extraction of fibres and their
fabrication into textiles, it is difficult to consider the two aspects separately. The use of
parchment little affects the issue, but leatherworking is clearly distinct from manufacture.[13] In the case of pottery—although still involving a relatively simple transformation by heat of a material that remains basically itself—there are a number of
different aspects ranging from the geological through the technicalities of the wheel to
the chemical effects of firing. Similarly the manufacture, application and setting properties of plasters and mortars require separate but integrated consideration.[14]

The production of totally new and 'unnatural' materials provides the climax in this
development. From the selection of raw materials to the final anneal, the making of a
glass vessel involves several highly specialized activities which all have to be taken into
account when devising a programme for investigation. This applies even more in the
case of metals where the extraction processes involve additional complexities, and
fabrication virtually provides another degree of freedom.

Certain features emerge from a consideration of the problem as a whole. Most specialist examinations have various tools and approaches in common. Thus the microscope is
universal, and indeed symbolic, as a first step. It suggests the number of materials
involved and defines the limits of the problem. This is clearly essential from the start.
Any one item, even when not a composite assembly, may require several specialists,
and there will be an optimum order in which they should see it. This order will depend
on whether the specific value of the artifact is intrinsic or relative, largely typological
or scientific, or lies in its use as dating evidence. But many of these factors will remain
obscure until after microscopic examination.

This may be followed by one or more of the many non-destructive tests now available,[15] before proper specialist investigation begins. Among these X-radiography has
proved to have a wide range of usefulness,[16] particularly marked in the case of 'iron
objects' of uncertain shape and doubtful stability.[16,17] There is here a vital distinction
between *revelation* of significant evidence and its (attempted) *exposure* by some form of
'cleaning'. It is theoretically impossible to return to the original surface by any cleaning
method. Radiography and similar techniques can almost always provide the required
information, and more simply and quickly, without removing any evidence which
might come to be regarded as valuable in the future. Any cleaning must always be to

some extent both destructive and subjective. This clearly indicates how intimately examination is related to conservation in almost all cases. While the latter introduces fresh aspects[18] it is entirely dependent on the former. On the other hand, conservation in the widest sense must be a primary factor in decisions from the start wherever there is any risk of losing evidence by exposure.

Results of specialist investigations on artifacts are most useful in separate reports, by the specialists, rather than as extracts quoted in the main text. Even when it must be restricted to a short note, the specialist contribution should be clearly recognizable and unedited, otherwise its value may be considerably reduced, to the detriment of future work. When no scientific examination is possible, at least a brief specialist description should be sought. Specialist reports on artifacts have been systematically abstracted since 1934.[19-21]

At the same time, all scientific evidence from artifacts, and indeed from all other aspects, of any one site greatly benefits by co-ordination at a scientific level. It is now widely accepted that, to ensure its full recognition, all material should be submitted to specialist examination. But the significance of any one artifact may not be clear even to the specialist until he knows about all the others. Precise distinctions—as for instance between various 'slags', over-fired pottery and certain forms of lava, which bear a family resemblance to each other—may become vital and require further work. However, the principal advantage of such co-ordination lies in its provision of an over-all scientific picture which to everyone concerned is of far greater value than the algebraic sum of the individual features.

REFERENCES

1 IVERSEN, J. 1954. *Arch. Newsletter*, May, 8; *Ill. Lond. News*, 1st May, 722; and see p. 141 above
2 RIEHM, K. 1961. *Antiquity* 35, 181–91
3 JEWELL, P. A. 1958. *Adv. Sci.* 14, 165–72. See also [31] p. 112 above
4 COGHLAN, H. H. 1956. *Notes on the Prehistoric Metallurgy of Copper and Bronze in the Old World*, Oxford
5 —— 1960. *Sibrium* 5, 145–52
6 OAKLEY, K. P. 1955a. *Proc. Third Pan-African Congr. on Prehistory*, London, 385–6
7 —— 1955b. *Proc. Prehist. Soc.* 21, 36–48
8 CHILDE, V. G. 1956. *Piecing Together the Past*, London, 162–3
9 FOX, LADY (A.) 1957. *Trans. Devon Assn. Adv. Sci. Lit. Art*, 89, 33 and 73–5
10 OAKLEY, K. P. 1949. *Man the Toolmaker*, London
11 BIEK, L. 1959. In RICHARDSON, K. M. *Arch. J.* 116, 107–9
12 —— 196–. In RAHTZ, P. A. *Chew Valley Lake*, London
13 WATERER, J. W. 1956. In SINGER, C. (ed.), *History of Technology*, London, II, 147–90
14 DAVEY, N. 1961. *A History of Building Materials*, London
15 HALL, E. T. 1959. *Archaeometry* 2, 43–52; HINSLEY J. F. 1959 *Non-Destructive Testing*, London; Moss, A. A. 1954. *Museum Techniques: The Application of X-Rays, Gamma-Rays, U. V. and I. R. Rays to the Study of Antiquities*, London
16 BIEK, L. 1963. *Archaeology and the Microscope*, London

17 LOOSE, L.; KOZLOWSKI, R. 1960. *Studs. Conserv.* 5, 85–8; 89–101
18 PLENDERLEITH, H. J. 1956. *The Conservation of Antiquities and Works of Art*, Oxford
19 STOUT, L. and GETTENS, R. J. (ed.) 1932–42. *Technical Studies in the Field of the Fine Arts*, Harvard
20 GETTENS, R. J. and USILTON, B. M. (ed.) 1955. *Abstracts of Technical Studies in Art and Archaeology, 1943–1952*, Washington
21 International Institute for Conservation of Historic and Artistic Works From 1955. *Abstracts of the Technical Literature on Archaeology and the Fine Arts*

45 A Statistical Analysis of Flint Artifacts

A. BOHMERS

FOR AN ADEQUATE SURVEY of the large number of artifacts usually found on a Palaeolithic, Mesolithic or even Neolithic site the use of statistical methods is essential. Such methods are particularly important in the comparison of large assemblages from a number of sites belonging to the same culture and of the utmost value if one wishes to compare two groups of sites belonging to different cultures.

For the study of Upper Palaeolithic, Mesolithic and *Bandkeramik* sites of north-west Europe the author uses the statistical method described below.

This method is based on the comparison of the percentages of a number of clearly defined types of artifact, combined with the mean measurements of these types. The whole is worked graphically into a series of vertical histograms, which are placed alongside one another (Figs. 67, 68).

A histogram of this type has the following advantages over the cumulative graph, which has often been used:

(1) Several sites can be indicated clearly and simultaneously. Sometimes entire cultures can even be compared (Fig. 67). A cumulative graph can combine a maximum of only four sites.

(2) The percentages of the types of artifact, the dimensions of the artifacts and their indices can all be combined; this is impossible on a cumulative graph.

(3) A histogram is 'open': one can alter the number of types and their measurements; a cumulative graph is 'closed'.

(4) The percentages of the various types can be read more easily.

Flint artifacts can be measured in many ways; for example length, breadth and thickness, or ratio of length to breadth; or angles such as the angle of the cutting edge of a scraper or graver; or the height of the scraper-edge. Some measurements are important in one culture or group of sites, others in another.

The application of this method in the study of a great deal of highly diverse material from many cultures belonging to different parts of Europe has enabled the formation of a picture of the full possibilities of this method.

Thus, for example, we know that the height of the scraper-edge is an important measurement in the *Bandkeramik* culture; that the size of the scraper-angle can be used to divide Upper Palaeolithic and Epi-Palaeolithic cultures; that the measurement of the graver-angle is generally important in the Palaeolithic; that the breadth of the cutting-edge of a graver is an important measurement in the Perigordian and that the index $\frac{\text{Length}}{\text{Breadth} \times \text{Thickness}} \times 100$ gives particularly interesting results when applied to Mesolithic blades.

The raw material used certainly influences the measurements of the artifacts, and a good gauge of its quality is the size of the unbroken blades, indicated on each histogram. Long, narrow blades, for example, indicate high-quality flint. In several cases it has been found that Palaeolithic peoples went to great trouble to search for and select a particular sort of material which they were used to working with. Thus the Hamburgians searched laboriously for the flint of superior quality found only spasmodically in the north Netherlands and so extended the Magdalenian tradition, while the bearers of the Tjongerian in the north Netherlands used the flint of poorer quality, thus extending the Azilian tradition.

The first requirement for the preparation of a diagram is a list of the various types to be defined. For obvious reasons it is strongly recommended that different investigators choose their types in consultation with one another. However certain types inevitably belong to particular regions and cultures; the list given in Fig. 67 represents the Upper Palaeolithic of continental north-west Europe, that in Fig. 68 the Mesolithic of the same area.

The types given in the main graphs are listed below, each with its graph number and a brief description which is not intended as a full definition of the type, but merely as a statement of the most important criteria used to distinguish it. We also give for each type a description of the measurements which are diagrammed in the supplementary graphs.

UPPER PALAEOLITHIC (Fig. 67)

Points type B (1). See description p. 475.

Gravette points (3). I formerly[1] grouped all points made from blades with one straight, curved or angular steeply retouched side under the heading of Gravette points. I now believe that they can profitably be subdivided.

These implements are, in my opinion, points rather than knives. It appears best to employ the term Gravette point, first introduced by Breuil, for the long, slender, more or less symmetrical examples, with a straight or nearly straight back. On these the point is normally situated near or on the long axis.

Chatelperron points are broader, and have a strongly curved back. Since this name has always been used for the larger implements of this type, I would suggest that Chatelperron points less than 50 mm in length be designated as *micro-Chatelperron points* or *Tjonger points* (2). This seems necessary because one finds in various cultures many examples which are so small (e.g. between 30 and 40 mm) that the name Chatelperron point would hardly be applied to them; and yet they correspond exactly to Chatelperron points in form. Indeed, many of these were found at the type-site of Chatelperron itself.

I would also suggest that points of Chatelperron or Tjonger type of crescentic form, that is, with a more regularly curved back and two distinctly pointed ends, be termed *Azilian points* (4).

Creswell points (5). In the Creswellian, and at the related sites, in the Netherlands, such as Neer II, we find points similar to Tjonger points, but with a single angle on the back. For these I propose the name Creswell points (5), after the sites at Creswell Crags.

Cheddar points (6). Implements similar to the Tjonger points, but with two angles on the back, were found especially at the site of Zeyen in the Netherlands. A site with an industry corresponding to it in many respects was found at Gough's Cave near Cheddar in the west of England. Since the main concentration of sites yielding such points appears to be in that region, I propose the name Cheddar points. Other sites with this type have been discovered in north Germany and in south Belgium.

Shouldered points (7, 8) (Ger.: *Kerbspitzen*; Fr.: *pointes à cran atypiques*). The retouch of the upper part of the point may or may not meet the retouch of the shoulder. There may be retouch at or near the base of the blade opposite the shoulder. In addition to the shoulder there may be one or more 'hafting notches'. The notching and the shoulder may appear on the bulbar face or on the reverse face. The retouch of the point and of the notch may appear either on the left or on the right edge; usually they are on the same edge (type I) (7) but occasionally on opposite edges (type II) (8). The implement is made on a blade.

Tanged points (9). (Ger.: *Stielspitzen*; Fr.: *pointes pédonculées*).

Gravers (11–16). Gravers are here classified primarily according to the form of the worked end rather than according to the position of the cutting-edge in relation to the long axis.

On most gravers the worked end is either blunted by retouch or simply broken. This appears to me to be more important (at least for our material) than whether the cutting-edge is found on or near the long axis (median graver; *Mittelstichel*) or eccentrically (*burin d'angle*; *Eckstichel*). An initial classification according to the form of the worked end can be carried out easily and objectively while the distinction between median gravers and angle gravers is often somewhat subjective because of the frequent occurrence of intermediate forms which are not easily assignable to one or the other category. The median graver-angle graver classification is however retained as a secondary division if only because it is almost universally used in the literature.

Thus we have the following types:

1. Gravers with a broken (or flaked-off) worked end, in short: removed-end or AA-gravers (11, 12) (Fr.: *Burin dièdre*).

2. Gravers with a blunted or retouched upper end, in short: blunted-end or RA-gravers (13, 14) (Fr.: *burin sur troncature retouchée*).

3. Gravers with a graver facet which does not descend from a previously prepared, broken or retouched end, but from an ordinary, unworked, blade or flake edge (or, rarely, from the striking platform). In this type of graver the graver-facet sometimes runs along the length of one edge of the flake, and not, as in most other graver types, at an angle to the edge. The name plane graver, single blow graver (Ger.: *Seitenstichel*), has accordingly come into use. We should like to call this type A-graver (15).

The gravers in Group 2 are often also called single blow gravers (Ger.: *Einschlagstichel*); those in Group 1, double blow gravers (Ger.: *Zweischlagstichel*). I prefer to discontinue the use of these terms, since the classification into single and double blow gravers is not really correct. Gravers are most often made by striking off a series of flakes to form the cutting-edge.

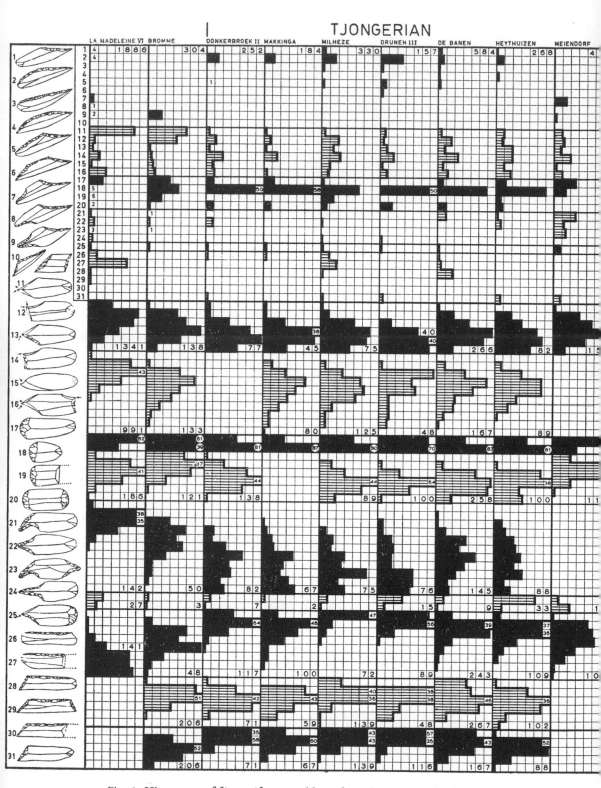

Fig. 67 Histograms of flint artifact assemblages from the Upper Palaeolithic of NW Europe.

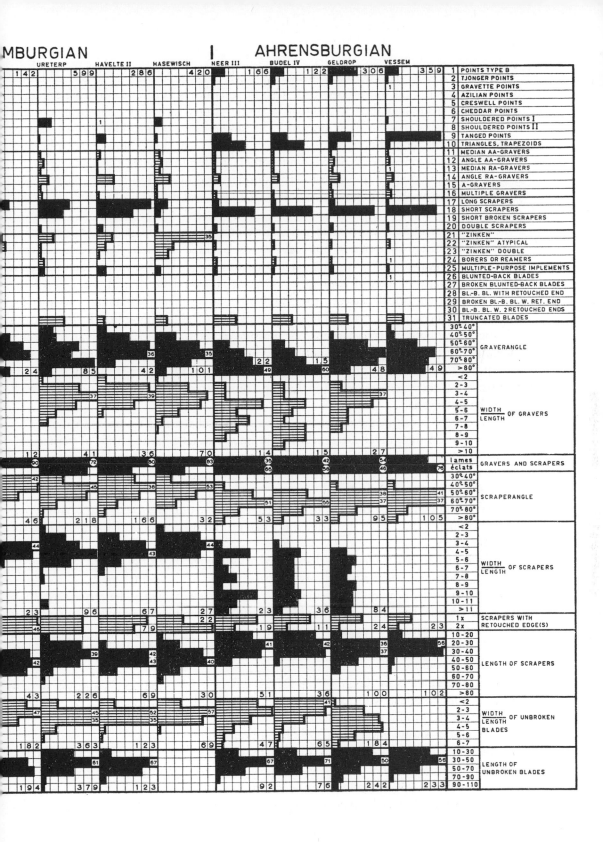

The cutting-edge is often resharpened by fresh graver-blows. The so-called double blow gravers are thus not produced by two graver-blows, but rather by first breaking the original blade and then striking off a single graver facet from the broken edge. They are therefore single blow gravers. The single-blow double-blow nomenclature gives rise to much confusion. Some observers use the term single blow gravers because they show only one graver blow, while others prefer to reserve the same term for gravers with a retouched upper end. Others understand by the term single blow graver the type`which we call A-gravers, without an upper end that is broken off, retouched or blunted.

No special treatment is given to polyhedric and/or prismatic gravers, which are in any case rare in our material. In our region most of these are merely core-gravers with a number of graver blows coming off the cutting-edge, but essentially belonging in Group 1. A separate classification of these gravers would be difficult because of the many forms transitional between these and other types. One would have to specify, for example, how many graver blows descend from the cutting-edge. In many cases it is merely a question of resharpened or massive gravers. It seems preferable to specify the nature of the resharpening or polyhedry in each individual case. We give therefore sometimes the number of graver facets descending from the cutting-edge, and also the number of earlier graver facets (no longer connected with the cutting-edge) which are to be observed.

Gravers with a retouched upper end can also be resharpened by fresh retouch. This is easily seen on the graver facet, which will have lost its negative bulb of percussion.

Core-gravers are often difficult to recognize, since there is every degree of transition between gravers deliberately made on a core and ordinary cores which have been utilized as cutting or graving implements.

They are not given in the graph, so as to avoid introducing too great a subjective element which would have an undue influence on the proportions of the more exactly definable types.

Multiple gravers (16) have more than one working edge on a single implement. These working edges can belong to gravers of the same or of different types.

Scrapers (17–20). Scrapers are divided into *long scrapers* (17), with a length greater than twice the width, *short scrapers* (18), with a length-width ratio of less than 2:1, and *short broken scrapers* (19). *Double scrapers* (20) are also counted. Scrapers with gravers or *Zinken* or with notches, or with the end opposite the scraping-edge blunted, are counted as multiple-purpose tools.

For all the scrapers the angle of the scraper-edges is measured as well as the length along the long axis, the width at right angles to it, and the thickness, given in groups as indicated on the graph. On double scrapers the angles of both scraping-edges are given. The graph also shows the percentage of retouched scraper-edges.

Zinken (21–23). As Rust demonstrated, these are not borers but implements for working antler and bone. The beak-like projection is appropriately large and thick, with a triangular or plano-convex cross-section. On *typical Zinken* (21) the beak is rather long and distinctly curved; on *atypical Zinken* (22) it may be more or less straight, and is sometimes so worn down by use that no curvature remains. In the sites one often finds *double Zinken* (23).

Borers and Reamers (24). True borers, with straight boring points, usually slightly (but sometimes heavily) retouched on the reverse face, are very rare on our sites. Here are also included the reamers (Fr.: *alésoirs*).

Multiple-purpose implements (25). Gravers with scrapers, with *Zinken*, with notches, or with blunted or retouched end opposite the graver working edge, are counted as multiple-purpose implements.

Blunted-back blades (26–30). See p. 478 for description.

Truncated blades (31).

MESOLITHIC (Fig. 68).

Points Type A (2) *and B* (1). The points that we distinguish as Type A and Type B are mostly asymmetrical and have always one steeply retouched edge. In the points of the Type A the edge-retouch extends to the base. In the points of the Type B it does not; the retouch stops short of the base, and the unretouched portion of the edge often makes a more or less distinct angle with the retouched portion. Absence of the angle does not, however, remove the point from Type B, as long as there is an unretouched portion of the edge. On neither of these types is there ever basal retouch. In both types of points the lower end may be a narrow or naturally pointed end, or it may be broad, for example a broken-off blade end. In the latter case the point will be tend to be triangular in form. There is, however, never a retouched base. This permits the more triangular points to be distinguished at once from Tardenoisian points. The larger and wider points of the Type B have often been classified with the Zonhoven points. In sites transitional between Palaeolithic and Mesolithic, points longer than 30 mm are counted as Palaeolithic types (see description, pp. 470–1) and shorter than 30 mm as Mesolithic types.

Points Type C (3) (Tardenoisian points; Ger.: *Tardenoisspitzen*; Fr.: *Pointes de Tar-denois*). Points of Type C are more or less symmetrical. They are triangular, with a straight or somewhat concave base which is always retouched. Basal retouch may also occur on the bulbar face. Retouch may also occur on one or both of the edges.

Sauveterrean points (4). Points of this kind sometimes have both ends intentionally worked to a point, and they are also retouched on both edges.

Double points (5). Two intentionally pointed ends also occur on the double points with surface retouch (Ger.: *Doppelspitzen mit Oberflächenretusche*; Fr.: *pointes doubles à retouches empiétantes*; *feuilles de gui*). For the most part these have a very distinctive form, with one or two rather convex edges and one rather blunted or rounded point.

Leaf-shaped points (6). In the group of broader points we include the leaf-shaped points (Ger.: *blattförmige Spitzen*; Fr.: *pointes foliacées*). They are more or less symmetrical, with the point on the longitudinal axis, and have a rounded lower end. They occur with or without surface retouch.

Fig. 68 Histograms of flint artifact assemblages from the Mesolithic of NW Europe (see over).

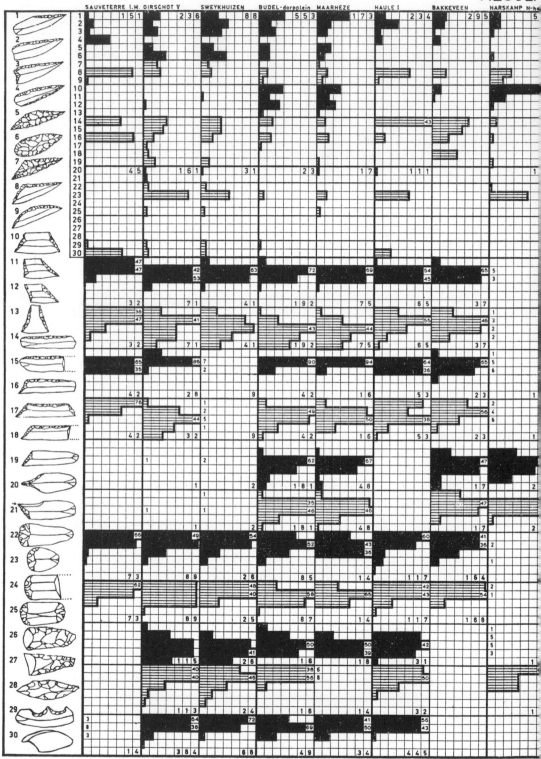

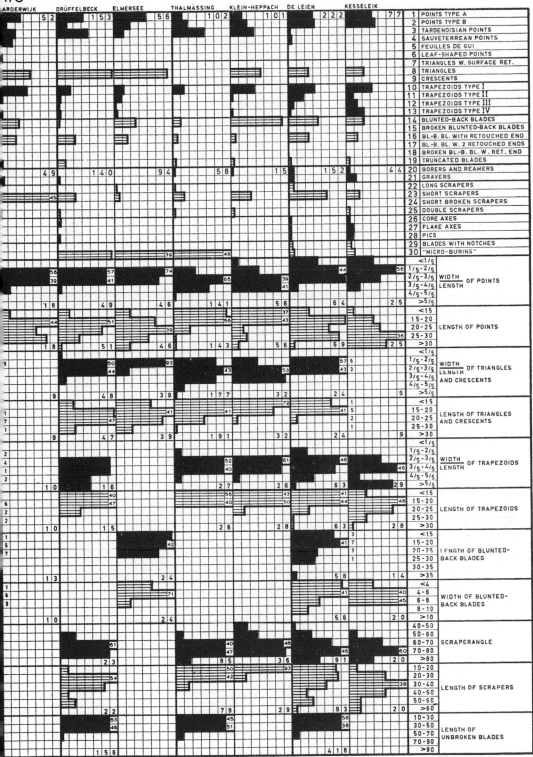

Column headers (left to right): ARDERWIJK, DRÜFFELBECK, ELMERSEE, THALMÄSSING, KLEIN-HEPPACH, DE LEIEN, KESSELEIK

1	POINTS TYPE A
2	POINTS TYPE B
3	TARDENOISIAN POINTS
4	SAUVETERREAN POINTS
5	FEUILLES DE GUI
6	LEAF-SHAPED POINTS
7	TRIANGLES W. SURFACE RET.
8	TRIANGLES
9	CRESCENTS
10	TRAPEZOIDS TYPE I
11	TRAPEZOIDS TYPE II
12	TRAPEZOIDS TYPE III
13	TRAPEZOIDS TYPE IV
14	BLUNTED-BACK BLADES
15	BROKEN BLUNTED-BACK BLADES
16	BL.-B. BL. WITH RETOUCHED END
17	BL.-B. BL. W. 2 RETOUCHED ENDS
18	BROKEN BL.-B. BL. W. RET. END
19	TRUNCATED BLADES
20	BORERS AND REAMERS
21	GRAVERS
22	LONG SCRAPERS
23	SHORT SCRAPERS
24	SHORT BROKEN SCRAPERS
25	DOUBLE SCRAPERS
26	CORE AXES
27	FLAKE AXES
28	PICS
29	BLADES WITH NOTCHES
30	"MICRO-BURINS"

WIDTH/LENGTH OF POINTS: <1/5, 1/5-2/5, 2/5-3/5, 3/5-4/5, 4/5-5/5, >5/5

LENGTH OF POINTS: <15, 15-20, 20-25, 25-30, >30

WIDTH/LENGTH OF TRIANGLES AND CRESCENTS: <1/5, 1/5-2/5, 2/5-3/5, 3/5-4/5, 4/5-5/5, >5/5

LENGTH OF TRIANGLES AND CRESCENTS: <15, 15-20, 20-25, 25-30, >30

WIDTH/LENGTH OF TRAPEZOIDS: <1/5, 1/5-2/5, 2/5-3/5, 3/5-4/5, 4/5-5/5, >5/5

LENGTH OF TRAPEZOIDS: <15, 15-20, 20-25, 25-30, >30

LENGTH OF BLUNTED-BACK BLADES: <15, 15-20, 20-25, 25-30, 30-35, >35

WIDTH OF BLUNTED-BACK BLADES: <4, 4-6, 6-8, 8-10, >10

SCRAPERANGLE: 40-50, 50-60, 60-70, 70-80, >80

LENGTH OF SCRAPERS: 10-20, 20-30, 30-40, 40-50, 50-60, >60

LENGTH OF UNBROKEN BLADES: 10-30, 30-50, 50-70, 70-90, >90

478

ARTIFACTS

Triangles (7, 8). Triangles are divided into *triangles with surface retouch* (7) and *ordinary triangles*. In both types there must be three distinctly worked angles. It is not always easy to distinguish rather long and symmetrical triangles with a basal angle approaching a right angle from Tardenoisian points. In such cases the thickness becomes a criterion. Tardenoisian points show no great variation in their thickness at the base, which is usually thin to facilitate shafting. With the triangles, on the contrary, the thickness at the base is often much greater at the angle with the retouched side than it is on the angle with the unretouched side.

Triangular implements with one natural end which is not deliberately pointed, i.e. without three clearly defined angles, are not counted as triangles, but as blunted-back blades with retouched ends (see below).

Crescents (9) (Ger.: *Kreisabschnitte*; Fr.: *segments de cercle*). Crescents always have two distinctly worked pointed ends and an arched back.

We suggest dropping the terms *trapeze, Zonhoven point with basal retouch,* and *quer-schneidige Pfeilspitzen* and substituting for all these the name *trapezoids.* We found it impossible, for example, to separate Zonhoven points with basal retouch from trapezes.

Trapezoids (10–13). The trapezoids are most readily subdivided by regarding them purely geometrically, orienting them so that the longer unretouched edge forms the horizontal base. Then we have in the first instance those with a width greater than their height, and secondly those with a height greater than their width. The trapezoids with a greater length than height can be subdivided into *trapezoids with two acute basal angles* I (10), *trapezoids with one or two basal right angles* II (11), and *trapezoids with one obtuse basal angle* III (12), The trapezoids with a height greater than their width are called *narrow trapezoids* IV (13). This gives four clear and easily distinguishable varieties of trapezoids.

Blunted-back blades (14–18). (Ger.: *Messerchen*; Fr.: *lamelles à dos abattus*). Blunted-back blades[14] may or may not have straight or diagonal retouch; if so they belong to a distinct group, *blunted-back blades with one* (15) or *two* (16) *retouched ends.* Some of these have a more or less triangular form, with the diagonally retouched end distinctly broader than the other end, which is usually the natural end of a blade. The bulb of percussion was thus in the direction of the diagonally retouched end. *Broken blunted-back blades* are also counted. They are divided into those with (18) and without (15) retouched ends.

Truncated blades (19) are classified as in the Palaeolithic.

Borers (20). As borers we have grouped all implements with a borer-like form, including the so-called reamers (Ger.: *Räumer*; Fr.: *alésoirs*). In the Mesolithic we find many atypical borer-like points; these are all counted together.

Gravers (21). Since they are rather rare in the Mesolithic the gravers are counted together.

Scrapers (22–25). The scrapers are classified as in the Palaeolithic.

Core axes (26), *flake axes* (27) and *triangular implements* (or *picks*) (28). These implements are not further differentiated in the present publication, partly because we are here concerned principally to explain the method, but also because they are rare in the sites here described.

Notched blades (29) are classified as in the Palaeolithic. It should be noted that there are often small notched blades which can be regarded as unsuccessful products of the 'micro-burin technique'. For the most part they have a small but deep notch on one side just above the bulb of percussion.

Micro-burins (30) are counted but not further distinguished.

If we wish to include here the Upper Palaeolithic of France we have to add several types to this list. The type-list for the Mesolithic is fairly complete however; for central France we would have to add a *pointe de Vielle*, a *pointe à recurrence basale* and a *trapezoid with surface retouch*.

In the Palaeolithic and Mesolithic diagrams (Figs. 67, 68) one square represents a value of 5 per cent. Each type is converted into a percentage and plotted.

In the Mesolithic diagram (Fig. 68) all microliths (types 1 to 19) are first calculated as percentages. Next the macroliths are calculated as percentages, and these are added to the microliths. In the case of a site from which only the microlithic assemblage has been collected, a statistical comparison with another, complete site is impossible unless the microliths from the latter are calculated separately. The microlithic percentages are generally the most important characteristics of a Mesolithic site.

Dimensions of length, breadth and thickness are always taken at their maximal values, on the main axes of the implement. The angle of a scraper edge is measured not on the finely retouched cutting-edge, but on the surface of one of the coarser central retouch scars. The graver angle is always measured at right-angles to the graver edge, and not more than 10 mm from it. The measurements of angles are grouped at 10° intervals; this diminishes the subjective differences which always occur to a certain extent in measuring angles.

The absolute number of measured implements is always indicated in the diagram, and must always be borne in mind, as on it the relative significance of the diagram largely depends.

The implements are best measured with an instrument of the type illustrated in *Palaeohistoria 5*, Fig. 1; here the dimensions of each individual artifact are not determined separately. With sufficient time to study a site, each artifact can be measured separately and the measurements processed by an electronic computor specially programmed for the purpose. No further calculations need be made as the machine automatically computes the reproduced histograms, and many others also, if one so wishes. All the data relevant to one site can thus be stored on a roll of tape five inches in diameter.

Figs. 67 and 68 are examples of the results of the statistical method, representing a number of assemblages from Upper Palaeolithic and Mesolithic sites in the Netherlands and Belgium.

The Mesolithic of continental north-west Europe can be divided into a number of groups. One of these is characterized by the presence of microliths with surface retouch (5–7), either without trapezoids (10–12) (Oirschot V; Schweykhuizen), or with trapezoids (Budel; Maarheze). This group of sites stretches into the Paris Basin and the Ruhr region; the centre however, with the most numerous and the largest sites, is in the south Netherlands, in Brabant. Radiocarbon dates are: Oirschot V, $7,970\pm75$ (Gro. 1559); Ermelo, $7,775\pm60$ (Gro. 1637). These sites are therefore *not* of Neolithic age, as has been supposed.

Another group, O (Haule I; Bakkeveen), stretches over the north Netherlands and north-west Germany. This group also shows a phase with trapezoids and a phase without. The many blunted-back blades and small microliths are typical. Radiocarbon dates for this group are: Haule I, $7,525 \pm 200$ (Gro. 128); Waskemeer, $7,435 \pm 120$ (Gro. 615); Siegerswoude, $7,720 \pm 70$ (Gro. 1509); Duurswoude I, $7,460 \pm 100$ (Gro. 1173); Drouwener Zand, $7,635 \pm 90$ (Gro. 1513).

A third group stretches over the Veluwe, the centre of the Netherlands. This group (Harskamp; Harderwijk) contains particularly numerous trapezoids.

Yet another example is a Mesolithic group from south Germany (Klein-Heppach; Thalmässig) with, among other things, particularly broad microliths. In contrast, the classical Sauveterrian of Le Martinet Sauveterre-la-Lémance, is characterized by particularly small microliths.

It would take far too long here to compare all characteristics of these Mesolithic groups point by point against each other. This is quite possible however with the help of the diagrams.

The sites Kesseleik and the Leien, in the south and the north of the Netherlands respectively, belong to a kind of Maglemosian-Campignian with some axes and many microliths, among which trapezoids of type IV occur. Radiocarbon dates for the Leien are $6,960 \pm 140$ (Gro. 68) and $6,990 \pm 65$ (Gro. 1683).

The Mesolithic of Europe is, in my opinion, most complex; to arrive at a division into groups, a great number of sites must first be counted and measured in this manner. Sometimes the differences between the groups are best established with the help of the measurements, sometimes with the help of type-percentages, frequently however with both. Sometimes, also, local differences can be better established with the help of the measurements.

A number of Late-Palaeolithic sites are represented on the diagram, Fig. 68. The Hamburgian, which stretches over the north Netherlands and north-west Germany, is found below, and therefore is earlier than, the Alleröd oscillation; the Tjongerian, which we find in north Belgium, the entire Netherlands, and a culture closely connected with this in north and west Germany, is nearly always found in the Alleröd oscillation; the Ahrensburgian ($\pm$ 8,800 BC), which stretches over the Netherlands and north Germany, is generally found just above the Alleröd oscillation.

The Tjongerian contains Tjonger and Azilian points; the Hamburgian and the Late Magdalenian shouldered points and the Ahrensburgian tanged points. The Brommian, a Danish culture from the Alleröd, contains tanged points of the Lyngby type.

The Hamburgian and the Late Magdalenian have more long than short scrapers, whilst the other cultures mentioned above have more short than long. This coincides with the fact, also deducible from the diagram, that the scrapers and gravers of the first-mentioned cultures are mainly obtained from blades, while those of the latter-mentioned cultures are mainly obtained from flakes.

In the two first-mentioned cultures, and in the Brommian, the scraper-angles and the graver-angles are sharper than in the others.

The Hamburgian has many typical *Zinken*, which contrasts with the other groups, with the exception of the Late Magdalenian, which has a few.

In the Late Magdalenian and the Hamburgian the blades, the scrapers and the gravers are narrower, in terms of their breadth/length ratios, than in the other groups.

There are also differences between the Ahrensburgian and the Tjongerian, as there are between the different groups within the Ahrensburgian. For example, compare the graphs of Neer III and Budel IV with those of Geldrop and Vessem. The first two have many triangles and trapezoids, fewer B-points, fewer gravers and shorter scrapers than the latter two. Furthermore the gravers of Neer III and Budel IV are blunter than those of Geldrop and Vessem. This also applies to the variations within the Tjongerian. Thus the Donkerbroek-Makkinga variation differs considerably from that of Milheze-Drunen III of the south Netherlands, and these two differ again from the Heythuizen-de Baanen variation, also from the south Netherlands. The Milheze-Drunen III variation has very small implements with obtuse angles; the Donkerbroek-Makkinga variation has more scrapers than the Heythuizen-de Baanen variation in comparison with the gravers.

After studying a great deal of material from all parts of Europe in this manner, the author has come to the conclusion that an extended statistical method, in which use is also made of measurements and comparisons, promises important results in the study of the Palaeolithic, the Mesolithic and also some of the Neolithic cultures.

REFERENCES

1 BOHMERS, A. 1957. *Palaeohistoria* 5, 7–25
2 —— and WOUTERS, A. 1957. *Ibid.* 27–38
3 —— and BRUYN, A. 1958–59. *Ibid.* 6–7, 183–211
4 —— 1960. *Antiquités nationales et internationales* 3–4, 51–56
5 —— 1961. *Palaeohistoria* 8, 15–37
6 VERHEYLEWEGHEN, J. 1961. *Ibid.* 39–58

46 Petrological Examination

F. W. SHOTTON

ON PAGE 778 OF WILLIAM DUGDALE's *Antiquities of Warwickshire*, published in 1656, there is an excellent engraving of a small stone axe, shaped by chipping except for ground surfaces meeting at the cutting edge. It is stated to be in the possession of Sir Elias Ashmole, though it is apparently not now in the Ashmolean Museum. The illustration accompanies a reference to an earthwork at Oldbury, near Nuneaton, and Dugdale writes: 'On the North part of this Fort, have been found, by plowing, divers Flint stones, about four inches and a half in length, curiously wrought by grinding, or some such way, into the form here exprest: the one end shaped much like the edge of a Pole-Axe, which makes me conjecture that, considering there is no flint in all this part of the Countrie, nor within more than xl. miles from hence, they being at first so made by the native Britans, and put into a hole, boared through the side of a staff, were made use of for weapons, inasmuch as they had not then attained to the knowledge of working iron or brass to such uses.'

We have here, I think, not only the earliest recognition in Britain of a prehistoric stone implement but also the first use of petrology for deducing that the object had been imported from some considerable distance. From the sapient way Dugdale writes, one feels that he was able to recognize flint and that he knew it occurred in the Chalk of eastern England. Geological knowledge was so embryonic in his time that we cannot object that his 'more than forty miles' is actually not less than seventy-five.

Nevertheless we have to wait until this century before we find the petrological examination of stone objects becoming an important aid to archaeological deduction. One of the more famous pioneering examples was the demonstration by Dr H. H. Thomas that the circle of small stones (the 'blue stones') at Stonehenge came from Carn Meini in the Presely Mountains of Carmarthenshire.[10] Archaeologists since then have exercised their minds on the dual problems of what particular significance this stone had (we know it was also used for axe-making) and how the boulders were transported a distance which is 140 miles as the crow flies but certainly far longer as Early-Bronze Age man went.

It is only within the last twenty years that the petrological examination of small objects has been systematically pursued, prompted particularly by the Council for British Archaeology's investigation of stone axes. Under this scheme, a comprehensive account has been given for the counties of Cornwall, Devon, Somerset, Gloucester, Wiltshire, Dorset and Hampshire,[4,8,9] and interim accounts for Hereford, Shropshire, Worcester, Warwick and South Staffordshire [6,7] but there is also a steadily-accumulating store of knowledge about the rest of Britain which is not yet published. Slowly the detail is being filled in to the complex picture of axe-making factories and the dissemination of their products by trade during the Neolithic and Bronze Age. In the tools of earlier times, exact recognition of the nature of the rock is less rewarding, for in general

Palaeolithic man used local materials—flint where he could get it, though often from river or glacial gravels, but in default of this, chert from the Carboniferous Limestone or quartzite pebbles from the Bunter or glacial gravels.

It should not be thought that petrological examination is important only in the case of axes. It is useful for all tools, particularly for such objects as hones which were often made ·from highly-prized stone carried long distances. Querns, millstones, building stone and roofing slate are examples of other objects where understanding is enhanced if an exact knowledge of the rock is obtained.

The preparation of a microscope slide of a rock—a 'thin section'—follows practice which is standard in all departments of geology. Initially a thin slice is removed from the object by two parallel cuts of a diamond wheel. Inevitably this leaves a gap in the specimen which may be 4 mm wide and 15–20 mm deep, but this is a price which has to be paid if a thin section is to be made. The injury can be filled with plaster and if painted skilfully it may be difficult to detect that anything has been removed. Indeed, the writer has on more than one occasion received from museum curators axes for sectioning which had already been so treated.

The cut-out rock fragment is smoothed on one side which is then attached to a glass slide by a transparent cement such as Canada Balsam or 'Lakeside'. The rock is now rubbed away with suitable abrasives until it is only 0·03 mm thick, when a cover glass is cemented upon it. Thus a thin section is prepared but the reader will appreciate that this bald account conceals a considerable amount of technical skill and experience on the part of the preparator. At this thickness the majority of the minerals found in rocks are transparent, some colourless, some with typical colours, and only a few still remain opaque. Moreover, as the section can be looked at in ordinary, plane-polarized and cross-polarized light and the investigator can use various accessories of the petrological microscope, mineral identification can nearly always be made with precision. Not only, then, can a rock be placed into its fundamental class of igneous, sedimentary, meta-morphic or pyroclastic (and often this is impossible on simple examination by eye), but the further identification of the minerals present, their shape and size, relative proportions and textural relations to each other, gives to a rock a uniqueness which can be described and recognized when it is met with again in another specimen. Reference to the illustration of a thin section (Plate XXIII) will show how many distinctive features it has, even when the reproduction takes no account of colour.

THE PETROLOGICAL EXAMINATION OF STONE AXES

The nation-wide survey of stone axes has not, so far, attempted to differentiate those made of flint. A thin section of this rock is quite distinctive, but we do not need such a section to tell us that the material is flint. On the other hand, no one has yet found micro-characteristics which will enable us to separate the flints of Yorkshire from those of Lincolnshire, Suffolk, Kent, Sussex or Antrim, still less to be more precise in localization, so that thin section work in this direction is unrewarding.

The case of the non-flint axes and hammers (often loosely spoken of as 'stone' axes) is quite different. Up to the present, about 21 petrological categories or 'Groups' have

been defined, with some further subdivided. Not all these groups are of equal significance, for a few have been based on only two or three similar specimens in a restricted
region and such a group may not be recognized further afield as work extends over the
country. Most of the groups, however, include many examples and their number
steadily increases as the area of investigation widens.

THE PRODUCTS OF KNOWN AXE-FACTORIES

Before the idea of petrological examination had really started, Hazzledine Warren had
discovered the litter of flakes and rough-out cores at Graig Lwyd and recognized that
it marked a Neolithic factory site. Since then other working sites have been located
elsewhere. To the rocks used at these factories, group numbers have been allocated,
as follows:

VI.   Great Langdale, Westmorland.
VII.   Graig Lwyd, near Penmaenmawr, Caernarvonshire.
IX.   Tievebulliagh and Rathlin Island, Antrim.
XXI.   Mynydd Rhiw, Lleyn, Caernarvonshire.

There are now also known to be a number of working sites around Scafell in various
Ordovician ashes not unlike but still not the same as Group VI.

The *Langdale* rock is a fine-banded, epidotized andesitic ash—the result of a shower
of volcanic dust into the Ordovician sea. In the writer's opinion it produces the finest
of all axes and it was widely disseminated by trade throughout the land. So highly
prized was the rock that numerous working places were set up on the screes below the
outcrop of the stratum, itself about two thousand feet above sea level.[1]

The *Graig Lwyd* factory is also now known to be a series of working sites. The rock
in this case is igneous—to give it its technical name, an epidotized micro-granodiorite—
which congealed within the neck of an old volcano.

Mynydd Rhiw has only recently been discovered[2] and appears not to have been as
extensive as the two mentioned previously. Like Group VI, the rock is a compact
Ordovician volcanic ash but its details are very different from Langdale and there is
no possibility of confusion.

The factory sites in Antrim perhaps illustrate better than any others how carefully
prehistoric man chose the material for his tools. The rock at *Tievebulliagh* is a dark grey,
fine-textured, very hard stone of unmistakable appearance in thin section (Plate XXIIIc),
breaking rather like flint and restricted to a small outcrop—as well it might be in view
of the special way in which it arose. Everyone knows the Tertiary basalt flows of
Northern Ireland, typified by the Giant's Causeway, but fewer are aware that the lavas
flowed out when the region enjoyed a moist tropical climate, so that the tops of individual flows are often weathered into bright red laterite soil. These red surfaces of varying
thickness can be seen separating the flows. Now at Tievebulliagh a volcanic neck
pierces a succession of these lava flows, the neck being also filled with a plug of basalt.
The heat of this, when molten, could do nothing to the unweathered lava flows, but it
baked the red soils, in particular one thicker than the rest, and for a short distance the
neck produced this black flint-like rock which was so attractive to prehistoric man for

the purpose of axe-making. In more recent years another factory has been discovered at *Rathlin Island* and its products are indistinguishable from Tievebulliagh because exactly the same geological situation has been chosen and the end-product is therefore similar. Axes from these factories abound in Ireland but are also found, though in much reduced numbers, across the Irish Sea.[3]

PETROLOGICAL GROUPS OF UNDISCOVERED FACTORIES

There are bound to be numbers of implements made from the same rock and to which, therefore, a Petrological Group number can be given, even though no factory site is known. It is obvious also that, working from geological advice, it might be possible to pin-point the place from which the rock came and then to discover the working site. So far it has to be admitted that no success of this kind has yet been achieved but there is no doubt that it ultimately will be.

Group I is a most distinctive rock which in the past would have been simply called 'greenstone', but now 'uralitized gabbro'. It is the type of rock which we would expect in Cornwall and although examples of this axe have been found almost all over England, there is such an overwhelming preponderance of finds near Penzance that there can be no doubt of the approximate source. Because an exact match to the rock could not be found at any known outcrop, Keiller, Piggot and Wallis[4] suggested that the factory site was low-lying and had been drowned by the post-Neolithic rise of sea level. In these days of exploration of the sea-floor by skin divers, there is still a prospect of the site being found.

Group VIII is a fine rhyolitic ash much used for axes, particularly for many found in South Wales, but there is a strong suspicion that several closely similar rocks have been included in this group and the products of more than one factory, perhaps widely separated, may have been confused.

Group XII is the best example of a most distinctive rock—picrite—which has been matched exactly with a source.[7] It occurs in Hyssington parish in Montgomeryshire. How distinctive the rock is in its minerals and texture and how exactly it matches the parent source is apparent in Plate XXIIIa, b. We now know that there are two small out-crops of picrite separated by about a mile and indistinguishable from each other. At either or both the rock could have been worked by Bronze Age man, but from it he made only perforated axe-hammers by a process of pecking and grinding and to find the factory waste will be far more difficult than in such cases as Langdale or Graig Lwyd where thousands of flakes litter the site. It is significant that two implements with their perforations not yet finished have been found in the same parish as the alleged parent source.

Group XIII is 'preselite'—the well-known spotted dolerite from the Prescelly Hills which was used in the Stonehenge ring of smaller stones and also for a modest number of axes and axe-hammers. Although the parent outcrop is quite restricted, the site of the factory is still unknown.

Group XIV is a small one—only about eight axe-hammers have yet been put into this group—but the rock is so distinctive that we can be certain that a small factory worked a sill of camptonite in the Cambrian rocks of Griff, near Nuneaton.[6]

Group XV is a form of sandstone used extensively, mainly for axe-hammers and perforated adzes, and this is a good example of a rock which, though distinctive, occurs over such a large outcrop that we can do no more than suggest a source, or sources, in the southern part of the Lake District.[6]

Group XVIII is widespread, a distinctive quartz-dolerite which can be matched with some dykes in Scotland and north England but even more obviously with the Great Whin Sill which outcrops along more than a hundred miles of massive crags in Northumberland and Westmorland, in Teesdale and the Farne Islands. These great scars must have been a constant invitation to tool-making man but he had so much to choose from that his factory sites will be difficult to find.

Group XX is a coarse epidotized volcanic ash which is being recognized in increasing numbers now that work is being done in the north Midlands. Charnwood Forest is the probable parent source.[6]

OTHER USES FOR MICROSCOPICAL PETROLOGY

Hones have been in common use for sharpening steel since Roman times. June E. Morey and K. C. Dunham[5] have shown that amongst a collection of medieval whetstones in Yorkshire half are made from one type of rock, a fine-grained quartz-mica granulite, which they suggest came from Aberdeenshire. This indicates how carefully raw material was selected and the extent to which it was traded.

Querns and *millstones* need rocks of special characteristics—they must be made of hard minerals and yet they must have a limited proportion of softer grains or crystals which wear away to maintain a rough pitted surface on the stone. The grits of the Carboniferous formation appropriately enough known as the Millstone Grit, which occurs dominantly in Yorkshire, Lancashire, north Staffordshire and Derbyshire, is preeminently suitable in this country. The Romans certainly knew this, for petrologists constantly recognize this rock at sites far removed from the outcrops.

It is very obvious that the advice of the geologist will often be sought about the materials used in construction—*building stone, slates* and *natural tiles, tesserae, road metals* and so on. At times it is worthwhile making a thin section to look for special features of diagnostic significance, but in many cases it is the larger-scale features of bedding, grain size, colour and identification of contained fossils which are of more use.

Petrological examination need not be restricted to natural raw materials. Although comparatively little work has been done on *ceramics*, thin sections of pottery, bricks or tiles will reveal the size and nature of the gritty component of the clay and may enable conclusions to be drawn about the origin of this, whilst the mineralogy may give an indication of the temperature of kilning. The petrology of *slags*, too, is a highly specialized study, but exact identification of the crystalline part of these can indicate what product was being produced and perhaps what type of ore was being smelted.

Again, it is the trained mineralogist who will identify the minerals used in jewellery and suggest from where they might have come. Here he may well encounter extra-British imports. Particularly is this the case with amber which, in quantity, will always suggest physical links with the Baltic countries.

There are, of course, other cases of importation across the sea, particularly in and after the Roman occupation. The Romans brought in their most-prized ornamental stones, such as the imperial purple porphyry from Egypt, and they rather strangely had a predilection for slabs of basalt from the region of Niedermendig in the Eifel. In pre-Roman times, examples of sea commerce are less numerous, though the occurrence of northern Irish (Group IX) axes in England and Scotland has been noted. We occasionally meet axes of jadeite which probably are not British and the most unexpected case concerns a few axes rich in corundum (emery) which have been matched in Crete. Perhaps we are more prepared for such a conclusion after the evidence of the carved daggers at Stonehenge showing Minoan influence.

Finally it must be emphasized that the petrologist is engaged in a fascinating sort of detective work which can be used equally well to detect fraud (or perhaps one should say, to prevent misrepresentation, since archaeological fraud is seldom deliberate). Amongst the axes which are sent in from all sorts of collections or circumstances of finding, a small proportion look 'wrong'—their typology is non-British, or they are of exotic-looking stone. Petrological examination can sometimes indicate that the rock comes from a known distant source, and very often it can at least suggest that the raw material is most unlikely to be British. Amongst such dubious examples are specimens from museums where curating has been poor and labels which have become detached have been wrongly stuck on again, or private collections where the owner relies on his memory. When such specimens are dug up, it is reassuring to find how often they are in the garden of a house once occupied by the local doctor or parson who was an enthusiastic collector, but whose surviving relatives had little respect for his 'old junk'.

Nevertheless, the writer has met a few cases where the circumstances of discovery have been given in great detail, though usually at second-hand and certainly quite erroneously. One of these concerned a beautiful flint dagger or spear-head. The sister of the finder recalled the exact spot on the farm in Warwickshire where it had been ploughed up, yet it was made of an unusual finely-banded coloured flint which exactly matched the artifacts of the Ohio Indians and nothing else. One can cite also a block of sandstone carrying a Roman inscription, originally in a Birmingham garden, where the possibility of its being of local origin had to be balanced against the chance of its being an imported collector's piece. Petrological examination came down clearly on the side of the second possibility, for the thin section revealed fossil foraminifera which were identified as probably Miocene in age. The sandstone could not have been British, but it could easily have been Mediterranean. Last of all may be mentioned part of a 'stone' statue, typically Roman and found near to a known Roman site—but it showed the unmistakable texture and mineralogy of concrete and was undoubtedly a Victorian copy.

REFERENCES

1 BUNCH, B. AND FELL, C. 1949. *Proc. Prehist. Soc. 15*, 1
2 HOULDER, C. H. 1960. *Trans. Caern. Hist. Soc. 21*, 1-5
3 JOPE, E. M. 1953. *Ulster J. Arch. 15*, 31
4 KEILLER, A., PIGGOT, S. and WALLIS, F. S. 1941. *Proc. Prehist. Soc. 7*, 50

5 MOREY, J. E. and DUNHAM, K. C. 1953. *Proc. Yorks. Geo. Soc. 29*, 141
6 SHOTTON, F. W. 1959. *Proc. Prehist. Soc. 25*, 135
7 —— CHITTY, L. F. and SEABY, W. A. 1951. *Ibid. 17*, 159
8 STONE, J. F. S. and WALLIS, F. S. 1947. *Ibid. 13*, 47
9 —— —— 1951. *Ibid. 17*, 99
10 THOMAS, H. H. 1923. *Ant. J. 3*, 239

47 Some Aspects of Ceramic Technology

FREDERICK R. MATSON

THE POTTERY FOUND IN MOST archaeological sites that were occupied by man after he began to farm and to settle on the land has changed very little in its appearance since it was fired and used. Although most excavated vessels are broken or exist only as remnants in the form of one or more potsherds, they serve as important evidences of the people who made and used them. Sherds are little affected by burial in the earth—they endure while metals corrode and disintegrate, and objects made of bark, wood or skin decay. Pottery preserves in its shape, decoration and physical properties a permanent though very fragmentary record of some of man's activities. Therefore, it must be studied intensively if the archaeologist is to reclaim from it all that is possible of the record remaining in such objects, and of their associations with other materials, in his excavations of ancient villages and towns.

If the mineralogical, physical and chemical properties of pottery are selectively determined in the light of the archaeological problem being studied, information can be obtained about the raw materials selected and used by the potter, their treatment before being formed into pots, the manner of fashioning the vessels and of firing them, and perhaps the uses to which they were put. The role of the potter as the active and controlling agent in these procedures must be kept in mind, and the function of his products in his community cannot be overlooked. We are concerned with the analytical data of products made by man, data which will help us better to understand this man's culture. Each study increases our historical knowledge of technological developments in areas of the world where ceramic products have been manufactured through long periods of time.

It is not necessary to have available expensive equipment in well-arranged laboratories in order to undertake the basic technological examination of pottery and other ceramic objects. Careful observations by one understanding the ceramic processes of pottery forming and firing can produce valuable information of direct use in the archaeological study of the wares. In this paper simple procedures requiring little laboratory equipment will be discussed first, followed by examples of the spectacular results obtained with special analytical equipment. Although technological pottery studies are the subject of this discussion, it should be recognized that similar approaches can be used in the examination of other important ceramic materials used by man such as brick, glass, glaze, enamel, faience, pigments, cement and plaster.

A close examination of the interior and exterior surfaces of sherds and of freshly fractured cross-sections through body walls can tell much about the ware and its production if one has some understanding of the properties of clays and the changes that occur as the surface of a semi-dried vessel is worked to its final condition by the potter, and as the well-dried ware is fired. A hand lens or a low-power binocular micro-scope helps one see the details sought, especially if oblique lighting can be arranged so that shadows are cast which emphasize the surface striations and textural variations. It is desirable to examine all of the sherds excavated at a site in this manner, if possible, after they have been washed, catalogued and assembled as parts of restorable vessels. When the latter is not possible, they should be sorted as to wares and then grouped according to the vessel area from which they came—rims, bases, shoulders, handles, body pieces, etc. By examining the entire ceramic production in groupings one can most effectively evaluate the materials and select characteristic as well as unique items for more intensive study. It is misleading to choose a sample for further analysis unless the selection is made with a background knowledge of the variations within the site's ceramic spectrum. In this connexion an appreciation of elementary statistical procedures and methods of sampling are useful.

One further step is desirable for the ceramic examiner. He should have a practical knowledge of the local clays available to the potters, and in his off hours of relaxation at the dig he should have sought such clays, tempered them with water, considered their textural variations, and attempted to make simple pots from them. I have done this with some success in Iraq, Iran and the eastern United States, and have found that this experience helped me to understand the ancient potter at work as I studied his sherds.

In the first sortings it is helpful to check the broken edges for fracture patterns transverse and parallel to the body walls that might indicate how the vessels were formed. In a large collection of sherds it is usually possible to find a few whose fractures show evidence of the junction of the body walls and the base, the joining of coils of clay while building the walls, or the addition of a rim to the formed vessels. The absence of such breaks in the fabric does not necessarily show more than that the potter was skilful, yet it could, with small pots, indicate that each was formed from one lump of clay.

If a paddle and anvil technique was used in the final shaping of the vessel to compact its walls, round out its base and prevent serious cracks from forming as the pot dried, its use can sometimes be recognized by the slight depressions on the interior surface that were caused by the rounded anvil, and by paddle marks on the exterior. When a wooden paddle has a carved design on its surface or a piece of coarse textile has been wrapped around it as in some parts of North America and the Far East, to mention but two areas of the world, it is easy to recognize this technique. If a smooth paddle is used, however, the surface must be carefully examined. I have seen the walls of olive jars in the Lebanon thinned and the bases of water jugs in Afghanistan rounded by the use of the paddle and anvil, and have been impressed by the force of the blows given as well as by the tough resiliency of the clay. This technique has probably been used far more frequently in the past than has been recognized.

Ridgings and striations on the exterior and interior surfaces of body sherds and the finishing marks on both faces of basal sherds can indicate whether or not the vessel was formed on a potter's wheel. This is not a simple matter to determine when examin-ing sherds from the time period when the wheel was first being used as in the Uruk period in the ancient Near East—very roughly about 3,000 BC. It is possible to fashion a pot by hand and then add a wheel-turned rim as has been done in Upper Egypt in recent times. It is also possible to rework the surface of a partly dried vessel on a simple wheel or lathe, scraping off the surface irregularities. This treatment leaves parallel striations on the smoothed surface, scratch marks caused by the dragging of mineral inclusions along under the scraping tool as it moves across the slightly moist clay surface. Usually the interior of narrow-mouthed vessels is not as well finished as the exterior, and the basic techniques of forming the piece can often be seen there.

A slip is sometimes applied to the surface of jars and to one or both surfaces of bowls. If this is a red slip on a clay body that fires to a brown or yellow colour there is no trouble in recognizing it. Such slips appear on pottery in the Near East from the very earliest ceramic strata of simple agricultural villages that were occupied well before 4,000 BC. They were also common on pottery made in Europe and the Americas in later times. The red burning clay was available in the Near East on the mountain slopes, but it may have been enriched with abraded powder from soft ferruginous rocks, for well-worn fragments of such rocks are found in some of the excavations. Often, however, a yellow, tan or red surfacing is termed a slip when in reality its colour is due to a concentration of salts on the surface of the vessel or is caused by the wet hand of the potter as she smooths the surface of the piece she is fashioning. Wet smoothing concentrates the finest clay particles in a thin layer at the surface where they may develop a more intense colour when fired because the diluting effect of the coarser ingredients is masked by this fine-textured layer. Such a film, termed by Childe a 'self-slip', may be described by a hasty observer as an intentionally applied slip. If it cannot be determined whether or not a slip is present from the careful examination of a significant series of sherds and this information would be useful, then a thin section of a characteristic sherd, should be prepared. When it is examined under a petrographic microscope it will usually show whether or not there is a layer of foreign material on the surface.

Freshly fractured edges of sherds uncontaminated by adhering clay or lime deposits will show clearly the textural variations in the ware and the degree to which it has been fired. When sherds are sorted under a binocular microscope with respect to texture, one quickly learns to recognize major variations in the quantity and size of the mineral grains present and is able to classify the sherds into one or more fabrics. If the core of the sherds is black or grey in colour, care is necessary so that one is not misled by the colour contrast between the mineral grains in the dark core and those in the tan to red oxidized clay zones near the surfaces. Whether the mineral inclusions were intentionally added as tempering material or occur naturally in the clay is a question of some interest that can be answered when one is familiar with the local clays and the possible variations from gravel admixtures through sandy to very fine that occur in them. The local deposits of sandy clays used for pottery in glaciated regions can often be traced to river banks of flood plains. Some such clays must be washed to remove the coarsest inclusions before they can be used successfully. If shell has been added to the clay as was done by some North American Indians, or straw was included as in many agricultural areas of the world, there is no difficulty in recognizing the intentional admixture.

A correlation between the size and shape of the vessels and the purity of the clay from which they were formed may at times be of interest. Fine-textured clay, naturally river-washed or intentionally levigated, may have been used for the smaller and finer wares while large storage jars and the coarser, thicker domestic wares may tend to contain more mineral grains, for they give structural strength to the plastic vessel as it is shaped, and help prevent excessive cracking during drying. Detailed identification of the mineral inclusions and the study of sherds whose texture and appearance suggest that they are foreign to the site can best be done under a petrographic microscope by a mineralogist.

Estimates of the weight percentage of the tempering inclusions in the clay may be desirable if the textural variations seem significant in the study of the kinds of pottery made. If so, it is a simple matter to prepare briquettes as comparison standards. The series shown in Plate XXIVa have been useful when studying shell-tempered pottery. Crushed shell that had passed through a 14-mesh sieve but was retained on one of 20 mesh was mixed with a fine clay in the weight percentages shown, and the tempered clay was formed into small briquettes. After firing, the test pieces were broken in half. Those shown in the left-hand column were then ground to a smooth flat surface while those in the right-hand column were retained in their fractured form similar to that of the edges of sherds. This scale greatly aided in the classification and analysis of shell-tempered pottery. The thickness of the briquettes approximated that of the pottery being studied. The ground surfaces in the first column suggest that a similar treatment of some sherds might be of use, through the study of the orientation of the shell platelets, in determining how the pottery was fashioned. Similar series tempered with sand, straw, asbestos or other materials used by the potters can be prepared when needed. They give a degree of precision to the work and are particularly useful when one tries to replicate and understand the potter's procedures. However, too fine steps in the scale must be avoided as they can cause confusion and may lead to a degree of precision that is false, since the early potters were not necessarily consistent in their product as made in many households over long periods of time. Compositional limits for tempering within which the potters worked can be determined, because they were controlled by the desirable working properties of the tempered clay and also by the successful production of fired pots.

The dark core that appears in many sherds can be used as a means of studying the manner and degree of low-temperature firing of pottery. Dark-cored wares occur in all parts of the world and do not necessarily indicate a primitive stage of ceramic development. All they really show is that the pottery had been fired insufficiently with respect to both temperature and duration of the firing to eliminate this dark zone. Usually this will mean that a kiln was not used. With many clays a low firing temperature will not impair the usefulness of the vessels, and it certainly requires less fuel. Since all clays contain some organic matter derived from decomposing plant materials, they will turn black in the initial stages of firing but will then become lighter and lighter greys as the carbonized organic material is removed through oxidation. The natural colour developments of this carbon-freed clay, now no longer under strong internal reducing conditions, can then be seen. The surface regions will quickly brighten in colour, but it may take quite a while to eliminate the black or grey zone in the core, as its oxidation is dependent upon the porosity of the clay body—a sandy clay being much more open in structure than a very fine-textured untempered one. Then too, some clay minerals hold more strongly than do others the adsorbed organic matter. The total amount of organic material present is of course an important consideration, for in addition to the naturally occurring carbonaceous ingredients, some peoples have added dung to their potting clay to make it more plastic. In such cases it will take a longer time at a given temperature to oxidize all of the carbon if the ware is not very porous.

The series of test briquettes shown in Plate XXIVb illustrate the phenomena just described. Prepared pieces of a sandy Tigris River clay from south of Baghdad were fired at 500°C in an oxidizing atmosphere, one trial piece being drawn from the kiln every five minutes for half an hour. When cool, the briquettes were cut in half and the core faces were ground smooth so that their colour zones could be compared. As can be seen in the left-hand column, the clay first darkened and then became progressively lighter in colour as the firing progressed, yet a grey core remained after half an hour. Some of the Tigris clay was then levigated to remove much of the sand that it contained, and a series of fine-textured briquettes was prepared. Both sandy and fine clay test pieces were then fired at 600°C in the same manner as in the preceding series. A faint trace of a grey core remained in the sandy clay after 25 minutes, but had completely disappeared after half an hour. The black core of the fine clay remained massively present, however. Similar test firings at 700° and 800°C did not entirely remove the black core from the fine clay.

This experiment emphasizes the effect of texture and porosity on the rate at which a clay can be oxidized. Since time and temperature are interrelated variables in all ceramic firings, it can be seen that with longer firing periods at the test temperature the core can be oxidized, but not always to the same colour as the surfaces. When one has the data at hand that such experiments provide, one can make some reasonable estimates concerning the firing processes used by the potter. When doing so, the core colour of the rim, body and basal sherds must be carefully considered for they may differ greatly in one vessel as well as from jar to jar. It is sometimes possible to determine the probable manner of firing the pots—upside-down, right-side-up, several in one firing, etc. Such studies provide good training for student archaeologists.

Similar experiments showing the colour developments at higher temperatures can be carried out under both oxidizing and reducing conditions for a local or an imported clay, and a firing temperature scale can thus be developed that is useful when studying kiln-fired wares. I have discussed the results of such higher temperature studies elsewhere.[5]

In the preceding pages it has been shown that one can learn much about the technological aspects of ancient pottery by comparatively simple means and thus gain an insight into the problems the potters faced and solved in selecting their materials and in shaping and firing their wares. More refined and detailed analytical methods are available, and can be used when the questions they may help answer have been co-operatively proposed by the archaeologist and the technologist, and the sherds to be so tested have been carefully selected. Examples will illustrate some analytical approaches, many of which are still in their exploratory stages of development.

The petrographic microscope is one of the most useful tools of the ceramic technologist. Carefully prepared paper-thin slices of sherds, about 0·03 mm in thickness, can be studied at high magnifications. These thin sections can be used to identify and compare the mineral inclusions in the sherds with those of local clays. If the two differ significantly in their mineral fabric the sherds may represent imported wares which can then be described in mineralogical terms. It is then possible to prepare and analyse thin sections of sherds of the areas from which the importation is suspected in the light of one's knowledge of ancient trade and of the geological nature of the regions. This technique is useful only if there are readily recognizable differences in the mineral inclusions in the clays from the regions in question. Thin sections can also be checked for the orientation of the particles with respect to the surfaces of the sherd; this may yield information about the manufacture of the pottery, while the grain-size distribution, knowing that of the local clays, can suggest whether or not the clay had been levigated before use. The addition of tempering materials can often be recognized, and changes in the degree of oxidation of some minerals may help show the extent to which the pottery had been fired. Experience with the mineralogy of sedimentary materials is a most useful preparation for one who wishes to study petrographic thin sections.

An example of the identification of an imported ware at the long-occupied pueblo of Pecos, New Mexico, and the location of its place of origin will illustrate one application of petrographic methods, in this case to a ware tempered with crushed potsherds. Miss Shepard, who has conducted many successful petrographic analyses, summarizes the results of one aspect of her Pecos studies as follows in her useful volume, *Ceramics for the Archaeologist* (pp. 383–384):[11]

'A black-on-white type at Pecos has the same finish and style as the black-on-white pottery of the Galisteo Basin, some 30 miles away. Was the Pecos pottery imported or made locally? The potsherd temper seemed at first to offer little hope of answering the question, but thin sections showed that many of the temper particles were from culinary ware (blackened and coarse textured), tempered with rock—andesite or diorite. Galisteo culinary ware is tempered with this kind of rock, that of Pecos is sand-tempered. The sherd temper is, therefore, from Galisteo, for Pecos people obviously would not go 30 miles for sherds when there was an abundance of them on their own trash heaps, and this type of sherd-tempered pottery must have been brought into Pecos.' This information was then used by Miss Shepard and A. V. Kidder in the study of the trade relationship in its many aspects between Pecos and the Galisteo Basin.

Spectrographic analyses have long been used to determine the relative proportions of the elements present in trace amounts or in small quantities in ancient metals and glasses. They are now being used with success in studies of the regional distribution of some kinds of pottery. The small powdered sample of a body that is to be analysed is ignited in an electrode arc and the elements that are present in relatively small amounts can be identified by the characteristic spectra of light that they emit. In coarse-textured pottery it is difficult or impossible to obtain a representative sample for such analysis because of the variation in the quantity and size of the mineral grains of several types that will be present in each sample chosen. Two sherds from the same pot could differ markedly in their overall composition and in the relative amounts of the less frequent elements that are present, depending on the chance distribution of the coarser mineral grains in each sample analysed. This difficulty does not apply to all wares, so within limits, emission spectroscopy can be useful in pottery studies. Quantitative spectrographic analyses can at times be made if one can prepare a set of samples of known chemical composition as standards that approximate the compositions of the specimens being tested.

Sayre[9] (pp. 156–157) has made quantitative spectrographic analyses of powdered samples of the clays from fifteen wine jars of unknown provenance that were excavated in the Agora, the ancient market place of Athens. Many wine amphorae have a tax stamp impressed on one of their handles while the clay is still plastic which shows the place of manufacture and presumably the source of the wine. Sayre also analysed clays from stamped jars of known origin, and found that of the fifteen just mentioned, eleven had a composition like that of jars made on the island of Knidos, while the remaining four agreed in composition with jars from Rhodes. His work can aid materially in tracing the ramifications of the Aegean wine trade in classical times.

Mrs E. E. Richards[7] has been making a series of spectrographic analyses of Romano-British mortaria, searching for ranges of concentration for certain elements that may be characteristic for samples known to come from specific kiln sites. Her preliminary work has already met with success.

Physicists are now working with archaeologists in several countries in trying to apply some of the newer analytical techniques to the solution of archaeological problems. The Research Laboratory for Archaeology and the History of Art at Oxford which has excellent research physicists interested in instrument design and application on its staff is a good example of this effective interaction between members of the two disciplines. Each type of instrumental analysis presents certain advantages within certain ranges of application, and these limits are still being determined and in some cases modified by further refinements in instrument design. A few examples of recent work will illustrate the imaginative application of some of the newer techniques.

Nuclear bombardment and activation of archaeological materials has produced interesting results. At the invitation of Dr Robert Oppenheimer, a small discussion group composed of archaeologists and physicists met at the Institute for Advanced Study at Princeton, New Jersey, in 1956 to consider the possibility of applying nuclear analytical techniques to the solution of archaeological problems. As a result of this meeting, E. V. Sayre and his associates at the Brookhaven National Laboratories studied carefully selected sherd groups whose places of origin were questioned on archaeological grounds. One problem selected was that of the Fine Orange Ware, a distinctive type in Mesoamerica that occurs at several Mayan sites. A small quantity of this ware was found among the sherds in the excavations at Piedras Negras, but it was an important ceramic item at Kixpec, a site some distance away. Was the pottery of this type found at Piedras

Negras imported from the region of Kixpec? Bowl fragments of Fine Orange Ware from both sites as well as the normal Piedras Negras pottery were exposed to neutron irradiation in the Brookhaven nuclear reactor in order to produce neutron activation in the test pieces. The artificially induced neutron activity of materials that have been exposed in an atomic pile under the same conditions will decrease at a rate determined by the relative amounts of the activated chemical elements present in the sample. Therefore, the decay rate is a means of characterizing the chemical composition of a sample. The gamma rays emitted are suitable for such measurements. The rates of decrease in the gamma ray activity of these artificially activated Mayan sherds showed that the Fine Orange Ware from both sites had the same relative concentration of chemical elements, while the typical Piedras Negras pottery was quite different in its decay rate. These results confirmed the archaeologists' assumption that the Kixpec region was the centre of manufacture for the Fine Orange Ware.

Another problem investigated by Sayre was that of one type of Roman *terra sigillata*, the Arretine ware, which often was stamped when formed so as to show its place of manufacture. Stamped Arretine sherds known to have come from bowls made at Arretium received nuclear bombardment with similar ware of uncertain origin that was found in other regions. Some of the pieces from foreign regions had the same decay rate as those from Arretium, while others that Howard Comfort, who defined the problem and supplied the materials, suspected because of differences in texture as having been ancient forgeries—though they bore the stamp ARRET so that they would have greater market value—were found to differ from the true Arretine pieces. It is likely that this analytical technique will be used to help trace the place of origin of many of the Roman wares widely dispersed throughout Europe and the Mediterranean countries, and can probably be applied with success to the study of Greek trade in its widespread ramifications. Preliminary studies of Gaulish Samian pottery at the Research Laboratory for Archaeology, Oxford, by Miss Emeleus and Miss Simpson [2,12] have made it possible to group the samples 'in a manner that is understandable both geographically and archaeologically'.

A great advantage of this technique of nuclear bombardment is that it is non-destructive. Museum pieces from which chips cannot be removed for other forms of analysis can be exposed in a nuclear reactor, and after the necessary decay rate measurements have been made they can be stored in a protected place until their radioactivity has disappeared or is negligible. They can then again be safely exhibited or handled in study collections.

Another non-destructive technique is that of X-ray fluorescent spectrometry which has been successfully used at the Boston Museum of Fine Arts and at Oxford. The equipment is now available in many university and industrial laboratories so it should be fairly accessible to archaeologists. The test specimen is bombarded with X-rays and the characteristic fluorescence that is then emitted by chemical elements receiving this induced activation can be measured spectrometrically and the elements can be identified.

Young and Whitmore [13] have used this instrument at Boston to characterize the composition of certain types of Japanese and Chinese wares through the use of sherds that have been excavated at known kiln sites. Such work will help in the specific identification of some of the Far Eastern wares from regions where little controlled archaeological excavation has yet been done although beautiful objects from these areas have long appeared on the markets and in private collections and now grace museums throughout the world. Hall[3] discusses the advantages and limitations of X-ray fluorescent spectrometry, and points out that the analysis is largely of elements occurring very close to the test surface, so weathered or corroded surfaces can seriously affect the usefulness of the measurements.

A new tool that is still being refined and rebuilt on both sides of the Atlantic in order to attain greater effectiveness and smaller areas of analysis is the electron probe which can identify the elements present in a spot as small as five microns in diameter. Its use in archaeological studies is largely potential although Roberts[8] describes his 'electron gun', an X-ray microanalyser.

There are other new techniques being tried in archaeological studies which are of direct application in the broad field of ceramic technology, particularly when glasses and glazes are considered. Many of these techniques are discussed in the papers in the volume on the Boston Seminar that was edited by Young.[9] Current work in progress is effectively reported in the small annual bulletin, *Archaeometry*, published by the Research Laboratory for Archaeology and the History of Art, Oxford.

Ceramic technological studies have been conducted on a limited scale for a long while. In 1883 Anatole Bamps[1] presented a paper at the Fifth International Congress of Americanists in which he pointed out the usefulness of microscopic studies with particular reference to Peruvian pottery. He summarized the microscopic studies of Wilhelm Prinz which showed that some black and red pottery were made from the same paste and that the colour bands seen in cross sections of sherds did not indicate the building up of successive layers of different clays but showed the degree of firing. Bamps also recognized the value of microscopic work in tracing the origin of widely distributed wares and pointed out the danger of drawing conclusions from the chemical analyses of pottery when the mineralogical composition of the pastes was not considered. These points are still valid today and must repeatedly be emphasized.

Over the past eighty years many technological studies have appeared in widely scattered publications, often as little known appendices or footnotes in archaeological reports. Lucas's valuable volume, *Ancient Egyptian Materials and Industries*[4] summarizes his long years of distinguished work in Egypt. Miss Shepard's *Ceramics for the Archaeologist*[11] provides a detailed introduction to the nature of ceramic materials and processes as well as to many aspects of ceramic analyses. Its examples are drawn chiefly from the south-western United States and Central America, the two regions in which she has worked with great distinction. Her bibliography and those in Matson's papers of 1955 and 1960 will suggest a basic set of references for those interested in further reading.

In this paper it has not been possible to consider all aspects of the technological study of pottery. The surface decoration of wares in terms of pigments, vitrified slips and glazes has not been discussed. There have been several excellent studies of the nature and replication of the so-called Greek 'glaze' found on the red figured and black figured wares. A citation of the recent literature in this field is available (Matson,[6] p. 50). The higher fired wares leading to the development of stoneware and porcelain form another subject of immediate interest to students of Far Eastern and post-medieval European ceramics.

Technological studies can be carried out most effectively when the field archaeologist is aware of the potentialities of such work and systematically collects samples of the possible raw materials that were used and saves for study more of the miscellaneous items that occur in excavations. Lumps of tempered unfired potter's clay, for example, have been found in American Indian sites, crucible fragments and refuse slag appear in the Near East, and kiln-site wasters abound in the Far East. Ceramic technological studies based on carefully collected field samples and the identification of well-defined problems can significantly advance our knowledge of man's development and his ways of life.

REFERENCES

1 BAMPS, A. 1883. *C. R. Congres. int. des Americanistes*, 5ᵉ Sess, Copenhagen, 274 ff.
2 EMELEUS, V. M. 1960. *Archaeometry 3*, 16–19
3 HALL, E. T. 1960. *Ibid. 3*, 29–35
4 LUCAS, A. 1948. *Ancient Egyptian Materials and Industries*, London, 3rd ed.
5 MATSON, F. R. 1955. *The American Ceramic Society Bulletin 34*, 33–44
6 —— 1960. The Quantitative Study of Ceramic Materials; in HEIZER, R. F. and COOK, S. F. (ed.) 'The Application of Quantitative Methods in Archaeology', *Viking Fund Publications in Anthropology 28*, 34–59
7 RICHARDS, E. E. 1959. *Archaeometry 2*, 23–31
8 ROBERTS, G. 1960. *Ibid. 3*, 36–37
9 SAYRE, E. V. 1959. Studies in Ancient Ceramic Objects by Means of Neutron Bombardment and Emission Spectroscopy; *Application of Science in the Examination of Works of Art*, 153–180; proc. of seminar (Sept. 15–18, 1958) Research Laboratory, Mus. of Fine Arts, Boston
10 —— MURRENHOFF, A. and WEICK, C. F. 1958. The Nondestructive Analysis of Ancient Potsherds through Neutron Activation; *Brookhaven Nat. Lab. Rep.* no. 508
11 SHEPARD, A. O. 1956. Ceramics for the Archaeologist. *Carnegie Inst. of Washington*, Publ. 609
12 SIMPSON, G. 1960. *Archaeometry 3*, 20–24
13 YOUNG, W. J. and WHITMORE, F. E. 1957. *Far Eastern Ceramic Bulletin 9*, 1–27

48 Optical Emission Spectroscopy and the Study of Metallurgy in the European Bronze Age

DENNIS BRITTON and EVA E. RICHARDS

THE FRAMEWORK OF THE LATER PREHISTORY of Europe has long been standardized in the sequence: Neolithic, Bronze Age and Iron Age. But within it our interpretations are constantly shifting. More and more, for example, are we appreciating that in many regions the first use of metal comes already among cultures generally styled 'Neolithic'.[1] This metal is not bronze but copper, as spectroscopic analyses have proved, and so a sort of 'Copper Age' forms a prelude to the Bronze Age itself. For the next thousand years, roughly from 1600 BC to 600 BC, bronze was the metal chiefly used for tools, weapons and ornaments through most of Europe.

But spectroscopic analyses do more than modify our view of the traditional 'Three Ages' system. The technology of copper and its alloys holds a crucial position in the early industrial history of Europe, and the extensive trade that a Bronze Age of necessity implies formed a major step in our economic development. If we are to appreciate this story in all its aspects every means of study must be applied, and one of these is analysis by optical emission spectroscopy. Yet this is no magic key to open all doors. On the contrary, an uncritical use of its results would soon lead us astray. Our best hope of a right understanding lies in using the various methods together, wherever possible checking their conclusions against each other. So in focusing our attention on one approach, we shall nevertheless refer to others, some based purely on archaeology and some of a technological kind. First the technique itself is described, then the problems of interpretation discussed, and finally a short review is given of some notable applications.

THE PRINCIPLES AND TECHNIQUE OF OPTICAL EMISSION SPECTROSCOPY

Of the methods which may be used to analyse a material for the chemical elements contained in it, spectroscopy offers a combination of advantages which make it specially suitable for the study of archaeological specimens. Sometimes from a single experiment on no more than 10 milligrams of a substance, the elements present may be identified and their relative amounts measured. Few other analytical procedures have the ability simultaneously to identify as many as a score of constituents and to estimate their concentrations over a range as wide as four orders of magnitude (i.e. from 0·001% to 10%). An outline of the principles underlying the method and some of the practical aspects will be described here.

The transmission of energy by radiation is familiar to everyone: the heat from the sun reaches us as light; the wireless programmes reach us by radio-frequency radiation; X-rays are well known to be a very penetrating form of radiation. All these forms of radiation are fundamentally the same phenomenon, in that they can be regarded as wave motion. They differ from one another only in their wavelength. Furthermore, the radiation which we perceive visually we call visible radiation or light. The different colours of the rainbow, into which white light is split when it passes through the water droplets acting as minute prisms, are again different in wavelength. The corresponding experiment in a laboratory, the resolution of light into colours by means of a prism, was achieved by Newton three hundred years ago.

In 1817 Frauenhofer set up the first spectroscope, consisting of a slit, prism and theodolite which enabled him to observe separately light of different colours. With this instrument he observed spectral lines in the light of the sun. Before the middle of the nineteenth century Fox Talbot, the inventor of photography, applied this invention to the recording of spectra. He was also the first to observe that the light emitted by certain elements when introduced into an electric arc consisted of characteristically coloured rays. By 1861, the basis of the spectroscopic method of analysis was firmly established by Kirchoff and Bunsen. They showed that the spectrum of an element consists of a number of lines (rays of light of different wavelengths) which are characteristic of that element and at the same time independent of its state of chemical combination.[2]

The lines of a spectrum have different intrinsic intensities, more light is emitted at certain wavelengths than at others under a given set of circumstances. The most important factor which determines the intensity of the spectrum as a whole is the concentration of the element producing it. Qualitative spectrographic analysis consists of the comparison of the wavelength of the lines in the spectrum of the sample with the spectra of the pure elements. Quantitative analysis depends on the measurement of the intensity of a chosen line for each of the elements whose concentration in the sample is required. The intensities of the same lines in the spectra of synthetic or chemically analysed samples are used for comparison. It is important that the reference material, whose composition is known, should be similar in kind to the samples of unknown composition.

The general layout of a spectrograph is shown in Fig. 69. The light emitted by the source (A) is gathered into a narrower beam by a lens (L) outside the spectrometer. It then passes through a narrow slit (S) (0·01–0·02 mm), is then reflected through a right angle and falls on the collimating lens (C). This is so placed that the beam reaching the prism (P) or grating consists of parallel rays. The light is refracted by the prism or diffracted by the grating. In either case the light which returns to the photographic plate (E) is spread out: different wavelengths are focused at different points along the photographic plate.

The source of light is an electric discharge between two electrodes maintained either at a high, alternating (spark) or low, direct (arc) voltage with respect to one another. It is the collision of the atoms, present in the gaseous state, with the electrons of the discharge which leads to the emission of light characteristic of these atoms. There are a number of ways of introducing the sample to be analysed into the discharge. The electrodes are usually made of graphite. The bronze may be converted into a mixture of

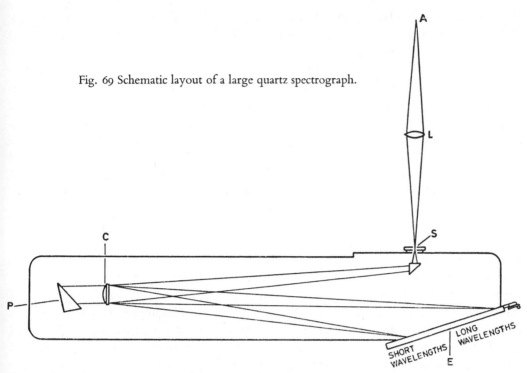

Fig. 69 Schematic layout of a large quartz spectrograph.

the oxides of its constituents; this is mixed with pure graphite powder in known proportion and packed into the cup hollowed out of the lower electrode. This method is
also suitable for the analysis of ore and mineral samples. At the high temperatures
generated in an electric arc, the mixture volatilizes. The dimensions of this cup are
critical, and a new one has to be used for each exposure. Alternatively, the metallic
sample is cast into a small globule and it is this which is placed into the electrode cup.
In yet another method a solution of the bronze (0·2 ml of a 2·5% weight/volume
solution) is placed into a thin-bottomed cup, which constitutes the upper electrode. The
solution seeps through the porous graphite and the minute droplets volatilize into the
park discharge.

In all methods the electrical characteristics of the discharge, the shape and distance
from one another of the electrodes are critical and must be strictly controlled in order
to obtain reproducible results. The quantitative determination of as many as twenty
elements in one, or possibly two experiments, requiring between 2 and 10 mg of
bronze, is quite feasible as a routine operation, by suitable initial choice of experimental
conditions.

It is for this reason that spectrochemical analysis is the most widely used method in
industry for the determination and control of the composition of alloys of all kinds.
It is also widely used in the routine analysis of minerals, rocks and ores. Several
hundred papers are published each year describing the optimum conditions for the
spectrochemical analysis of particular materials. It is impossible to summarize here the
various methods recommended for copper alloys, but critical reports are published by

the British Non-Ferrous Metals Research Association, and by the American Society for the Testing of Materials. Most of the methods which have been used for archaeological work are quoted by Pittioni.[3]

If the spectrum is recorded on a photographic plate, only a narrow horizontal strip is exposed to the light, so that spectra of many (in some spectrographs up to 30) samples can be recorded on the same plate. Since the elements likely to be present in a bronze emit light mostly in the near ultra-violet and blue region of the spectrum, ordinary, unsensitized plates are satisfactory. These are fast and simple to process, but again, for quantitative work the conditions for development must be standardized. An enlarged photograph of the spectrum of a bronze is reproduced in Plate XXV. Some of the lines which have been found suitable for quantitative estimation of the main elements present are marked. The wavelengths are measured in Ångstrom units, one hundred million of which are equal to one centimetre.

If only qualitative information is required, such as for instance the presence or absence of lead in scrapings from a mould which had been used to cast bronze objects, then all that is required are spectra of the elements looked for, photographed through the same spectrograph. The plate with the reference spectra and that of the unknown are placed in a comparator. This apparatus enables one to view simultaneously two spectra on two different plates alongside one another either through a microscope or projected on a screen. Either way, coincidences can be picked out which show the presence of particular elements. If reference spectra are not available, then the wavelengths of un-identified lines can be computed from their position on the plate with respect to known lines. Compilations of all known lines of all the elements are available and can be used for identification in these cases.

The complete spectrum of an element is unique, although occasionally one or more of its lines may have a wavelength so nearly the same as that of some other elements that they will not be resolved in an ordinary spectrograph. For this reason it is customary in identification work not to rely on a single coincidence between the reference and unknown sample. The most sensitive lines of the elements, which are not necessarily the strongest ones, will persist down to concentrations as low as 1 part per million (0·0001%) for the consumption of as little as 1 mg of the specimen. This means that many elements can be detected when there was no more than one millionth of a gram present in the discharge. Quantitative work at these concentration levels is possible but difficult.

Although in the most modern equipment for routine spectrochemical analysis the photographic plate has been replaced by direct reading facilities, most of the analyses of archaeological interest have been done with the more conventional type of spectro-graph. Since the amount of illumination at a particular wavelength depends on the amount of the element emitting at that wavelength, the amount of blackening produced by a particular spectral line has to be measured. Visual estimates of the blackening are used for semiquantitative work, but as the variation in intensity is usually continuous it is difficult to decide where the boundary between such terms as medium and strong etc. will lie. The numerical evaluation of the blackening is carried out by means of a photoelectric device called a microphotometer. As the blackening produced is not strictly proportional to the amount of illumination, due to the peculiarities of the photographic process, fairly elaborate calibrations have to be carried out when the method is first set up. By means of these calibrations the blackening of the lines is converted into percentages of the appropriate elements.

It adds greatly to the value of these analytical results if the overall experimental error, as observed by replicating experiments, is assessed by a standard statistical method.

Most of the conclusions reached about archaeological material on the basis of composition relies on *differences* in the concentrations of particular constituents arising from differences in origin, date, method of manufacture and purpose. It is most important that no finer distinctions should be drawn than are warranted by the accuracy of the analysis. If for instance it is found that the standard deviation (this is the statistical definition of error due to random causes) of the determination of lead by a particular procedure is 10% and supposing that 5·0% of lead is found in a bronze, then the actual value has an even chance of being within 0·3 of this figure, while the odds against the real value being less than 4·2 or more than 5·8 are 9 to 1, and it has only one chance in a hundred of lying outside the range 3·7–6·3. These probabilities should be considered when the bronze is to be distinguished from another on the basis of its lead content.

When developing the analytical method it is important to ensure that the experimental error is less than the intrinsic variations in composition within the archaeological groups which are to be compared. On the other hand, extreme accuracy involves considerable expenditure of time. In archaeological work it is usually necessary to accumulate analytical data about a large number of samples. A compromise between sufficient accuracy and reasonable speed has therefore to be reached. This compromise will vary from problem to problem.

PROBLEMS OF INTERPRETATION

The information provided by optical spectroscopy is essentially descriptive. It tells us things we could never know merely by looking, but it leaves in our hands the problem of using this extra knowledge as a source for prehistory. In practice, interpretation involves two steps, the first in terms of technology, the second by way of archaeological reconstruction.

From the analysis we try to follow back the sequence of processes which led to the finished product. Our first question is: did the smith use copper by itself or did he aim at the deliberate production of an alloy? Some objects are of very pure copper and the traces of other metals in them may be regarded as impurities derived from the ore. But during the full Bronze Age alloys were in general use, the extra components being arsenic, tin, or tin and lead. Whenever the proportion of these rises much above 1% the possibility of intentional alloying must be considered.[4] To define the exact processes by which these alloys were made is often difficult and may be in part impossible. In any case, other evidence besides the analyses themselves must be taken into account, in particular the experience of geologists and metallurgists. For example, could the alloy be derived from selected kinds of copper ore, perhaps with skilful control of the smelting processes? The arsenical coppers of the later Neolithic and the Early Bronze Age probably originated in that way.[5] Or should we rather suppose that the other components were smelted from their own ores? This is certainly the usual explanation for the alloys of copper with tin and with tin and lead.[6]

When the main components shown by the analysis have been considered, others remain which presumably came in as impurities from the ore or ores. If the material is unalloyed copper, clearly all these are derived from the copper ore. Even in the alloys of copper with tin and lead, the ores of copper are again the likely source for most of the impurities. With the arsenical alloys, as already mentioned, the arsenic itself is very probably an impurity of this kind. It seems that the ores of copper are the sources for the bulk of the impurities, and from this arises a fascinating possibility. The combination of impurities in the smelted copper will broadly reflect that of the parent ore. Further, both objects and ores can be grouped according to their impurities, again taken not individually but in their recurrent combinations. Can knowledge of this kind enable us unambiguously to match finished objects with specific ore deposits? If it can, then we might learn a great deal about the economic organization of these early industries. The regions where copper was extracted could be compared with the overall dispersion of the products, and the importance of the various deposits at different periods could be assessed. Besides we should greatly increase our chances of discovering the sites of early mining and smelting, about which so little of a definite kind is known outside Austria.

But the obstacles are indeed formidable. First there are theoretical difficulties. The correlation between ores and the copper smelted from them is in terms of the combination of certain elements in both. But a direct quantitative comparison is hazardous and perhaps without meaning, since the several elements will pass over from the ore to the smelted metal in differing proportions, and these ratios might in fact have varied with the process used: how uniform were the extractive techniques and how standardized a product was achieved? Then it is known that the composition of the ore body itself varies from place to place through its depth, and into the bronze-smith's melt might even go ingot metal or scrap from more than one source. The practical difficulties lie in the assembly of all the information needed. Even if we suppose that the objects in question each contain copper from only one ore deposit, it is obvious that the comparisons of single analyses are of no value. What is needed is a soundly based assessment of the range of variation likely in the copper from all the probable ore sites, some of which may have been worked out long ago. The objects too must be grouped in terms of ranges of variation in their composition. It is doubtful if valid results can be achieved except by great numbers of analyses, and these may require statistical evaluation before they are used as evidence. If such problems are to be tackled effectively, it is certain that patient and long-term study on a considerable scale is necessary. At least outside Austria, which we shall mention again below, it is questionable whether or not these exacting conditions have been fulfilled so far.

In terms of technology two kinds of information are yielded by the study of spectroscopic analyses. The first is the definition of the metals used, and within the limits of the method, the results are direct and unequivocal. The second concerns the sources of copper, and here the difficulties involved mean, at present, conclusions of a rather tentative sort for most regions of Europe. When historical reconstructions are attempted, we should keep in mind the very different character of these kinds of evidence, and to start with at least consider them separately. It is also valuable to form our ideas of what happened first of all from the archaeological standpoint alone. Then the new data from the side of technology, with an independent source, can be compared. But if all the evidence is thrown together at the beginning, we lose helpful possibilities of cross-checking our interpretations, and indeed may easily succumb to arguments that are essentially circular.

SOME EXAMPLES OF APPLICATION

Single analyses are of little value and may easily mislead: conclusions with real meaning must be based on large series of results. Awareness of this fact has been rather slow in taking root generally, although systematic research has been done on several aspects of the European Bronze Age.[7] Here some of the main examples are mentioned, with a few details to illustrate the different kinds of approach.

The pioneers of this method were W. Witter and H. Otto, whose researches in connection with the Landesmuseum of Halle/Saale had started already in 1931.[8] They were concerned with the beginnings of metallurgy in central Europe and by 1952 had completed about 1,500 analyses. Both the sequence of metals used and possible sources of copper were studied, and they realized the need for a knowledge of the likely ore deposits. Their conclusions are of great interest but call for checking by further work. The correlations between objects and ores require more detailed information about copper deposits—they did not themselves study samples of ores, and their broader historical suggestions should be viewed against comparative evidence from other regions. This applies particularly to the possibility of an independent growth of bronze metallurgy in central Germany.

It is in Austria that the systematic study of both objects and ore deposits has been pursued intensively and with notable success. This work began slightly later than that of Witter and Otto, about 1935, and it is particularly due to H. Pesta and R. Pittioni.[9] The other aspects of the story have also been given special attention, particularly the problems connected with early mining, and the treatment and smelting of the ore. Research has been concentrated on the regions of early exploitation in Salzburg and the Tyrol, where all the major deposits of copper ore have now been examined. Care has been taken to analyse samples from different depths in the deposit so as to define correctly the range of impurities characteristic of the ore-body as a whole. By 1959, Pittioni had available no less than 1,925 analyses of ores and material from ancient smelting places.

On this very substantial basis, study can now, it is claimed, be directed with confidence to the problem of correlating the ore deposits with likely products. Several aspects of the Copper Age, Bronze Age and the Urnfield Period have been studied in detail and these analyses are yielding results of great interest for the early economic history of central Europe. Two instances must suffice. Hoards of ingots are well known in the Early Bronze Age of the *Voralpenland*, and on the basis of 452 analyses the ores of Slovakia are suggested as the likely origin for much of this metal. On the other hand an intensive study of material from the Urnfields of the North Tyrol (581 samples) points to a major source in the copper deposits of the Bertagrube near Schwaz. In his review of 1959, Pittioni was able to report a grand total of 3,391 analyses, and added reassuringly that the possibilities of research were by no means exhausted!

It is a familiar paradox that the splendour of Bronze Age metal-working in Scandinavia rested entirely on imported materials. Here there is no challenge to locate ores exploited in remote antiquity but great opportunities for the study of technological development. The magisterial work of A. Oldeberg on this theme[10] covers the later periods as well: we are concerned only with the Bronze Age sections. Oldeberg deals with each metal in turn as it occurred in the north. Frequent illustrations are drawn from the long series of analyses incorporated in the book—747 from all periods. For the earliest use of copper and its alloys he relies much on the work of Witter and pursues for Scandinavia his suggestions about the sequence of metals and sources of copper. But Oldeberg's interests carry him right through the Bronze Age, and for the later phases too he has much to say on possible sources of metals. Particularly valuable is his study of the development of metallurgical techniques through successive periods of Scandinavian antiquity. In both these fields, he has used perceptively the results of spectroscopic analysis as a basic source for prehistory.

Since 1949 a very extensive survey has been undertaken at Stuttgart through the collaboration of S. Junghans, E. Sangmeister, E. Scheufele, H. Klein, and M. Schröder.[11] The programme now embraces the same chronological span as that of Otto and Witter but is expanded to consider the original spread of metallurgy in copper and bronze from the first centres in the Near East throughout Europe. From this wider view it is hoped that historical conclusions can be drawn that are of real validity. The results of the first six years' work, based on 2,302 analyses, were published in 1960 and deal with central and western Europe.[12] Other regions will be the subject of future publications. By 1960, 2,700 new analyses could be claimed, with samples collected for a further 3,000.

Great care has been taken to set out separately the general picture of cultural development for each region as derived from the usual methods of archaeology. Only then are the results of the analyses considered. One major theme is the origin and spread of true tin bronze metallurgy. Amost everywhere in central and western Europe a distinct phase is revealed in which copper alone was used, and then the new and superior alloy spreads throughout Europe—to all appearances, quite suddenly. Its earliest use in the regions so far considered is said to be in the *Schlaner Gruppe* of the Aunjetitz Culture in Bohemia, probably about 1700 BC. Only future work will show whether an independent invention is involved or diffusion from the south-east.

The other main field of inquiry concerns the groups of copper as defined by their impurities. The work of Otto and Witter is greatly refined, with statistical evaluations to fix precisely the boundaries of the groups. Thirteen groups emerge and account for almost all the results. The occurrence of these groups is then plotted geographically and the main concentrations of each determined. Also their utilization by the different archaeological cultures is studied, in both space and time. Only when all parts of Europe have been thus examined will the problem of locating the sources be taken up in detail.

From all this comes the basis for a broad historical sketch in which the original account derived purely from archaeological techniques is combined with the new knowledge. What emerges is a general sequence in three stages. In the first, well before 2000 BC, knowledge of metal-working is confined to the extreme south-east and south-west of Europe. From these two regions metallurgy spreads in the early second millennium to many parts of central and western Europe, and a number of new copper groups appear, suggesting the exploitation of fresh sources. The initial schools of metal-working were masters of quite complex methods of casting, but these skills were lost in the spread of the craft, and most of the earliest products in temperate Europe were made simply in open moulds, often with much subsequent forging (*Blechstil*). Only in the third phase, and significantly just with the diffusion of bronze metallurgy, was the older competence transcended and closed mould casting—for which the new metal was so well suited—became very general. About this time too, in the seventeenth century BC and later, the exploitation of new ore deposits is indicated, and these have been identified with sources in the Bavarian and Austrian Alps. By the end of the Early Bronze Age this 'alpine copper' had in many regions come to dominate the market.

Our final example brings us at last to Britain and shows the way in which we may apply to familiar material information about the kind of metal used. The evidence for Middle Bronze Age metalwork, especially in southern Britain, was recently studied in detail by the usual archaeological methods of typology and association.[13] These showed its place in the prehistory of the region and related it to the independent sequences of the Continent. The material so defined was contrasted archaeologically with another group, which is broadly its successor and used to delimit our Late Bronze Age. Large numbers of specimens from both these assemblages, a total of 471, were analysed.[14,15] In each group tin had been added in rather variable amounts to the copper, but the Late Bronze Age material alone had as well an addition of lead, also variable but hardly ever absent (Fig. 70).

This interesting information is in some ways rather puzzling. For certain purposes the leaded alloy has technical advantages: the melting point is lower, and the molten metal would flow more easily into long or complex moulds. These properties might suit very well many of the typical forms of the Late Bronze Age and also its aspect of mass-production. But compared with plain tin bronze the castings would certainly be poorer in mechanical qualities. Perhaps economic factors were involved too, and we should recall that over much of southern Britain all the constituents would have to be imported. Besides an intriguing technological point, the analyses have proved for the first time an ancillary industry of some importance and uncovered a fresh aspect of Bronze Age trade. But they do not strictly provide a new method of dating—of deciding what is Middle and what Late Bronze Age. Those terms properly refer to assemblages defined by archaeological criteria. The reality of these groupings is buttressed by the analyses, though the sequence of alloys does not by itself furnish a yardstick for chronology.

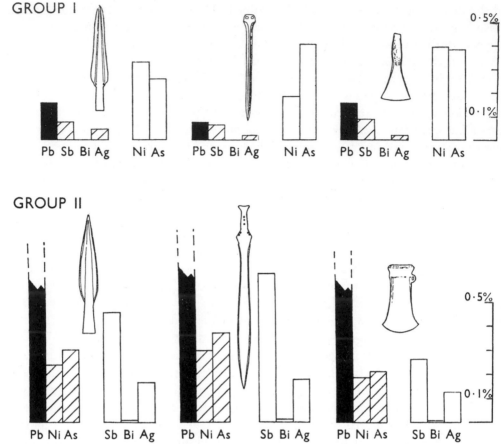

Fig. 70 Significant elements (other than copper and tin) in samples of spearheads, rapiers, swords, and axes from Britain. GROUP I: Middle Bronze Age; GROUP II: Late Bronze Age. From Brown and Blin-Stoyle.[14]

This picture for the Middle and Late Bronze Age of southern Britain is being complemented by studies of the earlier phases. The initial contribution was the notable work by H. H. Coghlan and H. J. Case on the first metallurgy in the British Isles.[16] For southern Britain the material between this programme and the Middle Bronze Age has recently been sampled.[17] It is in the later Neolithic, perhaps from about 2000 BC on, that the first metal objects are known, in particular the tanged flat daggers from Beaker graves. The metal here seems always to be copper, though sometimes so arsenical as to suggest deliberate choice of ores and perhaps control of the smelting. The broad butt flat axes that probably belong to the same period are of similar material. The clearest light on the start of a real Bronze Age is shed by the sequence of graves in the Wessex culture.[18] The earliest burials include six-rivet daggers, flat or with a midrib. Some of these are of copper—again this may be arsenical, but others are truly of bronze, containing a deliberate addition of tin, which rises once above 12%. In later graves, marked by two- or three-rivet daggers, bronze seems universal, and in 14 out of 22 daggers of this kind so far analysed the tin content is above 12%. The same alloy, with abundant tin, is found consistently in the hoards with flanged axes which belong to this second phase, and perhaps date from about 1550 BC onwards.

These results document very clearly the growth of knowledge in the alloying of copper (Plate XXVa). They show as well an interesting relation between the kind of metal and the methods of casting like that already observed for the Continent. Here too the first forms are of copper and cast flat in open moulds, with subsequent hammering and grinding. Next the first closed mould forms appear, cast in low tin bronze or the arsenical copper which has many of its advantages. Then bronze with rather higher tin content becomes standard and remains so throughout the Middle Bronze Age, until it was supplanted in its turn, sometime after 1000 BC, by the leaded alloy of the Late Bronze Age.

REFERENCES AND NOTES

1 JUNGHANS, S., SANGMEISTER, E. and SCHRÖDER, M. 1960. *Metallanalysen kupferzeitlicher und frühbronze-zeitlicher Bodenfunde aus Europa.* Berlin, 8–34, and Beilage 1

2 TWYMAN, F. 1951. *Metal Spectroscopy,* London

3 PITTIONI, R. 1959. *Archaeologia Austriaca 26,* 67–95

4 JUNGHANS, S. *et al., op. cit.,* 57ff.

5 COGHLAN, H. H. and CASE, H. 1957. *Proc. Prehist. Soc. 23,* 96

6 —— 1956. *Notes on the prehistoric metallurgy of copper and bronze in the Old World,* Oxford, 16–18, 23–25. The analysis of ingot metal might be instructive and show at what stage the lead became part of the mixture.

7 PITTIONI, R. *op. cit.*

8 OTTO, H. and WITTER, W. 1952. *Handbuch der ältesten vorgeschichtlichen Metallurgie in Mitteleuropa,* Leipzig

9 PITTIONI, R. *op. cit.* 69ff., 93ff.

10 OLDEBERG, A. 1942–3. *Metallteknik under förhistorisk Tid,* Lund

11 *Bericht der Röm.-German. Komm. 35* (1954) 77 ff.; *Germania 35* (1957) 11 ff.

12 JUNGHANS, S. *et. al., op. cit.*

13 SMITH, M. A. 1959. *Proc. Prehist. Soc. 25,* 144–187

14 BROWN, M. A. and BLIN-STOYLE, A. E. 1959. *Ibid.* 188–208

15 *Archaeometry 2,* 1959, supplement

16 *Proc. Prehist. Soc. 23* (1957) 91–123

17 BRITTON, D. and RICHARDS, E. E. 1962. *Archaeometry 4*

18 APSIMON, A. 1954. *10th Ann. Rep. London University Inst. of Archaeology,* 37–62

49 Microscopic Studies of Ancient Metals

F. C. THOMPSON

EVEN TODAY IT IS IMPOSSIBLE to produce any metal in a state of absolute purity, in other words all our metals are in reality alloys. So long, however, as the impurity content does not exceed that which is characteristic of the extraction technique used, they may, for all normal purposes, be regarded as commercially pure materials. Thus a copper of the later third millennium BC[1] which contained only 97·4% of copper with 0·87% of tin, over 0·5% of lead and more than 1% of other impurities would to the metallurgist be merely an impure copper despite the tin which is present. When the impurities exceed the amount inevitably present in view of the works practice of the age, the presumption is that deliberate additions had been made and the term alloy then becomes justifiable.

With the exception of the metals which are found native, mainly iron, copper and gold, all the metallic articles *except* those of iron or steel had, until very recently, started life in the liquid state. In that condition most metals are miscible in each other in all proportions—lead being the main exception—but on solidification one of three things may happen. In the first place the metals in solution in each other in the molten state may remain in solution in the solid, yielding an alloy of the 'solid solution' type. Secondly, they may separate out more or less completely, giving what is termed a 'eutectic' in which both metals have frozen out simultaneously to produce a constituent which is a mechanical mixture of the two. Finally, the metals may combine to form compounds which are just as definite chemical compounds as is common salt. On which of these types of alloy has been formed depend both the microstructure and the properties.

As far as the properties are concerned, the solid solutions are by far the most important since they are harder than the metals of which they consist but yet have sufficient ductility to enable them to be worked both hot and cold. Further, when cold-worked the hardness is still further increased. The eutectics, being merely mixtures of the component metals, have broadly the properties of a metal, i.e. are relatively soft as compared with the solid solution. They have, however, relatively low melting points and are the essential constituents of the lower melting point solders. The intermetallic compounds are all characterized by high hardness and extreme brittleness, are unworkable and have rarely found any real field of application. When present in an alloy consisting mainly of a solid solution, however, they may exert a useful influence by providing a hard scaffold and thus increasing the strength appreciably. This is effected, however, at the expense of some loss of ductility, i.e. workability. As typical of these three classes of alloy structure may be mentioned the brasses with less than thirty-five per cent or so of zinc (solid solutions), soft solders (eutectics) and high-tin bronzes of the speculum metal type which may consist almost entirely of the copper-tin compound $Cu_{31} Sn_8$.

Although special microscopic equipment is produced for metallurgical work, the basic necessities are neither complicated nor expensive. Since for all practical purposes it is impossible to produce metallic sections so thin as to be transparent, such structures must be viewed by reflected light and the main, indeed almost the only essential piece of apparatus additional to the microscope itself is a 'vertical illuminator' by means of which the surface to be examined may be conveniently illuminated. Light from a reasonably intense source enters through a hole in the side of the illuminator A, Fig. 71, strikes a reflecting surface B and is concentrated by the objective, C, on to the specimen D. After reflection it again passes through the objective and travels up the microscope tube to the eye-piece. In some ways this arrangement is even simpler than that employed for transparent slides since the objective forms its own condenser. Two forms of reflector are in common use, one a plain glass cover slip which reflects a proportion of the incident light and later transmits a part up the tube. It will be apparent that this involves a considerable

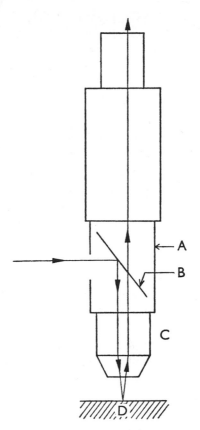

Fig. 71 Microscope with vertical illuminator.

loss of illuminating power but it has the advantage that, since the whole aperture of the lens is available for the formation of the image, a high degree of resolution is obtained. In the other type the reflection is effected by means of a prism which covers half the field of the objective with a corresponding loss of resolution in one direction but with the formation of a much brighter image. Except where high resolution at high magnifications is required, and this rarely happens in the sort of work with which we are concerned here, there is not much to choose between the two methods.

To obtain a surface suitable for examination, an area of the metal must first be given a mirror polish. This area need not in general be large and for many purposes a $\frac{1}{8}$ in. circle is sufficient, though there are cases where a more extensive examination may be desirable. Where hand-polishing is used, a flat is ground or filed on the article and the marks gradually eliminated by rubbing on specially prepared emery papers of finer and finer grade. On changing from one paper to the next the direction in which the rubbing is done is changed through 90° so that the scratches due to the coarser papers are removed each time. The Blue Back papers I.G. to 4/0, available from the English

Abrasives Corporation Ltd., provide a suitable series for most purposes. One word of warning may be given. The surface of the specimen can become quite hot if too much pressure is used in the rubbing down and, especially in the case of a quenched steel, the temperature may rise to an extent which will bring about quite appreciable changes in the structure of the metal.

Having obtained a surface which is flat and covered only by the finest scratches, these in their turn must be removed by polishing. This may be done by rubbing the specimen, after having most carefully washed off every trace of grit, on damp selvyt cloth stretched on plate glass and dressed with Silvo or Brasso for non-ferrous metals or specially prepared alumina for iron or steel. Diamond powder is even more effective but is more expensive. Among the brands of alumina powder on sale the 5/20 grade supplied by Griffin and George may be recommended. Since the clarity of the final structure depends entirely on the care and skill used in carrying out these processes, it will be apparent that there is much virtue in the old saying 'More haste, less speed'.

At this stage a pure metal if examined under the microscope would appear a structure-less blank and to develop the structure etching with some appropriate reagent which will dissolve away the polished surface is required. Before doing this, however, it is in the highest degree desirable to examine the sample in this unetched state. Flaws of all kinds such as the cracks in age-embrittled silver, Plate XXVIa, inclusions of slag, the presence of insoluble particles of lead, etc. are far more clearly revealed at this stage than is the case when the etching treatment has developed other structural features.

The final part of the preparation, the etching itself, is done with a reagent chosen according to the nature of the material under examination, and very many reagents are used by the specialist. For perhaps 99% of normal investigations two will however be found adequate: for non-ferrous metals and alloys a solution of 10% ferric chloride acidified with 2% hydrochloric acid, and for iron and steel a 2% solution of nitric acid in alcohol are commonly used. (Pour the nitric acid slowly into the alcohol in an open dish.) It is worth bearing in mind that it is always possible to re-etch a specimen if the structure is not sufficiently clearly developed but that if over-etched it will mean going right back to the emery papers and starting all over again. After etching the specimen, it must be thoroughly washed in running water and then equally thoroughly dried in absolute alcohol or some similar dehydrating medium. All this may sound somewhat complicated, but with a little practice and patience there is nothing beyond the resources of anyone prepared to take the necessary trouble.

NON-FERROUS METALS

The structure of a pure metal in the as-cast state is shown in Plate XXVIb and consists of irregularly shaped grains separated by boundaries which show up dark after the etching. These grains are the individual crystals of varying orientations. Some etching reagents colour the crystals differentially according to their orientations (c), but this must not be taken to imply any difference of composition. The best safeguard here is to note that all sorts of degrees of colouration are to be observed. When cold-worked, e.g. by hammering the edge of a blade, these grains become elongated (d), and in addition are

(a) Axes of copper and bronze from Britain and Ireland (× 1 : 2). Left to right: flat axe of copper (Ireland, later Neolithic); flanged axe of tin bronze (Corkstown, Co. Tyrone, Early Bronze Age); palstave of tin bronze (Andover, Hants, Middle Bronze Age); socketed axe of leaded tin bronze (Hammersmith, London, Late Bronze Age). (Pitt Rivers Museum, Oxford.)

Sb 2598·1

Au 2676·0

Fe 2739·5

Cu 2768·9

As 2780·2

Pb 2833·1

Sn 2840·0

Ni 3050·9

Bi 3067·7

Zn 3345·9

Ag 3382·9

(b) Spectrum of a bronze in the near ultra-violet region.

(see page 499) PLATE XXV

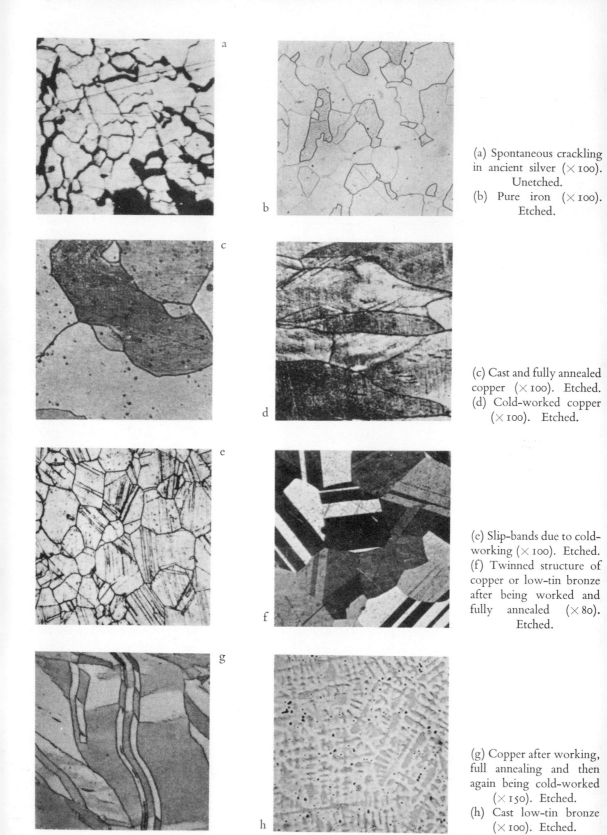

(a) Spontaneous crackling in ancient silver ($\times$ 100). Unetched.
(b) Pure iron ($\times$ 100). Etched.

(c) Cast and fully annealed copper ($\times$ 100). Etched.
(d) Cold-worked copper ($\times$ 100). Etched.

(e) Slip-bands due to cold-working ($\times$ 100). Etched.
(f) Twinned structure of copper or low-tin bronze after being worked and fully annealed ($\times$ 80). Etched.

(g) Copper after working, full annealing and then again being cold-worked ($\times$ 150). Etched.
(h) Cast low-tin bronze ($\times$ 100). Etched.

PLATE XXVI (see page 510)

(i) 'Burnt' structure in bronze (×100). Etched.
(j) Duplex structure in bronze. Typical of eutectic or the eutectic-like structure formed from solid solutions (×100). Etched.

(k) Eutectic in silver-copper alloy (×100). Etched.
(l) Widmannstätten pattern in meteorite (×10). Etched.

(m) Wrought iron (×200). Crystals of iron and streaks of slag. Etched.
(n) Superficially carburized iron (×100). Pearlite dark, ferrite light. Etched.

(o) Eutectoid structure of pearlite in slowly cooled steel (×00). Etched.
(p) Martensite in steel quenched from very high temperature (×250). Etched.

(q) 'Meteoric' structure in man-made steel heated to a yellow-heat and cooled in air (×100). Etched.
(r) Neumann bands (thin twins) in man-made iron (×100). Etched.

(see page 510) PLATE XXVII

(a) Part of the pneumatic tube system installed at the north face of the Brookhaven reactor. Here a small container, bearing sample material, is being inserted into one of the tubes. The container is then sped into the reactor under pneumatic pressure, for bombardment by neutrons. The sample, now radioactive, is quickly returned for use in some experiment. The system is useful in making radioactive isotopes of short half-life, which lose their radioactivity in seconds, or minutes. Delivery can be made either into this face of the reactor, or directly into one of several adjoining laboratories. Photo courtesy Brookhaven National Laboratory.

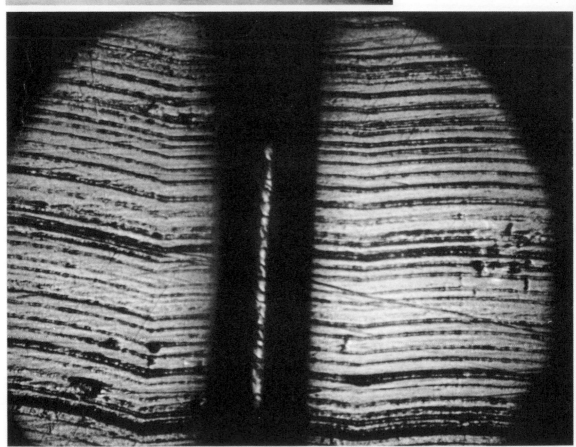

(b) Photomicrograph showing the laminar structure of a small piece of weathering crust on glass. The dark central band is a human hair placed across the layers to show the relative scale of sizes. Photo courtesy Corning Museum of Glass.

PLATE XXVIII (see page 519)

crossed by numerous straight lines called 'slip-bands' (e). On reheating such a worked metal the structure remains unaffected until a certain 'temperature of recrystallization' has been reached when new crystals make their appearance which are no longer elongated and in which slip-lines no longer occur. Such cold-worked and annealed material is, however, characterized by the broad bands shown in Plate XXVIf which are due to twinning of the crystals and which, with an appropriate etching technique, may separate light and dark areas within a single crystal. If the metal with such a twinned structure is again cold-worked, the grains are once more distorted and slip-bands formed anew. The evidence of the earlier twinning is not, however, eliminated but the originally straight twin boundaries are now bent and irregular (g). From this appearance under the microscope then it would be possible to say quite dogmatically that the sample in question was a non-ferrous metal which had been cold-worked and then annealed above the temperature of spontaneous recrystallization and, following this, had again been worked. It is not possible, however, to say how often the cold-work—annealing—cold-work cycle had been repeated; it might have been done twenty times and still yield exactly the same microstructure. However, should the working be done 'hot'—at a temperature above that of recrystallization—this amounts structurally to simultaneous working and annealing, and a twinned structure identical to that of Plate XXVIf will be obtained. This recrystallization temperature not only differs from metal to metal, but is also markedly influenced by the impurities present in solid solution, the temperature rising as the material becomes less and less pure. Some *very* pure metals, among them gold, copper and silver, will recrystallize spontaneously after cold-work even at ordinary temperatures in the course of time. Thus gold nuggets have been found to show a structure indistinguishable from that of Plate XXVIf due to grain-gold being autogenously welded into bigger and bigger masses under the hammering of the gravel in river beds and the spontaneous recrystallization in the course of millennia of the deformed grains. Further, the more severe the cold-work the more readily does the metal recrystallize. Once recrystallization is complete the initially small grains commence to grow, becoming larger and larger as both the temperature of annealing and the time at that temperature are increased. It is rarely possible, therefore, to do more than say in broad, general terms that the metal with the larger grain size has been heated to the higher temperature or, alternatively, that it has been kept there for a longer time.

NON-FERROUS ALLOYS

Passing on now to the non-ferrous alloys which form a single solid solution much of what has just been said also applies. Plate XXVIf for instance might equally well be either a pure metal or a solid solution in the cold-worked and annealed state. There are, however, two cases in which the structures are not the same. A solid solution in the as-cast state shows the structure of (h) whilst the pure metal is shown in (b). The 'dendritic' structure of (h) results from changes in composition of the solid solution which occur during the solidification process together with the curious manner in which it passes from the liquid to the solid state. Unlike a material such as common salt which forms a minute cubic crystal which grows as a cube, metals start from a crystal nucleus and grow by throwing out solid arms usually in three directions at right angles to each other. From these other branches grow until the whole mass is solid. In the alloy the primary arms are of the purest composition, the impurities increasing as solidification goes on. On annealing at a sufficiently high temperature and for a sufficiently long time, the variations of composition are wiped out by diffusion and finally the structure of the cast and fully annealed alloy differs in no way from that of (b). This diffusion is a process requiring time, and alloys are frequently found in which the dendritic pattern is still incompletely removed even when the material has been worked and then fully recrystallized by annealing.

It will be apparent from the identities of most of the structures of similarly treated pure metals and solid solutions that the microscope is not a substitute for chemical analysis although in some cases an approximation to the composition can be given. Its real function is to enable the treatment, thermal and mechanical, to which the alloy has been subjected to be determined, and, with certain exceptions, this can often be done with certainty.

Another feature of the structure of a solid solution, not found with pure metals, is that which results from heating it to a temperature at which partial fusion has taken place, i.e. the material has been 'burnt'. Just as the alloy freezes over a range of temperature, so does it melt progressively as the temperature rises. In (i) is shown a typical structure obtained when fusion has just commenced, the duplex constituent, a eutectic, forming initially at the grain boundaries where the impurities tend to concentrate.

Although, as has already been mentioned, some metals do dissolve in each other in all proportions even in the solid state, in most cases there is only a limited range of solid solubility after which another constituent, or 'phase', is formed. In the brasses for instance the solid copper can dissolve not more than 39% of zinc, above which a second phase makes its appearance. For our purposes, however, the more interesting case is provided by the alloys of copper and tin, the bronzes. With low tin contents that element remains in solution, yielding in the case of a casting the structure of (h). As the amount of tin increases another, eutectic-like, constituent makes its appearance (j). These structures in the bronzes are greatly influenced by the rate of cooling from high temperatures and it is, therefore, dangerous to attempt to predict the composition from an isolated microscopic structure.

Another interesting example of a eutectic structure is found in the silver–copper system. The maximum amount of copper which solid silver can dissolve is about 9% and usually it is less. When the silver becomes saturated with copper any increase in the copper content results in the appearance of the silver–copper eutectic whose structure is shown in (k). The higher the copper content the more of the eutectic is present until at about 30% the whole alloy is composed of this constituent. Since the eutectic has the lowest melting point of any alloy of these metals, it forms the essential constituent of the silver solders and has in fact been recognized as such in a plated coin of Neapolis[2] of about 300 BC.

Since with the exception of 'speculum metal' the intermetallic compounds found little or no application in ancient metallurgy, this brief account of the structures of the non-ferrous metals and alloys fairly covers the period from man's first use of native copper down to around the Middle Bronze Age. An exception occurs, however, in connection with the very curious alloys containing appreciable amounts of arsenic, lead, antimony or iron which seem to usher in the true bronzes—in the metallurgical sense—in which a fairly constant tin content of some 10–12% was used. These rather remarkable alloys, which suggest deliberate research [3] on the part of the craftsmen of the time, weld together the earlier use of varying and relatively low additions of tin and the later, more sophisticated alloys, and often have more complicated structures which cannot be discussed here.

IRON AND STEEL

That the earliest iron known to and used by man was of meteoric origin there can be no doubt, and the belief that such iron is too brittle to be worked into usable forms was effectively disposed of by Zimmer [4] when he showed that of the metallic meteorites known in 1916 no less than 99% possessed sufficient ductility to permit them to be forged down either hot or cold. It is well known that meteoric iron may be distinguished from the early man-made iron by invariably containing nickel from about 3% to around 35%, often together with not inappreciable amounts of cobalt. Terrestrial iron itself is, however, often made from ores which contain small amounts of nickel much of which will find its way into the metal. The presence, therefore, in such iron of some 1% or so of nickel must *not* be taken as any indication of a meteoric origin. There is, however, one problem which still awaits a complete solution. When meteoric iron corrodes away entirely what happens to the nickel originally present? Does it remain in the rust and so still provide evidence of its origin or does it pass away as soluble salts in the water responsible for the corrosion? An answer to these questions might at times be of immense value.

The characteristic structure (Plate XXVIII) of certain types of meteorite is well known. It must not be overlooked, however, that this structure is *not* typical of all, or perhaps even of the majority, of metallic meteorites. Further, when a meteorite with this structure is reheated to a good red heat transformations occur as a result of which it is permanently eradicated, the structure then becoming quite indistinguishable from that of a man-made metal of the same composition.

Since the whole of the man-made iron, and later steel, manufactured in antiquity had a totally different origin from that of the copper and bronzes, it is not surprising that corresponding differences are to be found in the microstructures. None of this iron or steel was ever molten, the product of the furnaces being merely a crumbly, coke-like lump of semi-solid particles of iron.

When the 'ball' of spongy iron is withdrawn from the furnace the metal is admixed with molten slag, bits of charcoal, etc. which are in part, but in part only, expelled during the subsequent heatings and hammerings. It follows that the bars produced still contain some slag which has been drawn out into threads by the working, the whole structure under low magnifications almost resembling a whirlpool. At higher magnification (m) the structure consists of light grains of iron, called 'ferrite' by the metallographer, and slag. Such iron is soft and is incapable of being hardened by quenching, though some degree of hardening can be induced by cold-work. It is to such iron that Polybius refers in his description[5] of the Roman defeat of the Celts at the battle of Addua where, discussing the long Celtic swords, he says that these were 'easily bent, and would only give one downward cut with any effect, but that after this the edges got so turned and the blades so bent, that, unless they had time to straighten them with the foot against the ground, they could not deliver a second blow'.

An enormous step forward was taken when it was realized that when this iron was heated in glowing charcoal something happened as a result of which the metal became much stronger and far more capable of retaining a sharp cutting edge. The explanation is provided by Plate XXVIIn in which it will be seen that in addition to the soft, white ferrite there is now a second, dark-etching constituent 'pearlite' which, at a sufficiently high magnification, shows a duplex structure of iron and iron carbide, Fe_3C, very much like that of a eutectic (o). It is in fact a 'eutectoid', i.e. a eutectic but formed from a solid, as distinct from a liquid solution. The carbon which has been absorbed during the heating in very hot charcoal is found entirely in these pearlitic areas which, therefore, increase in amount as the time and temperature of the carburization have increased. With this increase in the proportion of pearlite to ferrite goes a corresponding increase in the hardness. By controlling the treatment it was, as (n) shows, possible to carburize a cutting edge but still leave a soft but tough backing, or alternatively to convert the whole article into steel.

In addition to this increase of hardness, such steely iron (steel is only iron into which varying amounts of carbon have been introduced) possesses a further, and even more important, property, namely that of being hardened much more intensely if it be heated to a temperature above about $750°C$, a red heat, in a reducing atmosphere and then quenched in cold water. The explanation of such quench-hardening is evident from (p). The duplex, pearlitic structure of the unhardened steel has disappeared and in its place a new phase 'martensite' with a needle-like structure has been induced. Lightly etched in the alcoholic nitric acid solution—a few seconds are normally adequate— martensite appears as a light brown constituent and it is to the formation of this intensely hard material that the hardening is attributable. The early smiths must have discovered very soon that just as the carburization was possible only in the atmosphere within the mass of glowing charcoal, so any reheating of the steel in an oxidizing atmosphere would, by burning out the carbon, undo all the good which had been obtained by the previous treatment, by leaving a soft and unhardenable skin of practically pure iron.

When the degree of carburization had been substantial, and when the quenching was drastic, as in cold water, a blade although very hard would be distinctly brittle and liable to break. To reduce this brittleness the quenched steel may either be reheated to a low temperature—even boiling water will have some effect—or alternatively the quenching may be made slightly less severe. There can be no doubt that the latter technique was that adopted by the earliest workers and from this fact were derived the remarkable quenching fluids which were used. The symbolism of the belief in the efficiency of the urine of a red-headed boy is fairly obvious, and such nostrums persisted until well after the Middle Ages. Indeed, when the writer was a student, he was informed that there was an old-established Sheffield firm that still imported barrels of camels' urine from Egypt for this purpose. As the tempering treatment is carried out at progressively higher temperatures the rate of etching of the martensite becomes faster and faster until instead of the light, straw-coloured martensite a black-etching, microscopically structureless constituent is produced.

The technical details which must be satisfied if the best results are to be obtained are of the utmost importance. Learning by experience was quite evidently slow and it is to the unusual skill of certain smiths that blades to which magical properties were ascribed were due. The well-known letter of the Hittite king Hattusilis III (1275–1250 BC) probably to the king of Assyria[6] must refer to a quenched steel worked with all the skill and art available anywhere at that time: 'They will produce good iron, but as yet they will not have finished. When they have finished I shall send it to you. Today now I am dispatching an iron dagger-blade to you.' A single blade of sufficient value to be an appropriate present from one important king to another was most certainly not 'iron', and almost as certainly was a carburized and quenched steel with a microstructure not dissimilar from that of (p).

In conclusion two other typical structures may be discussed. Although all ancient steels in the unhardened state contain pearlite usually with more or less ferrite, the distribution of these constituents is by no means constant even when the amount of carbon present is the same. When the steel has been cooled down from a relatively low temperature, say a dullish red heat, the pearlite areas are small and arranged in a purely higgledy-piggledy manner. As the temperature to which the steel was heated gets higher and higher the size of the pearlite regions increases and a triangular pattern analogous to the Widmanstätten structure in meteorites is gradually formed (q). By itself, however, this pattern is no evidence of a meteoric origin and can be induced in any steel by appropriate very high-temperature treatment; it merely shows that the last time the specimen cooled down it was from a very high temperature—a yellow heat in the case of (q)—a rate of cooling that was reasonably slow and without any mechanical treatment such as hammering.

The final structure to be considered (r) shows crystals of ferrite crossed by relatively straight bands all parallel with one another within a given grain but changing direction from one crystal to the next. These Neumann bands are found only in the ferrite and afford evidence of some slight distortion of the material, usually by sudden stresses such as might occur on the edge of an axe. First found in meteorites, they are sometimes believed, erroneously, to provide proof that the material is in fact meteoric in origin. This is not the case since such Neumann bands are by no means uncommon in more or less pure, man-made iron especially if the metal is somewhat brittle due, for instance, to a rather high content of phosphorus.

The treatment given here has necessarily been sketchy and only the simplest examples have been discussed. It is hoped however that it may have provided sufficient evidence of the sort of assistance, often obtainable in no other way, which the microscope can give in the examination of ancient metals, and at the same time of showing how desirable it is when more complicated structures do occur of calling on the aid, usually gladly given, of someone more experienced in the interpretation of metallographic evidence.

ACKNOWLEDGEMENTS

The thanks of the writer are due to the President and Council of the Royal Numismatic Society for permission to use several of the illustrations from his paper published in the *Numismatic Chronicle*, Sixth Series, Vol. XVI, p. 329, 1956, and to Dr E. S. Hedges of the Tin Research Institute for Plate XXVIh and Plate XXVIIi and j.

REFERENCES

1 BURTON-BROWN, T. 1951. *Excavations in Azarbaijan, 1948*, London, 193
2 THOMPSON, F. C. and CHATTERJEE, A. K. 1951. *Nature 168*, 158
3 —— 1958. *Man 58*, 1
4 ZIMMER, G. F. 1916. *J. Iron and Steel Inst. 94*, 306
5 NEWTON FRIEND, J. 1923. Iron in Antiquity; *J. Iron and Steel Inst. Carnegie Schol. Mem. 12*, 219
6 GURNEY, O. R. 1952. *The Hittites*, Harmondsworth, 83

50 The Analytical Study of Glass in Archaeology

RAY W. SMITH

GLASS HAS TRADITIONALLY been neglected by archaeologists, and its historical development has been only imperfectly understood. Thus, only in rare cases has the archaeologist been able to date graves by glass found in them. Usually it is the association of glass with other materials, such as ceramics and coins, that permits its dating. Now, with the technical study of ancient glass receiving more attention than ever before, there is a good prospect that the situation will be rectified.

Technological research on ancient glass presents several particularly difficult problems. One of these, due to the special nature of the substance, is the determination of the raw materials used. In view of the amorphous character of glass, one might say that its components have lost their individual identity, and crystallographic observations, for example, give no clue to the types of materials that were placed in the glassmaker's crucible.

It has been observed, moreover, that glassmaking formulae were virtually identical through centuries on end and across vast areas. As a result, the most piercing and accurate analyses attainable are essential to the full determination of regional and chronological differentiations. Fortunately, methods are becoming available which will surely elevate technological research on ancient glass to a new level of effectiveness.

It should be pointed out forthwith that an 'analysis' of a specimen does not necessarily justify the effort put into it. It has been long known that nearly all ancient glass is of the soda–lime variety. If an analysis is so sketchy that it reveals no more than this fact it obviously contributes nothing to our knowledge. To carry significance, a chemical analysis of ancient glass must reveal in what respects the specimen conforms to or departs from the characteristics of the various recognizable groups of glass in antiquity.

Unless and until there is a comprehensive and well-organized backdrop of analytical data against which analyses can be compared and thus interpreted, they are of only limited usefulness. But this is a prodigious commitment. There are well over one hundred 'area-periods' in ancient glass, so that several thousand reliable and accurate analyses in great depth, of well-authenticated specimens of known origin in time and place, will have to be available before any single analysis can justify a narrow definitive attribution.

It is clear that the first phase[7] of a research programme should be the organized accumulation of data. Investigation of highly specialized problems could well be deferred in some cases to a later date.

A good beginning has been made at the Brookhaven National Laboratory in the United States, where Dr Edward V. Sayre has studied several hundred specimens of ancient glass.[4] This work has revealed (see Fig. 72, Table A) that ancient glass in the

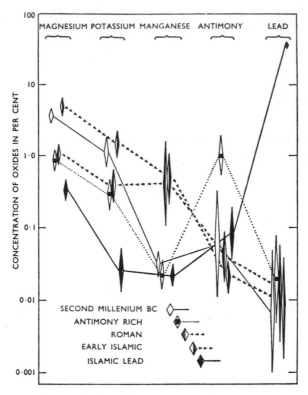

Fig. 72 Standard deviation ranges for concentration
of various metal oxides in the five main categories of
western ancient glass.

TABLE A

Mean concentration of the oxides that best characterize ancient glass.

Glass group	No. of Specimens	Mean percent concentrations and standard deviation ranges				
		Magnesium MgO	Potassium K_2O	Manganese* MnO	Antimony Sb_2O_5	Lead PbO
Second millennium BC	15	3·6 (4·6–2·9)	1·13 (1·89–0·69)	0·032 (0·046–0·021)	0·058 (0·32–0·011)	0·0068 (0·048–0·0010)
Antimony rich	34	0·86 (1·24–0·60)	0·29 (0·47–0·17)	0·022 (0·035–0·014)	1·01 (1·93–0·53)	0·019 (0·077–0·0047)
Roman	73	1·04 (1·47–0·73)	0·38 (0·63–0·22)	0·41 (1·60–0·10)	0·040 (0·089–0·018)	0·014 (0·057–0·0033)
Early Islamic	66	4·9 (6·5–3·6)	1·45 (2·2–0·94)	0·47 (1·07–0·21)	0·021 (0·035–0·012)	0·0088 (0·047–0·0016)
Islamic lead	6	0·33 (0·47–0·24)	0·026 (0·051–0·013)	0·022 (0·031–0·016)	0·081 (0·19–0·035)	36 (40–33)

★ Some glasses with a characteristic dark blue or violet colour contain considerably more manganese
than colourless glasses of the same type. It has been assumed that manganese was added deliberately to such
glasses as a colorant, and they have been excluded in calculating the average manganese values.

Occident was divided into five major compositional groups, which were sufficiently distinct from each other that in nearly every instance a single analysis can clearly assign an ojbect to one of them.

With the exception of Islamic lead-glass, the groups are soda-lime glass. The categories are described in terms of the expected ranges of concentrations of the five elements, magnesium, potassium, manganese, antimony, and lead, which most clearly differentiate the groups.

Glass of the second millennium BC group (fifteenth century BC to about seventh century BC), wherever found, has a high magnesium content. Glass of the antimony-rich group (about sixth century BC to about fourth century AD) is characterized by a lower potassium and magnesium content and by the consistent appearance of antimony in high concentration. From the earliest production of hollow glassware antimony was used deliberately in colour chemistry, but only sporadically. About the sixth century BC it began to be widely used as a decolorant. The high-antimony formula apparently became the standard composition in Greece, Asia Minor, and Persia during the fifth and fourth centuries BC, and the type continued to be used from the Euphrates valley eastward during the ascendancy of Rome.

Farther to the west, the picture was different. The great glassmaking centres of the Syrian coast began to use another composition, which we now call the Roman group. It differed from the antimony-rich group chiefly in its much lower antimony content, and usually in its correspondingly higher manganese content. This suggests that the distinction represented simply the use of one decolorant instead of another.

The Roman group is also found in the production of glass centres in Eygpt, Byzantium, Italy, and the Western Provinces, remaining with little change through the Byzantine, Frankish, and Saxon periods. Whereas there is as yet no case known of the antimony-rich formula being used in southern Syria and on the Syrian coast, it does occur, and sometimes frequently, in all areas farther to the west.

The emergent story of antimony and manganese in Italy and the Western Provinces is as follows. Manganese seems to have been the only decolorant used until towards the end of the first century AD, when antimony was introduced. During the remaining Roman centuries both decolorants were used, sometimes together, sometimes singly, and occasionally glass was made without a deliberate decolorant.

By the fourth century antimony was on its way out, and with the fifth century it apparently ceased to be used, both in the West and very likely elsewhere.

During its use as a decolorant, antimony must have been preferred to manganese, as it is an incomparably better decolorant. Presumably manganese was used through considerations of economy and availability. In any case, antimony must have been considered by the ancient glassmaker as a magic and mysterious substance, for here was a product which could impart both deep and luxurious colour to his product, as well as eliminate all signs of unwanted tints, producing a sparkling, limpid, crystal glass.

The early-Islamic group (introduced eighth–tenth century AD, or earlier) is marked by a return to the higher magnesium and potassium concentrations of the second millennium BC group, but, in general, without showing the low manganese content of the early glass. This glass is sufficiently similar to that of the second millennium BC group that the assumption has been voiced of an uninterrupted continuation of the same glassmaking tradition. The present analyses, however, would suggest that a lapse of many centuries occurred between the production of these two categories of glass. Certainly, glasses of both the antimony-rich and Roman groups were produced in some of the areas destined to become Islamic. The possibility, however, that the early formula was used without interruption in certain regions (Mesopotamia, Parthia, or Central Asia?) merits investigation.

The identification of the Islamic lead-glass group (introduced eighth–tenth century AD?) is based upon only six analyses, but the six glasses came from a variety of sources and yet possess remarkably similar compositions. Islamic lead-glass contains considerably more lead and less alkali and lime than most of the occasional New Kingdom high-lead glass. It is distinctly different from the lead-barium Chinese glass reported by Seligman and Beck,[5] and also from the two main types of eleventh–thirteenth century AD Russian lead-glasses described by Bezborodov.[1]

Two extensions of the foregoing findings are urgently needed. The initial and terminal dates of each group must be closely established, and it will be important to determine where each major change in glass composition first appeared, as well as to uncover the reasons for the changes. We do not yet understand, for example, the considerable decrease in potassium and magnesium around the middle of the first millennium BC and the increase in these elements again after the middle of the first millennium AD. The minor differentiations, moreover, which must surely exist within a group, either on a regional or a chronological basis, need to be exhaustively explored.

A few regional differentiations have already emerged. The antimony-rich Achaemenian glass from Persepolis, for example, shows systematically somewhat less titanium, zirconium and lead than early high-antimony glass from Greece (Phidias workshop) and Asia Minor. Early Islamic glass from north-eastern Iran seems to differ from material found in other parts of Iran, and clearly there is significantly less manganese in glass of the same group from sites in Mesopotamia and north-western Iran than in finds from other Islamic areas.

The most useful single technique in this work has been arc spectrography. While there is nothing novel in the use of this method in glass analysis, it produced for years simply qualitative results. Sayre,[4] however, had developed his methodology to the point where results are reproducible with standard deviations within twenty per cent of reported values. Arc spectrography offers the advantage that it is rapid, recording the concentrations of a large number of elements with one or two exposures. A disadvantage is that the operation consumes the specimen. Certain elements, also, do not show up satisfactorily in arc spectrography, for example phosphorus.

X-ray fluorescence has also proved its usefulness for our purposes. It is non-destructive, and either powdered samples or complete specimens of considerable size can be examined. In the latter case, a coloured spot may be caused by the exposure, but it is easily eliminated by moderate heating. The data produced by X-ray fluorescence is valid only for that portion of a specimen which lies close to the surface, a fact that must be considered if there is any surface contamination, decay, or lack of homogeneity. It has been determined that X-ray fluorescence is able to handle somewhat smaller samples than those required by arc spectrography, and that it can satisfactorily measure the concentrations of the five elements of Table A.

An important refinement of X-ray fluorescence, called the electron microbeam probe, is now available. This apparatus focuses its beam on an area only one micron in diameter, and can thus be used on extremely small specimens. Although the method has already been applied to archaeological problems, very little, if any, use of it has been made with ancient glass.

Several applications of the electron microbeam probe in respect to archaeological glass suggest themselves readily. One of them might well reveal the identity of a component material in glass of the fifth century AD. At that time glassmaking competence was in retrogression almost everywhere. Through carelessness or inability the impure matrix of a vessel frequently showed red streaks. The phenomenon was particularly frequent in the Rhineland. It is assumed that the glassmakers did not melt their batches at a sufficiently high temperature to achieve complete homogeneity, and that the red streaks represent movement of one of the imperfectly fused materials during the inflation of the paraison on the master's blowpipe.

If the microscopic beam of the electron probe were passed across the surface of such a vessel, there would be a sudden increase in the recording of concentrations for some elements and decreases for others at the moment the scanning cuts across one of the hairlines of these red streaks. This evidence might establish the approximate composition of one of the substances going into the batch, and lead to its identification with some type of natural deposit available to the ancients.

Another valuable use for the electron microbeam probe would be in determining the colour chemistry of fused mosaic plaques.[6] These precious tiny slices sometimes carry six or more colours of glass, both opaque and transparent, in closely spaced, minute areas. A scanning with the microbeam probe would quickly reveal the oxides by which each colour effect was set up. If one or two colours showed a divergence in its basic composition from the others, the possibility would have to be considered that the glass factory, unable to produce certain colours, had to go afield for these special shades.

Supplementing arc spectrography and the X-ray fluorescence equipment, flame photometry and colorimetry have been used with success for special purposes. Older methods of wet chemistry are still used effectively in the examination of archaeological glass specimens, and will continue to be applied, particularly to specialized problems involving small numbers of specimens. As the newer techniques are further refined and become more rapid, sensitive, accurate and economical, they are likely to be increasingly used. This will certainly be the case in larger programmes where extensive series of specimens are to be examined.

There can be little doubt that future research on ancient glass will turn to still unused, advanced methods of analysis. Sayre, for example, has already used the atomic reactor at Brookhaven with success on Greek pottery, and his preliminary investigations of ancient glass with the same neutron activation method show that certain patterns in the rare earths are present and can be uncovered in this way. Neutron activation can work with concentrations below the limits of spectrographic sensitivity, in fact can detect and measure some elements down to concentrations of a few parts per million million. The method is thus advantageous in the study of 'trace-trace' elements. As it is arduous and time-consuming, however, its use is likely to be confined for the present to problems beyond the reach of other methods.

Before examining further the probable future course of technological research on ancient glass, it is advisable to consider the proper objectives of this research. As the available basic analytical data expand, which is rapidly occurring, the archaeologist will expect the technologist to submit his findings in a form susceptible of far-reaching interpretation.

We have seen that a specimen of ancient glass can now be assigned to a compositional group on the basis of its analysis. This is analytical dating of a sort, but is only useful to the extent that the range in time of a group is not inordinately long. It is not enough to be able to determine, shall we say, that a given specimen belongs to the antimony-rich group and was made somewhere between the sixth century BC and fourth century AD. The span of a thousand years must be reduced to a century or less. The archaeologist, moreover, will insist on knowing where the specimen was produced.

Actually, there is a widespread misconception about the importance of 'dating techniques'. As valuable as it frequently is for the technologist to tell the archaeologist how ancient an object is, it would be obviously absurd to conclude that the usefulness of a method begins and ends with its ability to 'date'. The period of production of much ancient glass is already known from such circumstances as style, inscriptions, and association with other dated objects.

What we are after is much more basic and comprehensive. The objective is no less than that of archaeology itself—the advancement of human knowledge through the study of ancient cultures. We believe that man's understanding of himself, his future and his relationship to the order of things will immensely benefit from an expanded comprehension of his origins and his past. To be sure, the improved ability to date our objects will be an important result of the current technological advances. But this is only a small segment, albeit a significant one, of the range of benefits that technology is busily preparing.

We must at long last determine which substances were used as raw materials in each period. Little progress has been made in this direction. It is still moot, for example, whether plant ashes or soda deposits were used as the necessary alkalis. The resolution of these questions will open the way for an attack on a problem of far-reaching significance—the identification of individual deposits. If this can be accomplished, the door will open for significant new light to be shed on trade routes in antiquity.

A hint of these possibilities is contained in the recent observation that the basic composition of glass did not change in the Western Provinces with the break-up of Roman power in the fourth century AD. The analysis of a piece of Frankish glass from the Rhineland, for example, of the seventh century AD, is very little divergent from that of a beaker found at Pompeii from the first century. As it is commonly believed that no local source of soda alkali was available to the glassmakers in the West, it would appear that commercial traffic on the Mediterranean continued to be active, despite the political dislocations attendant on the events of the fourth century.

Ancient glass and its manufacturing background will not be adequately understood until more is known of furnace design and shop techniques. At each juncture of development there was a maximum level of accomplishment, determined in some measure by the highest attainable furnace temperature. This was dependent in turn on the type of fuel used as well as on furnace design. It is likely that changes in these practical conditions will have coincided at times with new departures in glass composition and with marked changes, up or down, in the quality of the product.

Firing circumstances in ancient glass furnaces, that is, the existence or absence of reducing conditions, will have profoundly affected the level of glass competence. And finally, chemistry of decolorization and the achievement of an extensive glass palette are matters that should be fully explored.

Research on the shop traditions of ancient glassmakers necessitates an ambitious pilot plant programme. We can learn with certainty how the ancients made their products in no other way than by doing it ourselves. When the raw materials used in antiquity are positively identified by careful analytical research, they should be melted down in the proportions used for the known ancient groups, and each type of glass fashioned under conditions duplicating as closely as possible the confirmed or presumed circumstances that obtained in these early shops.

This means constructing crucibles and furnaces and the use exclusively of tools and shop equipment which, in the absence of direct knowledge, may be assumed to have been available in the early periods of the art. The results of this exercise will surely be astonishing in given instances. Before drawing any conclusions as to how a type of glass was fashioned, every possible bit of evidence must be derived from the objects themselves. Visual examination can reveal tool and mould marks. The study of ancient glass surfaces, using the microscope if necessary, frequently produces clear evidence of an object's manipulative background.

No inquisitive observation of ancient glass should proceed without close attention to its bubble pattern. These virtually always-present flaws speak volumes. The size, shape, orientation and distribution of bubbles illuminate the handling of an object from the time an incandescent blob of fused raw materials is withdrawn from the crucible until hardening of the matrix on the blowpipe or pontil, or within a mould, precludes any further fashioning except by the cold technique of abrasion. The behaviour of bubbles in viscous glass is still only imperfectly understood. Full interpretation of bubble evidence cannot be achieved until all contributing factors have been precisely determined at the laboratory level.

One of the end products of forthcoming research on ancient glass will be some understanding of the structure of the vast industry that created it. We need to know whether it was competitive or monopolistic, whether it controlled its sources of raw materials or had to bid against other consumers for its basic substances. And where was the fountainhead at each period, whence came the epochal advances of early glass history.

It will be valuable to determine, for example, whether there were several 'sides' to the industry at any given period. Did the expansion of the industry in the first century AD occur from a Syrian and an Egyptian base separately? Or was there indeed any distinction, organizationally or technically, between the glassmaking of Sidon and Alexandria? How revealing it would be to determine that two distinct types of glass, compositionally speaking, were being made concurrently in the Rhineland at the end of the second century AD, and that one of them was identical with Syrian, the other with Egyptian production of the same time.

How, then, are these matters to be settled? Probably not by sole reliance on analytical methods presently in use. Many of the differentiations, albeit systematic ones, that will be the keys to important problems, will be found only in the extremely low concentrations of 'trace-trace' elements, or in subtle differences in the amounts of larger constituents. Thus an even greater degree of sensitivity and accuracy will be required in analytical methods. Neutron activation, for example, is likely to be increasingly used.

A purely hypothetical case will illustrate the possibilities of 'trace-trace' analysis. When analysed by normal methods, glass found at Pompeii from the first century AD is indistinguishable in composition from that made at Sidon. It may well be that both were made from the same materials with a common source. A systematic distinction might still be present if the crucibles were made from local clays in each instance. In Pompeii, shall we say, the corrosive action of the hot furnaces drew a minute concentration of an element from the crucibles into the batch, whereas this element, not being present in the clay used for Sidonian crucibles, cannot be found in glass from Sidon. The point is that such a minor systematic distinction would be impossible to detect except by 'trace-trace' methods.

There is good reason to believe that isotopic studies will have to be applied to the analysis of archaeological specimens. It is known that systematic isotopic ratio differences for some elements are to be found in nature, according to the geologic history of a substance or other circumstances, and that in some cases one or more isotopic ratios will accordingly vary from deposit to deposit. In any case, the availablity of the mass spectrometer suggests that isotopic research in various directions could benefit research on ancient glass.

The perfection of an ingenious new direct dating technique for glass will be watched with keen interest. Brill and Hood[2] have announced that decay in buried glass specimens proceeds under the influence of annual temperature or humidity cycles in such a manner that visible discontinuities in the cross-section of a layer of decay can be counted under the microscope as one would count the rings on a sawed tree trunk. Four specimens of ancient glass have thus far been examined in this way. They were found at ancient sites in Nishapur (Iran) and Sardis (Turkey). In all cases the number of layers counted corresponded approximately to the presumed age of the specimens on the basis of other evidence. The technique will be useful on glass which acquires a tight layer of decay, permitting cross-sections to be prepared.

The Brill-Hood method will be particularly valuable in special cases. For example, there are periods where the date of glass is seldom known. This is true of glass made between the seventh and eleventh centuries AD in the Middle East. Such specimens are not found in graves, and usually come from refuse heaps or other places which are disturbed or otherwise unsuitable for normal stratification dating. Due to these difficulties it has not been possible thus far to determine when and where the early Islamic composition was introduced. We know that it was not used in Egypt on glass weights and vessel stamps until the tenth century. It is further demonstrable that it was in use in Mesopotamia and Persia by the tenth century and probably in the ninth. But it occurs in certain objects from these areas which may well be earlier, their dates being still uncertain.

If the Brill-Hood technique can be perfected, it could be used to date with certainty a series of glass objects embracing a cross-section of glass accomplishment in various Islamic areas during these difficult centuries. This should provide the answer to the riddle of when and where the older 'Roman' composition was first abandoned in favour of a newer and doubtless more advanced glassmaking formula.

Meanwhile, excellent progress has been made with some of the specialized problems of glass research. Turner, for example, has been particularly active in exploring the methods used by the ancients to produce opacity and a range of desirable colours and in investigating other aspects of ancient glassmaking. Bezborodov[1] has analysed large numbers of specimens found in southern Russia, of which only a part qualify as ancient under the arbitrary definition of Sayre and Smith.[4]

As early as 1938 Seligman and Beck[5] examined numerous ancient Chinese glass objects, revealing that many such objects are rich in lead and others in barium, the latter not occurring in occidental glass except in traces. Caley[3] has now published a comprehensive résumé of analytical work on ancient glass.

The developing surge of research on ancient glass can proceed, as we have seen, on the basis of extensive preliminary published work. Perhaps there is danger that it will move forward too impetuously in some respects. Certainly there is need for much basic research before many of the ultimate projects are undertaken. Some of these necessary preparatory investigations have been mentioned. Others are:

(a) A searching study of the phenomenon of ageing, including the process of surface decay of buried and submerged glass. Some good work has been done in this direction, but little progress has been made in determining the precise relationships through which physical and chemical situations within the glass produce different types of decay at various rates when in contact with given soil conditions.

(b) Investigation of the selective absorption by plants of elements in the soils in which they grow.

(c) A survey of the raw materials which might have served the glass industries of antiquity in all areas accessible to presumed glass-manufacturing centres. This must include not only conventional chemical analysis, but the determination of 'trace-trace' concentrations and the investigation of isotopic ratios of possible usefulness in glass research.

(d) The detection and measurement of the maximum number of chemical elements which can be found in ancient glass, using a limited and carefully selected series of specimens typical of all periods and areas. In this work the most sensitive methods known should be used, irrespective of cost. This broad investigation should precede any extensive 'trace-trace' analyses in specific projects. Certainly many more elements than have been reported can be detected in ancient glass, and until the basic work has been performed it will be impossible to estimate where the most promising 'trace-trace' research can be undertaken.

The basic work alone that lies ahead is an immense commitment. It cannot all be done soon, and some of it will have to wait until the results accrue incidentally from programmes unrelated to glass research.

The stage is thus being set for large-scale research on ancient glass, work that will illuminate the field to a degree still visualized by few. It is doubtful, indeed it is perhaps not desirable, that such a programme will be authoritatively directed from any central point. Certainly the magnitude of the task will require the participation of numerous laboratories. It is to be hoped, in any case, that ample cross-contacts will be maintained between those undertaking glass research so that each contributes the most significant and effective work possible within the limitations of his facilities and resources, and that the programme as a whole advances purposefully towards its worthwhile goals.

REFERENCES

1 BEZBORODOV, M. A. 1956. Glass manufacturing in ancient Russia (in Russian), *Izdatel, Akad. Nauk Belarus S.S.R.*, no. 4758, Minsk
2 BRILL, R. H. and HOOD, H. P. 1961. *Nature 189*, 12–14
3 CALEY, E. R. 1961. Analyses of Ancient Glasses, 1790–1957; *Corning Mus. of Glass, Publ. Mon.*, Vol. 1
4 SAYRE, E. V. and SMITH, R. W. 1962. *Science 133*, 1824–26
5 SELIGMAN, C. G. and BECK, H. C. 1938. *Mus. Far East. Antiq., Bull.* no. 10, Stockholm
6 SMITH, R. W. 1957. Glass from the Ancient World. *Corning Mus. of Glass Publ.* nos. 98–121
7 —— 1958. *Archaeology 11*, 111–116

(a) Wool off a piece of skin from a frozen burial mound in the Altai Mountains; fourth or fifth century BC. (b) Fine-wool fibre in parchment from the Dead Sea Scrolls. (c) Medium-wool fibre in parchment from the Dead Sea Scrolls.

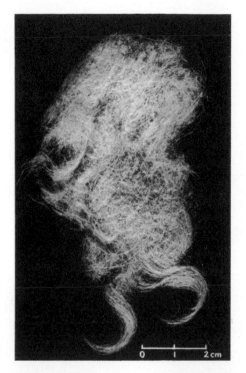
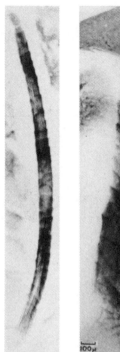

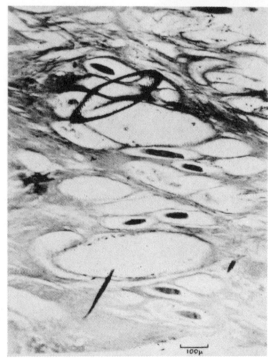

(d) Follicle group from a hairy sheep in a parchment from Hatfield, Yorkshire, dated AD 1403. Note the coarse fibre with a latticed medulla displaced from the primary follicle, and fine fibres in secondary follicles. From Ryder.[22]

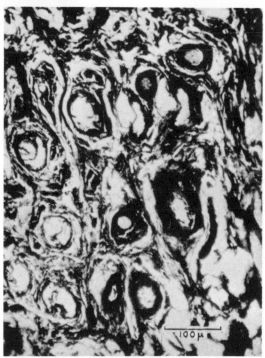

(e) Follicle remains characteristic of cattle skin in a specimen of medieval shoe leather from excavations in York; three of the follicles contain hairs.

(see page 529) PLATE XXIX

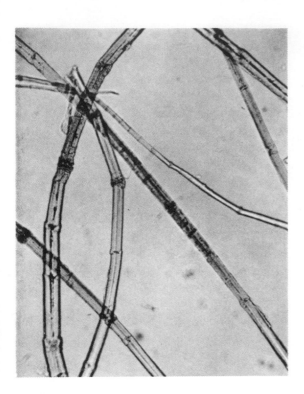

(a) Whole mount of fibres from sixth-century Turkish tombs ($\times 200$).

(b) Section of parchment from the Dead Sea Scrolls ($\times 88$).

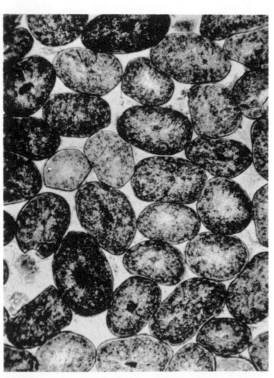

(c) Cross-section of unspun fibres from Ghirza ($\times 200$).

PLATE XXX (see page 545)

(a) Cross-section of fibres from Fonaby: packing of wool fibres (×190).

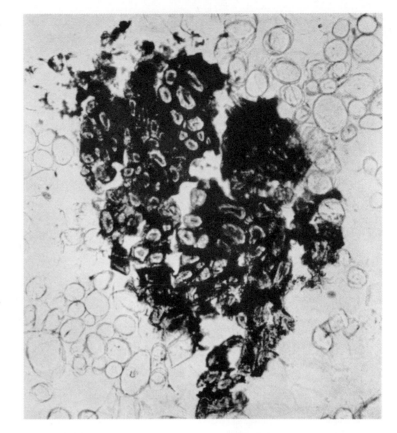

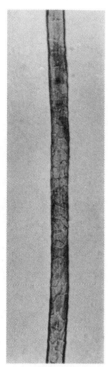

(b) Whole mount of fibres from Muraba'-ât (×200).

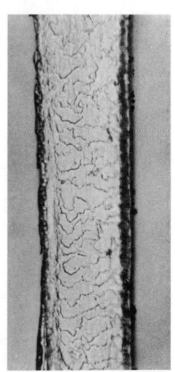

(c) Whole mount of pigmented fibres from Taplow Barrow (×210).

(d) Scale cast of fibre from Muraba'-ât. (×400)

(see page 545) PLATE XXXI

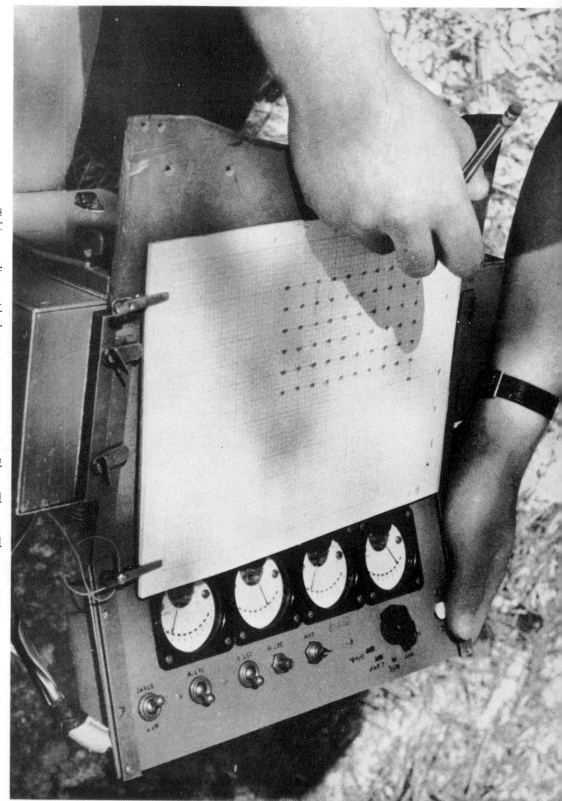

Taking readings with the proton magnetometer Photo Thomas Thompson.

PLATE XXXII (see page 555)

51 Remains Derived from Skin

M. L. RYDER

THIS CHAPTER discusses the microscopic examination of skin, leather and parchment, and the light it throws on the history of domestic animals. Among animal remains on archaeological sites, skin and hair are preserved less often than bone. They, and textiles derived from them (see chapter by Appleyard and Wildman), decay rapidly in the damp climate of northern Europe, and are destroyed by alkaline soil, but are well preserved in acid waterlogged conditions such as peat bogs. Skin is preserved well in the dry climate of the Near East, good examples being ancient Egyptian leather, and the parchment from the Dead Sea Scrolls. Another classic example of preservation is that of skin in the frozen wastes of central Asia. The frozen burial mounds of the local Early Iron Age (about the fifth to the first centuries BC) that have been excavated in the Altai Mountains have yielded skins of sheep and goats, and the hair of yaks, in addition to leather, carpets, and fur, wool and silk clothing.[1]

The animal from which skin remains have come has mainly been identified from any hairs remaining above the surface. Leather has been identified from the characteristic pattern on the skin surface, known as the grain pattern, which varies with species.[2] According to Plenderleith[3] it is almost impossible from the appearance of a parchment to identify the animal from which it has been derived. The method described here, which depends on the microscopic examination of hair remaining in the skin, provides a useful new approach to the study of ancient specimens.

This method was derived from one of the lines I followed in wool research at the Wool Industries Research Association, Leeds, which is to make a microscopic study of the size, numbers and grouping of wool fibres in specimens of skin from different breeds of sheep. In this way differences in the skin that cause differences in the fleece can be determined. In order to examine tissues under the microscope, they have to be cut into sections (thin slices) with a microtome (an instrument rather like a bacon slicer). In order to study the number and grouping of wool fibres in the skin, the sections are cut horizontally, i.e. parallel to the skin surface. The sections are then mounted on glass slides and stained to make the different parts visible before being examined under the microscope.

The skin is first treated with a fixative which precipitates the proteins of the living cells. Then, as the fixative is usually dissolved in water, and as the tissue is supported during the cutting by being embedded in wax, it has to be dehydrated before it can be put into the wax. This is done by passing the tissue gradually through alcoholic solutions of increasing strength, until absolute alcohol is reached. Then the tissue is passed through a solvent such as xylol which will mix with both alcohol and wax.

This histological method has been detailed so that the reader will appreciate the preparation that is necessary before a fresh specimen can be examined. The essential first stage, in order to obtain good microscopic detail, is considered to be the fixation, and this must be carried out soon after death. I was therefore surprised to find that dried skin gave almost as good preparations of the microscopic structure of the follicles in which hairs and wool fibres grow, as fresh skin that had been fixed. This came about when my interests widened to include wild sheep and the history of domestic sheep,[4,5] and it happened that the only source of skin from some of the wild sheep was from dried skins in museum collections. The good preparations obtained from dried skin in turn suggested that, if archaeological material was available, the method might be used to study the evolution of domestic animals towards the different breeds in existence today. Ancient specimens of skin, that might show what the coats of primitive domestic animals were like, were therefore sought.

Skin from the sheep that the ancient Egyptians mummified would have been ideal for this, but according to the British Museum no mummified sheep are available in Britain. In addition, with sheep, the body was apparently not mummified whole; the different bones of the body are found jumbled together in a basket of papyrus, to one corner of which is attached the head, so that the whole resembles the shape of a sheep.[6] It would seem unlikely therefore that much, if any, skin would be preserved with this method. Dr A. T. Sandison kindly sent me a leg from an Egyptian mummified cat and good preparations were obtained from the brittle skin on this (see below). This mummy was from Bubastes and is of the Ptolemaic period (323–30 BC).

A few specimens of ancient leather have been examined and most of these had evidence of having been made from cattle skin; they either contained cow hairs, or follicle remains characteristic of cattle. The idea of using parchment came to me when I was studying local history in Yorkshire by examining old parchment documents, and discovered that many had a well-defined hair pattern which I later found was well known to archivists. It was fortunate that the first specimens that came available were fragments of the Dead Sea Scrolls,[4] which were provided by Professor D. Burton and Dr R. Reed of Leeds University. The results obtained from these stimulated the provision of other material for study. Only a short strip of parchment 1 cm wide is required and this can often be taken from the junction of a membrane without spoiling the appearance of a document. A sample can sometimes be taken from the end of a sealing tag, and book-bindings can be sampled from the part folded inside the cover.

THE STRUCTURE OF SKIN

The skin of mammals consists of two main layers: a thin, outer, epidermis, and a thicker, inner layer known as the dermis or corium (Fig. 73). This is composed mainly of fibres of the protein collagen, which is quite distinct from the protein keratin which is the substance of hairs, nails and horns. The hairs grow from pits in the skin called follicles, and these, and their associated glands, are derived as downgrowths from the epidermis. The layer of the dermis in which the follicles are enclosed is known as the papillary layer. This is the layer that gives leather its characteristic grain. Beneath the papillary layer the collagen fibres of the dermis are coarser, forming a more open network, and this layer is known as the reticular layer. At the base of the dermis, many animals, e.g. cattle,

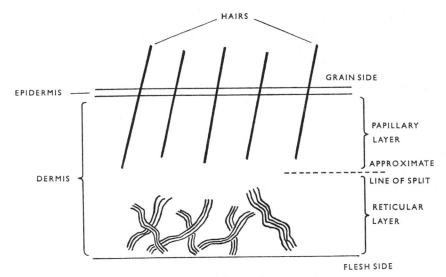

Fig. 73 Vertical section of skin to show main layers.

have a fatty layer. During the preparation of leather and parchment the hairs and the epidermis are removed, and today, in order to obtain a thinner product, the skin is often split in a region roughly corresponding to the boundary between the papillary and reticular layers.

METHODS OF PRESERVING AND TANNING SKIN

Skin may be left untreated, as with rawhide and parchment, or it may be tanned to produce leather. Tanning is a chemical process that preserves the skin, tending to make it impervious to water, but retaining the natural pliability. The main tanning methods involve (a) oils, (b) vegetable extracts, and (c) minerals.[2] Oil tannage is probably the oldest method and may go back to Palaeolithic times; the Eskimos have probably used fish oil since prehistoric times. Milk, butter and egg yolk were used by Asiatic peoples, and they, and the Indians of North America, used brains to emulsify the oil. Oil-tanned skin can be readily washed, and was used for cheap clothing in the past, which was sometimes made from old parchments.[7] Oil is still used in the preparation of chamois leather, which is made from the flesh side of a split sheepskin. The tanning action of smoke, which depends on substances such as aldehydes, was used by primitive peoples, and persisted until recently in Siberia and China.

Further west, vegetable tanning was probably used by Neolithic times. In ancient Egypt, acacia pods provided the tanning material, whereas in northern Europe tanning was done with an infusion of oak bark. The process became more elaborate, and involved dehairing and defatting the skin. Alkali is necessary to remove the hair, and lime has probably been used for at least 2,000 years, but the first materials were probably urine, and later, ashes. The chemical effect of combination with the skin proteins in vegetable tanning is different from that of oil, but is similar to that of the chromium salts used in the modern mineral tanning process. The only mineral process of ancient times was alum dressing (tawing). This was probably used first in the Near East where alum was available, and it gives a lighter-coloured product than vegetable tanning. Alum dressing is still used for woolskins and gloves, but it is a reversible process because the alum will wash out.

PARCHMENT

From remote times, hides, first raw, and according to Latour,[8] later tanned, were used as a writing material by the peoples of the Near East. The first mention of documents written on skins occurs in the time of the Egyptian IVth Dynasty (c. 2600–2500 BC).[9] Next, Ctesias quoted by Diodorus Siculus (died AD 34) relates that skins were used by the Persians for historical records. The 'writer on skin' was depicted on Assyrian monuments from the eighth century BC and Herodotus (fifth century BC) said that skins of sheep and goats were once used for writing by the Ionians, and added that barbarians still used them. Driver lists the extant Egyptian documents, and considers that at least some are on leather, but it is not clear whether or not he makes a distinction between leather and parchment. Mongait,[1] listing some documents of the eighth century AD found in a Sogdian castle in Tajikistan, mentions paper and leather but not parchment. True parchment did not appear until the second century BC. The word parchment Latin: pergamena) is in fact derived from Pergamum, the name of the city in Asia Minor in which parchment was developed. The development of parchment was probably the result of a gradual improvement in methods of preparing skin for writing. But the high cost of papyrus may have acted as a stimulus; it is said that parchment was invented by Eumenes II (197–159 BC) of Pergamum as a substitute because the Egyptian pharaoh had forbidden the export of papyrus to Eumenes' country in the hope of preventing the growth of the famous library at Pergamum.

The manufacture of parchment has changed little through the ages. The skin is limed in order to loosen the hair or wool which is then scraped away with a curved knife. Any remaining flesh or fat is scraped from the under-surface (flesh side); the skin is then stretched on a frame, and the scraping continued. Parchment was originally made from the entire skin, but in more recent times it was (and still is) made from the flesh side of a split skin, the grain side (containing the hair roots) being used for bookbinding. Apart from the liming, which is often repeated to remove the grease, and which according to Plenderleith[3] leaves the parchment in an alkaline condition, the skin receives no further chemical treatment, i.e. it is not tanned. The manufacture of this very durable material therefore involves little more than drying under tension, during which it is rubbed with pumice in order to obtain a smooth surface. But despite this, the flesh side can usually be distinguished from the grain side by its rougher texture, and in books, the pages are usually mounted grain to grain and flesh to flesh in order to give a uniform appearance.

According to Plenderleith[3] the most common source of parchment is sheepskin, and my studies confirm this. Saxl,[7] on the other hand, claims that among medieval parchments, whereas those from sheep predominated in England, those from goats predominated on the Continent. I have not yet had the opportunity to examine continental parchments, so have no evidence about the source of parchments there. Calf parchment, for which the term vellum should strictly be reserved, is usually thicker and harder than sheep or goat parchment, and is used for bookbinding rather than writing.

DATING

In the Leeds University Department of Leather Industries a method has been evolved which gives a rough indication of the date at which leather or parchment was made.[10] This depends on the shrinkage temperature of collagen fibres from the material. Samples are rehydrated in distilled water for an hour, fibres are teased from them, and mounted between cover-slips on the heating stage of a microscope. Heat is applied and the temperature at which the fibres begin to shrink (ranging from about 25° to 60°C) is noted. In general, older specimens have a lower shrinkage temperature. Fragments from the Dead Sea Scrolls were found to have shrinkage temperatures comparable with other ancient specimens of known age, and so a date was indicated which was in agreement with that obtained by palaeographic and radiocarbon methods.

HISTOLOGICAL METHOD

The first specimens of dried skin were merely softened in carbolic xylol (25 g. phenol in 75 ml. xylol) before being embedded in wax prior to sectioning. Then Sandison's softening fluid was found to give better results.[4] This consists of 90% alcohol—30 vols; 1% formaldehyde—50 vols; 5% aqueous sodium carbonate—20 vols.[11] The effect is for the dilute alkali (sodium carbonate) to attack the skin slightly and swell it, while the alcohol and formaldehyde act as fixatives. The more delicate material such as ancient parchments was left in this fluid for only 20 mins., whereas the harder material (leather and recent parchments) was softened for 24 hours. Specimens were dehydrated in the usual way, left in carbolic xylol overnight, and wax embedded *in vacuo* for 30 mins.

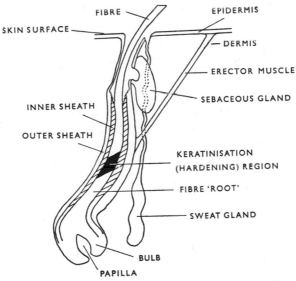

Fig. 74 Primary wool follicle in vertical section. From Ryder.[14]

Sections were stained with the Sacpic method. In this the cell nuclei are stained purple-black with haematolylin, and there are two other dyes, red basic fuchsin, and green, acid picro-indigo-carmine, which is in fact a mixture of yellow picric acid and blue indigo-carmine. This staining method shows the different structural features of the skin and follicles; for example, hairs and wool fibres in the skin show three successive zones representing stages of growth (Fig. 74). The soft root part of the fibre is acidophil and stains green with picro-indigo-carmine; then there is a keratinization (hardening) zone which is basiphil, and stains red with basic fuchsin; and finally the fully formed part of the fibre, composed of keratin, stains yellow with picric acid. Part of the inner sheath stains red and other parts of the follicle and skin stain varying shades of green.

STAINING REACTIONS AND STRUCTURAL DETAILS

Modern dried wool-skins from museum collections gave the same staining reactions as fixed, fresh skin. The taxidermist in preparing such skins may preserve them with salt, alum or oil, or not at all. At least one specimen known to have been preserved with alum gave the same staining reactions as fresh skin. Cells and their nuclei were visible, but the detail was naturally not as good as in fixed, fresh skin. The collagen of the dermis in sections of modern chamois leather (oil tanned) stained blue-green, as in fresh skin, and there were no follicle remains because this leather is made from the flesh side of the skin.

According to Sandison[12] hair and follicles in the skin of human *mummies* are often well preserved, and he found[13] (see chapter by Sandison) that the eyelids, including hair follicles and eyelashes, were remarkably well preserved.* Early in the series of sections of skin from the mummified cat that Dr Sandison sent me, the sections showed hairs cut above the skin surface. These had stained blue or mauve instead of the usual yellow, and they were somewhat degenerate and swollen, which may have come about during the softening treatment. However, the ladder-type medulla[14] (central core) of the fibre was frequently visible. In the skin the dermis stained dark green, but had the appearance of having coagulated so that no trace remained of its original fibrous nature. Within the skin the hairs had stained red, indicating increased basophilia. The follicle walls stained a paler shade of green than in fresh skin, and no cellular detail remained.

Old *parchment* stained in a similar way to fresh skin, and although the collagen of the dermis sometimes seemed to have coagulated, most specimens retained their fibrous nature. The dermis usually stained green, and sometimes yellow, but occasional patches, usually thicker areas, stained red. Wool fibres seen in vertical section usually showed the normal transition from a root stained green, through a red keratinization region, to a yellow fully-keratinized part. This frequently stained orange, instead of yellow, and often red, and on at least one occasion a blue fibre was seen. Cellular detail was very variable and not necessarily associated with age, although eighteenth-century parchments probably showed the most detail of all. Sections of parchment often showed maroon debris around the edge which may be similar to the maroon staining of leather mentioned below. Parchments lacking follicle remains, and having an open mesh of

* Natron (sodium sesquicarbonate) was used in the embalming process.

coarse collagen fibres suggesting the flesh side of a split skin, were found as early as the thirteenth century, but they only became common from the sixteenth century onwards. It would be interesting to find an historical record of the period at which the splitting of skins began. Apparently the earliest method of making a skin thinner was to shave away the flesh side.[15]

Archaeological specimens of presumably vegetable-tanned *leather* usually appeared brown or black before sectioning, and often stained maroon throughout. This maroon stain seemed to be a convenient method of distinguishing leather from untanned skin or parchment, supplementing chemical tests for tanning. But as most specimens examined were from excavations, and had therefore been in contact with soil, some modern (strop) leather was examined to see whether the maroon stain was due to tanning or to decay. In fact the collagen fibres at the flesh side of the skin stained a dirty blue-green, with parts yellow, red and maroon. The grain side was darker, the collagen fibres being mainly grey-blue and the follicle remains maroon. The darker blue-green staining was confirmed in some modern Egyptian sheep or goat leather and in some modern 'Morocco' bookbinding made from the grain side of sheep skin. Thus, whereas untanned skin tends to retain the bright blue-green stain of fresh skin, leather stains darker and has a tendency to stain maroon.

Next it was decided to determine which component of the stain gave the maroon result, and this was carried out with a medieval specimen, by staining different sections separately with each of the different stains. The sections were a pale brown colour before staining, and this colour was apparently unchanged by haematoxylin. Picro-indigo-carmine on the other hand stained the collagen fibres olive green (cf. the flesh side of the strop leather) while the follicles remained brown. Basic fuchsin stained the whole skin bright maroon; the maroon colour therefore derives from this stain, and indicates an increased basophilia in leather, particularly after degradation. The hairs, too, in leather often stained maroon, but surprisingly they were sometimes colourless, i.e. completely unstained, and sometimes stained bright blue.

IDENTIFICATION OF ANCIENT SPECIMENS

Until about the middle of the last century it was thought that hairs had no particular arrangement in the skin. Then it was found that they were arranged in characteristic groups, and towards the end of the century it was found that many mammals had two kinds of hair follicle within the group. But it was not until about the nineteen-twenties that the full significance of this difference as it affects the fleeces of sheep was realized: one type of follicle tends to grow finer wool fibres than the other. The two kinds of follicles are now known as primary follicles and secondary follicles. The primaries, formed first in the foetus, are usually the largest, and are arranged in rows in the skin often of three primaries each. The secondaries are more numerous and lie to one side of the primaries. The primary trio with its associated secondary follicles constitutes the follicle group which is the unit of the fleece (Fig. 75). The fundamental difference that distinguishes them in the skin is that the primaries have a sweat gland and erector muscle, whereas the secondaries have neither of these. Both types do, however, have

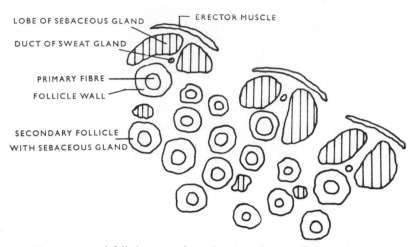

Fig. 75 Typical follicle group from domestic sheep in horizontal section.

sebaceous glands, the glands that produce wool grease. The secondaries being usually the smallest follicles tend to grow finer fibres than the primaries, and therefore the more secondary follicles a sheep has in its skin, the finer on the whole will be the fleece. The relative number of secondary follicles is expressed as the secondary-primary follicle ratio, or S/P ratio; in general the higher the S/P ratio the finer is the fleece.

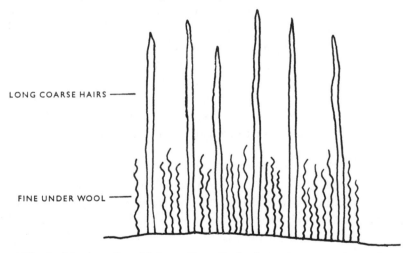

Fig. 76 The double coat of a wild sheep. From Ryder (*New Scientist*, 27th October 1960).

Wild sheep from which the domestic sheep arose have a double coat consisting of an outer-coat of very coarse, hairy fibres known as kemps, and a short, under-coat of very fine woolly fibres[5] (Fig. 76). And as the outer-coat kemps grow from the primary follicles, and the under-coat wool grows from the secondaries, examination of the skin shows considerable difference in size between the primary and secondary follicles. There is an apparent fundamental difference in the arrangement of the follicles in the skin between wild sheep and domestic sheep. In wild sheep (Fig. 77b) the secondary

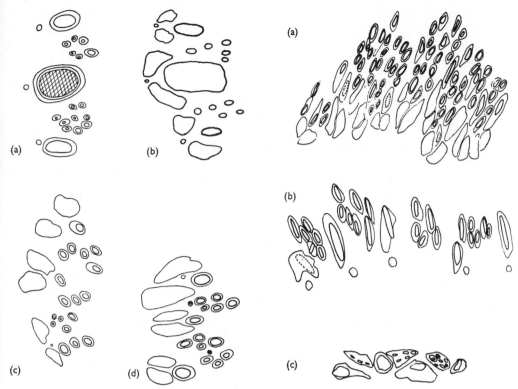

Fig. 77 Follicle groups from (a) domestic goat; (b) wild (mouflon) sheep; (c) Shetland sheep; (d) Soay sheep. (a, c, d) From Ryder.[4]

Fig. 78 Follicle groups from the Dead Sea Scrolls; (a) fine-wooled sheep; (b) medium-wooled sheep or hairy sheep (see text); (c) hairy sheep. From Ryder.[4]

follicles frequently lie between the primaries, whereas in most domestic sheep, as already mentioned (Fig. 75), the secondaries are usually grouped to one side of the primaries.[4]

The hairy primitive sheep such as those belonging to the Near Eastern and Asiatic breeds, which are among the most primitive in existence today, have a somewhat intermediate grouping with the secondaries beginning to move from between the primaries (Fig. 78c). These are still much larger than the secondaries, and produce the hairiest fibres of the fleece. This arrangement is similar to that in the goat (Fig. 77a), but the goat has fewer secondaries. Woolly primitive domestic sheep, such as the Soay and Shetland, have appreciable difference in diameter between the primaries and secondaries, and the secondaries are grouped in a wedge, only the points of which are between the primaries (Figs. 77c and d). Such an arrangement is often found in the coarser-fleeced British breeds such as the Scottish Blackface, the long hairy fibres of which make them somewhat similar to the sheep of the hairy primitive group (cf. Plate XXIXd). In the more highly evolved domestic sheep the secondaries have spread out beyond the wedge and in general become grouped at one side of the primaries. Modern medium-wooled sheep, e.g. the longwools and down breeds, have less difference in diameter between the primaries and secondaries. Fine-wooled sheep, e.g. the Merino, have large fibre groups with many secondaries, and hardly any difference in diameter between the primaries and secondaries (cf. Fig. 78a). The evolutionary trend after domestication therefore seems to have been a movement of the secondaries from between the primaries, accompanied by a tendency for the primaries to become smaller, and to grow less hairy fibres. As more secondaries have developed in finer-wooled types, these have spread away from the primaries.

Knowledge of hair type in different breeds of cattle is not as advanced as it is in sheep. All follicles in cattle are comparable with the primaries in sheep, i.e. they have sweat glands and erector muscles, and they are distributed at random in the skin. But there are differences in size, the *first-formed* follicles and fibres being larger than the *later-formed* follicles and fibres.[16]

Saxl[7] made attempts to use the hair follicle pattern on the surface of parchments to identify the animal from which the parchment was made, but her material was such (e.g. The Book of Durrow) that she could not check her identifications by sectioning. I found that examination of the surface pattern did not give a sufficiently clear picture, and that the impression gained from the surface was often quite different from that gained from the examination of sections. In addition, a pattern on the surface did not necessarily indicate that there would be good wool fibre remains within the parchment, neither did lack of pattern on the surface necessarily mean that it contained no wool or hair remains. Sometimes my preparations showed short lengths of fibres in which the scaly surface was visible. The surface scale pattern of a fibre provides an additional feature to help identification[14] (see chapter by Wildman and Appleyard).

One of the oldest specimens examined[4] was from some Aramaic documents originating in Egypt in the fifth century BC.[9] The specimen stained bright green, so it could be parchment or could have been preserved with oil or alum, but it had apparently not been vegetable tanned. There were traces of large follicles, as well as fine fibres, suggesting a hairy sheep or goat. Remains of follicle bulbs showed cell nuclei, and the fine fibres were apparently not pigmented and had scales visible. Two of these had a diameter of 12 microns, and two more had diameters of 14 and 18 microns respectively.*

All available evidence suggests that the sheep was domesticated in south-west Asia, possibly as early as 7000 BC.[17] It is not known what the fleeces of the earliest domestic sheep were like, but it has always been assumed that they were hairy and pigmented brown or black like wild sheep. The next specimen to be described was therefore of even greater interest than the last. This was a piece of sheepskin from Scythian excavations in the Altai Mountains.[18] It came from frozen burial mound No. 5 at Pazyryk, and was kindly supplied by N. J. Merpert, Scientific Secretary of the Institute of Archaeology in Moscow. The sample was taken from the shoulder region of the skin, and was dated as being of the fourth or fifth century BC. The wool was intact (Plate XXIXa) and had a slight yellow-brown discoloration; the microscopic preparations confirmed that

* Diameter measurements were made with a Lanameter projection microscope.

it was not pigmented.[19] This therefore compares with the whiteness of Iron Age wool in the west. Cloth from the Roman period apparently had fewer pigmented fibres than wool from the Bronze Age oak-coffin burials of Denmark.[20]

The fleece was double coated with hairs extending in a shallow curl 4 cm beyond the under-wool to a length of 12 cm. This was the maximum staple length (in fact comparable with the maximum in wild sheep)[5] because the hairs in the skin had brush ends that are formed preparatory to moulting. These were the coarsest fibres; a goat is likely to have had coarser fibres: there were no kemps. The under-coat wool was dense and mixed with the hair, and had no staple crimp (cf. wild sheep).[5] A whole mount of the coat fibres showed hairs that were typical of those found in sheep, i.e. the central medulla or core of the fibre occupied no more than about half the width of the fibre, and they were roughly 75–90 microns in diameter. The surface scale edges were prominent, and the scale pattern was apparently an irregular mosaic. The fine, non-medullated fibres were typical fine wool fibres, having smooth, near, scale margins, and a few were as fine as 12 microns, but most of them had a diameter between 20 and 26 microns. This is comparable with the under-wool of modern hairy sheep; the under-coat of the goat tends to be finer, as in the last specimen. There were also a few non-medullated fibres of medium diameter, i.e. about 40 microns. These had an irregular waved mosaic, being like wool from a down breed, and some of them had the more diagonal scale edges that have a tendency to occur in lustre longwools (fibres of down breeds and longwools are illustrated in Appleyard,[21] p. 113).

Sections of the skin stained bright green and the wool fibres stained bright yellow. These were well preserved, having a clear scale pattern. Some of the sebaceous glands remained as a grey mass near a wool fibre. Despite particles of earth in the wool attached to the skin there was no maroon staining; the skin may have been preserved with butter. Vertical sections of the skin showed that the follicles had an acute slope, which is a primitive feature, and that there was a well-developed fat layer, which in my experience is uncommon in sheep. The follicle grouping seen in horizontal sections was that of a hairy, primitive animal. The secondaries formed a wedge between the primaries, and their relatively large number and their lack of extreme fineness are in accordance with the specimen being from a sheep rather than a goat. The secondary fibres occasionally showed the bilateral staining characteristic of crimped fibres.[14] The primaries were narrower within the skin than above it, and had lost their medulla, because they had formed brush ends preparatory to moulting.

The overall picture obtained from this specimen was of a hairy primitive sheep with some generalized characters. The moulting and short staple length are primitive features; e.g. the staple length was comparable with some modern Asiatic, hairy breeds, but was only about one-third as long as the fleece of the modern Scottish Blackface. However, the specimen was comparable in fineness with the less hairy grades of Scottish Blackface wool, the hairs in particular being much finer than the coarse kemps of the coarse Scottish Blackface fleeces, and of the wild sheep. This fineness, lack of pigment, and the wider range of fibre types than in the wild sheep, are interesting in a sheep that is apparently primitive. There is a tendency today for the different fibre types to be associated with different breed types, but most of the range of fibre types are still found in breeds such as the Scottish Blackface.

Sections of a sample of Egyptian leather dated 300 BC stained blue-green with maroon patches, suggesting vegetable tanning, and the fibrous nature of the skin had mainly been lost. There were fine fibres (one had a diameter of 8 microns) and larger, pigmented follicle remains. Occasionally these had medium fibres (about 50 microns in diameter) and some of them had a narrow medulla. This specimen seemed to be from calf.

Some twenty fragments of parchment from the Dead Sea Scrolls were examined,[4] and five from the nearby site of Muraba'ât, which are grouped here with the Dead Sea Scrolls for convenience, although, whereas the Dead Sea Scrolls are generally agreed to date roughly from the time of Christ, the Muraba'ât parchment came from caves used during the Jewish revolt of AD 132–135; these are situated to the south of those in which the Dead Sea Scrolls were found.

Only four parchments had clear groups; one of these was a calf and this and another calf specimen were the only ones with pigmented fibres. The others are shown in Fig. 78, a fine-wooled sheep (a), a medium-wooled sheep (b), and a hairy animal (c) that could have been a sheep or a goat, although the relatively large number of secondaries suggested that it was from a sheep. Three other samples had both fine and coarse fibres, and were therefore hairy animals. One of these had two fine fibres 12 microns in diameter, and a larger non-medullated fibre 42 microns in diameter. Another had fine fibres, 6, 8 and 12 microns in diameter, and a fibre with a diameter of 16 microns in which there was a medulla 12 microns wide. Medullae occupying such a large proportion of the fibre usually only occur in coarser fibres, and a similar unidentified fine animal fibre in a Bronze Age textile specimen from Amesbury was found to have a wide medulla by Appleyard.[22]

The medium-wooled type had appreciable difference between the diameter of the primary and secondary fibres, and a Soay-type grouping in which there was a wedge of secondaries pointing between the primaries (Fig. 78b). Short lengths of fibres had a scale pattern with diagonal scale edges (not found in the Soay) suggesting a longwool type (Plate XXIXc). Six other samples had fibres of medium-wool size (primaries ranging in diameter from 32 to 42 microns and secondaries around 20 microns in diameter) and three of these had diagonal scale edges. The intact wool of the Altai sample has enabled a reassessment to be made of these findings published in 1958.[4] First, the group (Fig. 78b) was similar to that of the Altai specimen and the primary fibres had brush ends. Therefore instead of being medium wool these fibres may be hairs that had narrowed preparatory to moulting. Second, the significance of the apparent long-wool type fibres may lie more in these fibres being present in a hairy type, as in the Altai specimen, than their indication of a primitive long-wool type. It is only as more specimens become available that answers to these problems will be found.*

* Leather and wool recently supplied by Prof. Y. Yadin from the Cave of the Letters, in Judea (AD 135) confirm the existence of a medium-wooled sheep, with a high proportion of fine fibres, which was the predominant type in that time and place.

The fine-wooled type is even more interesting. This had large groups of fine fibres that are found today, in even larger groups, in Merino sheep. Two other samples had fibres as fine as this one (12–16 microns in diameter) and these had a scale pattern that was suggestive of the Merino (Plate XXIXb). It is known that modern Merinos came from Spain about 200 years ago, but little is known of their history before that.[6] These findings support hints that the Merino originated in the Near East. One fragment from the Dead Sea Scrolls, although apparently parchment, was found to consist of plant tissue when sectioned, and so was presumably papyrus.

The only specimen linking the ancient with the medieval specimens was some Egyptian leather of the Coptic period (seventh to twelfth century AD) from the British Museum. This had a well-defined grain pattern on the surface, and was clearly leather which the museum authorities thought was pigskin. In fact when sectioned it was found to be from a hairy sheep or a goat. The collagen stained a dirty green, but there was hardly any maroon staining, the original brown colour of the unstained sections remained in the follicle walls. The follicles had pigmented cells and the fibres were moderately pigmented, so the skin was from a brown animal or a brown patch on an animal. Some of the coarser fibres had a latticed medulla and of three fibres that could be measured one had a diameter of 94 microns with a medulla 64 microns wide; the figures for another fibre were 58 and 34 microns respectively, and a third, non-medullated fibre had a diameter of 34 microns. These measurements are more comparable with those of a hairy sheep than a goat.

MEDIEVAL AND RECENT SPECIMENS

Parchment. The study of the Dead Sea Scrolls stimulated provision of further material for investigation, and about 150 British parchments ranging in date from 1193 to 1871 have been examined.[23] The source of most of these was known, and there were three collections: from Hereford, Yorkshire and Scotland. The assumption has been made that parchment was made in the region of the place in which the document was written. However, certainly as early as the seventeen-nineties, it was clear that the parchment had not necessarily been made locally: a parchment of that date from Hereford bore the name of a London stationer. Also, there is evidence of livestock movement as early as the Middle Ages. One of the medieval sources of parchment was the Royal Manor of Hatfield, Yorkshire, and there is a record of AD 1323 of sheep being taken from East Anglia to re-stock Royal Manors in the north.[24]

Only one of these British parchments showed a clear follicle grouping, so the identifications were made mainly from individual fibres. Even those with many well-preserved follicles or fibres did not show the follicle arrangement. The remains in the medieval parchments were on the whole no better preserved than those in the Dead Sea Scrolls, possibly owing to the wetter British climate, although many of the medieval parchments were of excellent quality. The seventeenth- and eighteenth-century ones were on the whole of the worst quality, being the thickest, but showed most histological detail, e.g. cell nuclei in the follicle bulbs and surface scale patterns on the wool fibres. The nineteenth-century ones were the thinnest, and contained the fewest remains. This is possibly owing to increased efficiency in the removal of wool fibres from the skin before manufacture, or to the practice of using only the flesh side of the skin to make parchment.

The criterion of fibre diameter used for identification led to descriptions: fine (7–18 microns), fine to medium (about 18 microns to about 35 microns) and medium (about 35–60 microns). These descriptions give no indication of breed, which is the main interest in this period when the different breed types must have been evolving. Sometimes, however, further information could be gained from indications of follicle grouping and fibre scale pattern so that suggestions of type, e.g. down breed (in the fine to medium group) and longwool (in the medium group), could be added. But too few specimens have yet been examined to indicate the distribution of these types. However, the Scottish parchments, which were from the fifteenth to seventeenth centuries, had pigmented follicle remains suggesting the primitive domestic Soay sheep. This is of interest because it tends to confirm the scanty evidence that this breed remained in Scotland until as late as the eighteenth century. Three of the medieval English parchments had pigmented fibres closely resembling those of the Soay.

Hairy types were easily distinguished because of the presence of both coarse and fine fibres, and hairy sheep could usually be distinguished from goats, e.g. modern goat primary fibres are about 160 microns in diameter compared with about 80 to 100 microns in the Herdwick sheep, and the secondary fibres of the goat are as fine as 10 to 15 microns, whereas those of the Herdwick are around 20 microns in diameter, e.g. a parchment from Hatfield dated 1403 had a primary fibre 108 microns in diameter with a medulla 100 microns wide, and three secondaries 18, 20 and 22 microns in diameter (Plate XXIXd). A parchment from Startforth, Yorkshire, dated 1727 was identified as goat from the scale pattern of the fibres actually protruding for about half an inch above the parchment surface. One of the two Dead Sea Scroll samples identified as calf had a patch of hairs above the surface. The only British parchments that was certainly from calf was from the cover of a book from Fountains Abbey dated 1450. This had pigmented hairs, and although the cover appeared like parchment, there were areas of maroon staining in the skin suggesting a form of preservation.

Hairy sheep were apparently kept in all periods. Whereas most of the fine wools came from the medieval period, the medium wools became more common in the sixteenth century and predominated after that date, those of the eighteenth century being the coarsest, e.g. 50 to 60 microns in diameter. The findings so far therefore support the doubtful historical records of the extreme fineness of medieval wool. And as many of the medium wools are likely to have been longwools, historical evidence[25] for an increased supply of long wool during the sixteenth and seventeenth centuries is also supported. There was evidence, however, of the existence of medium and fine to medium-wooled sheep in the Middle Ages that could have been the ancestors of the longwool, the origin of which has recently been much discussed.[24–27]

In the hope of throwing light on the early Merino in Australia six specimens of parchment from the covers of nineteenth-century account books in the archives of New England University library have been examined, although the parchment may not have been made in Australia; none of the samples had any wool fibre remains.

Leather. The earliest medieval samples of leather came from a tenth-century shoe found in excavations at the South Corner Tower of the Roman Fortress at York.[28] The leather was examined by Miss Betty M. Haines of the British Leather Manufacturers Research Association who, using vertical sections, identified it as being made from cattle hide, and said that the leather had a break in the middle which had arisen from incomplete penetration of tan. My own (horizontal) preparations from a black, brittle fragment showed follicle remains which confirmed that the leather was from cattle, but only a few degraded hairs remained.

Another sample from York came from excavations carried out in Petergate by Mr L. P. Wenham in 1957 and 1958. The finds dated from the eleventh to the fourteenth century, and among many animal bones (see my chapter on fish remains) were found a number of shoes which were described by Mr. J. H. Thornton of Northampton College of Technology. The fragment of leather examined[29] was black and moderately brittle, but sections showed many follicle remains with a few well-preserved cattle hairs (Plate XXIXe). The hairs had little pigment, and so could have come from a white (or grey) animal (or patch on an animal). Some hairs stained the usual yellow colour, others stained green or blue and some were colourless. Some pieces of stitching from the shoes were clearly leather, but some could possibly have been bits of yarn made from flax fibres. However, when these were mounted on a microscope slide the fibres could not be separated easily as they can be in a yarn, and when a piece was sectioned and stained, a microscopic examination confirmed that the fibres were collagen fibres (stained maroon) from leather, and not flax fibres.

Another piece of medieval leather examined was found during excavations at Pontefract Priory in 1959.[30] This was attached to a buckle of thirteenth to fourteenth century date, and microscopic examination showed follicles characteristic of cattle skin, but no hairs. Two specimens of shoe leather supplied by Dr A. E. Werner of the British Museum research laboratory were examined. One came from the boat found at Kentmere in the Lake District, possibly dated to between AD 1000–1800, and the other came from a fifteenth-century grave at Lincoln Cathedral. Both were made from cattle skin; the Kentmere leather showed clear traces of follicles, whereas the Lincoln leather had less well-defined follicles, but had a few degraded hairs.

Finally, I was recently sent a specimen by Mr D. M. D. Thacker of Llantilio Crossenny, Monmouthshire. This came from under the hinge of a door leading to the Chapel of the Pyx at Westminster Abbey. The door had once been covered with skin which was reputed to be that of Richard de Podlicote, a monk who in 1303 robbed the king's treasury and was flayed when caught. The specimen appeared like parchment, but was thicker than sheep or goat parchments and more comparable with a calf parchment. The hairs lacked pigment completely, which is unusual for human hair, and they had a moderately dense arrangement even for the scalp. Comparison with both human and cattle skin led this to be identified as calf.

A microscopic examination of skin remains can therefore often reveal details that give a surprising amount of information that is of interest to biologists, as well as to archaeologists and agricultural historians.

REFERENCES

1 MONGAIT, A. 1959. *Archaeology in the USSR*, Moscow. 1961. Harmondsworth
2 GANSSER, A. 1950. *Ciba Review* (81) 2938–2964
3 PLENDERLEITH, H. J. 1956. *The Conservation of Antiquities and Works of Art*, Oxford
4 RYDER, M. L. 1958. *Nature 182*, 781–783
5 —— 1960. *Proc. Zool. Soc. Lond. 135*, 387–408
6 —— 1959. *Wool Knowledge 4* (12), 10–14
7 SAXL, H. 1954. *An investigation of the Qualities, the Methods of Manufacture and the Preservation of Historic Parchment and Vellum with a View to Identifying the Species of Animal used*; M.Sc. Thesis, Leeds University
8 LATOUR, A. 1949. *Ciba Review* (72) 2630
9 DRIVER, G. R. 1957. *Aramaic Documents of the Fifth Century BC*, Oxford
10 BURTON, D., POOLE, J. B. and REED, R. 1959. *Nature 184*, 533–534
11 SANDISON, A. T. 1955. *Stain Technol. 30*, 277–283
12 —— Personal communication
13 —— 1957. *Medical History 1*, 336–339
14 RYDER, M. L. 1962. A Survey of the Gross Structure of Protein Fibres; in HEARLE, J. W. S. and PETERS, R. H. (ed.), *Fibre Structure*, London
15 WATERER, J. W. 1956. Leather; in SINGER, C. *et al.* (ed.), *A History of Technology*, Oxford, vol. II
16 LYNE, A. G. and HEIDEMAN, MARGARET, G. 1959. *Austral. J. Biol. Sci. 12*, 72–95
17 RYDER, M. L. 1959. The Domestication of Sheep. *Wool Knowledge 4* (10), 19–23
18 RUDENKO, S. I. 1953. *Kul'tura Nasileniia Gornogo Altaia v. Skitskoe Vremia*, Moscow
19 RYDER, M. L. 1961. *Austral. J. Sci. 24*, 246–248
20 CLARK, J. G. D. 1936. *The Mesolithic Settlement of Northern Europe*, Cambridge, 117
21 APPLEYARD, H. M. 1960. *Guide to the Identification of Animal Fibres*, Leeds
22 —— Personal communication
23 RYDER, M. L. 1960. *Nature 187*, 130–132
24 TROW-SMITH, R. 1957. *A History of British Livestock Husbandry to 1700*, London
25 BOWDEN, P. J. 1956. *Econ. Hist. Rev. 9*, 44–58
26 RYDER, M. L. 1959. *Agric. History Rev. 7*, 1–5
27 —— 1960. Sheep Breeds in History. *Year Book of the National Sheep Breeders' Assoc.*
28 STEAD, I. M. 1958. *Yorks Arch. J. 39*, 515–537
29 RYDER, M. L. 1962. In WENHAM, L. P. Excavations in Petergate York. *Ibid.*, in press
30 BELLAMY, C. V. 1962. Excavations at Pontefract Priory. *Ibid.*, forthcoming

52 Fibres of Archaeological Interest: Their Examination and Identification

H. M. APPLEYARD and A. B. WILDMAN

THIS CHAPTER IS CONCERNED WITH the fibres which are found at archaeological sites, whether they are from fabrics or skins and with particular emphasis on any diagnostic features of their microstructure. Garments and the construction of fabric remains have already been adequately described elsewhere.[2,5] We have not taken part in any of the field work connected with these discoveries but have examined samples of fabrics, yarns or loose fibres for those who have been directly connected with the excavations or who are responsible for the preservation of the finds.

For the dating of the samples reliance has been placed upon the information supplied with them. The date of these samples must be determined by other relics found on the same site. Unaccompanied textile remains are very difficult to date.

All animal fibres of archaeological interest examined by us have had one common feature, they were all stained various shades of brown ranging from a light yellowish-brown to a very dark brown; this also applied to most of the vegetable fibres. Difficulty has therefore been experienced in commenting on the colour of many of these fibres, that is whether or not they have been dyed or whether the colour is due to natural processes in the course of the years in storage.

Some fabrics may have been bleached originally but it is not possible now to say if they had any treatments comparable to present-day finishing processes. It is known that bleaching and scouring processes did exist in ancient times; there are references to bleaching and scouring of cloth dating back to Roman and early Egyptian times.[7] One of the early works on bleaching is a review by Dr Francis Home of the methods used in Britain and Holland.[8]

THE PREPARATION OF FIBRES FOR EXAMINATION

In this chapter the names given to different types of cuticular-scale pattern and other structural features of mammalian fibres are from Wildman's classification.[11] The manner in which the sample of fibres is manipulated depends upon several factors but particularly upon its size and state of preservation. The historical value of excavated garments, coverings and skins or fragments of these means that in almost all instances samples which are available for fibre examination and identification are necessarily small; usually, therefore, extremely little material is available for any chemical tests, cross-sectioning and other manipulations. The whole sample is generally used for these examinations and the process of preparing representative sub-samples of archaeological material, so necessary for samples of modern textiles, is not usually carried out: when, for example, a small sample of cloth is in a very poor state of preservation it will easily disintegrate and cannot be handled to the extent of sub-sampling; special measures have in fact to be taken to protect the sample from the effects of even the minimum necessary manipulation. Frequently samples consist of a few scraps of degraded warp and weft thread or even just a tiny collection of fibre fragments. In addition to the samples already mentioned fragments of skin and hair are occasionally received from archaeological sites.

First of all, if the sample is fabric with a recognizable weave, the type of weave is noted in the manner set forth in the detailed descriptions of some samples given later in this paper. When the fabric piece is extremely fragile it is treated prior to laboratory manipulation with polyvinyl acetate solution to hold it together and prevent it breaking into small fragments.

A small amount of any sample suspected of consisting wholly or partly of fibres of vegetable origin is submitted to staining and solubility tests designed to reveal their presence. Reference is made later in the paper to the preparation for examination of fibres of vegetable origin.

Small samples of fabric are examined dry through stereoscopic binoculars using objectives with magnifications of from $\times 1 \cdot 25$ to $\times 10$, to observe the weave and general cloth construction.

The preparation of fibre whole mounts. Whole mounts of fibres are often made and their preparation is a routine operation with each sample submitted; indeed where the sample is very fragile it may be the only kind of mount possible for examination microscopically. Washing or cleaning the fibres in ether or benzene is not usually possible with archaeological samples and the fibres are therefore mounted straight away in the mounting medium.

The best medium for this purpose is liquid paraffin, its refractive index $(1 \cdot 470)$ being sufficiently different from that of the keratin of animal fibres $(1 \cdot 548)$ to allow cuticular-scale margins to be visible but not so far different to produce undesirable optical effects; the relatively high viscosity of paraffin is also an advantage in helping to hold fragile fibres, preventing them from disintegrating on the microscope slide.

Whole mounts reveal the relative thickness of fibres, the presence of pigment, its type and distribution and sometimes also the medulla and the pattern formed by the external margins of the cuticular scales.

Cross-sections of fibres. Sometimes information provided by whole-mount examination is not sufficient to identify fibres: transverse sections of fibres show more precisely the type and distribution of natural pigment, the relative thickness of the cuticle and the structure of the medulla. These characteristics constitute very useful evidence for fibre identification: furthermore it is usually possible to obtain cross-sections of even the most fragile fibres (Plate XXXc). Good cross-sections of fibres at thicknesses of approximately 20–25 μ may be cut using a Hardy type hand microtome which is described elsewhere.[11] The fibres, again without cleaning in any way, are inserted with celloidin in the slot of the microtome and cut in the ordinary way; if the fibres available are very few in number they may be surrounded in the slot by wool or other available fibres which then form a packing material.

Preparation of fibres to show their cuticular-scale patterns. The patterns formed by the external margins of the cuticular scales are among the most important aids to the identification of mammalian fibres; this is particularly so where the fibres are of sufficient length to facilitate the observation of pattern sequences along their lengths: fibres in archaeological samples are often rather short and broken and therefore less precise identifications are possible than with fibres of more recent origin which are not so degraded. Nevertheless, and this will be demonstrated later in the chapter, the cuticular scale pattern of even short lengths of fibres can be a valuable clue to their identity, and fortunately it is possible to obtain casts of the scale patterns of some of these fibres. Methods of making such casts are described elsewhere in detail:[1] perhaps the best method for these fibres is the one in which the fibres are placed between two slides one of which is coated with a thin film of polyvinyl acetate (PVA): the whole preparation receives slight pressure in a light press which incorporates a warm plate whilst being warmed to the melting point of the PVA. The preparation is then cooled, the slides separated and the fibres peeled out leaving a cast of the surface of the fibres in the PVA (Plate XXXId). When the fibres are too fragile even for this treatment, the semi-embedding technique is employed; in this method the fibre remains on a microscope slide, and a medium with a refractive index near that of keratin, e.g. celluloid solution or glycerine yellow, is allowed to drain along both sides of the fibre. The upper surface is not covered and only the under half of the fibre is in contact with the medium. Sometimes PVA is used for this purpose. Where possible the scale-cast method is employed, because this eliminates from the preparation pigment and other fibre details which otherwise may obscure the scale margins.

THE IDENTIFICATION OF FIBRES FROM ARCHAEOLOGICAL SITES

Mammalian fibres can only be identified by methods of microscopy: keratin is common to all of them and therefore chemical and staining methods are of no use. Fibres from different families and orders or groups of mammals can be distinguished microscopically but those from different animals of the same species naturally resemble each other in many features: however, as elaborated below, it is sometimes possible to distinguish fibres as originating from, for example, a variety of sheep such as Down, mountain or lustre type when it is not possible to specify the precise breed of origin. From whole mounts alone one may in some instances determine the origin of a fibre; some animal fibres, such as, for example, mohair, camel hair and cashmere, are very uniform in fibre thickness along their lengths as opposed to wool fibres which are very variable along their lengths. If, for example, in addition to a very uniform fibre thickness, the scale pattern can be seen in the whole mount to be an irregular waved mosaic (Fig. 80a), with the characteristic steeply-sloping margins of fine camel hair, then the fibre may be identified immediately. However, the scale margins cannot always be seen in whole mounts of archaeological specimens and usually it is best where possible to cut cross-sections and also prepare casts of the cuticular surface. Evidence such as the distribution of pigment, relative thickness of cuticle, type of medulla and pattern of scale margins can be built up from these different preparations and a more accurate diagnosis made.

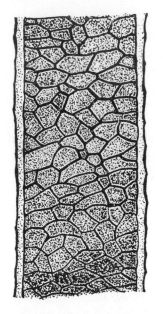

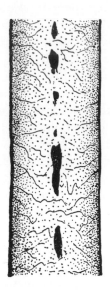

(a) Lattice medulla   (b) Fragmental medulla   (c) Broken medulla

Fig. 79 Types of medulla.

An example of the diagnostic value, with some fibres, of cross-sections is provided by Plate XXXc. These fibres were identified as human hair because of the dense concentration of pigment granules towards the cuticle and the characteristic shape of the narrow medulla.

We have stated that where the scale margins of fibres can be seen their pattern even on short lengths of fibre, together with evidence from whole mounts and perhaps cross-sections, enables a statement of their possible origins to be made with some confidence. Fibres may be identified as originating for example from certain groups of sheep: the cuticular-scale pattern of coarse outer-coat fibres from mountain sheep, e.g. Scottish Blackface, is of the type known as irregular mosaic (Fig. 80b) and this together with the presence of a coarse lattice type medulla (Fig. 79a) is characteristic. Again, the scale margins of medium to coarse lustre wool fibres form an irregular mosaic pattern of a rather different kind,[11] the fibres being either non-medullated or with a narrow interrupted or fragmental medulla (Fig. 79b). Fine wool fibres, for example from Down sheep which are quite common in medieval remains in Britain, are non-medullated with a cuticular-scale pattern of the irregular mosaic type with smooth margins and often of the waved variety (Fig. 80a).

Skin fragments. Fragments of skin which have been used for a variety of purposes, such as clothing, burial wrapping, sheaths for weapons and as parchment, can usually be readily identified by an experienced investigator. Pieces of material thought to be skin may be softened and relaxed in softening fluids and they may be sectioned on a microtome. The sections when stained by any of several nuclear and cytoplasmic stains show portions of epidermis connective tissue and root sheaths of follicles; they may even show follicle bulbs at the base of several follicles. The presence of fibre follicles may even be detected in softened fragments without any necessity for staining. Plate XXXb is a photograph of a section of parchment from the Dead Sea Scrolls in which fibres in their follicles may be seen.

There is an element of danger in attempting to identify fibre remains in parchment: these fibres are usually very short and each consists of the basal portion only of the original fibre: only one type of scale pattern therefore is shown. Several types of fibres have a similar scale pattern in this basal region, the pattern changing to a more distinctive and characteristic one further up the fibre.

DESCRIPTIONS OF SAMPLES EXAMINED

Fibres of vegetable origin. Fibres of vegetable origin often decay faster than animal fibres. This is particularly noticeable on sites where the soil is acidic. Examples of fabrics have been unearthed which contained fragments of vegetable fibres in the weft direction. Such examples are usually from cloths made chiefly from animal fibres and decorated with a weft yarn made from vegetable fibres. In some of these fabrics the animal fibres have been comparatively well preserved but gaps have occurred in the weft direction where the vegetable fibres had been. Vegetable fibres from some sites where the conditions have been favourable for preservation have been unearthed.

The earliest examples of vegetable fibres have been from Jutish and Saxon sites in Britain and from a sixth-century site in Turkey. The example from the Jutish site consisted of a few strands of fibres attached to the back of a brooch. These fibres were very fragile and could only be examined in whole mount; the fibres were not strong enough for other preparations, and were too discoloured for staining tests to be of any use. All that could be said of these fibres was that they were of vegetable origin.

Fibres from the Saxon site were quite well preserved. These were from very small fragments of woven cloth, but unfortunately they were very dark in colour so that

Fig. 80 Some cuticular-scale patterns.   (a) Irregular mosaic: waved   (b) Irregular mosaic

staining tests were of no value; their microscopical appearance showed that they were bast fibres and were very similar to flax.

A stronger and better-preserved sample of vegetable fibres from a plain-weave cloth was found among unstratified material at an Anglo-Saxon cemetery at Fonaby.[4] This sample was dark in colour and was strong enough to withstand sectioning. The cross-sectional shape of these fibres and the shape and size of the lumen suggested that they were flax; microscopical evidence only could be obtained from this sample (Plate XXXIa).

By far the best examples of vegetable fibres so far examined came from sixth-century Turkish tombs. These were from samples of cloth in plain weave which had been decorated with coloured silks. Several samples were examined and all were very well preserved; the weft from one was very clearly cotton. All the other samples had a similar appearance when viewed in whole mount; only one, however, was unstained and staining tests listed by the Textile Institute were used.[10] From these tests, appearance in whole mount and cross-section it was reasonably certain that this particular yarn consisted of flax fibres. The other yarns were certainly made from bast fibres and from microscopical preparations they were similar to flax (Plate XXXIa).

Fibres of animal origin. Animal fibres, especially wool fibres, are particularly interesting because they provide evidence of the different types of fibres used by peoples in early periods of history. In view of the very wide range of types and qualities of wool used in the textile trade today it is most interesting to discover what types of wool have been produced in former days. Britain today produces many types of wool from the fine Southdown to the coarse mattress type of wool grown by the Scottish Blackface sheep. Leggett states that there were both wild and semi-domesticated sheep in Britain at the time of the Roman invasion, and suggested that the Romans introduced improved methods of breeding.[9]

The production of wool became of great importance to the economy of England and, according to Carus-Wilson,[1] in the thirteenth century English wool was in demand by the Continental weavers because of its good quality, especially wool from the Lindsay region of Lincolnshire which was required for fine-quality cloth in Flanders. Historians suggest that the sheep in England in these early periods were of the fine-wooled varieties, and evidence to support this has been found in some of the samples we have examined.

There is also evidence to support the idea that there were at least two types of sheep in Britain, even as early as the date of the Roman invasion. Roman historians reporting on conditions in Britain at the beginning of their occupation claimed that two kinds of cloth were woven by the natives in the eastern part of England, one a thick, harsh cloth, the other a fine-spun wool cloth woven in a check design in different colours.

Only a few samples from the Bronze Age have been examined and these were not very rewarding; one sample, preserved in PVA, was so badly damaged that it was not possible even to say whether the fibres were of animal or vegetable origin. Another sample, also preserved in PVA, was recognized as being of animal fibres, but there was not enough evidence to say what type of animal fibre. The only interesting feature in these fibres was that they were medullated, the medulla being very wide in comparison with the diameter of the fibres which was 12–15 μ. A third sample from the Bronze Age was most tantalizing; they were animal fibres; cross-sections were made and one very short length of scale pattern was found, but did not provide sufficient evidence for identification purposes. The thickness ranged from approximately 10–30 μ, the finer fibres were not medullated but some of the coarse fibres had a fine lattice type medulla, all were pigmented and in some fibres the pigment granules were arranged bi-laterally.

Roman site. Work on a Roman site at Ghirza in Tripolitania revealed two samples of pigmented animal fibres, one, a repp cloth consisting of fibres of medium thickness with interrupted medulla in some fibres. In whole mount the fibres were seen to be too regular in thickness along their length for wool fibres. Scale casts were made of fibres where the scale pattern still remained, the scale margins were crenate and the patterns were very similar in appearance to those seen on fibres from the common goat. The second sample from this site was of unspun hair, and this example serves to show the value of observing the pigment distribution. In cross-section the distribution of pigment granules and the size and shape of the medulla were clearly visible. When these sections were compared with sections of known human hair the chief difference was in the thickness of the layer of cuticular scales. Human hair has a thick layer of cuticle whereas the fibres in the sample had a thinner layer than one would expect to find on human hair; this could have been the result of degradation of the outer surface. Other factors, that is, distribution of pigment and the size and shape of medulla, matched those seen in human hair. Pigment in human hair is often densest near the cuticle, becoming less dense near the medulla. Where the scale pattern could be seen on these fibres it was of the same type as that seen along the length of human hair, i.e. waved, crenate with near to close margins. There was, therefore, enough evidence to be as definite as one can be on these samples to identify these fibres as being of human origin (Plate XXXc).

Samples from the caves at Muraba'ât. Several samples from the caves at Muraba'ât in Jordan were examined some time ago. The fabrics from which these samples were taken were described by Crowfoot,[2] some were plain weave, some fine tapestry and some regular tapestry. The probable date of these is given as AD 132 and onwards. Some of these fibres were very badly degraded and were beyond recognition, others were comparatively well preserved and there was sufficient evidence to indicate their origin. Of the samples examined two could not be identified, four were identified as wool and another probably wool, two were almost certainly camel hair and one was goat hair; the last three samples provided the greatest interest.

Some of the fibres were coarse and had a continuous medulla and streaky pigment distribution characteristics of camel hair, others were fine and had scale patterns similar to those seen on fine fibres from the camel. A difficulty arose with one of these samples of coarse fibres. It had been suggested that this sample could possibly be goat hair; now some coarse fibres from the common goat have features which are similar to those of coarse fibres from other animals. One feature which makes the identification of goat hair certain is a scale pattern on some coarse fibres which is transitional between smooth and rippled-crenate margins. To find this pattern it is necessary to make casts of as long a piece of fibre as possible; the small size of the available piece of yarn and the condition of the surface of the fibres made it difficult to find this particular pattern.

Cross-sections of these fibres were cut and several were found which had contours similar to some goat fibres. The distribution of pigment in these fibres was significant; in a number of goat fibres the pigment is in large aggregates arranged in a radial pattern, and this distribution was found in some fibres in this particular sample. It was this evidence which led to the conclusion that the original suggestion that the sample was made from goat hair was correct.

Saxon period. A short piece of yarn from a Saxon cemetery was one of the few samples which was made from coarse wool fibres. The scale margins were easily seen and the scale patterns were similar to those seen on coarse fibres from present-day British mountain breeds and on the coarse fibres from some of the primitive breeds of sheep such as the Mouflon and Urial.

The form of the fabrics found at Sutton Hoo and Broomfield Barrow were in good condition and were described by Crowfoot[3] as diamond twill, twill in two colours and tablet weave. Unfortunately the fibres were not in such good condition. The weaves were also described as being similar to those of Scandinavian origin, particularly from Denmark. In only one of these samples could the fibres be identified as being wool; the scale pattern was clear on some fibres, and a few were medullated. Fibres in the other samples were too badly degraded for a full identification; they could be described only as being of animal origin.

Anglo-Saxon period. Two samples from Taplow Barrow consisted of both coarse and fine fibres. One fragment of cloth was a 2/2 twill and thought to have been part of a cloak, the other was a plain weave. Unfortunately fibres from these samples were badly degraded and very little detail could be found on the surface of the fibres. The coarse fibres had the wide lattice-type of medulla found in the coarse fibres from British mountain wools and coarse fibres from primitive breeds.

This example and the previous one from the Saxon period suggest that at these periods in British agriculture double-coated breeds of sheep were extant, that is sheep with long coarse outer-coat fibres and short fine under-coat fibres.

The sample thought to be from a cloak also contained a number of pigmented fibres, some very densely pigmented and others only sparsely. This was also a feature of both primitive breeds and some of our present-day British mountain breeds.

Several samples from a site at Fonaby in Lincolnshire were examined; some could only be identified as being of animal origin. One of these samples from unstratified material, labelled US95b by Hawkes,[4] was of particular interest. This was a tuft of hair found lying on but not attached to a sample of cloth in plain weave (US95a).[4] Some of these fibres were pigmented and parts of the fibre follicles were still attached to the root ends. No scale patterns could be found on these fibres but they were strong enough for sections to be cut. It was seen from these cross-sections that the fibres had contours and shape and size of medullae similar to those of body hair from cattle. The shape of cattle body hair is elliptical in cross-section; the medulla is also elliptical and concentric with the outer edge of the fibre.

The root ends of these fibres were similar to those on fibres which are removed from pieces of skin. There is a trade practice in use at the present time of obtaining wool from small pieces of skin by leaving a pile of skin pieces to stand in a moist condition until the skin has rotted away leaving the wool fibres intact for use in textiles. The presence of this type of root end on the tuft of fibres (US95b) suggests that they could have come from a hide used as a covering.

Sixteenth-century sample from Northern Ireland. An example of wool fibres being preserved in a bog was found at Flanders Farm, Dungiven. The sample, part of a fabric, was well preserved. The fibres were degraded but it was possible to make quite good casts which showed wool-type scale patterns. In whole mount most of the fibres were seen to be fine, others were of medium diameter and had broken medullae, some of the fibres were densely pigmented.

Archaeological field experiment. An archaeological field experiment is being organized by the British Association at Overton Down, near Marlborough. Textile fabrics are being buried in an earthwork on a chalk site and samples of fabrics will be recovered at intervals. Samples of wool cloth have been supplied by the Wool Industries Research Association and the recovered samples will be examined and compared with control samples in the Association's laboratories. It is hoped that this experiment will provide some of the answers to problems relating to the preservation of textiles, including degradation and discoloration of fibres. Archaeologists of the future will be able to reap the benefits of this experiment.

APPENDIX

An interesting sample of fibres was sent to us by Dr M. L. Ryder of the University of New England, Armidale, Australia. This sample was from a whole skin found in a frozen burial mound in Siberia; it was dated 500 BC. The skin was thought to be from sheep or goat. The fibres were in a remarkably good state of preservation; the scale structure was exceedingly clear, as clear as on newly grown wool fibres. The features of the fibres showed quite clearly that they were wool. The sample included fine non-medullated fibres of approximately 15 μ diameter, fibres of medium thickness, non-medullated and approximately 40 μ in diameter, and some coarse medullated fibres of approximately 85 μ diameter. An interesting feature of these coarse fibres was the width of the medulla; it was much narrower than one would expect in wool fibres of this thickness. These coarse fibres were dissimilar from those of known primitive breeds which have a wide lattice type medulla.

ACKNOWLEDGEMENTS

The authors wish to thank Miss E. Crowfoot and Miss A. S. Henshall for supplying the material for examination, Mrs S. E. Hawkes for permission to refer to the samples from Fonaby and to Mr R. L. S. Bruce-Mitford of the British Museum, for permission to refer to the samples from Sutton Hoo and Taplow Barrow. We are indebted to Professor Burton, formerly of the Leather Department of the University of Leeds, and his colleagues for samples of parchment from the Dead Sea Scrolls. We thank also

Dr D. J. Smith and Mrs Olwen Brogan, Department of Classics and Ancient History, King's College, Newcastle upon Tyne, for permission to refer to the samples from Ghirza. The technical assistance given by various members of the staff of the Biology Department of the Wool Industries Research Association is highly appreciated.

REFERENCES

1 CARUS-WILSON, E. 1952. The Woollen Industry; in POSTAN, M. and RICH, E. E. (ed.) *Cambridge Economic History of Europe*, Cambridge
2 CROWFOOT, E. 1961. Les Grottes de Murabaat, *Discoveries in the Judaean Desert*, Oxford, II
3 CROWFOOT, G. M. Personal communication
4 HAWKES, S. E. Forthcoming publication
5 HENSHALL, A. S. 1951–52. Early Textiles Found in Scotland. *Proc. Soc. Ant. Scot.*
6 —— Forthcoming publication
7 HIGGINS, S. E. 1924. *A History of Bleaching*, London
8 HOME, F. 1771. *Experiments on Bleaching*, Dublin
9 LEGGETT, W. F. 1947. *The Story of Wool*, New York
10 TEXTILE INSTITUTE. 1958. *Identification of Textile Materials*
11 WILDMAN, A. B. 1954. The Microscopy of Animal Textile Fibres, *Wool Ind. Res. Ass.*

SECTION V PROSPECTING

53 *Magnetic Location*

MARTIN AITKEN

MAN HAS BEEN GUIDED by the earth's magnetism for many centuries, certainly since the tenth century AD when the laws of Gottland prescribed penalties for Baltic sailors who tampered with the compass.* Ancient mariners knew too that compass directions were liable to be erratic near to certain coasts and that this was due to deposits of lodestone—fragments of which formed the active element of early compasses. A particular form of iron oxide (*magnetite*, Fe_3O_4) is responsible for the strong magnetic properties of lodestone and towards the end of the nineteenth century mineral prospectors in Sweden began to use *anomalous* compass readings—checked by reference to the sun or to the pole-star—as a method of locating rich iron-ore deposits.

Magnetic surveying is now an important and highly developed aspect of geological prospecting and very sensitive measuring techniques are used. One of these is the *proton magnetometer*, developed from the magnetic property of the nucleus termed 'free precession', which was first observed experimentally only in 1954.[9] By adapting the proton magnetometer for archaeological use it is possible to detect the following categories of buried remains:

(1) iron objects;
(2) fired structures such as kilns, furnaces, ovens and hearths;
(3) pits and ditches filled with top-soil or rubbish; and, in some circumstances:
(4) walls, foundations, roads and tombs.

The detection of iron objects hardly needs explanation; no one who has tried to take a compass bearing close to an iron fence will doubt the reality of the magnetic disturbance (or anomaly) from it. The disturbances from the other categories listed are very much weaker and arise because of subtle magnetic effects produced by fire and high humus-content. This means that the greater the involvement of a site with the basic human activities of smelting, cultivation, pottery-making, cooking, excretion, etc., the greater is the ability of the proton magnetometer to locate its various features.

The particular advantages of the proton magnetometer compared to more conventional magnetic field instruments, and compared too to resistivity surveying, are the ease and rapidity with which measurements can be made. An acre can be covered in upwards of four hours, depending on how many features are found. Plate XXXII shows

---

* Breathing over the compass after eating onions is one of the practices specifically condemned.

the instrument developed by the Oxford Archaeological Research Laboratory. Each measurement is initiated by pressing the white push-button and the digits subsequently indicated by the four meter-dials are recorded directly in plan form by the operator. A second operator moves the detector over the area being surveyed; this is temporarily marked out, 50 ft by 50 ft at a time, by a string net of 10 ft mesh. The chart of readings obtained from an area containing two pottery kilns and a ditch is shown in Fig. 81.

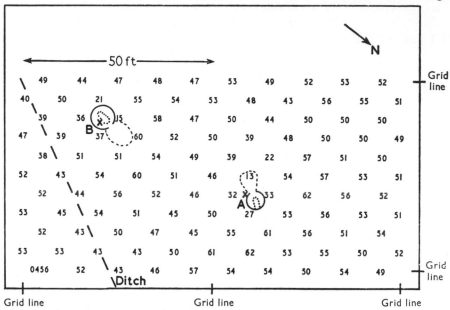

Fig. 81 Sample readings from proton magnetometer survey at Water Newton. The readings shown cover two unit squares each 50 ft by 50 ft. The detector-bottle was at 3 ft above ground level. Fig. 84 shows detailed measurements on traverses through 'A' and 'B'; Romano-British pottery kilns were found beneath these points. From Aitken.[3]

The simplicity of operation of the proton magnetometer is only achieved at the cost of complex electronics, and the instrument is expensive—upwards of £600. Another instrument based on the nuclear free-precession phenomenon is the proton *gradiometer*. This is a little cheaper to construct, and in its simplest form—the 'Bleeper', which is adequate for most types of archaeological site—the cost should be only £150. The *fluxgate* magnetometer is another alternative to the proton magnetometer or gradiometer. It has important advantages but is not at present available in a form suitable for archaeological surveys. Its cost seems likely to be comparable to that of the proton magnetometer.

PRINCIPLES

Thermo-remanent magnetism. A lump of crude clay heated to a dull red heat (about 700°C) acquires a weak *permanent* magnetism on cooling—the phenomenon is termed *thermo-remanent* magnetism. It is the basis of magnetic dating (see pp. 59–71), and was first investigated towards the end of the nineteenth century.[5] The same effect occurs with soil and stones, as long as a small percentage of iron oxide is present—which is nearly always the case (among rocks, chalk is an obvious exception). The effect can be very simply demonstrated by holding an ordinary builder's brick close to a compass: the thermo-remanent magnetism is sufficient to cause a deflection of half a degree or more. On a larger scale, the thermo-remanent magnetism acquired by volcanic lava as it cools from the molten state gives rise to an appreciable magnetic anomaly in the region of a volcano. Thermo-remanent magnetism is carried by all types of igneous rocks, being strongest in recently-formed basalts and weakest in granites.

The thermo-remanent magnetism of baked clay has been exhaustively studied experimentally by Thellier[10] and a theoretical interpretation given by Néel.[8] The effect results from the *ferrimagnetism* of *magnetite* (Fe_3O_4) and *haematite* (α-Fe_2O_3). The average iron oxide content of the earth's crust is 6·8 per cent, and most soil, clay and rocks can be expected to contain significant quantities of magnetite and/or haematite, uniformly dispersed in fine grains. Each grain of haematite forms a magnetic *domain*; within a domain the magnetization is uniform. In unbaked clay (soil, or rock) the domains point in random directions (Fig. 82a), and because of mutual annulment, their net magnetic effect is very small. At a high temperature however, the intrinsic magnetization of each domain weakens and thermal agitation permits some of the domains to be lined up along the lines of force of the earth's magnetic field (Fig. 82b). On cooling, the domains remain 'frozen' in this lined-up situation. At the same time the intrinsic domain magnetization returns to its normal value and the net magnetic effect is now appreciable—simply because the magnetic fields from the domains now add together instead of cancelling out.

Fig. 82 Acquisition of thermo-
remanent magnetism.

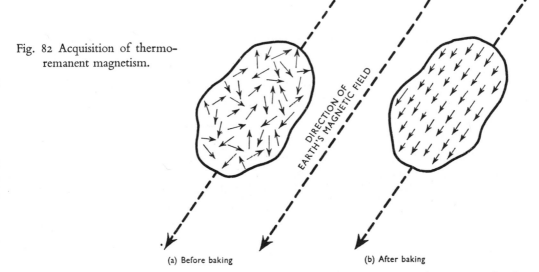

(a) Before baking   (b) After baking

As long as the temperature has reached 675°C (a dull red heat) there is no further increase in the subsequent thermo-remanent magnetism. The duration of heating is unimportant. The effect produced by heating to a lower temperature than 675°C depends on the clay; for a typical clay the effect would be 10% of maximum after cooling from 200°C, 30% after 400°C, 50% after 500°C and 90% after 600°C.

In the case of magnetite the grains are larger than can be occupied by a single domain and explanation is more complex. However, the experimental behaviour is similar to that of haematite except that the degree of magnetization acquired is very much stronger, although the stability of the 'frozen-in' domains is not so hard. The latter factor only matters in magnetic dating, but the former gives rise to a wide variation in the strengths of the anomaly to be expected from fired structures. The specific remanent magnetization of clay cooled from dull red heat can vary between 0·0001 and 0·1 e.m.u. per gram of clay (for refined clays, such as china clay, relatively free from iron, the figures are very much lower). The lower limit applies to red, highly oxidized clay in which conversion of iron oxide to haematite is nearly complete, and the upper limit to grey reduced clay in which magnetite is predominant.

Enhancement of soil susceptibility. The anomalies from pits and ditches arise from a different effect from thermo-remanent magnetism. It is not quite true to say that at ordinary temperatures the magnetic domains are unaffected by the external magnetic field. Some degree of alignment does occur, and a small magnetization results.

Magnetic *susceptibility* expresses the magnetization *induced* in 1 gram of the sample when it is placed in a magnetic field of 1 oersted, *without any heat treatment.* (The specific magnetization is obtained by multiplying the susceptibility by the earth's field strength—about 0·47 oersted in Britain). Induced magnetization is essentially temporary; in whatever direction a sample is turned, the magnetization always lies along the direction of the lines of force of the earth's magnetic field. Consequently disarrangement of the filling of a pit or ditch does not greatly* affect the strength of the anomaly from it. This is not the case for the thermo-remanent magnetism of a burnt structure.

The anomaly from a pit or ditch arises because the susceptibility of the filling is greater than that of the adjacent sub-stratum into which the pit or ditch has been dug, thereby creating a magnetic discontinuity. In general, the less sterile the filling the stronger is the anomaly.

The enhanced magnetic susceptibility of top-soil compared with that of the underlying sub-stratum has been studied by Le Borgne.[6,7] The enhancement is related to the concentration of organic matter in the soils and results from the conversion of the iron oxide from its weakly ferrimagnetic form, haematite (α-Fe_2O_3), to the strongly ferrimagnetic form of maghaemite (γ-Fe_2O_3). The conversion proceeds by reduction to magnetite and subsequent reoxidation to maghaemite.

Two possible mechanisms have been suggested. The first[6] occurs at ordinary temperatures and is favoured by alternating periods of humidity (for reduction) and dryness (for oxidation): a period of high humidity must not last for too long however. The second mechanism put forward[7] is the cumulative effect of fire on the soil—ground clearance by burning being postulated as inherent in the methods of cultivation employed in ancient times. Although high temperatures have intervened in this case, the anomaly is due to enhancement of instantaneous susceptibility rather than thermo-remanent

---

* There is some growth of anomaly with time if the filling is left undisturbed. This effect is due to viscous magnetism. With soils, the viscous component is not usually as great as the instantaneously induced component, although it may be of a comparable magnitude.

magnetization since the latter is subsequently destroyed by disarrangement as cultivation of the ground proceeds. Le Borgne has shown that burning can produce a rapid enhancement of susceptibility and to a higher degree than can be achieved with the first mechanism.

The susceptibility of artificially produced magnetite (dispersed in kaolin) and maghaemite (dispersed in sand) is of the order of 0·001 e.m.u. per gram for concentrations of 1%.[7] However, the susceptibilities found in natural soil samples will differ widely for the same concentrations due to variations in the grain size of the magnetic particles. On most archaeological sites visited by the author the susceptibility of the top-soil has been between 0·00005 and 0·0002 e.m.u. per gram. Sites with top-soils below and above these limits are described as 'weak' and 'strong' respectively.

In general the susceptibilities of samples taken from the filling of an archaeological feature are greater than that of the top-soil. This is presumably due either to the higher humus concentration in the pit (particularly in the case of a rubbish pit, latrine and food-storage pit that has gone foul) or to the greater degree of burning that the filling has suffered as a result of its close association with occupation.

The creation of an anomaly depends not only on the actual value of the susceptibility but also on the magnetic *contrast* between the feature and the material that surrounds it. Fig. 83 gives the susceptibility of specific magnetization, as appropriate, for some common materials. The question of contrast is important in respect of

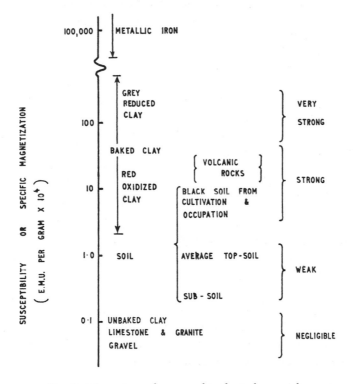

Fig. 83 Magnetism of some archaeological materials.

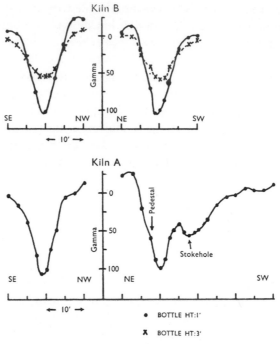

Fig. 84 Magnetic anomalies from kilns. From Aitken.[3]

walls. Although the susceptibility of a limestone wall is negligible, it can create a detectable anomaly if it is buried in top-soil of appreciable susceptibility: however the anomaly is in the reverse sense and is due to the absence of top-soil rather than to the presence of wall.

Anomaly detection. The thermo-remanent magnetism of a kiln, or the greater depth of high-susceptibility top-soil in a pit, distorts the earth's magnetic field from normal in the vicinity of the feature (the effect is strongly localized and doubling the distance from the feature can, in extreme cases, reduce the strength of the anomaly by a factor of eight). However, the effect from archaeological features is too small to cause a detectable error in the compass; instead, the deviation from normal of the *magnetic intensity* (or *field strength*) is measured. The unit of measurement is the gamma,★ and the normal value of magnetic intensity in Britain is about 47,000 gamma. In some equatorial regions the value falls to below 30,000 gamma, while at the poles the value reaches 70,000 gamma. The proton magnetometer can detect changes of 1 gamma without difficulty.

The distortion caused by an archaeological feature is not easy to calculate because it results from the vector addition of the field due to the feature and the normal earth's field. However there are four general rules which are worth bearing in mind. These are applicable only where the angle of dip is between 60° and 70°N as is the case for Britain. Elsewhere modification is needed.[3] The rules are:

★ 100,000 gamma = 1 oersted (CGS e.m.u.) = 79·6 ampere-metre^{-1} (MKS).

(a) The maximum of the anomaly lies to the *south* of the feature. The displacement is not greater than one-third of the depth of the centre of the feature.

(b) The separation between the two points, in a straight-line traverse, at which the anomaly has half its maximum value, is not less than the depth of the feature.

(c) A *reverse* anomaly may occur to the *north* of the feature at a distance equal to the depth. The reverse anomaly does not exceed 10 per cent of the maximum anomaly strength, except where the cause is modern iron.

(d) The anomaly is very small (less than 2%) at distances greater than three times the depth of the feature.

Actual traverses above two Romano-British kilns are shown in Fig. 84. The anomaly is shown as a dip rather than a peak as this corresponds to the sense of the proton magnetometer indication (*infra*); the anomaly does in fact represent an *increase* above the normal magnetic intensity.

The above rules apply primarily to isolated features such as kilns and pits. For linear features such as ditches, the anomaly depends upon the orientation. The anomaly for a ditch running north–south is nearly twice as great as that for an identical ditch running east–west. For an east–west ditch the reverse anomaly (lying to the north) may amount to 60% of the anomaly maximum, and should not be mistaken for a wall or rampart.

The sensitivity of magnetic surveying to iron is inconveniently high, and although, by detailed measurements, it is possible to distinguish between anomalies from iron lying in the surface and those due to genuine features, such measurements impede progress. Surface iron is most readily identified by measuring the width of the anomaly (rule (b)); if this width is not much greater than the height of the detector above the ground then clearly the cause lies close to the surface. Widespread iron (such as chicken netting) produces an irregular anomaly and is easy to recognize. The magnetic gradients produced by iron are often too strong for the proton magnetometer to operate satisfactorily and a 'killed signal' is another sympton of iron.

INSTRUMENTS

The proton magnetometer. The detector consists of a half-pint bottle of water or alcohol around which a 1,000-turn electrical coil is wound. The magnetic intensity is deduced from the behaviour of the protons which form the nuclei of hydrogen atoms in the water or alcohol. An essential preliminary to measurement is the three-second *polarizing period*. During this, a current of an amp is passed through the coil thereby producing a magnetic field of several hundred oersteds along the axis. This aligns a majority of the protons in that direction. When the polarizing current is cut off the protons try to align themselves along the lines of force of the earth's field. However, because they can be regarded as miniature gyroscopes, they perform gyrations about that directon instead. The frequency of gyration is exactly proportional to the magnetic intensity of the earth's field.

The proton gyrations are detectable because when gyrating in phase they produce an alternating voltage of about a microvolt in the coil around the bottle. This is fed, via a flexible cable which can be several hundred feet long, to the low-noise, highly-selective amplifier in the instrument itself. The use of special transistor techniques enables the frequency to be measured to an accuracy of 1 part in 50,000 within half a second; this corresponds to a sensitivity of 1 gamma. Greater sensitivity, say, down to 0·2 gamma, can be obtained without difficulty, though for archaeological application this is rarely required. The polarizing period is timed automatically within the instrument. At its conclusion frequency measurement takes place; the answer shown on the indicating meters is proportional to the reciprocal of the magnetic intensity. The greater the magnetic intensity, the lower the number indicated.

The polarization period is necessary before each measurement because internal magnetic inhomogeneities within the liquid cause the proton signal to die away after three or four seconds. This normal duration of signal may be reduced by an external magnetic gradient such as exists close to a piece of iron. Observation of the duration of the proton signal can be a useful check of whether an anomaly is due to iron. In some cases the signal decays too quickly for the frequency measurement to be performed—hence the term 'killed signal'.

Detailed circuits for the proton magnetometer have been described by Waters and Francis[11] and by Bradshaw.[4] An instrument suitable for archaeological work is manufactured by the Littlemore Scientific Engineering Co., Oxford. Field instruments are also manufactured in the United States by Varian Associates, California, and in Canada by Barringer Research Ltd., Toronto. The sensitivity of these two latter is only 10 gamma; although this is adequate for kiln detection it is barely enough for pits and ditches.

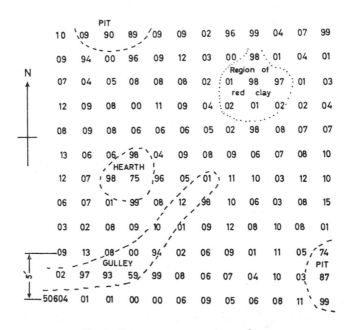

Fig. 85 Proton magnetometer readings.

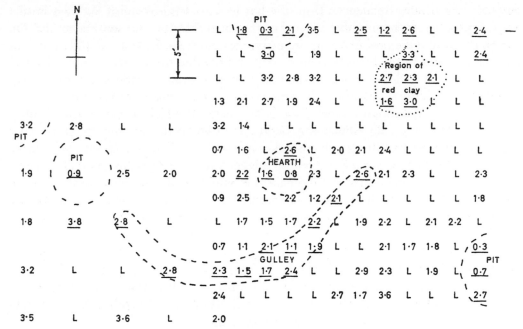

Fig. 86 Proton gradiometer readings.

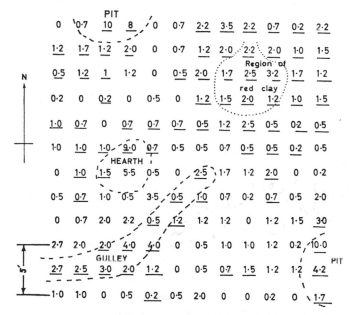

Fig. 87 Fluxgate gradiometer readings.

The proton gradiometer. This instrument uses the same basic nuclear phenomenon of proton free-precession. Two bottles are used in this case, carried at either end of a vertically-held staff which is five feet or more long. In the absence of a magnetic anomaly the proton frequencies from the bottles are identical and if the two bottles are fed, in series, to an amplifier a signal of the usual three or four seconds results. On the other hand in the presence of an anomaly, the two frequencies are slightly different and the two signals gradually get out of step and the duration of the combined signal ceases prematurely. The stronger the anomaly the shorter the duration, and the reading given by the instrument indicates the time taken for the signal to reach zero.

The 'bleeper' is a simplification of the gradiometer in which measurement of signal duration is left to human estimation.[3] Besides the two bottle-detectors the instrument consists only of an amplifier and loudspeaker or earphone. Consequently it can be made for a fraction of the cost of the proton magnetometer or gradiometer. The name 'bleeper' arises because when the anomaly is strong enough, the two signals move in and out of phase while their individual amplitudes are still appreciable and 'bleeps' are heard (technically these are 'beats' so that a more precise nomenclature would be 'beat gradiometer').

By making the height of the upper bottle greater than the dimensions of the expected features and keeping the lower bottle fairly close to the ground (say at 1 ft) the results with the gradiometer or bleeper are easily comparable with those of the standard (or absolute) magnetometer. Because of the sharp fall-off of anomaly with increasing height the upper bottle acts as a reference with which the frequency of the lower bottle is compared. The system has the definite advantage that it discriminates in favour of small-scale disturbances and tends to ignore more widespread anomalies such as originate from geological causes. Also, it is unaffected by magnetic storms or the proximity of DC-driven trains and trams.

Gradiometer measurements can be converted to anomaly strengths in gamma as follows:

> Signal duration of 2 seconds—6·25 gamma
> Signal duration of 1 second—2·5 gamma
> Signal duration of 0·5 second—25 gamma
>   etc., etc.
>
> 1 bleep per second—25 gamma
> 2 bleeps per second—50 gamma
> 3 bleeps per second—75 gamma
>   etc. etc.

The differential fluxgate magnetometer. This works on a completely different principle, the detecting elements being small strips of mu-metal. As with the proton gradiometer the two detectors are carried vertically above one another and the difference in magnetic intensities is indicated on a meter. An instrument of this type developed by the signals and Research Development Establishment, Christchurch, uses detectors spaced 2 ft apart and can measure gradients of as little as 0·2 gamma per foot. The results of some comparative trials of this and the two preceding instruments are shown in Figs. 85–87.

The fluxgate has two immediate advantages over the proton-type instruments. Firstly the reading is continuous. Secondly the fluxgate magnetometer, because of the small size of its detecting elements, can be used in strong magnetic gradients which preclude use of the proton magnetometer. Like the proton gradiometer it ignores widespread anomalies, magnetic storms and DC trains and trams.

Against these advantages must be balanced a greater complication in initial setting-up and in operation, and the fact that it has not yet been developed in a lightweight form suitable for archaeological use.

SURVEY LOGISTICS

Magnetic surveying is only a means to an end and to be worthwhile, the time and effort expended must be negligible compared to that required to trial-trench the same area. Consequently competent organization is vital. It is also important that the survey is carried out scientifically; measurements made solely to test out a preconceived archaeological idea can all too easily produce false support for that idea.

The standard procedure employed by the author is as follows. The area is first marked out with stout pegs (which must of course be free from nails!) so as to form a grid of 50 ft squares. Each square is covered in turn by a net stretched between the four corner pegs; the mesh size of the net is 10 ft and the middle of each 10 ft length is marked with a coloured tag. These enable the bottle to be moved over the square on a 5 ft mesh; this involves 100 measurements per square, approximately 1,800 per acre. In order to avoid shrinkage in wet weather it is essential that the string used for constructing the net is plastic-covered.*

Each square takes approximately 10 minutes to complete. Any abnormal readings are then investigated by more closely spaced measurements, firstly in order to determine the maximum strength of the anomaly, secondly to find its spatial extent, and thirdly to pin-point its centre on the ground.

A significant proportion of sites present serious handicaps to surveying. Trees, undergrowth, long grass, clover, nettles and thistles, etc. may impede movement of the cable and net so seriously as to rule out a survey. The proximity of AC electrical power cables and of radio transmitting stations is liable to cause interference with operation of the instrument. Iron litter on the surface, water pipes and gas mains, wire fences (to within 30 ft) produce their own disturbances which may mask, or simulate, archaeological features. Differentiation can be made with careful detailed measurements but this impedes progress. Another, more fundamental, difficulty occurs with sites on igneous geological formations. As mentioned earlier, igneous rocks have acquired an appreciable thermo-remanent magnetism as they cooled from the molten state. From recent basalts (of the Tertiary) the magnetic disturbance is far too strong to permit detection of archaeological features. In older basalts (10 million years or greater), and in granites, the effect is much weaker and archaeological surveying is possible.

The presence of DC power lines (such as are associated with DC trains and trams) creates difficulty only with the proton magnetometer. With the gradiometer and with the fluxgate the magnetic field associated with DC current affects both detectors equally

---

* Obtainable from James Lever, Box 6, Everlastic Rope Works, Bolton, Lancs.

and so cancels out. The same is true of transient variations of the magnetic intensity due to ionization currents in the upper atmosphere. On 'magnetic storm days' changes of upwards of 10 gamma may occur within 10 minutes even though the detector is kept at the same point. To survey with the proton magnetometer under such conditions it is necessary to have a second reference detector-bottle at a fixed position on the site and make check measurements with it at frequent intervals.

RESULTS

Some forty archaeological sites have now been surveyed with the proton magnetometer. With two or three exceptions these surveys have been highly successful, though it must be emphasized that the sites were chosen with increasing discretion as experience accumulated. The magnetic effects from various types of feature are summarized in the following sections. Unless stated to the contrary anomaly strengths refer to measurements with the detector-bottle 1 ft above ground level.

Kilns. No difficulty has ever been experienced in finding kilns. Pottery kilns have been detected magnetically and confirmed by excavation, on the following sites: Brill, Downpatrick, Hartshill, Rossington Bridge, Savernake, Wappenbury, Water Newton. Of these the most outstanding was Hartshill where two dozen Romano-British kilns were located in advance of quarrying operations.

The anomaly strength from a kiln is usually 100 gamma or more, depending on the depth. In the sites covered, the depth of the old ground surface below the present-day surface has not been greater than 4 ft. At Hartshill the kilns were so close to the surface that the magnetic gradients were strong enough to give a 'killed signal'. This suggested surface iron but as soon as the turf was removed in order to confirm this on the first anomaly, the distinctive red upper rim of a pottery kiln was evident. On the other hand at Water Newton, where the old ground surface was about 2 ft down, the anomalies from kilns were not decisively different from that from a highly humus-laden pit (cf. Figs. 84 and 88).

Hearths. There is much less baked clay in a hearth so that the anomaly is smaller and hearths can escape detection. At High Rocks hill-fort an anomaly strength of 40 gamma was obtained from a hearth about eighteen inches below the surface whereas at Gwithian a hearth 1 ft down produced only 20 gamma. At Rainsborough hill-fort a hearth 9 in down produced an anomaly of 35 gamma (see Fig. 85).

Pits. Magnetic surveying was originated as a method of finding kilns. It is equally efficacious in finding pits and there is no known case of a pit going undetected. The strength of the anomaly is variable, depending on the susceptibility of the filling. This in turn depends on the degree of burning and humifaction—the 'dirtiness' of the filling—as well as on the basic iron content of the soil. Of the sites visited six stand out as examples of the immense value that magnetic surveying has in exploring the visually blank interiors of forts and camps: Barley, Burrough, Danes Camp, Madmarston, Rainsborough, Waddon Hill. Except for the first and last, these sites are on limestone and conditions are evidently suitable for formation of high-susceptibility top-soil apart from any added enhancement due to archaeological occupation. Soil susceptibilities in

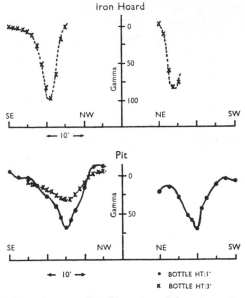

Fig. 88 Magnetic anomalies from pit and from iron. From Aitken.[3]

the range 0·0001 to 0·001 e.m.u. per gram were encountered, and pit anomalies as high as 100 gamma. At Barley, on chalk, the average soil susceptibility was lower and consequently the anomalies were smaller—not greater than 30 gamma from a pit 5 ft across, 3 ft deep beneath eighteen inches of overlay. A difficulty with sites on chalk is the presence of irregularities in the surface of the chalk, which because of the consequent greater depth of top-soil give rise to anomalies. Such anomalies can usually be distinguished from genuine pit anomalies because of the better-defined shape of the latter, found when investigated with a detailed traverse.

Ditches. In general ditch-fillings are more sterile than pit-fillings. In some cases the filling is entirely rampart fall-in with little silting of top-soil. The anomaly may then be too small for detection. A compensating factor with ditches is their geometrical form. Anomalies, which considered in isolation would be indistinguishable from random fluctuations due for example to natural variations in the condition and depth of the top-soil, may acquire significance when seen in plan form. This is similar to recognition of geometrical features in aerial photography.

The classic example of magnetic ditch location is at Verulamium,[1,2] where an inner fosse, sectioned near to Bluehouse Hill, was followed for over half a mile. Closely-spaced traverses were necessary (traverses 10 ft apart, readings 2 ft apart along each traverse) in order to keep track of the ditch when it passed through other magnetic features. The anomaly varied between 5 and 20 gamma, presumably depending on the condition of the fill. The magnetic indications were confirmed by sectioning near either end; the ditch was about 15 ft across and deep. The ditch was followed along three sides of an approximate rectangle; one of the corners happened to lie exactly between the wickets of the corporation cricket-pitch—clearly out-of-bounds to digging!

Comparative surveys using different instruments. Figs. 85, 86 and 87 show the readings obtained over the same area by using a proton magnetometer, a proton gradiometer, and a fluxgate gradiometer respectively. Subsequently the area was stripped and the archaeological features examined. This was carried out in the course of the excavation of the Iron-Age hill-fort at Rainsborough by the Oxford University Archaeological Society in 1961.

The area covered in detail by all three instruments was 25 ft by 25 ft. Part of the standard-spaced survey using 100 readings per square of 50 ft by 50 ft is also shown in Fig. 86. For the proton magnetometer the detector-bottle was at 1 ft above ground level, for the proton gradiometer the lower bottle was at 1 ft and the upper bottle at 7 ft, and for the fluxgate gradiometer the lower detector was at 1 ft and the upper at 3 ft. In all cases the reading as obtained directly from the instrument is recorded. For the proton magnetometer (Fig. 85) only the digits from the two most sensitive meters are recorded; a change from 00 to 99 is only a change of 1 unit, that is an *intensification* of the magnetic intensity by 1 gamma.

For the proton gradiometer (Fig. 86) the readings represent the time (in seconds) for the proton signal to reach zero (see sub-section on the proton gradiometer). Where this exceeds 3·5 seconds, 'L' is recorded. Readings indicative of an anomaly of normal polarity (i.e. an increase in intensity) are underlined. Clearly a more immediate picture of the anomalies is obtained with the gradiometer and this compensates for its more tedious operation. This is also the case for the fluxgate gradiometer (Fig. 87), where the readings indicate the vertical magnetic gradient in gamma per foot, underlining having the same significance as before.

REFERENCES

1 AITKEN, M. J. 1960. The magnetic survey; Appendix to FRERE, S. S. *Excavations at Verulamium 1959, 5th Interim Report Antiq. 40*, 21–24
2 —— 1961a. The magnetic survey. Appendix to FRERE, S. S. *Excavations at Verulamium 1959, 6th Interim Report 41*, in press
3 —— 1961b. *Physics and Archaeology*, London and New York
4 BRADSHAW, C. G. 1957. A versatile 100 Kc/s transistor counter chronometer for frequency measurement; *SRDE Report no.* 1106
5 FOLGHERAITER, G. 1899. *Arch. Sci. phys. nat. 8*, 5–16
6 LE BORGNE, E. 1955. *Ann. Géophys. 11*, 399–419
7 —— 1960. *Ibid. 16*, 159–195
8 NÉEL, L. 1955. *Advances in Physics 4*, 191–243
9 PACKARD, M. and VARIAN, R. 1954. *Phys. Rev. 93*, 941
10 THELLIER, E. and THELLIER, O. 1959. *Ann. Géophys. 15*, 285–376
11 WATERS, G. S. and FRANCIS, P. D. 1958. *J. sci. Instrum. 35*, 88–93

ANTHONY CLARK

THE DETECTION of buried archaeological remains by measurement of the electrical resistivity of the soil is a well-established technique that has been in use for fifteen years. Instrument design and the theory of resistivity measurement have recently been concisely summarized by Aitken,[1] but the last general description of field technique in English appeared in 1953,[2] since when experience has been gained in this subtle aspect of the subject, and some novel ideas have been advanced in scattered papers; also instruments are now more freely available to the amateur. The bias of this review will therefore be towards problems of survey and interpretation.

Soil resistivity measurement has been used as a geological and civil engineering aid since the second decade of this century, but it occurred to no one to apply it in archaeology until 1946, when Atkinson first used the method in his excavation of a group of Neolithic henge monuments at Dorchester, Oxfordshire. The technique was tried because of the need to locate as quickly as possible filled-in ditches and pits visible only as crop marks from the air, and not closely related to reference points on the ground. The success of the method was remarkable, and led to its enthusiastic application on other sites, but results were sometimes disappointing and development was slow for the next ten years.

Clearly Atkinson's first surveys had chanced to be made in almost ideal conditions, and refinements of interpretation and technique would be necessary before some other types of site could be tackled. Also the first instruments tried for archaeology were naturally those already available for commercial earth testing and geophysics. These are generally designed for work on a larger scale and are commensurately substantial and expensive, and not adapted for the archaeological requirement of rapid traversing along a straight line. Resistivity survey therefore tended to remain in the hands of a few specialists.

In 1956 the writer had the opportunity to use a simple two-terminal transistorized resistance meter designed by the Distillers Company Instrumentation Laboratory. This was tried prior to the first excavation of the Romano-British township of Mildenhall-Cunetio, Wiltshire, and readily detected the foundation of the town wall.[3] The extreme compactness, relative cheapness and low current consumption of a transistorized circuit seemed eminently desirable archaeologically, and such an instrument, using the conventional four-terminal system, was designed by John Martin and the writer. The successive excavations at Cunetio served as testing ground and control, and the instrument became commercially available in 1960.

The advent of magnetic detection in 1958 provided the archaeological armoury with a powerful new weapon. Whereas resistivity surveys are most conveniently made in straight lines, an area can be quickly examined with a magnetometer, which is also unaffected by the dampness of the soil. Magnetic measurement is superior in its ability to locate isolated, and often small, objects with magnetic fields, such as refuse pits, iron objects and baked-clay structures such as kilns. Resistivity, however, is particularly at home with linear features such as ditches and is more reliable for the detection of buildings and stone structures generally; and the apparatus is usually much cheaper at present. Resistivity can also be used in towns and close to power lines, where stray fields interfere with magnetic measurement. Clearly magnetic and resistance detection will remain supplementary to each other, although it should be remembered that most things that can be detected with a magnetometer can also be detected with a resistivity meter, if sometimes more tediously.

What of the future of resistivity measurement technique? At present, all meters require a hand operation in order to obtain a reading, and attempts will probably be made in the future to develop circuits giving instantaneous readings. Instruments that do not require the insertion of probes are also possible.[4]

PRINCIPLES OF SOIL RESISTIVITY MEASUREMENT

The ability of a mass of soil or rock to conduct electricity is due to water in the interstices which contains salts dissolved from the material and humic acids of biological origin. If an electrical potential (voltage) is applied between two electrodes connected to different points on the mass, the solution will separate into positive and negative ions by the process of electrolysis, and these will flow respectively to the negative and positive electrodes thereby setting up an electric current. The ratio of the applied voltage to the magnitude of the current is known as the resistance between the electrodes, and varies with the compactness and dampness of the mass and on the solubility and quantity of the salts and acid.

A crude soil resistivity meter can be made by inserting two metal probes a few inches into the ground, say a foot or more apart, connecting a battery across them, and measuring the ratio of the voltage to the current that flows between the probes. Not being constrained as in a wire, the current does not pass straight from probe to probe, but spreads out into many curving paths through the earth, some of it going considerably deeper than the horizontal separation of the probes. Herein lies the great power of resistivity measurement: the deep current penetration obtainable with only a short length of probe insertion. However, the readings of such a simple instrument are adversely affected by (i) probe polarization, the accumulation of oppositely charged ions close to each electrode, causing a continuous rise in resistance reading; (ii) probe contact resistance, which is usually much greater than the resistance value for the bulk of the soil between the probes and can vary considerably from one insertion to another; and (iii) natural earth currents and voltages of chemical origin where the probes make contact with the ground. Replacement of the battery by an alternating current power source obviates all these troubles except (ii), but this is overcome by using a four-probe system[5] as shown in Fig. 89. In this an AC current flows between the two outer probes, and the resultant voltage difference between the two inner detector probes is measured by a system which draws no current from them. The instrument is arranged to divide

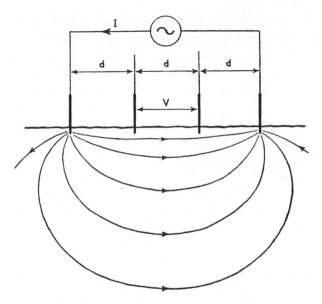

Fig. 89 The Wenner four-probe arrangement, showing
spread of current paths through homogeneous soil.

the voltage, V, by the current, I. This gives a resistance value, R, which, by the
formula

$$\rho = 2\pi dR \quad . \quad . \quad . \quad . \quad . \quad . \quad . \quad . \quad . \quad . \quad . \quad (1)$$

where d is the spacing between the probes, gives an average specific resistivity, ρ, which
is assumed to apply at the centre point of the electrode system to a depth of about $1\cdot5d$,
providing the soil is fairly homogeneous. ρ is in ohm-centimetres, ohm-feet, etc.,
depending on the unit used to measure d. In most archaeological work, d is kept constant and the whole of the multiplying factor $2\pi d$ becomes a constant and ρ is proportional to R, so that there is no need to work out this expression for comparative readings
taken with equal spacing along a line. The presence of media more or less resistive than
the normal soil causes distortion of the regular current pattern shown in Fig. 90, and

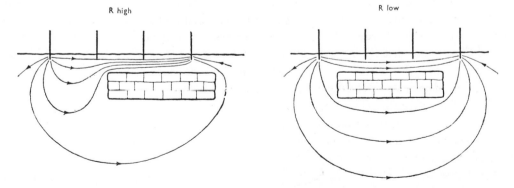

Fig. 90 Approximate indication of the distortion of current paths as the probe assembly passes over a
high resistance feature, showing how a low reading can be obtained over the centre of the feature.

consequent anomalies in a continuous line of readings. A high value of R is due to a high value of V relative to I which one can picture as being caused by current lines crowded near the surface by a high resistance intrusion such as masonry; conversely, a conductive anomaly, such as a pit with a moist filling cut into subsoil rock, draws the current lines to a greater depth, so that few pass the voltage probes and a low reading is registered.

The normal linear traverse with constant probe separation has already been alluded to. Another procedure, much used in geological work but more rarely in archaeology, is known as the expanding electrode system. If a reasonably homogeneous top layer is underlain by one of different resistivity, it is possible to determine the depth of the lower layer by making use of the increasing current penetration obtained as the probe spacing is increased. For each value of d, equation (1) must be worked out. This will give a fairly constant value for ρ until d is large enough for the current pattern to reach and be distorted by the lower layer. ρ will now increase more rapidly if the lower layer is more resistive than the upper, or will fall if it is less resistive. It is worthwhile to plot a graph of ρ against d. Where the lower layer is much more resistive than the upper, d approximates to its depth when ρ has increased to $1 \cdot 5$ times its original value.

INSTRUMENTS

The Megger Earth Tester.[6] This instrument was used by Atkinson for the first archaeological resistivity trials in 1946. It has the advantage over others that the reading is obtained by direct observation of a dial, although the operator must generate the working voltage by turning a handle. The Megger is a substantial wooden instrument mounted on a tripod. One disadvantage is that its accuracy is more readily affected by dry conditions than is the case with null balance instruments such as those described below. Atkinson devised for the Megger a switching system which operates in conjunction with five probes to enable consecutive four-probe readings to be taken along a line with the minimum of probe movement and time loss (see below).

The Tellohm.[7] This instrument is available in two forms, one designed for general use, the other a larger and more sensitive version for geophysical work. The latter seems usually to be chosen by archaeologists, although the writer can see little objection to the more compact model. The instruments are well finished and accurate, the power being derived from self-contained dry batteries, and the reading taken by adjusting a calibrated dial to give a zero (or null) reading on a meter. Using a Geophysical Tellohm, the United Kingdom Ministry of Works Test Branch have developed a system for making rapid area surveys which will be described below.

The Gossen Geohm.[8] This instrument, much used in Germany, is similar to the Tellohm in form and action, but more compact and extremely reasonably priced in Europe. Unfortunately, like all the meters so far considered, it lacks a rapid changeover switch, which must be supplied by the user.

The Martin-Clark Meter.[9] This is the first instrument specifically designed for archaeological work. Unlike the other instruments, which use rotary choppers or vibrating systems, the AC voltage is derived from a transistor oscillator which applies only a small voltage to the earth, but this is compensated for by the use of a very sensitive amplifier so that only light leads need be used and the battery is very long-lasting. The instrument is of the null-balance type. The compactness of the M–C meter enables the operator to hold it in one hand: he can thus follow the probes as they are moved so that the leads need only be of minimal length. Perhaps the most useful feature of the instrument is the changeover switch invented by Martin. This consists of four fixed spring contacts within the instrument and a rotating turret with five contacts and leads outside. At any setting of the switch, the four lower leads (1, 2, 3 and 4 in Fig. 91) are in use in the order in which they are seen from above, the top being spare. When the

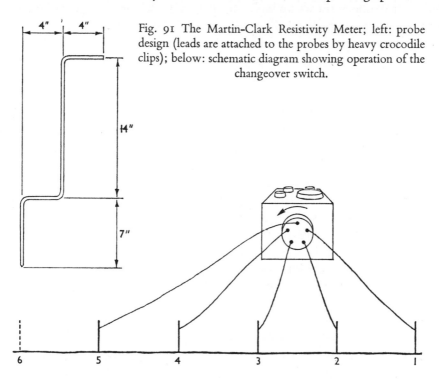

Fig. 91 The Martin-Clark Resistivity Meter; left: probe design (leads are attached to the probes by heavy crocodile clips); below: schematic diagram showing operation of the changeover switch.

turret is rotated one-fifth of a turn in the direction of movement, the former spare lead (5) becomes the leading one of the next group of four and, while the second reading is being taken, the new spare lead (1) is moved by the probe handler (to position 6) ready for the third reading. Thus both instrument operator and probe handler work simultaneously without time-wasting intervals. This method of working is exactly the same as that devised by Atkinson, but the switch is much simpler than his and, being rotated in the direction of movement, counteracts the twisting of the leads that is inherent in this method of moving the probes. Probes and leads are colour coded and, as the instrument operator works close to the probes, no instructions have to be exchanged with the probe handler.[10]

The probes, of ⅜ in mild steel, are also designed for compactness combined with easy removal and easy and accurate insertion, and the design is recommended for use with any instrument (Fig. 91). The upper crank is used as a handle, and for insertion the foot is placed on the lower crank which also acts as a depth stop.

SUITABILITY OF CONDITIONS

As already stated, the ability of a soil mass to conduct electricity depends on the presence of salts and acids in water solution. The best agricultural land is usually a rich loam upon a well-drained subsoil, such as Chalk or gravel, and such conditions can be expected to give good resistivity results, especially for revealing filled ditches and pits. In clay, the subsoil often differs little in resistivity from the top soil, so that the latter are difficult to detect, but masonry shows up well, and the writer has accurately detected a Roman building at a depth of about 2 ft in a clay soil awash with rainwater.

At the other extreme are sandy soils. In elevated positions such as the Greensand hills of the Weald, these often develop podsol conditions in which all soluble material has been dissolved out of the upper part of the subsoil, and top soil is scant indeed. Not only is the ground then practically incapable of conducting electricity, especially in a drought, but a similar fate sometimes overtakes the silting of archaeological disturbances and prevents their being detected. Such land often becomes more tractable after prolonged cultivation. Although most modern resistivity meters are compensated for probe contact resistance to a remarkable degree, their accuracy can be affected in very dry conditions, which also reduce the sensitivity of all types of instrument. Stony soils, besides making the insertion of probes physically difficult, are liable to exhibit both poor and variable contact conditions, quite apart from soil inhomogeneity, all of which factors tend to produce erratic resistivity results.

Difficulties also naturally arise where a deceptively uniform top soil overlies an inhomogeneous subsoil. The writer experienced such conditions on a survey in Norfolk, where the subsoil consisted of the mixed glacial material loosely known as Boulder Clay, and extra readings and interpretative care were necessary to separate the geological and archaeological effects. In such a situation, the filtering methods used by Scollar (see below, p. 581) would probably be worth while.

The resistivity surveyor must also pay attention to the surface condition of the ground. Soil fairly freshly ploughed is usually well aerated and loose in texture. This tends to give high and erratic probe contact resistance because such well-ventilated soils tend to be dry, and included air pockets, being of infinite resistance, have the same effect as stones. It is therefore important to try to push the probes well down to furrow level, or to compact the soil around them with the foot. In a grass field on a Chalk subsoil, the writer found that a little-used track smoothed by wheeled vehicles and by people walking gave resistivity values on an average only two-thirds as great as the field generally. This can be accounted for by the small surface area of the compressed soil, resulting in a low water evaporation rate, and by the moisture absorbed and expired by the more luxuriant growth of grass in the rest of the field. Scollar found that a field of beet gave lower values than a rye field because of the protection against evaporation afforded by the broad leaves of the beet. Fertilizers probably also have an effect. To sum up: an absolute change of top-soil resistivity can be expected from one field to another, or from one part to another of a single field. This may be due to a change of soil depth, or of surface condition, or crops growing or recently harvested, but such effects should not inhibit the indication of buried remains.

A little rain before a survey is often useful in improving contact conditions, and the short circuiting effect of even heavy rain is often less than might be expected, as the instance cited above of the survey on clay demonstrated; and the onset of heavy rain halfway through a survey has also had no immediate effect. This is probably because freshly fallen rain first passes through the uppermost layer of the soil from which most electrolytes have already been dissolved, and the process of solution must also take some time, so that the water is at first hardly more conductive than distilled water; the first rain after a drought probably has more effect. Even prolonged rain for several days has not affected the ease with which the foundation of the Roman wall of Cunetio (soil: loam on Clay-with-flints on Chalk) can be detected, although the magnitude of the indication is not as great as in drier weather; on the other hand, similar conditions have almost completely masked the much more subtle indications of small Neolithic ditches in the light loam on Chalk soil of Salisbury Plain. The converse conditions of general drying out of the soil will also suppress any resistivity contrast. Scollar has observed that the indications of a Roman town wall, which normally have the expected high values with respect to the surrounding soil, can become completely reversed to give lower values after much rain, presumably because water collects on top of the relatively impermeable masonry.

Generally masonry and brick will give relatively high, and silted ditches and pits low, resistivity readings, but there are exceptions. For instance, apart from the rather abnormal case above, a wall may be represented by a robber trench filled with low resistivity material, and a ditch may be wholly or partly filled with loose stones, especially when the filling has been deliberate.

CHOICE OF PROBE SEPARATION

This is a problem which the resistivity surveyor must consider very carefully on each site if he is to obtain the maximum information. The accepted rough rule is that a measurement, using the equidistant Wenner probe spacing, will detect remains down to a depth about equal to the horizontal probe spacing, d. Thus, if the probes are too close together, deeper features may be missed; on the other hand wider spacing, although giving deeper penetration, reduces the precision of location and, as the current spreads through a larger volume of soil, may fail to detect the smaller features and tends to suppress the effect of large ones. There is, of course, no definite limit to the penetration, the current falling off gradually with increasing depth.

Some workers recommend preliminary tests by the expanding electrode procedure (see above) at points away from the remains and, if their position is known at all, over part of the remains themselves, so as to ascertain the spacing likely to give the greatest contrast between remains and soil, and any variations of subsoil depth over the area of the site. If one is searching for filled ditches or pits expected to show as interruptions in the subsoil, a spacing must be chosen which is greater than that at which the subsoil begins to affect the preliminary readings appreciably; on the other hand, masonry often rises well above subsoil level, perhaps to the lowest ploughing depth, and in such cases can be detected with a much narrower spacing which is also valuable for the definition of individual small walls.

In practice, however, the top soil is often too shallow for this procedure to have much value; and there is usually regrettably little time for such preliminary work, and the surveyor must choose his spacing more rapidly and arbitrarily. This is often quite easy. For instance, remains which have been discovered by aerial photography, or ground observation, of crop marks or soil marks, are rarely much below plough depth (say 1–2 ft), especially if the crop mark has given a well-defined picture; and conditions that give a good crop mark can usually be relied upon to produce good resistivity results. Other sites are found by chance or intent during excavation. If such indications are supplemented by some preliminary work with the humble but neglected auger, or even by simple probing, a suitable spacing can be reliably chosen. An auger of some type is a most valuable addition to the resistivity surveyor's equipment.[11]

To prevent a survey from being too time consuming, it may be necessary to make preliminary traverses with a greater probe spacing than the ideal, but once the broad position of remains has been defined, traverses with smaller spacing can be made at selected places. However little preliminary work is done, a spacing of 1 metre, or 3–4 ft, can almost always be relied upon to produce results on the average site. Such spacings give fairly precise horizontal location of remains, with a limit of detection in the region of 4–5 ft and sites with a greater overburden than this are rare. Nevertheless, to take an example, care must be exercised where lyncheting has occurred, that is, the accumulation of soil at the lower end of a sloping field. Air photography may reveal remains close to the surface at the top of such a field, but lower down these indications are often masked by the deeper soil. In such a case the deeper penetration obtainable by resistivity measurement is particularly useful as a supplement to the aerial indications, but the probe spacing must be related to the maximum depth of the soil which can often be estimated by inspection of the field boundary.

SURVEY PROCEDURE

The simplest type of survey is the straight line traverse using the five-probe system described above. This is particularly useful when tracing a linear feature such as a wall or ditch. A plastic or metallized linen measuring tape (not a metal tape or chain because of their conductivity) is laid along the ground as nearly as possible at right angles to the feature, and to start the five probes are placed in line along it from the zero point. If a 100 ft tape is used, with a 4 ft probe spacing, this will mean that the first reading occurs at 6 ft along the tape, and the last at 94 ft. In order to allow for this, and to obtain a representative idea of the resistivity level of the undisturbed ground, the tape should be amply extended on either side of the buried feature: this will help greatly in deciding whether a resistance anomaly is due to the feature sought or to variable ground resistivity. The results should be written down and plotted as a graph with resistance as abscissa and distance as ordinate. If an area survey is contemplated, individual traverses of this type give a useful preliminary indication of whether remains are clearly enough defined. When a fairly wide spacing has to be used, intermediate readings can be obtained by repeating a traverse with the zero point advanced by a distance equal to half the probe spacing ($d/2$). This halves the reading interval and gives a more complete resistivity picture. If even closer coverage is required, the whole probe assembly (without the fifth probe) can be moved a very short distance between readings, but there is rarely much advantage in this.

Although our two-dimensional diagrams do not show it, the current spreads sideways as well as downwards; therefore some effect can be expected from features not actually crossed by the line of survey, and care should be taken to keep traverses at least a distance of $1\cdot5d$ from any modern anomaly such as an excavation trench.

An area survey is a more elaborate approach with which the approximate plan of remains can be defined in good conditions. The readings are obtained by making a series of parallel simple traverses, usually separated by a distance equal to the probe spacing. This will give a square grid of resistance values which should be plotted to scale in plan form. Staggering alternate traverses by a distance equal to half the probe spacing (see Fig. 92e) gives a slightly more even coverage of the ground, but the extra trouble in laying out hardly seems justified. 'Contours' of equal resistance are then sketched in sparingly and should give an approximate outline of the remains. (Various inelegant terms have been coined for these 'iso-resistance' lines, but 'contour', although not strictly accurate, is generally understood and sufficiently unambiguous.) The choice of contour interval can usually be made by inspection, those passing through regions of steeper resistance gradient being generally the most useful. Contours drawn where resistance changes are small tend to wander aimlessly about the plan and are distracting and best omitted.[12]

As a quicker alternative to contouring, the writer and Schwarz have independently devised systems whereby each reading on the plan is replaced by a shaded mark in which the density of shading is related to the resistivity at the point. In a published plan Schwarz places a small circle at each point: a clear circle indicates a resistivity range of 75–95 ohm-metres, a circle with one quadrant blackened, 96–120, two quadrants, 121–160, three quadrants, 161–220, and completely blackened, 221–300 ohm-metres. This method of presentation gives a useful broad indication of the anomalies present.

An interesting alternative method of area surveying is used by the United Kingdom Ministry of Works Test Branch. To quote Aitken's description: the system 'employs a dozen or so probes each connected to a terminal on a multi-bank switch on the instrument; this successively energizes consecutive sets of four probes down the line. When a probe has served its purpose on one traverse it is moved to the corresponding position on the parallel traverse adjacent.' This is probably the quickest way to make an area survey, its only drawbacks being that there is a considerable mass of equipment and the system is not convenient for long linear surveys. The equipment includes a board carrying a specially printed sheet on which readings are marked directly, so that contours can be inserted as soon as the survey has been finished.

In the case of a building, such as a Roman villa, once a survey of either of the above types has located the broad position of remains, the potential excavator will probably require the indication of individual walls which may be ill defined if a fairly large probe spacing has been used for the original survey. If the building lies just below the tilth, a probe spacing of 1 ft should be suitable for this, and if it is required to locate the centre of the wall with great precision, the electrode assembly should be advanced as a whole by steps of 6 in or less, instead of in the usual way, so that the fifth probe becomes super-fluous. Note, however, that if such a high resistance anomaly, embedded in a generally less resistive medium, is smaller in width than about $6d$, the readings may not rise to a simple maximum at the centre of the wall, but will have two peaks symmetrically disposed about the centre, giving an 'M' pattern. This is probably because, as indicated in Fig. 90, some of the current passes beneath the feature when the current electrodes are close to its edges, so that the voltage drop measured by the inner probes is too small. If this effect does not occur, one may assume that the wall is set in a dry subsoil or flooring. An inversion of this phenomenon, a 'W' effect, occurs with narrow features of relatively low resistivity, but these are less frequently encountered. To avoid these effects, and to obtain the sharpest possible indication of a narrow feature, the 'broadside on' approach advocated by Palmer can be used.[13] In this, the group of four electrodes is set out at right angles to the line of travel, and remains parallel to the linear feature as it is moved across it.

When using a probe spacing of only 1 ft, particular care should be taken to maintain accurate spacing. Aitken has calculated that, to keep the total error in the measured resistance within 14%, the probes must be inserted to within $\frac{1}{2}$ in of their correct positions. This is particularly difficult in stony ground, and probably explains why narrow-spacing resistivity is less often used than might be expected. In view of this, and the frequent need to move the electrode group as a whole, it seems logical to mount the four probes on a single insulator only 3 ft long, and it is curious that no successful trials of such a system have been reported. Such a probe system would probably have little ground penetration, but in moderately damp conditions most modern instruments should be capable of overcoming the contact resistance.

The permissible error in probe placing increases proportionally to d. Variations of a few inches in probe insertion and deviations from the straight line have negligible effect on the value of R, but it is worth while to keep the former as constant as possible to avoid excessive variations in contact resistance.[14]

Examples of rapid survey methods. In tracing the exact positions of circular ditches revealed by air photography, Atkinson has used the following method: linear traverses are made across the approximate position of the feature, and when one of these produces a double ditch type anomaly, it is assumed to be a chord of the circle. Halfway between the anomalies, another traverse is laid out at right angles: this should be a diameter of the circle, which is confirmed if two anomalies at suitable spacing are again recorded. The halfway distance between the two new anomalies is assumed to be the centre of the circle, and a second diametrical traverse is laid out at 45° to the first to check this. At Cunetio (Fig. 92), Annable and the writer have traced the external bastions of the

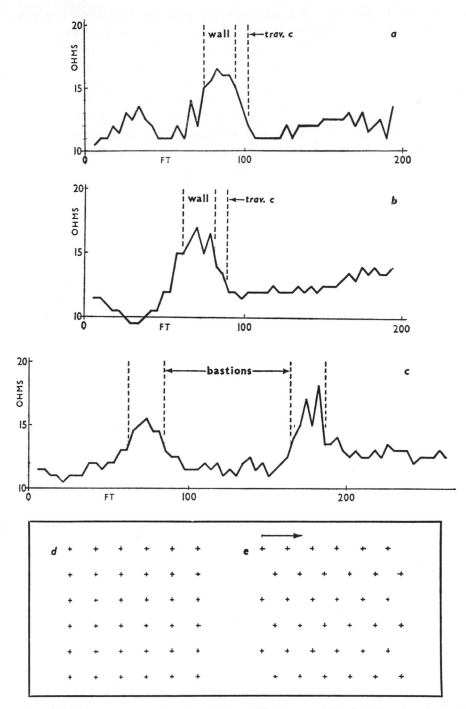

Fig. 92 a, b, c: The three traverses used to locate two wall bastions at Mildenhall-Cunetio; $d = 4$ ft; d, e: two ways of arranging measuring points in an area survey; e, in which the arrow indicates the direction of traversing, gives a slightly more even ground coverage.

town wall as follows. The line of the wall was established with two long traverses (a and b) at right angles to its line. Using information derived from a trench cut elsewhere, the exact width of the wall was superimposed upon the graphs of these traverses, and the front face line of the wall thus established marked on the ground with pegs 8 ft away from these pegs, a new traverse (c) was laid out at right angles to the first two, in other words 8 ft outside the wall and parallel with it. Measurements along this immediately revealed the positions of two bastions, and a trench was laid out over half of the one giving the strongest indication after its distance of projection from the wall had been determined with a fourth traverse. The survey took two men about one hour including the plotting of the results, and the trench gave precisely the information required without any adjustment.[15]

ALTERNATIVE ELECTRODE ARRANGEMENTS

One of the difficulties in resistivity measurement in low resistance conditions such as clay or boggy soil is that readings are often very low (in the region of 1 ohm) and the variations caused by buried remains proportionately small. Some instruments have poor discrimination in this region, and Palmer has proposed that the normal Wenner probe configuration be modified so that the inner voltage probes are closer to the current probes. This increases the voltage measured and gives higher values of R more suitable for the instrument and easier to read. Aitken considers that such a configuration increases errors due to the voltage probe penetration, and probe location certainly becomes more critical, although Palmer has solved this by linking the adjacent probes with insulators. An objection to this approach is that it reduces the power of the method to provide accurate positional information. Dr A. I. Rees[16] favours the opposite approach of closing up the inner probe spacing, relying on improvements being made in instruments. His preliminary field measurements have given results superior in definition to the Wenner arrangement but, here again, probe spacing is more critical. With special switches the rapid traversing method used with equal spacing could be adapted to both this and Palmer's configuration.

IMPROVEMENT OF RESULTS

However good the instrument, and however carefully the measurements are made, all soil resistivity measurements are subject to a greater or lesser degree to fluctuations superimposed upon the archaeological indications and complicating the picture. These variations—'noise', to use the conveniently short electronic jargon word—may be due to variations in the dampness, nature or depth of the soil containing the remains. Even a modest inhomogeneity in the top soil can affect the passage of current past the voltage probes, and on this current depends the measured value of R. Therefore, providing the remains sought are large compared with the probe spacing, there is no objection to smoothing the results of a linear traverse by averaging each value obtained with the value on either side of it, i.e. in overlapping groups of three. This slightly suppresses and spreads the extrema, but it does save the eye some of the work of extracting significant deviations, and helps to normalize the 'M' and 'W' effects already referred to.

Scollar has paid special attention to the problem of separating archaeological effects from those of subsoil variation. One of his methods is to literally filter archaeological variations from the broader soil variations, and is used to produce 'background free' plots of area surveys. Another, useful for linear surveys over inhomogeneous subsoil, involves covering the traverse twice with two different probe separations, giving coincident readings. Dividing one set of readings by the other gives fairly constant values except where archaeological features have a greater effect on one of the two sets of readings. These and other precedures he suggests are mathematically sound and effective, but sometimes involve making assumptions about the size of the remains beneath the ground and need to be used with caution. Analytical procedures involve a lot of arithmetic, for which there is often little time or justification—in the end one must simply dig.

REFERENCES

1 AITKEN, M. J. 1961. *Physics and Archaeology*, London and New York, 60; this includes a useful bibliography
2 ATKINSON, R. J. C. 1953. *Field Archaeology*, London, 2nd ed., 32
3 *Illustrated London News*, 1 June 1957, 900
4 G. T. SCHWARZ claims good results from an apparatus using only one moving electrode which is simply placed on the ground: *Jahrbuch der Schweizerischen Gesellschaft für Urgeschichte* 47, 1958–59, 96
5 Known as the Wenner configuration. Originally derived by F. Wenner, 1916. *Bulletin of the U.S. Bureau of Standards* 12, 469
6 Made by Evershed & Vignoles Ltd., Acton Lane Works, Chiswick, London, W.4, who publish a useful booklet (no. 245/1) on resistivity prospecting
7 Made by Nash & Thompson Ltd., Oakcroft Road, Chessington, Surrey
8 Made by P. Gossen & Co., Erlangen, Bayern, West Germany
9 Made by Martin-Clark Instruments, 1 The Drive, Farnham Road, Guildford, Surrey
10 An advantage of Atkinson's original switch is that it can be made up from standard wafer switch components. Details will be supplied by Atkinson on request, and a circuit diagram is given by Irwin Scollar in an important paper in *Bonner Jahrbücher* 159 (1959), 284
11 A very useful auger, consisting of a slotted steel probe, is made by And. Mattson, Mora, Sweden, and available from J. H. Steward Ltd., 406 Strand, London, W.C.2; it is made in two sizes, the smaller having the innocent appearance of a walking stick
12 SCOLLAR avoids guesswork by using a contour interval of half the mean standard deviation
13 PALMER, L. S. 1960. *Proc. Prehist. Soc.* 26, 64
14 AITKEN examines the effect of such errors in some detail
15 ANNABLE, F. K. 1958. *Wiltshire Archaeological Magazine* 207, 233
16 Lecture at CBA Conference on Prospecting in Archaeology by Geophysical Methods, 1961

Index of Sites

General Index